NO TURNING BACK

MARGARET POWERS MILARDO

EVENING STREET PRESS
SACRAMENTO, CA

Evening Street Press

January, 2017
Sacramento, CA

Library of Congress Control Number: 2016962759

ISBN: 978-1-937347-38-3

Acknowledgements

So many people have been instrumental in bringing this novel to publication that I am bound to leave out someone's name. I apologize ahead of time for any omissions. There are people who encouraged me to write another novel, and there are those who offered suggestions. Some of my students offered their comments and even their photographs. Some read early drafts, making helpful suggestions. Others read the drafts for errors. My publisher guided the book to its publication. Thank you all.

I hope those whose names I have omitted will forgive me.

In alphabetical order:

Barbara Bergmann, Deborah Downs, John Drake, Gordon Grigsby, Nancy Jordan, Sebastian Milardo, Bruce Miller, Edward Rielly, Bill Stauffer, Students from my writing classes, Colleen Tierney

Table of Contents

Prologue

October
Boston

I never finished my first drink. One minute I was sitting on a couch, sipping a sweetish-tasting drink in a tall glass that some guy had handed me as he sat beside me. The next thing I remembered was lying on a bed in the dark.

About that time I realized two things: my body hurt all over, and I was naked. I managed to mumble, "I think I'm going to be sick."

Suddenly, strong arms pulled me off the bed, and I was half-pushed, half-dragged down a hall into the bathroom. As I retched, I felt someone holding me over the toilet, pushing my head down while pulling back my hair so I didn't get vomit on it. I wasn't aware of much else just then, except that this person was not familiar.

When I stopped being sick, mystery man, for the person was a guy, walked me back to the bedroom. I still was unsteady on my feet as he started dressing me. He picked up my panties. Unbalanced and still shaky, I couldn't do much to help him put them on me. It seemed as if things were happening around me, that I wasn't quite present in the situation.

I heard a tearing sound and thought that, in pulling on the underwear, he had forced a leg opening over my torso and ripped the material. I was aware but unable to react. I stood dumbly while this stranger continued to dress me.

Neither of us said a thing. I was too woozy, but I wanted him to talk to me in the worst way. I desperately needed to know if anything had happened, yet I couldn't focus my brain to say anything to him. I stood mute and aching while he finished dressing me and used his fingers to smooth the tangles in my hair.

He guided me downstairs and found Julia, who told him my address. Then he called a cab. When it arrived, he handed me into the back seat, gave the cabbie the address and some money and shut the door. As the cab left the curb, I realized he had not said a single word to me, and I had no idea who he was. What had happened? Had I been raped? Or had I willingly submitted? How had I come to act so irresponsibly? In my foggy state, I managed to blame the events of the past summer for the present circumstances...

Chapter One

June
Olietta College

1

I accepted a summer internship at Olietta College because I thought it would provide me good experience for my senior year at my own college in Boston. I had applied for a summer internship for a couple of reasons. I wanted to gain more experience in legal work, since I hope to go to law school after graduation. I also wanted to have some time to devote to my writing. I'm not a fabulous writer or anything, but I hope to be good someday and know I need to write a lot to get better.

Olietta, I discovered, is small and rather preppy, in its students and in the campus itself. Many of the girls on campus in the summer seemed so young and fresh. They wore make-up and never seemed to leave their dorms without lots of attention to detail about clothes and hair. For instance, one girl I noticed early on—her name was Lindsay—had long, blond hair; it seems there were more blondes than anything else at Olietta, guys as well as girls.

Lindsay often had a long, tiny braid or two drifting through her hair on one side or the other. She used colored thread or maybe ribbons twisted in the braid or even tied around the ends. The colors always matched something she was wearing. It could have been a top or a belt or even her shoes. Now I have long, sort of blondish hair, but I don't take time to do more to it than brush it before I leave my room. Lindsay's hairdo had to take a lot of her time whenever she did it, and she often had a change of colors in the braid more than once a day.

Lindsay was maybe an extreme, but I noticed that some of the young women looked like they were modeling outfits for fashion magazines rather than going to classes and studying. I'm sure they studied, too, but it was such a shift from the way my friends and I dressed at our school. I mean we took care of ourselves and we usually looked nice, but these girls were like perfection addicts.

2

The college was preppy, too, in my eyes. I'd been around Boston for three years and grown to be comfortable with the city. Olietta was an enclave within an enclave. The town was small, pretty rural, and enclosed on three sides by either lake or river. The college nestled inside its own brick walls, doubly protected from the world.

There were paths, a mixture of brick and gravel, with some newer cement walkways. The paths cut through vast areas of grass—lawns, fields, and occasional gardens. Statues, metal, marble, cement, any number of different materials, appeared in unexpected places. Benches had been set among shrubbery or along a path, as if placed to beckon lovers to sit together or dreamers to idle away life's encroachments..

I loved the contrast from my school. Both were beautiful. Olietta oozed security and nostalgia, I thought, while my college was grounded in the present and rushing toward the future, a breezy, sometimes frenzied place. I expected Olietta to be safe, peaceful and placid. Boy, as it turned out, I was wrong.

3

The summer session began smoothly. I was anxious to get started in my internship as quickly as possible. I had to get settled in my room in one of the student houses and meet the other students living there during the summer. The house was magnificent. It was white-painted brick, three stories high and huge. The main part, a colonial style with tall windows, sat nearly on the curb, with only a small area of grass in front. A long ell extended from the back of the house into a large yard surrounded by high wooden fencing.

My room was on the third floor at the front of the main part of the house. It was a spacious, airy room with two large windows overlooking a side-street and a cemetery beyond. While normally a double, I was the only person staying in it that summer. The bathroom was used jointly with another room, but that room was unoccupied, so I enjoyed a private bathroom. In contrast, my quarters at my college in Boston were small, and I shared that room with two other girls.

The walk to central campus was an easy ten minutes. I passed a few other houses for upperclassmen, both male and female. Some classroom buildings and the library were situated in the block beyond. Next came the student center, which, for some unknown reason, was called the "Pit." Finally, there were a few more classroom buildings and an old dormitory before the grounds opened up into roughly a two-block square of lawn dotted with trees.

Almost in the center of the square was Irwin Bell Tower, actually a church-like structure that had a few offices and rooms for upper level classes or seminars and boasted a tall cupola with a liberty bell facsimile at the top. Even though it was not in the exact middle of the campus, since the eye gravitated to it as the highest building and the most striking, literally, the Bell Tower attracted people's attention and presence. For all intents, Irwin Tower was the center of campus.

Chapter Two

Summer Tutorials and Me

1

Ever since I was in high school, I've worked, both for free and for pay, at a few law firms. I also started writing years ago, when I was a rebellious teen. In fact, I even had to write, as part of a court thing, but that's another story. I'd been writing for years about all kinds of stuff, mostly somewhat personal and centered on social issues, so I'm comfortable writing in most any situation. Something I heard attributed to Gloria Steinem seems true for me, too: writing is one of the few things I can do and not feel like I should be doing something else.

When I received the internship, I was delighted. I came to Olietta anticipating working with a local law firm connected with the college and rooted in advocating for the underprivileged, particularly children. Why would a college be interested in young children, you might ask. Well, that's one of Olietta's unique qualities. It is very involved in the community.

For instance, it has a swimming program for at-risk teens, where they come to the pool twice a week and learn competitive swimming. Then they travel to meets in the state and compete. Everything is free. Of course, not all of the children are underprivileged, since anyone in the area can try out; those who are needy never would get the chance to do a program like that without the kind of help the college provides. Part of my duties included working with the swimming program.

2

There are other reasons the internship appealed to me. First of all, my adopted mother, Muriel Buckman, lives right across the lake from the college, less than half an hour away. So I knew I could drop by often to see her or get recharged at home. Then, I found out that the attorney assigned by the law firm to the college was a personal friend of Brian McKee! Now, Brian McKee was a very close friend, actually more than a friend, of Mure (that was what I call my mother most of the time). More than that, he is the lawyer who helped me so much during my terrible times. I even worked for him when I was in high school. So I already felt a connection to Mr. Dunfey, the college's attorney, before I even met him.

My primary role as an intern was to tutor a few students and to record my work on the project. This consisted of keeping notes and writing about the things I did, including the tutorials. I wrote up what I learned, and if I was asked, what I thought might be done concerning some issue.

So my journal, as I came to call it, was pretty much my brainchild. This entire intern project struck me as both challenging and rewarding. I knew I would learn a lot, and I hoped I would contribute something meaningful.

3

My tutorial excited me tremendously. I was assigned three students to work with over the course of the summer. There were students who were accepted to the first-year class who were required to attend the summer program because they had low scores on the writing portion of the SATs. My role was to be a writing tutor to three students. I would meet separately with each two or three times a week. Exactly what writing they did was my decision, so I decided I would design my assignments around each student.

I was given a small room on the first floor of Irwin Bell Tower, right in the center of the campus. It contained a desk and a chair for me, as well as a long table with four chairs that I could use for both the students and me. On the floor was an old Oriental rug. There was a large window beside my desk that looked onto a colorful garden and the lawn beyond.

Chapter Three

Student One and Someone Else

1

The first student I met was Lindsay, the girl I mentioned earlier when I was talking about the types of girls at Olietta. I described her as typical of the preppie girls I encountered as first year students. Lindsay walked into the room I was using for my office.

"Well, I'm here, but I don't know why," she said, looking at a spot somewhere to the right of my head. Without saying anything else, she sat down at one of the chairs and slid down so her sandaled feet protruded beyond the table toward me. I noticed that her toenails were colored a dark purple, which matched her tank top and the colored threads woven through the braid on the side of her head.

I began by saying, "Hi, I'm Brandi, and I think you are here because you probably did not do as well on the SAT writing sample as required by the college." Before I could say anything more, she cut in.

"Yeah, I know that. But it doesn't mean anything. I don't write much, don't care about it, since I'm not gonna be an English major. I don't need to learn from a tutor. I have a computer to do what I need; it has spell-check. That's enough. I'm going to major in liberal studies, maybe, or else management and I don't need to write. Anyway, I'll end up working for my dad until I get married. So writing isn't important."

"Are you engaged?"

"Not yet, but I figure I'll find somebody here. That's my plan."

"Oh," I said. Not knowing what else to say, I changed the subject. "What does your father do for business?"

"He owns a construction company. I work there sometimes. I usually answer the phone or take clients around, stuff like that. I don't need to write anything." While Lindsay was talking, she twirled the braid in her hair or picked at her nails, which were painted purple, also. She did not look at me.

"Well, for my own information, I would like it if you would write a page or two about yourself," I said.

"What for? I can tell you what you wanna know."

"I think, if you put something down on paper, you might tell me some interesting ideas you have or a little about your family, friends, things you have done and might like to do."

"Do I have to?"

I took a breath before I answered her. I was reminded of myself as a teen and how uncooperative and even belligerent I sometimes was. I decided it would be better if I didn't confront Lindsay, and maybe she would come around. After all, the tutorial was supposed to be a positive experience, so my acting like a big boss might turn her off more or even send her away. "You don't have to do anything you don't want to do. You're here at college because you want to be here, I presume. The college has devised this program for your benefit, and I am the tutor assigned to you. The guidelines suggest you write something for me to read, and then we go from there. Is that all right with you?"

Lindsay looked me in the eye for the first time. Then she sat up straight and spoke. "I'm not here because I wanna be. My mother wants me to go to college, so my dad said okay. She promised she'd make it worth my while if I try."

"So will you try it by writing something for me to read?"

"Yeah, I guess so. Can I leave now? I have some stuff to do."

I looked at Lindsay and said, "I thought you could write here now, and then we'd meet again in a couple of days."

"I can write better in my room. My computer's there, and I have stuff I need to do now." She got up from the chair and moved toward the door. "I'll come back in a couple days."

Before I could say yes or no, Lindsay was out the door in a few long strides.

After that introduction to the first student in my tutorial program, I sat back in my chair and considered my options. Lindsay was not what I was expecting a tutorial student to be. In my excitement and naiveté, I anticipated an enthusiastic person desiring to get some tips on learning to write better. She would want to sit down with me and write something immediately. Obviously, I had been projecting my own expectations about the project onto an unknown student. I vowed right then to tamp down my expectations before the next student came to see me. In the meantime, I gathered my papers together into a neat stack and left the room. I had an appointment to meet with Mr. Dunfey to talk about my duties with him in outreach for community children.

2

Climbing the steps of the Administration Building, I thought about the upcoming meeting. I had met Mr. Dunfey once with Brian McKee, at the courthouse in Portland. He was an older man, sort of a grandfather type. I wasn't sure if he would remember me; I had been working as an intern for Brian, who would take me with him to court once in a while.

I entered the room designated to be the meeting place for me with the community outreach program. At the end of the room, with his back to me, stood a tall man who was looking out the large window onto the lawn. As he turned, I realized it was not Mr. Dunfey. This man was younger, much younger, maybe thirty or even less. He smiled, and I realized he was quite good-looking, handsome even. His hair was short and blondish, and his eyes seemed to be green. I started to excuse myself. "I'm sorry," I said. "I think I got the room number mixed up. I thought I was supposed to meet Mr. Dunfey here."

"You're in the right place, Miss Buckman. I'm Colin Dunfey's assistant, Jay Bingham. I'm working on the community outreach program this summer. I hope it's all right with you and that you won't be too disappointed not to be working with Colin.

He may join us when he can make it, though."

I was a little flustered. This guy was too cool by a mile. Being around older men like Brian and Mr. Dunfey and working for them felt safe. Jay Bingham didn't look particularly safe to me. "Oh, that's fine. I mean whatever you and Mr. Dunfey decided. I just thought he'd be here, you would be …" I stopped; I figured I'd better quit before I made a bigger fool of myself.

"I understand," Jay said. "It can be disconcerting when you have preconceived plans, and they turn out to be different." He smiled again. Boy, he certainly knew how to fire up the wattage. "Anyway, Brandi, if it's okay with you, I thought we would take a look at the general guidelines that were set up last year for selecting candidates for the programs at the college. Is that all right with you? I think it's probably a good place to start; I'm new to the outreach program, too. "

"Yes; I would like to know more about the program. I didn't know you hadn't done it before," I said.

"I'm new to the firm of Atkinson, Dunfey and Jeffers, so this is my first time at the college. It seems like a warm and welcoming place. I think the young people who get a chance to be in the program should benefit from the experience. Don't you?"

"Most likely," I said. "But sometimes it's complicated with troubled kids. They need all the help they can get, but they have to decide they want it and then accept the help."

Jay looked at me and cocked his head. "You sound as if you've had first-hand experience yourself in this area."

I had managed to regain my composure, and I didn't want to get into the horror show of my adolescence, so I changed the subject. "A story for another time. How about I show you around the campus after we look at the guidelines. I know my way around pretty well, and I can take you by the pool and the art studio."

"Sounds like a plan, Brandi." Jay smiled again.

We spent a while reading and talking about the guidelines, making comments on the pamphlet when we had a question or wanted clarification on something. Sitting next to Jay was a bit unnerving. I couldn't put my finger on why, exactly. I had dated several guys after Dean's death—a long time after, but I finally was able to go out casually with other men without fearing I would crumble like a sugar cookie being near any date. Dean was everything, and, at first, I had to force myself to socialize with other guys. I started because I knew he would want me to do that. We'd promised each other we would get out and do things when we were at our different colleges because it would make us more interesting to each other. Only Dean never had a chance to get beyond high school graduation night before his father killed his wonderful future.

After a long grieving period, I wondered if I'd ever get over wanting to die myself. I finally stopped wallowing in self-pity and decided I'd live an active life to help make up for what Dean couldn't do. I dated different guys and even learned to have fun, but I never grew close to any of them. I'd become something I read, which goes a little like this: A female needs a man like a fish needs a bicycle. That's a pretty dismissive statement, but I pretty much felt that way myself. Guys were sometimes sleek and racy, but I didn't find them especially useful, so I was confused as to why I was flustered around Jay. I had no problem around boys my age or older men, so I thought maybe it was because he was older than college guys but younger than the professors and the lawyers I knew. Was I suddenly attracted to a bike and thought I needed one now?

We walked around the campus, and I started to feel a little more at ease with Jay. It helped that we were walking beside each other, and I wasn't looking into his eyes—or he looking at me. After about an hour, Jay said he had to get back to Portland to meet with a client, and he asked me if I would give him my phone number so he could call me to set up our next meeting. Then we said goodbye, and I watched as he walked to the parking lot. Then I headed to the house to have lunch and settle into some writing of my own.

Chapter Four

Student Two and That Someone Again

1

A couple of days later I met my second tutorial student. His name was Randall. I looked up from my seat behind my desk, and up, and up. The young man walking into the room was tall, 6'6", I guessed, or maybe even taller than that. His hair was red-auburn, his eyes blue, his frame skinny, and his stride a shuffle-step. He was dressed in gym shorts and a tank top, with a college logo cap on his head. The sneakers on his feet were huge, and, though I thought they were fairly new by the looks of the laces and the tops, they were scuffed around the toes. I guessed I was looking at a first-year basketball player.

"Hello, Randall?" I asked and smiled at the boy.

"Randy's my name. I hate Randall." He scowled as he spoke.

"Randy it is, then; I'm Brandi Buckman. You must be here for the writing tutorial."

"Coach said I hafta come and do what you say. I'm not here because I wanna be, but I'll do what you want. Otherwise, I'll get into trouble and wouldn't be able to play ball."

Bless the coach, I thought. The college is very strict about its athletes attending to academics, as well. Coaches work hard and have good teams who do well in their college conference, but they are sticklers about their athletes working to their ability in the classroom, as well as on the field, so I knew this kid at least would do what I asked of him. If he didn't, one email from me to his coach would set a fire under him. He'd also have to do double study hall in the evening, I knew. "Well, okay, then. I think we'll do just fine. First, I'd like to get a writing sample from you so that I can determine your strengths and weaknesses in writing. Would you mind writing about a page for me? I've got paper and either pencil or pen here for you—whichever you prefer."

"You mean you don't care if I use a pencil? My high school teachers wouldn't read anything in pencil, and it's harder to fix mistakes."

"No; pencil is fine with me."

"Okay," Randy said, as he took a pencil and a piece of paper from me. Then he sat at the table. I was glad I had asked for a table and chairs rather than desks; I don't think he would have fit into a normal-sized desk and chair set. "What should I write about?"

"I mostly want to see how you write. So you may write whatever you wish. Anything about you is fine. Usually, it's easiest to write about what you know. "

Randy looked out the window for a minute or so, then started writing. He stopped once or twice, but he seemed attentive. About fifteen minutes later, he rose from his chair and ambled to my desk. "Here ya go."

"Thank you, Randy. I'll see you in a couple of days, same time, and same place."

"Okay, Ms." He answered and was out the door in two loping strides.

After Randy was gone, I looked at his paper. The writing was blocky but neat:

> I'm a great basketball player. That's all I want to do. I am the best of any player at my own school. So far from what I see of the team I am the best here too. I hope to go at least semi-pro, maybe even before I finish college. I would of tried right after graduation but my father wants me to go to school first. He said if I came here he would buy me a new car so I came here.

The paper was short, but at least he wrote something, and I could get a sense of his writing. Next time he came in, I would have some place to start.

2

I had just finished dinner at the house when my cell phone rang. I answered it and heard a deep, masculine voice on the other end. I knew before he identified himself who it was and felt something like the sound of a bicycle bell ting in my stomach. "Hello, Brandi; this is Jay. I hope I didn't disturb you. How are you?"

"Oh, hi, Jay. No, you didn't disturb me at all, and I'm fine, thank you. How are you?" Despite the tingle, I thought I sounded pretty composed.

"Just great. I like hearing your voice. I hope you are enjoying yourself at Olietta. I wonder if you would like to get together, perhaps tomorrow evening. There is a new restaurant that's opened in Portland. We can try the food, and it will give us a chance to talk some more about the program. What do you think?"

I thought it was a neat idea, more seeing him than talking shop, but I didn't say that. "That sounds like a nice idea, Jay."

"Great. I'll pick you up about seven, if that's okay. It's a casual restaurant, so wear whatever is comfortable."

"Seven is fine. I'll see you then."

"Great, Brandi. Till then."

And he was gone. My stomach slowly returned to normal. What was the deal with this guy? All he did was call and ask me to a dinner meeting; it was nothing, really, yet I reacted like a kid accepting a first date with the most popular guy in school. Get a grip, Brandi, I thought. You've got plenty on your plate without mooning around about some guy who's too old for you, anyway. I shook my head to get back to normal and headed outside to take a walk before going over the background material on the swimming program so I would appear intelligent and informed at dinner tomorrow.

17

Chapter Five

Student Three and Him, Again

1

The next morning I was scheduled to meet the last tutorial student. The name was Chriz. I was pondering whether there was a typo on the paper, when there was a knock against the door. I looked up and saw a tall— average tall, not super tall like Randy—young man standing in the open doorway. "Good morning, Miss. I am Chriz. May I come in, please?"

"Yes, of course. Please come in and sit down," I said, thinking that his name probably was spelled right on the paper. Apparently, he was one of the foreign or exchange students at the college, since obviously he was not American. His accent seemed British; he was dark-skinned with wavy black hair and dark brown eyes. Maybe he was from Africa. At any rate, he certainly had good manners.

After he had taken a seat, Chriz looked at me and smiled. Against his black skin, his teeth were so gleamingly white. I thought of the cliché about needing sunglasses because they were so bright. They were still teeth, not brilliant pearls or some equally silly metaphor; they just were quite white in contrast, and I noted the attractiveness of his face.

"My name is Brandi Buckman, and I am the writing tutor. I would like to have you write a short essay, about a page, so that I may assess your writing. Then I will be able to see where your strengths are and in what areas of writing you might benefit from help. Would you mind writing a short piece now? You can write about whatever you want; yourself or a topic you are familiar with would be good."

"I will be very happy to write for you, Miss. I want to improve my writing as much as possible. I want to become a writer, and I need to learn as much as I can about good writing."

"That's great, Chriz. And you don't need to call me Miss; Brandi is fine. This is an informal setting." To my ears, I sounded like a jerk. This was just another tutorial student, yet I felt something else, something more significant about him. Good grief, Brandi, I told myself, you are going loopy over good-looking guys lately, and this one is only a first-year. Looking at him, I just smiled.

He smiled back, a blazing, white-toothed Colgate smile. "Thank you, Miss Buckman, Brandi," he said.

"Okay, then. You can get started. I have paper and pencils or pens."

"Oh, thank you, but I brought my own materials." He pulled a notebook from his backpack, as well as a pen. "I wanted to come prepared to work."

Well, that was a pleasant change from the other two students. "Excellent, Chriz. You may get started, then." I sat back and waited while he set up his paper and began writing almost immediately.

When Chriz finished his writing, he rose and brought the paper to me. "I did not write too much, Brandi, just a page as you suggested. I hope it is sufficient for your examination. Is there anything else required today?"

"Thank you, Chriz. No, that's all for now. I will see you again at our next scheduled session. Have a good day."

"Yes, Miss Buckman...Brandi...you, too. Goodbye." He left the room, and I sighed. This student would be a real pleasure to work with. As I picked up his paper, I hoped that his writing wouldn't be too lacking in good form. I didn't know what kind of background he had in writing in the English language:

> My name is Chriz. The spelling is close to the American Chris. That is what most people think my name is, so they call me Chris or Chris-with-a-z. It is okay to me because I think it is easy for them. When I am not at school I live in Portland with my aunt and uncle and their three childrens, my cousins. They are 8, 11, and 13. I went to

high school three years in the city. Before that I was in Egypt waiting to get a visa to go to America. Before that I lived in Sudan with my father, my mother, and my three little brothers. I am glad finally to be here in college. It has been a dream I had since I was a young school boy to go to college to learn many things. I want to be able to write about the things I have seen, and I want to make monies to help my family. Next time I will write about why I left Sudan and came here to live. I am twenty-two years old.

Respectfully, Chriz

No wonder I was feeling odd around Chriz. He was older than I was! And he probably was smarter than I. Plus he was a good writer already. All I saw was some wording that most likely was odd because of his previous schooling. I wasn't sure I could be of much help on his writing skills, but I knew I wanted to try. Chriz certainly had ability and motivation. Now I had to do what I could to help him the way he wanted.

2

After dinner at the restaurant in Portland, we sat over iced coffees, and I listened as Jay talked about his day. He was working closely with Mr. Dunfey on some of his cases and had spent part of the afternoon in court with him. He was doing what I hoped to do in a few years. Jay told me he had begun his job only a few weeks before he met me.

"I have been in New Haven for three years. I graduated, moved to Portland and started at the firm all in a matter of three days. It was quite a whirlwind. My mother wanted me to take a break before jumping right in to work, but I was eager to get started."

"Does your mother live in Portland?" I asked.

"No. She lives in New York. She wants me to visit her this summer. I'll get there once or twice, if the work doesn't pile up too high. Where do you live when you aren't at school, Brandi?"

"On the other side of the lake from Olietta," I answered, thinking that Jay wasn't as old as I thought. He was maybe three or no more than four years older. Shut up, Brandi, I said to myself; you think too much.

"Well, that's very convenient for times you just want to get away for a while. Are you and your mother close?"

Much as I might be a bit interested in the guy, I didn't feel like telling Jay my life story yet. Some lady smarter than I am said that the truth doesn't set you free; it just makes you weird, or something like that. I didn't want to reveal myself as weird, not right off the bat, anyway. So I just said, "Yeah; we're pretty close. We get along well, and she is supportive." I didn't want to get into like how she saved my life when I was a kid and then again when Dean died; like how she loved me when nobody else did and adopted me and gave me my first real home. No. I wouldn't share that until I knew him better. For now, we were hardly more than working colleagues or friendly acquaintances.

"That sounds pretty nice. How about your dad?"

"My father died a long time ago." I felt myself stiffen reflexively. Jay much have sensed my reticence, because he drew back and changed the subject.

"I'm sorry. Say; since it's such a nice evening, why don't we walk along the pier. We can look at the boats and the people out and about around there." He rose from the table and reached for my hand.

We spent about an hour walking slowly through the Old Port and the pier, looking in shop windows, noticing people, and checking out the yachts docked at the marina. Jay held my hand most of the time, and I found myself enjoying the experience.

Finally, he drove me back to campus; all the while we listened to a great music mix on the awesome sound system in his shiny Mercedes. I wondered how he could afford such a fancy car when he was just out of law school, but then I thought maybe he leased it. I knew a few people, from my working with Brian McKee, who leased expensive cars to make a good impression on clients. Maybe that's what Jay did, too.

The evening had been just perfect, and Jay didn't try to overdo it when he left me at the door. He gave me a hug and a quick kiss on the top of my head, and he said he'd check his schedule to see what day we could meet next to work on the project.

Chapter Six

Muriel, Brian and a Surprise

1

When I got out of bed Sunday morning and saw the blue sky unblemished by clouds, I called Mure and told her I wanted to come over for the day if she wasn't busy.

"And pray tell, what would keep me too busy to see you, Brandi? Get yourself over here, and we'll enjoy ourselves catching up. I haven't seen you in almost two weeks; you've been so busy. We can have lunch on the deck and go out on the lake afterwards."

Excited by her enthusiasm, I rushed around getting ready, and then I drove around the lake to the house. As I stepped up onto the deck, Mure came through the doorway from the kitchen. Behind her came Brian McKee, with a big smile on his face. He's here pretty early for him, I thought. If he came out on a Sunday, it usually wasn't until early afternoon. It was hardly after 11 o'clock. Then it hit me like a ton of bricks: he'd slept over!

"Hey, my girl," Mure said, as she grabbed me in a bear hug. "It's about time you came to see your long-suffering mother."

"You don't look to me like you are suffering much. Hi, Brian," I said. I put my hands on my hips, but the smile fell out of my mouth across my face, so I just laughed.

"Caught us, didn't you?" said Brian.

"We've got things to talk to you about," Mure said, almost at the same time.

"Maybe I've been away too long. Let me sit down first, though," I said. I knew that Muriel and Brian had been seeing a lot of each other, and I supposed I also knew the relationship was more than platonic. It was a surprise to me, though, but I also realized right then that I liked the idea. Brian is a really solid person, kind and generous, and he's a good provider, too! "Before you hem and haw too much, I think I got the picture, and I'm all in favor of whatever your plans are."

Mure laughed, and Brian looked at her before he said, "Well, that makes it much easier for us, doesn't it, Muriel?"

"Brian and I are going to get married, that is, if it meets with your approval. It means you would inherit a step-father."

"If you'd want me, of course," Brian winked as he spoke.

"All I want to know is when? And can I be the maid of honor? I hope it's going to be this summer."

"We thought Labor Day Weekend, here, and I would not want anyone else for my beautiful maid of honor," Mure said. I noticed her eyes were very glisteny. This was a big deal, I realized. She almost never shed a tear, and here she was nearly crying.

"Wow! That doesn't give you guys much time to plan a wedding."

"We've been planning it for months; we just haven't told anybody. You're the first to find out. There isn't a lot to do, either," Muriel said. "We're having a simple ceremony and only a few people in attendance."

"Are you going on a honeymoon?" I asked. "I think you should have a honeymoon,"

"Well, thank you, Dear," Mure said. "Yes, we are going on a honeymoon. We're going down the coast, and then we're going on a windjammer cruise out of Rockport."

"Oooh," I actually squealed, "just like you and I did that time."

"Well, yes, like we did; but, not like we did, either," Mure said. "Brian and I will be on our honeymoon. That trip you and I took, Brandi, was necessary for your recovery from a terrible experience. Brian was involved that time, too, but he didn't go on the cruise. We think this is the right way for us to celebrate our good fortune and all the happiness we share. Now I'm going to stop before I get too worked up."

"Absolutely," chimed in Brian. He looked like a happy, cuddly bear. His arms were draped around Mure's shoulders. Mure had more sparkles in her eyes. I almost laughed to think my tough mother could feel so weepy. Then I shut off the chuckle that was rising up; she deserved this happiness more than anybody. I couldn't think of two people who were better for each other.

"I'm so excited for you. This is so great. I got a great mother, and now I'm going to get a great father."

Brian grabbed me and hugged me so tight I gasped. "I think I loved you almost the minute I met you," he said. He seemed a little choked up, too.

"Well, I don't think I was so loveable when you first met me. But it's nice of you to say so," I teased. "I love you, too, Brian."

"All right; enough. It's time to have lunch. Then we're going out in the boat and cruise around the lake," Mure said.

2

The rest of the day at the lake was wonderful. The three of us had a great time. I played my Adele songs at high volume while Brian had the boat at full-throttle. Finally, they both begged me to lower the volume and to change the artist. "Not that we don't like Adele, Brandi; we do. But enough of her for one afternoon, and please play something else," Muriel said. When she reached for my IPhone, I upped the volume and segued into "Moondance," just for a moment, to calm the waters; and then I shut off the music altogether.

As we settled into a more sedate speed, I told them what had been happening with me at the college. I mentioned going out on a casual date, but I didn't elaborate, and they didn't ask. After our time in the boat, we hung out on the deck at the house for a while; even though we really weren't hungry, we ate some of the salads left over from lunch and grilled a few hot dogs. Before I knew it, it was time for me to head back. I wanted to gather my materials and my thoughts for the week ahead.

After I set up my datebook and took a few notes for my

tutorial, I sat on my window seat, looking out at the cemetery. There was a full moon which cast some long shadows among the stones; I found the effect relaxing. The summer at Olietta seemed off to a fine beginning for me. My tutorial students were interesting. Lindsay might be a challenge, but that was okay. I thought I was capable of meeting the challenge. The other two students were going to be easier to work with, since they both were motivated, even if for different reasons. I liked the ideas contained in the swimming program and looked forward to working with Jay Bingham. That he was not Mr. Dunfey no longer concerned me. Jay seemed very capable, and the fact that he was good-looking with a nice personality made it that much easier to accept the change.

Chapter Seven

More Tutorials in a Busy Week

1

The second week began well. I sat in on a political science seminar for seniors, taught by the department chairman, Dr. Maddox. He was energetic and inspired his students to speak their opinions. The atmosphere encouraged people to argue, albeit in a friendly manner, with each other and Prof. Maddox. All he seemed to require was that a student had a factual basis for any argument he presented. He introduced me to the class at the start, and then he seemed satisfied to have me simply observe and listen. So, I sat back and enjoyed the hour, taking a note here and there just to make sure I could say something intelligent if Prof. Maddox asked me later.

When class was over and the students had left the room, I went up to Dr. Maddox and thanked him for an enjoyable experience in the class. "I found the give-and-take among the students stimulating. I realized that I need to read up on some of the issues you discussed today," I said.

"Ah, well, that's nice of you to say, Brandi. I do love this seminar. Everyone is so engaged. Here is a copy of the book we are using. I can put together some articles you might like to peruse in your spare time. They'll offer some background on the topics we're pursuing in the course."

"That would be great; thank you."

"Feel free to come by as much as you are can," he said. "I know you will be very busy with your duties, so just visit us when the time allows."

I thanked Prof. Maddox and left for my office at Irwin Tower.

I had settled into my chair, looking through the book that Dr. Maddox gave me, when I looked up and noticed the time on my desk clock. Lindsay was late; I was hoping she would appear soon. Then she came around the corner, sashayed into the room and slipped into the chair closest to the door and farthest from me.

"Hi, Lindsay," I said. "How are you this morning?"

"I'm tired. I don't like to get up early, especially in the summer. I tried to fix my fall class schedule so most of my classes are in the afternoon, but everything was set. I even have an eight o'clock three days a week. I'm going to get it changed, if I can. Otherwise, I'd have to get up before six and skip breakfast to make an eight o'clock."

"Well, maybe you could eat a piece of fruit before class and have breakfast after class. The dining hall is open all morning and serves breakfast until eleven, I think," I said. "Couldn't you get up about seven or so, then, and make it to class all right?" I asked.

"I don't think the school takes into consideration how long it takes to get ready in the morning. It takes me over an hour and a half, even without eating," she practically whined.

Lindsay was a pretty girl and would look fine if she just showered and brushed her teeth. But I held my tongue. "What did you do in high school? It starts a lot earlier than eight."

"My mom helped me get my schedule so I didn't have a class first period, and second period was study hall, so I didn't have to get to school until ten. And my mom took me 'til I got my license, and then I drove myself. I thought college would be a lot easier about classes and times and all." Her voice petered out.

"I'm sure everything will work out," I said, hoping to get us on the track of writing. "Did you bring me a writing sample today?'

"Oh, I forgot. I was kinda busy this weekend. I could do one for next time, though," she said and actually smiled at me.

"I'm afraid I really need you to write a short essay right now."

"I'm not good at writing like that. I told you." Now she was pouting.

"It doesn't matter, Lindsay," I said. "As I told you, I want a sample of your writing—normal writing, not something you work over—so whatever you write this morning will be fine. It will give me an idea of the things we should emphasize in the tutorial." Before she could argue with me, I rose and handed her a couple of pieces of lined paper and a pencil. She struck me as the pencil type, not the pen type.

"All right, but I don't think this will be very good. If you let me do it at the dorm…"

I didn't wait for her to finish her sentence but interrupted, saying, "I understand, but it's fine. Please write about a page or so about whatever you want. It may be about your family, your life story, or anything else that you feel like writing. Just show me how you write." Before she had a chance to disagree, I turned away and walked to my desk. "Take about twenty minutes or so, really, as long as you want. When you're done, just give me the paper, and then you can leave."

I sat down, picked up a piece of paper and began writing, anything to take my attention away from Lindsay. She would see that I had work to do, so she would get to work herself, I hoped.

Barely fifteen minutes went by when Lindsay spoke. "Okay. I'm done. I don't have anything else to say. Can I leave now?" She reached her hand toward me, holding out the piece of paper.

"Thanks, Lindsay. Of course you may leave now. I'll see you next tutorial," I said. She was out the door before I finished speaking. I went back to my desk and took a look at her paper:

> There aren't many people on campus this summer so it's pretty boring. I use the pool most afternoons. I met a couple of guys who are jocks. They don't have much time, they are practicing all the time. They asked me to come watch a practice tomorrow, so I think I might since I have nothing else to do. The girls I met so far are okay. I hope it

will be better when there are more people here when school starts.

Well, I thought, at least she wrote something. I decided that I would come up with some possible writing prompts for Lindsay. Maybe, if she had a kind of assignment, she would write a little more purposefully. I thought we'd probably do all right, as she got used to the idea of sitting with me and writing.

3

Things settled into a routine. I looked forward to the tutorial sessions. True, Lindsay was a challenge, but at least she had started to write each session, and I thought she would improve in her skills. She sometimes was defensive ("I never learned that in high school." "Well, I'm doin' it the way I always did."). But she corrected her work and continued to write, and that's all I asked.

Randy usually wrote something about basketball. If I had been interested in learning how to play well, I certainly could have gained quite a lot from his essays. He told me about all of the positions on the team, what each person did in each position, what position was most important (his, whatever position he happened to be playing), how to hold the ball, how to dribble the ball, how to throw the ball; you get the idea. The topics got rather boring, but it didn't matter because Randy wrote enough so that I could work with him on his writing skills, which was the purpose of the tutorial, after all.

Chriz was another story altogether. I so anticipated his visits. He arrived early and full of enthusiasm, making me feel that I really contributed to his writing. Every time he came to the room, Chriz greeted me cordially and then settled in his seat to write. Usually we chatted a bit first; then he wrote, sometimes for half an hour or more. After he finished, either we would go over what he wrote right then or else we would talk about various things, school, his studies, usually light topics. He was more likely to commit to paper the more serious things about himself and his life. When he left, I was a little sad to have him leave. Chriz brought a brightness to the room; the glow lasted much of the day.

In his second essay, he related how he came to the States and then to Olietta College:

I was 14 years old when they came for me on the playing field at school. My father, my uncle (another uncle not the one I live with now) and another man friend ran to me while I was playing football. (I have learned that this sport is called soccer in America, so I will try to use that word.) You must come with us now they told me. Hurry, I ran and ran with them until we finally stopped. People were coming to my village to take all the young men like me. My father had a way to get me away and his man friend and my uncle would help me. He had to go back to my mother and the little boys or the people would think something was not right. We spent a lot of time moving at night and waiting in the day. Sometimes we had a hut to wait in, and then I could sleep. Other times we had to hide on the ground or sometimes in bushes. Later we got to a place where a truck picked us up. My uncle went back then, and my father's friend went with me on the truck. After a long time, we changed to another truck and drove many distances. At last we got to a camp. Some of my mother's peoples were there, and they took me in with them. It was crowded in the tent. There were 10 peoples already, but they told me to stay with them. They were happy to see me.

Then I waited. There was not a real school there but there were books and I read a lot. One man helped me with maths. He taught some other boys and me, from 2 books he had brought with him to the camp, and from his head. I think he had more in his head than both of those books.

After 3 years, some of it in another kind of camp in Egypt, I received papers and permission to go to America at last. I left and came to America to live with my relatives.

My uncle (the other one) and his family lived in the Portland City so I started school there. It was very hard at first. I knew English because we learned it in my school in Sudan, but my speech was a little different. Some peoples laughed and teased me but mostly peoples were kind and some peoples helped me very much. Pretty soon my speech was like Americans speak English. Now I think I speak almost perfect.

Writing was hard also but I had a tutor who taught me to write better. I was very good at maths. I always was so I did not have problems with maths or with chemistry too at the high school. So that is why I want to major in maths and chemistry. I want to go to Pharmacy school in Boston in 3 or 4 years. After that I think I can help other peoples at the same time I take care of my family.

Chriz

I was beginning to understand more about Chriz from his writing. I know I had some tough times growing up, and I was lucky to make it, mostly because of Mure and a few other people. So I could identify with Chriz's gratitude in getting help from family and friends. But I was blown away by the situation he lived in in Sudan and in the camp, wherever that was. Then Egypt— I certainly didn't identify with the dangers he faced. I had some big problems, yeah; but I don't think I ever really was in grave danger for my life.

I never had to struggle to get the chance to learn, either. In fact, I almost threw it away a couple of times. Chriz's ability is amazing. He is right; he speaks English like he's lived here all his life. And his writing is better than some of my college friends' writing. I have heard around that he is brilliant in math (maths, as he calls it—I think that's cute!). I am fortunate to have met him and to have the chance to work with him. He is an amazing guy.

Chapter Eight

Mike and the Swim Team

1

Another week sped by. I spent some time at the pool, learning about the swimming program and meeting the kids involved in the community outreach project. There were eight or ten of them, and they spent their days working out in the gym and swimming. They got instruction and some pointers on team competition from Mike Simmons, who was in charge of the team. They were preparing for the first of their meets, which would be at Olietta at the end of the week.

I was impressed by Mike's rapport with the kids. He was a co-captain of the Olietta College team and a champion diver. He was strict, but he also had a great sense of humor. One of the biggest jokes was on me. Mike loved to fool around, and everyone knew it, except me. He also had a fiancée, Kristen. She was a senior at Olietta, but she recently had left for a swimming conference in Indiana. The kids on the swim team had met her before she left, but I had not. Since the kids knew that Mike and Kristen were engaged, they played along with his little joke. As I walked up to him, Mike got down on one knee. He pretended to be smitten, saying, "Oh, you are so beautiful, Brandi, I don't think I can stand it." Then he fell over onto the concrete, and the kids howled. A couple of the boys started singing Justin Bibber's, "I Want to Be Your Boyfriend."

At first I was flustered, but then I remembered the pretty girl I had seen Mike with several days before. They were standing a distance from me, but I still saw the sparkly ring on her finger. After a second, I caught on to Mike's joke, so I placed my foot on his belly, raised my fist and yelled, "Another conquest!" Everyone laughed, and Mike jumped up and grabbed my hand.

"Hi, Brandi. I'm so glad you're a good sport. I probably

shouldn't have done that, but it was too tempting. When the kids saw you, they thought you were pretty cute and thought it would be funny if I "swooned" over you. Welcome to the Super Summer Swim Team. You're an official honorary member." Then the kids gathered around Mike and me, laughing and "high-fiving."

Mike turned from cut-up to serious instructor quickly. He called the kids together and sent some of them into the pool to do laps. The others he gathered around him as he talked about his expectations for them to prepare for the meet. I had taken a seat on the bleachers to watch, when I sensed a presence.

2

I looked toward the pool entrance and caught a flash of white and blue. In walked Jay in a brilliant white golf shirt, pressed jeans and boat mocs. I saw a couple of girls look up from Mike's huddle and nudge each other.

Jay looked around, spotted me and strode over. "When I didn't find you in your office, I thought you might be here," he said. Then he smiled and sat down next to me.

The huddle around Mike disintegrated. "Whoa, daddy," one of the girls shouted. Another gave a wolf whistle.

"Hey, Mike," said a lanky girl in a tee shirt and sweat shorts. "You got competition, baby. I think Brandi's got a man."

"Wow," said another. "He's hot stuff. Hey, hi there, Hot Stuff."

The boys didn't say anything, but they were looking at Jay.

Then Mike spoke. "Okay, ladies and gentlemen. We're here to practice. Now, switch places. Girls, go in the water and start your laps. Guys, out of the pool and head to the locker room and change. Start calisthenics next."

As everybody moved, I noticed that one girl did not get into the pool. She sat on the edge and swung her legs, wetting her feet. Mike bent over her and said something into her ear. The girl shook her head. Mike left her and came over to us, sitting down next to

Jay.

Holding out his hand, he said, "You must be Jay Bingham, the lawyer with the committee. I've heard about you from the Dean. I'm pleased to meet you, and ignore the giddy girls. They don't see enough good male role models."

Jay shook Mike's hand and said, "Actually, they're a refreshing change from the stodgy office and the nervous, unhappy people in court. Why isn't that girl going into the pool? Is she ill?"

"She says she has a headache. I don't know, but I usually give the kids the benefit of the doubt unless it becomes a hobby with them. She's usually a hard worker and pretty serious about the swim team."

I looked at the girl again. She was chubby but cute, with dark, curly hair. "Why don't I try talking to her," I said to Mike. "What's her name?"

"Shondra"

While Jay and Mike chatted, I went over to Shondra and sat down beside her on the edge of the pool. "Hi," I said.

"Hi."

"I hope you'll feel better soon. You must not like missing practice."

"Well, I'm gonna quit the team, anyway," she said.

"Oh, but Mike says you really like the team and work very hard. Why do you want to quit the team?"

Shondra lowered her voice. "I don't want to; I have to." Then she started to sob.

I stood up. "C'mon. Let's go into the girls' locker room for a minute."

Shondra pushed herself up, and together we left the pool area.

3

Once in the locker room, I led Shondra to an empty office and guided her to a chair. She was crying in earnest now. I picked up a box of Kleenex from the desk and handed it to her.

When her crying stopped and she wiped at her eyes and nose, I asked, "Are things bad at home?"

"Yeah, they're real bad."

"Maybe they seem that way now, but maybe talking about it might help," I said.

"It won't help. Nothin's gonna get better. I've been thrown out. I don't know where to go."

"Did you have a fight with your parents?"

"I only have a mom. She lives with a guy; he's not my father," she whispered. "Besides, it's my fault they threw me out."

"Why do you say that, Shondra?"

"Because it is." She started crying again. I leaned in and put my arms around her. At first, she stiffened; then she relaxed and put her arms around me. "I don't know what to do. I can't go home. They told me to get out and stay out. My mom threw my clothes out the door in a garbage bag."

I thought for a bit, while Shondra continued crying softly. "Stay right here for a couple of minutes," I said. "I'll be right back."

I went back to the pool and told Mike not to let the girls into the locker room until we came back out. Then I told Jay that something came up, and I would be busy with Shondra for a while, so we'd have to postpone our meeting for now. I told both of them that I would call them when I knew more

Back in the locker room office, I said to Shondra, "Okay; let's get out of here and take a walk. We'll go out the back way. Bring your clothes bag with you."

We left the sports complex and walked over to my office.

4

Once we were sitting in my office, Shondra calmed down. She had stopped crying while we walked across the campus. The room was peacefully quiet, contrasted to the pool. Shondra had washed her face and cleaned up in the bathroom. She took some clothes from the garbage bag and was now dressed in shorts and a loose tee shirt. Although her eyes were red and a little puffy, she looked calmer. She really was a cute kid, with blue eyes and freckles, a short nose and round cheeks. Watching her, I decided to jump right in.

"I know you just met me, Shondra, but if you want to tell me what happened, I'll see if I can help. You can tell me whatever you want or nothing at all. We can just sit here till you feel better. Do you think you might want to talk to me?"

"I don't know. There isn't that much to say."

"Yeah, sometimes it doesn't seem like talking about it helps. I got thrown out of my house, too. I got thrown out of two houses and disowned by my foster parents, and I even ended up at the Youth Detention Center in Portland."

Shondra looked me in the eye. "Naw, you never. I don't believe you."

"Why? You think you're the only one who can screw up?"

"You look like nothing bad ever happened to you. You must have a perfect life."

"Well, Shondra," I said, "Think again. My father died before I was born, my mother died when I was a little kid, and I got bounced around foster homes. I ran away, lived on the street, tried to hang myself, stole, hit somebody, and spent time at the Youth Center. And all this happened before I was your age. Can you top that?"

"You really tried to kill yourself? What happened?"

"The rope broke."

"Oh," she said.

"Well, I'm sure you feel pretty bad. But nothing you tell me will shock me, and I can promise you I'll keep my mouth shut."

"You didn't get pregnant, did you?"

"No, but some of the things I did were a lot worse."

Shondra put her head down. "There's nothin' I can do." I saw the tears start again.

"I think maybe I can help. Are you pregnant?"

She started crying in earnest, again. "Yeah," she barely whispered.

"Well, now that I know, I can start thinking about some ways to help you," I said. "I guess your parents threw you out because they found out."

"He's not my parent."

"I'm sorry. Your mother and her boyfriend."

"Yeah. She told me I was a slut. And she was so mad. I already told you she threw my clothes in that bag and then threw it out the door and told me to go with it and never come back."

"Do you think she'll let you go back tonight?"

Shondra shook her head. "No, she meant it, I know. Earl and her talked about me before. I knew she was getting sick of it. So I know she won't let me back. She does whatever she wants for her and him, not me."

I thought for a minute. "Okay, I know what we can do for tonight. You can stay with me."

Shondra's head shot up. "With you?"

"Sure. I have two beds in my room at the house. You can be my sleep-over friend tonight. Then we'll figure out some plan. I could use a little help from Jay, that guy who came into the gym just before we left. He's a lawyer, and he helps the college with stuff. He can make sure we help you the right way. If you let me, I'll talk to Jay. I promise nobody else will know unless it's all right with you. And if you don't want to do what we find out we can do to help you, of course you don't have to."

"Oh. A lawyer. Am I in trouble?"

"Of course not. You can think about it for a while. Right now, let's go to the house. You can take a shower or a bath and get comfy in my room. We'll have dinner and hang out, so you have time to decide if you want my help."

"Ok."

We left the office and walked toward the house. "After you think about it, you can let me know if I can ask Jay for help. Maybe you want to meet him first. If you do, we can see him tomorrow."

"Will you be there with me if I see him?"

"I won't leave you for a minute, kiddo," I said.

Chapter Nine

Complications

1

Shondra settled in at the house. After a shower and a nap in my extra bed, she looked, if not happy, at least refreshed. Since she was my height, I let her go through my clothes and pick out something to wear for dinner. She flipped through the clothes and chose a short, loose-fitting dress, which fit her fine.

While Shondra had been bathing and resting, I went downstairs and made a couple of phone calls. First I called Jay, and, without telling him Shondra's condition, I let him know that she had been put out of her house and was staying with me for the night. "I need some legal advice. Since you are part of the college and the swim team, I was hoping you could talk to us."

"I'm certainly able to do that, Brandi," Jay said. "You haven't told me much, though."

"How about if we meet tomorrow morning, here at the house? We'll have privacy, and Shondra can decide what she wants to tell you. I think she'll tell you everything, once she sees what a great guy you are," I said and then laughed.

There was a pause. "I'm just checking my schedule. Glad you think I'm a great guy. Okay; I can be there by 10 in the morning, if that's okay with you. What are you doing tonight?"

"I'm hanging out with Shondra. I don't want her to get nervous about staying here, so I might just take her for a ride or something. I want her to feel comfortable with me."

"I'm sorry I can't see you tonight, but that sounds like a good idea. So, I'll see you both in the morning."

"Ok; so long. And thanks, Jay."

"My job, and my pleasure, too. 'Til tomorrow."

The second call I made was to Muriel. Without telling her very much, I said that I was coming by if it was okay, and I was bringing a young friend with me.

"Of course, you can come by any time you want to. This is your home. I get the sense that there is something going on with this girl and you are looking for some advice or some help."

"That's why I love you, Mure. You are so perceptive."

"No, you are so obvious sometimes. And I know you so well. I hope my so-called perception is not the only reason you love me."

"You know it isn't," I said and laughed. Mure always can make things better for me. "We'll be there around seven."

"I'll make some cookies. Young friends always like cookies, and snacks usually make it easier to talk."

"You're great. See you soon"

3

As we pulled up to Muriel's house on the lake, Shondra sat up straight in the seat. "You live here? You must be rich."

Getting out of the car, I said, "The house belongs to my mother, Muriel Buckman. She went to college and worked in a good job for many years. She earned enough money to buy this house. She also has an interesting story about her teen years."

"Like she got pregnant when she was fifteen?"

"I'll let her tell her own story. Here she is now."

Muriel came out the kitchen door and met us on the deck. She hugged and kissed me, and then she turned to Shondra. She didn't hug or kiss her, but she took the girl's arm and smiled at her. "You must be Brandi's friend. I'm so happy to meet you. Let's sit on the deck and watch the boats."

Muriel was so casual that I saw Shondra visibly relax, and, with Muriel's arm across her shoulder, she walked with my mother to the front deck, where they both sat down in lounge chairs. A pitcher of lemonade sat on a low bench in front of them.

"Brandi, I forgot the cookies and the fruit in the kitchen. Will you go in and get them, Dear?" Mure asked.

I went inside and looked around. I didn't see prepared fruit or cookies, but I did see a large bowl with fruit in it, a cookie jar and a note next to it. The note said, "Brandi, you need to cut up the fruit. Then put it in the large green bowl and pour over it the syrup I made. It's in the fridge. Get the small fruit dishes and some spoons. Then put the cookies on the yellow plate, and put everything on the teak tray and bring it out to the deck. Do a good job and don't hurry. M."

When I finished preparing the fruit and arranging everything, I brought it out to the deck. Mure and Shondra were deep in conversation. My mother must have gotten right to the core of the issue because, as soon as I sat down, she said, "Shondra has shared her concerns with me, and I've suggested that she stay here with me, starting tomorrow. You can't have overnight guests all the time. You like the idea, Shondra?" she asked.

Shondra smiled at Muriel. "Yes, Mrs. Buckman."

"Well, you settled that fast," I said. "But don't we need to get some legal advice first?"

"We'll get that started as soon as Brian gets home," Muriel said. She looked at Shondra. "Brian helped me when I adopted Brandi. Brian and I are getting married at the end of the summer, too. Maybe you might be here for that."

"Oh," Shondra said.

"I thought I might get Jay's help, if Shondra is agreeable," I said.

"Since Jay's firm represents the college, he can make the decision to have Brian assist him," Muriel said.

Just then a car door slammed, and Brian called out, "I'm back. And I see Brandi is here." He came onto the deck and gave Muriel a hug and a kiss. Then he put me in a bearhug and looked over my shoulder at Shondra. "Another beautiful lady. How are you, my dear? You must be a friend of Brandi's."

After the introductions, Muriel said, "Okay, Brandi, why don't you show Shondra around. You can swim or take the canoe out. I'll want to talk to Brian, and then maybe we can go out in the boat, if it's not too late."

I showed Shondra around the house first, and then we took a walk down to the dock and sat with our feet dangling over the water. She was quiet, so I didn't talk, either. We just sat next to each other. I felt better now that someone else shared my concern. I knew that Muriel and Brian would decide what was best.

Less than half an hour later, Muriel and Brian joined us on the dock. "Everything is set." Muriel said. "Well, it's not all set, but it is for the time-being. Shondra is staying with you tonight, as your house guest. Tomorrow you and she can see Brian and Jay at the college in the morning. After that, Shondra, you can go to the pool. I think you can continue to swim for a while, anyway. You can stay here starting tomorrow night. Brian and Jay can take care of the legal concerns. You don't need to worry about any of that right now. We can take one day at a time. So, as I said, we're all set for now. Anyone want to take a ride in the boat with Brian and me?"

Shondra jumped to her feet. I moved a little more slowly, and Brian reached for my hand, winking at me as he did so. Muriel was the first to the boat, assisting Shondra over the gunwale. I got in after her. Brian started the motor, Muriel cast off, and we headed over the water toward our favorite place to watch the sun set.

Chapter Ten

Shondra in the Center

1

I learned later that, when Brian and Jay arrived at the college house around ten, they already had had a couple of meetings about Shondra earlier that morning. Neither of them said anything other than Brian's comment that, "Everything is in place where it needs to be, so we can concern ourselves with some practical details."

I thought he would tell us more once we sat down in the living room, but he introduced Jay to Shondra instead. "Shondra, I would like you to meet Jay Bingham, who is a colleague of mine and another lawyer. Brandi already knows him because she is working with him for her internship."

Jay stood and offered his hand to Shondra. He smiled and said, "I am very happy to meet you, Shondra. I hear you are an excellent swimmer. I used to swim competitively in high school, so I'm hoping to go to one of your team meets this summer."

"Oh, how did you...thank you." She shook Jay's hand and smiled in return. I needn't have worried that Shondra would be overwhelmed by two lawyers jumping into her business so quickly. The time we spent with Brian last night must have helped dispel any nervousness toward him. Plus he had that air about him that I called his "Teddy Bear Daddy" look. And Jay, with that dazzling smile, worked his magic. I had no idea he was a competitive swimmer; he never told me. But Shondra sat down and looked from Jay to Brian. She seemed completely at ease.

Our meeting was not what I had expected. Instead of asking Shondra questions about herself or her situation, Brian chatted with her about the lake and Muriel. Then Jay really got her interested talking about music. He seemed to know all the groups she liked. I was wondering when the serious questions would begin, when Brian said, "Well, you need to get to the pool, Brandi has work at her office, and I need to go to Portland. Jay, you probably have something to do, too. So I'll say so long for now, and we'll see each other again soon, Shondra."

Without saying anything else, Brian was off the couch and out the door almost before I could say goodbye to him. Jay stopped long enough to say he would call me later. Then he asked Shondra if she would mind him stopping by the pool to watch a practice. "I'll let you know before I go there, so you can tell me if it's a good time. Is that all right with you?"

Shondra answered him with a, "Yes," and another smile. Then Jay was gone, too. Shondra and I looked at each other. "They're both so nice. You know really nice people."

"I do, Shondra. I'm very lucky. And both of them like you and are going to help you."

"I don't know why."

"Because you're a good person, and you need help. That's why. Same for me."

"Oh. Thanks." She ducked her head a bit, then looked at me and smiled.

I took her hand and squeezed it; she squeezed back. We gathered our things, her gym bag and my books, and headed out the door.

2

The next time I saw Jay, he told me why our meeting with Shondra had been so casual. He and Brian had begun their morning at 7 a.m. Jay's first meeting was with the Dean of the college, and Jay met with Human Services in Portland. Between the two of them, they also contacted Mike, the Portland Police and some judge. By the time they saw Shondra and me at ten, they had gathered all the information they needed. By noon, they had started formal proceedings to assure Shondra's welfare and her safety. Her temporary living arrangement with Muriel was set up legally by the end of that day.

"What do you mean, 'Safety?' Is Shondra in some kind of danger?" I asked Jay. We were sitting in a little dockside restaurant in Portland, eating fried clams and drinking beer; that is, Jay was drinking beer, and I was having an iced tea.

"Look, Brandi. I don't want to put you into a difficult position. The less you know that isn't necessary to your relationship with Shondra, the better for now. She most needs a friend, and you can be that without all the baggage. Brian and I will handle that part. Believe me, if there is something you should know, for her sake or for your own, he or I will tell you."

"You're making this sound mysterious, mysterious and unsavory."

"It really isn't quite either. But it's serious and unpleasant. All you need to know to be helpful to Shondra is that her mother is a drug addict who has been in and out of rehab and probably won't live a whole lot longer. Her stepfather seems to be a ne'er-do-well."

"So there's no support for her there, I take it. Are they a threat to her?"

"The mother is a sad case. She is quite ill from drug abuse and its ramifications. The stepfather seems to do her bidding. He gets the drugs for her, and he seems to keep Shondra on edge. He's the mother's enabler."

"Is he the father of the baby? Did he rape Shondra?"

"We don't know yet. Look, Brandi. Brian and I are working on this. If there's anything you should know, he certainly will tell you. I feel more comfortable if he does the talking with you. I'm not trying to blow you off. I really think you have enough to do and to think about without taking on the legal battle for Shondra. Let us do that. Okay?"

"Okay, as long as you promise you'll tell me if there's something I should know –you or Brian."

"I promise, Brandi." Jay flashed me one of his incredible smiles.

The next morning before I saw Lindsay, I called Muriel. I wanted to visit with Shondra that evening.

"That's a great idea, Brandi. Why don't you come for dinner; say sevenish. And bring Jay with you."

"How do you know about Jay?"

"We talked before he and Brian set up the foster care arrangements. Then Jay came out here so I could sign the papers…"

"He was out there? You met him? Nobody told me."

"Jay brought out the paperwork for me, so of course I met him. Nobody told you because it's only been a few days, and we've all been busy– you, too, dear."

"But I just saw Jay last night, and he didn't say a word about meeting you."

"Maybe he had other things to talk about with you, Brandi. By the way, he seems like a very nice young man. So you went out with him last night? Where did you go?"

"You're deliberately changing the subject, Mure," I said. "We went to the Dry Dock. I don't even know how Shondra is doing. Is she happier now being with you?"

"Well, that's nice you and Jay went to the Dry Dock. I've always liked that place; it's very Old Portland. When you and Jay come over tonight, you can see for yourself how Shondra is. I really have to go now, dear. I have to drive Shondra to swimming. I'll see you soon; I love you."

"Love you, too." I barely got the words out before Mure ended the call. I wanted to be upset with her, but I smiled inside instead.

Chapter Eleven

Tutoring and Other Activities

1

Lindsay didn't display much enthusiasm when she came to my office, but now, at least, she accepted the routine of writing during each meeting. This time she arrived wearing a short denim skirt and a tight, dark blue tank top. Protruding from her blue flip-flops were bright blue toenails. Her fingernails were the same color, and the index fingernails each had a silver star over the polish. Her hair was done into two braids and secured at the ends with blue elastics.

As she took a seat, she said, "Hi. I have something to write about today."

"Hi, Lindsay. Oh, that's good. Would you like to chat first, or do you want to start writing?"

"We could talk, but I better write first, or I might not want to if I wait," she said.

"All right. That's fine." I gave her some paper, and she produced a pen from her blue book bag. Then she started writing.

When Lindsay finished her essay, she said she had to leave. "I don't have time to talk right now. I have an appointment. So is it okay if we talk next time?"

"We'll talk about your writing next time, then. Don't make any appointments right after our session so we will have enough time."

"Okay, 'Bye."

"'Bye, Lindsay. Have a nice day." I watched her leave, and then I picked up the paper she had dropped on my desk:

I met a guy at the basketball scrimmage I went to the other day. His name is Randy. Hes not real good-looking, but hes not bad. His hair is red, and he has blue eyes. Hes really really tall – like maybe going on 7 feet. I

48

never knew a guy so tall before. Maybe that's why he's so good playing basketball. Anyway, he asked me to wait while he showered after the scrimmage. I wasn't going to but he said then he would take me for a ride in his new Jeep. So I said ok. We went to the Tasty Freeze and got sundaes. I didnt finish mine but he ate his and then the rest of mine too. Mostly he just talked about his Jeep. Boy is he in love with that car. It's ok but its just a car. But he asked me to go to Portland with him tomorrow night to some movie or something. Probly it wont be bars. He said he doesn't drink cuz he an athlete. Whatever.

How interesting, I thought. Lindsay and Randy are going out together. I wondered what to make of the two of them together. I guessed I would find out, eventually.

2

Because I got overly busy when I first got involved with Shondra and because of Randy's basketball practice schedule, my tutorial meeting with Randy was set for soon after Lindsay's meeting. I just had time to review the things I wanted to talk with Randy about, when he appeared at the doorway. I smiled and started to greet him, but he cut me off.

"Hey, I just saw Lindsay outside the building. She said she was coming from your office. You tutor her, too?"

"Hi, Randy. Yes, that's right. Lindsay is one of my students, too. I understand you are dating. That's nice," I said.

"Did she say that?" He smiled. "Yeah; I guess we are. It's cool with you? We can see each other even if we're both getting tutored by you? I thought maybe it wasn't allowed or something."

"Oh, no; it's perfectly fine. Our writing tutorials are totally separate from your social life."

"Okay; great. I'm all set then. I was going to write about my Jeep, but maybe I'll write about Lindsay first."

"Why don't you write about your car today and maybe Lindsay next time," I said. "But let's look at your paper from last time first. I just want to go over a couple of grammatical rules."

"Okay." Randy sat down at the table. I went over a few writing tips with him, and then he started riffling in his pack. "I got a notebook like you suggested, and I got a bunch of pencils so I'd have plenty of sharp points. I got a pen, too, just in case I get good enough that I don't make a hundred mistakes every line. Ha, ha." He also pulled out what looked like some magazine pages and said, "I brought some stuff about the Jeep Wrangler so I could write about it better. Is that okay?"

"Sure it is," I said. "Just take the information and put it in your own words. You can add personal things, too."

"Okay."

Once he was writing, I took some notes on Lindsay's two recent papers. I wanted to make sure we talked about them at the next meeting. I really wanted her to do rewrites, as well. That would be an issue for her, I was pretty sure, but I'd figure out something by her next visit.

Randy wrote for over half an hour without stopping. Finally, he put his pencil down and looked up at me. "Wow! I never wrote that much at one time before. My hand is sore. That's something new. My legs get tired after games sometimes, but I never had a hand hurt before."

"Well, thank you for writing so much. I'll read it, and we can talk about it next time."

"Great. I love to talk about my Jeep almost as much as I love to drive it." After ripping out the pages and handing them to me, he put his notebook and the pencils back into his pack. "Gotta run. I don't want to be late for practice. We have to do extra laps if we're late. See you, Miss Buckman."

"See you, Randy."

I decided to get a salad at the Pit and read Randy's essay at the same time. It was sunny and a little breezy outside. It felt good to get some fresh air, so I took my time both walking to the Pit and returning. I decided to sit on a bench outside Irwin Tower while I ate my salad and read Randy's paper:

Jeep Wrangler Unlimited

The Jeep Wrangler Unlimited is the four wheeler of the year every year. It's a tough authentic legend born to rule the trails and the urban jungle. The Jeep Wrangler is made to make every day behind the wheel, a thrilling experience.

It has embroidered cloth seats and embroidered leather trim. It has 18 inch wheels that are silver sparkled and a electric rearview mirror with LED lights.

It has premium tire pressure monitoring and a electronic deep information center.

The Jeep Wrangler comes in 9 colors. Black, White, Commando Green, Deep Cherry Red Crystal Pearl, Silver, Blue Pearl, Dune, Rock Lobster, and Rugged Brown. I thought it would be cool to get the Rock Lobster cuz I live in Maine. But its pretty orange and my dad said it would look awful in no time. So I decided to get either the Dune or the Deep Cherry red Crystal Pearl. After I saw both Jeeps, I decided the Dune looked more Macho so I got that.

The inside is rugged and refined. The seat says Sahara on the top. That's why I decided the Dune color is better. Its more like the Dessert.

There's improved Noise, Vibration, and Horse-power (NWH). The front seats are heated. It has illuminated cup holders. That's good cuz I like to get a coffee when I drive at night and its easy to find the cup holder to put the cup back in. There is lighting near the floor so if you drop something you can find it okay.

The instrument panel has Technical aviation appearance. There are drain plugs on the floor so I can wash it when it gets dirty. My friends get in with dirty shoes and don't clean them off first. So its ok cuz I can hose the floor down after we get done driving around.

The Jeep Wrangler has auxiliary Juice too. That means theres an extra 115 volt outlet and 3 plugs to put in a GPS, a laptop if I want to, my battery charger, and my IPad. Im all set for anything! Oh, it also has a leather steering wheel which is nice for my hands and automatic speed control that is good on the Turnpike so I don't speed.

I hope I am not boring you but I love to talk about my Jeep Wrangler. And Im here at school partly because of it. So far I'm glad I came and Im very glad I got my Jeep Wrangler Unlimited Sahara.

Randy

When I finished reading, I decided I knew far more about the Jeep Wrangler Unlimited than I ever wished to know. But I was happy that something besides basketball motivated Randy to write. There was plenty to work on in the essay, and I was confident we could work together to improve his skills.

Chapter Twelve

Shondra Again

1

Jay and I pulled into Mure's driveway at the same time as Brian. We got out of the cars together. Brian came around to me, planting a kiss on my forehead. "Hi, Honey, Jay. I meant to be here before you two, but I got delayed at the office. It's been a bit hectic these last few days. But I think that a cold drink, some of Muriel's food, and a boat ride will put me—all of us—in a place we want to be."

Mure came out onto the deck, with Shondra behind her. They both waved, and Mure called, "Hello, everyone. You're just in time for a cool drink before dinner. I'm grilling chicken, and it's almost done. Shondra made potato salad, and we put together a salad from the garden, with a little help from the farmers' market."

The three of us headed to the deck. Jay and I sat down in Adirondack chairs, but Brian stood. "I am going to take a quick shower before I sit. Relax, and have something to drink."

"Here, Shondra, please take the tray and set it on that side table. Help yourself to iced tea, if you like. You've done enough, so sit down and relax. There's beer in the refrigerator, if you want one, Jay. If you want something stronger, Brandi can show you where things are. I want to tell Brian something; then I'll be back. I'll try to hurry him along, too, so we can eat. I'm sure everyone's as hungry as I am."

I looked out over the lake while I was sipping my wine. I truly loved this place. It brought back so many memories of my troubled time, when Mure took me in and saved me from the horrible path I was on. Once I finished law school, I thought, I could be very happy living here—or perhaps near here, now that Mure and Brian were getting married. I was sure they'd rather not have me under foot all the time.

"…and you seem to be adjusting well with Muriel, too." I

heard the end of what Jay was saying to Shondra.

"Oh, yes. She is such a nice lady. She takes me to the college every morning and picks me up in the afternoon. We've been doing stuff together, too. We even picked strawberries on the way home. She showed me how to clean and prepare them. Then she showed me how to make shortcake for tonight's strawberry shortcake. I've never cooked anything before, and I made two things today!"

"Wow! That's so fine, Shondra. I take it swimming practice is going well?"

"Yeah. I'm going to be on the relay team for the next meet. Coach said I am a good starter; either I'll do that or be the second person to swim. I'm practicing both."

I wondered if her pregnancy had anything to do with what Coach Mike would have her swim, but I didn't say anything. I knew Mike had been informed and that he would handle the situation well.

Just then Muriel came out onto the deck, with Brian trailing behind her, a beer in his hand. "Okay, sorry about the delay," he said. "Let's eat.

2

The evening had been a pleasant break from my tutorials, my writing, and my concerns about Shondra. When Jay and I returned to campus, we sat in the car in front of the house. I wanted to ask him more about the case with Shondra, but I knew he'd rather that Brian talked to me, instead, so I didn't say anything. Instead, I commented that the evening had been relaxing and a nice break.

"You're being charitable, Brandi. Having that girl at her house is a real imposition for Muriel, and for Brian, too, for that matter."

"What do you mean?" I asked. "Muriel seems to enjoy her. It's not awfully dissimilar to what she did when I was in trouble.

Plus you seemed to enjoy talking to Shondra. You certainly drew her out."

"It's part of my job to draw out people and get them to like and trust me. But do not confuse your past situation with Shondra's. She isn't anything like you. I have a suspicion about Shondra: that girl is a manipulator, and she's exactly where she wants to be."

"What are you talking about?" I must have raised my voice, because Jay put his hands out and took mine.

"I'm sorry, Brandi. I shouldn't have said that. I shouldn't have said anything. I want to help the situation as much as the rest of you. I especially want to assist Brian however I can. He's in charge. And you all are so welcoming and generous."

"Then, what's wrong, Jay?"

"I don't have good vibes about Shondra. I'm finding it hard to like her. Maybe I'm wrong, and everything will turn out fine. I hope so. Let's just leave it at that for now. Okay?"

"Okay."

Jay put his arms around me and drew me to him. I settled against his chest. Then he lifted my chin and kissed me, a long, full kiss that left me breathless. "I'd rather think about you," he whispered. Then he tucked my head between his shoulder and his chest. I could smell the residue of his cologne on his shirt, even after a long day. I closed my eyes and sighed, feeling pretty much at peace.

3

It was several days before I saw Brian alone. He came to the college for something and dropped by my little office. I was surprised and happy to see him. He sat down at the table; I took a seat across from him.

"This is a cozy set-up you have here, young lady. I think you found where you belong."

"I'm so glad you stopped by. I haven't seen a lot of you,

only at Mure's the other day. I do love it here. I'm very busy, but I like working with the students I'm tutoring. And, of course, I love having a writing project. The only thing that's a little disturbing is the Shondra situation."

"That's partly why I stopped by," Brian said. I frowned. "Oh, I wanted to see you and see where you work, too. You are going to be my real stepdaughter soon." He laughed. "I'm very proud of that, Brandi. You're so special to me, in case you didn't know."

I felt tears come into my eyes. I really loved this chubby man. "You are just as special to me, Brian. You know that I love you—almost as much as I love Mure."

"Ah, yes; I'm destined to remain second fiddle. But that's all right. She had first dibs on you."

"Always the jokester. But at least you stopped the waterworks from coming."

"Well, my girl. Now that we will be a real family, I think that you understand, under my joking, I have serious fatherly feelings for you."

"I know. I do, too. Daughterly feelings, that is."

"Which brings me to something I wanted to say…"

"Oh, I knew you had another motive for this visit," I said.

"Well, Jay mentioned to me that you asked about Shondra's circumstances. He also said he indicated that he doesn't quite trust her; he's sorry he said that, but there it is. I don't want you to get yourself overly concerned here. I am handling it, and I have Jay's very competent assistance. But I think you deserve to know a few things, to keep it all in perspective. Muriel agrees."

"Does she know everything?"

"Everything Jay and I do. It's her business to know. She is Shondra's legal guardian, at least for the time being. We decided there are some things you should know, without overburdening you."

"You make it all sound so sleazy."

"I'll start at the beginning. First, Shondra isn't fourteen; she's almost seventeen. Second, her stepfather is her biological uncle, and I think she knows that. Third, he did not throw her out of the house. In fact, he wanted her to stay. She left of her own volition. We don't know the whole story yet, but we think his questionable actions have to do with the mother only, not with Shondra. And it might even be that he was trying to protect her from the mother."

"I thought her mother was so far gone in her addiction that she may not live a lot longer," I said.

"That appears to be true. But in her more lucid times, apparently she could become violent, both to Shondra and to the uncle."

"Good grief," I said. "What more should I know?"

I looked at Brian and then turned my head toward the window. I couldn't help thinking I had started this whole thing by taking Shondra to Muriel in the first place.

"Brandi!" Brian's raised voice caused me to turn to him in alarm. "I know what you are thinking, and it's not true. You did nothing to cause any harm. You acted in a kind and generous manner, nothing less than I would have expected from you. At the very most, your actions simply brought a troubling situation to the attention of people who can address it. Do you understand me?"

"Yes, I guess so."

"Good. Now there is something I want you to do. I want you to treat Shondra just as you have. That may be harder now; that's one reason I didn't want to tell you. But nothing will be accomplished by ostracizing her, either to her face or even in your mind. There are reasons she is acting as she is, and we will find out. I hope we can succeed in helping her, too. I need you to help me here. Can you do that for me?"

"It will be hard, but I will make sure I do it—for you, Brian, not for her."

"That's all I ask. Now I better get to work. If you have any concerns, call me anytime, honey. I don't want you worrying alone." Brian hugged me, and I hugged him back hard, not wanting to let him go.

Chapter Thirteen

A Halcyon Time

1

"I want to take you out on a date by ourselves and with no concerns about anybody's issues," Jay had said to me several days before.

So here we were on a Saturday night, walking around Old Orchard Beach, eating junk food and joking about the wonderful tackiness of the place. I wanted onion rings, so we got those. They were greasy and delicious. Next, Jay wanted Bill's pizza. As we gobbled the slices, he got cheese and sauce all over his hands, and I dribbled sauce down my chin. Jay used a napkin to wipe my chin, and then he kissed my lips, licking them. I jumped back.

He laughed. "Relax, girl. I'm just getting the sauce off your mouth. You look like a clown."

"Okay, smart guy. I dropped a piece of pepperoni on my toe. Why don't you clean that off, too? Ha!" I punched him on the arm and took off at a fast shuffle through the crowd.

"You don't get away that easily," he said when he caught up to me. "Hold up your foot. I'm not going to lick it, but I'm going to wipe that embarrassing mess off you. I don't want folks to see me in public with a girl who has pepperoni and sauce on her toes; it clashes with her pink nail polish." As he grabbed my leg, I leaned on his other arm, and he actually wiped off my toes and my whole foot, not with his tongue, though. He used a napkin.

Most of the evening went that way. We laughed our way through ice cream on a stick, which both of us dripped all over our hands and the sidewalk. We gargled our tart-tasting, fresh lemonades, pretending we were using mouthwash. After topping off the meal with vinegary French fries, we called a halt to eating and headed to the rides.

"I want to go on the merry-go-round," I said.

"That's such a baby ride. I'm not going on it unless you go on the Cobra after that," Jay said.

"What if I barf?"

"Well, do it on yourself, not on me. I challenge you."

"Okay, you're on," I said, as I ran toward the beautiful carousel. It had just stopped, so I signaled to the attendant that Jay had my ticket, and I rushed to a stately golden horse before anyone else could claim it. Jay gave the man our tickets and picked the black and white creature next to mine.

"You won't be able to grab for the brass ring if you sit there," I told him.

"I don't need any brass ring," he said. "I've got better than that right here." He leered at me and crossed his eyes. Laughing so hard, I almost fell off my horse, just as it started moving.

Of course, I missed the brass ring every time I tried, and Jay made weird sounds when I complained. The ride was over too quickly, and, as we headed away from the carousel, he said, "Okay, now the Cobra."

"Ugh," I said.

"A promise is a promise. You have to keep it."

"Or what"

"Or I'll make a scene right here."

"You wouldn't dare. You are too professional and mature to do that."

"Watch me." Suddenly, Jay stooped down, grabbed my skirt and tugged. "No, no, Leslie, you can't leave me. And for that spoiled Albert Cranberry? I can't let you go. I still owe $300 on your ring." As if his actions weren't bad enough, he was practically shouting. People were staring, and a few had started to gather around.

"Stop it," I hissed.

"Only if you come quietly, Leslie—we can make up on the Cobra." His eyes glittered, and I couldn't help but laugh.

"All right, Vernie. But you have to do the laundry for the next week."

"Anything for you, Leslie."

59

We got to the Cobra line just as it was moving, thank goodness. I didn't want to have to stand around with all those gawkers any longer. We made it onto the platform and got the last empty car. I looked at Jay and said, "If I do barf, it will be red and pink and brown, and I'm going to do it all over that nice blue shirt and those beautifully creased pants."

"I'll take my chances."

The ride was as crazy and loud as I remembered it from a few years ago, but I didn't get sick. In fact, I didn't even feel sick. For the first time in my life, I really enjoyed the Cobra.

2

Jay put the top down on his car for the drive back to the college. He put some jazz in the CD player and drove one-handed, with his right hand holding my hand. The evening was still warm, and I put my head against the soft leather of the seat-back. I closed my eyes, but then I opened them so I could look up at the stars. We were far enough out into the country so that they shone brightly. The moon was a lovely crescent. When I saw a falling star, I said, "You have to make a wish on a falling star."

"Does it still count if I didn't actually see it?"

"Since you have to keep your eyes on the road, you get an exemption. So, yeah, it counts."

"Okay, I wish for …"

"No," I said and squeezed Jay's hand. "You mustn't say what you wish or it won't come true."

"Oh, I didn't know that."

"Didn't you ever wish on stars when you were a kid?'

"Yeah, but we always told each other what we wished for. Say, maybe that's why nothing I ever wished for came true." Jay looked at me and smirked.

"Oh, you are such a big tease. Well, I made my wish, and I hope it comes true. I'm not going to tell you, either. "

"Will you tell me if it comes true?"

I laughed. "You'll know if it comes true."

"Oh, that sounds pretty interesting. I can wait."

Jay parked the car by the side of the house and turned to me. "Do you think people watch us when we park here?"

"I think they are so used to college kids making out in cars in front of dorms and houses that they don't care," I said.

"If that's the case, then, I'm going to kiss you long and slow." Then Jay kissed me, and I was speechless. "Brandi, I had a great time with you tonight. I want to do this again soon. You are enchanting. And now I'm going to walk you to your door and walk away like a well-behaved gentleman."

I said nothing because that was the end of a perfect date with a perfect gentleman, and I was truly smitten.

3

For the next several days, I was on Cloud Nine. Jay was the first guy since Dean that I felt relaxed enough around to be myself, fool around, and not worry that I was being dishonest. When we talked about forever, I had told Dean he was my forever. He said he felt that way about me, too, but he said it didn't always work out that way. Boy, was he right, dammit. He said that, if something should happen to him, I shouldn't close myself off from people. He told me I should go out with lots of people and find someone to share things with.

For a long time, I did hide from life. Then I got myself into activities and accomplishments. I also started engaging people again. But I never really let myself get close to another guy. Jay's arrival in my life was beginning to change that.

After Dean died, I wrote to him all the time, using my grief like pages of anger. Finally, the grief and the anger mellowed, but I kept writing, and I still was writing that summer.

I wrote to him, as well as about him. I still blamed him for dying on me, but I had learned to live with the loss. Part of me left with him, but my "Dean" writing kept him close, and kept me strong.

After that wonderful evening with Jay, I turned to my journals –
there were many now, not just "a journal" —to help me understand
my feelings about Jay and how they fit into the scope of my
forever love of Dean. I found a poem I'd written before I came
back for the summer. It seemed to contain the essence of...of
something that would help me deal with my conflicted desires. I
desired to keep Dean and his love pure, but I also desired to build
something with Jay. When I wrote the poem, I hadn't met Jay, but
something in it hinted at his arrival in my life:

> Future
> All the dreams concocted in the lazy days,
> Celebrated as our defining halcyon days,
> Scattered slowly, inevitably becoming cloud memories,
> Misting into wisps of a new reality.

I copied the poem to a fresh page of my current journal and
added my present thoughts:

> Dean, I can't let you go away. I won't let that
> happen. But, is it possible that you remain, even as Jay
> emerges from those memories as another beginning? Can I
> keep you close, and maybe even bring you closer, as I let
> Jay become a serious part of my life? For the first time
> since your death, I think I want to start a relationship. I
> know you would want me to; I have to discover if Jay is
> worthy to follow in your path. Is he as genuine as you
> were?

Chapter Fourteen

Company of Three

1

Walking across campus to my office, I saw Chriz coming toward me. He smiled and waved, and I called, "Hi, Chriz."

"Hello, Brandi. How are you today?"

"I'm just fine, thank you. Where are you headed?"

"I'm going to take a coffee break before I go back to my studies. Would you like to have a coffee or a tea with me? If that is proper, of course, for a professor and a student."

"I'm not a professor, Chriz. I'm just your tutor. And I'm really a student, too. Sure, I'd like an iced tea. It will be a nice stop."

We walked over to the Pit, bought our drinks and took them to a table on the deck. "Thank you for paying for my tea, Chriz. It'll be my treat next time," I said.

"In my upbringing, the man always pays for the lady."

"Well, we'll see. How are things going on campus? Have you met many people? I know there are not a whole lot of students here, but there still are quite a few."

"I have met my professors, of course, and the students in my classes. Everyone is pleasant. But I study most of the time, so I have not gone out socially much. I try to sit with different people at dinner, and I have met more students that way."

"I hope you don't study all the time. There are other things to do here."

"I take a walk every evening, usually after I have finished studying. I also attend the films that are shown in the college theater. They are very good, and they are helping me improve my American English, I think."

"I don't know how much you've improved," I said, "but your English is excellent."

"I am trying to understand slang and American humor. I want to understand casual talk and not speak only formal English."

"Well, that's a good way to go about it, I guess. You probably can learn a lot from the dialogue in movies. I've never thought about it myself."

Chriz looked at me and laughed. "I do not think there would be any reason for you to study film dialogue. You are an American and speak American English."

"Yeah, you're right." I smiled and said, "Well, I'd better get going and get some work done before it's afternoon. Thank you for the tea."

As I got up, Chriz rose from his chair, too, and said, "Thank you for sharing your drink break with me. May we do this again?"

"Only if you let me pay next time. Deal?"

"All right; it will be our deal," he said.

"So long," I said, and I waved goodbye.

2

The next time I saw Chriz was at our tutorial session. After we talked about the comments I had made on his last paper, we talked briefly about American English and British English. I assured him that his British English was not a detriment; I thought he spoke English beautifully.

"Do you think I should not study casual American speech in films, then?" he asked.

"Oh, no," I said. "I think that's a great idea. Just don't worry about how you sound. The speech you hear in films, and when you talk to people anywhere on campus, will start to rub off on you."

"Rub off?" he asked and frowned.

I laughed. "See, that's what I mean. You pick things up just chatting with people. 'Rub off' means like you will hear different things people say, and then you will start to use those phrases yourself. They will become a part of your speech; they will 'rub off' on you."

"Oh, I think I see. Nothing actually rubs off. I just start to use these sayings in my own talking."

"Yes, that's right."

We stopped chatting then, and Chriz settled into writing his essay. After he finished, we said goodbye, and he left my office. A short time later, I read his paper:

> I have met some other students. I went to a party that the Sciences Department held for all the summer students taking maths or science. I am taking both maths and chemistry, so I attended. The reception, as it was called, was on the lawn near the shore of the lake. I was standing by a swing with many people in it. The swing was like ones we have in my country but the people here call it a hammick (I do not know if you spell it like that but I will look for it in my Webster's New Dictionary). Okay it is hammock. I almost spelled it right and I found it in the Dictionary. Well, I looked at the faces of the people in it. Most of them got up and left to get some food but I looked down and saw a girl. She was very pretty in the American way. By that I mean she had long blond hair and blue eyes and was not wearing a lot of clothes. Her legs and arms were exposed and they had freckles on them. I was embarrassed (I did not have to look for that word in the Dictionary. I learned that in high school from so many girls wearing so little clothes. People, boys, told me I looked embarrassed and I had to find out what the word meant. I still get embarrassed). She looked at me. I tried not to be embarrassed and I smiled. I guess that was the right thing to do because she smiled back and said hi and told me her name was Lindsay. I told her mine and then she asked me if I wanted to get something to drink and some food. I said yes. She got meats in buns but I ate the salad and some vegetables that were placed around a large plate. We talked

about what we were doing at school until a very tall man with reddish colored hair came up to us. Lindsay introduced him to me. His name is Randy. She told him my name, and we shook hands. Then Randy said he had to go and would Lindsay go with him. She said yes, so they said goodbye to me and left the party. I stayed many minutes longer; I talked to a few students from my maths class. Then I said goodbye and went to my room to study for a maths quiz. I see Lindsay sometimes on the campus.
Respectfully, Chriz

3

Well, I thought, after I read Chriz's essay, the plot was thickening, as a mystery writer might say. But this wasn't a mystery; it was my recollection of that summer. Anyway, now Lindsay, Randy and Chriz all knew each other, and I was tutoring the three of them. I wondered what that might mean, if anything.

I decided to drop by the pool and see how things were going there. At the first meet, the team had not won, but they performed decently. I was sure Mike was working on their individual strengths and moving them around if he thought someone would do better in a different position.

I was curious about Shondra. I hadn't seen her since Brian and I talked about her. I tried to put her out of mind, the way Brian had asked me to do. And it hadn't been that hard, what with Jay taking up most of my thoughts—him and Dean.

The pool area was noisy. Some of the kids were swimming, some running around (so much for those signs on the walls saying, "No running in pool area"). A small group seemed to be doing some kind of calisthenics off to one side of the room. Mike was talking to a huddle of boys near the bleachers.

Shondra was in the pool, doing laps, it looked to me. She had a strong, steady stroke and moved through the water gracefully. There were girls in the lanes on either side of her; one was ahead of Shondra by about a body length, and the other one was behind the same distance. I guessed they were pacing each other.

I sat down on the bleachers, and soon Mike came over and sat down next to me. "Hey, Brandi. Haven't seen you lately. You must be really busy. How's everything going?"

"Hi, Mike. Everything's going well. Yeah, I am pretty busy. My tutorial students are writing a lot now, and they're doing nicely. I've been writing some myself, and I guess time just gets away from me."

"Some of that time gets taken up with Jay, I understand."

"How do you know that?" I asked.

"Shondra keeps me informed. She says you've been to your mother's house with him."

"Oh. Well, yeah, she's right, I guess. We see each other about the program, and we've been out a couple of times."

"That's great. It's none of my business, of course, but Jay seems like a nice guy. So that's good."

"Good, yes. Speaking of good, it looks to me like Shondra is a good swimmer."

Mike looked at the pool, where the three girls were still swimming in their lanes. "Yes, she is good. She's here every morning; hasn't missed one practice. That's at least partly because of Muriel, your mother. I met her, too. Shondra wanted us to meet. She's a super lady."

"She is. Is Shondra's condition going to be a factor for the team? When she starts to show, what's going to happen?"

"I'm staying completely out of it. If it becomes an issue, or when it does, then Shondra or Muriel will deal with it. Muriel told me they would handle it. Between you and me, I'm relieved. I don't want to try to figure that one out."

"Oh," I said. I was a little surprised that Muriel had taken charge of working out the swimming and the pregnancy thing. On second thought, I guess I wasn't surprised. She always seemed to decide the most sensible things to do in any situation. "But what if the kids start talking when she starts showing? Won't that be a problem?"

"I don't know. But Muriel said to let it ride, unless and until there is something to worry about. Then call her, and the three of us will figure it out."

"The three of us?" I was confused; did Mike mean I would have to get involved then?

"Muriel, Shondra and me," he said. "So far, though, nothing's happened. And Shondra is good enough that no one wants to lose her on the team. So, even if anybody has any suspicion, nobody has said anything."

"So Shondra is a good team member, I take it."

"She's great, Brandi. She is competitive and also cares about the team. She does whatever I suggest without complaining. I can't say that about all the kids. She's not the best swimmer, but she's one of the best girls here."

Shondra was still swimming laps when I realized I needed to get back to my office. I waved in her direction, said, "'Bye," to Mike and went outside into the hot sun.

I wondered what was going on about Shondra's pregnancy. Mure was going to "handle it," Mike said. What was that supposed to mean? Was she going to have an abortion? Who was the father, anyway? I wanted to know exactly what this was all about, and everyone seemed to be pretending there wasn't anything to think about. I determined to find out before too long.

Chapter Fifteen

Expectations

1

Randy came into the office and greeted me with a big smile. "Hi, Ms. Brandi."

"Hi, yourself. You look really happy about something," I said.

"I had a great practice, yeah. I always thought I was the best player. Coach never acted that way, though. Today he said I'm really doing terrific. So I stopped at the Pit on the way over and got a big slush. I don't usually drink that stuff; it's not good for my regimen. But it was special to get Coach's praise. I got one for you, too. Here," he said, handing me a large paper cup of crushed ice and purple liquid.

"Thanks for the slush. That's wonderful about Coach, Randy. I'm glad he appreciates you. I know you care a lot about basketball."

"I sure do. It's the only thing that really matters to me. Everything else I do is because of the game."

"That's fine. Just don't forget to keep studying. You can't play basketball if your grades aren't good enough."

"Oh, I know that," Randy said. "The second thing I do after basketball is study. I wouldn't have my Jeep, either, without staying in school. And you know how much I love my Jeep. I almost bored you to death making you read all about it. I'm having a little problem, but I plan to solve it today. Maybe I'll write about it so I get my head in gear. Is it okay if I write about something personal? Nobody's going to see it except you, right?"

"That's right. Unless you write about causing physical harm to someone or about selling drugs, I will not divulge a word. That's our privacy policy."

"Good." Randy laughed. "I'm not going to hurt anybody.

I'd never do that. It'd only happen if I accidently did it on the ball court. Or maybe if somebody was trying to kill a friend or a little kid or something. I'd try to save them. But I'd never purposely hurt another person. And I don't do drugs or alcohol. It takes away my edge in the game."

"I'm sure you wouldn't deliberately hurt someone. You seem too happy and friendly. I don't think I've heard an unkind word from you," I said.

"I like everybody. And as long as I can play basketball, I'll do anything anybody wants. I'm so happy, even in a pick-up game. But being on a good team is the best thing." Randy grinned at me and ducked his head. "Okay, then. I'm going to start my paper now. I want to get back to the gym pretty quick."

2

Later, I read Randy's essay, hoping he hadn't been too personal. There were some things I really would rather not know about him and Lindsay:

> I love it here. I love the basketball team and the coach. I don't mind my classes cuz they are nessasery to take so I can play ball. I like my room and my roommate Barry. He doesn't play basketball, but he is a nice guy to share a room with. He is easygoing like me. Everything at the college is cool. There is just one thing that isn't quite right. Acktually its not a thing. It's a girl. Shes real nice and cute and everything but she wants me to spend all my time with her. And I cant do that. I like her fine but I'm to busy to spend all the time I'm not on the ball court with her. She doesn't understand how important it is to me. I know I have to study a lot to get good enough grades. So I need to study every night and even some of the weekends. Shes not like you, you understand that studying is nessasery if I want to stay here and be on the team. You even remind me to study.

She thinks its stupid to study so much. Those were her words the other night. Its stupid to study so much. Boy if I didn't have to study I wouldn't but Im not like those really smart guys who don't have to study much and get good grades. Lindsay Woops, I wasn't going to say her name but you know it anyway cuz you know weve been going out. Lindsay is fun to go out with but just not every night. I think I can handle once a week and once on the weekend if I really hit the books the rest of the time. I wanna be able to drive my Jeep a little bit too. I think I will tell her what I think when I see her. I told her I couldn't see her tonight. I have a quiz tomorrow in my math class and I really have to study more for it. Its hard. I'll tell her that I can see her tomorrow and then we'll go for a ride and I can tell her then. She likes to ride in my Jeep. She likes it so much she keeps bugging me to let her drive it. So far I haven't let any one drive it except my dad of course. He bought it so he can drive it. But hes not at school so now Im the only one driving it. I want to keep it that way. I never spent much time with girls in high school. I was too busy playing basketball and a little football and a little baseball before I stopped to spend all my time on basketball. I was popular though. I went to the proms and the big school parties. If I didn't ask some girl then some girl asked me so I went to all those. But I didn't have a girlfriend. No time for that. This thing with Lindsay is new to me. Now I know why guys say girls are a problem. I don't think they meant it in the same way I do. But it's still a problem. Well I think I decided what to do to fix it. Ill tell Lindsay we can go out once during the week and once on the weekend as long as theres still enough time for practice, games and studying. Wish me luck Ms. Brandi. Wish I was going out with a girl as smart at you who knows you have to study a lot to keep playing ball.

I had thought that Lindsay might be a high-maintenance

type of girl. It looked like Randy had his hands full with her. I hoped he'd be able to extricate himself from her demands easily.

3

The cheering was raucous. It didn't seem to emanate from any particular side, or from winning or losing teams. Everyone was full of energy. The swimming meet seemed to be an excuse for clapping, whistles and cheers.

Jay and I were sitting in the bleachers next to Muriel. "I don't know much of anything about competition swimming, only what I've seen of the Olympics on TV," I said.

"There isn't a lot you need to know about rules. Just watch, and you'll pretty much figure out what's going on," said Jay. "The beauty is that it's easy to follow. What you see is pretty much what you get."

"I don't know about the rules," Muriel said. "I probably know even less than you, Brandi. But I do know it's a good, wholesome sport. Shondra has really taken to the team effort. She thinks the world of Mike, and she likes the girls on the team, too."

"So Shondra is getting along all right? "

"She's doing very well. Her whole attitude has changed since she moved in and got settled. Besides loving swimming, she is eager to help me, especially in the kitchen and in the garden."

"Well, that's good," I said and looked at Jay. He smiled but didn't say anything. "What?" I asked.

"Nothing."

I started to challenge him to tell me what he meant, but then a loud roar went up from both the teams and the spectators. The meet was over. As we walked toward Mike and the kids, Muriel said, "Don't forget the picnic this weekend. If you want to stay overnight, your room is waiting for you, Brandi. Jay, you can bunk on the sleeping porch."

"We'll be there," I said.

We stood near the team. Mike was in their midst, giving

and receiving high-fives from all the kids. Even those who didn't place in an event were whooping and laughing. Probably they were excited just to be a part of a school team, even a summer one.

I heard Mike say, "I'm proud of all of you. Everybody looked good out there. We got a few first finishes, and we came in fourth overall, out of ten teams. That's terrific sportsmanship. It means all of you tried your best. That's what really counts. Now all of you hit the showers. Then we'll take the van and head to the Dairy Delight."

A louder cheer went up from the kids. Then they dashed toward the locker room to shower and dress. Mike came over to us. "That was a great effort by those kids. I think they really are working well together. Do you want to go to the D.D. with us? I'll spring for the sundaes."

I started to say yes, just as Jay spoke over me. "Thanks for asking us, Mike. But we had prior plans. Maybe we can go with you next time. Tell the kids we think they did a great job, too. Right, Brandi?"

"Oh, yes, of course," I said. "Thanks, Mike. Maybe I'll see you tomorrow."

We said goodbye to Muriel. Heading toward Jay's car, I wondered what this was all about. We didn't have any prior plans that I knew of. I also had wanted to congratulate Shondra and her relay teammates; they almost won their heat. Since I hadn't seen much of her lately, I was thinking that this was a good time to catch up with her.

Once inside the car, I asked Jay, "Why the big rush out? I didn't think we had any plans. It might have been fun to go with the team. They were in such high spirits. I would have liked to congratulate Shondra, too."

"That's exactly why I didn't want to go out with them."

"What do you mean? You didn't want me to talk to Shondra?"

"That, too. I knew, if you did, she'd monopolize you. And I'd like to spend some quality time alone. We don't get enough of that."

73

"I thought we'd been doing a pretty good job of seeing each other regularly."

"We've had some nice times alone. But more often it's seeing each other for a quick talk before you have your students or I have to get to a meeting. Tonight I want to go somewhere where there aren't a bunch of loud teenagers constantly wanting our attention."

"Okay; I see your point. So where do you want to go?"

"I heard about a little place on the river near the locks. It has live music most nights. I thought we'd check it out, see what it's like. I'm hoping it's dark and relaxing. Want to try it?"

"I've heard of it. I think it's one of those places that caters to the summer residents and vacationers. They even bring in groups from away. It sounds good, so let's go." I said.

Chapter Sixteen

To Know You Better

1

The place was called Faro. It was located on the main road halfway between the lake and the river outlet. The nightclub was about a half-mile from the locks which serviced the Maine River Queen. The Queen was a tour boat that plied the waters from the lake along the river to the next lake in the chain.

Faro was small and dark inside. As our eyes adjusted, we looked around and saw an empty table on one side along the wall. We made our way to it and sat down just as a guy in a black tee and black jeans arrived. "Hi," he said. "You have just enough time to order before the next set. We don't serve during sets. It's distracting for everybody, the musicians and the folks listening. We are proud of the musicians we get here at Faro."

"That's fine with us. We'll have a carafe of the house red wine. That okay with you, Brandi?" When I nodded, Jay continued. "Could you bring a couple of appetizers—whatever you think is good—from the kitchen."

"Will do," the waiter said and left us.

Our chairs were side-by-side, facing the small stage at the front of the room. Jay moved his closer to mine, and our thighs touched. I looked at him and smiled, and he winked.

Although the room was small, it held about a dozen tables, with either two or four chairs at each table. A battery-operated candle sat in the middle of the table, and there were similar candles attached to the walls at intervals. I knew there was a fire code prohibiting the use of real candles in nightclubs. I guess the danger of fire, and the fires that had occurred at some nightclubs, had brought about stiffer codes. There had to be more than one exit and adequate access, including staff to help customers exit in an emergency. I thought the candles were a nice touch because they looked pretty real.

The waiter returned with our order just as the music started. On the stage were three people, two men and a woman. The guys were dressed in tight jeans and loose black shirts. The woman, not much more than a teen by the looks of her, wore a long black skirt and black peasant-style blouse with silver threading that glistened in the dim lighting.

They were good. The guitar player handled himself well. The bass player broke into an accomplished solo. But the standout of the group was the girl. Her voice was smoky and smooth, and very strong. She nearly moaned in places, then broke into a wail that put shivers down my spine. Hardly changing a beat, she shifted effortlessly into a steady, rhythmic croon. It wasn't a male kind of croon; it was all female, but it was intoxicating. Amazingly, I could understand the words, too. Most of the time in a bar, I found the words indecipherable, either because of the acoustics, the music itself, or the singer's voice.

Jay and I listened intently. After the first sip of wine, I didn't lift my glass again while the girl was singing. I forgot to sample the appetizers. I was entranced. The songs were unknown to me. Maybe they wrote them themselves. I didn't know, and I didn't care. I loved them.

Jay put his arm across the back of my chair and laid his hand on my shoulder. He started fiddling with the ends of my hair. I felt more shivers go down my spine. Then, with his other hand, he took mine and squeezed it. I heard one of those little bicycle bell trills again. I was getting a little distracted from the music. More accurately, the stirring music was becoming background to the stirring of my body.

2

The group finished their set and left the stage for a break. I let out a breathy sigh. "Wow," I whispered.

"Nice, huh?" Jay released my hand and turned my face

toward his. "This is the evening I wanted for us, Brandi. Now do you see why I wanted us to be alone?"

"I'm so glad you did. This is perfect. How did you find out about this place?"

"A client at the firm told me about it, so I checked it out."

"You mean you've been here before? So I'm not the first date you've brought here?"

"Hold on there, tiger. Don't claw me yet. I wanted to see if it was a place I'd want to bring you. So I came myself about a week ago. The group playing was different, but they were also good. I even talked to the manager. He says they use a musical booking group out of New York, so he gets high caliber groups. Some of them are famous."

"How can he afford to do that? I know this is a summer resort area, but still."

"It's like a lot of business conglomerates. The people who own this place own a stake in the Maine River Queen. They also are sole owners of the Lake Princess Resort and co-own a couple of other hotels and a restaurant or two. They don't make a profit on Faro. But the other businesses are quite profitable, so the owner takes a loss on Faro but gets to have the music and the groups he likes when he's here in the summer.

"Sounds like a sweet set-up," I said. "Is the owner from New York, too?"

"New York and Los Angeles and maybe other places, too. He's a wealthy man."

"Well, I'm glad he opened this place. I'd like us to come here often this summer."

"I hoped you'd feel that way. Let's come every week," Jay said. The group returned to the stage, and we settled back to enjoy another set.

3

Jay stopped the car about a block from my college house

and turned off the motor.

"Have you tired of being the evening attraction for my neighbors?" I asked.

"Actually, I get a kick out of thinking I may be giving some old guy a thrill. But, no, tonight I want to talk to you about something important. I also don't want to be interrupted by any of the girls from the house coming back and waving to us."

I laughed. "There are a couple of them who like to do that, don't they? Especially Marcia. But what's so important you want to talk about tonight?"

"Us."

"Us? I don't understand. I thought we were getting along fine. Are you breaking up with me? Was that lovely evening at Faro your gentle let-down?' I was flustered, and I could feel myself getting red in the face.

"Of course not, Brandi. Don't be silly. You know that I care about you. I really care about you. In fact, I'm falling in love with you."

I gasped.

"You must have had some idea how I feel."

"I know you like me a lot, and I know we have fun together. I hoped you cared more than that. But you haven't tried anything, and you haven't asked me to come to your apartment. I don't know much about your past love-life or what you've done. You could have been with tons of girls for all I know."

"I've been with some girls, but not tons. I've done things, but it's different with you."

"Why?"

"Because I am very serious about you, and I don't want to ruin our chances by going too fast or giving you the wrong signals."

"What do you mean by that?"

"You have a past, Brandi. That past includes a ghost."

"What are you talking about?" I nearly yelled. "Dean isn't a ghost. And what do you know, anyway?"

"I know most of the story about you and about Dean."

78

"We've never talked about it...Oh, Mure. Muriel talked to you. How dare she? How dare you?" I turned in my seat, as I felt hot tears start to fall.

"Muriel loves you more than anybody, even Brian. She would protect you from any hurt she could. And she saw me as a potential danger to your well-being. So she talked to me. She talked to me so long and so hard that, if I didn't really, really have deep feelings for you, I would have run away as fast as I could. That woman can be scary."

In spite of my tears, I started to laugh. It was a choky, kinda gurgled sound that came out.

"Are you all right?" Jay turned toward me and put his hand on my shoulder.

I left the hand there. It felt good. "I'm going to be just fine, thank you. I suddenly had an image of Muriel talking to you. You're right; Mure can be scary. You'd have to care about what she's saying to hang around listening. She can be tough when she wants to be. So, what was she telling you about me and Dean, and what did you say?"

"First, Muriel wanted to know my intentions..."

"Ha. That sounds like my mother. If that didn't send you packing, I guess you aren't just looking for a good time."

"Oh, I am looking for a good time, and I've found one. But let's stay on the topic here. Muriel wanted to be sure I was upstanding. Don't laugh, Brandi. I knew what she meant. She told me that you had suffered enough heartache for a lifetime. She also said she would give her life if she could prevent you from suffering again."

"Oh. What else did she tell you? All about Dean and what happened to us?"

"Only the sketchiest outline. She mentioned a little about your past and her and Brian's involvement in helping you. She also said Dean and you had a once-in-a-lifetime relationship and that he died a tragic death."

"That's all she said?"

"She gave me a few details, but only enough that I could

see it was serious and she was serious for a good reason. She said she'd be around to watch what went on and to help me if I was sincere."

"Wow. She said that? She must think a lot of you or she wouldn't have said she'd help you."

"She didn't tell me everything about you. She said that would have to come from you, and it wouldn't happen until you trusted me completely. But I did tell her most everything about me, more than even you would care about knowing. I told her the good and the bad and plenty in between. I think that's why she finally said she would help me."

"Okay." I sat back against the door. "That's a lot to digest. I guess it makes sense. That must be why you never made a serious pass at me, in case it would upset the applecart, or the Brandi glass—ha. Now where do we go from here?"

"I was afraid to go too fast, to push you into something and find out later what an ass I'd been. I want you, Brandi. I want you every time I see you. I want you right now. Feel my pants, if you think I'm kidding. No! Don't really do that."

I had reached toward his crotch, but he grabbed my hand and held it away from him. Then he put it on his chest. "I want you, but it has to be the right time for both of us. Muriel knows all about me, but you don't. I want to tell you all about me."

"I want to know all about you, too. I didn't ask because I thought then I'd have to tell you all about me."

"When you are ready, you can tell me. You can take as long as you want. I'm not going anywhere, Brandi, unless you tell me to."

"I'm not going to do that. I want to know all about you, whatever you want to tell me. And I'll try to tell you about me— most of it, anyway. I can start with me, first; that's easier than talking about Dean. But, if we stay together, you need to know it all."

"Thank you, love. I'm honored you'd say that. I will always try to live up to your trust in me." Now Jay had tears in his eyes.

"Okay. That's settled. I'm falling in love with you, too, Jay Bingham. We'd better stop talking about this right now before we fill up your beautiful car with our waterworks."

"That's a good idea for tonight, except for one thing."

"Now, what's that?' I asked.

There was no more talking, and, when I went into the house, my lips were tingling.

Chapter Seventeen

Sunday at the Lake

1

It was a gorgeous summer morning in Maine. Jay and I were driving to Muriel's house for the big weekend party. We had decided to take Mure's suggestion and stay there overnight. I thought Jay might not want to spend all that time with the others, but he seemed as happy about the idea as I was. We wouldn't have to drive back and forth to the lake two days in a row, and he wouldn't have to go all the way to Portland each evening. I was looking forward to a relaxing weekend—with Jay, with Mure and Brian, and with Shondra.

In the first days after I met her, I thought that I would have more time to share with Shondra. I had overextended myself, with my internship, with the time needed to tutor Lindsay, Randy and Chriz properly, and with my involvement with Jay. My intentions to visit Dr. Maddox's class on a regular basis had fallen of late. I failed to find much time for Shondra; that and the warning I got from Brian steered me away from her. I thought I might catch up on things with her, at least a little, this weekend. I also missed talking to Mure; we hadn't been connecting, even on the phone, nearly as much as we used to do.

"Penny for your thoughts," Jay spoke and broke me from my reverie. "You've been awfully quiet, girl. I wonder where you are right now. You don't seem to be with me."

"Oh, Jay, I'm sorry. I really am very much with you. I want us to have plenty of time to spend together these next two days," I said.

"That's good, because I do, too. But I sense there's more going on in that mind of yours than just contemplating the two of us."

"You are a perceptive attorney, Mr. Bingham. I am guilty

as charged. I was thinking about us, that's true. But I also was hoping I'd get to spend a little time with Mure; I've been neglecting her. And I also thought I might get to talk to Shondra."

"I'm all for you spending as much time as you want with Muriel. I'd enjoy some time with Brian, myself. He is a grand person. I hope you get some time with Shondra, too."

"I'm not planning to set up meetings with people or anything. I was just musing about seeing everyone. Things have changed between us since the last time we all were together at the lake. I wonder about the best way to tell Muriel and Brian."

"I bet you an ice cream at Dairy Delight that you won't have to say a thing. We both feel different, and I'm guessing we'll look different to them. People in love have a way of showing it without saying anything."

"You may be right. But I bet you that ice cream, anyway," I said.

When we got to the lake, Jay and I greeted Muriel and Brian sitting on the deck. We said hello, and I hugged them. Jay shook Brian's hand and gave Muriel a light kiss on the cheek. Then we sat in a couple of lounge chairs.

"Well, don't those two look like a pair of cats that just found the canary, Brian?" Muriel said. "Something's going on."

"Yep; I'd say plenty is going on. You two finally found each other, I take it. I wondered how long you were going to circle before you jumped right in."

"Jumped right into what, Brian?" I asked.

"Ah, well, in my day, they called it falling in love. I imagine that hasn't changed." He looked at Muriel, and they both laughed.

"It's that obvious?"

"Yes, Brandi, dear, it's pretty obvious. "

I looked at Jay, and he said, "I think I will have a triple sundae, please." Then he started laughing, too. I joined in; this weekend was going to be memorable.

After lunch we decided to take the boat to Sand Bar Island, a small mound of rock and a little grass that sat atop a sand bar out in the middle of the lake. It was a popular place for boaters to go for swimming and drifting about. The water was shallow around the island, with a gradual drop to deep water.

There were several boats anchored near the sandbar when we arrived. Some people were sitting in their boats, eating or drinking, or just relaxing. Quite a number of folks were in the water. A few of them had tubes or other water floats.

Brian and Jay anchored the boat in a spot not too congested. "Before anybody dives, somebody get out and check the depth of the water. I don't want any of you diving until you know how deep it is here. I can move out farther if it's too shallow."

Jay jumped overboard, with Shondra right behind him. They both disappeared amid bubbles. When they came up almost at the same time, Jay said, "It's plenty deep enough here for diving. Come on, Shondra. Let's check all around the boat as far as we can dive; I'll look under the boat, too."

The two of them swam around the boat, diving to check for rocks or shallows. Jay swam under the boat, and Shondra followed him. They came up at the other end, sputtering and laughing. "That was my foot you grabbed down there," Jay said.

Shondra splashed him. "Well, you pulled my hair."

"Never. That must have been a shark."

"Yeah, right, Mr. Smarty." Shondra pulled herself over the side of the boat; Jay followed. They both shook water over Mure, Brian, and me.

"Both of you can get right back out, if you're going to do that," Muriel said. Almost immediately, Jay dived over the side into the water, Shondra right behind him. They both were excellent swimmers; they looked so comfortable in the water.

"I'm going in," said Brian. He did a shallow dive; then

Muriel jumped in after him. I dived in last. The water was cool in contrast to the hot sun. Immediately, I felt refreshed.

Jay and Shondra were still at it: splashing each other, spitting water, kicking their feet. I swam over and joined in for a few minutes. I definitely was getting the worst of it, so I headed back to the boat. Muriel and Brian were climbing up the ladder.

Once we were in the boat, Jay and Shondra came back, too. They both flipped themselves over the side of the boat, not bothering with the ladder. Muriel handed out towels, and we rubbed ourselves.

"I have some cold drinks. Brian and I don't drink any alcohol when we are boating, but I have a couple of beers if you and Brandi want one, Jay. I also have some soda, some ice water, and some iced tea. Shondra, do you want a Coke?"

"Yes, please. That sounds good."

Jay said, "I'll stick with soda, too. I'll wait till we're back at the house to have a beer. Brandi?'

"I want some water first," I said. "Then I'll have a soda. I'd like some wine, but it's too hot. Later it will taste good."

We sat drinking our sodas and soaking up the sun. The boat was rocking gently. My eyes started closing, when Jay suddenly pushed me and half-jumped, half dived into the water. "Hey," I said. Then Shondra pushed me the other way and went over the side of the boat right behind Jay. "What's going on?"

I turned to see what they were doing. Jay had come up to a young boy who was half-submerged, his head above water level, his mouth about at it, and his arms pretty much in the water. He grabbed the boy and pulled him up. Shondra caught up and helped Jay, as they headed toward shore.

The three of them were on the shore by the time I swam there. Muriel and Brian came out of the water behind me. There was a young woman standing in front of Jay and the boy. Her fists were practically in her mouth. Then she rushed at the boy and held him to her.

"He was drowning, Ma'am. That's what drowning looks like. It's not what you see on TV, with people screaming and thrashing around. They don't have the breath to do that. He's all right, since he can cry so hardily. He swallowed some water, but he'll be fine. Just keep him out of the water for the rest of the day, and make him rest."

The woman looked at Jay. I think maybe she thought he was a lifeguard. She nodded her head at him and whispered, "Thank you."

The boy, who was about six or seven, grabbed a towel someone held out and wrapped it around himself. He was shivering. The woman led him to a blanket; they both sat down. A few people joined them, and we headed back to the boat.

"Thanks, Shondra," Jay said. "That was smart thinking. I probably could have got him to shore, but you really helped me. You recognized he was drowning, too."

"Yeah. I saw a video at the club where I used to swim. They made us watch it a couple of times so we'd know what drowning looked like. He looked just like the video."

We all sat for a minute. Then Jay said, "Okay; I'm ready for that triple sundae you owe me, Brandi. How about it? Let's all go back and change. Then we'll hit the Dairy Delight. Does everyone want a triple sundae? It's on Brandi." He laughed and punched my arm.

Brian started the motor and pointed the boat in the direction of the house.

3

The parking lot of the Dairy Delight was crowded with cars and a few motorcycles. Brian parked off to the side of the lot. The lines at the two order windows were long. Brian and Muriel got in one line and Jay and I in the other.

"I have to go to the bathroom," Shondra said. "Please order me what everybody else gets." She walked around the side of the building where the restrooms were located.

"We've certainly had enough excitement for one day," said

Muriel. "I'll be glad to go back home and relax on the deck."

"I'm with you, my dear," Brian said.

"How about you two take it easy. We can pick up lobsters on the way back, and Brandi and I can cook them."

"Why, that's a nice idea, Jay. Thank you. I've got some corn, and I made macaroni salad this morning. We'll be all set."

"I like this having dessert first," I said.

"Does this sundae really count? I thought we still would have dessert," Brian said.

Just then I heard some yelling and looked past the end of the building. Shondra was flailing her arms and pulling away from a couple of guys who had hold of her. They seemed to be half dragging her toward the end of the parking lot. "Oh, my god," I cried. "Someone's kidnapping Shondra."

Jay took off running toward Shondra and the men, with the three of us behind him. Muriel had her phone out and was already talking into it. Jay moved fast and had nearly caught up to them. Suddenly, a car appeared by them, with a third guy in the driver's seat.

Everything happened fast then. One of the men opened the rear door, and the second one shoved Shondra inside, getting in after her. The first man started to get into the front just as Jay caught up to him. Jay pulled the man back, but he hung on to the doorframe and kicked at Jay; then he pulled the door toward him and swung it back hard at Jay. The driver starting moving while the other guy swung himself on the door, trying to get into the car.

Jay was up and running at them. The driver swerved the car and hit Jay, who went down hard. By this time, I could hear sirens. The driver swerved again, gaining speed as he went.

The car was out on the main road now. It was going so fast that it fishtailed. It disappeared around a corner and was gone. Then we heard a crashing noise.

Chapter Eighteen

Déjà vu

1

I had reached the spot where Jay lay, not moving. He was bloody. I didn't know what to do. Muriel came up behind me, and she still had her cell phone out. Other people were congregating around us.

Then a couple of policemen pushed people back. A man said he was a doctor, and they let him through. Soon, there were uniformed rescue workers rushing to Jay.

After checking him, one of them said, "Let's get him on the stretcher." They moved quickly and started toward an ambulance. All I could think of was Dean. He had lain in that dirty alley in a pool of his blood. Please, God, if you are there, don't let this happen to Jay, too.

"I'm coming with him," I said, getting up.

"Only family can ride in the ambulance. Are you family?" The rescue people had taken Dean away in an ambulance, and I never saw him again. The casket at the funeral didn't count. I was not going to let Jay leave me the same way.

"Yes; I'm his fiancée," I said. I was running along behind them, and I climbed into the ambulance before they could object.

Just before the doors closed, Muriel called to me. "We'll meet you at the hospital, Brandi."

I sat inside the rescue truck, numb to anything other than Jay. I was holding his hand in one of my hands and stroking his head with the other. "Wake up, Jay. You can't die on me, too. I love you."

Jay stirred and opened his eyes. "Hey, Brandi," he sort of mumbled. "I'm not going anywhere." He closed his eyes, but he held on to my hand.

I started sobbing. The medic sat back. I hoped it was because he wasn't so worried now that Jay was conscious. Time had stopped for me, and I didn't register anything until the ambulance doors burst open. Hospital people helped move the stretcher from the truck to the ground and through the hospital doors.

Once inside, they took Jay away, but he gave me a cockeyed smile before he disappeared behind some more doors. I stood at that spot until Muriel and Brian appeared and guided me to the waiting room with the awful orange chairs. Muriel left Brian and me; she returned a while later.

"Jay's going to be all right. He's pretty bruised, and he probably suffered a mild concussion. He's completely conscious and talking to the doctor now. They're going to do some more tests. We'll be able to see him shortly."

"Oh, Mure. I thought he was dead. He looked just like Dean did. I got so scared."

"I know, Brandi. He's very lucky. You stay with Brian. When they let you see him, you both can go into the room. I am going to see what I can find out about Shondra. A couple more ambulances came in after Jay."

Brian and I sat together. I was clutching his hand. He had his arm around me but didn't talk, thank goodness. We just sort of held on to each other. It seemed we sat there for a long time; then a nurse came over and told us we could see Jay.

2

He was still banged up and bloody. I guess nobody was in a hurry to clean him up. There was a needle in his arm and a tube running from it. But his eyes were open, and he was smiling.

"Oh, Jay; you're alive." I said, as I clutched his free arm.

"I couldn't bail. I thought I heard an angel say she was my fiancée, and I have to find her," he said. His smile was large as life. "I feel like I was run over by a car, though. Poor joke. I'm fine, Brandi, just a little worked over. Where is Shondra? Did those guys get away with her?"

89

Until he mentioned Shondra, I hadn't thought of her since I saw Jay get hit. I looked at Brian. "I don't know," I said.

Brian said, "The car was moving so fast, the driver missed a sharp turn in the road. The car hit a tree. So many people had called 911 that the police got there right away. The ambulances were right behind them. Shondra and the three men were brought here in two or three ambulances. We don't know anything about Shondra yet. Muriel went to find out what she can. You're staying the night, I imagine. They probably want to monitor the concussion."

"Hell, no. I'm going home with you. If anybody needs to monitor me, Brandi can do it, right, Brandi?" Jay tried to laugh, but he winced and stopped.

I was shaking a bit, but I hugged him. "I'll stay up night and day, just as long as you are okay."

"We'll wait and see what the doctor decides. We'll all do whatever he says," said Brian.

Just then Muriel walked into the room. The look on her face was enough to give us pause.

"Did you find out about Shondra? Is she all right?' Brian asked.

"Maybe we should go back to the waiting room. Shouldn't Jay be resting?" Muriel said.

"I've got plenty of time to rest, and I'll do it better knowing how Shondra is," he said. "What did you find out?"

"All right, everybody. Sit down if you can find a place, and I'll tell you from the beginning."

I sat on the bed, as close to Jay as I could get without actually sitting on him.

"First, the car was going fast enough that, when it hit the tree, the back door on the driver's side came open, and Shondra was thrown from the car." I gasped. "Hold on. That may be what saved her life, so far, anyway, because the car burst into flames from the rear—maybe the gas tank. The boy in the back is badly burned. He's been airlifted to Boston."

90

Nobody said anything for a minute. Muriel continued. "The man who was half in and half out of the passenger's side was thrown from the car. He's dead. The driver hit the steering wheel. He has some broken bones, a possible punctured lung and other internal injuries. They're running tests on him."

"What about Shondra?" Jay asked.

"We don't know. So far, she's alive, but she is unconscious. The doctors are still determining the extent of her injuries. There's internal bleeding."

"Oh," I said.

We sat together, saying nothing then. I don't know how long it was before a doctor came into the room. We all stiffened, I think; I know that I did. I was so afraid to hear any more bad news.

"We are going to need to get you cleaned up, Mr. Bingham. Then we want to do a couple more tests," the doctor said.

"Then will I be able to leave?" Jay asked.

"We want to watch you for a while. It would be good for you to stay the night. You have a mild concussion. But we'll see. If the tests come out good and if you have someone to attend to you for the next twenty-four hours, we might release you. You might get more rest at home."

"I can tend to him," I said. "And my mother will, too. And my father."

The doctor looked at Muriel and Brian. They both nodded. "Of course."

"Okay, then. If the other tests check out, we will release you to them."

"Thank you," Jay said. "Can you tell us any more about Shondra?"

"The girl from the accident? I don't know. But when we do know something, someone will be in to tell you." The doctor left, and we continued to sit.

A couple of hours passed. Jay left to have the tests and returned. We sat quietly, except for simple conversation. I don't think any of us wanted to think about the accident or who the men were and why they tried to kidnap Shondra. All that seemed to matter right then was that Jay got rested enough to leave and that we got an update on Shondra's condition. I know I felt too shocked to think past that.

Eventually, the doctor returned and said that Jay was cleared to go home. He didn't have anything to wear besides his bloody, torn clothes, and he refused to wear a hospital gown outside. Finally, a nurse found him a pair of scrubs to wear. Brian helped him dress while Mure and I waited in the hall.

Once at the house, Muriel got one of the guest rooms cleared out while Brian helped Jay in the bathroom. Finally, he was settled in the bed, and Muriel and Brian left the room, promising to spell me in a couple of hours. I didn't want them to have to get up in the middle of the night; I knew I wouldn't be able to sleep anyway. But I didn't say anything because Mure would do what she wanted. So I just nodded my head.

Jay had a light tan and some sunburn from the boating earlier in the day. Under that color, though, he looked pale. Below his closed eyes were dark smudges. I thought he might be dozing, so I pulled up a chair and sat next to him. I closed my eyes, but I wasn't worried about falling asleep on my watch; I was too keyed up.

Then, Jay whispered, "Get into bed with me, angel."

I climbed onto the bed. "Where should I sit? I don't want to hurt you," I said.

"Put your head on the pillow next to me. You can stretch out beside me. Just don't press on my body; everything hurts."

I lay down beside him, putting my body against his but not using any pressure. One arm I lifted over his head to sort of cup it, and I touched his hair with my hand. The other hand I lay carefully over his heart. "Does that hurt? I'll move it if it does."

He shook his head. "That feels so good, Brandi."

We lay that way for a while. Then Jay spoke. "You know, it was strange. I felt like I was sliding down a tunnel or something slanted. From far away I heard a voice say, 'I love you,' and I knew I had to go back up that chute and get to the voice." He paused for almost a minute, and I thought he was going to sleep. "I think you might have saved my life, Brandi. Moving down that tunnel was easy. It was releasing me from pain or something hard. But your voice made me try to get back up. Do you think I was dying? If I'd let myself slide down the tunnel, would I be dead now?"

I started to shiver, even though it was not cold in the room. "Oh, Jay. I don't know. That's an awful thought. Could you have died if you only had a concussion?"

"I've heard of instances when people who aren't all that badly hurt just give up. Maybe it's too hard to fight back to consciousness. I don't know. But I do know that your words changed everything for me."

"Seeing you lying still on the ground changed things for me, too."

"I told you I was falling in love with you. Before the accident, I didn't know how you felt, if I was wasting my time. When you said you loved me, it was like I said before. An angel cares, and I have a whole new world to live for. I liked my life before you. It's not that I wasn't happy, but I guess I wasn't fulfilled, and I was looking for something. You. Does that make any sense?"

"Oh, yes, it does. I had feelings there on the ground next to you, too. But mine were fearful ones. Dean's death flashed by, and I think right then I realized that I did love you. I do love you. I know that because I thought then that I couldn't go on living if I lost you, too. So that meant I love you."

"Funny it took a near-death experience to wake us both up," Jay said.

"Everything would be perfect now, if only Shondra is

okay."

"It's ironic," he said. "I was finally getting to like her. She really showed brains and courage when that kid was drowning. I could have got him to shore myself, but her help got us there faster. Everybody around the boy was either oblivious to his plight or else too shocked to move. She is a good kid."

"Yeah," was all I said because Brian came into the room then.

"Okay, you two. Party's over. You're supposed to keep him awake, Brandi, but you don't have to entertain him, too." We all laughed at that comment. "Brandi, go get some sleep. You'll have all day tomorrow to babysit him. I'll keep you awake now, Jay, but I'm not getting into bed with you."

Chapter Nineteen

Aftermath

1

Jay and I were sitting in deck chairs, watching late morning boat traffic on the lake. There were skiffs, some high-powered racing boats, several jet-skis, a couple of pontoon boats, and, close to shore, a few canoes and kayaks. It was a busy Sunday.

Muriel came toward us from the house; Brian was behind her. We snapped out of our lethargy and looked at her face as if we could read in her expression the information she had received from the hospital. She sat down in a chair in front of us, and Brian pulled up another one.

"Have you found out about Shondra?' I asked.

"She is still in the ICU and on the critical list, but she made it through the night. The doctor said that's a good sign. She's still unconscious, but he said that is neither good nor bad. The longer she holds on, the better her chances are," Muriel said.

"Are you going to go into the hospital? I'm sure you are."

"Brian and I both are going, unless you need one of us here," she said. "I can't do anything, but I think she might be able to sense my presence, just like Jay did with you. Maybe it won't matter, but I have to try."

"We're fine here. We aren't leaving the deck, unless Jay wants to lie down in his bed. After being awake so long, he must be awfully tired. Aren't you, Jay?"

Brian cut in with a laugh. "Are you talking about sleeping or bunking together? Maybe you need a chaperone."

"We will behave ourselves, Brian; I promise," Jay said. "It's important for you to go with Muriel, I think. If I do go to bed, I won't let Brandi climb in like she did last night. I will make her behave."

"Oh, thanks. Now it's my fault. Seriously, Mure, go. But

call us as soon as you know anything. Or even if you don't, call us, anyway. They have to find out something today, I hope. Did they tell you what all her injuries are?" I asked.

"You know, they did not, and I didn't ask. Last night was so traumatic. This morning I was relieved just to know Shondra is still alive. I'm sure they'll tell us when we see the doctor today, and one of us will call you."

2

Jay and I stayed in the lounge chairs on the deck. We didn't bother to eat lunch. Jay said he wasn't hungry, and I didn't feel like moving. The breeze off the lake was pleasant; it helped both of us relax.

"Brandi, when things settle down, I want us to talk. We're both too tired and too stressed about Shondra right now, but, when everything is sorted out, we should take the time to talk to each other."

"I'd like that," That's all I said, and I think we both fell asleep. The sound of ringing came from far away. I jerked in the chair, reaching for the cell phone on the table. "Hi, Mure."

"It's Brian, Brandi. I have Muriel's phone. She's in Shondra's room. Shondra is conscious now. She woke a little while ago."

I put the phone on speaker so Jay could hear, too. "Oh, Brian, that's great. She's going to be all right, then? How bad are her injuries?"

"It's pretty amazing, considering that she was thrown from the car. She is covered in cuts and bruises, she has a concussion and she cracked a couple of ribs."

"What about the internal bleeding? Was that from the ribs?" I asked.

There was a long pause on the line. Then Brian said, "No. Shondra lost the baby."

I stared at the phone. Jay touched my shoulder. "Oh," I

said. "Oh, wow." I knew Shondra was pregnant, but it had been in the abstract to me. I hadn't thought about a baby. It still seemed unreal.

"Does she know?" Jay asked.

"I don't think she does yet. Although she is conscious, she's groggy and has a lot of medication in her system. Muriel is going to stay with her, at least through the evening and maybe overnight. It depends on Shondra. Look; I'm coming home. I need to pick up a few things for Muriel, and then I'll go back to the hospital. I'll tell you everything we know when I get there."

3

The three of us were sitting in the kitchen. Brian had picked up some take-out food; the remnants were scattered on the table.

"We just found out that something else happened yesterday, and Muriel is concerned how Shondra will react when she finds out. Her mother died."

We knew she was really ill, but I didn't think she would die so soon. "I wonder what that will mean for Shondra," I said. "There's her stepfather, or father, or whoever he is. Are there other relatives?"

Brian said, "We don't know. Nobody has had time to get any information together. Nothing was done when Muriel became Shondra's temporary guardian. Records were sketchy, and no other relatives were listed on any forms. It remains to be discovered; things will get done in due time. What's most important now is that Shondra recover." He shook his head. "It's too bad all of this happened just when she was doing so well."

I wondered about so many things: Shondra's background, Jay's and Brian's questions about her in the beginning and now the kidnapping. "Do the police know anything more about the kidnapping? And what about the guys?"

"The police are still investigating the incident. We found out that only one of the kidnappers is over twenty-one: the one who grabbed her."

"Is he the one who was burned?" Jay asked.

"Yes, and there's no word yet on his condition. The driver is still in critical condition in the ICU. He is twenty, and the one who died was nineteen."

"Did Shondra know them?" I asked.

"We don't know. The police haven't been able to question the two guys; either they aren't conscious or they're too unstable. I've got to go back to the hospital now."

"It's getting late," Jay said. "Do you want us to go with you? You might fall asleep coming back."

"I'm not coming back tonight. I'll give Muriel her things, and I'll stay at my condominium tonight. In the morning, I'll check at the hospital; then I'll call you."

"We both have work tomorrow," I said.

"Keep your cell phones on. And make sure you take it slow tomorrow, Jay. You're still pretty banged up."

Chapter Twenty

The Day After

1

Monday was one confusing day. Muriel called me on my cell phone soon after I arrived at my office. "Hi, Brandi. I'm not going to try to tell you much except that Shondra is in stable condition now and has been moved out of the ICU to a regular room. She'll be in the hospital a couple more days, at least. I'll be with her most of today. I'll talk to you and Jay either Tuesday or Wednesday evening. I'll call you if I have anything in particular to tell you before then. Brian will be in and out of the office and probably will stay in his condo the next couple of nights. I have to go now. I love you."

"I love you, too," I said.

I barely had time to digest Muriel's one-sided conversation when Lindsay walked in. I could tell by her slumped posture and the scowl on her face that she wasn't in a good mood. I supposed attending to her would ease my concern about Shondra. "Hi, Lindsay," I said.

"Hi."

"Did you have a nice weekend?"

"No. It sucked."

I asked, "Did something bad happen?"

"My boyfriend broke up with me." Lindsay dropped into a chair at the table.

"Oh, I'm sorry. That must have been a shock."

"Yeah; well, I thought he was really into me. Now he says he doesn't have time."

"So he broke off your relationship?"

"No," she said. "He said he just doesn't want to spend all of the time together. He has to practice basketball all day and study most evenings. We can go out once or twice a week."

"Well, that doesn't sound like breaking up to me. It sounds like he is very serious about his sport and keeping up his grades. He would have to do that to stay in school," I said.

"What a crock. If he wanted to, he could spend more time with me. I have to figure out a way to get him to pay more attention to me—make him jealous or something."

"Oh," I said. I decided to stop talking about this topic, since I knew a little bit about the issue from Randy's paper last week. "Well, shall we go over your last paper? Then you can write today's essay."

"I suppose I have to, or I won't get out of here."

I sat next to Lindsay, and I showed her some places in the last essay where I thought she could improve the writing. She didn't argue with me, which was unusual. Either she agreed with me, or she wasn't paying attention. I decided not to question her and suggested she start writing.

While Lindsay was working, I mused about Randy's last essay. He said he planned to tell Lindsay basically what she told me he said. I remembered that he thought it was a good compromise; he hadn't said anything about breaking off the relationship. Apparently, Lindsay wanted more than going out a couple of times a week. I imagined they would work out their differences.

"Okay; I'm done." Lindsay rose from the chair, handed me the paper, and started for the door.

"Thanks, Lindsay. Have a good rest of the day, and I'll see you at our next meeting," I said.

"Whatever," was her reply.

2

Lindsay did not write much in her essay. It was very messy, with doodles in the margins and what looked like stabbing motions with the pencil tip. There were little dots all over the paper, and some of them went all the way through:

This weekend really sucked. I thought Randy and I were going to have a great time. Instead he wanted to talk. He says we're seeing too much of each other. He says he needs more time for his basketball. Boy, that's a waste of time. I told him that too. Then he said he needs to spend more time on studying. It's only summer school I said. It doesn't matter but he said it does to him. He is so wrapped around his basketball crap and making sure he gets good grades so he can keep playing the stupid game. I told him Id think about it. I'm so mad. I will think about it and I'll come up with something to get his attention.

3

I decided to give myself a break from thinking about Lindsay and go over to the pool. I wanted to see what Mike knew about Shondra's accident. Mike was talking to a few students when I walked in, but he broke away and came over to me.

"Hi, Brandi. How's it going?" he asked.

"I'm fine, Mike. Did you have a nice weekend?"

"I did, thanks. It went too fast though."

"Yes, I know what you mean," I said. Usually I felt that way, but this past weekend seemed to have lasted forever. Now it seemed to be a lifetime away. "Did you hear about Shondra?"

"I heard from the Dean's office that she was in an accident and will be out for several days. The secretary said she'd keep me posted."

Brian or Jay must have contacted the Administration and told them the bare minimum. "I heard that, too, Mike. She's in the hospital, but I haven't heard how long she'll be there."

"It's too bad. I hope she'll be better soon and can get back to swimming. She's been doing so well on the team."

"I hope so, too," I said. We chatted a little more; then Mike went back to the kids, and I started to leave the gym.

Just inside the door, I nearly ran right into Jay. "I thought I might find you here when you weren't in your office," he said. "I want to talk to Mike and the team—give them a little spiel about Shondra. Nothing was in the papers or on the news about her, so we decided to keep the information to a minimum. I have a lot to do after that, but we should be getting together this evening. I don't know where yet; it could be here at school or at the hospital or wherever Brian or Muriel decides. Brian says Muriel wants to talk to us. Oh, I miss you, and I'd like to kiss you right now, but I guess that would be a bad idea."

"Well, hi, yourself. You mean making out in front of all these kids might give them the wrong idea? Yeah, I think you're right. How come you aren't home resting the way you're supposed to be? I know you're really busy or you wouldn't be running around like this, so I'll let you go. By the way, I hope you have a good excuse for the condition of your face. The kids will ask you for sure."

"I'll think of something. I can think fast on my feet," he said.

"I'm sure you can. Depending on what Mure wants to say to us, maybe we can get a minute alone tonight."

"I plan on it. I'll take a rain check on that kiss, but I'm holding you to it." Jay touched my shoulder and headed toward Mike.

Chapter Twenty-one

Beginnings

1

I noticed Chriz standing outside Irwin Hall. As usual, he was dressed in a clean, ironed shirt and creased pants. It wasn't time for our tutoring session. I didn't really want to take time to talk; there were too many things I wanted to do. But I didn't want to be rude, either. So I said, "Hello."

"Hello, Brandi. I brought you an iced tea. I know you are busy, so I won't waste your time. I am on my way to the chemistry lab."

"Thank you, Chriz. That's so nice of you."

"I thought that later, if you have some time, maybe we could have lunch together. You have to eat lunch, and so do I."

"Oh," I said, "I hadn't thought about lunch. I'm actually not hungry."

"Perhaps you will be hungry in an hour or so. I can stop at the Pit and pick up salads and sandwiches after I finish at the lab."

"Well, I guess I do have to eat. That's really nice of you, Chriz. But only if you let me give you the money for my lunch."

"I would like to buy your lunch."

I knew that Chriz didn't have money to squander. "I don't want you to spend your money on me." I took a ten-dollar bill out of my purse and handed it to Chriz. "Get me whatever looks good. I'll see you in an hour or so. And, thanks, Chriz."

2

We were sitting on a bench outside my office, eating the sandwiches Chriz brought. It was a lovely day, and several people were eating nearby. Four or five squirrels had gathered and were moving among the people, competing for scraps. I threw a piece of bread in the direction of one squirrel, but a blue jay swooped down, grabbed it and flew off before the squirrel could get to the morsel.

"Thank you for agreeing to eat lunch with me, Brandi," Chriz said. "I do not have many friends; I am becoming friendly with Lindsay, but I do not find it easy to talk with her the way I do with you. She does not understand things in the same way. I wanted to talk with a friend like you. I hope you do not mind."

"I don't mind at all, Chriz," I said. He sure was right on about Lindsay not thinking the way the rest of us do. "Sometimes I just feel like I don't have enough time to take a break like this. It's nice, though. What did you want to talk about?"

"I do not want to talk about anything particular, Brandi. I just wanted to talk to someone, and I like talking to you. You are easy to be around, and you seem to understand things much the way I do. I can relax when I am around you."

"Oh," I said. "Well, thanks. I hope you can get to meet more people who think like you and you can be comfortable with. I guess it's hard when you come to a new place like this, especially in the summer. There aren't a lot of people here. In the fall, there will be more students. Then I think you will be able to find different kinds of people."

"Yes, I am trying, but, as you say, it is hard. I do see people in the dormitory and at dinner. I see other students in my classes, of course. Everyone is in a hurry, though. Then I am studying so much. So we do not take the time to talk and to visit."

"Chriz, why don't you try the same thing you did with me today? Ask a guy or a girl in one of your classes to get together for lunch. You each pay for your own, and you can get to know someone a little better. Even if you only do it once or twice a week, you'll start to know more people."

"Yes, that's a good idea. Thank you. I will try that."

We sat together for a while longer, talking about school and things in general. I told Chriz a little about my classes in Boston, my living arrangements there and my roommates. He told me about his high school experience in Portland. After half an hour or so, he left for an afternoon class and a lab, and I returned to my office.

I was reading when my phone rang. Mure said she would be home later, and she was hoping that I could come there with Jay so that she could talk with us about Shondra. She said that she had asked Jay already and that he would be happy to pick me up. She also asked me to bring clothes for the morning because she hoped we'd stay the night. My mother could be pretty bossy when she had an agenda.

3

We heated and ate the pizzas Brian had brought with him from Portland. The day still was warm, and Brian said he was going swimming before we sat down to talk. Muriel said she would go with him.

After they left the house, Jay pulled me into a tight hug. "I missed you all day. I kept thinking about kissing you."

"Do you think Mure and Brian left us alone on purpose?" I asked.

"I don't know, but I do know I'm taking advantage of it."

It didn't seem like we had been alone for more than a minute before we heard the back door slam. "We're back!" Mure called. "Don't you two want to take a swim? The water's so refreshing right now."

We joined them in the kitchen. "Do we have enough time?" I asked. "Do you have a lot to tell us?"

"I'm going to change. If you just take a dip and keep the fooling around to a minimum, you have time," Brian said.

I walked into the water up to my shoulders and felt the coolness penetrate my body. Jay came in and wrapped himself around me from behind. Suddenly my bikini top slipped down, and I realized Jay had undone the tie around my neck. His hands

105

touched my breasts; the bike bell went off in my stomach, and my whole body shivered, too. His fingers barely touched me, but I was feeling tingly. "Jay…," I started to say, but he cut me off.

"Shh." He turned me around, and we kissed, a long, slow, soft kiss. My head was dizzy.

"I told you I'm going to take it as slow as you want. I'm not here to hook up with you for a summer fling. I intend to stay, so I can wait as long as it takes. I'm committed to you, Brandi."

Just then, Brian called out from the deck. "Okay, you two; time to get in here."

Jay retied my top, and we emerged from the water. As we neared the deck, Brian threw us a couple of towels. We dried ourselves and patted down our suits. Then we changed back into our clothes in the cabana and went into the house.

When we were seated in the den, Jay and I on the couch and Mure and Brian in the two easy chairs, Brian said, "Shondra and Muriel have been doing a lot of talking. Shondra has told her what's been going on. She trusts Muriel, but she's understandably cautious and pretty weak, too, so it's taken her a while to get things out. Muriel's going back every day until Shondra is released, which could be as long as a week."

"Then what's going to happen?" I asked.

"We don't know," Mure said. "But she'll come back here for the time being. She needs to rest and be watched. After we know more, we'll see. Brian and I both think you should know what Shondra told me. I've told Brian already, and it's going to upset you."

Chapter Twenty-two

Shondra's Story as Told through Muriel

1

Shondra is sixteen years old. She lied about her age because she thought she would have a better chance of getting into the swim program at Olietta College. Although her correct age was on her school records, the swim club she belonged to in Portland did not keep age records. When she applied for the swim team at Olietta, she simply wrote fifteen as her age. The Olietta program did not require school records, so Shondra's age was not verified.

Shondra has been an average student in school, neither a problem nor outstanding in any way. She is one of those kids who gets lost in the pack. Except for swimming, she did not shine, but she did not get into trouble, either. Shondra seems to have done her school work, practiced at the swim club and pretty much kept to herself. She did not join activities at the school.

Growing up has not been easy for Shondra, but she and her mother managed for a long time. The difficulty for Shondra began when her mother's drug habit started to take over the woman's life. For several years she was able to handle it; she managed to keep a job that paid their modest rent and provided sufficient food. Gradually, however, the mother succumbed to her addiction. The mother did not apply for social services of any kind; she also did not belong to any church.

Shondra did not have any friends in her neighborhood. She kept to herself there. The few friends she made were from school, but they were not close. Until she asked to stay with a couple of the girls, she had not been to their homes.

The man whom Shondra called her stepfather is, in fact, her uncle. He is the younger brother of her father, who died in an accident of some sort; the details are sketchy. It began as a bar fight and ended in a traffic accident. People were arrested, but no one was charged with anything more serious then assault and DUI. Her father died about five years ago.

Apparently, the uncle tried to fill the breach after the father's death. A couple of years ago, he moved into the apartment and used his income to keep things going. He works as a fisherman's helper, when he can.

Contrary to Shondra's original accusation that the uncle hit her or threatened her, he actually was the one trying to hold it together, especially for Shondra, as her mother got worse. But he got caught up in the mother's plight. He'd been sweet on her for years, so he had a hard time refusing to help her get drugs. The more he helped, the worse it got. The mother became sicker, he had a hard time keeping a job, and the money he earned was not enough.

The three young men who tried to kidnap Shondra were the uncle's suppliers. The oldest one was the actual supplier; the other two were his "collectors." They came with him to intimidate people to pay what they owed. All of them were high school dropouts. The two older men also had criminal records.

One evening they showed up at the apartment, and the uncle was not there. The mother was in the bedroom in a stupor. Shondra answered the door.

They took out their payment on her. The supplier raped her; then he offered her to his buddies to do the same. When they left, they threatened her not to tell anyone or they would be back with worse.

Shondra was too frightened to tell her uncle. When she realized she was pregnant, she left and made up the story about her mother and her uncle putting her out because the "boyfriend" didn't want Shondra around.

She managed to stay with a couple of friends a few nights here and there. She'd been accepted into Olietta's swimming program, and she contrived to get to the college. The rest is a bit vague.

Shondra apparently knew who I was. She'd heard of Muriel Buckman from a school counselor. Somehow she got enough information to figure out that Brandi was my daughter. Brandi was at the college, too, so Shondra managed to get to Brandi when she came to the pool. By concocting that story about getting thrown out of her apartment because she was pregnant, she played on Brandi's conscience. When Brandi took her in, Shondra was half-way to achieving her goal of getting to me, Muriel.

She knew enough about me that she figured she had a chance, actually the only possible one she could think of, to get herself out of her predicament, at least in the short run. When she was invited to stay at my house, Shondra decided her prayers had been answered. Between that arrangement and the swim program, she thought she might be able to get away from the situation and those men.

Then they saw her at the Dairy Delight. That was an unfortunate coincidence. I guess they planned to take her and then use her to force the uncle to get them more money. They probably thought he would be desperate enough to steal it somewhere. In the meantime, I guess they thought they would use Shondra. Thank goodness we saw them and Jay helped stop them.

Shondra will heal physically. What will happen next is uncertain. There is a lot to sort out. There is no other family on the uncle's side. No information is available about the mother. Whether she had any family in the state is not known.

Chapter Twenty-three

Thinking

1

I was thinking about Shondra. Knowing her background explained a lot about her behavior. I thought I understood why she lied her way onto the Olietta swimming team. She needed to get away from her apartment and from that neighborhood. Those young men were dangerous.

Now that she was injured and could not compete on the team, I wondered what would happen. Would she have to leave Olietta? That would be tough on her. At least she still had Muriel and could continue to live with her for a while. But then what?

I didn't know if her uncle was still in the picture. No one had said anything about him. Maybe he was going to jail. Even worse, Shondra's mother had died. How was that going to affect her? Were there relatives of her mother who might want to become involved?

The situation was complicated. I knew that Muriel and Brian would handle it in the best interests of Shondra, whatever occurred.

I wanted to visit Shondra at the hospital. It had been a few days, and the last time I saw her, those guys were dragging her away and she was screaming. I wanted to see her in a safe place, even if she was weak and injured. I also wanted her to know that I care about her. We weren't alike or anything, but she'd had a rough time, too.

Maybe I could put in a word for her at the college. She was doing a really good job on the swim team, and what happened was not because of anything she did. What if I talked to Mike and got him to vouch for her? Maybe we both could convince the school to keep her on the team. She could be a student manager or something like that. Maybe I was worrying too much; maybe they would keep her because she was already in the program.

2

I also was thinking about my tutorial students. I wished I had more time to spend with Chriz. He seemed lonely. It must be hard to be from another country and a different culture, and then try to fit in to something you don't really understand.

There certainly were things I could do if I got the time. I could talk to his professors and find out who was in his classes. Maybe they would have some ideas about getting Chriz more involved with other students in his class.

I wondered about his budding relationship with Lindsay. She was a handful for anyone, and Chriz was not experienced with girls. I wanted to warn him about her, but, really, what would I say? Be careful, Chriz, Lindsay might be a man-eater? That wouldn't help him much. I didn't think he had any idea what a mousy girl was like, let alone a tough cookie like her.

Thinking of Chriz with Lindsay made me think about her in her own right. She was a tough cookie, but she seemed awfully young to me. Was she ready for college? By her own admission, she didn't want to be there. She wasn't interested in improving her writing skills. I guessed she wasn't interested in any academic work.

Immaturity was written all over her pout. She was after a guy to put on a leash and parade around for her own pleasure. I recalled that she wanted to marry a rich man, so that should put Chriz out of the picture. But that certainly left Randy as a perfect target.

I thought that Randy probably could take care of himself, even with a girl like Lindsay. He was mild-mannered, and, by his own admission, he hadn't dated girls. But he did not seem the kind of guy to fall into a "man-trap" like Lindsay. Already, he had told her he couldn't spend the kind of time she expected from a boyfriend. Probably he would let her down slowly. She'd move on

111

to another rich boy and leave him to his basketball and his studying.

My three tutorial students could use more attention from me. I wanted to give it to them, but I was feeling my own pressures. There just wasn't enough time in a day. I trusted they each would find their way.

3

My thoughts drifted to Jay and stayed on him. The situation between us was powerful for me. I had never felt so strongly about someone from the opposite sex except for Dean. My present feelings were mixed.

There were more differences than similarities between Dean and Jay. I had known Dean as a casual friend before he became my boyfriend. We grew into each other. In the beginning I had no physical feelings toward him. Those came later.

I also knew all there was to know about Dean—no mystery. I knew his mother and his father. I knew about the drugs, the dealing, the beatings from his father. Dean's anger and his desperation became a part of me, too. The two of us grew a bond that was unbreakable, except by his death. We were joined at the heart.

There was more I didn't know about Jay than I did know. What I knew was pretty slim, as information goes. He certainly was very different from Dean; that I definitely knew.

Jay had attended prep school and gone to Ivy League colleges. Probably he was wealthy. Probably I was being naïve when I thought he leased that fancy Mercedes with its incredible sound system. Probably he got it as a graduation present.

What kind of upbringing did he have? Obviously, it wasn't anything like Dean's. I knew his father had died. I knew his mother lived in New York City. Maybe he grew up there. From what I'd heard about people living in NYC, you had to be pretty well-off to live there. Did Jay's family have servants?

If they had money, where did it come from now that his dad was dead? Jay hadn't mentioned that his mother worked; somehow I didn't think she did. I knew Jay cared for me, but could we really be compatible when our backgrounds were so different? How could an orphan and a graduate of reform school, and a street person, to boot, find lasting happiness with possibly a blue blood heir to a family fortune? Or, more to the point, how could he settle for me?

The physical attraction was different with Jay than it had been with Dean. I loved touching Dean, and I would have made love with him if he'd let me. But what happened to his mother made him decide he wouldn't have sex until we were married. I knew it wasn't going to happen, so we just enjoyed playing around with each other.

That's not to say I wasn't attracted to him and he to me. But, because we knew we weren't going to go all the way, there wasn't any tension around making out; we just had fun.

Things were different with Jay. I knew he said he would wait, but what was he waiting for, exactly? I didn't even know what that meant. I knew Dean meant marriage. But Jay and I had known each other a couple of months. So that couldn't mean he was waiting to marry me.

To complicate an already complicated situation, I felt a lot of sexual tension with Jay. The waiting could mean anything; perhaps the next time we were alone and felt these urges could mean he would decide the waiting was over.

And what did I want, anyway? Part of me expected to honor the pact Dean and I had made—no sex before marriage. I wanted to keep that promise, no matter who would become my husband. But was that fair to Jay?

Could I even do that? Was I strong enough? When he touched me, it felt so erotic that I wasn't sure I didn't want Jay to make love to me at that moment. The realization scared me. The issue of sex had to wait, though.

A bigger question was did I want to marry Jay? I almost didn't know where that idea came from. I was just getting to know

113

him and moving along smoothly before he changed the tempo. I didn't even know if I loved him. There certainly was something there, however, what with that bicycle bell going off in my belly, the dizzy feeling in my brain, and the general tingly sensation when he touched me.

I knew that Jay and I needed to talk. I had to know all about him, but that also meant I had to tell him everything about me, too. Muriel had told him enough that it shouldn't be too hard for me to fill in the details. I could do that, I thought. I had to do it for all our sakes—for Dean, for me, and for Jay.

Chapter Twenty-four

Talking

1

"When am I going to meet your mother?" I asked.

"I want to talk to you about that. I know you had a hard upbringing until Muriel took you in. But, as I see it now, you and Muriel and Brian have a close relationship. You are a real family. Actually, I envy what you have." Jay stopped talking and looked away. After a minute, I got the impression he was somewhere else. I was surprised; I thought everything was so normal for him.

"Hey, Jay; if you don't want to talk about it, it's okay. I know who you are. I trust you, and that's enough for me, at least for now."

"Oh, Brandi; it's not like that."

"Well, I don't need to meet your mother, if it's not something you want to do right now. But, if we stay together, I'd like to meet her sometime."

"No, it's not that exactly. I want you to meet her, but you need to know that it's going to be different from your family situation. My mother and I aren't close. It's a long story, and I want to tell you. But it's going to take a while. Neither my mother nor I act very normal around each other."

I was surprised by Jay's comment. I expected he came from a close family. He had told me his dad was dead, but I thought that made him closer to his mother. I wasn't sure what to say in response.

He shook his head. "I haven't been fair to you. It's past time I told you at least some things about me. And after I tell you the rest, I'll arrange for us to visit my mother, if you still want to."

"But why wouldn't I want to, Jay?"

"Wait until you've heard the story, and you can decide for yourself. We'll have to figure out a time to talk. It's going to take a while, and I want to do it where we won't have any interruptions."

"Okay; that's fine, Jay." I said to myself that I, of all people, should realize that surface appearances, just as often as not, are nothing like the way things really are.

"What if we take Saturday for ourselves? I know a quiet place we can go to down the coast; then we'll have time to talk, just the two of us."

"I would like that," I said.

2

I went to Muriel's house a couple of days after Shondra returned from the hospital. When I saw her, she looked frail. There still was some bruising on her face, and she walked slowly and delicately, I thought, as if she were in pain.

Before I could say anything, she came up to me, her head down, and spoke in a low voice, hardly above a whisper, "I'm sorry I lied to you. I wouldn't blame you if you hate me now and don't want anything to do with me." She stopped talking and made a gulping sound.

"Shondra." I put my arms around her, and she practically fell into my embrace. We hugged; then she was crying. "I don't hate you. You were in a horrible situation. I think you were brave. You did what you thought was best when you left the apartment and then sought out Muriel and me. Maybe you might have told me the truth, but you didn't know how I would react. I understand. The accident was awful. I'm so glad you are going to be all right."

I let her go, and we both sat down on the couch. My arm was around her shoulders, and her head was leaning against my shoulder. We sat that way for a while.

"You can tell me whatever you want to, Shondra. I'm not going to judge you. And, anyway, Muriel is the one who matters. You and she should make your decisions together."

"I know," she said. "But I tricked you into caring about me. I hope I can make it up to you."

"You already have. You've been honest and told Muriel everything. You have, haven't you?"

"Yes."

"Then that's most important. No more secrets. Plus you apologized to me. I accept your apology, so we can start fresh."

Shondra looked at me and smiled. "Thanks, Brandi."

"No problem. If and when you want to tell me anything, about your life or about swimming or your miscarriage or anything else, don't be afraid. I'm not perfect by a long shot, and I don't have any answers, but I promise I'll try to be a good listener. That's only if you want to."

"I do. Only right now I feel so talked out with Muriel. And I'm so tired."

Almost as if she had been waiting in the wings for her cue, Muriel walked into the room. "Okay; I'm glad you two had a chance to visit. Now I think you need to rest, Shondra. You're still very weak. You have enough time before dinner to take a nap."

"Will you still be here when I get up, Brandi?"

"I will."

"Okay. Then I'll see you a little later." Shondra rose from the couch and walked slowly from the room.

Muriel gave me a kiss on my cheek. "That was nice of you, Brandi. I think your talk did her a world of good."

"Were you listening?"

"Only toward the end. It's less what you said than what you did. You spent a little time with her and were supportive. That's what counts."

I followed Muriel into the kitchen to help her make dinner. Once we were settled into our tasks, I asked, "So what happens with Shondra now?"

"As far as her living here, everything stays the same. If there is anything legal to deal with, Brian and Jay can handle that. We'll take one step at a time."

"What about the swimming team and the college?" I asked.

"I don't know the details. But I do know she'll stay in the program. Why don't you talk to Mike? He probably has figured out

117

something to do with Shondra. Just remember, when you talk to him, though, that only the five of us know the whole story about the accident: Shondra, Brian, Jay, you, and me. Even the college knows only that she was in an accident. Let's keep it that way."

"That sounds fine by me."

3

The next day on campus felt odd for me. The place seemed so tranquil. All the things that had been happening left me feeling jittery, definitely at odds with the outward calm of the school.

I went to my office to check my schedule before I headed to the athletic center. I had upcoming meetings, and I needed to get my head in the right place to work constructively. Talking to Mike would help me settle down. Once I found out his thoughts about Shondra, I would be able to put that issue aside for a while.

Mike was his usual ebullient self. Just seeing him in action with the kids on the swim team refreshed me. I felt myself relax.

"Hi, Brandi. How are you?" Mike called to me, as he moved across the floor.

"I'm good, Mike. I wanted to say hi to you and see how you and the team are doing."

"We're doing great. We all talked about Shondra and made a decision together. As soon as she's able to, we want her back with us. She can be our student manager until she's well enough to swim."

"Oh, that sounds like a good idea."

"Yeah; she can be in the middle of things that way. She'll know what's going on. And she'll be able to work out a little in the pool as soon as her doctor says it's okay."

We talked a few minutes longer about general things going on—strengths of the team, upcoming meets. I'd learned what I wanted to know about Shondra's place on the team, and I left the pool feeling less stressed.

Chapter Twenty-five

The Tutorial Students

1

As usual, Chriz was punctual and upbeat when he arrived for his tutorial. We chatted for a bit, and then we went over his last essay.

"I hope to do better each time, Brandi. I don't know if I am advancing as much as I should; I seem to make many of the same mistakes."

"I think you are progressing very well, Chriz. The more you write, the better you get."

"Thank you, Brandi. Your confidence in me helps me try hard."

Chriz settled into his writing. I had planned to use this time to read material that Dr. Maddox, the professor whose class I sat in on occasionally, had given me. Instead, I spent the time reviewing my lesson plans for the three tutorials. Chriz had that effect on me: I wanted to do the best job I could, for his benefit as much as for my own.

When Chriz finished his essay, he brought it to me and said, "I tried very hard to write correctly. I hope I succeeded."

"If you did your best, that's all that matters. Anyway, I'm sure you did a fine job. Your writing really is quite good, Chriz."

"Thank you, Brandi. You seem very busy today, but I was hoping you have time to join me for a tea."

"Oh, Chriz, I do have a lot to do, but I'll make time."

"That would be nice. I wanted to tell you that I have been practicing my speaking, too. I am trying not to sound so foreign, so I'm using more colloquial English. Did I use that word right? I looked it up in my Webster's."

I laughed. "You are doing fantastic, Chriz. You can practice on me right now."

"It's a deal, Brandi. Thanks."

Chriz and I chatted on our way to the Pit. He was an engaging talker; I loved hearing his stories about Africa. Today he told me an old tale about a lion and a young warrior. He walked back with me to my office.

"I guess that story was not the best one for practicing informal English," he said.

"Maybe not, but I enjoyed it. Just keep practicing in all your conversations. You'll only improve."

We said goodbye at the office door. He left, and I went inside to read his essay:

> I've been working very hard; I am testing my limits. I want to excel in my studies so I will be accepted by an important university where I can achieve recognition. It is not the recognition that is my goal. If I am recognized as a prominent maths and sciences scholar, then I will be able to achieve more opportunities to make a better life for myself and then for my people. By "my people" I mean people suffering in my homeland, but I also mean any people suffering in my adopted land, too. How are they suffering? They want for food and a home; they want for education and a job; they suffer most for lack of dignity. I hope I can extend my good fortune to any people suffering. I must stay focused on purpose. Sometimes I fear distractions from enticements.
> Respectfully, Chriz

After I read Chriz's essay, I was struck by its heavy tone. He certainly had written clearly and well, but he also seemed worried about other things, too. What did "distractions from enticements" mean? What was he afraid might hinder him from serious study? Something was bothering him; I told myself I should ask him next time when we were going over the essay.

I really was thick sometimes. How could I not have guessed immediately what— who— the enticement was?

When she strolled into my office the next day, I nearly exclaimed out loud, "Of course!" Who else but Lindsay would be the temptress?

Damn, I thought. Chriz didn't need her complicating his life. She was a recipe for disaster; or at least she was a lousy partner for someone as academically ambitious and as emotionally vulnerable as Chriz.

Looking her over, I was not impressed. But I knew she attracted the opposite sex like a light attracts a moth. And she'd be just as lethal for somebody like Chriz.

I wanted to warn him, but I wasn't sure how to go about it in a way that was subtle and wouldn't offend him but would succeed in separating him from her advances. Also, I had to be careful that I didn't overstep my bounds with Lindsay.

Randy seemed to have disentangled himself from her clutches, as far as I knew, anyway. Maybe Chriz had the fortitude to keep Lindsay at a distance and focus on his studies, just as Randy concentrated on basketball first.

I shook my head to dispel my negative projections of Lindsay. After all, both young men were capable of sorting out what was most meaningful for them. And Lindsay was one of my charges, too. I owed her my best intentions just as much as I did Chriz and Randy.

As it turned out, Lindsay and I spent extra time going over her last essay and working on some specific areas of grammar and composition that she needed to develop. Since she was amenable to work-shopping her writing, I devoted my energy to helping her in that area.

I told her she could write a short essay, since she'd worked so hard. "Oh, thanks, Brandi. That's good because I've got some things to do right after this. It's going to be for a special occasion."

"Oh. Why don't you tell me about it in a short essay, then,"

I said.

"Okay." Lindsay began writing in her notebook.

A few minutes later, she was done. "That was quick," I said.

"Well, I wrote what I wanted to. I've got to go. See you."

It didn't take me long to read what she wrote:

> I finally thought of a way to get Randy's attention. He's so in love with that stupid Jeep; I'm going to surprise him and get it detailed. I'm going to this place today to find out all the options and how much it costs and stuff. After that, I have to figure out how to get him to let me borrow his precious car to take it to the detailing place. Wish me luck!
> Lindsay

Good luck, indeed, I thought. I wondered who really needed the luck. But at least Lindsay's essay, short as it was, was well-written in comparison to most of her others.

Randy arrived for his session soon after Lindsay left. I wondered if they crossed paths as she left and he was coming in. He seemed a little out of sorts, but, when I asked him, he said, "I'm fine. I've had some days that were better than others in the past week. I'll write about it."

"That's a good idea. I want to go over the last essay first. Your writing is getting better. There are a couple of areas where punctuation is inconsistent. Let's take a look at those."

When I had completed my critique, Randy got right to work. When he finished the essay, he seemed in a hurry to leave. "I'm all done now. I'm going to shoot some hoops before practice starts. I'll see you next time," he said and was gone.

I picked up his essay to read right after he left:

> I've had some good days and some not bad but not as good days these past days. The good stuff comes from

basketball, of course. It's always good. I practiced hard and I played hard in our game. We won. That was great. But the best part was we all worked as a team and that's how we won. It looked like we would lose to this other team. But then coach told us to think how we worked together in our practice and to do it right then against this other team. And we did and it worked and we won and we were so pumped. Our practices have been great now. I also had a good day the day of my science quiz. I really studied for it some every day from the day the prof told us we'd have a quiz. And I did okay—better than okay. I got a 88. Now it makes me want to study more all the time. The badder day was when Lindsay got really mad because I broke a date with her to study for that science quiz. Boy can she scream. And use a lot of foul words too. I don't like to swear. I could write more about all this but my hand hurts. And I want to go practice and then study. You probably don't want to read all this anyway. It's probably boring.

Randy

3

I was musing about the odd triangle of Lindsay, Chriz and Randy when Jay picked me up Saturday morning for our drive down the coast. The weather was beautiful, he had the top down on the car, and he'd brought a picnic for us. I put all thoughts of the others out of my mind. This day was going to be for us.

We sang to a mix Jay had, as we drove along Route 1. There was a lot of traffic, but it didn't matter, at least not to me. I was happy sitting in that beautiful car next to Jay, singing to Neil Young and Eric Clapton and even a couple of Bee Gees songs.

Jay had chosen to take us to the botanical gardens, which occupied many acres of land along the shore near Boothbay. The place was a gardener's delight, with flowers, trees and shrubs, and sculptures. Lovely paths and trails virtually beckoned visitors to follow them through meadows, woods, and along the water. There also were many benches for sitting and little nooks and crannies to rest in; they afforded plenty of privacy.

We meandered through some of the flower gardens, admiring the multitude of blooms and variety of colors. We ate our picnic in a birch grove that offered a view of the bay and some islands. Jay had packed cheese and pâté and some great bread from a local bakery in Portland, as well as peaches, plums and wine. I only dared have one glass of wine, especially in the middle of the day. Naturally, Jay had thought to put in a bottle of water, too.

Finally, we ended up sitting on a bench that was tucked among a lot of shrubbery in a wooded area off a path. I caught a glimpse of the ocean through some of the trees. It was time to talk.

"Brandi, I've thought and thought about what I want you to understand about me. I need to tell a little about my childhood, I think, so you will know me better. It's not easy for me to talk about this, but I have to. Otherwise, it's always going to be a barrier between us."

"Whatever you decide to tell me is what I want to hear, Jay," I said. I don't know why, but I was a little scared. I wanted to know all there was to know about Jay Bingham, but I was afraid things might change between us. Once you tell something, you can't take it back.

"I'm just going to start talking, and, when I finish, you can say whatever you want."

Chapter Twenty-six

Jay

1

I adored my father. When he came home from the office, he would walk in the door and give his briefcase and his coat to Roland. Then he would stoop down and open his arms for me to run into them. He would twirl me around and around till I was so dizzy that I'd yell, "Stop, Daddy, stop."

He'd fall onto the couch with me on top of him. We'd laugh and laugh. This would happen every night of the week except Saturday and Sunday.

On Friday night we would go to the house in the country; we would be together most of the time there. Usually, he only left me to play tennis, and even then he usually let me come with him. Mrs. Judson, my nanny, came, too, but I liked her so I didn't mind. I was with my father.

Some Saturday evenings Mother and Father socialized at their club. Those Saturday nights I didn't like very much. Mrs. Judson tried to amuse me, though, with games and stories.

Many Saturday nights my parents had people come to dinner instead of going to the club. My father did that because of me, I think. He told my mother he would rather be near me than at the club. They disagreed about it; I heard them sometimes. My mother said he was spoiling me. She wanted to go out instead of entertain at home. My father said that the staff did all the work. All she had to do was look beautiful and be his partner.

Mother still didn't like it, though. She told my father he coddled me. She said I would turn out weak, but he just laughed. "Don't worry about Jay; he's a strong little boy, and he'll grow up to be a strong man."

My father owned a small, prestigious investment firm that his grandfather had founded and his father had managed after him.

My mother was beautiful, just as my father had said. She was tall and blond, with blue eyes. My father was fair and blue-eyed, too, but he was large-boned and ruddy-faced, while my mother had a delicate frame and pale skin.

They met at her debutante coming-out ball. My father told me she was so beautiful that he proposed to her that night. They didn't get married for a while, though. He said she made him wait until she dated all the other suitors; then she decided that he would be the one she would marry.

I think they were happy. My mother continued to live the way she always had before the marriage; she did what she wanted. We lived in a huge apartment in Manhattan and had a staff to take care of everything. She had charities she worked at, and she rode her horse almost every day. She also had me, but I don't think I interfered much with her routine.

I think she loved me the way her own mother loved her. She was aloof, not like my father, with his physical boisterousness and cuddling. But she kissed me and hugged me and was kind. I felt loved by both parents.

2

My father died when I was six. He went to work one day, and he didn't come back. I remember feeling lost then.

The following days were a blur. I know I cried a lot. I remember that, when people came to the apartment, Mrs. Judson would take me upstairs to my playroom. We would spend the time reading or doing projects. Sometimes she would talk to me, about my father and about other things, too. I knew she was trying to make me feel better. I didn't, though.

Less than a year later, my mother remarried. Conrad Skinner was a friend of both my parents. He was a widower. I knew him as Dr. Skinner; I had never seen him with a woman, and I guessed that his wife had been dead for some time. Conrad was a lot older than my mother.

I was too young to understand very much. We moved to a different apartment on the other side of Central Park. It was just as big and had a doorman, and there were many servants there, too. But it was different, and I felt alone and lonely.

Mrs. Judson was gone. Conrad said I didn't need a nanny anymore; I was old enough. I missed her very much, but it was true that I didn't need her. Yet I missed her presence and her devotion to me.

The biggest change was Alma. She was Conrad's daughter. Alma was fifteen and went to a day school in the city. She had blue eyes like my mother and me, but her hair was very dark and curly. She was not very tall, but she had strong legs and stood very straight, like a dancer. She was a dancer.

Alma took dance lessons and had a studio in the apartment for practicing. The dance instructor came there sometimes, and other times Alma traveled downtown to her studio.

The problem began with the dancing, I think. At least the problem for her did—that and Conrad's attentions to my mother. For me, the problem was Alma.

Before my father died, my life had been full of laughter, physical closeness and love. Other than the laughter, it was a quiet home. I never heard either of my parents raise their voice at anyone.

Conrad's home was loud and rancorous. It seemed the dissension centered on Alma. I watched it quietly and from a distance, both physical, when I could keep out of the way, and mental, when I would will myself to think of pleasant things from the past.

But I could not distance myself emotionally. I grieved for my father, I missed my mother's former serenity, I disliked Conrad's overbearance, and I hated Alma. It's a terrible thing to say you hate another person, but it was true. My seven- and eight-year-old self was miserable, and I blamed Alma.

I remember many arguments about Alma's body. She hardly ate, and Conrad grew more furious and impatient with her.

As she became thinner, their fighting became more intense. The last fight I remember vividly.

I couldn't exit the room in time. We were having dinner, and, as usual, Alma was not eating. Conrad would not stop shouting at her. She finally picked up her dinner plate and threw it at him.

I shrunk down in my seat and trembled. Things like this never happened in my real life, as I had started thinking of the life before my father died. Conrad rose from his chair and stepped over to Alma. He grabbed her by her arm and yanked her from her seat. Then he slapped her across the face.

My mother gasped, and I started to cry. But I made sure I did not make any noise.

Alma was not quiet, however.

She looked her father in the eye and screamed, "You bastard!" Then she spat at Conrad, hitting him on the cheek. The spittle ran a little before he picked up Alma's unused napkin from the table and wiped it off his face.

Conrad's demeanor changed then. My mother was sobbing quietly; I could hear her, even with my head now practically between my legs. I feared I would vomit.

I couldn't see them, but I think Conrad still was holding Alma because she did not leave the table. Otherwise, I thought she would have left the dining room.

When he spoke, his voice was controlled, controlled and cold. "You are a disappointment, Alma. I've given you everything since your mother died, but you are a consummately ungrateful child. I will not have you in this house while you disrespect your mother and are such a poor role model for your little brother. You will go to boarding school until you decide to act appropriately. There will be no more dance lessons, either."

"May I be excused to my room now?" Alma asked. Her voice was as controlled as his had been.

"Unless you plan to apologize to your mother for disrupting dinner, you may go to your room and put together your things to take to school."

Alma must have moved across the room. When she spoke, her voice came from farther away. "She's not my mother. My mother is dead. And you should be, too."

The door to the hallway slammed shut.

The room was quiet for a few minutes. Then my mother spoke. "Conrad, are you sure you want to send Alma away? Are you being too hasty?"

"I've been thinking about this for a while now," he said. "I even contacted the headmaster at the Mt. Brighton Academy in Maine. He's an old college friend. She can start there anytime."

"Maine? That's so far away."

"It's not that far. It will give her a chance to think. The place is strict; they won't put up with her antics. She'll get straightened out, and then she can come back."

Alma left early the next morning in the town car, driven by Leonard, Conrad's chauffeur.

I had had a hard time sleeping after the fight, and I overslept in the morning. No one woke me. Only my mother was in the dining room when I entered.

"Alma is gone, Jay," she said. "She left with Leonard."

"Did Conrad go with her?" I asked.

"No, only Leonard."

I said nothing, but I was glad. Now the apartment would be peaceful. I thought that my mother would pay more attention to me if Conrad was not so mad all the time.

3

After Alma left, things settled down at home. I was happier, my mother seemed satisfied, and Conrad calmed down.

At first, Conrad seemed relieved that Alma was not interfering with our lives. He said she was better off at school. My mother and he went out more often, to concerts, charity events and other social engagements. I didn't care for the fact that my mother was not there for me in the evenings. When they were home, however, our dinners were quiet affairs, for which I was grateful.

I went to school each day. Leonard drove me and picked me up. The school was all right. I made friends easily and did well in my lessons. My mother usually was at home when I returned from school,

Our life wasn't to stay calm and orderly for long, though. Things did not remain peaceful, as I had hoped. Even though Alma was not in the apartment, she still was a part of our life. Worse, she managed to disrupt it again.

Alma ran away from Mt. Brighton Academy. Conrad got a call in the middle of the night. She had been there less than a month.

No one told me the details, and I didn't ask. I didn't want to know. Things got bad again, and I wished Alma just would go away forever. My mother remained serene, on the outside, anyway, but Conrad became distraught. He went to Maine, and he hired someone to find her. The longer she was gone, the more upset he acted.

I don't know why, but the investigator didn't find her. Alma remained missing. My mother tried to soothe Conrad, assuring him she would turn up when she felt like it.

Over six months went by this way. My days continued as before, and my mother's activities with me didn't change. Dinners were not as relaxed as they had been right after Alma left, but Conrad was quieter. Everything was orderly; there were no raised voices or fighting. I didn't realize it then, but probably Conrad was drinking more. He always had had one or two cocktails before dinner, but now he seemed to start as soon as he came home and still had a glass in his hand when I went to my room around 8:30.

I was home alone one evening. My mother had persuaded Conrad to attend some charity function with her. The phone rang, and, when the housekeeper didn't answer it, I picked up the receiver.

"Skinner residence," I said.

"Daddy? Daddy, is that you? I want to come home.

Please."

It was Alma, and I thought she was crying.

I started to answer her, but I stopped. Instead, I set the receiver back in the cradle. Then I unplugged the phone from the wall.

I rushed up to my room, changed into my pajamas and got into bed. I would let Louise, the housekeeper, be blamed if anyone asked why the phone was unplugged. No one did, though. If Alma called again, nothing was said about it, so I didn't think she had.

Several days later, I was home alone after school. Conrad was at work, Louise was off for the day, and my mother had gone to one of her now infrequent afternoon appointments. The day's mail was on the table by the door. Looking through it, I saw a letter addressed to Conrad in familiar handwriting: Alma's.

I crumpled it and put it in my blazer pocket. Then I picked up a book of matches from a coffee table and went to my room. I took the letter from my pocket, carried it to my bathroom and dropped it into the sink. I lit a match and burned the letter. Then I scooped up all the charred pieces and flushed them down the toilet. I opened the window to let out the odor. Also, I sprayed some air freshener the cleaning lady kept under the sink.

I tried to forget about the phone call and the letter. Since I never saw any more letters, I thought Alma was over her homesickness or whatever it was. I knew that what I did was wrong, but I so wanted things to stay the way they were without Alma.

Then Conrad had a stroke, which totally incapacitated him. He could not speak, and he was paralyzed on one side of his body. At first my mother hired around-the-clock care for him. When he did not improve, she had him moved to a nursing home. Barely more than a month after that, Conrad died.

Almost immediately after the funeral, we moved back to the other side of Central Park, to a smaller apartment but one that was luxurious. My mother hired all new staff and changed her name back to Bingham. She seemed content. I was happier than I had been since my father died.

131

What I did was wrong. I knew that when I did it, but, as I got older, I realized how heinous the act was. I consoled myself, however, by deciding Alma was living somewhere far away and was happy. I thought that she probably had become a dancer. Mostly, though, I kept myself from thinking about her at all.

Chapter Twenty-seven

No Turning Back

1

When Jay had started talking, my first reaction was to hold him. I felt such compassion because his pain was so evident to me. I held his gaze at first, but then he turned his head slightly, and he seemed to focus on something far away. His voice varied. Some of the time, it was clipped; a couple of times his tone took on the cadence of a child—jerky, a little breathless, and tentative.

I knew Jay was aware I was there because we held hands, and I never loosened my grip on him. Yet, he seemed to travel somewhere beyond me.

Although I was startled by his story, it was not because of what he did as an eight-year-old boy. I could understand that behavior. What shocked me was that his innocence had not been protected by his family's wealth and position. He was as vulnerable to disaster as I had been.

We shared a commonality from our otherwise different childhoods. We both suffered the loss of a loved parent and turmoil, some caused by our own actions, but some thrust upon us by outside forces.

I was at a loss as to what to say. "Thank you, Jay, for sharing such a tumultuous experience. I can relate to some of your pain, but I'll tell you my story another time. I'm sure you're feeling pretty raw. What can I do to help?" I asked.

"Oh, Brandi. You are helping just being here with me and being you. I was afraid you might be disgusted after you heard my tale, that you would judge me a monster."

"Never. There's nothing disgusting or monstrous about it. You were a little kid. Did you ever talk to your mother about the phone call or the letter?"

"I did. I wasn't sleeping well. I would have dreams about

Alma, or about lost letters and missed phone calls, anyway. So one day, when we were alone, I finally blurted out what I had done."

"Admitting what you did to your mother was such an honorable thing to do. It must have helped both of you."

"Ironically, I think it had the opposite effect," Jay said. "She didn't seem either upset or surprised. I was surprised, though, that she already knew about the phone call and the letter. I was even more surprised when she said that she had received phone calls from Alma that she disconnected. She intercepted letters meant for Conrad and didn't tell him. I thought that, after we talked, we would have become closer then, but, instead, we grew away from each other."

"What happened?"

"At first, I wanted to talk about it and ask her questions. I wondered if she ignored Alma because she hated her, too. At the least, I wanted to confess my feelings toward Alma. But my mother closed the door on all conversation having to do with either Alma or Conrad. It was harder to talk to her about most things after that. Eventually, we hardly communicated."

"Oh, Jay. That must have been so painful. You loved your mother so much."

"It was. I learned to live that way, though. Over the years, I closed off that part of me. I love my mother, Brandi, because she's my mother. But I don't much like her. Probably the sentiment is mutual. We talk when it's necessary, which isn't often. She didn't come to my law school graduation. I haven't seen her in a few years."

"I'm so sorry; I really misunderstood. I just assumed you had a great relationship with her."

"Now you know. And I'm glad. Thanks for listening and being so sensitive. I think it's time to change the subject. We can talk about it again sometime, but now I want to do something fun with you."

We walked back to the car, Jay's arm around my shoulder and mine around his waist. I felt so close to him.

134

I ran to a beautifully painted horse on the covered carousel by the bay. Jay stood beside me. "Don't you want to get your own horse?" I asked.

"Nope. Yours looks like he might rear up and gallop off any minute. I better keep him in line while my girl's riding him."

We had walked from the huge parking lot at the marina to the center of the village, where the antique carousel stood. We had held hands and smooched a little while we waited in the long line for our turn.

The shadows had lengthened, and the evening was turning cool. When the ride was over, we wandered around, looking into shop windows and checking menus at a few restaurants.

We found a little place overlooking the water and considered ourselves lucky to get a table for two on the deck. As we sat down, Jay broke off a pink flower from the vase on the table, and, reaching over, he placed it behind my ear. "There. You look like a princess."

"And you are my Prince Charming."

The dinner was extravagant. The pasta was tasty, but the price was the real extravagance. When the waiter suggested dessert, I shook my head at Jay.

He paid the bill. Heading out, I suggested ice cream. "I saw a place up that street somewhere," I said.

"Well, that's precise. Let's go."

We walked up and down and around before we finally turned one more corner and found the ice cream shop. Jay bought us double scoops of ice cream in big Belgium waffle cones. He ate his quickly, but I was not making much headway with mine.

"If you don't start eating the ice cream soon, you're going to be wearing raspberry all over your white dress. And I'll be embarrassed being seen with you."

"Oh, yeah, smart guy? I don't think raspberry will look any better on your blue shirt, so you better be careful."

Just then, I saw a couple of kids, maybe twelve or thirteen.

They were holding hands and looking at us. "Hey," I said. "I can't eat this. And my boyfriend is going to smush it on my dress. Would you like it?"

The boy looked at this girlfriend; she nodded. "Well, yeah, sure, if you don't want it," he said.

As they took the cone and moved off, the girl looked back at us and said, "Thanks."

"Hey, that was nice of you, Brandi. By the looks of them, I don't think they had enough money between them to buy an ice cream."

"Not at the prices they charge here," I said. "And besides, now you won't be embarrassed to walk with me."

"I'll show you what else I'm not embarrassed to do." Jay picked me up and carried me over this little footbridge and put me down on the other side. "Do you think you might be ready for this?"

I looked around and realized we were standing before the entrance to a swanky-looking hotel alongside the marina. I think I let out a little gasp. Then I looked up at Jay.

"It's completely your decision, Brandi. Not counting my father when I was a little boy, I've never felt so close to anyone as I do to you. I told you I love you. I want to be with you— especially tonight. We don't have to do anything you don't want to. But I'd like to spend the night together." Jay spoke in a soft tone.

"Oh. But I don't have any clothes or anything." Then I looked at the backpack hanging off his shoulder. "Oh. Is that why you've been carting that around all evening?" He smiled. "Well, I can't let that effort go to waste. I want to see what's in it." I reached for the pack, but Jay pulled it back.

"Oh, no, you don't. Not till we get inside."

"Do I hide in the bushes until you register us as Mr. and Mrs. John Doe?"

He reached into his pants pocket and palmed a key. "Allow me to escort you to your suite."

"You certainly are full of surprises. When did you do this?"

"While we were having dinner. You went to the ladies room, remember?"

"Huh? How'd you do it so fast?"

Jay laughed. "That waiter figured you passed up dessert because you were 'hot to trot'."

"Oh, my gawd, Jay. You had him get the key and…oh, good grief; he must think I was your lady of the night."

"He only passed it to me. The concierge at the hotel sent someone over with it. Don't worry, though. It was in an envelope—a plain, sealed one. Nobody knows your secret."

I nodded. Jay scooped me up again and walked toward a small, cottage-like building to the side of the main building. He opened the door and carried me inside, closing the door with his foot.

3

Walking over to the bed, Jay dropped me onto it. Before I could react, he removed the backpack from his shoulder, upended it and dumped the contents in front of me. I noticed toiletries, including condoms, some underwear, a bright sundress and what appeared to be a skimpy nightie.

"Gee, looks like you came all prepared. If I'd said no, would you have picked up some lovely on the street?"

"That wouldn't have been a bad idea, but then you'd have had to thumb a ride home. And I'm a gentleman; I wouldn't have left you stranded." Jay took a dive and landed on the bed beside me. I punched him in the arm, and he started tickling me. Pretty soon, we were laughing and rolling around. Then Jay fell off the bed, and I rolled off on top of him. I sat up on him, looked into his eyes and we both stopped laughing.

"You are so easy to be around, Brandi," he said. "I want to make love to you, but I want you to enjoy yourself, too. I want our first time to be fun, not uncomfortable or alarming."

"Gee, Bingham, are you getting cold feet? You sound like

you want to bail on me."

"Oh, no, I didn't mean…" I stopped his talking by kissing him, just a long, slow and soft kiss on his lips.

"Be quiet," I said. "Just don't tickle me again, or I'll scream. And I'd rather kiss you and kiss you and then…" I sat up suddenly. "You know, I don't know what then. I'm at a loss what to do next."

"How about we just take it slow. I'll show you what I know, and you can let me know if you like it. Then I bet you can improvise; you are pretty innovative."

"Okay," We climbed back onto the bed; Jay pushed me down and kissed my neck. I squirmed.

"Hey," I said. "No tickling." I rolled over onto him, pulled up his shirt and kissed his bellybutton. He started laughing again and ran his fingers up and down my back.

We spent a lot of time playing around. I guess it was a form of foreplay, but it was so exciting and so much fun that I forgot to be scared about having sex for the first time. We segued into our passion naturally.

He went about it slowly, taking off my clothes one piece at a time. I wanted to remove at least some of his clothes, too, but he wouldn't let me. "I want to look at all of you and touch all of you first," he said. Finally, when I was anxious to become an active participant, he whispered, "Help me take off my clothes, now, Brandi."

Making love with Jay was a wonderful, private experience. I know I felt happy afterwards, and I felt closer to him, too. I think Jay was glad. He said, "I never thought two people could have such a good time making love. You are amazing. I find out something new about you all the time."

I don't want to make love with anyone else. I don't think that it could be so fulfilling. Now I'm glad Dean and I never made love. I never would want to start comparing him and Jay. It wouldn't be fair to either one. Dean and I share something no one can touch, but now Jay and I share something that is ours alone.

Chapter Twenty-eight

Love of Life

1

After the day and the night Jay and I spent together, I felt different. A perkiness and a spring in my steps evidenced an increased confidence. My self-esteem also had been growing since I met Muriel, and now Jay gave it a kick-start. It led me to believe that I could make more of an impact on the lives of others—that I could make more of a difference—especially with Lindsay, Randy and Chriz. I also thought I would be more effective in Shondra's life. I can't remember a time that I felt this good about myself.

Jay and I went to the lake on Sunday. The change in our demeanor was obvious to Muriel and Brian, but, wisely, they said nothing. I could tell, though, by the looks Mure gave me and her prolonged gazes at Jay. Once, when I caught her eye, she blushed. In my whole life, I never saw Muriel Buckman blush once. The fact that she didn't say anything to either of us was telling; I don't remember Mure ever being at a loss for words.

Brian acted overly-bubbly to me and buddy-buddy in the extreme toward Jay. He squeezed my arm or patted me on the back nearly every time we crossed paths. He made countless comments to Jay, such as, "Come and help me grill the steaks; it's men's work," or, "Let the ladies do their thing. We men have our own duties." Normally, Brian never talked this way.

I decided to say nothing, too. Jay and I hadn't discussed what we would or wouldn't say, and I think he was following my lead.

The only person who acted normal was Shondra. She didn't pay any more attention to us than she usually did. "Hi, Brandi, Hi, Jay," and comments such as, "I hope we can go in the boat," "Maybe I can try swimming a little later; the doctor said it would be okay as long as I don't strain myself or try racing yet," were typical of the things she said to us.

After lunch, we talked about going for a ride in the boat. Muriel and Brian declined, saying they had some pre-wedding things to attend to. "But you three go ahead. Brandi, I know you know how to drive the boat, and I'm sure you do, too, Jay. Don't you?"

"Oh yes."

"Just stay away from Sandbar Beach"

Jay nodded, and Shondra said, "Yeah. I don't ever want to go there."

I was skeptical that Mure and Brian had so much to do about the wedding that they would miss a chance to go out on the water, especially on such a hot day, but I didn't say anything. They must have had their reasons. The three of us headed out on the lake.

2

Jay drove the boat, and Shondra stood next to him. I happily stretched out on the rear seat; I wanted to work on my tan.

It was hard to talk over the sound of the motor, but Jay was gesturing to Shondra to take the wheel. He started showing her how to use the throttle, and he was pointing to the instrument panel. For basic instructions, it wasn't necessary to talk.

I must have dozed. Suddenly, the boat swerved, and I was thrown around the seat, nearly falling onto the floor of the boat. I looked toward Jay and Shondra. He cut the throttle, and the boat slowed to a crawl.

"What a crazy fool! That guy wasn't even looking where he was going," Jay said. "You reacted fast, Shondra. Have you had experience with boats before?"

"No, but I was watching all the boats around us, and I saw that one tear-assing toward us. I thought something was wrong, so I tried to get out of his way."

"That was good thinking." Jay patted her on the shoulder,

smiling down at her.

Shondra smiled back. "Thanks, Jay."

The rest of our ride was uneventful. We drove around near shore, looking at some of the camps and year-round houses. Then we headed back to Mure's house.

I didn't want to stay too late at the lake, but we decided to take a swim before we left. Jay and I dived off the dock. Shondra slipped into the water without diving; I guess she wasn't supposed to dive yet. Muriel and Brian walked into the water; she went in quickly. Brian took his time, sputtering and groaning all the way.

"Good grief; how do you people get in so fast? It's an assault on the body. Oh, my word! This is excruciating! I think I'm going to freeze before I make it in all the way." Finally, Brian kicked off the bottom and glided over to Muriel, who was treading water several feet away. He turned on his back and floated, kicking water all over Muriel.

"Hey," she said. Then she surface dived and came up under Brian, using her momentum to flip him over. He grabbed at her, they both went under and then they came up coughing and laughing.

Jay, Shondra and I swam toward the float. Jay arrived first and pulled himself up easily. Even though she was still recuperating, Shondra beat me. Jay reached out a hand and pulled her onto the float. I brought up the rear and was headed toward the ladder. Jay came over and pulled me up, too. We lay down, luxuriating in the feeling of the warm sun on our cool skin. The float rocked with the waves. I almost fell asleep again.

"I'm going to head in," Jay said. "You two staying or coming with me?"

Shondra and I looked at each other. "Let's stay a few more minutes," I said. Shondra nodded her head.

Jay dived into the water and swam quickly and gracefully back to the dock. He hoisted himself up and headed toward the house. Muriel and Brian already were stretched out in loungers on the deck.

"You must be feeling better, Shondra," I said. "You swam

fast out here."

"I'm a lot better. The doctor said I might be able to swim with the team by the end of next week. I won't be doing very much, but at least I can participate. I'll be glad to get back into it."

"Don't answer if you don't want to, and tell me not to ask if you'd rather not talk about it. But it happened, so I don't want to pretend nothing did happen. Are you okay about losing the baby? Tell me to mind my own business if I'm overstepping."

"No, it's all right. I never really thought about it as a baby. Those guys attacked me, and then I found out I was pregnant. I never even had a boyfriend before. I was so scared. I didn't know what to do. When they came after me again, I was mortified. Maybe I'm a bad person, but I'm not sorry they died."

"I thought one of them was still alive," I said.

"Yeah, but they don't think he'll make it. He's on a machine and in a coma. I guess Muriel didn't tell you yet. Maybe she forgot, but I don't think so. Maybe she didn't want to bring it up today. But I'm okay. Like I said, maybe I'm being bad, but it's a relief for me. I'll never forget any of it, but I want to go on with my life."

"I think I understand, Shondra. It's really been a trauma for you."

"Yeah. And I want to have a baby someday, but I want it to be with someone I love. I see the way you and Jay are. You love each other. I hope I can have a love like that."

"I hope you do, too. I hope you have many good experiences before that, too," I said.

Jay called from the dock, "Brandi, I think we should go soon. Are you ready to come in yet?"

"I'm coming," I said. "Thanks for talking to me, Shondra. And good luck next week on the team."

"Thanks, Brandi."

Both of us swam into shore. I got dressed, said my goodbyes to Mure and Brian, and Jay and I headed around the lake to my college house.

Driving along the lake in the car with Jay, I felt at peace. I was in love, Mure and Brian were in love and getting married soon, and Shondra was in a much better place than she had been two months ago.

I felt more relaxed about my tutorial students. They were young adults, and the interaction between Lindsay and the two guys would work itself out just fine, I thought. In a way, it was a little comical; maybe Lindsay would get dropped by both Chriz and Randy, and she would learn a lesson.

I leaned my head back on the headrest and looked over at Jay. He was watching me. "You better keep your eyes on the road, fella," I said.

"Don't worry; I'm a good driver. I was catching glimpses of you. You look so perfect right now. Are you happy?"

"I don't think I could be more happy. My life is good. And you're the best part of it."

"I'm glad because you are my life, the most important part of it now. I think I am as content as I'll ever be."

I said, "We are lucky we found each other."

"I think I found you. You didn't seem interested at first. But I knew I wanted you."

"What makes you think I wasn't interested? I had these bicycle bells going off in my belly every time I saw you."

"As in women needing men like a fish needs a bicycle?"

"You know the quote by Gloria Steinem?"

"I know the lyrics by U-2."

"Oh, I don't think I've ever heard that song."

"Hold on; I've got it right here somewhere. Open the glove box and take out that blue CD case. It's in there—the 'Achtung Baby' CD."

"Here it is," I said.

Jay put the CD into the player, and we drove along listening to, "Trying to Throw Your Arms around the World." When it was over, I said, "Wow. That was pretty incredible. I'm surprised I never heard it before."

"And you thought I had to read Steinem. By the way, does that mean you do need a bicycle, woman?"

"I don't need just any man. But, if you come with a bicycle, then, yes, I do. Because I need you."

"I'm getting a bicycle tomorrow, first thing," Jay said. We both laughed. "Hey, I saw you and Shondra talking. How did that go?"

"She was upfront about a lot of stuff. I'm glad we talked. You seemed to get along pretty well with her on the boat, letting her drive it and all. I thought you didn't trust her."

"I didn't in the beginning. I knew she was up to something. She had lied about herself, and I was suspicious of her reason for getting to Muriel. But, now that I know, I understand. I also think she's a pretty good kid, considering all she's been through. She's smart, too."

"Yeah, she is. I'm glad you like her now, because I do, too."

"I'm still reserving judgment, though. Time will tell with that girl."

Our evening ended with sweet kisses in the car. I hope the neighbors enjoyed the show.

Chapter Twenty-nine

A New Purpose

1

The next week I was energized by the change in my relationship with Jay. I felt light-hearted. My outlook was positive, and no task seemed difficult.

I looked forward to the meetings with my three tutorial students. I thought that each of them had improved in writing skills; they would be ready to take the required college writing course in the fall. I could concentrate on individual areas of weakness in the time remaining.

When Chriz approached me at the steps of the Irwin Bell Tower and invited me to have lunch with him early that afternoon, I accepted. "Sure, Chriz; that would be fun. I can meet you in the Pit about one," I said.

"One is good. But I was thinking of eating in the café instead. They have good lunches, too. It's smaller, and they play music. I could meet you there," he said.

"All right. We can do that. I'll see you about one, then."

"That's great. I hope you have a nice morning, Brandi."

"You, too, Chriz."

My good mood continued, even when Lindsay, with an attitude, showed up in my office a short while later. She stalked into the room and dropped her back pack, with a loud thunk, on the floor.

"Hi, Lindsay. You don't seem too happy this morning. Is something wrong?"

"I'll say there is. I tried to do something nice for Randy, and he totally blew it off."

"What happened?"

"Remember I wrote I was gonna surprise him and get his

Jeep detailed? Well, he wouldn't let me have the keys and borrow it. He said nobody drove his car. I got so mad that I told him why I wanted to borrow it. And he still wouldn't let me. He said his precious Jeep was "clean as a whistle" cuz he never let it get the least bit dirty or messy."

"Oh. Well, maybe you can use the money you saved to take him out."

"Like where would I take him?" she asked.

"You must have saved quite a bit for the detailing. So you could take him to a movie and pizza or a nice restaurant for dinner."

"I was gonna use my dad's credit card. I can use it for whatever I want. If he asked, I'd just tell him I had my car detailed. But dinner or a movie doesn't sound very special."

"Let's see. How about taking him to Old Orchard Beach? There's a lot to do there. You could go to the beach first. Then later you might eat some of the great junk food and go on a few rides. I bet that could be fun," I said.

"I don't know. Maybe."

We changed the conversation to a discussion of her last paper. Lindsay was inattentive. I had to repeat myself a few times. Finally, since she was so distracted, I ended the tutoring session and had her get to work on the next essay.

Lindsay tried to cut that time short, also. I told her she had to write for at least fifteen minutes more. I got a nasty look, but she did comply. When she handed me the essay, she didn't say goodbye; she practically stomped out of the room. So much for the writing calming her down, I thought.

The essay was a diatribe of venomous ridicule. I nearly laughed as I read it. Lindsay was so immature and self-centered. At least, putting all that anger on paper would get it out of her system, I hoped. I predicted that she'd be all lovey-dovey with Randy next time I saw her:

> I should burn that stupid Jeep up. It would
> serve him right. Nobody should be that attached to a

car. Especially not when you have a girlfriend and you already spend to much time playing basketball and studying. I should show him how lucky he is to have me as his girlfriend. I'll find something to make him sorry he doesn't treat me good enough.
Lindsay

2

The next day Randy came to see me. He was upbeat, so I presumed Lindsay and he had made up. We went over his previous essay. I told him how pleased I was with his improvement. Randy was attentive to my critique; he said he had come up with some ideas for improving his writing. He wrote about them in his essay:

I started rewriting my assignments for all my classes. And I'm using a dictionary now. I used to think you couldn't find a word if you couldn't spell it, but actually you can. Like I just looked up actually—I started to write it acktualy, but I knew it was wrong. So, when I couldn't find it, I took out the k and tried again. And I got it. I just needed to add another l. It takes me longer to write, but I don't mind so much. It makes me feel like I'm smarter when I can't spell a word and I look for it in the dictionary and then I find it. It's kinda like a shot that I might miss, and then thinking about it and the best way to do it, and then laying it up right and making the shot.
Randy

After reading Randy's essay, I felt proud of him. Before he started the tutorial class, he didn't care about writing or any academics. They only mattered insofar as they were necessary if he was going to be able to play basketball. Now, it seemed that he actually took pride in writing well. I was happy to think that I had a part, if only a small one, in helping Randy see the importance of good writing.

3

That same afternoon, Chriz showed up for his writing session a little early. "I hope it's okay if I start now, if I don't disrupt your schedule too much. I need to get to the bank, and it's off-campus. Lindsay said she'd take me, but it has to be before the bank closes. Will it be all right with you?"

"Oh, of course, Chriz. That was nice of Lindsay to offer. Are you seeing more of her now?"

"She comes by the room where I study and sometimes to the lab. I told her I can't go out; I need all my time to study. But she can come when I study, as long as she studies or at least is quiet. Once in a while, she brings a Coke or a shake or something for me."

"Sounds like she likes you."

"We are friendly, yes."

"Well, good. I'm glad you're making friends."

"I am, too, Brandi."

I showed Chriz a couple of short essays that I thought might interest him, both for their content and for their writing style. We talked about how he might use some of these methods in his writing. Then, Chriz wrote his essay for the day, and I read it after he left:

> I have been putting aside some of my money every week. I don't have much, so I can't save a lot. But this week I realized that I have saved enough to send it to my father. He is saving up money to send for my aunt, my mother's little sister. She is only a couple of years older than me. She was in a camp in Pakistan for a long time. Now she is in Egypt, like we were, but it is very dangerous there now. So my father is working to get her a visa and then pay her way to America. I will get a Banker's Check

148

from my bank to send to my father. Lindsay was nice to offer to drive me to get it. I am very happy that I can contribute some money to help my Aunt Amira.

    Respectfully,

    Chriz

Chapter Thirty

A Night at Muriel's

1

The morning was hot; I had an urge to go to the lake and visit Mure. When I called, she greeted me warmly and agreed that I should come to the house.

"Come this afternoon, if you can, and stay the night. Brian won't be home. He has some kind of meeting in Portland and is staying at the condo. Come right after lunch if you're free. We can spend some time together, just the two of us."

"Don't you have to pick up Shondra from swimming?"

"Not today. Dottie Winthrop is bringing her home. She works in the Dean's office. We switch off. Her daughter is taking a course and has a summer job there."

"Oh, okay. I don't have any students to see this afternoon. Jay is busy tonight, so I'll stay over, too."

"That's great. Then I'll see you shortly."

I said goodbye, thinking that I missed the times Mure and I spent together, without anyone else around. Those opportunities were few and far between these days.

I had thought that I would spend more of the summer hanging out with her. Things never traveled a straight path. She and Brian were living together now. Shondra had come into our lives and was staying with Muriel. And Jay had appeared to change my life. All of these things were good. But they meant that Mure and I saw each other less. I was looking forward to some quality time alone with her.

I skipped lunch and left the college around noon. The drive out to the lake was quick. Once there, I changed into my bathing suit, and the two of us went to the dock to sit in the sun.

For a while, we just lay there, basking in the warmth and enjoying the companionship. I might have dozed for a few minutes. Mure's voice brought me back.

2

"So tell me about Jay. I know something significant is going on; I saw it the last time you two were here."

"Yeah. I finally fell in love with someone else. I wondered if I ever would love anyone after Dean. Jay's different enough that I'm not comparing them."

"I'm glad. I think he's an upstanding young man. I gather this is more than a passing romance."

"I don't think I could have a casual love affair with anybody. No, you're right. I'm pretty serious. And Jay is, too."

"Have you talked to him about Dean?"

"Not yet. He knows what you told him about us." I looked at her and smiled. "It's okay that you did. I'm glad you did, actually, because it makes it easier when I tell him the rest."

"Are you planning to soon?"

"Pretty soon. He told me more about himself, some troubling things about his childhood. I feel much closer to him, and I want to share my past now."

"I think you make a nice couple."

"You know, we did it. We made love. I wondered if I'd ever be able to let myself do that with anyone. Dean was supposed to be my only lover, on our wedding day."

"I assumed as much. You told me about Dean, and I guessed about you and Jay the Sunday you came here after going off together the day before. Brian figured it out, too."

"It was pretty obvious, huh?"

"Both of you acted different. There was a closeness, a sweetness, between you that was new. I'm glad."

"Well, we don't have any commitment or anything."

"I shouldn't think so. It's a first step for you, maybe even for Jay. That I don't know. But I think it's a positive place for both of you to be. For now, I think you should enjoy yourselves and

151

each other."

"Oh, we are."

I heard the sound of a car door slam and voices. We looked at each other, and Mure said, "That will be Shondra."

3

Muriel called to Shondra, who came toward us. "Hi, Muriel. Hi, Brandi."

"Hi, Shondra," I said.

"Hello," Muriel said. "We're having a girls' night. Why don't you put you suit back on, and we'll all go in the water before we eat. Does anybody want to go shopping after that?"

We agreed we did want to shop. Muriel and Shondra wanted to look for school clothes for Shondra, and I just wanted to look at clothes; I hadn't been in a store in months.

Shondra had good luck finding several things she liked at Old Navy. She had some money of her own from babysitting for kids around the lake, and Muriel bought her a couple of items, sneakers and a jacket. I looked, but I didn't see anything I wanted.

On the way home, we picked up some ice cream. Muriel said she had cream and fresh peaches, so we could make sundaes.

"Let's put on our p.j.s, since we're alone. We can sit on the deck and talk girl talk," I said.

"Sounds good to me," Muriel said.

Shondra nodded her head. "I'm glad I'm here. Everything is so nice—people, the house, the lake—everything. This was fun tonight."

"You didn't have a lot of times like this before, I guess," I said.

"I didn't have any times like this. Before my mother got so sick with those drugs, she was nicer to me, but she was moody, too. She could fly off the handle for no reason. We didn't have much money, either. So we never went places."

"Do you miss her?" I asked.

"I miss my mother. But she was gone a long time before she died. That person was a crazy woman. I don't miss her."

"I don't even know; was there a funeral? If there was, did you go?"

"We both did," Muriel said.

"Yeah. I said I didn't want to go, but Muriel told me I'd probably regret it later if I didn't say goodbye. She was right. It did feel right. At first, I was scared, but now I want to get back to school."

"Did you see your uncle at the funeral?"

"Yeah, but only for a few minutes. Muriel stayed with me. He said he was sorry about everything. I don't know what to think. I don't hate him or anything. He never hurt me, but he didn't help me, either. I don't want to go live with him."

"You won't have to, Shondra," Muriel said. "We promised you. Brian is working on your case. It might be you can live here. You can stay here for now, anyway, and finish school in Portland. If you'd rather not, we can arrange to have you go to school out here."

"I'm not sure. I think Portland, but then I wonder how hard it will be to see kids I know there."

"We still have time. You don't have to decide tonight, or tomorrow, either."

We sat without talking for a few minutes. Then Muriel got up, saying she was turning in. We said goodnight. Shondra and I remained sitting. I could hear a boat out on the water and an occasional bird cry nearby.

Presently, Shondra started talking. "My mother ruined her life. I don't want that to happen to me. For a while, I thought it was going to happen."

"What do you mean?"

"She left home and got pregnant young. I did, too; I was younger, but I was raped. I don't know if she was or not. But I know she didn't love my father. And he may not have been my father.

"How do you know?"

"Sometimes they would fight about it. I would hear them. They fought a lot. That's what I remember when I was little. Later I could understand what they were saying."

"People sometimes say things they don't mean when they are angry or hurt," I said.

"They said the same things so many times that I know they were true. Sometimes I would cry at night, and he got up and comforted me. My mother would tell him I wasn't his. He'd say of course I was. Then she'd say, 'When there are four guys, you can't know who's the father.' Then he said, 'But I was the only one who loved you right from the beginning. I always loved you.' And she'd kinda snort and say, 'You always loved my body.' 'And I love our little girl, too, Alma.' And she'd say, 'That's a crock.'"

I interrupted Shondra. "What did he call her?"

"He called her Alma. That was her name."

I sat there, stunned. It couldn't be, could it? That was impossible. It was just a name.

Chapter Thirty-one

A Dilemma

1

Shondra continued to tell me about her mother. I sat, attentive, but asked no more questions.

"Anyway," she said, "That's why I think my father was not my real father. I mean, he's one of four guys she was having sex with at the same time. What kind of teenage girl does that? But I know now I won't be like her. It was a close call with those three creeps. And after getting a lucky break, I'll never let a guy near me till he marries me."

She stopped and then resumed talking. "I think calling it a lucky break, when those guys died and I miscarried the baby, must sound terrible to you. That whole scene was awful, and it's lousy what happened to those guys. But they were doing horrible things—not just what they did to me, but they sold drugs and beat up people and stole, too. They kinda set up their own ending.

"For me, it was a lucky break—after the rape, I mean. I found you and Muriel, and I lost their baby. Like I told you before, it never was a baby to me. You get babies when you love somebody and you make love together, not when three druggies rape you and make you pregnant. I definitely could have ended up like my mother if I had to marry one of those thugs. Ugh! My skin crawls just saying it.

"Well, I'm really tired, so I think I'll go to bed now. Thanks for listening to me, Brandi. 'Night."

After Shondra left, I stayed on the deck for a while. Then I got up and went into the house.

Tapping lightly on her door, I pushed it open and whispered, "Mure, are you awake?"

"Well, I am now. What's wrong?"

"I need to talk to you."

"All right." She pulled down the covers. "Hop in."

"Not here. Not in the house. We have to go outside where Shondra can't hear us."

"You can be mysterious in the middle of the night. I'll get some clothes on and meet you outdoors."

I waited in the driveway. A few minutes later, Muriel joined me. "We have to talk out here?" she asked.

"No, it's too chancy. Either we sit in the car or we take a walk down the road. Shondra could wake up and follow us out. She can't hear what I'm going to tell you."

"Okay. Let's walk down the road to the corner. I gather this is terribly important."

2

"I need your advice." I spoke softly, even after we were far from the house. "All of this is really sensitive, but I don't know what to do. So I have to tell you; you'll know what to do."

"You give me an awful lot of credit."

"I have a dilemma. Part of it has to do with Shondra and the other part with Jay. He told me something in confidence, so I wasn't going to say anything to anybody. But now Shondra told me something tonight that could be very important. It could be a coincidence, but, if it isn't, then maybe they need to know. If it's a coincidence, I look like a fool, and I've breached a trust with Jay— sort of, anyway. He didn't actually tell me to keep it a secret. But if it's true, and I don't say anything, it's still bound to come out sometime, and then it's maybe a bigger crisis."

"Brandi, stop it. You are rambling, and you're not making sense. I am your mother. You have every right to come to me for advice in a difficult situation. So, calm down, and start from the beginning. You can just give me the big picture; skip all the little details."

"Jay told me something about his childhood and his

156

mother. He had a stepsister who ran away when she was about fifteen and he was about eight. She tried to come back later. She wrote and called. But Jay hung up on her and burned the letter he found in the mail. He found out later his mother did almost the same thing. The stepsister's father never knew, and then he died."

"All right. And Shondra?"

"Tonight she told me some things about her childhood and her mother. The mother's name was Alma."

"Let me guess. Jay's stepsister was called Alma, too."

"Yes. I feel like I could be holding the lid on a pot that might boil over. What should I do?"

Just then we heard the sound of a car behind us and turned. The car pulled up beside us and stopped. "What in God's name are you two doing in the middle of the road at one o'clock in the morning?" Brian asked.

"Oh, you scared us. I thought you were staying in Portland tonight."

"*I* scared *you*? I couldn't imagine who would be out now. I finished up earlier than I expected and decided I wanted to come back here for a good night's sleep."

"Well, you must have ESP because we need your advice."

"Right now? I was hoping to go to bed in a house full of sleeping women. Oh, all right, I gather this is important or you wouldn't be wandering out here in the dark at this time of night. Let's go inside, and we can talk."

Muriel and I got into the car. "We can't go in the house, in case Shondra wakes up. We can talk in the car. Just go down the road a little ways and stop."

"You definitely have piqued my curiosity now. This seems like cloak and dagger stuff."

Muriel gave Brian a brief version of the issue. He sat quietly until she finished.

"Do you think I broke a trust with Jay?" I asked.

"By telling Muriel and me, I think you broke no trust. The two of us are deeply involved with Shondra, both legally and emotionally. We will keep the information confidential. I'll be able to look into the situation or get someone to do it discreetly. If the name is a coincidence, that's the end of the matter. It goes nowhere."

"What about Jay?"

"What about Jay?" Brian asked.

"Well, if he ever finds out anything, how do I defend what I did? If it's true, he'll have to know, and he'll want to know who started the whole thing. He'll realize that I went behind his back. If it turns out to be a coincidence, I've even done a worse thing, because sometime he will find out the name of Shondra's mother, probably the way I did. Then he'll ask questions."

"Brandi, stop," Muriel said. "You're rambling again."

Brian cut in. "And you're creating more of a problem in your head than there is realistically."

"What should I do?"

"Let's take it a step at a time," Brian said. "We are involved in checking the background of Shondra's family. So far, we have been focused on the uncle because, potentially, he could be a blood relative and have grounds to petition for guardianship. We've finished that investigation. The uncle's been ruled out. Shondra's presumed father, and the uncle's brother, was not her biological father. We've been able to verify that fact. And there's no record of any sort that would reveal paternity. Our next step is to look at the mother. We were ready to do that, anyway."

"What about Jay?" I asked.

"He did some work on the case of the uncle. So it's logical for me to enlist his help with regard to the mother's background."

"Am I supposed to pretend that I don't know about the

name? I feel like a traitor. And if he finds out I knew and didn't say anything to him after he shared his past with me…oh, man what a mess."

"Brandi, again, stop," Muriel said. "Don't keep building disasters in your mind."

Brian said, "First thing tomorrow, I will confer with Jay. I'll get him involved in the search of the mother's family background. You probably won't talk to him before nine or ten in the morning, Brandi. You can tell him you have something you want to tell him that may or may not be important, and you want to tell him in person rather than on the phone. Then, when you see him, you can tell him about your conversation with Shondra."

"What if he finds out we talked tonight?"

"Nobody knows what the three of us have talked about tonight. I'm so tired that I've already forgotten," Brian said.

"I think it's settled then," Muriel said.

"What if he freaks out when I tell him?"

"Don't invite problems, Brandi. Wait and see."

"Okay. I think I fixed your little drama," Brian said. "Now I just want to go to sleep."

Muriel punched him on the arm and pushed him out of the car. They walked to the house, arm in arm.

I sat a bit longer, musing. Muriel and Brian allayed much of my distress, but I still feared Jay's reaction when he learned that Shondra's mother's name was the same as his stepsister's name, the stepsister for whom he felt so much remorse.

Chapter Thirty-two

Hiatus

1

As it turned out, I didn't see Jay for several days. He called late on the afternoon after my midnight talk with Muriel and Brian. He told me he was going to be tied up for most of the week.

"I have some work I'm doing for my firm that my boss, Colin Dunfey, assigned to me. There are some meetings I have to attend in New York. Brian asked me to look into another matter for him while I'm there. So, I'll be busy. I hope I can get things wrapped up quickly, but I should be back by Friday night."

Part of me breathed a sigh of relief. As much as I would miss him, I was glad to prolong the moment when I'd have to tell him about the name coincidence. "That's okay, Jay," I said. "I will miss you. There's something I want to talk to you about; we can do it over the weekend."

"Can't you tell me now?"

"I want to tell you in person."

"That sounds ominous. You aren't planning to break up with me, are you, Brandi?"

"Oh, no, Jay. It's nothing about us. It has to do with something else entirely."

"Well, can't you give me a hint?"

"I'd rather tell you when we are together."

"Okay, as long as it's not bad news for us. I love you, Brandi, and I'm going to miss you."

"I'll miss you, too, Jay. Call me if you can."

"I'll call you at least once a day, if not ten times."

I laughed. "As long as I'm not tutoring one of my students, I'll answer on the first ring ten times a day."

After we said our goodbyes, I thought about the reprieve Jay's trip granted me. I felt a little guilty that I was more relieved that he would be away than I was sad that I wouldn't see him. I would use some time to plan the best way to tell him about Shondra's mother and her name.

2

I decided to spend some of my free time with Shondra. Another swim meet was scheduled for that week, and it was to be held at Olietta. I walked to the pool to tell Shondra I would attend. Mike was in the middle of a drill and just waved. I signaled that I wanted to see Shondra for a minute; he smiled, nodded and returned to the group of kids around him. Shondra was in the pool, and I approached the side to tell her my plan. She grinned and flashed me a thumbs up.

I spent a quiet night at my college house, eating dinner with the young women there, visiting a couple of their rooms and turning in early.

The swim meet turned out to be an enjoyable time. Muriel was there, so I sat with her. I told her that Jay would be away in New York all week.

"That'll give you plenty of time to decide how to tell him," she said.

"Do you know what Brian wants him to do there?"

"No, I don't want to know, and neither do you."

Shondra swam as the second in a relay of four girls. They came in first, and we all cheered heartily. Shondra was not quite as fast as she had been before the accident, but she swam strongly and looked comfortable. She must be healing well, I thought.

After the meet, Shondra came over to us and asked if I was coming to the lake again. I looked at Muriel; she said, "It's up to you, Brandi. You know that I always love having you there."

"Why not?" I answered. As long as there were no more dramas, it should be a relaxing visit.

Once there, I decided not to return to the college until morning. Dinner was casual. Brian was late, so we went swimming first. When we returned, he had arrived. He wanted a quick swim and a drink first, so Shondra and I decided to get ourselves showered and dressed for bed before we gathered to eat.

We spent an hour or so, eating, joking, and enjoying ourselves. Brian kidded us about being his "two little girls" sitting at the kitchen table, ready for bed.

For a minute, I felt a wave of jealousy. He was equating Shondra and me; I wanted to be his only "little girl," I thought. Then I chided myself for being childish. Brian was a sensitive and caring person. He knew I was Mure's daughter, for real, and almost his now, too. Shondra was not, and he wanted her to feel wanted.

Shondra and I went to bed early and left Muriel and Brian to themselves. I went to sleep, hoping the whole week would be so peaceful.

3

Randy came to see me the next afternoon, right on time for his appointment.

"How are you, Randy?" I asked.

"I'm great, Brandi. I love everything I'm doing. I hope you are good, too."

"Yes, thank you, I am."

We went over his last paper, and then he wrote his essay for the day. I decided to read it later and took it with me; I went to the pool again.

Today some of the kids were swimming laps, and a few were horsing around at one side of the pool. Mike was letting them relax after a great meet the day before.

I decided to stay on campus that evening and catch up on a few things I had let ride the past few weeks. Once I was done, I changed into my night clothes, settled in bed and read Randy's essay:

Summer practice will end too soon. It's been such a great time, I don't want it to stop. I really love the guys on the team. I wish we could all make the team in the fall. But it won't happen. There are too many when you combine our summer team and the guys coming back to the team from last year. I know I will make it. I am the best player here this summer. I said that when I got here, but I was really being cocky. But I've worked hard, and I can tell that I am stronger, faster and more accurate then the other guys. Now, though, I want to help them get better. We've been doing little practice drills together after dinner, 3 or 4 of us at a time. It makes me proud to do it. I get forgetful about other things when I'm doing the drill practices. Like the other day I left dinner in a rush. Later Lindsay was outside the gym when I was leaving. At first I was a little annoyed because I wanted to hang with the guys before I went back to my dorm to study. But then she started shaking keys and said, "Lose something?" I looked at the keys and saw they were mine. "You left them on the table at dinner. I happened to walk by and recognized them. They might have ended up in the garbage, with all the trash you guys left on the table." So I was glad after all. I had got careless. My mind has been on more than just basketball and my Jeep. So I thanked Lindsay, and I introduced her to a couple of the guys. Maybe one of them will ask her out. That would be good.
Randy

It had gotten so that I truly enjoyed reading Randy's essays. Not only had he improved in his skills; he also had matured in his attitude. I anticipated he'd do well at college, both on the basketball team and in his academic courses. And it looked like he might solve his Lindsay problem, too. Surely at least one of his teammates would find her alluring and ask her out.

Chapter Thirty-three

A Night Out

1

Lindsay skipped her tutorial the next day. Annoying as it was, I selfishly felt good not to have to deal with her. The week was going so nicely that I was glad that I didn't have to listen to her complain. Sometimes I found her behavior trying. She had a way of getting on my nerves. I used the time to read some of the material Dr. Maddox had given me for the class I was sitting in on with him.

Chriz came to his session, as usual. We worked a little, and he wrote his essay. When he was leaving, he asked me to have a "coffee-break" with him.

As we sat on the deck outside the Pit, we chatted about the upcoming fall semester. Chriz asked me when I was leaving Olietta for Boston.

"I'll be heading to school after Labor Day. My mother is getting married that weekend, and I'll be here for that. Then I leave."

"I will be sorry to see you go, Brandi. I will miss you."

"I'll miss you too, Chriz. I've really enjoyed getting to know you."

"Since your mother lives near here, do you think you will come back often?"

"I'd like to, but usually I get so busy with everything that I don't come back until Thanksgiving break, or maybe once before then."

"Oh, that's too bad. I would like to see you this fall. November is a long time away."

"Well, I'm sure the time will go quickly for you, Chriz," I said. "I imagine you'll become as busy as I am, if not more so. You'll have more classes, activities and friends, too, when everyone is on campus."

"Yes, I guess so."

2

We spent a short time talking; then I left, telling Chriz that I had to get back to my office. Before I quit for the afternoon, I read his essay:

It is hard for me to anticipate the end of summer. It means the close of my tutoring lessons and the beginning of my experience as an official student of the college. I have learned a great deal during my stay at Olietta College this summer. What I have learned the most is two things. I learned that I can succeed and grow in my skills if I work hard. I also learned that there are some special people who work very hard to help people like me. I am gratified for such kind people who share themselves with me. Sometimes I get lonely, even though this does not happen to me often. Most of the time, I maintain myself because I feel strong in my desire to achieve my goal of succeeding in America. The first thing I must do is excel in my classes, especially maths and chemistry. Then I will do more science classes. I am improving in my English writing. I have been writing a journal, as you suggested, Brandi. It helps me write better. I also can focus on important ideas or problems. I write them down, and then I read my journal later. It helps me decide how to act and what I should do next. I anticipate great things here at Olietta College for me.

Respectfully,

Chriz

I skipped out early, deciding to go to my college house, take a bath and freshen up before dinner. Then I headed into Portland for a little relaxation time.

The evening was warm, and the Exchange district was crowded with tourists. It was early yet for the young adults, who started hitting the bars around nine. I wasn't interested in joining that group, anyway. I wanted the evening for myself.

I walked through the streets, stopping to browse before a few store windows. Nothing caught my eye, so I kept walking.

Eventually, I decided to stop at one of the small restaurants that populated the area. Many of them had set up a few tables on the sidewalk outside their door. I picked one that faced Commercial Street and sat down, mostly to people-watch.

A glass of wine would taste good, I thought, but I decided against it because I was driving. So I ordered a cappuccino and a pastry. I didn't need the pastry, but I wanted something to go with the cappuccino.

Sitting practically in the throng of people, I was enjoying myself when two people, walking on the other side of the street, caught my eye. I recognized Lindsay and Chriz.

At first, I wondered what they were doing in the Old Port on Thursday night. I thought Chriz, at least, would be studying. Then I remembered that he'd mentioned he was taking money to his father to help his aunt come to the States. He'd said Lindsay was driving him to Portland. So their being in Portland made sense.

But it didn't make sense to me why they were in here rather than on the street where his father lived. I raised my hand to catch their attention, when they entered a bar across the street.

I was tempted to follow them, but I figured that it would appear I was checking up on them. Neither of them would appreciate that, I thought. Maybe Chriz had decided to go out with Lindsay, after all. She was underage, so I figured that she would not be allowed to stay. They would be exiting the bar anytime.

While I was pondering this idea, my phone rang. I answered it on the first ring, saying, "Hi."

"Hi, yourself, beautiful." Jay's voice caught my full attention, and I forgot about Chriz and Lindsay. "What are you doing?"

"Hi, Jay. I'm sitting outside Rajah's having cappuccino, watching the world whirl around me and wishing you were here," I said.

"I wish I were there, too. It's hot and sticky here and not any fun. I finished my meetings, though. Tomorrow I'll look into Brian's thing, and then I hope to fly home in the evening."

"Oh, good. If you get in early enough, maybe you could come by. Or I could meet you at the airport."

"That sounds like a great idea. You could stay at my condo tomorrow night. Would you?"

"If you're inviting me, I would," I said.

"That's a definite invitation. I'll call you when I get to LaGuardia, and we can plan our night."

"Okay. It's a date."

Once we said goodbye, I remembered I had an unpleasant story to tell Jay. I decided it would work out all right, one way or the other.

My drink had cooled off by then, so I paid my bill and left. The drive back to Olietta was easy; commuters had long gone, and most of the traffic was headed into the city.

I slept peacefully that night, dreaming of flying in a plane with Jay. When the phone woke me, I noticed the time was five a.m. Assuming it was Jay, I clicked the answer button and spoke.

Chapter Thirty-four

Pending Disaster

1

"Good morning," I said.

"Is this Brandi Buckman?" a woman's voice asked.

"Yes," I said, instantly wide awake. I sat up in bed and put my feet over onto the floor.

"This is Marcia Coburn, Dean of Students at the College. I need to talk to you."

"Okay, I'm listening."

"No, this is an emergency. I am parked outside your college house. Please dress professionally and meet me at my car as quickly as possible."

"What is this about?"

"I'll tell you on the drive to Portland. Hurry, though." The line went dead.

I dressed quickly and rushed downstairs and outside. A middle-aged woman, whom I recognized from her college directory photograph, was standing by a sedan with the Olietta College insignia on the front door. She got into the car as I approached.

Once seated inside, I asked again, "What is this about, Ms. Coburn?"

"There was an accident last night involving Olietta students. The driver of the vehicle has asked for you."

"Suddenly, my heart started pounding. Randy, Lindsay, who? "Who is it?"

"A freshman named Lindsay Ayers. Another student of yours, Chriz Saaed, was a passenger in the vehicle. They are both at Maine Medical Center; that's where we're going now."

I recalled seeing Lindsay and Chriz together in the Old Port last evening.

"Are they all right?"

"Yes and no. Lindsay has minor cuts and bruises and will be released to the police this morning. Chriz is in the Intensive Care Unit."

"How badly hurt is Chriz? And why are the police taking Lindsay?" I asked.

"The details are sketchy. Chriz is in critical condition. Lindsay is being held on several charges having to do with the accident. Apparently, she asked to see you. What can you tell me about these two? Since you've been tutoring them, you must know something about them."

I told the Dean what I knew of Lindsay and Chriz, leaving out the parts about Randy's car keys and my sighting of them last night.

"All right," she said. "Thank you."

We didn't say much else on the ride. We parked before the emergency entrance of the hospital and hurried from the car, through the automatic doors, into the lobby.

Ms. Coburn gave our names to the man at the information desk. Almost immediately, a police officer came around the counter. "I'm Sergeant Riordan. Follow me."

Instead of heading to the bank of elevators leading to patient rooms on the upper floors, he led us back though the examination cubicles of the Emergency Unit. We stopped at one, he opened the door, and we entered.

2

There sat Lindsay and two more police officers, one female. Seeing me, Lindsay started to rise, but the policewoman put a hand on her shoulder; Lindsay sat back in the plastic chair. Standing behind Lindsay was a man I did not recognize.

"Oh, Brandi," she called. She had been crying. Her face was splotchy, her eyes swollen, and her hair disheveled. There was a white rectangle of bandage taped across her forehead and another on her left arm, between the elbow and the wrist. "Please help me," she said, through sobs.

"I've cautioned Lindsay not to say anything without my okay," the man said, patting her shoulder. I'm Thomas Pelino, the attorney hired by Lindsay's parents, who will be here shortly."

I thought that this must be serious, if the parents had sent a lawyer so quickly. I moved toward Lindsay, but the second officer stepped in front of the small table and said, "Ms. Coburn, Ms. Buckman, please be seated."

We sat in the two remaining chairs, on the opposite side of the table. The policeman who'd escorted us to the room left, closing the door behind him.

Marcia Coburn began talking. "Thank you for calling me, Lieut. Donlon. Please tell us what has happened." She spoke to the male officer as if she knew him. He nodded at her.

"Surely, Ms. Coburn. First, this is my partner, Lieutenant Simone." We all nodded. "Next, this is a serious matter, unfortunately. So, bear with me as I try to relate what we know so far.

"Around 9:00 pm last evening, the dispatcher alerted patrol cars in the area that a stolen vehicle had been reported by a student at Olietta College. The vehicle was a 2015 Jeep Wrangler, license plate number MX1357.

"Around 10:00 pm, a squad car saw the vehicle at a stop light near the downtown entrance to the Interstate. As it approached the vehicle, the driver accelerated onto the entrance ramp, whereby the officers in the car engaged lights and siren and pursued the Jeep.

"The driver headed south, quickly gaining speed. The officers radioed their position, requesting backup. A high-speed chase ensued.

"The Jeep suddenly veered to the right, overcorrected, then spun and crashed into the guardrail. The Jeep rolled and came to a stop, upright, in the right-hand lane of the Interstate.

"Other police cars arrived at the scene, as well as a fire truck and ambulances. Both occupants were taken to the hospital by ambulance.

"Ms. Ayer, the driver, sustained minor cuts and bruises. The passenger, Mr. Saaed, is in critical condition. As we speak, he is in surgery."

"How badly is he hurt?" Ms. Coburn asked.

"We don't know yet. He was unconscious when taken from the vehicle, and, last we heard, he still is."

"Have his parents been notified?"

"His father is upstairs in the surgical waiting area."

I finally found my voice. "Oh, that is awful. But you're going to be all right, Lindsay—just minor injuries?"

Lindsay didn't answer me, but she started sobbing again.

"Actually, Ms. Buckman, Ms. Ayer seems to be in serious trouble. As I said, the vehicle was reported stolen last evening by its owner." He checked some papers in his hands. "A Randall Birmingham."

Oh, no, I thought. The so-called misplaced keys that Lindsay said she found were not mislaid at all. She must have taken the keys again, unbeknownst to Randy, and then taken the Jeep without his knowledge. When he couldn't find the keys, he must have gone to his car and discovered it was gone. Then he assumed someone had stolen it. I looked at Lindsay and started to say something. Before I could, Mr. Pelino cut me off.

"I will answer any questions for Ms. Ayers," he said. "I'm advising her not to say anything. Once her parents have arrived, we will make a statement."

The attorney was not tall, but he was imposing. His voice was deep, and he spoke with conviction. His suit was well-tailored, I thought; it fit him perfectly. The shirt was bright white, starched and crisp. He wore a burgundy tie with small, dark blue stripes. I felt intimidated by him, and I was glad Lindsay's parents had hired him. I wondered what she was being charged with that they had acted so quickly.

Ms. Coburn must have been thinking the same thing. "What are the charges?" she asked.

The policeman looked at his papers again. "Speeding,

driving to endanger, evading a police officer, driving without a valid driver's license, grand theft auto, and, depending on the outcome of the surgery and the status of the passenger, possible involuntary manslaughter."

I gasped. Lindsay started howling.

3

A couple of hours had gone by, and we still were waiting: waiting for surgery, waiting for Lindsay's parents, and waiting for word from Randy. He had been notified by the police that they found his Jeep, which had been wrecked in an accident. They did not tell him who was driving the vehicle, but they did tell him that someone from the school was responsible. If he went to the hospital, they told him, he could see the Dean of Students, and she might give him some news.

We were sitting in another room, on a different floor. It was larger and contained several more comfortable chairs, a couch, and a round table with plastic chairs. In the hall were vending machines. Lindsay and Mr. Pelino sat in two chairs, talking quietly. Ms. Coburn and I sat on either end of the couch. Detectives Donlon and Simone had disappeared, but a policewoman stood just outside the closed door of the room.

Lindsay's parents arrived, finally. They were well-dressed and well-groomed, but they had a harried look about them. Mrs. Ayer's face was pale except for two spots of ruddy color high on her cheeks. She had light brown hair and was very pretty, except for the pinched look about her. She stumbled as she entered the room, and her husband took her arm to steady her. He was tall, blond like Lindsay, and blue-eyed.

Mr. Ayer glanced at everyone in the room and headed toward Lindsay and Mr. Pelino. He hugged his daughter to him, and she cuddled into him; she was a tall girl, but he was much taller. Mrs. Ayer wrapped her arms around both of them. They stood like that for what seemed like several minutes. Nobody said anything.

172

Then Mr. Ayer disengaged himself from his wife and his daughter, who continued to embrace each other. Mr. Ayer shook hands with Mr. Pelino; then they moved to the round table in one corner of the room and sat down. When they spoke, their voices were too low for me to hear anything.

Ms. Coburn rose from the couch and approached Mrs. Ayer; I followed her. She introduced both of us. Mrs. Ayer looked at me, and then she spoke to Ms. Coburn. "Thank you for coming here. I'd like to talk with you, but I think I will wait until my husband and our attorney are done. Then perhaps we all can find a place to meet and discuss everything."

Ms. Coburn nodded. "I think that is a good idea. Brandi is Lindsay's writing tutor. Lindsay asked her to be here with us."

"How nice of you to come, Dear," said Mrs. Ayer. "Lindsay told me about you. She thinks the world of you."

I was surprised by her comment, but I said nothing other than, "How do you do, Mrs. Ayer. I'm sorry we are meeting under these circumstances."

Lindsay had been quiet all the time the three of us were talking. Now she took my hand and said, "Oh, Brandi. I'm so glad you are here. I want to talk to you."

Ms Coburn spoke before I could. "That's a fine idea. For now, though, I think we all should try to relax a little. Hopefully, we will hear from surgery soon. Why don't we sit over here?" With a nod of her head, she indicated the sofa and surrounding chairs.

Lindsay and her mother sat close together on the couch. Ms. Coburn took me aside and said, "I am going upstairs to see Mr. Saaed in the surgery waiting room. I'll be back shortly." She left the room, and I sat in a chair to the side of the couch.

The three of us were in these positions when, a short while later, the door flew open, and Randy stood there. He was dressed in sweatpants and a tee shirt, both rumpled. I wondered if he'd been asleep, when he was called, and came right from bed. He looked around the room, as all of us looked back. "What the heck…" he said.

Chapter Thirty-five

A Discrepancy

1

Ms. Coburn appeared in the entranceway behind Randy, stopping when she saw him. Before he moved, Lindsay jumped and ran toward him. "I'm so glad you're here," she said.

She tried to hug him, but he took a step back and said, "You stole my car?" It was a question more than a statement. "Why?"

"Oh, no, honey. I didn't take your car. Chriz did."

Everyone in the room came to attention. Mr. Pelino stopped talking to Mr. Ayer and moved closer to Lindsay. Ms. Coburn walked around the two students and turned so she could see their faces. The policewoman positioned outside the room entered.

'What?" Randy raised his voice.

"Yeah." Lindsay spoke fast. "He said you gave him the keys so he could take something to Portland. He asked me to go with him. I wasn't going to go, but he begged me. He said he didn't want to go alone. I guess he likes me."

"I don't get it," Randy said. "I didn't give anybody the keys to my Jeep. I'm the only one who drives it. "

"Well, you usually leave the key in your gym bag. Maybe Chriz knew it and took it when you weren't looking," Lindsay said.

Mr. Pelino went to Lindsay. "So this Chriz Saaed took the Jeep and drove it to Portland: You were just a passenger"'

"Yeah, he…"

He cut off Lindsay. "Okay, that's all I asked. You don't need to say anymore now, Lindsay. This fact changes everything. We will need to get you released to your parents." He looked at the policewoman. "You'd better get the detectives back down here."

The officer nodded. "I'll contact them." She pulled a device from her pocket. "We'd best all remain here until they arrive."

"I would like to go back to Mr. Saaed up in the surgical wing," Ms. Coburn said.

"I think that the detectives will contact him. They may want us all to be in the same place."

Just then, the detectives arrived. The policewoman told them what Lindsay had said. They looked at her and Randy, then at Mr. Pelino and Mr. Ayer. Finally, Lieutenant Donlon spoke. "We'll need to get statements from Ms. Ayer. We also want everyone in the same room, so we may have to move to the surgical area. Hold tight, everyone."

He left, but the other detective and the officer stayed with us. I looked at Ms. Coburn, and, with a nod of her head, she indicated a couple of chairs set a distance from the others. We went to them and sat down.

2

"What do you know about Chriz Saaed, Brandi? Would he steal Randall Birmingham's car and ask Lindsay to go off with him?" she asked.

My mind was racing. I was sure Lindsay was lying. Everything she'd written in her essays and everything Chriz had said in his essay contradicted her story. She had a crush on Randy; she had tried to use Chriz as a means to make Randy jealous. Randy had left his keys in the dining hall once, but it seemed more likely that Lindsay took them the second time, also. Chriz told me Lindsay had offered to drive him to Portland.

"I'm completely shocked by everything, Ms. Coburn." That was the truth. I was still shaky and worried about Chriz. That surgery was taking a long time. "I don't know what to think," I said.

Another policeman opened the door and entered the room. We all looked toward him. He told us to accompany him and the detective upstairs.

There was still no news about Chriz's condition. We gathered in a room separate from the general waiting area for surgeries.

Lieutenant Donlon spoke to the one person already in the room. "Mr. Saaed, it has come to our attention that it is possible your son took the vehicle from the college parking lot and drove it to Portland. Ms. Ayer was his passenger."

"Oh, no, sir," Mr. Saaed said. He was shorter than Chriz and gray but otherwise resembled him. "That could not be."

"Why not, sir?"

"My son does not know how to drive. We never have had a car. Before we came to America, we walked. Now we ride a bus, unless we must go somewhere that a bus does not run. Then we hire a taxi car or get a ride from a friend." Mr. Saaed's speech sounded faintly British and formal.

"Who is this guy to contradict my daughter? He's black but he's not an American? What are you? African? What in God's name were you doing anywhere near a black African boy, Lindsay?"

"I felt sorry for him, Daddy. He had no friends and no money. I just tried to be nice to him."

"Well, see what you get for your trouble. These people..." Mr. Ayer shook his fist at Chriz's father. Then he turned to the lawyer. "Pelino, get the charges against my daughter dropped. I want to take her home now."

Just then, a man in scrubs entered the room. "Mr. Saaed?" he asked, as he looked toward Chriz's father.

3

"My son, sir?"

"We finished the surgery. Now we have to wait and see."

"Will he be all right, sir?"

"The operation was a success. The young man is still unconscious; however, some of that is due to the medication. He

176

was heavily sedated. It will be several hours before that wears off. We hope he regains consciousness then," the doctor said. "Why don't you come with me? There are a few things I'd like to discuss with you. It will be clearer with the x-ray pictures."

"Go ahead, Mr. Saaed," said Detective Simone. "We'll talk to you later." Chriz's father left with the doctor.

Mr. Ayer started talking immediately. "Let's get out of here."

"I'm afraid Ms. Ayer has to come to the police station with us for booking."

"She's innocent; she told you. Pelino, tell them," said Mr. Ayer.

"It's procedure, Mr. Ayer," said the lawyer.

"The questions of car theft and the driver will have to wait to be resolved. In the meantime, there are still charges connected with speeding, driving to endanger, evading police, and the accident itself."

"I'll accompany Lindsay," said Mr. Pelino.

"My wife and I are coming with you," Lindsay's father said.

The detective told Randy that he could leave. "But stop by the station later. You'll need to fill out some forms."

"Okay," said Randy. "My father's going to call me as soon as he gets to the school. I can tell him to meet me here, and then we can go to the police station. I need to go downstairs to the lobby to tell my friend he can leave; he brought me here. Is that all right?"

"That's fine, son."

"Brandi, will you still be here when I come back? I want to talk to you, okay?" asked Randy.

"I'll be right here," I said.

Chapter Thirty-six

Varied Relationships

1

After Randy left, Ms. Coburn and I were alone in the room. She looked at me and smiled. "You've certainly had an initiation by fire to the tribulations of a College Dean's job. Are you all right?"

"I think so. You seem to know Detective Donlon pretty well. I guess you've had dealings with him about other students who get into trouble."

"It's one of the tasks of my office. I'm fortunate, though. Mike Donlon is an excellent police officer and great to work with. These kids are lucky to have him on the case."

"I'm concerned about all three students. But I'm especially worried about Chriz. The doctor really didn't say anything about his injuries, only that the operation went well. What does that mean? And Chriz's been unconscious well over twelve hours. I wonder if he is purposely keeping something from us," I said.

"My guess is that it's just too soon for him to go into details. Chriz's injuries are serious. I imagine the doctor does not want to discuss the case until he knows more. He did take Mr. Saaed into his office to show him x-rays and tell him more. Probably he is the only person right now who should know exactly what is going on. Then the police will be informed next."

"You sound like you've been through this kind of situation before."

"All of the medical or criminal incidents I've handled over the years are unique. But they always impact the kids and the families pretty hard. I remember one of the saddest I had to deal with. Sometimes, good things can come from terrible tragedies, however."

"What happened?" I asked.

"It was several years ago. Some first-year boys went out to

a bar and got served. The driver and his roommate were coming back together. I think there was another car, and they were racing, but no one ever came forward to admit anything. Of course the boy was speeding. You know how winding that back road to the campus is. Well, he missed a turn and drove headlong into a tree.

"The roommate was killed. The driver was not seriously injured, but he was charged with driving while under the influence of alcohol and held responsible for the other boy's death. He pleaded guilty. His eighteenth birthday was a week after the accident. He was sentenced to a year and a half in the county jail and then probation.

"Two professors from the college agreed to tutor the student in jail. An English professor and a philosophy professor went to the jail twice a week for two semesters. Once he had served his time, the student came back to the college. He took summer courses and graduated with his class."

"It sounds like people were awfully forgiving to let him do all of that," I said.

"Well, it averted a double tragedy, for one thing. The roommate had been the student's best friend. They grew up together, and both sets of parents were close. The boy attempted suicide soon after the accident.

"The judge, the parents and the college—everyone concerned—supported the idea. The boy is a psychologist today and works with at-risk youth. He also devotes much of his free time talking to college students about the risks of drinking, such as drinking and driving and binge drinking among others."

"Then I guess it really was the right decision."

"One life was lost to a foolish act. At least two weren't. And the dead boy's story probably has helped prevent some other needless losses of life. Sometimes common sense and a little compassion can be good."

Ms Coburn had finished talking when Randy returned. He had combed his hair and was wearing a clean, white golf shirt, and a pair of jeans. His white athletic socks showed below the bottom of the jeans.

"My buddy had these clothes in his car, and he lent them to me. They don't fit very well because he's shorter than I am, but they're clean. At least they look better than my sweats, I hope."

"You look fine, considering the circumstances," Ms. Coburn said.

"Thanks. Brandi," he asked, "do you know what's going on? Who took my Jeep, anyway? I don't know Chriz very well, except from the writing program. I don't know why he would take my Jeep."

"I don't, either, Randy," I said. "His father says he doesn't know how to drive. But it's going to make a difference. Whoever did will be charged with auto theft."

"I'm going to talk to my dad about that when he gets here. I know Chriz a little, and I dated Lindsay some, so I don't want to make things worse for them. If my dad agrees, I'm going to drop the car theft charge."

"That's really generous," said Ms. Coburn. "You know that your car has been destroyed, don't you?"

Randy hung his head. "Yeah, I know. It really stinks. But I have insurance, so, if I still can have the insurance for another car, I'd rather not make Lindsay or Chriz be arrested for that, too. And, if it's Lindsay who took the Jeep, she's already in a lot of trouble with the cops, so she doesn't need car theft, too."

"That's pretty kind of you. You'd best talk to your father first, though, before you say anything," Ms. Coburn said.

"Yeah, okay, I will."

"Randy." A tall, slender man with reddish gray hair walked into the room. I thought he looked like an older version of Randy. He grabbed Randy and put him into a bear hug. "You all right, son?" he asked.

"I'm fine, Dad. It's my friends who aren't, though. I'm so glad you're here. I need your advice, and I don't want to be alone in this. Where's Mom?"

"As long as I'm around, you'll never be alone. Your mom is with Sandy and the baby; she took Grammy to see them. She sends her love, though. Now then, introduce me to these women who are with you, please."

"Oh, yeah, I'm sorry. This is my dad, Randall Birmingham, Senior. This is Ms. Coburn, the Dean of Students at Olietta College, and this is Ms. Brandi Buckman, my writing tutor. I told you about her."

Mr. Birmingham shook our hands. "How do you do Ms. Coburn. I'm sorry to meet you under these circumstances, but I am glad to meet you, nonetheless." He turned to me. "Hello, Ms. Buckman. I feel as if I know you already. Randy has told me a lot about you; he raves about you in fact. And anyone who can make my son care about writing is a person I'm honored to meet."

"I'm glad to meet you, too, Mr. Birmingham. Please call me Brandi. Randy is such a fine young man. I enjoy working with him," I said.

Ms. Coburn added her greeting. Then the atmosphere got cooler, like a damp breeze coming in off the ocean.

"I understand that a serious accident occurred with Randy's car. Someone actually stole it, and a passenger in it is badly hurt. Is that correct?"

"Yes, it is. As the Dean, I am here in all the students' interests. We don't know all of the details yet, and we still don't know the condition of the injured student. I will be staying for a while longer." Ms. Coburn briefly told Randy's father of the discrepancy about the driver. Then she mentioned that the police wanted Randy to file a formal statement with them.

"We probably should do that right away," he said. "We can call the hospital about the injured passenger, or perhaps, Ms. Coburn, you might call us if any news breaks."

"I will do that," she said. They exchanged cell phone numbers. Then Ms. Coburn said, "Randy also wants to talk to you about filing charges, I think. Perhaps you might discuss that on the way to the police station."

"That sounds like a good idea. We'll go right now; then we can either return or go back to the college. We'll be in touch with you, anyway. It's a pleasure to have met both of you. I'm sure we'll see you soon. Randy, you can fill me in on all the details in the car."

After they left, I considered the contrast between Mr. Birmingham and Mr. Ayer. Randy and Lindsay certainly took after their respective parents. I shivered from a feeling that all would not turn out well.

Chapter Thirty-seven

Still More Bad News

1

The end of the week did not bring good news. Chriz was still in a coma; the doctors projected a, "We must be patient and wait for signs of progress," attitude. Lindsay was out on bail, pending any new evidence about the driver of Randy's Jeep from the college to Portland; she had left campus with her father. By Saturday morning, Jay had not called me; I had tried calling his cell, but it went immediately to voice mail. I left a message on my first call, but I didn't on several others. His lack of communication worried me. With so much else gone wrong, I feared something had happened in New York.

I had a hard time getting out of my own way. Most of the morning, I vacillated between going to my office to retrieve the student essays or driving to Muriel's house. I wanted to look at Randy's essays and Lindsay's, in particular; I also thought I should reread Chriz's recent essays. I craved some common sense advice from my mother, as well as legal advice from Brian.

It was nearly noon before I made up my mind that I would get the student essays and read the most recent parts. I wanted to see exactly what each of them said about cars, keys, and Portland. Then I would go to the lake and talk to Mure and Brian.

Making a decision energized me. I got dressed, made a sandwich in the kitchen and grabbed my purse and my keys. I walked over to Irwin Bell Tower, unlocked the main door and my office door. Inside, I got the files containing the essays from my desk drawer. Riffling through the pages to make sure I had everything, I sat in the desk chair. I meant to spend only a minute or two, but, once I sat down, I felt enervated. Finally, I shook my head to clear away the cloud of indecision.

I had to get a grip; I decided to call Muriel to make sure

she'd be home. She answered almost immediately and said she'd be home all afternoon. "I'd love to see you. Brian went to Portland early and probably won't be home till dinnertime. He dropped off Shondra at the pool for some kind of practice. So I'm here alone. Come on over."

I was closing the front door of the building, when my cell phone rang. I looked at the screen and saw Jay's name; thank goodness he was calling, finally. I opened the phone and said, "Hi, Jay. I'm so glad you called. I've been waiting."

"Um, hello; this isn't Jay," a strange voice said.

"Oh," I said. "This is his phone. Who are you?"

"My name is Joel Binder. I live in Manhattan. I was leaving my apartment for a run and noticed this phone on the sidewalk. So I pressed the first 'favorites' key. You answered."

2

I stifled a cry. Was something wrong? What had happened to Jay? Then I took a deep breath, telling myself to chill; he must have dropped it and not noticed, and then he couldn't find it because he didn't know where he dropped it. I forced myself to speak in a normal tone. To Joel Binder, I said, "Oh, I see. I'm a friend of Jay; Brandi Buckman is my name. Could you tell me the name of the street where you found it? You said you came out of your apartment. Was the phone in front of the apartment building? I'm in Maine, but I probably can get hold of someone who'll know where he is." I was thinking that Jay's office in Portland would know where he was going.

"Hello, Brandi Buckman. The phone was on the edge of the sidewalk, about half a block from my building on Park Avenue near 61st. He could have dropped it when he got into a taxi, maybe. There are some offices on either side of the apartment building. Maybe he came out of one of them."

He waited until I got a pen and some paper from my purse; then he gave me his cell phone number, so I could call him later,

184

when he was at home, and tell him where to send Jay's phone. I thanked him and said goodbye. I rushed back to the house to get my car, punching in Brian's cell number while I was running. I got his voice mail, so I left a message. I told him briefly what had just happened and to call me as soon as he got my message.

I drove too fast to Muriel's house. Luckily, there wasn't much traffic, and I didn't see a police car. That would have been like flying blind if I got a speeding ticket on top of everything else.

Muriel came out of the house, as I pulled into the driveway. I jumped out of the car, leaving the motor running and all of my stuff inside. Running to her, I wrapped my arms around her, and, in spite of my resolve to act mature, I started to bawl.

3

Mure always had an uncanny way of knowing what to do to make me feel better. She didn't say anything for a while. We went inside and sat together on her bed, my head on her shoulder and her arms loosely around me. When I stopped sniveling, she handed me a box of Kleenex. I blew my nose and wiped my face.

"Do you feel like talking now?" she asked.

"That's why I came over here; then I couldn't hold it all together. I need your advice."

"How about if we go sit by the water, where it's cool. Then you can tell me everything that's bothering you."

I felt better already, just having her near me. "I don't know where to start. There's Chriz and Randy and Lindsay. That's what I was going to ask you, and Brian, too, about. But then, just when I was leaving to come here, I got this call. And now Jay is missing." I started to cry. Mure handed me another Kleenex.

"Okay; since you seem most unsettled about Jay, why don't you start with him. Tell me how you know he is missing."

I told Muriel about the phone call from Joel Binder in New York. I started to shake, and then I was crying again. Muriel let me cry for a minute; then she said, "There are many reasons why Jay might have left his cell on the sidewalk, and most of them are not indicative of anything dangerous. So let's not jump to the worst conclusion before we know any more. How about I call Mr. Dunfey's number and start there?"

Mure always seemed to know how to cut through to the point of things. I loved her for taking charge; I didn't think I could talk to Mr. Dunfey without falling apart. She took her cell phone from her shorts pocket and punched in some numbers. She must have called his personal number, because she started the conversation by saying, "Hello, Colin."

When she hung up, she pursed her lips and looked out at the lake for a minute. "Colin says that Jay called him late yesterday and said he wanted to follow up on some information he'd obtained from an investigator. He didn't go into any details, but Jay told him he'd be back in the office Monday. Colin didn't seem concerned that he'd dropped his cell phone; if he was rushing to hail a cab, for instance, it could happen easily. Colin said he once had lost an entire brief case rushing for a cab before someone else took it."

"But why wouldn't Jay call me to tell me he wasn't coming home? We had a date."

"If he's at all like you, I'll bet he doesn't know any of the numbers of people he has programmed into his cell phone. And you said the fellow who found it called you because you were first on his 'favorites' list."

"Okay, I guess that's possible. Still, I would have thought he'd have someone call me for him."

"Who? Colin Dunfey? I don't think Jay would want to broadcast to his boss that he wanted him to be a messenger for him, especially to relay a message to his girlfriend. And maybe that's the only phone number he knew, or he might have called the office—he could get that number from information."

"You have an answer for everything," I said.

"That's because most of the possible answers are logical and mundane. Like I said before, there's no sense in thinking the worst where most of the possibilities are simple."

"You're right—as usual. I knew you could help me feel better about this. I'm still a little upset, but I won't go off the deep end now, thanks to you."

"Of course there are bad things that happen, Brandi. You of all people know that only too well. But, in this case, I think taking a wait and see approach is the best idea."

We sat, letting the breeze off the water flutter over our skin and cool it. I suspended any morbid thoughts about Jay, at least for the time-being. Then, Muriel broke the silence.

"You mentioned Chriz, Lindsay, and Randy. Has something happened with your tutorial students?"

I frowned, remembering my dilemma. I told Muriel that Randy's Jeep was stolen, either by Lindsay or Chriz, that there was an accident, and that Chriz was in the hospital in a coma. "All of this is so disturbing. But I also am torn about what I should do. I have the essays the three of them wrote, and they pretty much indicate that Lindsay stole the Jeep and did the driving, not Chriz. But I don't know if I am violating a trust if I show them to somebody."

"I think Brian is the best person to advise you. He'll be home soon. Why don't you either take a swim or go to your room for a short rest. I think you'll feel better able to talk about the problem with Brian."

I decided to take Muriel's advice. I took a short swim, and then I lay down on my bed, anticipating unburdening myself to Brian.

Chapter Thirty-eight

Then There Were Three Problems

1

When I finished telling about Randy's stolen car and the accident with Lindsay and Chriz, Brian sat rubbing his cheek. "Well, what do you think I should do? Should I tell the Dean or the police, or do I have an obligation to keep the essays confidential? I asked.

"Did you sign a confidentiality agreement with the students? Or did you sign anything with the college having to do with your writing assignments?"

"No."

"Then legally you are not bound to keep the information in the essays to yourself. Especially in light of the circumstances surrounding the stolen car and the accident, if the students' own writing can shed light on what happened, then you might be expected to come forward. Otherwise, you could be accused of withholding information."

"Oh. Then I probably should call Dean Coburn."

"You don't have to do it this minute; no one has called, so Chriz still must be unconscious," Muriel said.

"Why hasn't Jay taken care of your concerns, Brandi? He can answer them as well as I can. Why did you have to wait to ask me?"

"I didn't tell you this first, because I wanted to find out what I should do about the students' essays, and I knew you'd have a pretty fast answer. The other problem," I said and felt my eyes fill with tears, "is that Jay is missing. I don't know where he is, he didn't come home when he said he would, and he hasn't called me." I couldn't stop myself from crying.

Brian looked at Muriel. She filled him in on the phone call I'd gotten on Jay's cell and the information Mr. Dunfrey had given us. "Naturally, Brandi's upset, but I think it's too early to jump to

188

dire conclusions. If Jay was gathering more information for Colin, I suspect he'll return, and all will be well."

"Did Colin say he asked Jay to spend the weekend following up on something? It seems unlike Colin to have him stay away over the weekend, especially since Jay's working with the college, too. I would have thought he'd have Jay return to New York next week, if necessary."

"Then you think something's wrong?"

"I didn't say that. Let's follow Muriel's suggestion for now. In the meantime, I'll contact Colin and see what I can find out from him."

"By the way, weren't you supposed to pick up Shondra?" Muriel asked Brian.

"No. This morning she told me she was getting a ride from another parent."

"Do you know who?"

"No, but she said she would be home around dinnertime."

"Then she should be here soon. Brandi and I can get dinner ready while you're talking to Colin."

2

While Muriel put the finishing touches on a roast, I set the table. That chore accomplished, I wandered into my room and looked in the mirror. "Who are you?" I wondered.

My life seemed headed to such good things. I had a purpose with the tutorial; Randy's father said I taught Randy to care about writing. Chriz had become a friend. Lindsay was a lost cause, but it just took a look at her parents to know the reason why. I gave myself to Jay, the first guy I trusted after Dean. He said he loved me and wouldn't hurt me. Well, things sure didn't look so promising now.

I heard Muriel call me from the kitchen. I shook my head to clear it; feeling sorry for myself was something I'd quit doing a long time ago. I wasn't going to wallow in the pit of bad feelings,

189

especially when I had a mother and a soon-to-be father like Mure and Brian for support. Heading down the hall, I answered, "I'm coming."

"Shondra is nearly an hour late for dinner."

"Maybe she got delayed," said Brian.

"I would have expected her to call, then," Muriel said.

"Is there someone you can contact? Maybe that guy from the swim team?"

"Mike. He'll know who picked her up and when. I'll call him right now. You two start eating. I'll be back in a minute and join you. Shondra can eat when she gets here. "

I only picked at my dinner. Brian had solved the problem about the essays. I'd call Dean Coburn in the morning. But I was still worried about Jay. Maybe he wasn't hurt or anything, but something was wrong. He would have gotten in touch with me. If he didn't remember my cell number, he could have called information for Muriel's home phone number. He could have called her and given her a message for me. The distress was pounding at my brain like a jackhammer; I was starting to get a headache.

"You haven't eaten anything, Brandi," Brian said. "I've finished. I'll call Colin right now. I left my phone in my jacket in the car. Be right back."

"Thanks." I started to say something about Jay's dropped cell phone, but he was out the door. I sat, making shapes with the food on my plate. A few minutes later, Muriel came into the room, and I could tell by the look on her face that something wasn't right.

3

"What's the matter?" I asked.

Muriel pursed her lips. "Mike said he doesn't know who picked up Shondra. She disappeared in the mass exodus of all the kids, and he assumed I'd arrived to get her. He said she'd been

190

talking to one of the local boys quite a bit during the day. He thinks it might be connected, but he doesn't know. He said he's coming right over."

"What? Did she leave with some boy? That doesn't make sense. She'd know better than to do that," I said.

"I'm pretty sure she wouldn't do anything rash. But it's late, and I'm worried. It's not like her to go off without asking or telling me. I don't want to be an alarmist, though. We'll wait and see what Mike can tell us. Then we'll figure out what to do."

"That's a good idea. Let's hope Shondra appears soon. Meanwhile the questions keep piling up on our missing boy," Brian said. "I talked to Colin, and he doesn't know why Jay is still in New York. The task he sent him on is completed; Jay told him on the phone. He even sent Colin a short summary of the results."

"Well, then, why was he staying for the weekend?" I asked.

"Colin didn't know. All Jay said to him was that, since he was in New York, he wanted to check on a personal matter and he'd be back in the office on Monday. Colin didn't think anything about it."

I stood up. "But why didn't Jay ask Colin to tell me, if he couldn't find his cell phone?" I felt the jackhammer pounding harder. Jay missing, Shondra missing—what was going on?

Brian said, "Well, we don't know yet."

There was a knock at the door, and Muriel let Mike into the kitchen. The look on his face scared me. His eyes were like black coals, his cheeks were two spots of red, and his mouth was twisted sideways.

I sat down in the chair, hard—more like I fell into it. I put my elbows on the table and my hands around my head. I told myself to breathe slowly, but everything seemed to be spinning out of control.

Chapter Thirty-nine

More Questions, No Answers

1

Interlude

I'm a phony. I haven't always been. Even when I was a screwed up kid, I was real; I was honest with myself. Not always a nice person and not very diplomatic, but I never pretended to be anything I wasn't. I don't know when I started acting a role, being somebody I'm not. In high school, I was natural; especially with Dean, I was the realest person in the world. Even after everything fell apart, I didn't go over to the phony side. Of course, I had a lot of help, and I don't think Muriel would have let me get away with anything less than honesty. First year of college started out fine. I think sometime between then and this summer before senior year, I started to become someone else. I'm not involved with the people the way I used to be, the ones who kept me steady and sane. It takes a whole lot of work to make me be "in charge" every day. I can do it all on my own, but doing it all results in my being a different person, at least up front.

I've been planning to be a writer since high school, but I don't think anyone would think, ah, she's a good writer. I can't even say what I most want. I'm a phony in that category too. I never believed in pity parties before, either, so why am I starting now? The only piece left of the old Brandi is the habit of writing in my journal. I used to do it to keep me grounded, and I had a good friend who liked to read it, and that helped too. But I stopped letting people in since Dean died. Everybody except Jay. And now look what's happened with him. It's me who's gone away from everybody. I can't even find me.

How did this happen? Well, I wonder, too. But I have a pretty good idea of what went wrong; or rather, I went wrong, and

I have some notion of where and why. I just don't know how to get back, or if I can or even want to, when I get right down to the core.

It didn't happen overnight. It's taken a few years. And I have only myself, dear ol' Brandi, to blame. I took a golden opportunity and pissed it away. I guess you can take the freak out of the circus, but you can't turn her into a real lady.

What brought on this tirade? Well, I've messed up maybe three lives, and one of them may die. I should have seen the warning signs. I was so complacent. I thought I was such a raging success as a writing tutor, and I didn't take seriously what they were writing about. Now Chriz may die, and Lindsay may go to jail. And Randy probably won't recover cuz he's so sweet. Oh, and then there's Jay. I told him I loved him, and he up and disappears. That's a real ego-booster.

I'm already sick of trying to recreate my thoughts this way. I think I will try removing myself from the center of my life and pretend I'm another person. Heaven or hell knows I am another person. I'm the story of damaged goods who became everybody's sweetheart and reverted to the loser she was in the first place.

2

I woke up in my bed, screaming. Mure was sitting next to me, lightly rubbing my hands. She made a sort of smile. "Hey," she said.

"What happened?" I asked. I pushed myself up.

"You fainted, honey. I put you into bed. Then you must have had a bad dream. I heard you crying out, and I came in to wake you. Probably it was a combination of eating nothing all day, on top of your distress about Jay and the problems with your students. Then Shondra's disappearance was a bit too much," she said.

"Shondra. What did you find out from Mike? The last thing I remember is that awful look on his face. Has something happened to her?"

"Nothing has happened that we know of so far. Mike was really concerned because none of us knows where she is, and Mike tends to blame himself for not having kept a better eye on her. But it's not his fault. He and Brian have gone out to see if they can find out anything."

"Where are they going?"

"Well, first of all, Mike remembers Shondra spending more time than usual around a boy on the team who lives nearby. They're going to check with his folks to see what they know. Then they'll go from there."

"What does that mean?"

"Just what I said. If they find the boy at home, they will talk to him. If not, they'll follow any lead the parents may be able to give them. They also might call some of the other kids on the team, to see what they know, if anything. It might be a matter of tracking down possibilities."

"Are you going to call the police?"

"Not yet. We don't know that anything bad has happened to Shondra. We're going to look for more ordinary explanations first.

I let my head fall back onto the pillow. "I feel so useless. Here you are holding everything together, and I'm falling apart. I need to get up and help. But I don't know what to do."

"You can get yourself ready for bed and go back to sleep. It's fine if you do. But, if you want to, and I think it may make you feel better, you can come out to the kitchen and talk to me. You could help me troubleshoot the situation. We can talk about Jay, too. It might feel more useful to you than lying in bed."

"Okay. I guess you're right. You always are. What would I do without you?"

"You'd do all right—just differently."

"I don't think I could live without you, Mure."

"Well, you might have to."

I sat up like a flash of lightning. "What are you talking about? Is there something wrong with you?"

"No, there is nothing wrong with me. I plan to live for at

194

least another fifty years. I'm simply saying that unexpected things can happen. If something were to happen to me, you're provided for completely."

"What does that mean?"

"It means this house is yours, as well as all of my investments—everything I own will be yours. My estate is already set up that way."

"Gawd. Are you sure you're not trying to tell me something? And what about Brian? You two are getting married. Isn't everything you have his, too?"

"Brian is the one who's made sure I provided for you. He doesn't need anything material from me. Remember, he's been a bachelor, and he's a wise businessman. He has more than enough himself, even for both of us."

"Oh," I said. "Oh, thank you."

"Okay. Do you think it's time for you to get up and get going? I could use the support."

"Yes, ma'am," I said. "You're beginning to sound like that mean guard in the Youth Center."

"Well, then stop sounding like that half-civilized brat you were back then, dearie."

I got up and put my arms around Mure. We hugged tightly, and she kissed the top of my head. "Go wash your face, and come out to the kitchen. Brian and Mike should be back shortly."

3

Mure and I were drinking tea and eating some oatmeal cookies that she had made earlier in the day, when Brian and Mike came into the house. They both looked tired. Mike had droopy eyes, and his hair was a mess, sticking out all over the place. Brian's shirt was wrinkled, his tie was askew and his eyes were a little bloodshot.

"You gentlemen don't look too ready to dispense good news," Muriel said, as she took out a couple of mugs and poured hot tea into them. "Sit a minute before you tell us what you learned. And have a cookie. It will give you a nice sugar high."

Brian gave Muriel a kiss on the cheek and sat down at the table. Mike stood until Muriel bodily steered him to a chair and pushed him into it. He practically collapsed in the seat.

"All right, now. Start at the beginning, and tell us what you learned."

Brian set down his mug. He'd already eaten a cookie and was holding another. "There isn't a lot to tell. Nothing that's good, but nothing that's bad, either. The boy Shondra was talking to, Jarrod is his name, is a nice kid who lives in the village part of town. We talked to his parents; they are concerned about him, too, and wanted to call the police. He hasn't ever been in trouble. We told them to hold off until we checked a couple of other people who might know something."

Mike said, "We called a few of the kids on the swim team, but they didn't know much. One of the boys said Jarrod had been talking to Shondra a lot during the day. He seemed upset about something, but she's the only one he talked to. One of the girls told us that Jarrod isn't a love interest or anything to Shondra. So it must be about something else."

"When we couldn't find out any more information or come up with any leads, we went back to Jarrod's house. We waited while Mr. Carmichael, Jarrod's father, called the police. Then we waited with him and his wife until the police came. We all gave a statement. They will look around the area tonight and alert area police to watch for the two kids. So that's it in a nutshell," Brian said. "Oh, we also called the Dean. Since both kids disappeared from the college grounds, I decided the school should be informed." He finished the cookie he was holding.

I was sure that I was not going to be able to sleep that night. Muriel insisted I shower and at least put on pajamas, even if I was not going to go to bed. Brian said he was going to bed, since the police would call if they learned anything, and then he would need to be ready to react. Muriel said she was going to bed with him.

196

Mike left to go to his apartment. I sat around for a while by myself. My brain was being invaded by the jackhammer again, so I took an aspirin and decided to lie down on my bed. In spite of myself, I fell asleep and did not wake until the light was coming in under the window shade. Then, the phone rang.

Chapter Forty

Noises from Above

1

I rushed from my bedroom to the kitchen to find out who was calling. It turned out to be Jarrod's parents, wondering if Brian had heard anything from the police. I heard him promise to call them if or when he learned anything.

It still seemed too early to start to do anything, so I wondered why Muriel was dressed up, or at least wearing a dress and sandals. "What's going on?" I asked.

"I couldn't stay in bed any longer," Muriel said, "so I decided to go to early Mass. Maybe a few extra prayers will help. Want to come with me?"

Muriel didn't go to church all that much, especially in the summer. She said there were too many summer people who overfilled the church, and God didn't need her church attendance to know she was a believer. So I guessed she really was feeling more worried than she let on; it would be good for me to go with her. "Yeah, okay. I'll get ready now so we can beat the crowds and get a front seat," I said. "Are you going, too, Brian?"

"No; I'll stay here and monitor the house phone, just in case. When you two get back, I'll have breakfast for you. Then maybe you and I can go to your office, Brandi, and I can take a look at those essays before you call Dean Coburn."

"All right." I turned and went back to the bathroom to get ready for church. I showered and dried my hair. Then I went to my room to dress. I picked out a bright pink sundress; I thought that, if I dressed myself up a little, I would feel better, maybe. I put pink sea glass studs in my ears and a matching pendant around my neck. I jettisoned my usual flip-flops for a pair of heeled sandals, pink like my dress. Then I decided to add a little blusher to my cheeks and some rosy lip gloss to my lips. All I needed was a big, pink ribbon in my hair, and I could pass as a garish summer fool. Oh, well, Muriel would appreciate my effort.

We did not arrive at the church in time to be ahead of most of the parishioners who must have come early: all the aisle seats were filled, and most of the back. The only seats left were in the front, so we settled ourselves there. I had been kidding when I'd suggested the front row earlier, but Muriel took me seriously; or at least she decided that's where we were going to sit.

The early Mass was not very long, but I did have plenty of time to think about what might happen next, with Chriz and my students, with Shondra and, of course, with Jay. I really prayed hard for Chriz, for him to live, first, and then for him to be physically all right and not crippled or something. I prayed for Shondra to be okay, too. She'd already had enough trouble, what with the kidnapping and her hospitalization. I did wonder, though, if she'd done something stupid; after all, she was only fifteen.

I saved my thoughts, not prayers, for Jay till after Communion. I wasn't feeling as charitable about him as I was for the others. I still could not contemplate why he hadn't sent me some kind of message. It really was selfish of him—unless he had run into some kind of terrible incident. Before I could embarrass myself or Muriel and start sobbing like a drama queen, I pulled myself together, deciding I would set aside all possible conclusions I might draw from the lack of communication on his part. There would be an explanation sometime, and I hoped it would be neither tragic nor callous.

Brian had breakfast prepared for us, when we returned. Muriel drank coffee and ate toast and a boiled egg. I picked at my food, failing to eat much of anything. Brian managed to consume three eggs, two pieces of bacon, three slices of toast, two cups of coffee and a glass of orange juice, despite this troubling time. Boy, that man could eat. He wasn't slender, but he wasn't fat, either, for all the food he consumed. I knew he went to the gym every day; he must have sweated away all those calories.

After cleaning up the breakfast debris, Brian said he was ready to go with me to the college, so we headed out.

I unlocked the main door of Irwin Bell Tower Hall, and Brian held the heavy door, while I entered the foyer first. Turning my key in the lock on my office door, I opened the door and stepped inside. Brian came in behind me and looked around. "It's small, but it's quite nice," he said. "You have a lovely view of the grounds. It's very serene-looking."

I laughed. "That's pretty ironic, given the unserene things that have happened here lately," I said. I walked over to the filing drawer on one side of my desk and opened it. Pulling out three separate file folders, I set them on the desk. "These are the essays of the three students. I have them in chronological order in each individual's file; they go from the beginning of the tutorial program until now. I did that so I could watch the progress in their writing skills. Do you want to go over then together?"

"At least until I get the hang of it. But I don't need to see the earliest ones, unless they are relevant to the situation now. Why don't you show me where to start?"

We sat down side-by-side at my desk. I opened Chriz's folder and went to the part where he said he was planning to take money to his father. "Here; start here. This is Chriz's work."

Then I looked into Randy's folder. I decided that Brian should read more of his essays, so that he could get a sense of how Randy felt about his Jeep and about Lindsay. I wanted him to see that she was pursuing him, not the other way around. I set up the essays in sequence. "These essays are Randy's. There are more of these that I think you should read." I set the pile near Brian, but more toward the center of the desk. That way he had room for Chriz's file, and I had room to open Lindsay's folder in front of me.

As I started scanning her essays, I was struck by the transparency of her scorn for school and writing, as well as other people's interests. Her narcissism hit me in the face; it hadn't been so obvious when I read her comments earlier. In hindsight, I could see how she was working up to something unsavory. I got an unpleasant feeling in my gut, and I felt bile rising. Why didn't I notice this before? Why didn't I take her negativity more seriously?

Brian had finished reading Chriz's essays and was scanning Randy's work. "This kid is in love with his Jeep, that's for sure." I sat quietly while he continued reading. "Well, it's pretty clear he was trying to extricate himself from Lindsay's advances." He finished reading and put the papers down on the desk. "I have a good sense of this boy. He seems to be profiting from both your tutoring and his athletic activities. He did an about-face regarding studies. I'm impressed."

I didn't say anything; I knew Brian was right. I handed him Lindsay's folder, open to the first essay. "I think you should read all of hers; that way you'll get a more complete picture of the girl," I said.

Brian read quickly, frowning sometimes. He uttered a grunt at one point, and then he continued reading. I let my thoughts drift. I hoped the essays would help determine who took the keys and who drove the vehicle off-campus. I also harbored the wish that the writing would point to Lindsay; my dislike of her overshadowed any sympathy I might hold for her. My compassion was reserved for Chriz and Randy.

Brian closed Lindsay's folder and stood. "All right," he said. "These essays are pretty definitive. They certainly point to the probability that Lindsay took the keys and stole the Jeep. She seems to have offered to take Chriz to Portland."

"Yes, that's what I've been thinking ever since I was with them at the hospital"

"We need to make copies. I want to read them again. Is there a copier in the building?"

"Yes; it's upstairs, on the third floor."

"Well, let's go. We'll do all of them, just to be complete."

We headed up the stairs to the copy room. It was locked, but I had a key for it. All of the people in Irwin Tower had a key for several doors: front, one's office, kitchen, copy room and bell tower. Why the bell tower I had no idea, but it had come on the key ring.

3

Brian decided we should make two copies of everything. He would keep the second copy for the time being. "It may come in handy at some point. Also, I can make copies from it, if I need them. And I don't want you to hand originals to anyone, at least not without checking with me first."

"Do you think there will be trouble?"

"Honestly, yes. I think that Lindsay may be accused of stealing the truck."

"But Randy said he wasn't going to bring charges against either Lindsay or Chriz."

"It may not matter. If Chriz pulls through this perfectly, then there will be less of a problem. But if he is incapacitated, or worse, then everything, including who took the vehicle and drove it, will be extremely important."

We started with Lindsay's folder. The machine was slow; I guess it hadn't been replaced for quite a while. There was a lot to copy, too. We ran out of paper once and couldn't find any more in the copy room.

"I have a package downstairs in my desk," I said. "I got one at the beginning of the program, in case I had to copy things. I never did, so it's unopened. I'll go down and get it."

I ran down the stairs, my sandals banging on the bare wooden steps. Returning with the paper, I ran up the stairs again, so I was winded when I got to the copy room.

"Here, sit in that chair and catch your breath. After I fill the copier, I'll get some water, if you tell me where the kitchen is."

"Oh, I can get the water. I have a few bottles in the fridge. I keep them there for when I get thirsty or if one of the students wants one. Nobody ever takes anything; you can leave whatever you want in the kitchen."

I went across the hall to the kitchen. The key was hard to

202

turn, but I got the door open and went inside. Grabbing two bottles of water from the inside shelf on the door, I slammed the door shut. Something fell inside; I thought I'd heard a thump. I opened the door, and a glass bottle of juice rolled off the upper shelf onto the floor with a loud crash.

Red juice and glass exploded. I jumped out of the way, missing most of the juice and all of the glass. Lucky, I thought. I found some paper towels and mopped up the mess.

I was returning to the copy room when Brian poked his head out of the doorway. "What was that loud thumping noise I heard?"

"Oh, it was just me. A bottle fell from the fridge to the floor..."

"Not that noise. I heard that one. This was a thwacking, like someone using a baseball bat on something. There it goes again." He pointed up the stairs. "What's up there?"

"The Bell Tower." We both rushed up the stairs toward the door to the tower.

Chapter Forty-one

One Answer

1

I beat Brian to the tower door by a single step. It took three attempts to find the right key from the several on my ring. Now the banging was louder, almost in response to my twisting the key and shaking the door handle.

"Something's in there," Brian said. "Be careful opening the door."

I finally inserted the correct key, turned the handle and started to open the door slowly. It burst open from the inside, and I went flying into the tower. The momentum sent me halfway across the floor, and, in skidding and gyrating, trying not to fall on my face, I landed on my bottom in a heap.

"Holy Smokes," yelled Brian. "Shondra! It's you. What are you doing here? Never mind that now. You're all right? That's all that matters. We've been worried sick about you. We had the police searching and... Who's that with you? Jarrod?"

Brian was blathering. Shondra was trying to say something, but she couldn't get a word in edgewise. "Be quiet a minute, Brian," I said. "Let Shondra talk. Hey, Shondra."

"Hey. Boy, are we glad to see you. We've been locked in here since Saturday afternoon."

"Let's go to my office downstairs. Brian can take you, and I'll get some water out of the fridge. I think there are some energy bars in my top desk drawer. We can sit down, and you can eat and drink a little. You must be hungry," I said.

"We're starved. We had one Coke and two candy bars between us in our back packs, and that's all we've had since lunch yesterday," Shondra said.

Brian came out of his "state" and grabbed Shondra in a bear hug. She hugged him right back. "Oh, girl, we need to call

Muriel as soon as we get to the office. She's been so worried; your parents, also, Jarrod. We'll call them, too."

Shondra and Jarrod ate all the energy bars I had in my desk, a package of six. They drank the water. Then they raced each other to the bathroom.

Brian was on the phone to Muriel. "Yes, they're fine. They were locked in Irwin Hall Bell Tower. I don't know anything yet. They had to eat and drink something. Brandi found some energy bars and water for them. You might want to rustle up something for them. We'll be home shortly. Oh, and would you call the Carmichaels? Maybe they can meet us at the house. Okay, then. We'll be there shortly."

2

We were sitting around the table in Muriel's kitchen: the three of us and Shondra, Jarrod, and the Carmichaels. Muriel had set out tons of food; she must have been cooking from the time Brian and I left for the college. She had a turkey breast, homemade bread, cold cuts, condiments and a couple of pies. The two kids were putting away the food as if they'd been unfed for a week rather than little over a day.

Once they finished eating, Muriel said, "Okay, I've been waiting patiently. Now I want to hear what happened, from the beginning."

At that moment, there was a knocking on the front door. "Who could that be?" Brian asked.

"I'll get it," I said, walking through the living room to the front door. I opened the door, and two uniformed police officers stood there. "Hello," I said.

"Good evening. We were told that the two teenagers were found, and they are here now. May we come in?" the female officer asked.

"Well, of course. Please come into the kitchen. The kids finally finished eating, and they were just starting to tell us what happened."

3

The two of them worked like a tag team. Shondra would say something, and then Jarrod piped in. Back and forth they went until they had told us the whole story. It went something like this:

Jarrod used to hang out with a less-than-sterling group of boys. Since he'd been in the swimming program, he had stopped seeing them and had made friends with some of the boys on the team. He hadn't seen the former friends until Saturday morning.

He was running to the college, instead of getting his usual ride from his mother. He had been trying to run several miles a day to build up his strength; it helped with his stamina for swimming, he said. His parents were against him running on the highway, because the road was winding, and cars often sped along there. But Jarrod argued that he didn't have time to run before or after swimming practice, and, that particular day, he won the argument.

When he was almost to the college grounds, a car approached him and slowed. Then it went past and came back on the opposite side of the road. Jarrod recognized two of his old friends, but he kept running. They started taunting him, and the taunts turned into threats.

Jarrod started to worry that they might try something, so he cut into a wooded area that bordered the college. He started sprinting and made it onto the campus, where there was enough activity to dissuade the boys in the car from continuing their pursuit.

During the day, Jarrod and Shondra talked about his situation. Shondra suggested that, after practice, Jarrod and she go to Brandi's office on campus. They'd be safe there, and they could call his parents, as well as Muriel, to come and get them.

The plan started out well enough. The front door to Irwin Hall was unlocked, so they went inside. Brandi's office door was locked, though, so they tried others. The only door that was unlocked was the door to the bell tower. They went in and looked around.

The view was amazing; they could see for miles, it seemed. They spent some time chatting and pointing out things they recognized. Then they heard footsteps on the stairs, so they ducked behind some timber and waited.

There was a scratching at the door, and they realized suddenly that a key was being turned. The door had been unlocked when they had come in. Someone had locked the door and was descending the stairs.

Shondra was going to yell, but she was afraid they might get into trouble if they were found in the bell tower without permission. Even though she hadn't noticed one, she thought there must be a fire escape or some means of getting down from the tower. But there wasn't.

They thought the security guard might come back later, but he didn't. They sat talking for a while. Then they checked for food. They found nothing in the bell tower, but they ate their candy bars and shared the soda. It got chilly during the night, so they wrapped themselves around each other to keep warm.

When Shondra said this, Jarrod cleared his throat, and he blushed. Shondra spoke firmly and said that nothing was going on with them; they were friends—period. She said she had read in a survival book that, if people huddled together in the cold, they would keep warmer. She said you could do it even with a dog, if you happened to have one with you; and a dog usually gave off more heat than a human.

Mr. Carmichael seemed to relax after she spoke; I peeked at Muriel, and she was smiling. I figured she understood.

They were getting really worried, thinking they would have to wait until Monday morning, when someone opened the main door and faculty entered. Then they heard Brian and me making noise. They didn't know who it was, of course, but they decided they would be better off getting into a little trouble and getting out of there rather than waiting through another night.

They didn't call out, though, because they were a little

afraid of who might open the door. They wanted to attract help, but, at the same time, they were afraid to be identified. If someone opened the door, they thought that they might be able to rush by the person and get away, without revealing who they were.

The plan was silly, Shondra told them. But they were so scared; and, after being in the tower so long, they weren't thinking very clearly. Jarrod chimed in that the cold had them shivering during the night, and they still felt cold on Sunday morning.

So that was the mystery of Shondra and Jarrod's disappearance. We were relieved. When they finished talking, one of the police officers spoke up. "You kids were lucky. And I'd say you were smart to keep yourselves warm the way you did. You're right," he said to Shondra. "Sharing body heat is a good way to stay warmer longer. Do you go winter camping or something?"

"No, sir. I just read a lot."

"Well, I suggest you keep reading." He laughed. "Things seem under control here. I think we'll be going; glad you're all right. Oh, by the way, all the buildings on Olietta's campus are usually locked by security on Saturdays. I wonder why Irwin Hall wasn't."

"That's my fault, I think. Just as I was leaving early yesterday afternoon, I got a phone call which distracted me. I must have forgotten to lock the main door. I'm so sorry; I caused part of the problem," I said.

"Maybe so. But you kept these kids from running into the troublemakers," said the other officer. "You'll be glad to know they are out of commission for a while, anyway. We know the kids who scared you. We've been following up on complaints about them from several sources and were just waiting for a reason to nail them. They got picked up early this morning, speeding. The driver didn't have a license, and they had some drugs in the car. All of them were high. You won't have to worry about them this fall, at least."

We said our "thank-you" to the police as they left. Then the Carmichaels departed, as well. We were starting to clear the remains of Muriel's feast from the table when her phone rang. I looked at it and then at Muriel. She answered it.

"Hello. Oh, hello, Jay. Yes, Brandi's here. Hold on, and I'll get her."

I froze where I was. "I don't...," I started to say.

"Go in my bedroom, and take the call on the extension in there," she said.

I walked into Muriel's bedroom, sat down on the bed and picked up the receiver.

Chapter Forty-two

Jay's Explanation

1

"Hello, Jay," I said. My voice was cooler than I felt.

"Brandi. I am so sorry that I didn't get ahold of you sooner. I lost my phone and…"

I cut him off. "I know. You lost it Friday on Park Avenue in Manhattan."

"How do you know?"

"I got a call from the guy who found it on the sidewalk. Did you drop it getting into a taxi?" I knew I was succeeding in setting Jay off-balance; his voice was shaky.

"When I left, I got into a taxi. I must have dropped it then, yes."

"Anyway, you didn't try to call me at the college house or here at Muriel's. I worried that you were hurt or something, until Brian talked to Mr. Dunfey. So, where did you go that made you too busy to call me?" I hoped I was making him feel lousy.

"Brandi, I want to tell you everything, but not on the phone. Can I come over? Now?"

"A lot of things have been going on here. I don't think it's a good idea. I'm heading to the house on campus in a few minutes. Why don't we meet there? Then you can try to explain everything to me," I said.

"That's great. I'll see you in a little while. And, Brandi?"

"What?"

"I love you."

"Sure," I said and hung up.

Jay was waiting for me, when I got to my college house. He tried to kiss me, but I brushed past him and went inside. I led the way through the parlor to the sunroom off it. "The parlor probably is fine for talking, but the sunroom is better because nobody ever comes in here. People pass through the big room or stick their head in when they go by to see who's in there. We won't be disturbed or overheard in here," I said, as I sat in one of the wicker chairs.

"I owe you an apology. I know I should have called you," Jay said and sat near me on the wicker settee.

"Why don't you just start at the beginning and spare the niceties, Jay."

"All right. I'll begin when I learned Colin wanted me to go to New York for some office business. I decided to use the same time to look up the investigator Dr. Skinner had hired to track down Alma after she ran away.

"The investigator came to the apartment a couple of times to confer with my stepfather. I was only eight at the time, but I remembered his name, probably because it was so unusual. He was called Miles Weathers; that seemed a strange name to me then.

"Anyway, he was easy to locate, and, more surprising, he still was working as an investigator. I called him, we talked, and I visited him at his office. He remembered the case, and what he told me was so upsetting to me that I pretty much forgot everything else, including contacting you.

"Weathers told me that he remembered the case so well because of Mrs. Skinner. He was sure he could find Alma, and it wouldn't take very long, either. But Mrs. Skinner, that is, my mother, contacted him and cancelled the investigation. She said they were going about getting Alma back a different way, and she paid him a huge bonus for his 'trouble.' She also told him to keep the information to himself. He assumed the bonus money was primarily for that reason, hush money.

"I left Weathers' office and immediately went to my mother's apartment. She wasn't there. The housekeeper told me she was at her house in East Hampton. I left in a hurry to get a taxi and find a means to get to her house quickly; I planned to rent a car, if I had to—that's where the fellow found my phone; outside my mother's apartment building. I must have dropped it when I hailed the taxi, and I didn't notice it missing until after I'd rented a car and was on the Long Island Expressway.

"My mother was not home when I arrived, and I had to wait until the next day to see her. She was very surprised to see me. She was more surprised when I confronted her about the investigator and her role in squashing the search. Needless to say, our meeting was not pleasant, but I got her to admit she had done it. She said she did it for me, as well as for her. I didn't stick around long enough to hear any more from her.

"She didn't know that Weathers had given me a copy of the investigation file. He said it was so old and, since I was a blood relative—he didn't know Dr. Skinner was my stepfather and Alma my stepsister—he saw no reason not to let me have it.

"By the time I had returned to my hotel in Manhattan, it was late Saturday evening. I stayed up reading the file until early morning. Then I fell asleep and didn't wake up until late morning. I reread the file, and then I got a plane back to Portland. I only arrived just before I called you.

"My only excuse is that I was so distraught. My mother's actions had been worse than I ever suspected. But my own behavior back then, when Alma called and wrote, disgusted me. I was probably as responsible as she was for losing Alma forever. Even with Miles Weathers' report, I don't have anything substantial to go on. I should have called you, Brandi. All I can say is that I hope you will forgive me."

Jay looked as distraught as he said he was. His eyes were bloodshot, his skin mottled and his hands shaky. "I have two things to say, Jay. Of course, I forgive you. I'm sorry that I acted the way I did when you finally called. You were more than distracted; you had found out that your mother betrayed Dr. Skinner and Alma and lied to you. The other thing I have to say may or may not help you, but I think you better sit back down instead of pacing, before I tell you."

3

"I was going to tell you when we next saw each other, which was supposed to be Friday evening. If I'd known what you were going to do in Manhattan, I would have told you on the phone. Jay, Shondra's mother's name was Alma."

Jay leapt from the settee and stared down at me. "What? How do you know that?"

I worked at keeping my composure. It wouldn't help if both of us flew off the handle. "I had been talking to Shondra, and she told me. I remembered the name of your stepsister and wondered if there was a connection. That's what I was waiting to tell you Friday."

Jay started pacing the room again. Then he started for the doorway. "I have to talk to Shondra now."

"Wait a minute, Jay. Shondra had a hectic night and day. I'll tell you about it later. She is fine, and nothing happened, but she was exhausted, and Muriel made her go to bed. I think she'll sleep the night. Please let it wait until tomorrow."

"I can't," he said.

"Okay. Let's go over to Muriel's house and talk to her and Brian. Then you and they can decide if you should talk to Shondra tonight or tomorrow. Please?"

"Let's go, then."

Chapter Forty-three

What to Say

1

Back at Muriel's house, we discussed the appropriateness of talking to Shondra immediately. Jay was determined that she should know everything he knew, but Muriel put her foot down. "I won't allow it, Jay," she said.

Brian concurred. "Shondra has been through more trauma this summer than any kid should have to endure. Wait until we have more substantial information to go on before you spring this on her—and it's nothing more than conjecture now. She's too vulnerable."

"I think we should stop saying anything more about this now." I chimed in. "Shondra could wake up any time and overhear."

"Jay, I promise you that, the minute we have something conclusive, you can talk to Shondra. Certainly, she has the right to know, if there is a connection. Right now, we don't know. And if it turns out that your Alma is not her Alma, then I don't think there would be any reason to say anything to her."

"Maybe the three of us can work on this question together," Brian said. "I can nose around my colleagues; we attorneys store tons of information in our heads. Brandi can shoot the breeze with Shondra, see if there's anything more about her mother that might help. Muriel can do a little of both; she knows a lot of lawyers from her corrections work, and she and Shondra talk a lot about nothing all the time." He smiled at Muriel. "And Jay can comb the investigator's report to see if he missed a clue. Will that work?"

We all agreed that we would see what we could learn before we confronted Shondra with the possibility that her mother was Jay's stepsister.

I felt drained of all emotion as I walked through the

doorway. Jay drove me back to the college house and walked me to the door. I had no desire for a good-night kiss, so I pecked his cheek lightly and said I'd talk to him tomorrow.

2

I woke up early the next morning, not very refreshed from my sleep. I had an appointment with Dean Coburn first thing. After the traumas over Jay and Brandi, I felt estranged from the situation with my writing students. It was as if it happened a long time ago. Chriz was lying in the hospital in a coma, wavering between life and death. What happened to him would impact on both Lindsay and Randy. Yet it seemed as if a layer of pink wall insulation divided their plight from my own concerns.

I decided that, before I went to the Dean's office, I would look over the pertinent parts of the three students' essays and highlight what I thought was essential for Dean Coburn to read. I hoped she'd read all of each set of essays, but, even if she did, she might miss something that I thought was important.

When I finished my task, I called the Dean's office and made an appointment to see her later in the morning. I compartmentalized my mind, setting aside my concerns about Chriz, Lindsay and Randy for the time being. My head still was too full—of Jay, Shondra, and Jay and Shondra. What was the significance of the name Alma? It could be coincidental, or it could be like the elephant in the room: so obvious that one couldn't really grasp the ramifications.

If Shondra's mother was the same Alma as Jay's stepsister, then we were going to have more complications than any of us had bargained for. Shondra had barely gotten acclimated to living with Muriel; she was thinking about staying there and going to school in town. Muriel seemed happy with the idea, and Brian appeared content. I could tell he was getting attached to this girl. He was rattled when he thought that something had happened to her.

And what about Jay and me? Already, this situation had

sliced a chunk out of our closeness, no pun intended. Jay had lost his cool when he learned that his mother was responsible for the investigation's failure to find Alma. How would he act if he found out there was no connection between the two Almas?

More importantly, what if there was a connection, and Alma Skinner and Shondra's mother were one and the same? Then Jay would be the step-uncle. And how would he deal with that, knowing he'd played a role in Alma's tragedy, not to mention Shondra's rough life?

How did I feel about all of this? I was Muriel's only child. She adopted me and loved me deeply, I knew. But what would happen to our relationship if she had another "daughter"? I wouldn't put it past her to adopt Shondra, too. If Alma had been Jay's stepsister, then the emphasis shifted to him. What would he do?

If Jay decided he owed Shondra, then where did I fit in? He might decide he had to support her and even take her to live with him. I guess that Shondra would have something to say about that, but I knew she had grown to like Jay a lot. She might love living with him. Either way, I thought I would lose.

With the depressing thought in mind that I could end up bereft because of this mystery of Alma Skinner and Alma, Shondra's mother, I headed over to Dean Coburn's office for our meeting.

3

The Dean met me at the door. She looked nice in a light green sheath, with her hair pulled back by a green and yellow printed scarf. She had no idea that I probably was going to ruin her day.

"Hello, Brandi. It's good to see you. I hope you had a relaxing weekend," she said.

Ha, little did she know about my messy weekend; and I didn't intend to enlighten her. "It was fine, thanks. Has anything changed with Chriz?" I asked.

"Things are still pretty much the same."

"Dean, I want to show you something that may help us figure out the details of Friday."

"Come and sit down," she said. She took a seat next to me at a small, round table. "What have you got there?"

"These are the files containing essays Chriz, Lindsay, and Randy have written for me," I said. "I don't think they are confidential, and I think you should read them."

"All right. I will try to get to them this evening."

"I don't mean to be impertinent, but I think you should look through them now. I've highlighted things I think might answer some questions."

She looked at me. "This is serious, isn't it?"

"Yes, I think it is."

"All right. Why don't you stay here while I look at the essays? If I have a question, you can answer it."

I sat back in the chair and waited, clenching and unclenching my fists as she read. Dean Coburn didn't ask me any questions. When she finished reading, she looked up at me. "I think you understated the significance of these essays when you said they were important."

"Well," I said, "I'm glad you feel that way. That's why I didn't want you to put off reading them."

"As I see it, these essays exonerate Chriz from any culpability. Lindsay was lying, about everything from her relationship to the boys to her part in taking the car and driving it. The police have to see this. I'll call them right now. You'll need to come with me if they want us in Portland. Maybe they will come here, but, either way, I want you with me," she said.

Chapter Forty-four

My Students and Shondra

1

When Dean Coburn called the police, she spoke with Detective Donlon. He told her that he and Detective Simone would meet with us in the Dean's office.

Dean Coburn had a couple of other matters to attend to while we waited for the police, so I used the rest room and then sat in the reception area. I wondered why they would come to us rather than have us meet with them at the police station.

Detectives Donlon and Simone arrived quickly. The four of us sat around the table in the Dean's office, while she explained how the files of essays came to be. She sketched what they contained, without going into a lot of detail. "I don't know whether you think the material is pertinent to the situation involving the three students, but I thought you should see what the students wrote."

"Are they dated?" Detective Donlon asked.

I answered, "No, they aren't. But I kept a record of each time we met and the gist of what each person wrote. It was a part of my record-keeping."

"That's good," the detective said. "Why don't you point out the entries that you think are relevant." The Dean had the files I'd given her in her desk drawer. I'd given the detectives the plain copy I had with me. The Dean and I had decided it probably would be better for the police to draw their own conclusions from the essays, instead of showing them the highlighted ones.

We started with Chriz's file. When we finished, Detective Simone looked at Detective Donlon. "It doesn't look like Chriz was interested in Lindsay other than as a friend, someone he was nice to. He seems to care most about his studies," she said.

"He doesn't ask her to take him to Portland or offer to steal a car to take her. She offers to take him," Detective Donlon said. "Okay. Let's look at another file."

I gave them Randy's; I wanted to save Lindsay's for last because I thought that it showed the most contradiction from her statements to the police, as well as to her parents.

Setting down Randy's file after skimming it, Detective Donlon said, "This kid is in love with basketball and his Jeep. He's not after Lindsay; in fact, I'd say he was trying to let her down easy."

"Here's Lindsay's set of essays," I said, handing over her file. Both of them read it together. A couple of times, they exchanged glances.

Then Detective Donlon put down the page he was holding. "I think we've seen enough here to warrant paying a visit to Miss Ayer. We'll head over to her dorm room now; we know where it is. No need to announce us."

"Do you want me to accompany you?" Dean Coburn asked.

"We'll do this part ourselves. We'll want to speak more with you, though. We'll get in touch later. Thank you both for your help," the detective said. They left the office without shutting the door.

I looked at Dean Coburn and asked, "What do you think they're going to do?"

"I'm not sure," she answered. "I think it's possible they might arrest her."

2

I went back to my office. There weren't any tutorials on my schedule, but I didn't want to leave campus. I sat at my desk and mulled over what had happened. It seemed that my actions were the impetus for the police to confront Lindsay. I didn't feel good about that possibility. She was the one who probably committed a crime, but I felt like I was guilty of doing a bad thing.

I was so self-absorbed that I didn't realize anyone had

come to my office until I heard a knock on the open door. When I looked up, I saw Randy standing in the doorway. "Hi, Brandi. Am I disturbing you?"

"No, Randy. I was just sitting here. Please come in," I said.

"I don't have an appointment with you, but I wanted to talk to you, if that's okay."

"Sure it is; how are you doing?"

"I'm okay. I've been thinking about Lindsay and Chriz and what happened. I hope he's going to pull through. Have you heard anything about his condition?"

"The last I knew, Chriz was still in a coma. I haven't heard anything different," I said.

"That's so lousy. What about Lindsay?"

"I think the police plan to talk to her again, but that's all I know for sure," I said. I didn't feel like telling him that I'd shown their essays to the Dean, and she'd given them to the police.

"I hope she'll be okay, but I guess they'll charge her with something. My dad agreed that I didn't have to accuse her or Chriz of stealing my car. She's probably gonna be in enough trouble without that against her, and Chriz needs to pull through his injuries, not get charged with car theft. Anyway, I don't think he took my Jeep. Lindsay did, I think, but she didn't really steal it. I know she planned to bring it back; she just borrowed it without asking me first," Randy said.

"I think you're being very generous, Randy. Some people would want to make her pay for wrecking your car."

"Hey; it's only a car. Well, yeah, I loved it and all, but it's not anywhere near as important as a person. I wouldn't want anybody to go to jail or something because they took my Jeep. Lindsay is a friend of mine. She did something wrong, but I don't need to make it worse."

"As I said, you're very generous. You don't have a car anymore," I said.

"I don't," Randy said. "But my dad said that, when things get settled, I might be able to get another Jeep. For now, though, he's going to get me a cheap car so at least I will have wheels

220

when I need them."

"Your dad is pretty understanding."

"Yeah; he's the greatest. He really helped me this weekend. I knew what I wanted to do, but I was so glad to have him there. He said I was doing the right thing, and I made him proud. He made me proud of him; he's my best friend, except he's my dad, so I guess that's goofy," Randy said.

"I think that's very nice," I said. "You have a great relationship with your father. I think you both are fortunate."

"Me, too. Hey, thanks for talking to me, Brandi. I'm glad you're around here." Randy smiled, waved at me and left.

I felt better after talking with him. His attitude helped me shake off my funk. I decided to go to the pool and see what Shondra was doing.

3

The swim team was taking a break when I got to the pool. Shondra saw me and waved. Then she said something to the girls around her and came toward me. "Hi, Brandi," she said.

"Hi, yourself," I said. "How are things going?"

"Oh, fine. I'm a little tired, but that's all. Jarrod says he's pretty tired, too, but we both are okay, otherwise. I'm sure glad you came to your office when you did yesterday. Both of us were cold and starving; and we were getting pretty freaked."

"What are you doing this evening? I'll be at Muriel's for dinner and am planning to take a boat ride after we eat. I was wondering if you'd like to go with me. Are you interested?"

"Yeah, sure. That would be fun."

"I also have something I want to show you," I said. "Remember how I told you I never really got to know my mother, since she died when I was so young. But she gave me a locket; I keep it in a little velvet bag in my jewelry box. It's in my room in the college house. Would you like to see it?"

"Sure; I'd like to see it."

221

"Okay, then. When you're done here, walk over to the house, and I'll be there. You'll be all right walking by yourself, won't you?" I asked.

Shondra rolled her eyes. "Oh, yeah. All the bad guys are dead or in the Youth Center." She laughed. "Maybe not all, but, no, I'm okay. Besides, it's bright daytime, and there's lots of people around. The college is a good place to walk; it's safe here."

"All right," I said. "I'll see you later, then."

I started walking back to my college house, musing. If I showed Shondra my treasure from my mother, maybe she'd show me hers, if she had anything.

Chapter Forty-five

Mothers and Daughters

1

Shondra and I sat on the bed in my room at the college house. She was holding the locket with my baby picture and a picture of my mother. "This is all I have that ties my mother and me together," I said.

"What happened to your mother?" she asked.

"She died when I was very young."

"That's sad. Do you remember her?" Shondra asked.

"A little bit. I sort of remember picking blueberries with her; I think I was about three. That's it, though," I said. "Do you have any keepsake to help you remember your mother?"

"Yeah," she answered. "I have a little box she gave me a long time ago, before my father died and she got into drugs so bad."

"Well, that's something. Is there anything in it?"

"There's a little velvet bag, and it has some jewelry in it. She told me it was her mother's stuff. She took it from her bedroom after her mother died. Nobody knew."

"Oh," I said. "That's a good memento."

"After she started using drugs so much and we had no money, she told me to give it to her. But I wouldn't. She yelled and stuff, and my uncle wanted to know what she was talking about. But I just said she was talking crazy, and he believed me cuz she said really weird things a lot after she was sick."

"It must have been hard not to do what she asked you," I said.

"Well, yeah, it sorta was. But I knew she'd just have my uncle get her more drugs. She wouldn't have him buy food or anything with it. So I decided I'd keep it like she told me, when she gave me the box and wasn't sick."

"Was there a picture locket or anything with a likeness of her?"

"No. I don't have any pictures of her," she said.

I was quiet for a minute. Then I said, "Shondra, I'd love to see the box and the jewelry, if you want to show me."

"Sure. You showed me your treasure from your mom, so I'll let you see mine."

2

Shondra and I drove to Muriel's house and asked her about taking a ride in the boat before dinner. She said we had time if we didn't go out for too long. We urged her to go with us, but she said she had a few things she wanted to do before Brian came home, so we went out alone.

The lake was calm and quiet on a weekday afternoon, compared with the usual frenetic pace and the large number of power boats in action on the weekends. We cruised around for a little while; then I asked Shondra if she wanted to drive the boat. "You should have boating lessons, but I'll keep my hand on the wheel," I said.

Shondra smiled at me. "Hey, that's neat. I'd like to drive the boat."

We continued traveling around at a low speed. Shondra got the hang of steering and maneuvering the boat quickly. Too soon, it was time we returned to the dock, if we didn't want to be late for dinner.

After we secured the boat to the float, we walked to the house. Shondra said, "Thank you, Brandi, for taking me in the boat and letting me drive it. That was fun."

"You're welcome, Shondra. I had fun, too."

Inside, Muriel and Brian were standing by the stove. "Good," Muriel said. "You're just in time. Wash your hands, and sit down. We're ready to eat."

224

We did as we were told, and the four of us ate our meal, talking about everything and nothing. We seemed to be content just to be with each other. Brian seemed particularly solicitous of Shondra. He served her chicken, first asking her which piece she wanted. Then he made sure her glass was filled with lemonade. I almost said something to tease him, but I decided not to; maybe he was still coming down from his fear when she went missing overnight.

"Dinner was great," I said. We'll clean up, so you two can go outside and relax or swim or whatever."

"We can take care of it," Muriel said.

At the same time, Brian said, "Okay, that's a nice idea. We'll take the boat out for a spin, then. Thanks, girls."

Shondra and I loaded the dishwasher, washed and dried the pots and cleaned the counters. Then I asked her about her treasure box from her mother. "Come on in my room. I'll show it to you," she said.

3

I sat on Shondra's bed. She opened the night table drawer and pulled out a small box, which was quite beautiful. It looked like rosewood or something exotic; it wasn't like the boxes I'd seen around that were cherry or pine or maple. It definitely was different, not a Maine-looking wood. "That's a very pretty box," I said. "I've never seen one like it."

Sitting down next to me, Shondra opened the box. "My mom said it was her mother's box. She got it in Italy or something, when she was young. Then she gave it to my mom. I guess her family was rich or something, but that must have been a long time ago."

Lifting the cover of the box, Shondra removed a black velvet bag with a corded pull-tie that had tassels on the ends. "I haven't looked at these since my mom died." She stretched open the top of the bag and dumped the contents onto the bed.

I almost gasped. "What's the matter?" Shondra asked.

"Those are beautiful," I said, looking at a ring and a bracelet. The ring was what I thought was a platinum setting, holding a huge ruby stone, edged in diamonds. If it was real, it was worth a small fortune. The other piece of jewelry was a gold bracelet, encrusted with various colored stones. That, too, was worth a lot of money if it was real gold and real emeralds, sapphires and rubies.

"Yeah, they are pretty, aren't they? They'll all that's left of my mom." She put the ring on her middle finger and the bracelet around her wrist. "They sure do sparkle. Do you think they're real?"

"I'm pretty sure that they are. And, if they are, you should put them in a safe-deposit box or something like that. Brian can help you do it."

"You think so?" she asked.

"Well, let's ask him. I heard voices, so I think they're back from the boat."

We headed into the kitchen. I stopped short. Muriel and Brian were sitting at the table with Jay. He started to get up, saying, "Hi. I just dropped by to see if I could talk to you." His voice trailed off, as he glanced at Shondra. His eyes locked on her left hand. "What are you wearing?" His voice was sharp, and he left the chair. He moved to grab her arm.

Shondra didn't flinch, as Jay pulled her toward him, looking at the ring and the bracelet.

"Where did you get these, Shondra?" he asked.

"They were my mom's," she said. "She gave them to me a long time ago, and I've kept them. I don't ever wear them, but I was showing Brandi, and I put them on. We came out here to ask Brian if they are real and if I should put them in a bank safe or something."

"Take them off," he said.

"Okay, but why? Is something the matter?" She removed the ring, unclasped the bracelet and handed them to Jay.

He turned the ring so he could look on the inner side. Then

226

he ran his finger over the reverse side of the bracelet and looked at one of the stone settings. He stared at Shondra and nearly choked out the words, "These are Alma's."

"That's what I said. They were my mother's."

Chapter Forty-six

One Alma

1

Suddenly, the air in the room seemed too sparse for all of us to share. I inhaled as little as necessary. Jay was standing over Shondra.

"Who was your mother?" Jay looked at Shondra and then at the jewelry in his hand.

"I told you: Alma"

"What was her last name?"

"Reynolds; same as mine."

"No, I mean her maiden name. What was her last name before she married Reynolds?"

"I don't know. She never said." Shondra cocked her head and looked at the jewelry and then at Jay. "Why?"

"Did you ever hear her say the name Skinner?" Jay had eyes only for the jewelry and for Shondra. It was like nobody else was in the room.

"No. Like I said, why? What's the matter?" Shondra paused. Then she said, "Oh. You think she stole these; or maybe I did. Is that what you think?"

Jay ignored the question. "Did your mother keep it in a velvet bag inside a rosewood box?"

Shondra looked at me and then at Jay. "Yeah, she did. How do you know?"

"Alma was my step-sister's name. That's her jewelry. She used to put it on around the house, especially at dinner. She liked to make her father mad because he knew it bothered my mother to see her wear her dead mother's jewelry."

Shondra no longer was simply answering Jay's questions, like she was indulging an older person. Her body stiffened, and her voice came out hoarse. "Your step-sister's name is Alma? Where is she?"

"I don't know. She ran away when she was sixteen. I've never heard anything about her since then. That ring and that bracelet were her most precious possessions. After she left, no one could find them, and everyone thought she took them with her."

"Are you saying…" Shondra stopped talking for a moment. She cleared her throat and continued, "Are you saying your step-sister Alma was my mother Alma? Oh, my God." The color drained from her face, and she seemed to collapse rather than sit onto the floor.

2

Muriel got a glass of water and brought it to Shondra, holding it for her while she sipped from it. Nobody said anything. I peeked at Brian, whose face was nearly as white as Shondra's. Jay was staring back and forth between the jewelry and Shondra.

Brian moved over to Shondra and helped her up. "Why don't we all sit down at the table and have a cup of tea to settle us down?" he said.

"Okay," I managed to get my vocal cords working again.

"I'd rather have something stronger, if you don't mind," said Jay.

"Shondra, Brandi, and I will have some tea" Muriel said. "I'll make it. Brian, would you get the brandy for Jay, and, by the looks of you, you might like a little, as well."

Everyone sat except Muriel, who was making the tea and putting some brownies on a plate, and Jay, who was pacing the kitchen floor. Muriel finished her task and came to the table. "Sit down, Jay," she said.

Sitting in the vacant seat between Shondra and me, Jay put his hand in his hair and scratched his head. When he removed his hand, his usually neat hair looked like it had been whipped by an eggbeater. Part of me wanted to smooth his hair down and take his hand. But the other part of me was still angry that he had not called and confided in me when he was in Manhattan. The second part of me won out; I sat still.

For a while, no one spoke, as each of us with tea was giving undue attention to the teabags, the spoons, the sugar, and everything but the jewelry, which Jay had set on the table in front of him. He was staring at the pieces, and Brian was fumbling with the brandy bottle and the glasses. He actually spilled some while he was pouring it into one of the glasses; Brian prided himself on being neat and precise.

Muriel broke the silence first. "Why don't we talk about the two Almas, yours, Jay, and yours, Shondra? That is, Shondra, if you feel up to it; it might be better to clear up some things now rather than have them float around in your head, and yours, too, Jay, any longer. Would that be okay, Shondra?" she asked.

Brian reached over and took her hand and squeezed it. I noticed she squeezed his back. "Yeah, I would like to talk about it now. I'm really confused. How could my mother run away when she was sixteen and never be found by her family? How come she didn't just go home, especially when things got bad for her? If she was sixteen or seventeen when she left home, and I was born when she was nineteen or something, it wasn't cuz she was pregnant, at least not with me. So, what happened?"

I had to admire Shondra. There were a lot of different questions she could have asked, but she went right to the heart of the issue that Jay was grappling with; his mother, and he, too, had thwarted any attempt to get Alma home. I wondered what Jay was going to say.

"Before I try to answer all those questions, would you mind if I looked at the rosewood box?" Jay asked.

"Okay," Shondra said.

"I'll go get it," I said and left the room, returning with the box. "Here it is." I handed it to Shondra, who gave it to Jay.

He opened it, closed it, turned it over and then spoke. "I remember playing with this one afternoon. Alma was out, and, when she came back unexpectedly, I rushed to put it back where she kept it. I fell, and the box scraped along the floor. It got a scratch on it, but I got it put away before Alma caught me. She never said anything to me about the scratch. See, it's right here." With his finger, Jay traced a small line that discolored one side of the box.

"Shondra, I have so much to tell you about your mother, my step-sister. But I don't want to start by answering your questions. I'd rather tell you something about her. I also want you to know that she came from a very wealthy family. Her biological mother, the one who died, was an only child whose parents left her a fortune. Her father, Dr. Skinner, inherited wealth from his family. He was a notable doctor, who made another fortune of his own. As the granddaughter of Dr. Skinner, you are entitled to a part of the estate."

"Whoa," Brian interrupted. "Okay, but you're moving too fast, here, Jay. Shondra needs to absorb the initial shock of finding out who her mother was. I think that's the best place to start. The other issues can come later. What do you say, honey?" Brian addressed the question to Shondra.

"Yeah. Maybe you could tell me stuff you remember about her."

"I guess Brian's right. All right, Shondra. I can do that."

3

"Your mother was about eight years older than I was when my mother married her father, your grandfather; that's Dr. Skinner," Jay said. "We moved from the east side of the city to the west side, to his apartment. It was a large, beautiful place.

"My father had died suddenly, and I had been devastated. I was closer to my father than to my mother, but I loved them both. I thought we had the perfect family. Then he died, and I felt lost.

"My mother married Dr. Skinner not long after my father's death. His wife, your grandmother, had died a few years before. The Skinners and the Binghams had been social friends.

"I was not ready to have a new father, even less prepared to get a sister in the deal. Dr. Skinner tried to be close to me; he was a nice man. But I wouldn't let him. I was too unhappy, and I wasn't accepting of change.

"I don't think Alma was ready for a new mother, either. As I said, she was a lot older than I was, so she had different ways to react to the marriage. Where I withdrew and became quiet, she acted out and was outspoken to her father. She tended to dismiss my mother and talk around her rather than to her. I think my mother grew to dislike Alma. I'm not sure that's completely true; it's my impression now.

"Alma treated me all right. She probably wanted me around no more than I wanted her as a sibling, but she wasn't mean to me. It was more that she just moved around me. She was gone most of the day. She went to a private day school and then took private ballet lessons."

Shondra interrupted Jay's monologue. "I remember her dancing in the apartment when I was little. She told me she had wanted to be a dancer, and maybe I could be a dancer when I got older."

"She was serious about dancing. But then she and her father got angry at each other. Alma started treating my mother badly, too. Finally, Dr. Skinner sent her to a boarding school in Maine. She ran away from there, and we never saw her again."

"She was in Maine when she ran away?" Shondra asked. Jay nodded his head. "Then that's how she got here, huh? But why didn't her father send somebody to find her?"

"He did. But the investigator didn't find her at first."

Brian gave Jay a look, like he was afraid Jay was going to get into the details of the investigation and Jay's and his mother's parts in what happened. "What did Alma look like, Jay?" Brian asked. "Do you see any resemblance in Shondra?"

"I think you carry yourself like her. She was graceful because she was a dancer. Your swimming has made you graceful, too. She was a little taller than you, and her hair was lighter. It was long, and she often had it in a ponytail or a thing on top of her head, for dancing, I guess. But your eyes are similar. And I think

232

your smile is, too. She didn't smile a lot, though, and you do."

"What kind of clothes did she wear?" Shondra asked.

"Well, she wore a uniform to school. It was a red plaid, pleated skirt, a white shirt and a gray blazer, with gray knee socks and loafers. But around the house and for dance classes, she wore bright skirts and sweaters or leotards. And she wore a lot of tights with ballet slippers."

"That's nice," Shondra said. "Thank you, Jay." She looked at Brian and said, "I think I'd like to go to bed now and think about her a little. I'm really tired. But I hope you will tell me more soon."

"Soon, Shondra," Jay said. Shondra was out of the room before Jay finished his sentence. But I heard him mutter, "Then you'll really hate me."

Chapter Forty-seven

Serious Considerations

1

I looked toward Jay. His head was in his hands. I felt bad for him, but I also felt pretty worried for Shondra. So I got up and said, "I'm going to say good night to Shondra," and left the kitchen. I thought she could use my presence more. Besides, maybe Muriel or Brian had something to say to Jay, without me present. Brian certainly seemed emotional while Jay and Shondra were talking.

"Hey," I said, as I walked into Shondra's room. She had her pajamas in her hand and was headed toward the bathroom. "I wanted to say good night to you."

"Are you leaving?"

"I was planning to go back to the college, but I could stay here tonight, then we could go in together in the morning, if you want to."

"Yeah. I'd like that. I don't feel like talking much tonight, but I'd like to be with you tomorrow, if that's okay."

"It's more than okay. I'd like to be with you, too, Shondra."

"That's great," she said. "I'm going to take a shower and try to go to sleep."

"Sounds like a good idea. I'll see you in the morning. Sleep well."

"Thanks, Brandi."

Shondra went into the bathroom, and I walked, slowly, back to the kitchen. Muriel, Brian, and Jay were seated around the table. I started to sit down, when Jay spoke up. "Brandi, could we go outside and sit for a while? I'd like to talk."

"We're going to go to the bedroom, anyway," Muriel said. "I'm pretty drained, and tomorrow's a busy day."

"I'm staying tonight, Mure, so I'll take Shondra to swim practice when I go in the morning," I said.

"Oh, that would be helpful to me. Thanks, dear. Goodnight, both of you." She looked at Brian. "Are you coming with me?"

Brian took a moment to answer. "What? Oh, yes; I'm coming. 'Night, Brandi. 'Night, Jay."

"Good night," Jay said. Then he went to the door to the deck and held it open. I passed through the doorway ahead of him.

2

I sat in one of the chaise lounge chairs. Jay sat beside me. Neither of us spoke for a bit. I put my head back and closed my eyes. I was deciding where to start, when Jay spoke.

"I know things are strained between us, ever since I let you down on Friday. I should have called you. You were right that there was certainly some way to get ahold of you, through Muriel or even at the college house. I didn't try. My only excuse is that I was so angry when I found out that my mother cancelled the investigation to find Alma, and all I could think about was confronting her."

I cut in. "But you did stop long enough to call Mr. Dunfey. You remembered your professional obligations." I thought I was being a little harsh, but I wasn't quite able to "forgive and forget" just yet.

"Ouch, that smarts," Jay said. "But you're right. I thought about my boss, but I didn't consider you. I think I took you for granted. I'm so sorry. I will try never to do that again if you can see your way to forgive me."

I was melting fast. I felt the tears coming, and I blinked quickly to keep them from falling. "I still am hurt by that slight, Jay. But it isn't up to me to forgive you; I could do that easily. You have to make it right with yourself. As to forgetting, I think it will take longer to forget."

Jay leaned over, and I let him take me in his arms. "Come and sit with me, Brandi. I want to hold you close, and tell you again how much I love you. "

235

I half-slid, half-crawled onto Jay's chaise, and we hugged. He lifted my chin, looked at me and kissed me. We held the kiss for a long minute. I broke it off first. "Jay," I said, "there are two problems confronting us right now: Us and Shondra. I think we need to talk about each one separately. Maybe we should talk about us first. What do you think?"

"I think I won't be able to think straight unless we clear the air between us. Or, if you can't forget my transgressions, then at least we can decide how to deal with it so that we can move on. I want to have you on my side. I don't mean between Shondra or anybody; I mean I need to feel that you are there for me to talk to and to share things. If you give up on me, I don't know how I can cope with this mess about Alma. So, yes, I think we should talk about us."

"All right, then; I'm going to tell you a little bit about trust and how important it is to me.

3

"Before Muriel came into my life, I had no one I could trust. I never knew my father. My mother died when I was really little, about three, I think. From then on, I was shuffled around like the Old Maid in a deck of cards.

"I was adopted, but they didn't want me after a while; then I had foster parents. I was thrown out. I lived on the street in Portland for a while. I was kicked out of school for being a trouble-maker. I even spent time in the Youth Center for stealing and hitting a pregnant security guard at Macy's.

"At the Youth Center I met Muriel; she was my guard. I was awful to her for a long time, but it didn't stop her from starting to care about me. She changed my life. Probably, I'd be in jail now if she hadn't become my guardian and then my adoptive parent. She's never given me a hard time; I don't mean she's a pushover, because she's not. She's been strict. But she's solid. Every time I'd screw up, she was there. And she'd help me find my way back, not

236

with punishments or anything; she'd be honest, and she'd trust me to get it right the next time. I love her more than anything in the world.

"The other person who trusted me was Dean. We started out as friends. Then we fell in love. Dean never treated me badly. He believed in me, and we were planning a wonderful life together. He had just graduated from high school and had a scholarship to go to college in Boston when his father killed him. I thought I would die myself, too; but Mure brought me back to the living. She was patient, honest, like I said, and she believed in me, too. She trusted that I'd make it, and, with her help, I did.

"At the root of everything for me now is trust. So that is why I am so torn up about us right now. I never trusted anybody other than Mure after Dean died. When I met you, I knew there was something special about you. Remember, I told you I heard that crazy bicycle bell in my belly. I fell in love with you, and I trusted you to be honest always.

"So that's why I am at a loss right now. I'm stalled at this crossroads, like maybe my bicycle has a flat tire. The bell's a little rusty, too. I hope everything gets fixed, but I'm unsure how to go about fixing it. I guess I need time and a sign from you that I can trust you to be honest always."

Chapter Forty-eight

Complicating Factors

1

Jay put his head in my hair and whispered, "I know I really screwed up, Brandi. I think I got too complacent about us. I won't ever let that happen again. I forgot to pay closer attention to you, and I got too wrapped up in my own issues with my mother."

"I can understand that, Jay. The more we learn about each other, the more we will be better at trusting each other and being honest."

"Then you're not going to break it off between us?"

"I'm upset, but I'm not a quitter. I think we are worth fighting for. We have to work at it every day."

"That's what I want to do," Jay said, "and I will prove that you can trust me. More than ever, I really need you now. I feel so responsible for Alma's disastrous life. And Shondra's life has been tough because of what I did. Between what I did to them and what I did to you, I feel like shit, frankly."

"I understand some of your feelings about Alma and Shondra," I said. "But I think you need to remember that you were a little kid, eight years old. You had no idea of the ramifications of what you did. I think your reactions were pretty typical of a jealous, unhappy child. You know, it reminds me of a book that I read, where the young girl accused her brother's friend of a sexual act, partly because she was jealous and partly because she didn't understand what was going on. She never really had the chance to redeem herself with the brother's friend. You do, though. In fact, you've already started."

Jay hugged me tighter, until I grunted. "Oops; sorry. I didn't mean to hurt you. But you can see how much I need you. What you said helps. Even if you had to go literary on me! That's the charm of you. You can help me try to see the light at the end of this awful tunnel; maybe something good will come of it. But I don't know what yet."

"Give it time and thought," I said. "You and Shondra have plenty of that; you can talk a little bit here and there. I don't think you should dump your guilt on her, at least not right off the bat. Take it slow."

"But she already asked once what happened with the investigation."

"Well, the real culprit there was your mother. I don't know how you feel about telling Shondra about her actions, but I think she might want to know that part. And I think it's more relevant than what a little kid did. His actions probably had no bearing on the outcome, anyway. If your mother hadn't fired the investigator, he would have found Alma."

"Do you really think so? "

"Yes," I said, "I do. She wanted to be found, I think. She didn't come home because she was afraid, but the investigator would have convinced her that her father wanted her back, and then she would have come home."

"Hearing you talk puts the whole mess in a better perspective. You really do help me, Brandi."

"We need to help each other. But right now, we both need to get some sleep. I'm staying here. Are you all right to go back to Portland? Should you grab a couch and stay?"

"I'll be fine. I can use the driving time to think; you've given me a lot to digest."

"Morning should be calmer," I quipped, as we kissed goodnight.

2

Driving to the college with Shondra, I decided to ask her about her school intentions. "Summer will be over soon. Have you decided whether you'll go back to Portland High or go to the regional school out here?"

239

"I haven't quite decided yet," she said.

"Muriel and Brian's wedding is on Labor Day Weekend, and then they go on the windjammer cruise for a week. You start school the day after Labor Day, and they'll be gone. Muriel asked me about staying at the house while they're gone. I don't have to leave for Boston until the middle of the month. So I'll be around."

"Then, if I go to Regional, I can stay with you at the house?" she asked.

"You can stay there either way, I think. Probably, I can drive you to Portland, if you decide to go there. There may be other kids going there from around here, and we may be able to get up a carpool; so, either school should work out okay."

"Oh, that's good. But I don't think I'd need one after they come back from their honeymoon. Brian said he could take me back and forth if I go to Portland. Plus, Brian's been teaching me to drive, so I'll be able to get my learner's permit after my birthday."

"I didn't know that," I said. "You two are getting pretty close, I take it."

"We are. He's so good to me. And I really like him a ton. He's almost like a father, a real one who knows how to treat his kid." Shondra smiled.

"So you just have to make up your mind about which school, then. It sounds like you're leaning toward Portland."

"I'm not sure yet. Jarrod wants me to go to Regional. I'm not picking which school because of a boy, even if I'm starting to like him, though. But I'm keeping it in mind. Plus Regional is a new school for me; nobody knows about me, or my mother or anything."

"A new start can be a good thing, sometimes," I said.

I stopped the car outside the field house, and we said our goodbyes. I drove to my college house, got my things together and was heading to my office, when my cell phone rang.

When I answered, Dean Coburn spoke. "Good Morning, Brandi. How are you?"

"Hello, Dean. I'm fine," I said.

"I wonder if you can come to my office right away.

"Of course. What's up?" I asked.

"We'll talk when you get here. Oh, and, just so you are aware, the police are here."

3

When I walked into the Dean's office, the tension was thick enough to cut with scissors. Immediately, I felt my stomach clench. Something was wrong.

"Hello, Brandi," said Dean Coburn. "Please sit down. Everyone's acquainted here, so we can get started. The detectives have some alarming news, I'm afraid."

"There's no way to minimize it," Detective Donlon said. "When we went to Lindsay Ayer's room last week, she was not there. We then went to her home; no one was present at the house. Upon further investigation, we learned that Miss Ayer, accompanied by her father and her mother, had left the country."

I sucked in my breath, but I didn't say anything.

"Apparently, the family has financial and family ties in Switzerland," the detective continued. "The case is pretty much out of our hands now. Portland Police do not have the authority to go after someone in Switzerland. We have appealed to the Federal Government, but our case is small potatoes compared to some of the 'fat cat' financiers and convicted murderers who have fled to other countries. Miss Ayer's name is on a list somewhere, as are her parents' names, since she is under twenty-one and in their protection. For now, there is nothing else we can do."

"Don't we have some sort of agreement with the Swiss?" Ms. Coburn asked.

Detective Simone spoke up. "Yes and no; there is a treaty, but the Swiss pretty much do as they want, regardless. They often don't extradite."

"And this case is at the bottom of the pile, don't forget," Detective Donlon added.

"So they can stay there indefinitely?" I asked.

He said, "Apparently so. Mr. Ayer has several Swiss bank accounts, which, of course, no one else can access. His family has property there. There's a relative, distant by blood, but close by commitment, it seems."

"Is there anything else to be done?" asked Ms. Coburn.

"Our department isn't going to close the case, but we aren't going to be doing anything actively, either. "

"What about the stolen car. Did you decide who did it? Will Chriz be held responsible if he recovers?" I asked.

"From what we've learned, in good part from your student papers, as well as our own investigating, we're convinced that Miss Ayer stole the car. No one is pressing charges, anyway, so the issue is moot, as far as we're concerned." Detective Donlon frowned, and then he added, "We're off the case, unofficially. We stopped here to let you know."

The two police officers rose. Detective Simone said, "Thank you both for your help. We hope that the young man in the hospital recovers."

We exchanged handshakes and said goodbye; they left the office.

Dean Coburn looked at me and said, "I'm going into Portland to drop by the hospital. Care to come along?"

I nodded my head, and we left the office.

Chapter Forty-nine

Hopes and Wishes

1

Dean Coburn and I walked to Chriz's room and stopped outside. We heard a voice; I recognized it as Randy's, and I held my hand out to stop Dr. Coburn. I put a finger to my lips and signaled her to step back with me.

"That's Randy," I whispered.

We stood and waited in the hall. Just as we started to go into the room, Randy came through the doorway. He stopped when he saw us, and smiled a little. "Hi. I was talking to Chriz." He blushed as he spoke. "I've been coming here for the past few days—ever since my dad brought up a car for me. It's probably stupid, but I talk to him and think maybe he can hear me and he'll want to live. I've told him about Lindsay; I didn't tell him anything too bad, though. I told him she borrowed my car, and there was an accident. She's okay. Everything's okay. He just needs to wake up. I told him I'm gonna keep coming and yakking to him until he wakes up. So he better do it soon, or he'll die of boredom. Oh, that probably wasn't a smart thing to say." Randy lowered his head.

"Oh, Randy," I said. "That's wonderful. What a great thing to do. It certainly can't hurt, and it might help."

"I've read articles that say, when people are in comas, talking to them can be good. It's possible they hear it and react subconsciously," Dean Coburn said. "It's very good of you to come." She looked at me. "I'll let you two talk. I'm going to find the doctor and see what he says."

When she was gone, Randy and I started walking toward the elevators. "I haven't seen Lindsay around. Have you seen her?" he asked.

"I was told that she has gone away for a while," I said. "She and her family went on a vacation or something, I think, to visit relatives." I didn't lie; I just didn't elaborate, thinking Randy would learn more, as we all would, when the college rumor line got started.

"Oh, that sounds like a good idea for Lindsay. I don't think she liked it here. She talked about going somewhere else this fall. I'm sorry she didn't say 'bye to me, though. Probably she was embarrassed. Maybe I'll see her again sometime."

"She didn't tell me goodbye, either, Randy. So maybe we both will see her again."

The elevator had arrived, and Randy stepped into it. "I guess our sessions are done for the summer. But I'd like to come see you again before you leave for Boston. I'll be here cuz I have practice, and then school will start."

"I'd like that, Randy," I said. "Drop by, or call me." I gave him my cell phone number, and we hugged. The elevator doors closed, and I went back to Chriz's room.

2

I sat in the chair Randy had vacated and looked at Chriz. If I didn't know differently, I would assume he was asleep. His face was smooth and relaxed-looking. Someone must have been shaving him, because his skin was clean, no beard growing. I reached over and took his hand.

"I'm so glad that I got to know you, Chriz. You've brightened my life. You have so much to offer people, to offer the world. Please don't die. The doctors say that they can't find any physical reason for your coma. So maybe you have to decide to come back to us. I know Randy and I really want you back."

I knew I was going to start crying if I continued, so I stopped; but I kept hold of his hand. I squeezed it in mine, willing a response. I sat that way until Dean Coburn came into the room.

I stood up then and looked at her. "Did you find the doctor?"

"Yes, I did. His condition is still the same. By the way, I

244

wasn't eavesdropping, but I heard what you said. I think what you and Randy are doing is tremendous. Who knows if he hears you? He might, you know."

"I wish he did."

"Are you going to come back?"

I thought for a minute. "Well, one of my tutorial students is gone, and one is right here. Randy is the other, and he is coming every day. So maybe he and I can come together, at least some of the time, until his classes start and I go to Boston. Yes," I nodded my head. "I can come most days. Why not?'

"That is grand. Chriz's father comes most evenings. I can make it at least a couple of times a week. The doctor suggested that I encourage anyone who cares to come. Do you know anyone else who might want to see Chriz?"

"I don't offhand, but I can find out, I'm sure," I said.

"Good. Are you ready to go?"

I gave Chriz a quick hug, and we left. On the drive back to the college, neither of us said much about the situation. We talked about the college in general, instead.

I went to my office and looked up comas on the Internet, until Shondra came by after practice.

3

Shondra was in a talkative mood on the drive to the lake. "I was thinking about Jay while I was doing laps," she said.

"What about him?"

"It's pretty freaky that he and my mother were brother and sister, sort of."

"Step-brother and step-sister," I said. "His mother and her father."

"Yeah. So his step-father was my grandfather. That makes us pretty close, in some ways, I think."

"He lived with him and with your mother for two or three years. I imagine they got to know each other well."

245

"What did he mean about part of the estate being mine? What was that about?" she asked.

I thought for a minute before answering. "I guess his mother and your grandfather were very wealthy people. Since Dr. Skinner was your biological grandfather, and you are his only living relative, you are entitled to some of the estate, I think."

"Do you mean money?"

"I don't know whether it's money or stocks and bonds, real estate or what all. But, yes, I would guess there's money involved. But you should talk to Jay about this. I don't know any more than you do. I only heard about it last evening, same as you."

Shondra sat quietly for a few minutes. Then she said, "I'm going to talk to him as soon as I see him. Is he coming over tonight?"

"I don't know. I don't think so."

"Well, then I'm going to call him."

"You like him, don't you?"

"Oh, yeah," she said. "I've liked him for a long time. He's really cool. And now I like him better that I know he was part of a family with my mother. I want to find out as much as I can about her from him." She stopped and then continued. "But I like him for himself, first."

As soon as I stopped the car in the driveway, Shondra was out the door. She ran up the steps and into the house before I had gathered my things. When I got inside, she was talking on the phone. "Hey, Jay. I want to talk to you. Can you come over tonight?"

Chapter Fifty

Heart to Heart

1

"He wants to talk to you," Shondra said and handed me the phone.

"Hello," I said.

"Hi, Brandi," Jay said. "I've been talking to Shondra. I asked her if she'd like to come to Portland Friday after swim practice. I have to be there, and I'll pick her up. I want to know if you would come, too. We'll go out to dinner, and, if Muriel lets her, I'd like her and you to stay overnight. I have a guest bedroom and bath, and you two could bunk together. Oh, it's not bunk beds; I was just using a term. Anyway, what do you say?"

"Wow. Well, yes; it's all right with me. I'm sure we'd all enjoy it. Hold on a minute. There's a commotion going on here," I said. I put the receiver down and turned to the disturbance behind me.

"Can I?" Shondra was jumping up and down, beseeching Muriel.

"If Brandi is going, too, I suppose you can," Muriel said.

Brian spoke up. "Now, wait a minute. I'm not sure that's such a good idea."

Muriel shot Brian a look, and he stopped talking.

"As long as Shondra wants to go, and Brandi goes, too, I don't see why she shouldn't visit her uncle."

"Step-uncle," Brian said. His face was getting red, so I knew he was upset, but I wasn't sure why.

"Yes, he is," Muriel said. "And it's a good way for the two of them to start to know each other better. Are you going to go, Brandi?"

I looked at Brian. He didn't meet my gaze. I wondered what was concerning him, but I didn't see anything wrong with the plan. "Yes, I'll go," I said.

I picked up the receiver and spoke to Jay. "Okay; I think it's all set. Shondra and I would like to have dinner with you and stay overnight," I said. Then Jay told me he'd call me sometime the next day, and we could plan when we might see each other during the week. I hung up the phone, and, when I turned around, I noticed that Brian had left the room.

2

Dinner was uncomfortable for me. Shondra was her usual chatty self. She mentioned swim practice and Jarrod, but she spent more time talking about going to Jay's place on Friday. Muriel kept herself busy serving food, passing it around, and nodding in response to Shondra's comments or questions. Brian was unusually silent for most of the meal.

Shondra and Muriel said they'd clear away the dinner dishes, and Brian went outside. When Muriel declined my help cleaning up the kitchen, I followed Brian outdoors and found him down at the dock, fiddling with the boat.

"Hey," I said.

"Hey, yourself. Help me straighten out this line, will you?" I worked at the line; then Brian asked, "I'm going out for a short ride; want to come with me?"

"Sure," I said.

Brian got into the boat and started the motor. I undid the lines and hopped in; as we left the dock, I pulled up the fenders and tossed them inside the boat. We moved over the water at a steady pace.

The evening was lovely, and I was watching the sunset, when Brian cut the engine. We were in a quiet backwater, and he set out the anchor. Then he sat down on the bow cushion and patted his hand for me to sit next to him.

After a couple of minutes, he spoke. "I know I was acting like a horse's ass at dinner. I needed to get out of the house for a little while. I'm glad you came out because I want to talk to you; it'll help me put things into perspective. I hope you don't mind, Brandi."

"Of course, I don't. I could tell something was bothering you, but I don't know what."

"Before I get into it, I want to make it very clear that you are the second most important person in my life—a close second. Don't ever think that you don't mean the world to me. I had nobody until Muriel. She is the love of my life. Then you became the second love. I have been so blessed to be with her and with you. She is my soul mate, nothing less. And you are like my daughter; you will be my daughter when Muriel and I are married and I can adopt you. Do you still want that?"

"I've never stopped wanting it, ever since you and Muriel suggested it," I said. "Nothing has changed for me."

Brian scratched his arm; then he said, "I've harbored a funny feeling about Shondra since the beginning. She's a great kid, and she's really matured this summer. I've come to care deeply about her. But now I feel in a bind; I don't completely trust her."

"What do you mean? Trust her how?"

"I wonder about this jewelry stuff. Don't forget how she used you to get to Muriel. She's proved once that she's a manipulator."

"But Jay confirmed that the jewelry belonged to his step-sister, Alma," I said.

"Yes, he did. But maybe he's being too accepting of Shondra's word. Is it possible that Shondra's mother obtained the jewelry from someone else?"

I asked, "You mean she stole it?"

"Not necessarily; perhaps she found it when she lived around Portland with different young people. Either way, though, maybe Shondra's Alma is not Jay's Alma."

"Oh. I never thought about that. Jay is convinced."

"Jay has a soft center. He's a brilliant young man and a very capable lawyer. He's done many competent things, but I've noticed that he is not a hard-nosed man. That's why I was happy that you two hit it off. I know he's not going to let you down when it counts. He'll always put you first. You know that, don't you? He just got a little blind-sided in New York by his mother and forgot to call you."

"I know. I'm working up to forgiving him."

"Don't wait too long. Anyway, the quality that's so endearing when it comes to him treating you well is the same trait that keeps him from examining Shondra's story carefully. He wants to believe the best in people, and he wants to believe he's found his Alma's daughter."

"Are you going to investigate her and her mother's background?" I asked.

"I'm tempted, Brandi. And that's why I'm troubled. I don't want Jay taken for a chump. He's investing a great deal in this girl."

"Okay, but he seems to have a huge inheritance. He bought his condo outright, and it must be worth a small fortune."

"About a million dollars, and there's much more where that came from But it's not really his money that I'm concerned about. He's invested himself in the belief that Shondra is his step-niece; I'm worried; if it turns out she isn't, what will that do to him. You and he seem pretty solid; he did make one bad judgment call when he didn't telephone you, and that's minor compared to his basic goodness. But you are a new piece of his life. Alma is his past, and Shondra is the conduit to his redeeming himself in his mind. What happens if it's all a sham? I don't want to be the one who kills that dream of his."

I thought for a minute. "No wonder you're upset. You're damned if you do it and it turns out true, but you're equally damned if you don't and it turns out she's lying."

"What would you do, Brandi, if you had the means to find out the truth? Never mind, dear; that's a completely unfair question

250

to put to you." Brian touched my shoulder.

"No, that's okay," I said, giving him a little smile. "When you put it the way you have, I think I'd leave it be. Let Jay have his dream. If it turns out a false one, I think it's better that he figure it out by himself; if anyone else tries to influence him, Jay will resent that person, I think—even if it turns out true."

"I've been going back and forth about it, but talking to you helps. I think I agree with you. Even if it turns out Shondra's playing him, he might lose money, but, if he finds out about her from someone else, he'd lose his pride, not to mention his dignity. He can deal with it better if he's the one to 'unmask' her," Brian said.

"If there is anything to unmask," I said.

"Talking to you has been a tonic for me. You're a breath of freshness, my dear. Now we'd better get back before they send the patrol boat out after us."

Chapter Fifty-one

Shondra, Jay and Me

1

During the week, I thought of my conversation with Brian. We'd met each other about five years earlier, and I had interned for him at his law office when I was in high school. Monday evening was the first time I ever remembered him showing any self-doubt. Usually he was the epitome of self-containment and assurance. I was glad we had talked through the issue of Shondra's honesty.

Everyday Randy and I went into Portland to visit Chriz. I drove us the first day; I wasn't sure what kind of driver he was. But the second day, he pushed to let him take me, so I relented. I discovered that he was a very good driver, relaxed but conscientious.

Going back and forth to the hospital and spending time with Chriz took a couple of hours each day. I rationalized that the time I spent away from the college and my tutorial duties was justified. Lindsay was gone, and Chriz was incapacitated. Randy and I decided that he could write his essays wherever he chose, and then he would read them to me at Chriz's bedside. I'd also go over them with him there. Chriz was familiar with the tutoring process, so I knew that, if he was absorbing any conversation subconsciously, the essay reading and editing process would be familiar. The sound of voices could be comforting, too. Chriz didn't know Randy's voice that well, but he certainly knew mine.

I finished my journal/log of the tutorial program to submit to the college, but I also wanted to write a summary of my experience with the swim program. Jay served as liaison between his law firm and Olietta College, and he was in charge of submitting the formal report; I was simply adding the intern's involvement.

Jay called me Monday evening to set up a time for

coordinating our written conclusions. He had been to the college Monday morning, but he'd had to return to Portland for a meeting on another project he was involved in, so we hadn't crossed paths. He was tied up with office work that evening, as well, so we agreed to meet at the college pool later in the week for the final swim meet.

I stayed on campus most of the week, working on my write-ups. I met once with Dean Coburn to review my tutorial program, and we spent the time talking about the three students. Chriz was a question mark: we didn't know what would happen to him. She told me that the college would keep his place in the first-year class, and she promised to keep me apprised of his situation after I was in Boston.

Lindsay was gone; her status was questionable. She was no longer on the student roster. The Dean said her case was a police matter now. She would let me know if she heard anything, however.

Randy was the one true success story that came out of the tutorial program. He had developed his writing skills and proved himself to be a mature, responsible young man. The basketball coach was putting him on the first team, as well.

Dean Coburn assured me that, despite the problems that had occurred among the three students, my work had been more than good. Although I still felt some guilt, I accepted her praise. In my heart, though, I knew that I wouldn't believe I had done a good job if Chriz died; I believed that I could have prevented it.

2

We were quite the odd group of cheerleaders for Shondra at the final swim meet: Muriel, Brian, Jay and me. Brian never had seen a swimming competition before, so Muriel explained the basics to him. Jay sat next to me, but he spent most of the time shouting encouragement to Shondra, whenever she was in the pool. With my two main men otherwise occupied, I spent the time exercising my mind—my thoughts jumped around from Jay to Shondra, then to Lindsay, and finally to Randy and Chriz. I even spent a couple of minutes wondering about Brian and Muriel. I was relieved to know that his discontent on Sunday had nothing to do with any last-minute concerns about the wedding. Brian and Muriel acted as loving and considerate of each other as ever.

Jay broke my reverie. "Hey," he said. "You look much too serious. What's going on in that lovely mind of yours?"

I tossed my head to clear my brain from its wandering. "Oh, I was just reminiscing about everything that has happened this summer. The time has gone by too fast."

"I'll say. When do you have to leave for school?"

"I need to be in Boston by the fifteenth of September. I'll stay at Muriel's house while they're sailing Down East. I'll be Shondra's companion, and I'll also have a chance to get my things organized. It should be relaxing because my internship at the college ends before Labor Day."

"That's good. I hope we get to spend a lot of time together before you go. This week has been so busy, but I'm winding up a couple of things by the end of the week. I'll be done with the college project shortly, too."

"You're coming to the wedding, aren't you?" I asked.

"I wouldn't miss it. I'm hoping you and Shondra might stay with me at least a couple of times while Muriel and Brian are gone. That's why I asked Shondra to come this weekend."

"I don't think she decided yet which school she's attending, although she'd better figure it out quickly. Classes start right after Labor Day."

"Is anyone helping her make up her mind?" Jay asked.

"You know, I'm not sure. I've not said anything, because I really don't know which place would be better for her. I guess Muriel and Brian think either is fine; they've told her she can live at Muriel's, regardless."

"I think I'll talk to her about it when you two come to Portland Friday. I want to know how she plans to make her decision."

I asked, "Are you going to try to influence her one way or the other?"

"First, I want to see where her head is at on a couple of matters before I say anything," Jay said.

3

Shondra and I met Jay at his condominium on the Portland wharf early Friday evening. Both of us were impressed with the place. There aren't many condo buildings that sit on piers extending into the harbor, so these places are exclusive, as well as expensive, real estate. His condo was on the top floor of one of these buildings.

Jay greeted us in the parking garage, where we left my car for the weekend. Then we took the elevator to the fourth floor. When the doors opened, both Shondra and I gasped. We faced a wall of windows looking out over the harbor, with a view of Fort Gorges, pleasure boats, and islands.

The condo was decorated with a man's touch. The hardwood floors were carpeted in oriental rugs; the furniture was a combination of leather sofas and chairs, with a scattering of chrome and glass tables. The space was open and had walls of windows on either side; Jay's condo ran the width of the top floor.

"Holy moley," Shondra said. "Is this all yours? I guess your estate must be gigantic."

"I bought it when I knew I was moving to Maine because I thought it would be a good investment."

"It's gorgeous," she said, as she slowly spun around in a circle. "The kitchen looks pretty fancy, too."

The kitchen was visible from the main room, and it also stretched nearly the width of the building, with a hallway leading along one side. "Do you want to see your room, ladies?" Jay asked.

"Definitely," Shondra said, heading toward the hall. We followed, Jay directing her to turn at the first doorway on the left. Shondra stepped in, and I nearly ran into her because she had come to a standstill. "Oh, my gawd," she said. "This looks like something in a celebrity's house."

It was pretty incredible. The room was almost entirely white: walls, carpet, canopied bed, bureau and dressing table. There were touches of lilac and light green in the draperies and scattered pillows. I was as impressed as Shondra.

"The bathroom is through that door." Shondra headed in the direction Jay pointed and called out, "This is the most decadent bathroom I've ever seen. Can I use the Jacuzzi tonight?"

"The place is yours while you're here," Jay said. "Why don't you get your bag and Brandi's things and put them in here? You can change your clothes, and then we'll go to dinner. I have something I want to talk to you about later."

I assumed Jay was going to talk to Shondra about her school decision. While Shondra was getting ready in the bathroom, Jay showed me his room. A contrast to the guest room, it was done in shades of gray, with black and white accents: very masculine.

Before we left Jay's bedroom, he took me in his arms and kissed me. I kissed him back, and we held the embrace. "I wish you were sleeping in here with me," he said. "I don't think I'll sleep all night, knowing you are in the next room."

"I'd like to stay in here with you, too, but not with Shondra here. She might not like it, plus I want our first time together in your home to be when we are alone," I said.

Shondra called from the hallway, "Okay, you two lovebirds, stop smooching, and let's get going. I'm hungry."

I was hungry, too, but I was more interested in learning exactly what Jay was going to talk about to Shondra.

Chapter Fifty-two

Big Plans

1

Jay pulled out all the stops for our dinner. He took us to the Bay Grill, one of the best restaurants in a city full of great places to eat. "Okay, ladies," he said, "We're going to sample Maine's best treasures from the sea. Brandi, I know you've had all of these foods. But, Shondra, tell me if you see something you haven't eaten before, when the waiter brings a plate."

Shondra laughed. "Well, I've never eaten much fish or seafood, except what Muriel has given me this summer. I used to eat a lot of Hamburger Helper and hot dogs."

"Then you are in for a treat, I hope," Jay said. "But anything you don't want to eat, just say so."

"You really went over the top," I said to Jay, after we'd finished the appetizer course and the entrees. We had been served several kinds of oysters, clams, and mussels, as well as scallops, lobster, and a few different fish. "We did a pretty good job of demolishing this feast."

"You ate just about everything," Jay said to Shondra. "So you like seafood?"

"Wow; do I ever," she said. "There was only one thing I didn't like." She speared a purple-white, gelatinous mass and held it above her plate.

"Oh, squid. Yes, I think that's an acquired taste."

"Well, I don't want to acquire it, ever. That's grody."

Shondra excused herself to use the restroom, and I took the opportunity to tease Jay and to ask him a question, too. "You really are trying to snow the girl. What's the deal? Are you planning to tell her about your mother, or are you going to ask her to move to Portland and live with you?"

Jay's grin disappeared from his face. "Is it that obvious? I hoped to get her relaxed with being around me, and then, sometime tomorrow, I was going to broach the subject."

"Really?" I had been kidding when I mentioned the idea of Shondra living with Jay. The idea struck me as inappropriate. I was going to say something, but then I decided to wait and see before I jumped into the middle of Jay's moment with her. I'd wait and see what Shondra said and then decide how to approach the issue.

"I've been thinking about it since I learned she's my niece," he said.

"Step-niece."

"Forget the step part. She's Dr. Skinner's granddaughter."

"You're completely sure Alma was your step-sister?"

"Shondra's jewelry proves it; those were Alma's. I know we were a messed-up family, but I want to atone for all the mistakes. Do you think I'm being naïve, Brandi, to think I might be able to make amends to Shondra? "

"I think it's a generous and sweet gesture. I don't know how she'll respond, but you only can try. So far, she seems pretty smitten with you."

"Yeah, well she doesn't know about my mother and me yet."

"Are you going to tell her about your part, as well?"

"I've decided to be completely honest with her," he said. "What I did to Alma haunts me now and then, and I'll never be able to forget it. If I didn't tell her now, someday it will come out; and then it could ruin everything we might have built. If she hates me for my actions, better she hates me now, not a few years from now."

"It's pretty brave of you, Jay. You're risking yourself, and you could go crashing down. Shondra's had a great summer, and she's very upbeat most of the time. But she's had a terrible situation growing up. She might blame you for it. If her mother had come home, Shondra might have had a privileged childhood. So, I'd say it's a gamble for you."

"Well, I have to take that gamble."

Saturday morning Jay took us to the Casco Bay Ferry Terminal. We took the ten o'clock mailboat run, which sailed to several islands in the harbor. The ride would last over two hours, and, since the day was hot and sunny, we wore shorts and tee shirts. Jay brought along a picnic of fresh bakery bread, fruit, cheese and cold drinks.

I was content to sit in the bow, soaking up the sun, but Shondra and Jay wandered the boat from stem to stern and up and down the two levels. I saw them every once in a while, as they moved about, laughing. Then I didn't notice them anymore. Despite the noise, I was lulled by the rolling of the ferry and the warm breeze; I must have fallen asleep.

Shondra shook my shoulder, and I jerked awake. "Hey, no snoozing, Brandi. It's time to hit that picnic basket." She lifted the top and started removing and handing out the food and drinks. Jay sat down next to me and took the drink she offered him.

While we were eating, Shondra listed the sights Jay had pointed out to her. "We might kayak to Fort Gorges sometime soon; I think that would be fun. I want to go to Two Lights Park later today and see that lighthouse up close. Don't you think it would be fun to take that lobster tour boat sometime and learn how to catch lobsters?"

Her excitement was contagious. Jay held my hand, and I realized how happy I was. Part of the good feeling came from being with Jay, of course. But I also was glad for Shondra and Jay. Despite the odds, they had found each other, and I was hopeful that their relationship would grow.

After the ferry returned to the terminal, we decided to go to the lighthouse. Unfortunately, we couldn't climb up it, but the building was lovely to see close up, and its rocky surroundings were outstanding. The walking trail rambled through roses and edged dangerously close to the crashing sea. No wonder Two Lights was one of the most photographed and painted lighthouses around. Shondra gave us both a fright when she climbed down the rocks so close to the crashing waves that she nearly was swept into the surf. Luckily, a guy nearby grabbed her arm, and they both fell backwards, above the waterline.

We returned to the condo, and Jay made dinner. He impressed Shondra with his spaghetti and clams; actually, he impressed me, too. I had learned to cook from Muriel, and I considered myself pretty good, but I liked the way Jay prepared the entire meal, making everything come out ready at the same time. He and I had wine, and he let Shondra have a small glass, as well. He said, "A small amount of wine with a meal helps digestion; besides it tastes good, too."

We spent what was left of the evening listening to music—a mix of songs Shondra had on her phone and some of Jay's collection. Then we decided to get ready for bed; the next morning we were going to drive up the coast.

3

By midnight, Shondra and I were settled in the king-size bed in the guestroom. I was pretty tired, but she was too excited to settle down. I could tell that she had been waiting to talk to me.

"Guess what, Brandi? Jay asked me if I want to go to school in Portland and live here with him. I can't believe it!"

"What did you tell him?" I asked.

"I really want to. But I said I had to talk to Muriel first. It would be so great, but I think I need to have her tell me if it's okay."

"Why?"

"She's the one who saved me this summer. I owe her a lot, and I really care about her, too. I want to do what she thinks is right. I'm not going to just drop her and move in with Uncle Jay. I don't want to lose her caring about me. If she thinks it's better for me to stay at the lake, I will."

"That's showing a lot of consideration for Muriel's feelings, Shondra. I think that's great. Do you know if there are more advantages about school and swimming to choose one place over the other?"

"Well, if I live in Portland, it will be easier to be on Portland's swim team. But, then, Mike told me that he's going to continue something with some of the kids from the summer program at the college, and that team will meet at the college. It won't be every day, and the times will change because the college swimming team gets priority, naturally. Then it might be easier to be at Muriel's. So I'm not sure."

"I guess talking to Muriel is a good idea," I said. "She'll be happy you're thinking about her, and I'm sure she'll be able to give you some good advice."

"Yeah, I think so, too." She sighed. "Boy, Jay is really a great guy, isn't he? I'm so glad he's my uncle."

Step-uncle, I mumbled to myself. Aloud, I said, "He sure is, and you sure are."

Chapter Fifty-three

Endings and Beginnings

1

Labor Day Weekend signaled the end of summer. It meant the end of my stay at Olietta College, including the internship and writing tutorial. It meant the end of my daily trips with Randy to visit Chriz at the hospital; I meant to go a few more times before I left for Boston, but Randy would be starting classes after the weekend, so we would not ride together.

Labor Day Weekend also brought beginnings. Foremost, Muriel and Brian were getting married on Monday and leaving for Rockland to board their windjammer for the cruise Down East. I would be starting my final year as an undergraduate in Boston, interning at a law firm there and applying to law schools. Jay was committed to his job at the Dunfey law firm in Portland, as well as spending as much time with Shondra as possible. Randy was beginning his first year at Olietta, and he would be a starter on the basketball team. Jay and I were another story—an ending and a beginning both. But the wedding came first.

Monday was the big day. Muriel had wanted a small wedding, simple decorations and only closest friends. Shondra was the bridesmaid, and I was maid of honor. We wore hot pink dresses, the same shade but not matching. Shondra's was a short, ruffled sundress, and I wore a silk, A-line style dress that also was short, but it was more formal than Shondra's. We both put up our hair and had fresh flower crowns of pink and white roses and some other daisy-like flower, too. Since the ceremony was on the lawn, we all wore sandals.

Jay carried the rings, and he wore light beige linen pants and a Caribbean-style wedding shirt that was off-white and embroidered down the front. I thought he looked gorgeous, with his light tan and his golden hair.

Muriel was radiant. Her dress was white silk, very simple, cut on the bias and knee-length. She had lost a lot of weight since the first time I met her at the Youth Center. Now she wore a size eight; I knew because I had gone with her to the salon where she bought the dress. She was only one size larger than I was. Skinny Shondra wore a size zero. Muriel also wore a crown of roses, but hers was all white, and she had her hair done up in a French twist. I never had seen her look so lovely.

Brian wore a white linen suit, ruffled white shirt and white bow tie. He looked like a Polar teddy bear. I wanted to hug him to death, but I didn't because I didn't want to wrinkle the suit. He smiled through the whole ceremony.

The caterers who provided the food also put up the arbor that the bride and groom stood under. It was white wicker and had all kinds of flowers, mostly white but some pink, covering it. Muriel and Brian said their own vows and had a Justice of the Peace friend officiate.

We spent the time afterward eating, drinking champagne, and dancing to a string orchestra that had set up on the dock. There were white lights strung through the trees, but they didn't show up that much until after the happy couple left for Rockland. Later, when everyone was gone, Shondra, Jay, and I danced to his and her music, set up with portable speakers from the house. Shondra and Jay both had really good rhythm, and they were fun to watch. I didn't consider myself as good a dancer, but I danced under those lights, anyway, and enjoyed myself.

Jay had to go back to Portland because he had an early-morning meeting, so he left at a reasonable hour. Shondra had school the next day, so she went to bed. I had nothing I had to do the next day, so I dragged out a chaise lounge chair and sat under the arbor, sipping champagne, until the mosquitoes drove me inside. I went to bed, content that I had a mother and soon-to-be father heading off on their honeymoon.

The next morning the house felt too quiet with everyone gone, so I headed over to the college and went to my old office. No one had been assigned to it yet, so I went inside and sat at the desk. I hadn't been there very long when I heard the front door close and footsteps. When I looked up, Randy was standing in the doorway.

"Oh, I'm so glad you're here, Brandi," he said. "I just have to tell you something. Yesterday, when I was at the hospital, I was telling Chriz about school starting and how I was going to be on the starting team and what classes I was taking and stuff like that. I just happened to look down for a second, and I noticed his finger moving. I grabbed his hand and held his fingers. And he squeezed my hand."

"Oh," I said.

"It wasn't much of a squeeze or anything, but it was real. I know he did it. And, get this: he opened his eyes. Just a little bit, but they opened for a second. I'm so excited; I wanted to tell you right away."

"That's great. Did you tell the doctors?"

"I sure did. But they weren't quite as excited as I was. They said it was a good sign, but that I shouldn't make too much of it–at least not yet. But it's a start. And I believe it is a big deal. I think Chriz has heard you and me all this time, and he's getting ready to come out of the coma. What do you think?" he asked.

"I think we should go to the hospital now," I said, "unless you have practice and can't go."

"Oh, I can go right now. I was hoping you would want to come, too. I told Coach all about what happened to Chriz and how you and I have been going to see him and talk to him and everything. Coach said that's a wonderful thing, and he also said I can keep doing it, even with practice. I can't miss any of my academic classes, but he said he will excuse me from running laps and things I don't need to be at practice for, so I can get to the hospital almost every day. He thinks it's important to keep talking to Chriz."

"Wow; he's a pretty understanding coach. I'm surprised he would allow you to do that."

"Well, he said he had a kid who was in a coma from some kind of accident. Coach said he and his wife went to the hospital all the time and talked to their son. Finally, he came out of the coma. They think all their visiting and talking made it happen. So he is all for me doing it with Chriz."

"That's great," I said. "So, what are we waiting for? Let's go see Chriz."

The visit with Chriz was less dramatic than Randy's experience the day before. But, while we were talking, I saw Chriz's eyelids flutter. We talked to the doctor, and he was encouraging, actually. He said these things were good signs, although we shouldn't expect too much too fast. But I decided right then to continue my daily visits until I left for Boston. Then I would figure out a schedule when I could come to Portland to see him. I thought that I could combine it with visits to Jay; Randy and I could coordinate our days so that Chriz had someone visiting as much as possible. I also thought I might be able to get his father, who came most nights, to try reading the paper or something to Chriz. Maybe even Dean Coburn would be able to visit and talk to him some. Randy and I left the hospital excited and optimistic.

3

I saved the worst for last. Jay and I ended one phase of our relationship and began another. He was going to have a busy fall, what with the law practice, which he said would get busier now that summer is over. He'd be working early morning and late evenings. He also was committed to building the ties between Shondra and him.

For the time being, Shondra was going to the regional high school near the lake. She would live with Muriel and Brian and join the swim team Mike was coaching at the college. While it didn't meet every day, the team still would get in plenty of practice time. Shondra could swim at the high school, too, although she hadn't decided if she was joining that team.

Part of Jay's commitment to Shondra was that he would be available to take her to practices and such, when Muriel was unavailable. He also decided that they would spend part of every weekend together. That meant they might come to Boston to see me sometimes, but his priority would be Shondra.

I was pretty upset about this development. I thought that Jay would put me at the top of his list. So I was both hurt and angry when he told me that we would be spending less time together. I felt slighted. After talking to Muriel, I tried to be more understanding of Jay's feelings, as well as Shondra's, but I failed

Brian wanted to help me. "Let things run their course, Brandi. Jay needs to work through the situation with Shondra. If it turns out she is his step-niece, then they will reach equilibrium in the relationship. They might even become mildly bored with each other. Then he'll have most of his time and emotions to devote to you."

"And what if she's not his niece?" I asked.

"Jay will work that out for himself. Perhaps he'll turn to you. And, if you love him enough, you'll be there for him. He's the first man you've loved since Dean. He may be the one for your lifetime. But you have a lot ahead of you before that. This hiatus is good, I think. I'm a believer in things working out as they should in the end. Don't be in a rush. Live your life in Boston; let your relationship with Jay and his with Shondra play out."

So that's what I decided I was doing.

I planned to get involved in plenty of activities in Boston, both at school and through the internship. As I said, I'd made a commitment to come to Portland to see Chriz once a week, and that would involve an overnight. I said nothing to Jay because I believed that he should ask me, but I thought maybe I might stay overnight with him on the visits. If he didn't ask me over, I'd stay at Brian's condo.

Brian was right to say that I had much to do before I'd be

ready to commit myself to one man forever, anyway. Perhaps that one man was Jay, but I was willing to wait. And I planned to be busy with a lot of people in the meantime.

Epilogue

October

Once I got to Boston, I settled in at my apartment with my roommate, Julia. I refused to listen to the voice in my head; my bruised ego got the better of me. Julia was a very social person and had a group of fellow drinkers and party-goers. In the past I declined her invitations to join her in the revelry, but now I decided to get involved and go to a party with her.

The whole idea of it was foolish. I usually don't drink more than one beer or a glass of wine. The booze spilled over at the parties Julia went to with her friends, but I was feeling down, so I agreed to go.

The party was on a third-floor walkup and was filled with people and smoke when we got there. I didn't see Julia after the first ten minutes or so. Memory fails me after I had settled on the couch with a tall drink in my hand and some guy chattering at me and smiling like a gooney bird.

The next morning, when I woke up Julia was sitting on my bed. My head hurt.

"Glad to see you have your clothes on again," she said, as she handed me a cup of hot tea.

"Omygod, Julia, I really messed up."

"Well, you got drunk, but Marty took care of you."

I groaned and starting crying. "I'll say he did. I think he raped me."

"Don't be dramatic. Nothing happened. You got drunk—on one drink, I might add. You stood up, and you fell over. That's how you got the bruises." She pointed toward the side of my head, my left shoulder and my left hip.

"But…"

"Hold on. Let me finish. That jerk you were talking to, Jake, the one who doctored your drink…he might of tried to rape you. I guess he was doing his best when Marty found you two."

"What do you mean, found us?"

"When you fell, Jake took you upstairs to a bedroom. Marty had been watching Jake and you. He knows what Jake is like. The dirtbag has a reputation for taking advantage of tipsy ladies. If we hadn't gotten separated, I would have dragged you away from him before he descended on you.

"Anyway, Marty followed you. Jake had your clothes off already and was getting on top of you. But Marty hauled him off and shoved him out the door. Then he helped you. So nothing happened, and you have Marty to thank."

"Oh," I said.

"By the way, he told me he'd like to formally meet you. I think he likes your body." Julia started laughing but stopped when she saw the look on my face. "Well, anyway, he gave me this to give you and said maybe the three of us could have coffee together and you two could meet officially."

"Oh," I said. "I don't think so."

She dropped a business card into my lap. I picked it up, read it and dropped it. "Oh, no, not again."

"What's the matter?"

"It says here he's an attorney," I said and made a face.

"What's the matter with attorneys? Marty's really a good guy," Julia said.

"I don't have a good track record with attorneys," I said.

"Well, I don't know what that means. But I think you owe him a thank you, at least. You were a damsel in distress, and he saved you."

"Oh, I don't know how I could. He even saw me without any clothes. Oh, and he dressed me. Oh, gad..."

"And he still wants to meet you. Maybe that's why he does...just kidding. Well, I gotta go. Late for class. Think about it, Brandi. We'll talk later."

I decided I would think about it, at least. Dean would have seen the humor in the incident, and he would have told me to make every day count. This Marty couldn't be all bad. In fact, he sounded as upright as Jay, for what that was worth!

269

My life will go on, without Dean, but still with Jay sometimes, I hope, and maybe with this Marty. I'm not a fish; I want to get back on the bicycle.

THE INCOMPATIBLE ALLIES

A MEMOIR-HISTORY OF
GERMAN-SOVIET RELATIONS
1918–1941

THE MACMILLAN COMPANY
NEW YORK · CHICAGO
DALLAS · ATLANTA · SAN FRANCISCO

**THE MACMILLAN COMPANY
OF CANADA, LIMITED**
TORONTO

GUSTAV HILGER

ALFRED G. MEYER

The Incompatible Allies

A MEMOIR-HISTORY OF
GERMAN-SOVIET RELATIONS
1918–1941

NEW YORK · THE MACMILLAN COMPANY · 1953

To
MARIE HILGER
and
EVA R. MEYER

PREFACE

Writing memoirs has become an art in which professional social scientists have increasingly lent a helping hand. One recent example which the authors of this work follow in stepping forward as collaborators is that of Henry L. Stimson and McGeorge Bundy, who jointly wrote *On Active Service in Peace and War*.[1]

The aim of such joint authorship is to combine academic knowledge with personal experience so as to give a personal touch to historiography and to make personal reminiscences as useful as possible to the professional scholar. The authors of the present work wished to accomplish the dual task of writing personal memoirs which would at the same time constitute a history of German-Soviet relations.

The benefits derived by the academic historian through prolonged discussions with a person who has participated in making history are obvious, particularly if a young scholar is fortunate enough to team up with as knowledgeable, urbane, alert, and friendly a person as Gustav Hilger.

In the present case the historian's task was to act as the memoir writer's second self, to ask questions, raise challenges, construct a framework for the narrative, and provide the background information necessary to tie the story together. He considered himself to be Mr. Hilger's academic conscience whose purpose it would be to prod his memory, to elicit information he might have deemed irrelevant, to make him think out problems and puzzles that would not have presented themselves to him. Throughout, he endeavored to make Mr. Hilger reveal himself, his actions, motives, ideas, and general outlook, because Mr. Hilger was representative of an all-important group among those who helped to make German foreign policy in the twenties and thirties.

Efforts in this direction could not avoid meeting certain difficulties.

[1] New York, Harper & Brothers, 1948.

There is a limit to the extent to which any man will talk frankly and freely about his life, even when prodded by an academic conscience. The most thorough research in documents and published accounts will not always enable the scholar to check his collaborator's story for accuracy, so that distortions, omissions, and inaccuracies are bound to remain. There are, moreover, some opinions, incidents, and other matters which Mr. Hilger, out of consideration for many of his friends, decided not to reveal even though he sometimes felt free to discuss them with his co-author. Such reticence had, of course, to be respected.

A few words about the procedure that was followed in writing this book. The authors spent several months collecting and assembling Mr. Hilger's notes, correspondence, and other raw material for the memoirs, and reading published materials. Both authors then began writing independently, submitting their drafts to each other for comment and criticism. The cooperation on every part of the book was so close that it would be very difficult to distribute credits for any of the different sections. In general, it was only natural that Mr. Hilger would contribute those parts which dealt primarily with personalities and personal dealings, while the treatment of broader political developments was, in the main, allotted to his co-author. Even there, however, the latter took care to present the broad problems *as they appeared to Mr. Hilger* at the time, his aim being to bring out the considerations that were underlying German foreign policy toward the Soviet Union. The book was to be a revealing self-portrait of a diplomat and his environment. For this reason the authors decided to use the first person, singular, throughout. The omission of a bibliography, too, results from the desire to give the work as much as possible the personal flavor of memoirs.

The present work would not have been possible without the active interest and help of a great number of people. Thanks to the drive of Mr. George F. Kennan and Mr. John Gardner, the Carnegie Corporation of New York by a generous grant enabled the authors to devote their time to this work. The grant was administered by the Russian Research Center, Harvard University, which in its turn provided great conveniences and services. We owe deep gratitude to Professor Clyde Kluckhohn, who has read the entire manuscript; to Mrs. Helen W. Parsons for the cheerful aid she has given as office manager of the Russian Research Center; and to the many members

of the staff of the Russian Research Center who have contributed
their views, suggestions, and advice. Others who have read all or part
of the manuscript include E. H. Carr, Fritz T. Epstein, Alex Erlich,
Carl J. Friedrich, Barrington Moore, Jr., and Carmel Offie. Among
Mr. Hilger's friends, Paul Scheffer and Moritz Schlesinger have been
particularly kind in discussing the manuscript and offering valuable
advice. Mrs. Marie Hilger has helped to eliminate many a slip or
inaccuracy. She has shown great patience when the work on this book
took hold of her husband, and she has been a generous and gracious
hostess to his collaborator. Mrs. Meyer has borne her husband's prolonged spells of absence without complaint and has been a constant
source of strength and courage to him.

Although this study was made possible by funds granted by Carnegie Corporation of New York, that Corporation is not, however, to
be understood as approving by virtue of its grant any of the statements made or views expressed therein.

A. G. M.

Cambridge, Massachusetts
November, 1952

CONTENTS

CONTENTS

ILLUSTRATIONS

ILLUSTRATIONS

THE INCOMPATIBLE ALLIES

A MEMOIR-HISTORY OF
GERMAN-SOVIET RELATIONS
1918–1941

I PRELUDE

1. A MINISTER IS MURDERED

Shortly before five o'clock in the morning of June 22, 1941, Molotov and I shook hands for the last time and, together with Friedrich Werner Count von der Schulenburg, I left the Kremlin, knowing that I should never again enter its ancient gates. I shall never forget Molotov's drawn and tired face as he exchanged the last customary courtesy of the handshake with us, laboring hard to conceal his inner emotion. I myself was greatly perturbed by gloomy forebodings. It was not just an episodic parting; it was the end of my whole life's work; I knew that it was also the end of Germany. Count von der Schulenburg, the German ambassador, had just made a formal statement to the Soviet foreign minister announcing Hitler's invasion of Russia.

As we rode back to the embassy in the early dawn, I eagerly drank in the sight of my native Moscow, which I should never again behold. And, not unlike the proverbial drowning man who in a split second sees his entire life unroll once more before his mind, I recalled episode after episode from the five decades I had spent, with few interruptions, in that fascinating city. Many a house we passed, had it possessed the power of speech, could have told stories about my life, so rich in experiences, human contacts, and excitement. One familiar street turned my thoughts back to an afternoon almost exactly twenty-three years before that ominous June 22, 1941. Saturday, July 6, 1918, had been one of those brilliant days with which nature compensates the inhabitants of Moscow for the brief duration of the northern summer; eight months had passed since the October Revolution of 1917 in which the Bolsheviks had seized power. Intending to spend the week end with my wife and children in our *dacha* (summer cottage) in the country, I had packed a traveling bag

1

with a few necessities, had left my small apartment, and was just on my way to the railroad station when suddenly a colleague of mine came running after me, breathless and pallid, and told me that our minister to Russia had just been murdered.

Four months before, on March 3, 1918, representatives of the German Reich and the Russian Soviet Federative Socialist Republic had signed the peace treaty of Brest-Litovsk, a treaty which was dictated by the shortsighted belief of the victor that the benefits derived from it would be greater in proportion as the conditions imposed on the defeated were more severe. Nevertheless, Lenin felt himself constrained to accept these conditions; against serious opposition even within his own party he argued that the Bolshevik regime was in urgent need of a breather during which it might attempt to consolidate its position within Russia.

When the official representative of the policy of Brest-Litovsk, Count Mirbach-Harff, arrived in Moscow on April 25, 1918, the Soviet government included personalities who will go down in history as outstanding: Lenin, uncontested leader of the Bolshevik movement; Trotsky, who had the great gift of forcing the masses under his spell even though he lacked the abilities of a real statesman; Chicherin, who with his sharp dialectical mind rendered invaluable service to Soviet foreign policy; and many other outstanding men and women. Facing them in his capacity as German minister was this average diplomat, who may have been friendly, likable, and a valuable human being, but who had not had more than routine training. Beyond that he brought with him nothing that might have fitted him for the difficult task awaiting him in Moscow. Neither did he know the country where he was to work, nor did he master the Russian language, nor was he sufficiently familiar with the problems that had led and contributed to the Bolshevik revolution in Russia. His name would be little known today had not fate chosen him to be the victim of the domestic struggles which at that time were raging in Russia between the Bolsheviks, just recently come into power, and the Left Socialist Revolutionaries who were aiming their attacks against a sore point in Lenin's policies, the conclusion of the peace of Brest-Litovsk. The latter held the treaty to be a betrayal of the revolution as well as a shame for the Russian people. The assassination of the German minister, they thought, would be the surest means of involving the Soviet Republic once

more in war with Germany and of thus making the position of the Bolsheviks untenable. On Saturday, July 6, 1918, they proceeded to put their plan into execution.

The German mission at that time was situated in a quiet side street in Moscow's Arbat quarter. The luxurious palace had belonged to the Russian sugar magnate Berg, but the victorious Bolsheviks had declared it the property of the triumphant proletariat. In the spring of 1918 it had been given to the German government for its diplomatic representation. In size and in the magnificence of its interior furnishing, the Berg palace surpassed almost all the houses of its kind then in Moscow, a statement that means much, for the luxury with which the representatives of the rising Russian bourgeoisie surrounded themselves was proverbial. Ever since the nineties of the last century, it had far exceeded the style of life of the old Russian nobility which had yielded its place to the "third estate" of industrialists and merchants after the emancipation of the peasants in 1861. Enormous fortunes were concentrated in the hands of families who had a monopolistic hold on the trade in articles of consumption demanded by a population of 170,000,000, and who arbitrarily determined prices for grain, textiles, sugar, tea, and so on. They openly manifested their power and wealth in a manner which served to emphasize more than ever the social antagonism which had existed in Russia for ages.

Lunch, for which the minister daily invited the members of his personal staff and other prominent Germans temporarily in Moscow, had just ended. Some of the guests had already left the house when two men rang the bell at the main gate of the mission. They told the footman who opened the door that they were emissaries of the Cheka, the Extraordinary Commission for the Struggle Against Counter-Revolution, Sabotage, and Speculation, and that they had orders to talk to the minister personally in a matter of great importance. They produced identification cards, confirming their statements, signed by the head of the Cheka, Felix Dzerzhinsky, and were admitted. The cards had been forged. Only the names under which Blumkin and Andreyev gained access to the mission were genuine.

The two men were led through the hall into an anteroom, whose walls were covered with precious tapestries, and then through a huge dance hall into a drawing room. With its priceless Oriental rugs, its wall covering of crimson silk, and its heavy curtains of gold

brocade, the room might have served as the suitable setting for an Eastern potentate. On the wall opposite the window front, a low sofa stood behind a table which with its marble top and bronze ornament work was so heavy that a normal human being could not have moved it. A chair was standing at the small end of the table, and another to one side of it, with its back to the window.

The counselor of the mission, Dr. Riezler, and the minister's aide, a Lieutenant Mueller, received the two men and led them to the table. Blumkin must have surveyed the situation at once with the skilled eye of an experienced terrorist, for he sat down on the chair across from the sofa, with the window at his back. Consequently, the Germans had to sit on the sofa in order to leave the chair at the small end of the table free for Count Mirbach. Andreyev, who until now had not budged from Blumkin's side, sat on a chair that stood at the large folding door leading into the dance hall. From that vantage point he could survey the hall and cover the door leading to and from the drawing room. The dance hall was a room about seventy-five feet long and twenty-five feet wide. Two huge candelabras were suspended from its richly painted ceiling, and two windows looked into the street, which was separated from the building by a small front yard enclosed in a high grille of wrought iron.

After Riezler and Mueller had sat down opposite the Russian, and in so doing virtually seemed to be drowning in the soft pillows of the sofa, Blumkin made no immediate move to say anything about the purpose of his visit. He seemed to be awaiting the minister for whom he had said he had an important personal message. The latter was still taking leave of his last guests, but he appeared a few minutes later, obviously interested in getting personally acquainted with the emissaries of the Extraordinary Commission. He entered the room through the large door at which Andreyev was seated and, after a short exchange of greetings, sat down on the empty chair on Blumkin's left.

Blumkin opened the conversation by telling the minister that there was a Count Mirbach in a Russian prison camp who was probably a relative of his. If that were so, he said, the Soviet government would be pleased to release the man before his due turn if the minister would only express the wish. The latter replied that the prisoner of war was a very distant cousin from the Protestant branch of the

family (he himself was Catholic). Nevertheless, he would be grateful if everything possible were done to relieve the man's lot.

Blumkin then declared that his office had ordered him to inform the minister that the Cheka had uncovered a terrorist plan to murder him. He had brought papers, he said, which would give the count particulars about the plot and would convince him that he must be very careful. So saying, Blumkin put his right hand into his brief case, drew a pistol from it, stood up, and with lightning rapidity fired three shots, turning the weapon first toward the minister and then toward his two collaborators. All three of the shots missed. None of those present was even wounded.

Disputes later flared up about what happened in the subsequent seconds. How was it possible that the count's aides had not thrown themselves on the assassin in an attempt to disarm him? Blame was heaped particularly upon Lieutenant Mueller, a giant of more than six feet. Later, in attempting to solve the problem, I repeatedly tried to reconstruct the situation. I sat down on the sofa and found that the light coming in through the windows was blinding. Persons sitting on the sofa sank into its soft pillows. Moreover, any attempt to move the table behind which Riezler and Mueller had barricaded themselves would have been in vain. Even after overcoming the shock of the first second, the minister's aides were at a disadvantage because they did not have sufficient freedom to move.

Count Mirbach had jumped up at the first shot. He ran behind Blumkin to get out of the room, and was just about to run the length of the hall, obviously attempting to reach rooms in the back of the house, when Andreyev, who until now had sat without moving at the door to the hall, sent one bullet after him from a small-caliber pistol. The bullet entered the back of the minister's head and came out at the nose. He collapsed on the spot and was dead in a few moments.[1]

As Count Mirbach collapsed and residents of the house, alarmed

[1] The puddle of blood which formed on the hard wood floor of the hall left a stain which could not be removed in spite of all efforts. Therefore those who had been near the scene of the crime in 1918 could pin-point the exact spot at which the victim had breathed his last even twenty years afterward. When Italy recognized the Soviet government in 1924, the house was given to her embassy, which formed one of the centers of social life in the Moscow diplomatic corps. Though in the course of seventeen years I participated in many a festivity there, I was always conscious of the stain on the floor over which others danced in blissful ignorance.

by the shot, hurried to his assistance, an explosion shook the hall which damaged the candelabras and forced the windowpanes out of their frames. It came from two hand grenades which the assassins had hurled into the hall in order to create confusion and secure their flight. They jumped out of a window, climbed over the iron grille, and fled in a waiting car. All happened so quickly that the Germans had not yet regained their composure when the terrorists' car had already turned the corner and disappeared in the maze of Moscow's streets.

2. THE AFTERMATH

The assassination of the German minister was the signal for an insurrection staged during the following night by the Left Socialist Revolutionary party. Until Brest-Litovsk, power in the Soviet state had been shared by the Bolsheviks with the Left Socialist Revolutionaries. After the conclusion of the peace treaty, the latter had gone into opposition, and were tolerated as such by the Leninist regime; their revolt put an end to toleration. For several days Moscow was under a state of siege. Her streets were patrolled more vigilantly than ever, and all travel into and out of the city was prohibited. There was no trip to our *dacha* for me that week end! Within the next two weeks about two hundred persons were shot by the Cheka, although the assassination and the insurrection of the Left Socialist Revolutionaries were so closely linked that it is impossible to distinguish whether the shootings were meant to appease the Germans for the assassination or in punishment for the insurrection.

For the Bolsheviks the situation was very critical. They had to consider the possibility that the German government would use the assassination of its diplomatic representative as a pretext for a new declaration of war against the Soviet Republic, or at least for renewed political and economic pressure. For the Treaty of Brest-Litovsk, in the four months of its existence, had not yielded the German Reich all the advantages she had anticipated.

Lenin's attitude clearly showed that he was eager to appease Germany. Immediately after hearing about the murder, he appeared personally at the mission to express his and his government's sympathy. With him were Jacob Sverdlov, who as chairman of the Central Executive Committee topped the entire Soviet hierarchy and was

thus officially the head of the state; Lev Karakhan, the second Vice Commissar for Foreign Affairs; and Bonch-Bruyevich, the secretary of the Council of People's Commissars, as the Soviet cabinet was then called. In marked contrast to Foreign Commissar Chicherin, the first Soviet official to appear at the mission, Lenin was completely composed and master over his nerves. With cold politeness he expressed, in German, his and his government's sympathy to Dr. Riezler.

In spite of the political expediency which the Soviet authorities saw in making amends for the assassination, there were certain ideological concessions they were unwilling to make. Thus they staunchly refused to attend the religious ceremonies at the bier of the late minister. Chicherin also hinted that some of the leading accessories to the crime, like the veteran leader of the Left Socialist Revolutionary faction, Maria Spiridonova, had done too much for the revolution to be subjected to punitive action. The exchange of notes concerning amends to be made for the assassination lasted well into November, so that the matter remained unfinished by the time the two governments severed their diplomatic relations. As a matter of fact, German dissatisfaction with Soviet intransigence in the matter was one of the reasons advanced for the break.

More than thirty years have gone by since these events of 1918. And yet they stand before my eyes in all their detail. The body of the diplomat was to be transported to Germany. Before the procession to the railroad station began to move, all those attending spent more than an hour waiting in vain for the arrival of the People's Commissar for Foreign Affairs, G. V. Chicherin, who had explicitly promised to appear. Finally the cortege began to move without him. The car carrying the coffin was followed by a number of automobiles containing representatives of the many civilian and military offices which Germany then had in Moscow. The funeral party had already reached the broad Novinsky Boulevard when an open car came in the opposite direction. In it sat an insignificant, emaciated man with a pointed reddish beard, and without a hat. When the cortege came into his sight, he began to gesticulate to the chauffeur in great excitement. We saw then that one finger of his right hand carried a formless bandage which had not been changed for a very long time, as one could see from quite a distance. Obviously, the people's commissar was quite embarrassed to be late. After his car had joined

the procession, I constantly looked at Chicherin during the trip to the station. His bent figure and sorrowful mien were like an incarnation of the dire straits in which the Soviet Republic was in those days.

The insurrection that broke out during the night from July 6th to 7th severely tested the young Soviet state. The rebels had secured for themselves a number of key positions in the Cheka. They arrested Dzerzhinsky, who had shown considerable personal courage in going to the Left Socialist Revolutionaries' headquarters, and kept him prisoner for a night. Lenin himself barely escaped the same fate. But the strength of the rebels was insufficient, and their organization too poor, to withstand the Bolsheviks. The fanaticism of Socialist Revolutionary terrorists was no match for the determination of the party that had recently seized power in Russia.

This revolt of the Left Socialist Revolutionaries was the best organized and planned effort that has ever been made to overthrow the Communist regime from within. The conditions for success seemed extremely favorable. A moment had been chosen when the government had not yet consolidated into anything resembling the monolithic totalitarianism of the present regime. Moreover, subversive activities in the Soviet Republic were then still supported with the money and the agents of foreign embassies, mutually hostile but united in their opposition to the regime. In spite of these propitious circumstances, the revolt failed completely, thus adding to the well known argument that no revolution will ever succeed in overthrowing a modern totalitarian regime from within. Far from succeeding, a subversive movement could not even get started in such a regime today.

Nevertheless, the confusion created by the assassination and the insurrection enabled the two assassins to flee Moscow that same night and thus escape capture and execution. Hence, if they escaped the punishment on which the German government kept insisting, the Soviet government cannot be blamed for lack of intention to comply with the demand. On the contrary, it is an ironic fact that the murderers found refuge, not in a part of Russia which was under Bolshevik domination, but in the Ukraine, which was under German occupation. Their subsequent fate is known. Andreyev fell victim to a typhus epidemic which was raging in the Ukraine in 1919. After Germany's defeat Blumkin benefited from an amnesty the Soviet government had granted. By 1920 he was back in Moscow as a student

in the Military Academy of the Red Army. In his spare time he appeared publicly in talks in which he falsely boasted of having shot Count Mirbach. Since his accomplice was no longer alive, no one could, after all, contest him his "glory."

I notified Baron Ago von Maltzan, at that time the head of the Russian department in the German Foreign Ministry, of Blumkin's behavior, but chose the medium of a private letter in order to give him a possibility to refrain from taking any official steps should he think that to be more expedient. He replied that he had decided not to make any moves of protest against Blumkin's actions, in order not to jeopardize the German-Soviet rapprochement which was then in its beginning. Because of this tender regard, Blumkin remained in Moscow for many more years. One of his favorite haunts was the Club for Literature and Art, to which the then People's Commissar of Education, A. V. Lunacharsky, used to invite prominent foreigners. Imagine the consternation and helplessness of a German politician to whom Lunacharsky once pointed Blumkin out, with the pointedly tactless question, "Perhaps you would like to meet the man who shot your minister?" [2]

The Bolshevik success in suppressing the insurrection of the Left Socialist Revolutionaries, as well as the hesitating attitude of the German government after the death of the minister, served to strengthen the confidence and self-reliance of the Soviet government. They sincerely believed, moreover, that they had made sufficient amends for the incident by their expressions of sympathy and some payments of money. Hence they refused the request of the German government to garrison a battalion of German troops in Moscow for the protection of the mission. They were afraid that German armed forces in Moscow might help to overthrow the Bolshevik regime; on the other hand, they felt that Germany was no longer strong enough to insist on the fulfillment of her demands.

They had made a correct estimate of the situation. The German authorities dropped their demands, at least for the time being, and designated a successor to Count Mirbach, Karl Helfferich, a well known politician and financier. Later, in the early years of the Weimar Republic, Helfferich came to be an eminent and outspoken member of the extreme right-wing Nationalist party, which was un-

---

[2] In 1929 Blumkin was careless enough to look up Trotsky, then in exile on Prinkipo Island. For this he paid with his life after his return to the Soviet Union.

reconciled to Germany's defeat and the fall of the monarchy. His violent attack on the Reich's foreign policy on the floor of the Reichstag is said to have been the signal for the assassination of the then foreign minister, Walther Rathenau.

The new minister arrived in Moscow in late July, 1918. His conversations with representatives of the Soviet government soon convinced him that they were neither willing nor able to fulfill the material conditions imposed on them at Brest-Litovsk, which had been designed to aid the German war effort in the West. Moreover, the minister and his entourage lived in constant fear lest the forces that had removed his predecessor were still at work and might once again try to find a victim. His memoirs, published in December, 1921, revealed that he left the Berg palace only once during his stay in Moscow. Convinced that the Soviet regime would fall before long, he did not cherish the idea of being so uncomfortably near the scene of impending political catastrophe. Consequently, Helfferich left Moscow on his own initiative after a stay of only ten days. His flight from Moscow constituted a breach of discipline quite unusual in the history of diplomacy; and it was so regarded in the Foreign Ministry.[3]

My personal affairs were affected by Helfferich's sudden departure in that it caused me to urge my wife to leave Russia immediately, together with our children. I visualized that Bolshevik terror, combined with starvation and general misery, would soon make life in Russia impossible. But I myself had to remain in Moscow for another three months. The experiences I gathered in these months turned out to be very useful to me later. But before I tell about them, let me introduce myself to the reader by giving him a brief sketch of my family background and early life.

3. FAMILY BACKGROUND AND EARLY LIFE

I was born in 1886 in Moscow and received my primary and secondary education there. My parents were Germans belonging to that large colony of western European business and professional

---

[3] I was told this by Admiral Paul von Hintze when he visited Moscow in 1922. Von Hintze, erstwhile German military representative at the court of Nicholas II, was at that time interested in the post of ambassador, vacant after the conclusion of the Rapallo Treaty.

men who had found a second home in Russia. Every large city, particularly St. Petersburg and Moscow, contained such a colony of wealthy and highly respected foreigners who were in peaceful competition with one another while cultivating their languages and customs in their own churches and schools.

My ancestors had established a prosperous export business in the city of Remscheid in the Rhineland. My father himself had been sent to manage a branch office of the main house in Moscow. On my mother's side I can trace the origins of my family back to the late eighteenth century, when my mother's ancestors were prosperous manufacturers in Elberfeld. A wandering French journeyman had brought them the secret of the madder-root dye from France, and their factory was a valuable addition to Elberfeld's textile industries. An economic crisis in the 1830's induced my great-grandfather to move the factory to a place near Moscow on the Klyazma River, the water of which was said to be extremely suitable for dyeing. There my mother's grandfather and his descendants, who succeeded in developing the dyeing plant into a large textile enterprise, accumulated considerable wealth. The Russian Revolution has taken all of it away, and my cousins are spread all over the world as exiles.

After graduating from one of the German high schools in Moscow in 1903, I left for Germany, where I obtained a degree in engineering at the Darmstadt Technical University. For two years afterward I worked as a machine-construction engineer in Upper Silesia. I had just made up my mind to follow my father's advice and go to America, where a big farm-implement factory had an opening for me, when I received an invitation to return to Russia to work in a large fixtures plant belonging to a German born in Russia who subsequently became my father-in-law. In 1910, therefore, I returned to the country of my birth and worked for this "Russian Crane Company," rising quickly to more and more responsible positions. In 1912 I married the faithful companion to whom I have dedicated this book. She has actively shared all the experiences told in these pages.

During the years before the First World War, I traveled through the old Russian Empire in all its length and breadth, and became thoroughly acquainted with it. From my earliest youth I had been familiar with the Russian language and with the customs and ways of life of Russia's inhabitants. After I delivered a lengthy report to

Hitler in the spring of 1939, the Führer is said to have remarked that he thought me half a Russian.[4] At home, indeed, German influences were predominant, since my father was not only formally a citizen of the Reich but also took great pride in his German origin and sought to instill similar pride in me. He sent me to one of the German high schools in Moscow. But even in that school many of my classmates were sons of the Russian nobility and bourgeoisie, and both teachers and students wore the uniforms which marked them as members of the centralized tsarist school system. Anyone who is aware of the formative influence of history instruction in the secondary school in the acculturation of the adolescent will appreciate why I am in fact partly Russian in my culture. For although in the German school that I attended world history was taught in the German language, Russian history, which was taught from official tsarist textbooks, has remained more vividly impressed in my mind. Old Kievan Russia, Ivan the Formidable, and Pugachëv are more real, more familiar to me than the Holy Roman Empire, Charles V, or the German Peasant War. And the Russian classics, Griboyedov, Pushkin, Gogol, Tolstoi, and many others, are at least as familiar to me as Goethe, Heine, or Schiller. Looking back on my formative years, I am clearly aware that, depending on temporary influences, I was at times torn between Russian and German culture. In the end German influences far predominated; but it would not be wrong to say that I have always had two home countries, Germany as well as Russia. I am attached to both of them with affection and nostalgia.

The outbreak of the war and, later, the revolution, with its nationalization of private property and its political terror, abruptly severed the attachment binding the members of the foreign colonies to Russia. True, the Soviet government made temporary use of the services of numerous American and German technicians during the thirties; but few of those technicians have struck roots in the Soviet Union, not only because of the latent xenophobia of the regime but also because the Soviet conceptions of human dignity, morality, and liberty have remained foreign to most representatives of the West.

---

4 Perhaps he thought my square face with its high cheekbones, which you will often observe in Holland and northwestern Germany, to be typically Russian. Or he may have been puzzled by my curious dialect, which results from the fact that I speak German like someone from the Rhineland, but with a Russian *r*.

In August, 1914, at the very beginning of the war, I fell victim to the spy scare then gripping all warring countries. As I had undertaken a business trip to Germany shortly before the beginning of the war, I was arrested under the suspicion of having betrayed Russian military secrets. Although my firm was able to offer proof of the absurdity of the accusation, I was kept in solitary confinement. Thereupon my young and courageous wife decided to go personally to the dreaded chief of the tsarist secret police in Moscow, Colonel Martynov. Since this gentleman was inaccessible to ordinary mortals, she turned to the Moscow police chief Baron Budberg, whose daughter was her friend. But even Budberg could do no more than give my wife one of his calling cards, with the advice to make the best possible use of it.

Armed with the card, and with a ten-ruble gold coin, my wife went to the building of the Okhrana, worthy but comparatively mild and inefficient predecessor of the Bolshevik Cheka. The gold coin served to bribe the doorman, who otherwise would have refused to accept the police chief's calling card from an unknown woman. A few seconds later my wife was facing Colonel Martynov, who obviously did not wish to let the police chief wait. When instead of the latter he saw my wife before him, he decided that she must be a terrorist aiming for his life. He therefore took the precaution of raising both his hands, which was followed by my wife's copying his gesture. When mutual confidence had in this manner been established, a conversation developed which began with Martynov's remark that he could have me shot within twenty-four hours. After a correspondingly violent reaction on the part of my wife, the conversation ended with his promise that I would only be exiled into one of Russia's far-off provinces. First of all, therefore, I had two months' opportunity of getting acquainted with Russian jails and their inmates, as well as of making a number of other observations and gaining experience which broadened my knowledge of the country and its people. I found confirmation for much that theretofore I had known only from the writings of Tolstoi, Dostoyevsky, and others. The psychology of the inmates of Russian prisons, as well as the attitude of the population to them, was determined by the fact that the Russian people had for centuries lived under coercion and autocracy, thus generating the idea that jails are an institutionalization of human wickedness, and their inmates victims of man's injustice. This

is the mental attitude in which the priest of the Russian Orthodox Church included "all prisoners languishing in the jails" in his prayers. And on Sundays, after going to church, pious merchants' wives in Russian provincial towns gave freshly baked wheat bread to the inmates of the local prisons. During my sojourn in the Vologda jail in September, 1914, I also gratefully received such additions to my regular meager ration.

If twenty-five years ago I had had the time and the opportunity to tell about my imprisonment in Russia, I should probably not have spared the reader an account of the cells infested with bedbugs and lice, cells which were at times filled to double or triple their permitted capacity. I might have imposed on him to accompany me on a prison transport from Moscow through Vologda to Vyatka, then back to Vologda, and finally into a hamlet on the Sukhona River. I should have described how a dozen prisoners had to do with one mess kit; how I prevented only with great difficulty my being chained to a Russian convicted of first-degree murder; or the revolting scenes I had to witness during the night in the narrow hold of a small river steamer because female prisoners, as well as males, were entrusted to male guards; or finally how the deportees, after arriving at their destination, were left to their fate even though they had no money or shelter. It is not only the passing of time which makes these trying experiences seem pale but also the sad and revolting knowledge that since then crimes have been committed against humanity all over Europe which leave the sins of old Russia far behind.[5]

The majority of the German civilian internees in Russia were in most miserable circumstances, thus making it a natural duty for those who were in a better situation to help their compatriots as much as possible. In the beginning, before the aid of the American Consulate General set in, I used some of my own resources to aid my fellow internees; and for the subsequent three and a quarter

[5] These musings about the time of my internment in a far-off part of the Province of Vologda give me the welcome opportunity to remember the superb care which the then United States Consulate General in Petrograd gave the German internees in Russia. The United States had in the early years of the war undertaken to protect German interests in Russia. Should these lines by any chance fall into the hands of a Mr. Philip Chadbourn, I hope he sees from them that those who benefited by his aid still remember it gratefully after almost forty years.

years of my internment I devoted time and work to the assistance of my comrades-in-exile, without then foreseeing that my acts would have a deciding influence on my entire subsequent career.

Some thousand German civilian internees were distributed in small towns and villages of Vologda Province during World War I. The province was about as large as France is today, or about the size of California and Arkansas. The county in which I lived was as large as Belgium, or about half the size of West Virginia. But it had only *one* town, with three thousand inhabitants. There was only one physician available within a radius of sixty miles. In other counties of Vologda Province there were towns five hundred miles away from the nearest railroad station.

Radio did not exist at that time; the telephone had not yet penetrated deep enough into Russia to reach our province; and in the spring and fall the highways were at times impassable. It was all the more astonishing how rapidly and safely the news about world events reached us. Equally important was the fact that the administrative arm of the tsarist bureaucracy reached into the remotest corners of the vast country. Even in those years there was no escape from it. Legends telling about settlements in Russia or Siberia over which the First World War passed without leaving any traces thus do not stand up to serious investigation. They belong in the realm of sensationalist inventions. For instance, the local police supervising the internees possessed complete and precise information about every one of us. It was amazing to observe how quickly they were informed about escapes; and a minimum of time passed before repressive measures decreed by the government in St. Petersburg were felt in our hamlet, some hundred miles away from the nearest railroad station.

When in the course of 1917 the tsarist empire collapsed and the revolution developed toward the Bolshevik seizure of power, the principal events took place in Petrograd and Moscow. But in the far-off corners of the country the revolutionary events in the capitals were mirrored in processes during which the various social and political elements within the population played their successive roles. In my capacity as local trustee of the United States Consulate General representing the interests of the German civilian internees, I had faced tsarist county and police officers up to March, 1917. After the tsar's abdication they were replaced at first by bourgeois-liberal

representatives of the local zemstvo administration. These were followed by socialists. Finally, after the October Revolution, local authority in our little town was represented by a notorious good-for-nothing who documented his proletarian class consciousness by meeting me barefoot, and in unspeakably ragged clothes. I need hardly point out how difficult it was to make a good case for the material and spiritual needs of the internees to such people and in such times of upheaval.

Numerous German prisoners, both military and civilian, made use of the chaotic conditions brought about by the revolution. Either legally or illegally they left their exile and departed in a westerly direction in order to be nearer home in case the war should end. Through the efforts of my wife, who had returned to Moscow three months earlier, I obtained legal permission to leave Vologda Province, and in the beginning of 1918 I was back in Moscow.

After the United States entered the war, the Swedish Consulate General took over the function of protecting German interests. The enormous mass of prisoners of war collecting in Moscow gave the Swedes great difficulties. In view of this, the humanitarian zeal and conscientiousness with which they went about their task were beyond praise. Particular recognition is due to the activities of the representatives of the Swedish Red Cross who earned lasting credit in their travels to PW camps in eastern Russia and Siberia. The daughter of the Swedish minister in Petrograd, the late Elsa Brandström, has gone into the annals of that time as a shining symbol of genuine humanitarianism. The fame which the "Angel of Siberia" won among all those who enjoyed her care accompanied her many years later into the new country of her choice, the United States.

With the help of the Swedish consular officials, and in spite of the resistance shown by Bolshevik authorities, who regarded such help as an intrusion into their prerogatives, the first homes for prisoners of war were established in Moscow in January, 1918. In this work I placed myself at the disposal of the Swedes. By means of such establishments, the foundations for a systematic protection of German military and civilian prisoners in Russia were created even before the German diplomatic representation and the numerous German relief commissions arrived in Russia to be distributed throughout the country. These relief commissions, sent after the conclusion of the Brest-Litovsk Treaty, were subordinate to a Main Commission

in Moscow, which in turn was responsible to the Prussian War Ministry and the German Red Cross. Because of my previous experience in prisoner-of-war relief work, both of these agencies hired me to work for the Main Commission in Moscow. That is the reason why I became a witness of the events described in the preceding sections.

4. FROM MOSCOW TO BERLIN

My function in the Main Commission for Aid to Prisoners of War was to supervise and direct the entire evacuation work, a task which became more and more difficult as the months went by. The Soviet government became less and less co-operative when they perceived the impending collapse of the Imperial government. The approach of winter, with its rigors, and the growing lack of means of transportation meant added difficulties. On the railroad stations in Moscow's periphery, working daily and far into the night, I had to use all my vigor and persuasion in order to obtain railroad cars and locomotives, or to prevent wanton search and looting of prisoners' possessions. Driving back home through the unlit streets of Moscow after a day's work was a constant danger because of rifle and pistol shots whose origin and aim remained quite obscure.[6]

Terrorist acts of the Left Socialist Revolutionaries took on ever increasing dimensions. Two high Bolshevik functionaries, Volodarsky and Uritsky, were murdered in Petrograd, one shortly after the other, and Lenin barely escaped a similar fate. On the part of the Bolshevik leadership, this unleashed the so-called Red Terror, which began with its full fury after the attempt on Lenin's life on August 30, 1918. The lists of its victims published by the Bolsheviks at that time contained quite a few persons whom I knew personally.

During all this time official relations between the German Reich and Soviet Russia became increasingly strained. In the first months after the conclusion of the peace treaty and the resumption of diplomatic relations, the Soviet government had shown a substantial amount of good will. But its readiness to fulfill the conditions of the harsh treaty was continually on the decline in proportion as the

---

[6] Remembering the difficulties which we had to surmount, I cannot help mentioning my good friend and faithful colleague Carl Hecking, whose energy, circumspection, and selflessness, more than any other factor, helped us to conquer all obstacles.

coming German defeat loomed on the Western horizon. The strategy of the Soviet government was from the beginning aimed at gaining a rallying period. This period was, however, drawing to a close as the counter-revolutionary movement led by former tsarist generals gripped ever larger parts of Russia. The Civil War was beginning.

In turn, the German attitude toward the Soviet Republic was highly contradictory, to say the least. The continued maintenance of diplomatic ties with the regime was not much more than a convenient fiction. Simultaneously, opponents of the regime were actively supported by the numerous German agencies then in Moscow, while Bolshevik elements in the Ukraine were systematically persecuted and liquidated by the German occupation forces. Political tensions in the Ukraine, aggravated by the occupation, came to a head in the assassination of the German commander, Field Marshal Hermann von Eichhorn, on July 30, 1918. He too was a victim of Left Socialist Revolutionary terrorism. The assassin was later apprehended, tried, and condemned to death by the Soviet regime.

The German attitude of uncertainty toward Moscow expressed itself in the decision to move the embassy from Moscow to Pskov not long after Helfferich's departure. This amounted to its dissolution, since Pskov was situated in the area occupied by the German Army. Yet, because the Germans wished to preserve at least the semblance of continued diplomatic relations, the German consul general in Moscow, Hauschild, was entrusted with the fulfillment of diplomatic functions. However great Hauschild's personal decency, he was not up to the task which the situation demanded of him. At the same time it is at least doubtful whether any other German representatives could have done more for the interests of their country in view of the approaching German collapse in the West and the recklessness with which the Bolshevik partner came to disregard the provisions of the peace treaty.

What caused the greatest concern in Berlin was Moscow's increasing attempts to interfere in the domestic affairs of Germany. Simultaneously with the establishment of the German Embassy in Moscow in April, 1918, the Russian Socialist Federative Soviet Republic (RSFSR) had established its own diplomatic post in Berlin. This offered them the unprecedented opportunity to interfere in the internal political affairs of another country, under the cloak of diplomatic immunity, by spreading Communist propaganda material.

Money could be sent to the Soviet representative by official courier
mail. The German security organs thus faced a problem for which
there had been no precedent, and it paralyzed them for months.[7]
It was not until late in the fall of 1918, when the abuse of diplomatic
immunity became too obvious, that the German authorities decided
to make an end of this state of affairs, even if it should mean a rupture
of relations. At that time the German government did not, in any
case, regard continued relations with the Soviet government as
politically useful; on the contrary. In domestic politics all ties with
the Bolsheviks were highly dangerous, and in foreign politics, too,
they were regarded more and more as a liability. Realizing that the
German army had been beaten and that the war was lost, the policy
makers in Berlin began to search for means of securing a mild peace
from the Allies; and a rupture of relations with Russia may have
been an attempt to win their good graces. Agitation for a "peace of
understanding" with the West on the condition that Germany would
co-operate with them against Russian Bolshevism was one of the
many ideas and propositions with which German generals, politicians, and journalists then began to play frantically. At the same
time General Max Hoffmann seems to have been contemplating
a last-minute offensive against Petrograd. As Karl Radek put it in
his customarily acid way, "The corpse of the Soviet Republic was
meant to be the dowry toward a *mariage de convenance* between
Germany and the Entente." [8] As it turned out, the Western powers
accepted Germany's services for policing the East; German troops,
both regular and irregular, were ordered to remain in the Baltic
provinces until further notice. But this provision in the armistice
terms did not lead to any leniency in shaping the Treaty of Versailles.

A convenient reason for a break was easily found. When Soviet
courier packages were being unloaded at the Friedrichstrasse railroad station in Berlin in late October, 1918, some crates were "ac-
cidentally" dropped on their edges so that they broke open and re-

[7] The diplomatic representative whom the Soviet government had sent to Berlin
was Adolf Yoffe. The son of a wealthy Jewish family residing in the Crimea, he
had given the Bolshevik party his entire inherited property. He was highly educated, and his polished and tactful manners distinguished him favorably from
the average representative of the party. A personal friend and political associate of Trotsky, he would have fallen victim of the purges had he not taken
his own life in 1927 because of illness and disillusionment.

[8] Radek, *Die auswärtige Politik Sowjet-Russlands* (Hamburg, 1921, Bibliothek
der Kommunistischen Internationale), p. 72.

vealed as their contents revolutionary pamphlets in the German language.[9] Thereupon Wilhelm Solf, the Secretary of State for Foreign Affairs, demanded that the Soviet government recall its representative. This led to the mutual rupture of all diplomatic relations.

A few days later, on November 9th, the Kaiser's government collapsed. In its place stepped a Council of People's Deputies in which the Independent Socialist Hugo Haase took over the conduct of foreign relations. The Soviet government appears to have believed that the new German government, consisting exclusively of Social Democrats, would reverse the decision of its predecessor and re-establish diplomatic relations, especially since Yoffe had not yet departed from Berlin. But they were mistaken. On the contrary, Haase explicitly insisted on the recall of the Soviet representative, thus documenting the gulf separating even the extreme left-wing Independent Social Democrats from the Bolsheviks, and the continuity linking the new regime with the one that had just collapsed.

No more than twelve hours had passed since the arrival of the news about the revolution in Germany when a Central Revolutionary German Workers' and Soldiers' Council was formed in Moscow which enjoyed the full support of the Russian Communist party as well as the official Soviet authorities. It was headed by some left-wing German prisoners of war who had joined the Bolshevik movement, some out of conviction, others out of opportunism. The majority of the members of the Workers' and Soldiers' Council had during the preceding months infiltrated into the numerous German agencies in Moscow as office workers, messengers, and so on.[10] Thus they had become familiar with some of the internal affairs of these agencies. Their knowledge was later utilized by the Soviet government for propaganda purposes. They could accuse the German agencies of having participated in counter-revolutionary activities and of having undertaken illegal business transactions. As a matter of fact, the official German personnel in Moscow regarded the Bolshevik regime as a passing phenomenon, and considered it their

[9] The Soviet government has consistently claimed that the German authorities themselves must have placed these pamphlets in the crates.

[10] For instance, the commanding general of the Eastern Theater of Operations (*Oberost*), as well as the high command of the German Army, had a representative in Moscow. Serving them and a number of other German agencies was a German Army signal unit.

task to support the forces working toward the fall of the regime. This support was not only given in the form of money but also by smuggling counter-revolutionary leaders and agents out to Germany with prisoner-of-war transports. Moreover, former Russian diplomats and other members of the old high society who had fled to Germany would turn to their old friends in the German Foreign Ministry, requesting that help be given to their relatives still in Russia. Von Maltzan himself was swamped with requests of this sort, and he always tried to do as much as he could without jeopardizing his position and the aims he was pursuing.

As a consequence, the members of the German Consulate General, the relief commissions, and other agencies in Moscow found themselves in a very uncomfortable and embarrassing situation for the ten days between November 9th and the date of their departure from Moscow. Under the guidance and with the participation of Soviet functionaries, the Workers' and Soldiers' Council organized meetings for the German prisoners of war in Moscow. In these meetings flaming speeches were delivered, and the representatives of "reactionary imperial Germany" were told that they would be held to account for their inimical attitude toward the Soviet Republic. None of these threats was ever carried out. Perhaps this is due to the fact that the Soviet mission was then still in Berlin, and the Soviet government feared retaliation from the Germans.

Though I had never attempted to hide my anti-Bolshevik attitude, I had carefully refrained from any action out of keeping with my position and my duties. When I met the Soviet government and the German Workers' and Soldiers' Council again later, this fact considerably eased my official dealings with them.

On November 19, 1918, the German officials departed from Moscow. At about the same time the train carrying Yoffe and his large staff back to Soviet Russia was rolling out of Berlin. The exchange of missions was to take place at the line of demarcation separating the area occupied by Germany from the territory of the Soviet Republic. This line then ran through Orsha, about one hundred miles west of Smolensk on the railroad from Moscow to Brest-Litovsk. The Soviet authorities had furnished a train with upholstered seats to carry the official German personalities; for the remainder of the personnel and for those prisoners of war who preferred returning to a defeated Germany to remaining in Bolshevik Russia freight cars

had been added. Since I did not want to be separated from the prisoners of war, I, together with a few friends, decided to choose the freight cars. This gave me not only moral satisfaction but also the quite material advantage that the freight cars could be heated, whereas the passengers in the first-class compartments had to freeze miserably.

During the trip I was shaken to my heart by the pitiful sight of tens of thousands of Russian prisoners of war coming from the opposite direction. After the rupture of German-Soviet relations, the Soviet authorities had removed all facilities for the reception, sheltering, feeding, and transportation of returning prisoners from their side of the border. The German administration for prisoners of war was therefore well aware of the desperate situation in which returning Russian prisoners would find themselves once they crossed onto Russian territory. But in their German camps the Russians were extremely restive, clamored to be shipped home, and, in impotent resentment, began to wreck the camps in which they had languished so long. When, in addition, radical elements among them began to fraternize with German left-wingers, the German administration decided to continue shipping the prisoners out. They were transported to Orsha in sealed boxcars and then dumped into the laps of Soviet authorities completely unprepared for the rush. There was neither transportation nor food nor shelter available in Orsha. The prisoners, therefore, in spite of their miserable condition, set out on their eastward trek on foot. Because of lack of fuel and the breakdown of locomotives, our train was frequently forced to stop during the night. I can still hear today the shuffling sound of thousands of feet moving past the train on the right and left. Many of the Russians collapsed from hunger, cold, or exhaustion, and remained lying beside the tracks. Nor do I blame a small group of these unfortunate people for attempting to break into our warm boxcar by force. When they failed to do so, they decided to burn the car. In the last second, as though by a miracle, we escaped the danger of being burned alive when the train suddenly started to move once again.

When our train arrived at Orsha, the opposite train carrying the Soviet diplomats was waiting there. The Soviet ambassador refused, however, to consent to the exchange because two baggage cars be-

longing to the Soviets were missing. Two days were spent in negotiations until it was finally agreed that two baggage cars should be unhitched from one of the German trains to be kept as a pawn by the Soviet authorities until the missing cars arrived. Shortly afterward a railroad car slowly moved past me; from its middle window a pale face framed in a black beard was looking out. It was Yoffe, the first ambassador whom the young Soviet Republic had sent out into the world, and who was now returning after his mission had failed.

Our transport arrived in Berlin after another six days. Berlin seemed to be suffering severely from the consequences of war and revolution. But what impressed me most gravely was the sight of cars racing through the streets with red flags flying, and containing men in leather jackets armed to the teeth. They reminded me of the streets of Moscow at the beginning of the Bolshevik Revolution, and I saw in them an incarnation of the danger that in Germany, too, developments might take a turn toward the Bolshevik course. If this did not take place in spite of the ominous indications, credit must be given the German Social Democrats, men like Friedrich Ebert, Gustav Noske, Philipp Scheidemann, and others who succeeded in preventing Germany from going Communist in the years following World War I.

Among the problems then dominating the domestic situation in Germany, the prisoner-of-war question played a considerable role. The refusal of the Western Allies to allow the German prisoners of war then in their hands to return after the armistice had created considerable excitement among broad sections of the German population. A People's League for the Protection of German Military and Civilian Prisoners (Volksbund zum Schutze der deutschen Kriegs- und Zivilgefangenen) formed at the end of 1918 had rapidly developed into a mighty organization which not only sought to appeal to the world's conscience but at the same time was exerting strong pressure on the German government in order to hasten the return of the prisoners.

The German government was well aware of the political implications of the prisoner-of-war problem. Consequently, in the first days of January, 1919, it established a central agency, the Reich Central Office for Military and Civilian Prisoners (Reichszentralstelle für Kriegs- und Zivilgefangene), directly responsible to the Reich cabinet

and entrusted with all problems connected with the return of prisoners from foreign lands. The nominal head of the Reichszentralstelle was the Social Democratic Reichstag deputy Stücklen; the man, however, who gave the agency its soul and spirit was Moritz Schlesinger. A democratic Socialist by conviction, and therefore opposed to Communism, he was nevertheless an untypical representative of the Social Democratic party because of his acute feeling for political constellations and exigencies, unhindered by the doctrinairism hampering so many of his party comrades. He had not come up through the ranks of the party's trade-union bureaucracy, but had joined it only after the fall of the monarchy.

Although my own motives in working for close German-Soviet cooperation may have been of a much more sentimental nature, the common course Schlesinger and I were usually advocating served as a growing personal bond between us, which grew into warm friendship. When Ulrich Count Brockdorff-Rantzau entered the scene as ambassador, he knew the part played by the team Schlesinger-Hilger, and maintained close contact with us. Schlesinger often came to Moscow, and an almost ideal tricornered co-operation developed in the course of time between three men so utterly dissimilar in origin, training, and personal outlook. For many years Schlesinger and I corresponded frequently and regularly. This correspondence has become an important source for this book.

Schlesinger's immediate aim was to regain contact with Moscow in the interest of the German prisoners of war. In December, 1918, even before the founding of the Reichszentralstelle, he succeeded in having the Independent Socialist Reichstag deputy Dr. Oscar Cohn dispatched to Moscow for this purpose. Cohn had served as legal consultant in Adolf Yoffe's Soviet embassy in Berlin, and Schlesinger hoped that he would be able to reach Moscow and return to Berlin with a Soviet plenipotentiary who could negotiate about the fate of the German prisoners still in Russia. The plan misfired completely. When the Soviet government learned about Cohn's mission, it broadcast a wireless message containing the assertion that Cohn had been given large amounts of money by the Soviet government with which to support the German radical left. Upon this news General Hoffmann detained him in Kovno, and Cohn had to return to Berlin.

In January, 1919, the Allied powers assumed full supervision over

all Russian prisoners of war still in Germany and ordered the immediate cessation of all further transports to Russia, reserving for themselves the right to ship Russian prisoners anywhere they thought fit. The intention to press these Russians into service for the intervention against the Bolshevik regime was obvious. Recognizing it, Schlesinger strongly objected to the idea of transferring the prisoners from one master to another like cattle, without even asking their consent. Moreover, he feared that the Soviet authorities would, in such a case, take their vengeance on the German prisoners still in their hands, whose situation already defied description. He therefore decided to frustrate the plans of the Allies by intensifying, not stopping, the transport of Russian prisoners out of Germany, well aware of what hardships were awaiting them in Russia, and that they would at once be used by the Soviet government to help fight the Civil War. All this, he thought, would have to be the price paid for the benefit of the German prisoners in Russia.

I joined the Reichszentralstelle in the spring of 1919. My principal duty consisted of the supervision of all German prisoner-of-war camps containing Russian prisoners. Later I helped organize the systematic rehabilitation of German personnel returning from Russia and their reintegration into the German social fabric.

Thanks to Schlesinger's initiative, the Reichszentralstelle was requested in the first half of 1920 to enter into negotiations with the Soviet government concerning the further exchange of civilian and military prisoners still remaining in the two countries. Viktor Kopp, designated as the representative of the Soviet government for the purpose of these negotiations, arrived in Berlin in the spring, and an agreement was signed in that city on April 19, 1920. The agreement provided for the establishment by both governments of prisoner relief agencies on the territory of the other party, to be administered by persons especially designated for the work. Less than three months later, on July 7, 1920, a further agreement was signed which granted personal immunity to both of these plenipotentiaries. They were further given the right to maintain courier communications with their own governments, to use code, and to exercise consular functions. With this, both partners manifested their intention to revive the relations that had been ruptured in November, 1918. For this the exchange of prisoners of war furnished a welcome pretext.

On the part of the Soviet government, Viktor Kopp was made administrator plenipotentiary of the Soviet Relief Agency for Military and Civilian Prisoners. The German government designated me to be his counterpart in Moscow. Hence on June 7, 1920, I departed once more for Russia. The following chapters tell about the twenty-one years which I subsequently spent there.

II RELIEF AND RECONSTRUCTION WORK

1. EVACUATION OF PRISONERS OF WAR

MY TRIP TO MOSCOW AND THE
DISSOLUTION OF THE SOLDIERS' COUNCIL

In June, 1920, Soviet Russia was surrounded on its western border by a cordon of states which either had not yet regulated and defined their relation to the Soviet government or, like Poland, were still at war with it. The only exception was Estonia, which had concluded a peace treaty with the RSFSR in February of 1920. Her example was followed by Lithuania in July, Latvia in August, and Finland in October, 1920. But in order to reach Moscow from Germany in June, I had to travel by way of the Baltic and Estonia. Regular steamship runs between the Baltic ports of Germany and Estonia had not yet been opened. Hence, I had to take recourse to a small steamer the German overseas transport agency (Seetransportleitung) had chartered from a private steamship company in Stettin for the purpose of transporting military and civilian prisoners home from Russia. The Soviet organizations would transport these prisoners to the Soviet border near Yamburg; [1] there they were received by representatives of the International Red Cross and brought into a transit camp on the Estonian side of the border, in Narva. From there they resumed their homeward journey after a brief quarantine.

After a brief stay in Narva I traveled to the capital of the young Estonian Republic, Tallin. From there the official Russian "courier car" would go twice a week; it served as the connecting link between the Soviet representatives in Tallin and the governmental agencies

[1] Later named Kingisepp in honor of an Estonian Communist shot by his fellow countrymen.

27

in Moscow, and constituted the only possible means of getting across
the Soviet border legally.

The Soviet government was at that time represented in Estonia by
a certain Gukovsky, who had previously served in Moscow as People's Commissar for Finance, and who in this capacity had done
everything to speed the devaluation of the ruble. The Soviet government was then still maintaining the allegedly Marxist principle that
money is dispensable in a proletarian state and would soon disappear, being a bourgeois institution. In his outward appearance
Gukovsky was typical of the Bolshevik functionaries of that time.
Attempting to emphasize his Communist convictions by his proletarian appearance, he received me in shirt sleeves and without a neck-
tie, with a pair of worn-out house slippers on his feet.

Two questions became the subject of our conversation. The first
dealt with the desire of the Soviet government to obtain substantial
quantities of medicaments from Germany which were sorely needed
in Russia. The negotiations ran into difficulties when the German
suppliers insisted on advance payment in gold. I was the one who
had to inform Gukovsky of this condition; I told him that it was up
to him to have the gold transported to the seaport. From there it
could be shipped to Germany on one of the prisoner-of-war transport
ships. My words dealt a serious blow to Gukovsky. In great excitement he tried to make me see the impossibility of transporting the
required quantity of gold on horse-drawn wagons (the only means
of transportation he had available) from the railroad station to the
harbor, through the center of town. Tallin, he said, was lousy with
agents of the Entente observing every step of the Soviet representatives suspiciously. A Soviet gold transport to Germany would cause
the wildest rumors and would make the international situation of
both states even more difficult than it was already. To emphasize
his argument, Gukovsky asked me whether I knew how much weight
the amount of gold demanded by the Germans represented. With
these words he put his hand into the half-opened drawer of his desk
and drew out a sack filled with shining gold coins. He poured the
gold out before me and cried, "Half a pood of weight, and at that
it's only 10,000 gold rubles!" [2] And, with a gesture of contempt,
Gukovsky returned the sack to the desk, gave the drawer a kick, and

[2] 1 pood = approximately 36 American pounds; 10,000 gold rubles are the equivalent of about 5,000 gold dollars.

seemed to regard the matter as closed. The fact that the desk threatened to disintegrate of old age and the drawers were without locks did not appear to worry him in the least.[3]

The other matter which I took up with Gukovsky was about several crates containing a total of 15,000,000 rubles which I carried with me on orders from my government. The money was to cover the expenses of the Moscow relief agency and the cost of transporting the prisoners home. It consisted in part of notes printed by the Soviet government after the October Revolution, partly of tsarist bank notes, and for the rest, of so-called Kerensky notes, money that had been printed and circulated by the Provisional Government preceding the Bolsheviks. Tsarist money and Kerensky notes were at that time in great demand by those elements in Soviet Russia counting on a speedy fall of the Soviet government. They were valued much more highly than legal Soviet money. The tsarist ruble, worth about ten Soviet rubles when I arrived in Moscow, went up to eight times that much in March, 1921, only to drop to zero suddenly after the collapse of the Kronstadt revolt and the inauguration of the New Economic Policy (NEP). Luckily, this occurred at the very moment when our supplies of tsarist rubles had been exhausted, so that the relief agency suffered no heavy loss from the devaluation of the tsarist ruble.

Special crates had been constructed by experienced craftsmen in Berlin for the transport of the money. They had zinc linings, inlaid seals, and tight locks. Viktor Kopp, the Soviet representative in Berlin, had provided me with the necessary papers to get the fifteen million through the Soviet border and customs. Nevertheless, to be doubly careful, I asked Gukovsky whether he could not give me some additional written documents to prevent any possible difficulties at the border. His reaction to my request was typical of the attitude which the Bolsheviks at that time showed to money matters of all sorts. Gukovsky first of all made the proposition that I should leave the crates with all the paper money with him. In exchange he offered to make out a check on the State Bank in Moscow. Gukovsky's

[3] Soon after my conversation with Gukovsky, business interests in Germany desiring to resume trade relations with Russia established a Research Association for the Resumption of All Trade with the East (Studiengesellschaft für die Aufnahme des gesamten Handels mit dem Osten). Worried by the serious danger of disruptive epidemics, this association declared itself ready to ship drugs and medical supplies to Russia by sea and by air.

intentions were quite obvious, since tsarist money was in great demand in Estonia, too. Hence I declined his "generous" offer, stating that my government had ordered me to take the money to Moscow just as I had received it. Visibly peeved, Gukovsky wanted to find a release for his disappointment. "I can't understand all the fuss you make about money," he said. "Let me show you what we do with that stuff here." With these words he led me to a huge old wooden chest standing in the next room; it was one of those trunks used by Russian peasant women to store their belongings. Gukovsky gave the half-open lid a push, the chest opened, and I saw a most disorderly heap of Soviet paper money which had obviously never been counted; nor was there any control over its use. I could not hide my amazement; but Gukovsky, with a grand gesture, pointed to the trunk, exclaiming: "Well, how do you like that? After all, the stuff isn't worth any other treatment!"

The next day I departed for Moscow. My traveling companions were an official of the Soviet diplomatic representation in Estonia and the Russian left-wing Socialist Axelrod, who had been expelled from Germany and who was now returning to his home country after many years of exile. Apparently his feelings about returning to a Bolshevik Russia were mixed, particularly after the Bolshevik border control had paid excessive attention to his baggage, which was filled with the products of the capitalist world. The Soviet diplomatic official going to Moscow with us was Davtian, a man of elegant appearance, with a finely modeled face and polished European manners, all quite out of keeping with the impression his chief had made on me the day before. Nor was it easy to believe that this cultured gentleman belonged to an agency whose name is closely linked with all the horrors of the Red Terror.[4]

In Yamburg, the first station on the Soviet side of the border, the guard in charge of the courier car announced that a gentleman by the name of Sergei Koussevitzky wished to see me. I had previously met Koussevitzky in Moscow, where he had become well known first as a bass violinist, and later as a conductor. His wife came from one of the wealthiest and best known Russian merchant families;

[4] For the next seventeen years Davtian occupied a number of high and responsible positions in the Soviet Union. He was finally made ambassador in Warsaw, whence he was recalled to Moscow. He disappeared in the great purges of the mid-thirties.

through her he was connected with Moscow's leading society circles. In the hospitable villa of his father-in-law on Lake Geneva, my wife and I spent part of our honeymoon in the summer of 1912. Sergei Koussevitzky and his wife, it appeared, were being detained at the Soviet-Estonian border because the Cheka in Yamburg would not recognize as valid the exit permits they had obtained in Moscow. Neither I nor even Davtian could persuade the authorities to relent. Willy-nilly the Koussevitzkys had to go back to Moscow once more, an exceedingly difficult and exhausting trip at that time. There, after some efforts, I finally helped them to obtain papers with which they took leave of Soviet Russia forever. I had the further great satisfaction of being able to help them over the first days in Estonia with a few hundred Estonian crowns still in my possession.

On my way to Moscow I saw Petrograd again for the first time since the Bolshevik Revolution. This magnificent city, built by a tsar who used the most brutal and objectionable means for the purpose of doing great things for his country, was now terribly sad to behold. The faces of the population were modeled by starvation, misery, and desperation, no matter whether they were the sorry remnants of the dispossessed classes or representatives of the victorious proletariat. All had but one thought: To obtain a crust of bread. The food obtainable by means of official ration cards meant certain starvation. Not a single shop was open; no public means of conveyance was running; and much of the once famous wooden pavement of St. Petersburg had disappeared: the people had used it to fire their stoves.

In Petrograd was a branch office of the Moscow German Workers' and Soldiers' Council that had been established in a palace on the Moika River which before the revolution had been the property of a man carrying one of the more well known Russian noble names. The house itself and its interior furnishings, with their somewhat threadbare magnificence, were a reminder of the days portrayed for posterity by Lev Tolstoi in his immortal *War and Peace*. Its stylish marble ballroom seemed to symbolize an age in which a very thin layer of Russia's population enjoyed the highest products of spiritual culture and social grace at the expense of the vast peasant masses. Now the hall was hung with red banners bearing proclamations demanding the unity of the proletarians of all countries and the destruction of the bourgeoisie. They expressed the irreconcilable an-

tagonism between the old and the new social orders. Once more I became conscious of the difficulty of the compromise which I had decided to make for the sake of the lives of human beings entrusted to my care.

THE PROBLEM OF THE WORKERS' AND SOLDIERS' COUNCIL

The position held by the Central Revolutionary German Workers' and Soldiers' Council in Moscow and its provincial branches rested on the support given it by the Soviet government and the Russian Communist party. When the German agencies departed from Moscow in 1918, the council had taken over their entire property, consisting of buildings, motorcars, food stores, and so forth, and had been permitted to keep most of it. Since then its principal task had consisted of the Communist indoctrination of the German prisoners of war, in order to make them into the vanguard of the world revolution in Germany. For this purpose the Workers' and Soldiers' Council continued to maintain and operate the prisoner-of-war homes established by us in 1918, and, in its fashion, devoted itself to the spiritual and material care of the prisoners who were passing through these homes on their way to Germany.

During the conferences in Berlin that preceded my departure for Moscow, the Foreign Ministry expressed its expectation that I would, "of course," dissolve the Workers' and Soldiers' Council immediately upon my arrival in Moscow. In addition they thought it to be a matter of course that I should take care to prevent any further Communist propaganda among the German prisoners of war. I refused, however, to recognize these instructions as binding, for I knew that such procedure would at once set me into sharp antagonism with the Soviet government and with the Soldiers' Council. It would make my position impossible from the very beginning. I tried to demonstrate to the Foreign Ministry that we could not afford such an attitude since the Workers' and Soldiers' Council held in its hands all the material means necessary for the care of the prisoners. Moreover, I argued, the Soviet government was politically in no position to abandon the Workers' and Soldiers' Council for the sake of Germany. I finally succeeded in convincing the Foreign Ministry that after my arrival in Moscow I should at first have no choice except trying to bring about a *modus vivendi* with the Soldiers' Council

and to harness its apparatus for the purpose of getting the prisoners home. An agreement was reached, and the power of attorney given me by the Reichszentralstelle contained the following paragraph:

Herr Hilger is authorized to collaborate with the German organization still remaining in Moscow which has heretofore dealt with the care and evacuation of the prisoners; he may furthermore use his own dutiful judgment in creating suitable auxiliary agencies in other places in Russia or in allowing existing German organizations to continue as such auxiliary agencies and giving them specific orders.

The document is still in my possession today. It conceals the ominous name Workers' and Soldiers' Council under the harmless designation of "the German organization still remaining in Moscow." But the meaning and purpose of the agreement were not affected by this circumlocution, whereas I was covered against the danger of possible malicious attacks in the future; moreover, I was in a position to utilize not only the Soldiers' Council in Moscow but also its branches in the provinces for the tasks for which the prisoners-of-war exchange treaty provided.

Immediately after my arrival in Moscow, it became apparent how right I had been in predicting to the Foreign Ministry the attitude of the Soviet government concerning the Workers' and Soldiers' Council. The night after my arrival I paid a visit to Chicherin in order to introduce myself in my new capacity and present him an introductory letter from the German foreign minister. Chicherin, obviously supposing that my first demand would be the dissolution of the German Workers' and Soldiers' Council, seized the initiative. After expressing his satisfaction that Germany had decided, after an interruption of almost two years, to resume its relations with Soviet Russia, he declared that these relations could bear fruit only if Germany were to take the peculiar character of the Soviet regime into account. In saying this, he continued, in his fussy way of speaking, he had in mind the existence of a certain German Workers' and Soldiers' Council in Moscow. Admittedly, the existence of such an organization was unusual in view of the simultaneous presence of an official representative from the country in question. Nevertheless, he concluded, he saw himself obliged to state that I should create a very difficult situation if I were to demand the dissolution of the Workers' and Soldiers' Council. Indeed, such a demand on my part

would seriously jeopardize my entire purpose of caring for the prisoners. For political reasons the granting of such a request would be out of the question for his government; the Soviet government would refuse it even in the face of the danger that its refusal might once more disturb relations with Germany.

Chicherin was visibly relieved when I replied that it had not been my intention to demand of the Soviet government the dissolution of the German organization in Moscow. On the contrary, I told him that I had already found a *modus vivendi* with them.

The situation I had found in Moscow was what I had expected. Representatives of the Workers' and Soldiers' Council were waiting for me at the railroad station. Externally polite and correct in their forms, they nevertheless made me understand clearly that they had no intentions of letting me crowd them out of the picture, even though they would be perfectly willing to co-operate with me. There was no doubt that their behavior was based on orders from the Soviet government; similar directives must have been at the base of Chicherin's attitude.

Four men were at the head of the Workers' and Soldiers' Council at the time of my arrival in Moscow. Their chairman was a former foundry worker from Hamburg. Of the four, he was the only one who had joined the Communist movement from inner conviction. He was the one, therefore, whom I decided I had to remove from Moscow as soon as possible. Fortunately, he was intelligent enough to understand that after the arrival of an official German representative in Moscow the days of the Workers' and Soldiers' Council were, in the long run, numbered. To sugar-coat the bitter pill, I appointed him chief of the branch relief agency in Petrograd; he assented and moved to that city. I thought I could afford his making fiery revolutionary speeches before the German prisoners passing through Petrograd in view of the advantages I enjoyed from having rid myself of his presence in Moscow.

The other three were of petty-bourgeois origin and had been attracted to Communism by inferiority feelings and career reasons, motives I now sought to exploit. One of them had been a petty office clerk in Germany; his energy in work was matched by his craving for recognition and status. I appointed him chief of the evacuation department of the relief agency, so that he was now performing the work I had done in 1918. I sent the other man into the provinces.

The third one was a former Social Democrat who had done labor-union work. I appointed him to head the economic department, where he could give free play to his organizational talents.

It was a strange period of transition during which the two organizations not only co-existed peacefully side by side but also shared the same premises and were practically merged organizationally. A sign had been nailed beside the entrance door of our offices attesting to the presence of an official German agency; but next to it hung the red shield of the Communist Workers' and Soldiers' Council. The diarchy which had characterized the early months of the revolution was here repeated, as it were, in miniature. But whereas the diarchy of 1917, in which the Socialist Petrograd Soviet temporarily shared sovereign power with the bourgeois Provisional Government, had given way to the exclusive rule of the by now bolshevized Soviet, it was different in 1920. Now the bourgeois agency officially representing the German government succeeded at least in removing the last traces of Communist collaboration, especially after further steps had been taken to regulate and normalize German-Soviet relations. One night we quietly and unobtrusively removed the red sign of the Soldiers' Council from the door of our offices, symbolic indication that the diarchy in the German Relief Agency had come to an end. The Moscow *Rote Fahne*, official Communist paper in the German language, in February, 1921, calmly reported the dissolution of the Workers' and Soldiers' Council, not without praise for the "wise restraint and tact" I had shown in dealing with the problem.

NANSEN, EIDUCK, AND RAKOVSKY

Of the Soviet governmental agencies with which we had official dealings in our relief work, the most important was the Central Evacuation Office, entrusted with the job of evacuating all German prisoners. Tsentrevak, as it was briefly called, was headed by the Latvian Communist Alexandr Vladimirovich Eiduck, who had previously been an official of the Cheka and who must have had countless human lives on his conscience. The compulsion to have official dealings with this man, whom I loathed, was one of the more revolting aspects of my life in Moscow. Indeed, it seemed a paradox that he, of all people, had been put in charge of relief work. Together with Eiduck, I had to travel to Kovno in September, 1920. There a con-

ference concerning the evacuation of German, Austrian, and Hungarian prisoners of war from Russia was to take place under the chairmanship of the famous Norwegian Arctic explorer Fridtjof Nansen, whom the League of Nations had appointed high commissioner for dealing with all prisoner-of-war problems in Europe. Nansen had designated me as his representative for all Russia.

Nansen's human stature and the purity of his character raised him high above the environment in which the chaos of postwar Europe had placed him. Everything Nansen said and did was exclusively and without any compromise aimed toward the welfare of suffering mankind. He simply could not understand that people could regard problems like the evacuation of prisoners of war, the Russian refugee question, the desperate situation of the Armenians, or the famine in Russia from any other than purely humanitarian points of view; his whole being revolted against the idea that others might make these problems into objects of political deals. While his attitude on international conferences went counter to selfish political aims, the protagonists of such aims only laughed at his political naïveté. But for those who benefited from the services of his organizations or who came into direct touch with his great kindness or universal knowledge, Nansen was the incarnation of timeless ideals, of humanity, and international reconciliation.

Kovno, capital of Lithuania, had been chosen as the place for the prisoner-of-war conference because it was equally distant from Berlin and Moscow and because it could be reached on land routes by all participants. Lithuania had concluded a peace treaty with Soviet Russia on July 12, 1920, and had soon afterward resumed diplomatic relations with her. Nevertheless, railway traffic between Moscow and Kovno had not yet been restored by September, 1920. Poland and Soviet Russia were still at war with each other, and the Poles had just been cleared from the Lithuanian-Russian border area. Thus it took us a full three days and three nights to reach our destination, even though at every opportunity Eiduck underscored his demands for faster transportation with a pistol in his hand. Each change of locomotives took several hours, and the speed of the train seldom exceeded fifteen miles an hour because the locomotives were worn out and the only fuel available was damp wood. Several miles east of the Lithuanian border railroad connection stopped entirely, since

the tracks had either been removed entirely or changed to a narrower gauge. We traveled some of the remaining distance on foot and some of it on primitive peasant carts, until we reached a place where the Lithuanian railroad administration furnished us an old and decrepit passenger car which finally took us into Kovno.

At the Kovno conference a resolution was accepted which provided that the German prisoners interned in Siberia should be given priority in evacuation because of the adverse climate and severe conditions of life there. And since the capacity of the ships available in Narva was insufficient to evacuate prisoners from all parts of Russia at the same time, the German agencies agreed to postpone the evacuation of prisoners from the Ukraine for the time being.[5]

At the same time the Soviet government had from the very beginning of the evacuations demanded that the individual transports from Germany should contain prisoners of identical national origin (Great Russians, Ukrainians, or Siberians), so that they could be sent on to their destination in a body after arriving on Russian territory. The German authorities complied with this reasonable request, and henceforth every third contingent of Russian prisoners leaving Germany consisted exclusively of Ukrainians. The result was that all Ukrainian prisoners had already been returned to their home country at a time when the Germans in the Ukraine were still waiting to be evacuated. It was not until the end of the year, when the flow of prisoners from Siberia subsided, that I could approach Tsentrevak with the request to start making arrangements for the evacuation of German prisoners from the Ukraine. Deep was my indignation when Tsentrevak refused my request on the pretext that it had no jurisdiction in the Ukraine. They said I should have to go to the Commissariat for Foreign Affairs. But that office, too, declared that it had no power to do anything because the Ukraine was a sovereign state to which the government in Moscow could give no directives. The Ukrainian government, the commissariat told me, would surely be perfectly willing to release the prisoners as soon as the German government had concluded a similar treaty with it as it had with

[5] In January, 1921, the International Red Cross arranged for a conference in Riga in which I also participated. There arrangements were made for an overland connection between Germany and Russia. Riga was to serve as the place where German and Russian returnees were to be exchanged.

the RSFSR. My government, however, had no particular desire to grant recognition to the Ukrainian Communist government in this manner.

In vain I argued with the men of the commissariat that the prisoners-of-war exchange treaty of April 19, 1920, covered all prisoners who had fallen into Russian hands during the recent war.[6] The German government, I reminded them, had evacuated prisoners from all the nationalities of the former Russian Empire, including Ukrainians. Moscow's refusal to compel the Ukraine to release the German prisoners, I concluded, was a blatant violation not only of the above-mentioned treaty but also of the customary rules of fair play between treaty partners. Indeed, the Foreign Commissariat admitted the soundness of my objections but kept maintaining its position nevertheless, adding that the only way to clarify the matter would be direct negotiation between myself and Christian G. Rakovsky, chairman of the Council of People's Commissars in the Ukrainian Socialist Soviet Republic, who was expected to come to Moscow soon.

In this conference Rakovsky countered my arguments by saying that he could not see why the German government refused to conclude a treaty about the exchange of prisoners with the Ukrainian government. Even if other states refused to recognize the Ukraine, Germany, he thought, had the least reason of all, after supporting the erection of an independent Ukraine under the leadership of Hetman Skoropadsky in 1918. "Or does your government think an independent Ukraine under my leadership will be less likely to last than under Skoropadsky?" he concluded sarcastically.

Impatient and angry, I replied that neither the recognition of the Ukraine nor her ability to remain alive was under discussion at all. "The subject of our discussion," I continued, "is nothing else than the German demand that a treaty be carried out which was concluded in good faith, and with the understanding that it covered all prisoners who fell into Russian hands during the war. If you, Christian Georgievich, want to deny this now, I can only consider this an attempt at blackmail which the German government will not let pass

[6] Article IV of the treaty of April 19th said, " 'German prisoners of war' within the meaning of this agreement may be held to include all Germans or former subjects of the German Reich who have come into Russian hands fighting for the German Reich or against the Russian Soviet Republic."

under any circumstances. You are shamelessly trying to make deals on the backs of the suffering prisoners."

"Those are hard words," Rakovsky smiled wryly. "But a young state that wants to get things done has to make use of any means suitable to bring it closer to its goal." [7] Those were his exact words.

Face to face with such mentality, I became convinced that the plight of the prisoners made it obligatory for the German government to comply with the demands of the Ukrainian government for good or for bad. But several months passed before the German government overcame its objections. On April 23, 1921, however, a year and four days after the conclusion of the exchange treaty with the RSFSR, a treaty was concluded with the Ukrainian representative in Berlin which followed the former agreement almost word for word. It might almost be considered a mockery that the "Ukrainian" representative signing the treaty was none other than Viktor Kopp. Schlesinger signed for Germany. The treaty paved the way for the return of the last German prisoners still on the territory of the former Russian Empire.

2. FAMINE AND EPIDEMIC RELIEF WORK

FAMINE RELIEF WORK

In June, 1921, I obtained leave and returned to Germany for the first time. I was still there when news of a terrible famine in Russia began to arrive. The famine appeared to surpass everything of the kind the poor country had heretofore experienced, and it threatened to bring all the successes already attained by the NEP to naught. Faced with this catastrophe, the Soviet government decided to appeal to the outside world for help. In its appeal it gave the severe drought of the two preceding years as the only cause of the famine, remaining silent about one of the chief causes, the disastrous agrarian policy of the period known as War Communism which had made the intro-

---

[7] Readers not familiar with the Russian language might wonder why in this and subsequent conversations with Soviet officials I addressed them by their first names. In Russia it is customary to address all persons except children, servants, and complete strangers by their names and patronymics. I could not, after all, use the patently aristocratic title "Your Excellency," nor even the bourgeois "Mister," in talking to the head of a Soviet state. Thus, even Stalin was "Iosif Visarionovich" when I had to address him.

duction of the NEP necessary. At the same time the more moderate leaders of the party made use of the emergency for the purpose of justifying once more the turn toward moderation which had been taken with the introduction of the NEP.[8] To make it more attractive for bourgeois capitalist states to come to the aid of the Soviet Re-public, the Soviet government decided on a step designed to give the impression that Russia was now undergoing further political evolutions and was ready to make greater concessions. In actual fact the maneuver was nothing but bluff; as soon as it had achieved its desired effect it was called off. What the Soviet government did was to turn to what had remained of the political opposition parties in the country, with the proposition of some sort of "civic peace," and the suggestion to participate in the famine-relief operation. For this purpose the opposition elements were to form a committee of their own which would enjoy privileges similar to those enjoyed by corre-sponding foreign organizations.

With good-natured belief in the sincerity of the Soviet government, and hoping that they might again establish a political foothold in Russia, the surviving leaders in the opposition declared their readi-ness to collaborate. Leadership in the committee was taken by three persons who had played a role in Russia's political life during the time of the Provisional Government; all were known as irreconcilable enemies of Communism. They were the so-called "independent" So-cialists Professor Sergei N. Prokopovich and Katarina D. Kuskova, and the well known Moscow physician Kishkin, formerly a member of the Constitutional Democratic (Cadet) party. After the collapse of tsarism, and until the Bolshevik Revolution, Kishkin had headed the Moscow municipal administration.

The Cheka at first opposed the plan of collaboration with the political opposition, but then relented, possibly hoping to be able to strike a more effective blow at the proper time. The opportunity for doing so soon offered itself, for the opposition committee entered into direct relations with the foreign relief organizations that had meanwhile arrived in Russia, and began to publish a news sheet which in its outward appearance was an exact replica of the late *Russkiya Vedomosti,* a bourgeois-liberal newspaper which had stood

---

[8] Cf., for instance, the speeches of Kalinin, Semashko, and others at the Fourth Session of the Central Executive Committee (VTsIK) in early October, 1921.

in high esteem among the progressive Russian intelligentsia for decades. The government could not help regarding this as an open provocation, and decided to dissolve the committee. Its members were arrested and first of all deported to Siberia. When they were later expelled from Soviet Russia, Professor Prokopovich and Mrs. Kuskova found refuge in Switzerland, where they are still living today.

Many foreign organizations had put their services at the disposition of the Soviet government. Among them was the American Relief Administration, organized by Herbert Hoover, which dispensed large sums; the German Red Cross, the Swedish Red Cross, a Vatican relief mission, the Quakers, representatives of the International Children's Help, and many others. The various states and their relief organizations were eagerly competing with one another to secure a share in the work to aid the starving Russian population. They were not always motivated by the purest altruism; economic considerations played their role, as did the different governments' desire to obtain information about internal conditions in the Soviet Republic. The extent of these less altruistic motives probably differed in each case. The Communist press in Russia later spread the version that the Americans had participated in feeding the starving Russian population only because they wanted to get rid of their surplus wheat production so as to prevent a drop in grain prices; by this device they sought not only to pacify the radicals in their own midst, but what was much more important, to erase the impression foreign aid had made on the Russian population. That they succeeded in doing so is attested by occasional indignant comments we heard from members of the old ruling classes, condemning the "combination of charity with business." The fact remains, of course, that millions of human beings in Russia were saved from starvation by foreign aid.

Such suspicious allegations faltered only before the person of Fridtjof Nansen, for even the Communists did not dare question his lack of selfish motives. He had founded the Nansen Aid, headed by a committee of four, an Englishman, a Dutchman, an Italian, and myself. This committee not only organized the direct distribution of foodstuffs but also sent out food parcels collected from welfare organizations and generous individuals abroad. Outside Russia, Nansen was aided by two outstanding advisers, the Swiss Édouard A. Frick and the German Moritz Schlesinger, whose practical talents

and experienced skill in negotiations contributed essentially toward
transforming Nansen's noble humanitarian intentions into highly
useful and effective deeds.

One of Nansen's close collaborators would have been a bitter disappointment to him had he lived to follow his subsequent career.
This man was Vidkun Quisling, in whom Nansen placed particular
faith. Quisling was appointed chief of Nansen's branch organization
in Kharkov and was entrusted with important tasks in the field of
hunger relief. There I met him, in the fall of 1922, on a trip through
Russia which I had undertaken in order to survey the work of the
Nansen organization. At that time I saw in him a man who had a
deep understanding of the needs of the starving population and who
knew how to disarm even the distrust of the local Soviet authorities
by his thorough objectivity. I attribute the change that took place
in Quisling later to the influence of his Russian wife, a fanatical
anti-Communist, and also to the fact that Quisling, originally very
favorably disposed toward the Communist "experiment" in Russia,
had been utterly disappointed by its later development. He then
became obsessed by the fixed idea that Destiny had called him to
save Norway from the Communist peril, and he drifted into a mental
state in which he could no longer differentiate between means and
end. It was to be his undoing.

HUNGARIAN OFFICERS AND HUNGARIAN COMMUNISTS

In the fall of 1921 I was given an additional assignment which was
an indirect result of the Communist revolution in Hungary. The
Communists had come to power in Hungary in 1919, but their
regime collapsed after a short time. Only a few of its leading personalities had succeeded in fleeing from Hungary and finding refuge
in Russia, but among them was Béla Kun. The majority of the
participants in the Communist coup were still languishing in Hungarian jails, where they were subjected to treatment which cannot
be justified even by the understandable excitement of public opinion
over the atrocities of the Red Terror. The Soviet government, of
course, was not unconcerned about the fate of its Hungarian comrades. Béla Kun, too, made strenuous efforts to get them free. Upon
his suggestion the Soviet government committed a grave violation
of the rules of international law by declaring the Hungarian officers

still kept as Russian prisoners of war to be hostages; they were to be retained in Siberia until the Hungarian Communists were released and given an opportunity to emigrate to Russia.

No direct relations of any sort then existed between the Hungarian and the Soviet governments. The former therefore turned to the German government with the request to mediate between it and the Kremlin. This led to an agreement by which the Soviet government designated Schlesinger to represent the interests of the Communists jailed in Hungary, whereas the Hungarian government entrusted me with the task of negotiating with Moscow about the exchange of its officers for the Communists.

The Soviet authorities quite obviously wished to gain time because they did not want to send the Hungarian officers home in the sorry state in which they were; for this reason they deliberately let the negotiations drag on and on. The Foreign Commissariat suddenly declared that it had no jurisdiction in the matter, and suggested that I continue the negotiations with Béla Kun himself. I felt the suggestion to be an insulting imposition, because even during the short duration of his rule in Hungary, Kun had already attained the reputation of a mass-scale hangman. In the late fall and winter of 1920, moreover, he had been sent to the Crimea after the defeat of Baron Wrangel. There he had proceeded against the remainder of the Russian bourgeoisie with such brutality that even Lenin, who was never squeamish and knew no mercy in class struggle, took offense and ordered Béla Kun to be recalled. I am convinced that the Soviet government counted on my refusing any direct contact with Kun, which would have enabled them to make the Hungarians and myself responsible for the delay in the exchange. I decided, however, to defeat the Soviet plan and to negotiate with Béla Kun because, as I told myself, the saving of hundreds of human lives from certain death justified traffic even with the devil himself.

Further bitterness for me was added to my contact with Kun by the fact that, of all places, he had established himself in the former home of the head pastor of St. Michael's Protestant Church in Moscow. For more than three hundred years the church had been a religious center for the Germans in Moscow, and a school, to which I was bound by many memories of my youth, was connected with the church.

When Béla Kun received me, he was surrounded by his family,

on whom he wasted numerous tokens of affection as a tender husband and loving father. In this "idyllic" setting we traded in human lives—a memory that even today is still revolting to me. I have always been convinced that Kun's behavior was a deliberate trick designed to confuse me. I simply cannot believe that a man so notorious for his cruelties could harbor the personal affection for his family he showed when I visited him. But I was rewarded for all my tribulations by the success of my mission. One month after my talk with Béla Kun, the Hungarian officers came through Moscow on their homeward journey; and I saw that it was high time to rescue them from Siberia, for their condition confirmed my belief that I would have sinned against my conscience had I refused to negotiate with Kun.[9]

TYPHUS RELIEF WORK

By the fall of 1921 I had been relieved of some of my previous duties, among them, all consular business. In addition, the care of German prisoners meant much less work now that the bulk of them had been evacuated not only from Russia proper but also from the Ukraine. I could therefore comply with the request of the German Red Cross to assist them in their activities on behalf of the starving Russian population. Germany could furnish no foodstuffs to Russia, but the German Red Cross notified the Soviet government that it was ready to help in the fight against the epidemics which, owing to starvation conditions, had assumed terrifying proportions and were claiming millions of human lives. The German offer was accepted, and the German Red Cross appointed me its plenipotentiary for Russia. My first task was the conclusion of a treaty with the Soviet government defining the manner in which the German relief action was to be executed, and the rights and duties resulting for both parties. My partner in these negotiations was Lev B. Kamenev, whom the Soviet government had placed in charge of all problems connected with relief actions for the starving population. Kamenev was

[9] Of the Hungarian Communists released from jail at the same time, many have subsequently played important roles in the political, economic, and intellectual life of the Soviet Union, though the majority of them, including Béla Kun himself, later fell victims to the great purges. Among the few survivors is Eugene Varga, the well known economist, who was recently in disgrace because of his unorthodox appraisal of economic prospects in the United States.

married to Trotsky's sister, and was one of Lenin's closest collaborators. As a member of the Politburo, and chairman of the Moscow Soviet, he exercised considerable influence. Before the revolution he had lived abroad for many years, and as a Communist he was a "Westerner" by orientation. In the thirties he became one of the first victims of the great purge trials.

Because time was pressing the Soviet government, negotiations with Kamenev developed with comparative ease and led to a speedy agreement. The Russians were so much interested in getting foreign relief action quickly under way that they made remarkable concessions, granting the foreign relief workers freedom of movement and unhindered direct contact with the local authorities and public agencies, and guaranteeing effective support on the part of the central relief agency in Moscow.

Following this agreement, the German Red Cross in the fall of 1921 sent a group of German medical specialists to Russia. They went to Kazan, capital of the Tatar Autonomous Soviet Socialist Republic, to aid the local organizations in their fight against typhus by giving medical assistance and medicaments. Drugs and equipment were shipped to Petrograd on the steamship *Triton,* especially chartered for the occasion, and then taken to Kazan on a hospital train put at the disposal of the German physicians by the Soviet government as a headquarters and means of transportation. In Moscow the German Red Cross set up a bacteriological laboratory to make use of practical experiences in Kazan for scientific work, to maintain liaison with the Soviet physicians, and to provide the latter with scientific literature.[10]

I was in charge of the political, financial, and administrative affairs of the German Red Cross expedition. These were very difficult tasks because the means at our disposal were limited, and although general conditions in Russia had improved considerably after the introduction of the NEP they had taken another turn for the worse because of the famine. The transport system was in complete ruins, and what railroad travel still continued was disturbed by repeated attacks on moving trains.

At that time Trotsky was at the peak of his power and prestige, and his name was invariably linked with that of Lenin. I decided to

[10] The German physicians' delegation was headed by the late Professor Peter Mühlens, later appointed director of the Tropical Institute in Hamburg, in due recognition of his scientific merits.

secure his personal support by trying to interest him in the plans of the German Red Cross and the character of the German relief action. For this purpose I made use of a member of his staff, a former tsarist naval officer of high rank by the name of Berens, who had offered his services to the Soviet government, not out of sympathy for Communism, but, like many other tsarist officers, out of a mixture of opportunism and Russian patriotism. Upon Berens's suggestion Trotsky accepted my invitation to visit the establishments of the German Red Cross.

In preparation for the visit of the People's Commissar for Military and Naval Affairs, his aide appeared for a discussion in which the different steps of the inspection were planned in minute detail. Afterward, the aide made a rehearsal trip from Trotsky's headquarters to the bacteriological institute, and then to our hospital train. The trip had demonstrated, he advised me, that we had underestimated by a few minutes the time required for one of the routes and that these minutes would have to be subtracted from the time devoted to the inspection. I was floored by this unusual, un-Russian precision; but on the designated date Trotsky made me wait forty minutes for his appearance, and then threw all the previous careful arrangements overboard by staying far longer than planned.

Trotsky's unusual personality exerted a strange charm on all who came in contact with him. I too was impressed by his dexterity and poise, by the living interest he took in everything that was brought to his attention, and by his easy mastery of foreign languages. But an unstable spirit lurked behind his brilliant front; and Trotsky was bound to fail at the decisive crossroads of his life because he did not know how to act consistently and because he did not possess the gifts of a statesman. An acquaintance of mine, a Russian engineer with a fine feeling for human psychology, once offered me a fitting characterization of Trotsky's personality: "Brilliant fireworks; what remains is a small heap of ashes." Though Trotsky could fascinate his collaborators with numerous ideas, they had no lasting effect because he did not follow them through and did not know how to supervise their execution. At mass meetings he would rouse his audience to spontaneous enthusiasm by his brilliant oratory, but this availed him little since Stalin took care that his own obedient creatures passed resolutions carefully prepared long beforehand. The fundamental tragedy of Trotsky's personality lies in the fact that his own

failures helped a man like Stalin to a position of power from which he could threaten the entire Western World. I am inclined to believe that Trotsky's doctrinaire theories of "permanent revolution" would have been of far less danger to the world than Stalin's unscrupulous determination.

Trotsky was visibly impressed by the facilities of the German Red Cross that we showed to him. In turn, we basked in his flattering praise of "German efficiency, which the world ought to take as an example." Owing to defeat in the war, and to its political and economic consequences, German self-esteem had suffered to such an extent that Germans at that time welcomed every opportunity to re-establish it, a factor that played a considerable psychological role in the re-establishment of German-Russian relations after the First World War. German scientific, economic, and military circles felt rejected and avoided by former enemy countries. The Russians, however, seemed willing to give recognition to German achievements and to revive the relations of former times, thus opening what appeared to be a way out of Germany's isolation. The dangers of Soviet interference in Germany's internal developments were consciously disregarded; the general opinion seemed to be that the German people was immune against Communism, and that the New Economic Policy, moreover, was the beginning of an internal evolution in Russia away from revolutionary ambitions.

When Trotsky took leave, he asked me whether he might do us any favor. I replied that we were very much in need of a special car for our hospital train. But since the train was to leave for Kazan during the night, the car would have to be hitched on that same evening. Trotsky promised to make the necessary arrangements at once, and indeed, no more than a half-hour later, the chief of the military-transport administration, Arzhanov, appeared before me. He too was a former tsarist officer who had skillfully adjusted to the new rulers and, for the rest, made use of his position for the purpose of gaining material advantages. Clad in a smartly tailored uniform, with shining boots, and with a riding crop which he handled with emphasized nonchalance, he gave an appearance that was in oppressive contrast to the pitiful figures in his large entourage, most miserable among them the old engineers from the Railroad Commissariat. Arzhanov listened to our request and, with the tone of a master, commanded his subordinates to deliver the desired car at

once; but the latter declared that there was no such car to be found
in all the rail yards of Moscow. "Either the car is here in three
hours, or else . . ." These words, and a significant gesture with the
riding whip, silenced the engineers and painfully embarrassed me.
Sure enough, the special car was in our hands three hours later; but
I had ominous visions of the forms in which the system would develop further in Russia, if it wanted to succeed in the face of human
nature and material difficulties.

In Kazan the hospital train came upon the typhus epidemic with
all its horrors. I myself went to Kazan some months later, and what
I saw there belongs to the most terrible impressions of my life. The
hospitals were so overfilled with those caught by the epidemic, people reduced to ghostly skeletons, that two or even three patients had
to share one pallet, and there were others who had to lie on the bare
floor. The completely exhausted doctors and nurses had to climb
over them in order to get to the other patients. I was utterly dejected
by the awareness that all of our help was hardly more than a drop
in a great ocean of misery. A few years later my feeling of despair
gave way to admiration for the vitality of the Russian people, which
was astonishing the world by its rapid population increase as early
as 1924.

Typhus took its victims also from among the foreign relief personnel. Among the many people from my own immediate environment who were taken away was the English physician Dr. Farrar,
one of Fridtjof Nansen's companions on one of his trips into the
famine areas, and the rising young German scientist Dr. Gärtner,
who had performed his duty in the hospitals of Kazan in an exemplary
manner. I myself was infected with the dreaded disease by a typhus
louse in February, 1922, during an official trip to Petrograd, and
barely escaped death. My courageous wife hurried to Moscow immediately upon the news of my sickness; when she arrived, after a
fortnight, I had not yet regained consciousness. I owe my life to her
untiring care and to the skill of the experienced Moscow physician
Dr. Ling, but another four months had to pass before I could resume
my work.

III TOWARD THE RESUMPTION OF NORMAL GERMAN-SOVIET RELATIONS

1. INITIAL DIFFICULTIES

THE CORRESPONDENCE BETWEEN
DR. SIMONS AND G. V. CHICHERIN

Great as the satisfaction was which the humanitarian work of prisoner, famine, and epidemic relief afforded me, I had from the day of my departure for Moscow considered it my chief mission to contribute toward the normalization of general political and economic relations between Germany and Soviet Russia. Of course, back in the summer of 1920, the prospects of such a normalization were poor indeed; yet attempts were made repeatedly to disturb them. In the middle of July, for instance, the Paris edition of the *Chicago Tribune* bore the following headline: SOVIET GOVERNMENT DOOMED, and then, "It is only a question of time, asserts first German envoy." The article underneath began with the statement that the paper had obtained possession of the first private letter I had written from Moscow. The letter was said to contain a detailed account of the horrible conditions prevailing in Russia, and to have concluded with the prediction that the fate of the Soviet government was sealed and its fall was only a matter of time. The article further contained lengthy excerpts from a letter allegedly written by me, in which conditions in Russia were pictured in the blackest colors, and with fantastic exaggerations. Among other things, for instance, I was "quoted" as having said that Moscow was surrounded by an electrically charged barbed-wire enclosure severing all communication of the Moscow population with the outer world.

I had not written any private letters at all during the first four weeks of my stay in Moscow, and certainly not the one quoted by the paper. The *Chicago Tribune* article was therefore nothing more than an unscrupulous attempt to make my position vis-à-vis the Soviet government impossible from the very beginning and thus to sabotage the establishment of any relations between Germany and the Soviet Republic. Luckily, political friends of mine in Berlin called my attention to the article in time. This enabled me to prove to the Soviet government, even before they had learned of the matter, that the article was a vicious forgery, for my first mail from Moscow had not yet arrived in Berlin on the day the article was published in Paris. The hurry with which the article had been published enabled me to unmask the fraud, otherwise the Soviet government would probably have declined permission for me to stay on in Moscow.

A few days after I had this narrow escape, the then foreign minister, Dr. Walther Simons, wrote a long letter to Chicherin in which he expressed the wish of the German government to restore diplomatic relations with Soviet Russia. It seems that the immediate reason for the letter was Simons's desire to attach a German liaison officer to the right wing of the Soviet armies then rolling, unchecked, into Poland, for the purpose of preventing untoward incidents when the Red Army approached the old German border. But the long-range vista of renewed diplomatic relations which the letter opened was far more significant. This vista, in turn, was by no means unrelated to the immediate pretext on which the letter had been written. The rapid advance of the Red Army through Poland which took them almost to the gates of Warsaw and up to the borders of East Prussia had produced a state of near panic in Germany. In a few places, as a matter of fact, Soviet troops had actually crossed the borders of East Prussia, and in the border towns of Soldau and Strassburg attempts at the creation of a Soviet regime had been made. True, the Red Army units withdrew at once upon German protests; nevertheless, the foreign minister decided that Germany's relations with Soviet Russia could no longer remain unregulated and undefined as before.

In his letter to Chicherin, Dr. Simons combined his hopes for the resumption of diplomatic relations with a suggestion as to how the Soviet government might contribute to such a rapprochement. The

chief cause for the rupture of relations, he opined, had been the Soviet refusal to make sufficient amends for the assassination of Count Mirbach-Harff. Even though it would, admittedly, have been impossible to punish the murderers, the German people—he wrote—might at least expect some public satisfaction for the violation of its national honor. Therefore he suggested to the people's commissar that a ceremony be performed at which the German flag would solemnly be raised on top of the Berg palace while a company of Soviet troops, led by an officer, was to salute and subsequently parade in front of the building. "If you agree to such a ceremony, my dear people's commissar, you might at the same time make suggestions concerning the time and place for a joint conference about the resumption of diplomatic and economic relations." With words somewhat like these, the minister closed his letter.

Chicherin's handwritten reply, several pages long, in faultless German, was handed me a few days later for transmittal to Dr. Simons. He expressed his sincere satisfaction that the latter had provided an opportunity for renewed relations between the two countries. Frankly, he said, the Soviet government had been wondering why the possibility had been so long disregarded by Germany. After all, two underprivileged nations were natural partners, given mutual good will and understanding. He even indulged in a short ideological discourse to affirm that the Communist state had no intentions of forcing its way of life upon other nations. The Marxist theory of social development, he said, was an organic one; a Communist was far too realistic to make any foolish attempts to foster his ideas of social organization on an unwilling nation by force of arms. In short, he assured the foreign minister that Germany had nothing to fear from contacts with the Soviet state.

But when he came to discussing the suggested ceremony of atonement for the death of the ambassador, Chicherin was adamant. In actual fact, nothing would have been simpler for the Soviet government than to grant the German wish. The ceremony would have been held in a small side street of Moscow, which could have been closed to all other traffic to avoid a large audience. Thus attendance could have been limited to a restricted circle; the population at large need not have learned anything about it. But the suggestion seems to have been more than the Soviet insistence on the honor and prestige of the proletarian regime could stomach. In addition,

Chicherin or his superiors may have been overconfident of a speedy victory in Poland and thus believed, perhaps, that they could well afford to refuse the wooing of the German government. The victory of the French-Polish forces quickly reversed the situation. With the failure of Soviet dreams of carrying the proletarian revolution into the heart of Europe, it was now the Soviet government's turn to seek a rapprochement with Germany. But the ardor of the German foreign minister appeared to have cooled a bit. At the same time the defeat of Tukhachevsky's armies resulted in a marked sharpening of the Western Allies' attitude toward Germany, particularly in the question of reparations; and in reaction to Western intransigence a number of influential German politicians and statesmen began to reconsider the idea that the creation of better German-Soviet relations might be the most effective means of forcing the Entente powers into moderation.

Before following the subsequent events in the relations between Soviet-Russia and Germany, it is necessary, however, to cast a fleeting glance on conditions in Russia at the time.

"WILL THE BOLSHEVIKS RETAIN STATE POWER?"

A foreigner living in Moscow in 1920 had far better opportunities of finding out about the true situation in Soviet Russia than he would today. If our movements were severely restricted, this was due more to the breakdown of the communications system than to reasons of state security. The Soviet security organs had not yet thought it necessary at that time to prevent all contacts between the few foreigners residing in Moscow in an official capacity and the local population. Many personalities who had been prominent in the government, in society, or in intellectual circles of pre-Bolshevik Russia and who possessed rich knowledge and experience were still in Moscow and were only too glad to come together with foreigners. My office, its waiting room, and at times even the staircase were always crowded with oppositionists who came for help in personal matters, who wanted to talk to a non-Communist foreigner, or who attempted to draw me into anti-Bolshevik conspiracies. If there were any facts or rumors that reflected ill on the staying power of the regime, I was always sure to learn about them from these visitors. On the other hand, the government and the ruling party themselves

had not yet become so secretive and untouchable as they are today. Rival factions within the party were still permitted to publish their views concerning official party policy.

The period from the fall of 1918 to March, 1921, has become known by the name of "War Communism." This was the period during which the Bolshevik regime had to fight for its life continuously against seemingly heavy odds. The ruling party itself was seriously shaken by opposition movements within its ranks. Moreover, the activity of opposition parties had not yet been liquidated completely. Within the territory under its control, the loyalty of the peasantry had turned into passive resistance; even that of the urban proletariat was strained to the breaking point, and in March, 1921, it broke into open rebellion at Kronstadt. Around the periphery of Bolshevik-dominated territory, counter-revolutionary armies, supported by Allied intervention forces, were threatening, though most of the White Army was defeated by the middle of 1920.

The exigencies of this life-and-death struggle transformed Soviet Russia into a besieged fortress, and its economy into a war economy with the sole aim of helping to destroy the enemy. During this "Heroic Period of the Great Russian Revolution," as one Soviet writer has called it, the peasant was forced to give his entire produce, except for a small quantity far below the extreme subsistence minimum, to the state. The urban population was put on scanty rations which were distributed with great irregularity; frequently they were not given out at all. Lacking fuel and raw materials, most of the factories ceased to run. The workers fled into the country, where they hoped to keep from starving. Trade had virtually died, partly because of the increasing pace of nationalization and partly because commodities were lacking, and the currency was rapidly deteriorating.

These chaotic conditions were further aggravated, and at the same time their emergency character obscured, by the conviction current among Communist leaders at the time that such chaos would lead directly and quickly into real Communism. They thought that the social structure for which they had made the revolution was just around the corner. Their financial policy, based on the doctrine that money would "wither away" in the Communist society, illustrates their belief. The devaluation of the ruble was promoted systematically. The People's Commissar for Finance, Krestinsky, even pub-

lished a pamphlet under the title "How to Make the Ruble Drop to Zero Most Speedily."

The personal hardships under which everyone in Russia had to suffer were enormous, for the government paid no attention to the private needs of the population. Railroad trips, for instance, were subject to official approval, which was granted only if the state had an interest in the traveler's purpose. True, the railroads as well as the mails were operated gratis; but they were all the more unreliable in their operations. In our offices and homes, we of the German relief agency ran out of fuel early in 1921. Because deep snowdrifts that no one troubled to plow made it impossible for us to cart in fuel on our own vehicles, we shivered. Food rations were so scanty that some of my personnel were on the verge of collapse. Luckily, I seemed to be of stronger constitution; in any event I withstood the hardships of that winter rather well.

All news about the misery in Russia and the difficult situation of the Soviet government was eagerly reported by the press in the Western countries. In their attempt to demonstrate that the days of the Bolshevik regime were numbered, foreign newspapers would not only report its difficulties but also exaggerate them and invent additional ones. It was one of my continual tasks to correct the impression which this manner of reporting produced among my superiors in the German Foreign Office. Through the late fall of 1920, official German circles continued to hold that the Bolshevik regime could not last much longer, and they continued to overestimate the strength both of the internal opposition and of the Whites. And even some of those who later committed themselves entirely to the development of Soviet-German friendship continued in these early years to maintain active contact with White elements.

Some of the talk that the regime was about to fall to pieces could be supported by serious evidence, though hindsight shows today that even this evidence was insufficient. But some of the theories about the impending downfall of the regime were based on completely spurious arguments; for instance, there were people who asserted that a government with so many Jews in leading positions would never be tolerated by the Russian people. I shall not venture to guess how many of these opinions were based primarily on wishful thinking.

I wrote many a letter to Schlesinger and Baron von Maltzan, of

the Foreign Ministry, attempting to put the alarming news from Russia into proper perspective. I pointed out to them that the broad masses of the population were indeed fed up with Bolshevik rule, but that in spite of this there was no reason to suppose that any substantial part of the population desired a return to the prerevolutionary order.[1] And I warned them that, in spite of all news reporting the negative side of the Bolshevik regime, in spite of hunger, cold, and bitter feeling among the broad masses of the people, the Soviet government had so far emerged stronger and more consolidated from every crisis. The forces which in the beginning might have destroyed it from within were rapidly disappearing. All attempts to destroy the regime from the outside, by means of intervention, failed mainly because interventions had been undertaken with insufficient military means; the forces of intervention had been divided, and they had utterly failed to take the social needs of the Russian people into account. A politically conscious and militarily well equipped campaign, undertaken in common by all European states, might indeed make an end to the Soviet regime, I thought. But I did not think that Europe at that time was in any condition to muster the necessary material and ideological forces.

In short, my opinion was—and I did not hesitate to say so—that the Soviet government was firmly in the saddle, and that the German government would have to make this the basis of its actions. My interpretation met with so little understanding in Germany that well-meaning friends advised me to adapt my reports a little to prevailing attitudes; otherwise I might easily be suspected of harboring pro-Soviet views. I did not allow this to disturb me, however, and maintained the opinions which I thought were the correct ones. The justification of my position by later events recompensed me for the difficulties I had to surmount initially.

It is possible that my favorable reports concerning the staying power of the Soviet regime were based not only on a detached analysis of the situation but also on some wishful thinking It is true that, personally, I should have had a vested interest in the destruction of the Bolshevik regime and the restitution of private property. But

---

[1] That is the primary reason for the failure of the White Guardist movement, which offered the people no better prospects than return of the discredited tsarist regime. Their political stupidity gave Lenin a decisive hold over the masses.

from the point of view of German foreign policy, I saw certain advantages of a negative nature to be derived from the continued existence of the Soviet government. For I feared that this regime could be replaced only by a government which might make common cause with the Western Allies, thus adding new burdens to the ones imposed by the Versailles Treaty.

It was not until Soviet Russia had successfully come out of a war with Poland and had made an end to Baron Wrangel, the last of the White Guard generals, in October, that the growing consolidation of the regime was more and more recognized as a fact even in Berlin. And practical consequences had to be drawn from this fact in the interest of the Reich. How touchy a problem it was to draw such consequences will be shown by the following incident caused by the third anniversary of the Bolshevik seizure of power.

THE THIRD ANNIVERSARY OF THE OCTOBER REVOLUTION

Late in the afternoon on November 7, 1920, the People's Commissar for Foreign Affairs, Chicherin, sent me an invitation to an official dinner given for the foreign representatives in Moscow in the guest house of the commissariat. The occasion was the third anniversary of the October Revolution.[2] The guest house in those days was a magnificent palace situated on the right bank of the Moskva River, directly across from the Kremlin. Before the revolution it had belonged to a Ukrainian sugar magnate by the name of Kharitonenko. After the resumption of diplomatic relations with Great Britain, the Soviet government offered the building to the British Embassy, which is still occupying it today.

Chicherin's invitation subjected me to a grave dilemma. Until then there had been no precedent for the participation of an official representative of bourgeois democratic governments in an official celebration honoring the Bolshevik Revolution. Nevertheless, I decided to accept the invitation, since I argued that my failure to ap-

[2] The Bolshevik Revolution of 1917 has become known as the October Revolution because Lenin and his party proclaimed the Soviet Republic on a day which, according to the Julian calendar then effective in Russia, carried the date of October 25th. This calendar is thirteen days behind the Gregorian calendar accepted by the rest of the world, so that in the West the day was November 7th. Ever since the Gregorian calendar was introduced in Russia, in February, 1918, it is November 7th which is celebrated as the anniversary of the October Revolution.

pear would disturb my official relations with the Soviet government and jeopardize the interests of the German prisoners of war in Russia. I should not have acted differently even if I could have foreseen the political storm my attendance at the dinner unleashed in Germany.

It was a small group of persons that accepted Chicherin's invitation that evening, and one that corresponded to the limited extent of relations then existing between the Soviet state and the outside world. There were, besides myself, Prince Ali Gooli Khan, the ambassador of Persia, who for many years represented his country's interests in Moscow, shrewdly weighing the advantages and dangers of friendly relations between Soviet Russia and Persia; the ambassador of Afghanistan, General Mohammed Vali Khan, an outspoken foe of England who saw little danger in accepting help against Britain from the Soviet state; Sekkia-Bey, special envoy of Turkey; as well as representatives of the three Baltic States, without diplomatic status, who functioned as chiefs of citizenship and repatriation commissions. At the same time they devoted at least as much time and attention to their own little "businesses" as to problems of citizenship and resettlement which were a result of the separation of the Baltic States from the former Russian Empire. The only favorable exception was Lithuania's intelligent and cultured representative, Jurgis K. Baltrushaitis, a well known Russian lyric poet whom the Lithuanian government had appointed as its minister to Moscow because he was of Lithuanian origin and knew Russia like his own vest pocket. For many years to come Baltrushaitis was the best informed member of the Moscow diplomatic corps, until the G.P.U. finally sealed him off from the outside world, as it did all the others.

Persia and Afghanistan had been represented by ambassadors in Moscow ever since the late fall of 1920, even though formal treaties were not signed by these two countries until February, 1921. Their presence was an indication of the importance which the Soviet government attributed at that time to its southern and southeastern neighbors and mutual relations with them. The Soviet leaders started with the assumption that they needed security and cover in the East if they wished to realize their world-revolutionary aims in the West. At the same time, Persia, Afghanistan, and Turkey were seeking the protection of the Soviet Republic in the belief that only in this manner could they stand up against England as independent nations. Chicherin was very active in developing and pursuing this policy,

since he was convinced that England was the primary and immediate threat to the Soviet state; to counter the threat Russia would have to make use of its "natural allies," that is, those states which also felt themselves threatened by England.[3]

No contrast could be greater than that between the primitive and modest nature of the celebration of November 7, 1920, in the guest house of the Moscow Foreign Commissariat, and the brilliance and richness distinguishing official celebrations in the Soviet Union today. Our banquet began by Chicherin making his guests await his appearance for an hour and a half; the Orientals shrewdly commented that apparently the Communists had abolished even courtesy as a bourgeois prejudice. Furthermore, Chicherin on that evening disregarded all rules of protocol (with which he must have been familiar from old times), for he made me sit at his right, between himself and his assistant Litvinov, in order to give due emphasis to the presence of the first and only representative of a great power from the West.

Chicherin's second assistant, good-looking Lev Karakhan, sat across from the host, flanked by the ambassadors of Persia and Afghanistan. His smooth and assured dexterity was in marked contrast to the many little inadequacies of the banquet. For instance, the waiters, counter to the most elementary rules of their profession, consistently offered the food from the right, at the same time encouraging the guests with friendly words to take more; the quality of the food would not have honored even a second-rate restaurant; and, lacking another drink, the guests had to be satisfied with a thin raspberry lemonade. Chicherin and I poured for each other.

That very same evening the Soviet government announced to the world by radio that the Foreign Commissariat had given a dinner, in

---

[3] The idea that the rising nations of the East are the reserve army of the proletarian world revolution was just then being developed fully by Lenin and other ideologists of the Communist movement. I heard Chicherin expound it once at a dinner given in late February, 1921, by the Afghan Embassy in celebration of the third anniversary of Afghanistan's declaration of independence, and the accession to the throne of Amanullah-Khan.

Soviet friendship with Turkey at that time was complicated by the revolutionary events in Transcaucasia, especially Georgia, where a Social Democratic regime was fighting for its independence both from Communist Russia and from Turkey, the hereditary oppressor. It was a curious fact that monarchist Afghanistan was promised every possible assistance by Moscow, whereas the socialist Republic of Georgia was systematically strangled to death.

celebration of the anniversary of the October Revolution, at which all foreign representatives present in Moscow had participated and had expressed their best wishes for the continued well-being of the Soviet Republic. There followed the names of all persons who had attended the dinner, giving the states each one represented. My name, significantly, was at the head of the list.

The reaction which this announcement caused in Germany, particularly in the press of the extreme rightist German Folk party (Deutschvölkische Partei), was not long in coming. It began with angry notes to the German government demanding to know whether the cabinet was informed of the participation in this celebration of an "alleged" German representative in Moscow, or whether "Herr Hilger was making his own independent foreign policy." I was accused of having "sat down behind the same table, at the head of a horde of Asiatics, together with bloodstained murderers and hangmen, in order to discuss with them the prospects of world revolution, instead of caring about the fate of the tortured German prisoners of war in Russia." These ill tempered eruptions were followed by an interpellation made in the Reichstag by the German Folk party; its leader, a Major Henning, accused me of pro-Communist leanings and demanded my immediate recall from Moscow. The matter fizzled out after a matter-of-fact reply by Dr. Simons and the Reich commissar for prisoner-of-war relief, Stücklen. But similar attacks were to follow.

2. CRISIS AND RESOLUTION

Before German-Soviet relations could take a real turn for the better, my conviction that the Bolshevik regime was firmly and strongly in the saddle was to be tested by a severe crisis which not only marked a turn in the foreign relations of the Soviet government but also inaugurated an entirely new period in the history of the Russian Revolution.

The crisis of War Communism was evoked by the conditions in the country, which had become catastrophic when the peasants began to offer desperate resistance against the *prodrazverstka,* the forced requisition of all agricultural produce, which the government was carrying out mercilessly. The peasants began to attack and repulse the agents ordered to carry out the requisitions. Much worse was

the fate of the members of the punitive expeditions dispatched into the country by the government. Peasants who got hold of them would bury them alive up to the neck, cut out their eyes, tear out their tongues, and commit similar unspeakable atrocities, which only had the effect of fanning passions on both sides to greater heat. Peasant revolt spread over the entire country like a grass fire, and grain supplies virtually stopped coming into the cities.

The agrarian crisis found its political reflection in the Eighth All-Russian Congress of Soviets, which took place in the last week of December, 1920, in the Bolshoi Theater of Moscow. I attended the Congress as a visitor at the invitation of the Soviet government.[4] The Eighth Soviet Congress was the last at which an opposition party, the Menshevik party, was represented in addition to members of the Communist party and non-party elements regarded as absolutely trustworthy. During the following year the Menshevik party was eliminated from Soviet political life; its leaders were arrested and banished to Siberia or escaped into exile abroad. But the Eighth Congress was high-lighted by the last public discussion that has taken place in Russia between Mensheviks and Bolsheviks. I watched the event from the front row of the stage box, less than thirty feet from the speakers' rostrum. From my vantage point I could also observe the audience's reaction to the crowd filling the main floor.

The Menshevik party had sent forth Fëdor Dan, one of its leading intellects and best orators, to subject the Bolsheviks' agrarian policies to merciless criticism. With sharp words Dan castigated the methods of the Bolshevik rulers who were forcibly compelling the Russian peasant to give up his entire agricultural produce, not leaving him enough even to support his own frugal life. The speaker demonstrated convincingly that agricultural production would only continue to decrease, and that the rural population would perish miserably if present policies were continued. The only way out of the catastrophic situation, he declared, consisted of giving the peasantry an incentive to raise production. Instead of forcing the peasant to give up all his produce, the government should fix specific quantities

---

[4] At that time the All-Russian Congress of Soviets was, formally, the bearer of sovereign government authority in the RSFSR. When the Soviet Union was formed in 1923, this sovereignty was transferred to the All-Union Congress of Soviets. Today, according to the 1936 Constitution, formal sovereignty rests with the Supreme Soviet of the USSR.

to be delivered, leaving the peasant to dispose freely of his remaining surplus.

The applause following Dan's speech left no doubt that the overwhelming majority of the audience was in agreement with him; at the same time I felt clearly that, because of the physical and ideological pressure already being exerted on the population at that time, the speech had produced helplessness and consternation among the audience. This was immediately exploited by the chairman, who announced quickly that Lenin personally would give a proper reply to the speaker. The magic effect of the name strained the tension among the audience virtually to the breaking point. Dead silence prevailed in the auditorium while all eyes were directed toward the end of the aisle that had formed in the middle of the stage, for those sitting on the stage had moved closer together to leave a path for Lenin to come to the footlights. An overwhelming storm of applause and acclamation broke as soon as the crowd sighted Lenin, who hurried to the front of the stage with small, rapid steps.

After Lenin had begun speaking, I was at first disappointed. At first sight he seemed to have nothing to hold and inspire the masses. I saw a short man, with a pointed reddish beard and Mongolian features, who talked with a minor speech defect. But the longer he spoke, gripping the masses with a flood of eager, impressive eloquence, the more I became aware that the Bolsheviks might never have come to power without the spell exercised on the masses by Lenin. As an orator he possessed the particular gift of never allowing the attention of his audience to relax. Slowly and systematically, he built up his arguments until at last he delivered the decisive blow.

On this particular evening also, Lenin succeeded, by means of his superior dialectical skill, in quickly changing the minds of the audience. After first building up broadly conceived background arguments, he became more and more precise, and finally steered straight toward his real aim of revealing the preceding speaker as a traitor to the interests of the working class. He accused the Menshevik party of desiring nothing less than to throw the yoke of capitalism once more over the neck of the rural workingman by their proposal to let the peasants freely dispose of their surplus produce. When he closed his three-and-a-half-hour speech with the words, "The 'in-

centive' which this lackey of capitalism wants to sell you as the means of escaping from our present misery is nothing else than a return to the coercive rule of the tsars!" the crowd broke into a tumultuous ovation, completely forgetting—it seemed to me—that they had shortly before assented to the compelling logic of the Menshevik Dan.

Thus the Menshevik party suffered a decisive defeat at the Eighth Congress of Soviets. This defeat was sealed three months later, in March, 1921, when at the Tenth Communist Party Congress Lenin justified the introduction of the New Economic Policy with the same arguments Dan had adduced in December, 1920, in his attempt to convince the Soviet government of the necessity of changes in its agrarian policy. Nothing that Dan had said in vain at that time was missing from Lenin's speech at the Tenth Party Congress, beginning with an itemization of the mistakes that had been made, then going to the necessity of providing an "incentive" for the peasants to produce more, and ending with the demand to let the peasant dispose freely of the produce remaining in his hands after deduction of a fixed tax in kind. Here we have a classic example of the cynicism with which the Bolshevik party used to annihilate all opposition only to appropriate its arguments for its own benefit.

KRONSTADT AND THE NEP

Not only the agrarian crisis, but the entire crisis of War Communism came to a head when toward the end of February, 1921, a revolt broke out in the naval fortress of Kronstadt situated on the Gulf of Finland. Subsequent Soviet historiography has attempted to make counter-revolutionary elements responsible for the rebellion. In actual fact, it was made by the same radical sailors who in 1917 had played a decisive role in the Bolshevik seizure of power. Now they felt that they and their revolutionary ideals had been betrayed by the oppressive terror regime of War Communism, of which the agrarian policy was only one aspect. The men behind the Kronstadt rebellion were neither reactionaries nor even the unconscious tools of reaction; they were Socialists who led the struggle against Moscow under the slogan "For the Soviet system, but without the Communists." A friend of mine who was working at the University

of Moscow at the time told me of the enthusiasm with which the students who were party members went out to fight against the Kronstadt rebellion, convinced that they were dealing with enemies of the Russian people and the Russian Revolution; and of the dejection of those who returned to Moscow after they had learned the purely proletarian origin of this revolt.

The agrarian crisis and the Kronstadt rebellion evoked the widespread impression throughout the world that the days of Bolshevik rule were now, finally, at an end. But I, who had an opportunity to watch the development from within the country, observed daily how unswervingly the rulers in the Kremlin stuck to their aim, with what ruthless consistency they applied every means necessitated by the situation. At the same time there were many indications to show the inadequate organization, weakness, and disunity of those elements which believed they could challenge the Soviet government. I never had any doubts concerning the outcome of the unequal struggle.

However, before reports of my convictions arrived in Berlin, I received an order by telegraph demanding that I establish contact, at the earliest possible moment, with those individuals and groups that would soon step into the place of the Bolsheviks, so that there would be no interruption in my activities. For the immediate fall of the Soviet government was taken for granted. If there was no interruption in my activities in the end, this is due only to the fact that I paid no regard to my orders from Berlin, in spite of the quantity of alarming reports with which Moscow circles opposed to the regime provided me only too willingly. Had I followed Berlin's directions, I should have jeopardized my own position and delivered even more victims to the vengeance of the Soviet government.

With the introduction of the NEP, the previous system of *prodrazverstka* (forced grain requisitioning) was abolished and replaced by the *prodnalog,* a fixed tax in kind. The peasants were now obliged to give up only a specific portion of their produce, leaving them to dispose freely of all production in excess. Just as Dan had done, Lenin justified his own proposition with the necessity of giving the peasant an incentive to raise his production in the interest of supplying the urban population with food. Lenin countered any possible protests, according to which the right to dispose freely of surpluses might lead to a revival of commodity exchange on a capitalistic basis, by assur-

ing his comrades that state-controlled co-operatives were to buy up all agricultural produce flowing into the market. These same co-operatives would in turn provide the rural population with articles of consumption, and thus the development of capitalistic commodity trading by private individuals would be curbed. Soon it appeared, however, that the co-operatives were in no way up to their task. In order to obtain the required articles of consumption, it became necessary to uncover hidden private hoardings and to stimulate private enterprise and initiative to produce. There still were people who, in spite of two and a half years of Bolshevik rule, were in control of stores of commodities and capital, who possessed an enterprising spirit, and combined it with the deepest distrust of all measures undertaken by the Soviet government. They had to be put at ease concerning the character of the NEP by Lenin's assurance that the policy was being planned "seriously and for a long time."

The success of the NEP exceeded all expectations. Under the impact of the abolition of the *prodrazverstka,* the situation in the countryside took a sudden and radical turn. The revolts ceased, spring tilling was started immediately, and the hoarded stores of produce, up to then buried or otherwise hidden by the peasants, reappeared in surprising quantities. The abolition of all other obstacles to private trade, a natural corollary of the re-establishment of trade in agricultural produce, led to a flourishing of private initiative which after the shortest time filled the economic body of the Soviet Republic with new life after the deathly coma in which it had been lying. What developed in the first few months after the introduction of the NEP by far transcended the original intentions of the government, going far beyond the concessions which it had been ready to grant the population.

Once trade in agricultural produce had been permitted, the peasants had to be given an opportunity to exchange the money thus obtained for agricultural implements and articles of consumption. Trade in these commodities was therefore also permitted, and thus wide circles of the population were now drawn into the consequences of the NEP. This in turn created demands which the government had to take into account if it did not wish to jeopardize the outcome of the game from the start. And so it happened that within a few months richly stocked food stores, elegant restaurants, and even jewelers' shops mushroomed in a city like Moscow, where War Com-

munism had been in full swing as late as March, 1921, where the population had been put on the most pitiful rations, and where nothing, literally nothing, could have been purchased in the stores.

Soviet financial policies, too, had to be subjected to a speedy revision, since the demand, voiced theretofore, for a complete devaluation of the ruble and the abolition of all money had been carried to an absurdity by the NEP. Without hesitation the Soviet government threw principles that had until then guided its financial policies overboard and declared that the main task was the creation of a stable currency based on gold.

THE AGREEMENT OF MAY 6, 1921

As the Soviet government consolidated itself politically within Russia, Lenin saw that the most urgent task was the economic reconstruction of the country, which had been ruined by almost seven years of foreign and civil war. This could not be accomplished with the forces available in the country itself; foreign capital had to help. And it was one of the characteristic features of the NEP that it made concessions not only to private enterprise at home but also to foreign capitalism, encouraging traders and manufacturers in the capitalist countries to participate in the economic reconstruction of Soviet Russia.

Even before the introduction of the NEP, however, the German foreign minister had been persuaded that an economic and political rapprochement with Soviet Russia would be to Germany's advantage. The chief protagonists of such a rapprochement in the Foreign Ministry were the head of its Russian desk, Baron Ago von Maltzan, and the *de facto* head of the Reich Central Office for Military and Civilian Prisoners, Moritz Schlesinger. The latter had, in the spring of 1920, conducted the prisoner-exchange negotiations with the Soviet representative Viktor Kopp. Early in 1921 he had participated in talks with the Red Cross and League of Nations representatives concerning further questions of prisoner-of-war exchange that had taken place in Riga, and from Riga he went on to Moscow, on orders from the foreign minister, in order to attempt to find a basis for the resumption of German-Soviet diplomatic and economic relations. Schlesinger went to Moscow against the express wishes of the head of the Eastern Division in the Foreign Ministry, Ministerialdirektor Behrendt, who

was absolutely opposed to his conducting any negotiations transcending the framework of prisoner-of-war affairs.[5]

The mandate Dr. Simons had given Schlesinger for his trip to Moscow was as broad as it was indefinite. "See what you can do," the foreign minister had said in effect. Instructions such as these indicate how fluid and obscure the situation still was at that time. The conduct of international relations in such a situation is particularly exciting and rewarding. Here was an opportunity—rare in this age of mass communications that makes ambassadors into glorified messenger boys—for initiative, negotiating skill, imagination, and all the other virtues of diplomatic statesmanship. We had been placed in an exposed and responsible position and were now left to our own devices. In a sense, I look back upon this period as the happiest and most fruitful one of my life.

In retrospect, our negotiations of January and February, 1921, assume even somewhat of a piquant flavor by the fact that simultaneously Communist revolts shook Central Germany which we were convinced were actively being supported by the Soviet commission in Berlin. True enough, the piquancy is felt only in retrospect because the revolts of March, 1921, were suppressed. At the time it took great self-control to negotiate with people setting fire, as it were, to the very roof over our heads. We were all the while silently hoping for the defeat of the revolt, which would make the Soviet government more amenable.

The talks held in Moscow by Schlesinger, myself, and the Russians Kopp and Yakubovich resulted in the drafting, on February 19th, of a protocol containing a proposed agreement which, if accepted, would bring the two countries an important step closer toward full and normal political and economic relations. Just at that time the Soviet state was shaken by the severe crisis described above, and Berlin showed no interest in entering into the proposed agreement. But the regime in the Kremlin weathered the storm; and, immediately after the collapse of the Kronstadt rebellion and the proclamation of the NEP, interest for what Schlesinger and I had achieved in Moscow awakened in Berlin. In the last days of March, Dr. Simons instructed Behrendt urgently not to let the negotiations with the

[5] Behrendt was considered an expert on the economic aspects of Germany's foreign politics in eastern Europe because he had in previous years managed a prosperous grain business.

Russians be disrupted. Another strong impetus toward a definite agreement with the Soviet government was furnished by the fact that negotiations with the Russians were also going on in London at the same time. Finally, on May 6, 1921, the agreement was signed.

This "Provisional Agreement" concerning the "extension of the sphere of activities of the mutual prisoner-of-war-aid delegations" in effect converted the agencies Kopp and I had headed into political and consular missions by entrusting them with the protection of all their own nationals in the guest country, and by giving them a number of consular functions. Diplomatic privileges and immunities were extended to the missions' head plus seven members of their delegations. They were to be accredited to the Foreign Ministry of the guest country, and the commercial representatives to be attached to the missions were given authority to deal directly with other governmental agencies.

A number of provisions of the agreement reflected the abnormal nature of the times and of the Soviet state. Article 4, which permitted the German Mission to import strictly limited quantities of foodstuffs for their own use was a comment not only on the ruin of Russia's food economy but also on the unlimited opportunities this economy could have offered to black-market operations. Article 8 guaranteed to German businessmen entering Soviet Russia that any property they brought with them or would acquire legally was inviolate. In Article 15 both governments promised that their representatives would refrain from any agitation or propaganda against the government or governmental institutions of the guest country. Very important was a sentence in Article 1 by which the German government declared that it recognized no other agency as representing the Russian state in Germany; this amounted to a solemn reaffirmation of the *de jure* recognition which the Imperial German government had already granted the Leninist state in the Treaty of Brest-Litovsk.

Allied pressure on Germany in the reparations question reached another climax at the very same time that the Provisional Agreement was signed. The question whether or not Germany should accept the so-called London Ultimatum led to a cabinet crisis in early May; the cabinet resigned rather than accept the ultimatum, and a new cabinet, under the chancellorship of Dr. Wirth, leader of the Catholic Center party, was formed. This was a cabinet of "fulfill-

ment," that is, of submission to the Allied demands; and in this passive sense its orientation was purely Western. Hence it had no use for any ideas of a German-Russian rapprochement, nor for their exponents. The reign of the first Wirth cabinet and the term of office of its foreign minister, Dr. Friedrich Rosen, therefore brought with it far-reaching changes in personnel culminating in the removal of Baron von Maltzan from the Foreign Ministry. He was made German minister to Athens. Even before his removal attempts were made to eliminate me from the political scene in Moscow and relegate me to prisoner-of-war work and epidemic relief. For a moment it seemed as if an entirely new faction had taken hold of German affairs in Moscow.

The timidity and restraint with which Dr. Rosen approached the fulfillment of the agreement of May 6, 1921, was symbolized by the appointment of a completely unpolitical person as German representative in Moscow. Professor Kurt Wiedenfeld had been the chief of the Foreign Trade Division in the Foreign Ministry. He had made a study trip to Russia in 1912, had published a book about it, and had thus earned the reputation of being an expert on Russian economics. He possessed fine and valuable human traits, but he was little qualified to boost German-Soviet relations. Nor had he any intentions of doing so. Wary of any political rapprochement between the two countries, he interpreted his duties as narrowly restricted to economic relations; thus in his own eyes he was not much more than a glorified consul, and wished to be no more. Germany, he thought, was much too weak, conditions much too chaotic, and the revolution too great a threat. As he put it once, a country as weak as that internally could ill afford to see the red banner hoisted over an embassy in Berlin. If he had any political ideas concerning the aim of German-Soviet relations, they amounted to the belief that economic relations between Russia and the West might favor Russia's "internal evolution" away from Communism. A Westerner by orientation, he was firmly opposed to any arrangements which Germany alone might make with Russia; hence he welcomed the fact that the Provisional Agreement of May, 1921, had been preceded by a similar agreement between Russia and England in March of the same year. As a matter of fact there is some evidence that the German government remained in close informal touch with London while negotiating its agreement with Moscow. Wiedenfeld, for

one, seems to have believed that there was an understanding between London and Berlin to the effect that Germany in her relations with Russia would not go beyond any terms England had found with the Soviet state.

A man of my conviction could be of little use to Professor Wiedenfeld; and, as I have already said, in the end I was relieved of all political and consular duties I had heretofore fulfilled. This temporary eclipse of mine had been preceded by incessant sharp sniping from a whole faction of political antagonists and rivals. Personal ambitions, as well as honest political convictions, played their role in the struggle between two rival cliques; and the weapons used were of the nastiest kind: secret reports, unfounded accusations, insinuations and innuendo—in short, a typical smear campaign, during which I was accused of crimes ranging from pro-Communism to personal corruption. Many years later I happened to see a report sent to Berlin in which Schlesinger and I were accused of these and other things. There were broad hints at common intrigues against Berlin by the Schlesinger-Hilger clique jointly with equally corrupt individuals from the Foreign Commissariat; we were accused of using our offices for the purpose of lining our pockets or satisfying our insatiable political ambitions.

The report was written in September of 1921; seven or eight months earlier a similar assault to eliminate me had been made. Although enough men in the Wilhelmstrasse vouched for my loyalty and praised my talents and achievements to frustrate the attempt for the time being, some of the accusations made against me fell on fertile ground. In the spring of 1921 I learned reliably that the chief of the courier division was warning couriers being dispatched to Moscow against me; they were admonished to be extremely wary when dealing with me, as my political and general reliability was deemed highly questionable. When I returned to Berlin in June and reported to the foreign minister, Dr. Rosen received me with the words: "Good morning, Hilger. I understand you are a Communist." His lack of interest in, and understanding of, the problems of German-Soviet relations were in sharp contrast to the impression I had received shortly before from the Reich President, Friedrich Ebert, to whom I had reported immediately upon my arrival in Berlin. The former saddle maker showed much natural dignity and impressed me by the precision and pertinence of his questions. I

felt to my relief that this German Social Democrat, much reviled by Communists and German Rightists alike, had kept free from all personal and political resentment and was following the line he deemed correct with unshaken consistency. The cordiality and kindness with which Ebert thanked me for the work I had done in Moscow was ample reward for the difficulties and deprivations of the Moscow winter, and compensated me for the disappointment caused the next day by my interview with Rosen.

When I returned to Moscow in the fall of 1921, Germany and Soviet Russia were actively negotiating the exchange of official representatives for which the agreement had made provisions. Some of the difficulties encountered in these negotiations were characteristic of the strange relationship between the two countries. For one thing, Professor Wiedenfeld had not been the first choice of the German Foreign Ministry. Berlin had at first intended to send the Social Democrat August Müller; but had acquiesced, quite readily it seems, when the Kremlin categorically refused to receive a Social-Democrat. It proved far more difficult to come to terms on Wiedenfeld's Russian counterpart.

The Soviet government had asked Berlin to give its consent to the appointment of Nikolai N. Krestinsky, one of the oldest members of the Russian Communist party, up to then commissar of finance, secretary of the party's Central Committee, and one of the five members of the first Politburo. Great was the surprise and astonishment of the Soviet government when Kopp informed them that Berlin had refused to declare Krestinsky as *persona grata* for being "too prominent a member of the Communist party." Behrendt, who had formulated the phrase, could not have chosen a clumsier and less pertinent excuse for protesting against Krestinsky's appointment.

It would not have taken much more than this refusal to accept Krestinsky to let all previous efforts toward the normalization of German-Soviet relations fail completely. Karakhan told me officially that the Kremlin considered the reasons given for the refusal to accept Krestinsky as a grave insult. The German government, he said, seemed not yet to have found out that the Communist party was the ruling party in Russia. Krestinsky had been chosen to represent his government in Germany *because* he was a prominent member of the party, and thus wielded sufficient influence to enable him to further and develop German-Soviet relations for the benefit of both coun-

tries. Instead of recognizing the good intentions of the party and the Soviet government, the German authorities had adopted a point of view which the Soviet government and Lenin personally regarded as a slap in the face. While Karakhan made his declaration to me, Kopp brusquely requested the Foreign Ministry to retain the German representative in Germany. Wiedenfeld was just about to depart from Berlin for Moscow; but Kopp said the Soviet government could do without his presence in Moscow until the Krestinsky affair had found a satisfactory solution.

There is no doubt that the motivation behind Berlin's refusal to accept Krestinsky as representative of the RSFSR in Berlin was an important question of principle for the Communist party and the Soviet government. On the other hand, the rude manner in which they had prevented Professor Wiedenfeld's departure for Moscow had also damaged the prestige of the German government. Just after relations had so painfully been re-established, another break seemed threatening.

My task was to work for a settlement of the conflict on a basis acceptable to both parties. This was all the more difficult for me because I could not help accepting the Soviet objections as justified and logical. Hence I had no sound arguments at my disposal when the Foreign Commissariat announced that it could do no more in the affair after Lenin had personally taken a stand concerning it. I therefore had to try to appeal to Lenin's own intelligence, through an intermediary, and convince him that the German government had not intended to insult the Soviet state, and that the clumsy formulation could be explained by the excessive eagerness of a freshman official. It would not be the blundering civil servant who would pay the price of this lesson in the principles of the Soviet constitution, but the German and Russian peoples, whose interests would be affected unfavorably if normal relations were not restored. That is what I should have liked to say to Lenin.

The intermediary whose good offices I used on this occasion was a man whose destiny it was to play an important role—for good or for evil—in German-Soviet relations in the future. Karl Radek belonged to that group of Bolsheviks who had been in Switzerland together with Lenin when the Russian Revolution broke out, and to whom the Imperial German government had granted passage to enable them to return to Russia. Since that time Radek had been

a special confidant of Lenin, who appreciated his sharp mind and brilliant pen. Born in the Austrian part of Galicia, Radek had actively participated in the German Social Democratic movement ever since 1908. Linguistically and culturally he was bound much closer to Germany than to Russia, the country of his choice. His closeness and sympathy with the masses, his captivating wit and quick repartee inevitably earned him the hearty and spontaneous applause of working-class audiences, even though he never learned to master the Russian language and spoke it with a noticeable Polish accent.

Radek was known throughout Moscow for the reckless criticism to which he subjected people and things he disliked and for the stinging jokes he made about them. His biting quips would go from mouth to mouth, and after a while every anti-Soviet joke that was being told in Moscow was, justly or not, attributed to Radek. I believe that that is one of the reasons why Stalin, who had no sense of humor in such things, developed an intense hatred of this insolent jester whom he had never liked for being Lenin's favorite and a follower of Trotsky.

In 1927 Radek was excluded from the Communist party and banished to Siberia as a member of the Trotsky opposition. From his exile he did rueful penitence and swore away his sins, and it was not long before he was back in Moscow. By 1930 he had been taken back as a party member. When I saw him at that time he appeared to me to be a man who had lost every shred of belief in himself. What surprised me most, however, was the way in which he now talked about Stalin. He did not in the least hide the deep impression which Stalin's complete victory over all his antagonists had made on him, and the doubts and insecurity it had given him. But his inner change did not save him from his fate, the last act of which was staged in January, 1937, when Radek was one of the defendants in the second of the famous purge trials. But on that occasion he once more found his old self. I, who followed Radek's dialectics from among the audience, did not have the slightest doubt that his exaggerated confessions of repentance were not means by which he wanted to save his skin, but were appeals to the comrades abroad, in whose eyes he wanted to show up the true nature of Stalin's regime by his grotesque and absurd self-accusations. It was his last and unsuccessful gesture of desperation. After he was sentenced to a long prison term, nothing reliable was learned about his fate. I heard rumors,

which I was unable to confirm, about unusual liberties he supposedly enjoyed while serving his term; nor is there any verification of the story that he died of pneumonia during the war.

Until his fall from high position in 1927, Radek lived in the Great Kremlin Palace. His three-room apartment, quite sumptuous in that time of the Moscow housing shortage, was always so chock-full of books and periodicals, which lay about on shelves, tables, and chairs, that one could scarcely move around. I am sure my host had read most of them, for he could quote Clausewitz with the same assurance with which he discussed the newest books on international political and economic problems.

Mrs. Radek was an intelligent and likable Polish girl from Lódz, whom I first met in 1920 when she was Eiduck's assistant in Tsentrevak. They had a daughter, Sonia, whom Radek loved like the most precious thing on earth. Sonia was in the hands of a good old Russian service woman who had all the sterling qualities proverbially associated with her type. Whenever the conversation turned to the subject, Radek would never fail to praise the advantages of such a Russian *nyanya,* and with an impish twinkle in his eye he would add the story of how his own child, the daughter of Jewish parents and convinced atheists, had secretly been baptized in an Orthodox church because the *nyanya* could not bear the thought of caring for a girl who could not partake in the blessings of the Christian Church. I never could learn what later became of Sonia and her mother. Presumably they were sent to a camp in Siberia to share the sad fate of countless victims of Stalin's dictatorship.

There was great charm in dealing with Radek because of the brilliance and originality with which he would give his opinions, and the revealing frankness with which he would discuss even the most controversial and ticklish political problems. Most important for us, however, was the realization that this revolutionary by profession, this convinced internationalist, had one great weakness: Germany. The Polish Jew from Austrian Galicia felt himself tied to Germany by the closest cultural bonds, and he spoke German better than any other language.

Moreover, he was a most useful contact in Moscow. Even though his journalistic activity and his constant meddling in Germany's domestic affairs often put German-Soviet relations to a hard test, we could always count on him to help us in our dealings with the Soviet

government in difficult situations. This time, too, Radek understood
my embarrassing position and gave me his support.

For him, who was familiar with German mentality, Behrendt's
motivation was no ground for indignation, but only cause for biting
irony and a good laugh. His intervention with Lenin resulted in the
Soviet government's declaring the prevention of Wiedenfeld's departure to have been a "misunderstanding" which they now wished
to withdraw, whereupon the German government accepted Krestinsky as representative of the RSFSR with some similar explanation.
On September 19, 1921, Wiedenfeld was received by the Soviet "President," Kalinin, and gave the latter his credentials; polite speeches
were made; and thus Wiedenfeld's short term as German representative in Moscow had formally begun.

The first six or eight weeks of his presence in Russia coincided
with the lowest ebb in German-Soviet relations. It was about this
time that Maltzan was transferred, and the political influence of
Schlesinger and myself in Soviet-German affairs was never lower.
The Kremlin's disappointment over the development can be judged
by Radek's *Pravda* article of October 15, 1921, in which he made
nostalgic references to previous signs of German-Soviet friendship,
only to conclude that Germany had now completely sold out to the
victorious Western Allies. Three weeks later there was a decided
swing in the other direction. In accordance with the provisions of the
Versailles Treaty, the population of Upper Silesia, on March 20, had
voted in a plebiscite whether their little but economically important
land should belong to Poland or Germany. The plebiscite resulted
in 717,122 votes for Germany as against 483,154 for Poland. But now
the League Council decreed a partition by which Poland was given
the principal mining and industrial districts. The bitterness of German reaction against this violation of previously accepted rules resulted in a sharp turn from the policy of fulfillment. The cabinet
of Dr. Wirth resigned. In the new cabinet Wirth formed, he himself took over the Foreign Ministry, dropping Rosen, and Maltzan,
who had not yet departed for Athens, was promoted to head the Eastern Department of the Wilhelmstrasse, replacing Ministerial direktor
Behrendt. The German press correctly interpreted the changes as evidence that the government was considering a new rapprochement
with Soviet Russia. Comments in the Soviet press naturally expressed great satisfaction over this new turn, although Radek, in

Pravda, on November 11, 1921, emphasized that the reversal of opinion should not be exaggerated; he wrote that without doubt it was partly an attempt to frighten the Entente into leniency and concessions.[6] Yet he too did not conceal his pleasure. Wiedenfeld, on the other hand, was greatly perturbed by the sudden burst of pro-Soviet sentiment in the German press, since he feared that Germany would commit herself to a one-sided policy of friendship with Russia. Moscow, he felt, should always be the party seeking Germany's friendship; as soon as Berlin started courting her, Germany's position would be weakened.

The next months were a time of indecision during which the German government attempted to postpone or prevent any real decision concerning the orientation of Germany's foreign policy, while the Soviet leaders urged the German policy makers to answer French and English intransigence and hypocrisy by establishing a friendship of the two major underprivileged nations. In the long run their threats were perhaps more effective than their cajoling. On December 27, 1921, Radek, in another one of his *Pravda* articles, broadly hinted that Soviet Russia could, at any time she wished, accept the provisions of Versailles; under Article 116 of the treaty Russia could claim her share of reparations payments. In private conversations with Wiedenfeld and other members of the German Mission, Radek sought to soften the blow of his threat by explaining that Russia would do its utmost to avoid applying Article 116. Yet his government was baffled by Germany's vacillating attitude, he continued, and wished to use the threat to force Germany's hand. Such efforts of bullying Germany into friendship with Russia were unsuccessful at the time. They served only to reveal the nervous worry of the Soviet government lest they remain politically isolated. Another sign of nervousness was the sensitivity Soviet leaders displayed to the slightest indication that Germany might commit herself once more to a policy of appeasing the West. One occasion for such reaction was the appointment of Walther Rathenau to the post of foreign minister around the beginning of February, 1922. Chicherin displayed extreme excitement, asserting that the step clearly showed Germany had opted for the West; in Soviet circles Rathenau was then considered the father of a plan for an international financial consortium for trade with Russia, a plan stanchly opposed by the Russians on

[6] Cf. also *Izvestiya*, Nov. 9, 1921.

the grounds that it would have the aim of making Russia into a semicolonial object of exploitation for a united front of monopoly capitalists. Some remarks Rathenau had made at the Cannes Conference, characterizing Russia as an area open for Western colonization, were repeated pointedly by the men in the Commissariat for Foreign Affairs.

Their attempt to make a deal with Germany led the Soviet leaders to make yet another threat: proletarian revolution. An anonymous article in *Izvestiya* of February 5, 1922, hinted broadly that the Soviet government held the fate of the German bourgeoisie in its hand; for Soviet Russia need only get together with the Entente at the expense of Germany, on the basis of the famous Article 116, and the resulting impoverishment of Germany would boost the proletariat in its class warfare. The German bourgeoisie, this article said, were double-dealers, and the Soviet government should not be sentimental about their fate. Significantly, the editors of *Izvestiya* did not print the article without commenting, in a footnote, that they were not in agreement with it. The bogy of an understanding between Soviet Russia and the Western Allies, combined with the specter of the proletarian revolution, nevertheless continued to hang over Germany until a more permanent basis for German-Soviet relations was created at the Genoa Conference.

RAPALLO

The treaty which the German and Soviet delegations to the Genoa Conference signed, on April 16, 1922, at Rapallo came as a profound shock to the politicians of the West. Unknown to the West, the two signatory powers had toyed with the idea of such an agreement for at least four months. As early as December 12, 1921, Krestinsky, in a talk with the German foreign minister, had brought the problem of shaping political relations between the two countries up for discussion. At the same time men like Maltzan, Schlesinger, and the former foreign minister, Count Brockdorff-Rantzau, then in retirement, were discussing what they described as the urgent need for a decisive improvement in German-Soviet relations. Not that they had any bold plans for a one-sided political orientation toward the East; on the contrary, even these protagonists of the "Russian orientation" warned against political experiments of that sort, which

they thought could only benefit Soviet Russia and harm Germany. But they were insistent in their warnings that Germany should not let herself be abused, in regard to Russia, by the Entente powers. Moreover, they urgently advocated economic collaboration with Soviet Russia. A country as desperate for economic reconstruction as she could not afford to remain economically isolated and would attach herself to the first partner who would offer a modicum of advantages. In order to stay in power, they warned, the Soviet regime would not shrink, in the end, from selling Germany down the river by accepting the provisions of Article 116. About a year had now gone by since the introduction of the NEP had created the political and juridical basis for economic collaboration between Russia and the capitalist world; the men in Moscow would not wait much longer.

The history of the Rapallo Treaty has been treated exhaustively before, and I could add little or nothing to these accounts, particularly since I was at the time still removed from the political scene, slowly recuperating from typhus fever. Hence I have only indirect knowledge of the negotiations that went on in the early months of 1922, of Radek's frequent travels to Germany, of Chicherin's repeated suggestion that Germany and Russia decide on a common anti-Allied stand, and of the treaty drafted in Berlin by Maltzan and the Soviet delegation en route to Genoa.

In Genoa a development foreseen by Lloyd George actually came about. In March, 1919, the then Prime Minister had circulated a memorandum for the "Consideration of the Peace Conference" in Versailles, warning that an unduly harsh treatment of Germany might drive her into friendship with Bolshevik Russia. At the time the memorandum had little effect; Clemenceau is said to have replied that it was but a plea for placating Germany at French expense. Now, in March, 1922, on the eve of the Genoa Conference, Lloyd George released the text of his memorandum to the British press, presumably to dramatize the need for a more liberal treatment of Germany.[7] And once more his effort was in vain.

In Lenin's blunt phrase, Russia had gone to the conference—the first international conference at which a Soviet delegation participated—as a "trader," ready to bargain a certain share of her resources, market, labor, and investment opportunities for the aim

[7] Cf. Louis Fischer, *The Soviets in World Affairs* (Princeton, N.J., Princeton University Press, 1930), I, 178, 323.

of restoring her shattered economy to life. In his first speech before the conference, Chicherin made an obvious effort to stress the continuity linking the old with the new Russia, and by that token attempted to de-emphasize the crusading, ideological nature of the regime he represented. Germany, on the other hand, had gone to Genoa hoping to bargain for more liberal reparations terms. Thus both countries had gone with the resolve to make their peace with the Western Allies—for the time being and under certain minimum conditions.

The Russian efforts met open suspicion and hostility. It seems, indeed, that the Western powers were not in principle opposed to a policy of large-scale investments in Russia. But the Soviet Republic had no desire to be a passive object of economic exploitation on terms and to an extent determined by the investors; though ready to make substantial concessions in order to make foreign aid worth the capitalists' while, she was not prepared to relinquish an iota of her economic sovereignty. For this reason, too, the Soviet delegation refused to compromise on the delicate problem of repayment of tsarist debts. As for the German delegation, it saw itself virtually ignored, its pleas unheeded, by the statesmen from the victor states. Moreover, the constant fear of an agreement between the West and Russia lay heavily on their minds; and when the danger appeared to turn into an acute threat the Germans at last—and reluctantly enough—signed the treaty that had in substance been drafted already in Berlin.

In it, the two countries at one stroke cleaned the slate covered with claims and counter-claims accumulated in previous years. Both countries renounced all compensation for damages caused by war, intervention, and occupation, and for civil damages caused by Soviet measures of nationalization (Article 1). Thus the Damoclean sword of Article 116 was forever removed from above the heads of the German government. Article 2 gave Germany the right to bring up the question of Russian debts for re-examination in case the Soviet government satisfied similar claims of other states. This safety clause assured the Germans that they were not voluntarily incurring a decided disadvantage; on the other hand, it served to discourage severely any potential Soviet intentions to settle the debt question with other countries at Germany's expense. The treaty provided for the resumption of full diplomatic and consular relations (Article 3).

In Article 4 both countries granted each other the treatment given the most favored nation. Finally, in Article 5, the German government promised to assist German private firms in the extension of their contracts with the Soviet government. Obviously this was not a Grand Alliance nor an aggressive treaty; it was not even a treaty of non-aggression or even neutrality. Its principal aim was the removal of impediments to mutual understanding and goodwill created by the war and the revolution, thus making future friendly relations possible.

Nevertheless, its conclusion caused a flurry of indignation and accusations. For one thing, the scope and meaning of Rapallo were far exaggerated by its critics. Even in Germany rumors that it contained secret clauses providing for a formal political or military alliance persisted for many years, and are still heard every once in a while, even though at least formally they are groundless. Proving a negative statement is, of course, logically impossible; it is equally difficult to counter vague but sweeping accusations that Rapallo ran counter to "international morality," that Germany had violated the principle of mutual collaboration and consultation, that Rapallo meant a return to old-fashioned "secret diplomacy," or that the treaty had been concluded at an inopportune moment. Few if any of these criticisms could stand close examination. "International morality" is a most elusive concept, and even if it were better defined it would be difficult to brand the settling of mutual debts as "immoral," especially after the repeated efforts on the part of the Allies to free Russia of its debts to Germany unilaterally. The principle of mutual collaboration and consultation had, clearly, been violated first by the Western diplomats who kept the German delegation at the Genoa Conference in utter isolation; and the reproach of secrecy also boomeranged, for it is well established that Rathenau made repeated but unsuccessful attempts to get in touch with Lloyd George.

The choice of the proper moment for a political move can be the subject of interminable fruitless discussions. The opinion that Rapallo was concluded three and a half years too late is expressed in Arthur Rosenberg's *Geschichte der deutschen Republik* (page 130); he is correct in saying that a similar treaty made in December, 1918, might have given the domestic and international history of Germany a completely different turn, but few people shared his im-

plied view that such a turn would have been desirable. The contrary opinion holding that Rapallo constituted an untimely disturbance of the Genoa Conference was much more widespread. Count Brockdorff-Rantzau at that time held that the Foreign Ministry had shown unnecessary haste; assuming that the German delegation had allowed themselves to be ruled by sudden panic, he believed that they might have obtained even greater advantages by stalling. Even so, he acknowledged the great benefits Germany derived from the treaty not only by eliminating Russia as a claimant of reparations but also by securing most-favored-nation treatment for Germany in her relations with Soviet Russia. More generally, Rapallo meant that Germany had begun her slow road away from her position as a mere object of international politics. As such, it met with fairly broad approval throughout Germany.

Russia, in turn, had opened a breach in the wall of economic and political isolation heretofore surrounding her and had sharply reminded the West of her existence as a European power. At the same time Rapallo was an important precedent for a generous and favorable liquidation of the debts problem raised by the war and the revolution. Thus it was a substantial victory for the regime; as such, the treaty met some hostile criticism from political opponents of the regime within Russia who were in the habit of venting their dissatisfaction to members of the German representation. Remnants of the traditional anti-German attitude of moderate-liberal circles in Russia may have had their share of influencing such opinion. By this time, however, the people who paid attention to the remnants of the prerevolutionary society in Russia were becoming scarcer even in the German Foreign Ministry.

Rapallo did not bring with it a definite swing of German foreign policy away from the West, and toward a firm alliance with Soviet Russia. On the contrary, Walther Rathenau, the foreign minister, continued to make overtures to the Western powers even after the Genoa Conference; the hostile comments which Rapallo had occasioned in France increased his eagerness to show Germany's willingness to discuss the manner in which the provisions of Versailles might feasibly be fulfilled. But in vain. The French, at least, seemed not to be interested in talking to Germans about any easing of the reparations burden. When, on the eve of another payment, May 31,

1922, Chancellor Wirth asked for a loan or a moratorium, he was turned down. To many it seemed then that France was actually hoping Germany would not fulfill her obligations, thus providing a pretext for the application of stiff sanctions. Over this, in turn, the relations between France and England cooled appreciably. *Izvestiya* of September 2, 1922, went so far as to express confidence that England would soon be compelled to seek the friendship of Russia and Germany.

In Germany, meanwhile, Rathenau's and Wirth's attempts to come to terms with France were bitterly assailed from both extremes of the political spectrum. The right-wing press hurled accusations of appeasement and treason against the government. In its July 7th issue, the *Deutsche Allgemeine Zeitung,* mouthpiece of Hugo Stinnes's industrial empire, demanded that Germany abrogate the Versailles Treaty and refuse all further reparations payment. Two weeks before Rathenau had been assassinated while riding in his open car along a broad suburban avenue near his home. The murderers—henceforth to become heroes of German fascism—were members of a secret terrorist gang composed mainly of young officers and intellectuals unable to adjust to Germany's defeat. Small in number and actual political influence, they nevertheless had the tacit and not so tacit sympathy of broad sections of the population, the same sections that were to become the mainstay of National Socialism.

The Soviet leaders were not particularly sorry to see the death of the man who had been one of the chief protagonists of a Western orientation for Germany. Now that he was gone, an important obstacle in the way of a broad elaboration of the Rapallo relationship had been removed. The satisfaction of the Communist leaders was not, however, undisturbed. Any upsurge of right-wing extremism could not but produce serious apprehension in Moscow. For though the German counter-revolution may have been a convenient ally against English imperialism, it was also the most unreliable and dangerous ally the Soviet state could choose. The assassination was, therefore, not only a factor which might improve German-Soviet relations; it was at the same time regarded as an admonition that Communist vigilance must be sharpened. A revolutionary situation was ripening in Germany, and Communism should be on the alert. That was Moscow's reaction to the death of Rathenau. In order to

avert the reaction, Wiedenfeld, who was still in Moscow, tried his best to describe the assassination as the individual act of immature delinquents, to which no political significance should be ascribed.

Two months later an attack was made against the cabinet's policy of fulfillment, this time from the Left, the consequences of which demonstrate the fluid character and nervous tension of international politics in 1922, which was always close to a breaking point. On August 24th the German industrial and employees' unions sent an ultimatum to the Chancellor: The ruin of Germany's economy had progressed so far, and the burdens lying on the back of the people had grown so heavy, that the policy of fulfillment must cease at once. Coming from the trade-union movement, which commanded the allegiance of millions of voters, the ultimatum could be less easily disregarded than the deed of fascist murder gangs; and Dr. Wirth acted at once. He asked the German chargé d'affaires, von Radowitz, to notify the Soviet government immediately of the ultimatum. (Wiedenfeld had by that time returned to Germany.) Von Radowitz communicated the message to Karakhan on August 26th and elicited jubilation from the Russian over the sharp turn in German policy. Karakhan immediately talked about a German-Soviet united front against the Allies, and promised that the entire party and government press would at once be instructed to wage an intensive pro-German propaganda campaign.

Two days later von Radowitz received a wire from Dr. Simons in which he was told that any publication of the *démarche* he had made was highly undesirable. He said that Germany was adhering to the policy of fulfillment. Apparently the government had been able to appease the unions after Dr. Wirth's first panicky reaction to their ultimatum. But his panic had caused his representative in Moscow, as well as the entire foreign policy of Germany, serious embarrassment. Von Radowitz made desperate attempts to reach Karakhan so that the propaganda campaign could be canceled, but the latter "could not be reached." Perhaps he thought that Dr. Wirth's mistake, if it were allowed to become a *fait accompli*, could still be used to force his hand; perhaps his early enthusiasm had now given way to disappointment and disgust over German fickleness. In any event, I can imagine that he derived great amusement from watching von Radowitz try to wiggle out of the fix into which he had been put. Von Radowitz, in turn, complained bitterly to Berlin over his

contradictory orders. He finally got hold of Karakhan, who said he had been out of town, and the Russian promised that the press would not mention the incident. Nevertheless, two periodicals had, it seems, not been informed in time to cancel their comments; the August 31st numbers of *Ekonomicheskaya zhizn'* and *Rabochaya gazeta* featured detailed accounts of the German *démarche*.

IV PERSONALITIES AND PROBLEMS OF THE RAPALLO ERA

1. COUNT BROCKDORFF-RANTZAU

For the post of ambassador in Moscow re-created by the Rapallo Treaty, a personage of far greater political import than Professor Wiedenfeld was required. The Kremlin obviously had no problem of this kind, since Krestinsky was of first-rank prominence in the Communist party; his appointment to be the Soviet ambassador in Berlin—or representative plenipotentiary, as it was called in Soviet parlance, since prerevolutionary titles and hierarchies had been abolished—required little more than purely formal procedures and a change in his title. On August 2, 1922, he handed Ebert his credentials as Polpred (abbreviation of *Polnomochnyi Predstavitel'* [Representative Plenipotentiary]), a post he was to fill for eight years.

The new ambassadorship vacant in Moscow called for a man who should, ideally, have combined several traits almost never found together in one man. For one thing, no one could have been chosen who did not have the confidence of the moderate parties then dominant in the Weimar Republic, the Social Democrats, Democrats, and Centrists. Thus, anyone too far to the left or right was out of consideration, as was any man who had shown himself unreconciled to the fall of the monarchy and to democratic reforms; in any event, Moscow would probably have refused to accept an outright reactionary. But they would even more certainly refuse a Social Democrat, as the case of August Müller had shown in the previous year. The field of contenders thus seemed limited to men belonging, at least in their political allegiance, to the solid, respectable bourgeois center.

84

That was certainly not a formidable limitation in the Germany of the twenties. Yet it made it very difficult to fulfill a further desideratum: The new ambassador ought to be a man of long experience and proven ability in the diplomatic service—a career that had always been the preserve of able men from the high nobility.

Two men were seriously considered for the appointment. One was former Vice Admiral Paul von Hintze, who before the war had been the Kaiser's personal military representative in the tsar's personal suite, who had served as foreign secretary for a few weeks in 1918, and who now was an ardent advocate of close German-Soviet collaboration. The other, who was finally given the post, was a former Imperial German diplomat: Ulrich Count Brockdorff-Rantzau.

Born in the province of Schleswig on May 29, 1869, Rantzau—that is how he signed his dispatches—was the descendant of an old and proud noble family that could boast of many most illustrious ancestors. An aunt of his, a Countess Brockdorff, had bequeathed him her estate on the condition that he add her name to his own. But that did not prevent the count from using every opportunity to make clear that he was a scion of the much older, hence much nobler, tribe of the Rantzaus. One of his ancestors had been a Maréchal de France under Louis XIV; and gossip had it that he was not only the king's general but also the queen's lover. With characteristic cynicism the count would often hint that the last members of the Bourbon dynasty had really been bastards of the Rantzaus.

Count Ulrich had studied law and then, after a few years of service as an Army officer, entered the diplomatic service; he had been a secretary of legation in St. Petersburg, a counselor of embassy in Vienna, a consul general at Budapest, and had finally headed the German Mission in Copenhagen, an important listening post and center of ticklish intrigues during the war. Through his direct connections with the Socialist and adventurer Parvus, Rantzau had been one link in the chain of hands that had helped Lenin and his associates to return to Russia in the spring of 1917, and, in this minute detail, had helped to make the Russian Revolution. This is not, however, what earned him the epithets "Red Count" and *le comte malgré lui* by which he was known. He had acquired these during the war by his energetic advocacy of democratic and social reforms.

Rantzau was in no way preoccupied with "social justice" and paid no allegiance to political ideals like liberty and equality. The range

of values that mattered to his own inner personality might have seemed to be primarily aesthetic, not social. Nothing gave him greater pleasure than the enjoyment of fine *style,* be it in a masterpiece of fine arts from his exquisite collection, a literary gem, or in personal conduct. In the stress he laid on personal bearing and style of living, he was in every fiber an old aristocrat. The length to which he went in his sensitivity to style was indeed in the nature of an obsession; to some people it suggested the adjective "degenerate." Behind his sensitivity for style was a hypertrophied sense of personal dignity expressing itself as great arrogance. But Rantzau's arrogance was not simply the narrow ancestor-pride of the aristocrat who has nothing but noble forebears to boast of; his was the nervous, finicky arrogance of the aesthete who has absorbed the highest standards of his culture and abhors those unable to reach the same heights.

The unconcealed rebuffs he dealt to vulgarity—be it in politics or in personal bearing—might have created the impression that his sensitivity was really the essence of Rantzau's character. But he himself could be extremely vulgar among his confidants, and unspeakably rude to those he disliked. It was not simply vulgarity that repelled him; rather, his attitude to others was regulated chiefly by his own high estimate of himself and his origins. He did respect the personal dignity of persons beneath himself in his estimation. But their dignity had to be coupled with the humility befitting their lowly status. For that reason he could befriend Socialists and Jews, as long as they did not "presume" beyond their status, for instance, by becoming ambassadors or foreign ministers. That kind of career and duty was, in his mind, reserved for his own kind; hence he resented the spectacle of a successful businessman (Stresemann) or an eminent industrialist (Rathenau) daring to assume the ministerial office he had for a while occupied. He considered them usurpers of his own aristocratic functions, and they became the objects of an acrid sarcasm in which he became painfully personal. George Grosz has drawn a famous bitter cartoon of Rantzau, showing him as a degenerate Prussian aristocrat, which carries the caption "Hier riecht's nach Pöbel" (It smells of rabble here). This is, in a sense, a true portrait—and yet the epithet "Red Count" was no less fitting.

For the count advocated democratic and social reforms in spite of his disdain of the masses. Nor was his motive that of a self-seeking opportunist who aims to ride the wave of the future. He advocated

democratic reforms from the firm conviction that Germany could no more be governed in the old ways without inviting the most serious internal difficulties. Thus his vigorous espousal of social and democratic reforms stemmed from the desire to aid Germany's war effort by preventing internal convulsions. Moreover, sensing the coming defeat long before the majority of generals and politicians were ready to admit the possibility, Rantzau wanted to deprive the democratic enemies of Germany of the argument that Germany was a bastion of reaction. It was thus for reasons of political expediency, particularly for the sake of German foreign policy, that Rantzau proposed to institute his democratic reforms. This statement is in no way affected by the arguments he used to show that such reforms were possible. He argued that the loyalty shown by the German working class at the outbreak of the war had proved its political maturity and reliability far beyond the old clichés branding the proletarians as rabble without a country. Rantzau at first attempted to persuade the Kaiser and his regime to institute far-reaching reforms from above; he had visions of Wilhelm II transforming himself into a veritable "people's emperor." It was only when he met with persistent intransigence on the part of the emperor and his entourage that he abandoned the Hohenzollern dynasty as people whom the wheel of history would inevitably crush; and when Wilhelm II fled abroad after the war was lost, to spend his remaining years at Doorn mansion in Holland, Rantzau's political conviction merged with a deep personal resentment of the Kaiser's cowardice. Henceforth he would refer to him bitterly as the "deserter of Doorn." [1]

Rantzau's loyalty to the republic and his attitude to the Hohenzollerns is symbolized by the following episode: In December, 1918, shortly after the count had become the first foreign minister of the German Republic, the Council of People's Deputies discussed the disposal of the property of the former Kaiser's family. Rantzau suggested that it should neither be expropriated nor be handed back to be disposed of freely. Instead, the Kaiser's private property should be used by the German state to pay him and his family a life-long annuity that would enable them to live according to their status.

[1] This did not, by the way, cause him in any way to interfere with the activities of his twin brother, Ernst, who was devoted to his big brother like a shadow and followed his every hint. Ernst Count Rantzau had been a chamberlain at the Imperial German court, and now represented the material interests and the claims for compensation of the Hohenzollern family.

Rantzau wanted to prevent the house of Hohenzollern from using their tremendous fortunes to the detriment of the republic. The Social Democrats, on the other hand, maintained that the Kaiser and his family had the same rights as any other German citizen and that therefore the state could not deny them the free use of their private property.

During the war Rantzau had vigorously opposed unrestricted submarine warfare, and in political circles he was considered a "defeatist." This and his known views on domestic affairs made him one of the very few old-style diplomats in whom Liberals and Socialists had confidence. After the revolution of November, 1918, the Independent Socialist Haase, who was one of the six People's Deputies, went personally to Copenhagen to offer Rantzau the post of foreign minister. Thus the count became the first foreign minister of the German Republic.

Among the Social Democrats, Democrats, and representatives of the Center party in the first cabinet, he was conspicuous not only because of his aristocratic antecedents but also because he was the only cabinet member not affiliated with any party. Indeed, he identified himself in general with the Democrats, the party of liberal constitutional democracy which might be classified as slightly left of center; but he never formally joined them. The reason was that he was impatient with parliamentary party politics and wanted to be independent of it. As foreign minister he had no desire to share the adverse fate of any party during a cabinet crisis. Not that Rantzau failed to understand the nature of constitutional democracy and the principle of the cabinet's responsibility to parliament; as a matter of fact he understood these principles only too well. But he felt the rules of the constitutional game as an unwelcome fetter, at least in the field of foreign relations, which he thought should be above partisan strife—bipartisan, we call it today.

With this disdain for constitutional formalities of parliamentary government, the support Rantzau gave to the republic was, although by no means insincere, motivated only by political expediency, and not by a deeper faith in constitutional democracy. The count combined a sharp sense of reality with fervent patriotism. He knew that the majority of his own social set would call him a traitor to his class for entering the "revolutionary" cabinet. But instead of deterring him, this attitude drew only his scorn and derision. These

gentlemen were in his opinion doing the same thing they constantly attributed to the Socialists: They put the presumed interests of their class over those of the nation, whereas he had, with patriotic effort, put aside all instincts and predilections in placing himself at the disposal of the Council of People's Deputies.

As foreign minister, Rantzau headed the German delegation summoned to the Versailles Peace Conference; afterward he argued incessantly for rejecting the treaty document that had been handed to him, for he considered its provisions impossible of fulfillment. After bitter debates within the Constitutional Assembly and the cabinet at Weimar, he was overruled and resigned. The scar left on him by the personal and national humiliation of Versailles never healed. The treaty created or confirmed in Rantzau an implacable resentment against the French, which showed not only in his subsequent policies but also in a spiteful personal hostility toward French politicians and officials. He could neither forget nor forgive the treatment the German delegation had received at Versailles, and the barbed wire behind which they had been caged between negotiations. In spite of this, I cannot say that he identified himself with the traditional attitude of those Germans who considered France the "hereditary enemy," for he had absorbed too much of the fruits of French culture. Whereas he knew no English, he had a fluent mastery of French and loved to speak it. But, politically, he saw red when France or Versailles was mentioned.

With all his compromises to democratic realities, with all his ability to transcend the narrow arrogance of his fellow noblemen, Count Brockdorff-Rantzau was a much more genuine symbol of his class than the die-hard reactionaries of Prussian Junkerdom who spent themselves in futile attempts to reverse the trend toward greater influence of the common man on political affairs, only to pave the way for the rabble of Hitler's storm troops. Rantzau had no illusions of turning back the wheel of history. His conception of the well born leader's function was a positive one of leading a German people's state toward better days. Beneath these considerations a deep pessimism and despair were hiding; he seems to have been dimly aware that his idea of leadership in democracy was the last conceivable task left for the aristocracy before it would disappear altogether. Moreover, he must have had semiconscious doubts concerning Germany's ability to make a comeback. One often feels that what really

mattered to him was to see to it that Germany and the classes that had ruled her in the past would go down to their doom in style. Identifying himself with his country and his class, he felt himself to be a living corpse, a hero mortally wounded whose only concern was to die with dignity. "Do not mourn," he said to his twin brother a few hours before his death. "After all, I have really been dead ever since Versailles" (Ich bin ja schon in Versailles gestorben).

This is the man who was entrusted with the delicate task of implementing the Rapallo relationship as German ambassador in Moscow. The task attracted him mightily not only for its political significance but also because it called for a master diplomatist enamored of his work; for it he spent himself during the last years of his life, the outstanding living symbol of the Rapallo era.

Rantzau's appointment as ambassador was not officially announced until more than five months after the signing of the Treaty of Rapallo—months filled with hesitations and bickering over the appointment in high cabinet circles. Ebert, the Reich President, supported Rantzau's candidacy, and urged him to accept the appointment. The latter agreed in principle. In a series of memoranda submitted to Ebert, and in further conversations with him, he argued that Germany was compelled to seek a rapprochement with Russia even though the Soviet regime was, in his words, a "gang of criminals"; and he agreed to try his hand at the difficult task, even though he was going to go to Moscow without any illusions and with a good dose of almost morbid skepticism. Once this agreement was obtained, Ebert arranged meetings with Rantzau and the Chancellor, Dr. Wirth; but the blueblooded Prussian diplomat and the schoolteacher-politician from the South did not hit it off very well at first and established a *modus vivendi* only gradually. Unexpected stiff resistance against Rantzau's appointment suddenly came from the War Ministry in Bendlerstrasse. General Hans von Seeckt, the head of the Army staff, sternly rejected him as candidate for the post.

The personal enmity between von Seeckt and Brockdorff-Rantzau dated back to the days of the Paris Peace Conference. At that time von Seeckt had been the chief military expert in the German delegation, and he had seriously clashed with Rantzau, who as foreign minister was the head of the delegation. The memoranda the two men exchanged on May 26 and 27, 1919, now in von Seeckt's personal papers in the United States National Archives, show that they

disagreed over the attitude to be taken toward the proposed disarmament provisions of the draft treaty. Rantzau, traditionally opposed to the blunt militarists and power-politicians that had wielded a decisive influence in prewar Germany, proposed to recognize the military disaster Germany had suffered in the recent war, and was ready to direct the entire national effort toward non-military tasks of reconstruction. Hence he was prepared to offer only token resistance to the far-reaching disarmament provisions of Versailles. The general, on the other hand, regarded military power as the surest warranty of Germany's recovery, and he demanded a tooth-and-nail fight for every bit of a concession in the disarmament provisions. It is doubtful whether he would have succeeded in obtaining milder conditions; in any event he was overruled, to his great resentment. He believed that he had not been given the hearing due his position, and henceforth bore a deep grudge against the count, making him his scapegoat for the harsh peace treaty.

In turn, Rantzau focused on the general the wary suspicion he felt against highhanded military adventurism. It must be surmised that he suspected the existence of a secret deal between von Seeckt's Reichswehr and the Red Army; rumors that the Rapallo Treaty contained secret military clauses were widely discussed in Germany, and even if Rantzau gave them no credence he did believe that the treaty served to encourage such damaging rumors. In July, 1922, he wrote a lengthy *pro memoria* to the President and the Chancellor in which he warned even against the semblance of military agreements with the Soviet government, since such agreements would seriously jeopardize all remaining hopes of a rapprochement with the West and would draw England and France together in a united front against Germany. England's natural fear of France, he thought, could lead to German rearmament much more rapidly and safely than a deal with the Soviet regime. Only the latter could benefit from military agreements, for they would deliver Germany straight into Soviet hands. In the first place Russia could at any time reveal the existence of the secret relationship, and thereby discredit Germany; secondly, she could draw Germany into a hopeless war in the West by having the Red Army invade Poland. And if Russian troops then pushed farther into Germany, they would do so not to liberate her from the Entente, but to "push Asia's frontier as far as the Rhine." The memorandum closes with the admonition to wait for further develop-

ments in Russia and, meanwhile, seek England's friendship. In a way
it is not a typical representation of his views toward German-Soviet
policy, for it expressed only all the reservations he harbored against
Rapallo. Even earlier he had readily admitted that the treaty had
been a brilliant stroke; and after his appointment he did not spare
himself in working to cement the Rapallo relationship.

The *pro memoria* was given to von Seeckt on September 9, 1922.
Two days later Seeckt handed the Chancellor his reply, written in a
militant, aggressive tone.[2] The general began by stating point-blank
that Germany must conduct an *active* foreign policy entailing an aim
and a firm will, and struck a quick blow at Rantzau by saying that
"persons seeing only dangers . . . must be kept away from the
scene" of political action, as unfit to make policy. Germany needed
a Talleyrand or a Trotsky, he suggested.

Countering Rantzau's demand that Rapallo must be robbed of
its political implications by a narrow economic application, von
Seeckt stressed the treaty's political significance. The combination
with Russia, he said, had been the first and virtually only gain in
power and prestige Germany had made since Versailles. "There
are," he continued, "politicians afraid of a gain in an active German
policy when they see the danger of new and stronger counter-
measures from the Western enemies. That poses for them the question of Western versus Eastern orientation, a question they would
like to evade. But in actual fact this question has not come up at
all." The general then went on to show why in his opinion an
alliance with Soviet Russia would be the only means of strengthening Germany. A policy of fulfilling the provisions of Versailles was
hopeless; for France, he asserted, was bent on destroying Germany
and could not be appeased. England, he held, was drifting toward a
conflict with France, and no matter whether Germany was allied
with Soviet Russia or not, she was England's natural continental ally.
As a matter of fact, the stronger England found Germany, the more
she would be attracted to her. Poland was, for von Seeckt, the crux
of all problems in the East. Her further existence could not be
justified, he thought, taking the inevitability and desirability of a
fourth division of Poland for granted.

[2] The handwritten draft, together with Rantzau's memorandum, is among the
general's papers in the National Archives. Both memoranda have been published
by Julius Epstein in the November, 1948, number of *Der Monat*.

Once more making a jab at the count, von Seeckt said that anyone regarding Rapallo as a mistake was unfit for the post of ambassador in Moscow. By strengthening Russia, her potential future ally, Germany would strengthen herself, he wrote; and indicated that the process of strengthening should include military collaboration. Germany, he concluded, should not indulge in unrealistic dreams of staying out of possible future conflicts. Such dreams, he held, were suicidal; hence to talk about peace was tantamount to treason. Preparedness should be the slogan.

So much for the memoranda of the two antagonists. Even after Rantzau's appointment had been officially announced, von Seeckt made one final effort, in October, to get rid of him by openly casting aspersions on the count's patriotism and loyalty. But it was too late, and the attack had been overly rude. The general was in the end compelled to make a grudging and truculent withdrawal. The original draft of the retraction, in von Seeckt's personal archives, still contained a number of new insults which were, however, stricken out on second thought.

As a matter of fact, the entire campaign of the general against Rantzau's candidacy had been too late to prevent the appointment; negotiations between the count and the cabinet had already virtually committed the latter to their choice. They had been most extraordinary negotiations. Rantzau was so convinced of his prominence and suitability that he made some startling conditions before he would even consider accepting the post. In brief, he demanded that, if he were to take the post, he would be subject to no foreign minister, but subordinate himself only to the Reich Chancellor. Being a former foreign minister himself, he refused to pay obedience to anyone in the Foreign Ministry. In particular, he expressly refused to work under the direction of Walther Rathenau, whom he considered brilliant but without political sense. On June 24, 1922, Rathenau was assassinated and his portfolio was taken over by the Chancellor himself. This made it easier for Rantzau to accept the ambassadorship, since he considered Dr. Wirth comparatively innocuous because of his lack of experience in foreign affairs.

In addition, Rantzau demanded the special privilege of making reports to the Reich President directly, even over the head of the Chancellor. The amazing part of the story is not that the arrogant count requested this privilege of extra-channel communications but

that Ebert and Wirth gave in to his demands, even though they were constitutionally untenable.

Just as extraordinary as these conditions was a visit Rantzau paid on June 23, 1922, to Soviet Foreign Commissar Chicherin during one of the latter's frequent stays in Berlin. He introduced himself as the man being most actively considered for the post in Moscow, and then proceeded to lay his cards on the table with a disarming bluntness not customarily associated with the ways of diplomacy, outlining some of the problems he visualized and touching the most delicate issues of Soviet-German relations. Chicherin appears to have been delighted; the two men immediately hit it off marvelously and in this interview laid the foundations for a deep personal friendship ended only by Rantzau's death. They were drawn together not only by sharing many political likes and dislikes—the ideological gulf between them notwithstanding—but also by the similarity of their aristocratic past, by similar working habits (both used to do their work late at night, going to bed only at dawn), and even by suffering from identical ailments. They had similar predilections for the products of high culture—works of fine art, brilliant literary style, and choice wines. In their extensive private correspondence each tried to surpass the other in wit, style, and brilliance, and at public occasions they did not hesitate to pay each other the warmest tributes of personal friendship.

The closeness, not to say intimacy, of these two remarkable men often helped Rantzau to overcome the feeling of acute despair caused him by the intransigence of the Soviet government and the recklessness of their methods, which frequently brought him to the verge of giving up his post in Moscow. Moreover, even though he knew that a member of the Soviet government could not afford to show real sincerity and good will in his relations with a bourgeois diplomat, his hypertrophied sense of his own importance tricked him into abandoning that suspicion in the case of Chicherin, Kalinin, and a few other high-placed representatives of the Soviet state. He could not, it seems, doubt the sincerity of a government to which no less a person than he, Count Rantzau, had been accredited. However much he held the Communists in contempt, he resisted the temptation of subjecting, say, Kalinin, to the derision he instinctively felt for the men in the Kremlin. Similarly, the high esteem in which he held himself made it impossible for him to believe that Chicherin

might be insincere or ill willed. A misanthrope at heart, who encased himself in a carefully created glory of fear and admiration; a man with an almost psychotic distrust of his environment, who saw enemies lurking around every corner, Count Rantzau never lost his respect and his feeling of warm friendship for Chicherin. His last thoughts, dictated on his deathbed, express this belief in himself, his mission, and his friendship with the Soviet foreign commissar. This is the letter he dictated:

MY DEAR PEOPLE'S COMMISSAR:

My twin brother, Ambassador Count Brockdorff-Rantzau, had me called to his bedside this afternoon and requested me to convey the following to you, People's Commissar, and Mr. Litvinov: That, after the verdict of his physician, he was aware that he had to reckon with his sudden death any hour. That he was, in his hour of death, requesting me to tell both gentlemen that he had regarded it as his life's task to carry the policies pursued by him in the last years to the desired aim.

He further asked me to tell you that he thanks both Commissars, especially you, for the faith in collaboration that he has always found with you in the difficult years. His last and firm hope, he said, was that the German and Russian people may in common work attain the end they desire.

Berlin, September 8, 1928

ERNST COUNT RANTZAU

From the point of view of anyone working in the German Embassy, the years from 1922 to 1928 might well be called the Rantzau era, for the count dominated our political relations with Moscow and gave them their particular flavor. For him the Rapallo relationship had a decidedly romantic appeal; he saw in it the symbol of a curious but firm friendship between two nations whom the cruel course of history had converted into outlaws, forcing them together through thick and thin, breathing defiance against the satiated, victorious bourgeois world. His great disappointment was that neither his superiors in Berlin nor his Soviet counterparts in Moscow had as romantic a conception of this German-Soviet "community of fate" (*Schicksalsgemeinschaft*) as he. None the less, the spirit with which he went about his task of cementing that friendship sufficiently touched the sympathetic heartstrings of Russia's policy makers to make him their darling and their showpiece among all bourgeois diplomats in Moscow. They were enchanted to have captivated the

good will of such a colorful and important personality. In his obitu-
ary for Rantzau published in *Pravda* on September 11, 1928, the
Soviet journalist Kol'tsov wrote that "the ambitious, aristocratically
haughty Count turned out to be the most loyal, best-intentioned,
most accessible, and hence the most agreeable bourgeois ambassador
in Red Moscow." The Soviet officials who would see the "Old Count"
in the antechamber of the Foreign Commissariat, he wrote, "would
strangely feel no effect of violent class hatred, as would have been
proper at the sight of persons of noble blood." For "this Count had
grasped and never forgot that the Soviet Union, through whatever
eyes you may look at it, is a mighty power with which one must try to
live in friendship and concord. . . . Seek no quarrels, but maintain
friendship. . . . Stand behind this strong boy in case they gang up
on him. . . . This was the most important thing for the Old Count."
Certainly a one-sided account of the man who often described the
Moscow regime as a gang of thugs and blackmailers!

The judgment of Rantzau's associates about him was highly
contradictory. He had a large number of admirers, some of whom
were warmly attached to him as a human being. But many people
feared him or could not abide his overweening pride and his mordant
irony. Very few had sympathy with the pleasure Rantzau found in
embarrassing people with his biting wit. For instance, he loved to
ask young subordinates reporting to him for the first time whether
they knew the meaning of "subordination." After they had replied
by some obvious commonplace, he would disconcert them with his
own definition, according to which subordination is "the feeling of
shame that ought to creep into a subordinate when, facing a superior, he must appear more stupid than his superior is in fact."

Rantzau's morbid suspicion made the circle of collaborators who
were really close to him quite limited. Moreover, he lived the life
of a recluse; during the entire period of his six-year stay in Moscow
he did not once enter the office of the embassy. Forever accompanied
and shadowed by his devoted aid, he would see his counselors and
secretaries in his residence; and for routine work a small staff of
office employees would be available day and night. If he trusted a
particular subordinate, he would be a kind chief and take an active
interest in his advancement and well-being. But a chance incident or
even a completely imaginary *faux pas* would suffice to turn him
against the man with the stubborn finality of one suffering from a

persecution complex, so that neither efficiency nor ability availed the hapless outcast.

In July, 1922, Rantzau's counselor of embassy, von Radowitz, arrived in Moscow and took over the affairs of the embassy from Wiedenfeld, while the new ambassador still lingered in Germany to mend his political fences. It was not until November 2nd that the count finally arrived in the Soviet capital. The reception he got at the station was not particularly impressive; as a matter of fact I might call it shabby. "Like a high-class bootlegger," Rantzau characterized it. Obviously, his sense of personal and national dignity was sorely offended, and when he went to see Chicherin late that night he made no bones about his feelings. As a consequence, his reception in the Kremlin three days later, when he presented his papers of accreditation to Kalinin, was surrounded with all the pomp the Russians could muster; and when a detachment of Red Army troops passed in review before the dignitaries within the Kremlin walls the band sounded off with Rantzau's favorite march, the "Hohenfriedberger," which was allegedly composed by Frederick the Great himself.

At the railroad station Rantzau had had a few friendly words for me. The next day I had an interview with him which decided our subsequent relationship. It showed that our thinking in political and personal matters agreed to a sufficient extent that Rantzau soon afterward asked me to join the staff of his embassy. The decision was difficult for me because I was just then flirting with a return to business and had just received an attractive offer from the biggest German steamship company to manage their business in Russia. But the prospect opened by a position under Rantzau was too attractive. I agreed to work with him, and soon received a letter from him ending with the following wôrds: "I feel the urge of expressing my satisfaction that Your Excellency (*Euer Hochwohlgeboren*) has, upon my request, decided to devote your energies, which for years have been eminently proven in the cultivation of German-Russian relations, to the service of the German Reich and to assist me in the high task I have put myself as ambassador of the German Reich in Russia." The many tokens of friendship that Rantzau bestowed on me in the course of the next six years, and particularly the fact that he remembered me even on his deathbed, proved to me that I had not disappointed him.

2. *THE FOREIGN COMMISSARIAT*

In his treatise on the process of revolution, George S. Pettee maintains that a revolutionary regime and its counter-revolutionary neighbors are apt to conduct foreign relations very poorly owing to mutual ineptitude. The revolutionary, he maintains, is too much preoccupied with problems of domestic reforms or domestic changes to know much about foreign politics and its problems, whereas the conservative statesmen of the other states have never troubled to familiarize themselves with problems of a revolution, if only because their profession is so competitive that they have enough to do concentrating on problems of "normal" politics. As a result, he claims, foreign politics in both camps is handled by "rank amateurs" and "second-rate adventurers." [3]

As convincing as this argument may sound in the abstract, it is belied by the stature of Count Rantzau, as well as some of the foreign ministers of the German Republic who conducted German-Soviet relations. Nor were any of the people's commissars for foreign affairs of the Soviet state "rank amateurs" or second-rate adventurers. That applies certainly to the last three foreign commissars (or ministers), Litvinov, Molotov, and Vyshinsky, and with even greater emphasis to their two predecessors. Both Trotsky and Chicherin, who succeeded him in the spring of 1918, were among the best brains and most interesting personalities in the first period of the Russian Revolution. I have watched Andrei Yanuarievich Vyshinsky do his smooth and sinister work as presiding judge during the Shakhty trial and as public prosecutor in the more famous purge trials of the mid-thirties. My personal acquaintance with Trotsky has been confined to two meetings, one of which I have told in Chapter II. But for a great many years I had protracted official dealings with the other three Soviet foreign commissars, Chicherin, Litvinov, and Molotov. Of these, the first was on all counts the most colorful personality.

Born in 1872, hence two years younger than Lenin, Georgi Vasilyevich Chicherin was of Italian origin. His ancestors, originally named Ciceroni or Cicerini, emigrated to Russia centuries ago and, with the passing of time, married into the old established noble families.

[3] *The Process of Revolution* (New York, Harper & Brothers, 1938), pp. 139–141.

Thus, Chicherin's mother was born a Baroness Meyendorff, whereas his grandmother came from the house of Naryshkin, that old Boyar family which had produced the wife of Tsar Alexei, the second of the Romanov dynasty. Chicherin's father, Vasily, was an official in the Imperial Russian Ministry of Foreign Affairs, but played no role in the public life of tsarist Russia. His uncle, Boris, however, held a chair of Public Law at Moscow University and was a well known and well respected personality, richly blessed with earthly goods. Representing moderately liberal views, he fought for liberal reforms but opposed Socialism in his writings. He has made valuable contributions to Russian historiography. During the eighties of the last century, his estate, Karaul, situated in Kaluga Province, was one of the centers of Russian intellectual life, and famous for its magnificent Russian hospitality. Although young Georgi spent a good deal of his earliest youth in this environment, he later fell under the influence of radical circles and never severed his connections with them. True, in order to please his father, he entered into the Foreign Ministry after finishing his university studies, and served for a while in its archives; but in 1904 he was forced to flee to Germany in order to escape arrest by the tsarist secret police, who had become interested in his revolutionary connections. Abroad, he joined the Socialist movement. Breaking all relations with his family, he simultaneously renounced all of his very considerable inheritance claims, which would have given him possession, among other things, of his uncle's beautiful estate.

Lenin had recognized at an early time the benefits which Bolshevik foreign policy could gain by making use of this young idealist who could offer wide knowledge of history and world affairs, an inexhaustible memory, and a safe mastery of several European languages. And so, when Trotsky turned his back on foreign policy after the Treaty of Brest-Litovsk, Chicherin was made *Narkomindel* (Foreign Commissar) of the RSFSR, after he had entered the Bolshevik party.

The abilities that raised him far above the average of his environment were matched by some peculiarities of character which made life difficult for himself as well as for his subordinates. Among them was, particularly, a strange inability to differentiate between important and unimportant things. Little details of daily life very often played the same role for him as the vast problems of Soviet

foreign policy which he faced. A discerning collaborator of his, in a confidential conversation with me, once compared his brain with a photographic plate which indiscriminately takes all images offering themselves after or beside another. Consequently, Chicherin wore out his nerves on petty details and wasted his time by addressing envelopes or running about delivering handwritten notes. Deep in the early hours, when he used to do most of his work, you could have seen the people's commissar flitting back and forth across the corridors and stairways of the Foreign Commissariat, acting as his own messenger boy.

Chicherin showed genuine personal concern for those around him; and without the slightest hesitation he shared all the material needs and deprivations of those difficult times with his subordinates. This caused him to be very well liked among those who worked under him. At the same time he was at times so thoughtless and removed from realities that he could actually go so far as to phone a man at three o'clock in the morning and order him back to his office merely to ask him a question. The man may have trudged home several miles through the nastiest Moscow weather after a hard day's work until midnight; and yet it often happened that Chicherin had forgotten his question by the time the official, utterly exhausted, stood before him.

He was a very sick man, and his several ailments often kept him from his work for long periods, during which Maxim Litvinov, his first deputy, would act as foreign commissar. Ill health and the long years of exile and semistarvation had aged him far beyond his years. Altogether, he impressed the observer as a queer old man who was utterly helpless toward his immediate surroundings. Yet this little man was able to represent the interests of his country at international conferences with so much personal dignity, with such remarkable resourcefulness, brilliant repartee, and inner conviction, that even his opponents could not fail to give him their respect. Knowing these merits of his, valuing his acute political mind and the devastating dialectics of his diplomatic notes, Lenin indulgently overlooked his human frailties. Stalin may have had little understanding of Chicherin's intellectual world, but he appears to have valued his service. In any event, few if any commissars in the Soviet cabinet have served as long as he without interruption. It was only after the beginning of the first Five-Year Plan, when the Stalin regime, pre-

occupied with domestic problems, virtually abandoned foreign policy, screening its isolationism behind loudly proclaimed expectations of world revolution and intensified Comintern activities, that Chicherin ceased to be useful to the regime; the old man himself probably witnessed Stalin's "revolution from above" with despair and bewilderment. In the summer of 1929, while he was nursing his health in Wiesbaden, he was suddenly alarmed by rumors about machinations against him in Moscow. In open panic he determined not to return, and since he did not apparently mind talking about his decision it became somewhat of an open secret. The Kremlin physician, Dr. Levin, was dispatched to Germany to dissuade the foreign commissar from deserting his post; and when the doctor remained unsuccessful Karakhan himself undertook to bring him back. Shortly afterward, in the fall of 1929, Chicherin tendered his resignation, and in early 1930 he yielded his post to Litvinov. Since he was also not re-elected to the Central Committee of the Communist party, he was thus completely eliminated from the public affairs of the Soviet Union. He spent the last two years of his life in a modest Moscow flat, a sick and disillusioned man, seeking solace in Rhine wine and Beethoven.

The formal organizational structure of the Soviet governmental apparatus in the first years was founded on the principle of "collective responsibility." This meant that not a single individual was responsible for the activities of a ministry but a *kollegia* (board), the members of which were appointed by the Central Executive Committee (TsIK), the supreme organ in the Soviet pyramid. Thus the NKID (People's Commissariat for Foreign Affairs) was under the direction of the people's commissar, Chicherin, his two assistants, and two or three additional persons who were members of equal standing in the *kollegia*. In this board the people's commissar counted as no more than the *primus inter pares,* who had to comply with the decisions of the majority. Informally, his position in the party and the support he received from Lenin decided the extent to which the people's commissar could maintain his own views in the decision-making process of the *kollegia*.

Chicherin's position was made difficult by several circumstances. In the first place, he did not belong to the influential group of "Old Bolsheviks" who formed the ruling nucleus of the party; a Menshevik since 1905, he had joined Lenin's Communists only after

the October Revolution, in 1918. Seven years later the Fourteenth Party Congress elected him a member of the party's all-powerful Central Committee. Yet this high rank, the result of his able service plus the momentary political constellation of 1925, did not give him lasting influence over party policies. This was not so much because of Chicherin's personal career; rather it reflected the precarious position of the Foreign Commissariat within Soviet politics and the contradictory nature of Soviet foreign policy as a whole. To put it with exaggerated bluntness: The very pursuit of foreign relations, and the very existence of a Foreign Commissariat headed by a right-wing fellow traveler in the Communist party, were concessions grudgingly made by revolutionary Communism only under severe duress; and for many years the Soviet system as a whole struggled with great difficulty to absorb this alien body into its organism. The reason for this will become clear if we inquire into the motives behind Soviet Russia's dealings with the outside world.

Soviet foreign policy has always rested on two basic motivations: the extension of the proletarian revolution to other important countries, and the preservation and strengthening of the Soviet state. Only the second of these aims leads directly to the formulation of a foreign policy, that is, an attempt to regulate the relationship between the Soviet state and other states. The revolutionary ambitions of the Kremlin in themselves are rather a denial of all efforts to make foreign policy. Hence in the first months, when the revolutionary policies of Moscow were not only overriding all other considerations but were also thought to be immediately feasible and on the current agenda, the Bolshevik regime had no foreign policy proper; instead, its first international acts were exclusively designed to further the spread of revolution in Europe and Asia. Theoretically, such a fundamentally negative attitude to foreign policy as such is still the basic motive of Communist action; the party program of 1919 is based on the premise that "the era of world-wide proletarian Communist revolution has begun," and this program has never been abolished. But even before Bukharin wrote the first draft of the program, the Central Committee of the party had been compelled to think about the possibility that the spread of the revolution might be delayed. From the long-range point of view of historical materialism, this delay might not be a cause for concern; time is of no essence for anyone who approaches the broad stream of historical developments as

a contemplative observer. But for the party that had just won power in Russia, the timing of the world revolution was a matter of life and death. If in the boundless optimism that accompanied their accession to power the leaders were slow to realize this, it was dramatically driven home to them by the German offensive early in 1918, which rapidly knifed through the weakened and war-weary Russian front. Riga fell. Petrograd was threatened. And by thus raising the possibility that the capital and vital parts of the country would fall to the Germans, the offensive was a direct threat to the existence of the revolutionary regime of Lenin and his party.

This grave situation confronted the Communist party of Russia with an insoluble dilemma. If the new Socialist republic was to remain true to its internationalist traditions and Socialist ideals, the German offensive could be regarded only as an occasion for Communist propaganda and revolutionary resistance. The heroic struggle of the "Communards" of the October Revolution would either arouse the indignation of the proletariat in all the countries at war, or it would go into the annals of revolutionary history as a mighty, heroic example. Of course, none of the Communist leaders who advocated the proclamation of revolutionary war (and they were by far in the majority within the Central Committee) faced the prospect of heroic defeat lightheartedly. The Bolshevik fights not to lose but to win. Yet, weak as the Soviet-Russian state might be against the armies of Wilhelm II, the advocates of revolutionary war saw no alternative, for any other course of action would have necessitated compromises with proletarian orthodoxy. Specifically, a shameful peace would have to be concluded by the Socialist state with Imperial Germany.

This peace was actually concluded on March 3, 1918, at Brest-Litovsk, after the German armies had resumed their offensive and the Allies had remained silent to Russian requests for help. Lenin, almost alone against the great majority of his comrades, had pointed out to them that, in a bourgeois world, any act would in effect favor one or the other of the imperialist antagonists; hence attempts to preserve the proletarian purity of the party's actions were unrealistic and in effect threatened all the gains the revolution had made so far. In effect, Lenin argued that the most important achievement of the revolution so far was the Soviet state; hence to preserve and strengthen that state would be the most consistently revolutionary

course of action. The Manifesto of the Second Comintern Congress stated this very sharply by declaring that "the Communist International [that is, the self-styled representatives of the revolutionary world proletariat] has declared the cause of Soviet Russia to be its own cause." [4] With this, however, a Soviet *raison d'état* was born and a Soviet foreign policy began to be developed.

Trotsky, who had been opposed to the conclusion of a peace with Germany, resigned from his post as foreign commissar to become the top organizer and strategist of the Civil War; his former portfolio was taken over by a man who, although a veteran Marxist, tended much more to think in terms of old-style Russian foreign policy. It was quite fitting that Georgi V. Chicherin had served, however briefly, in the tsarist Foreign Office. On Lenin's suggestion, and against sharp opposition from the left-wing idealists who had drafted the party program, a passage was incorporated in its economic section which stated that it had now become "essential to look after the extension of economic collaboration and political connections with other nations. . . ." [5]

The sharpness of the turn must not be overstressed. True enough, in its desire to strengthen the Communist state the Kremlin was resolved to make a pact with any nation from among the imperialists. Yet another important method of Soviet foreign policy was still to invest, as it were, in proletarian revolution and other social unrest abroad, to support foreign movements of revolt, and to run the Communist International in which foreign Communist parties were organized. In this sense the world-revolutionary goals of Communism were incorporated into the new *raison d'état* of Bolshevik Russia. What a difference there is, however, between world-revolutionary activities which are part of a national policy and world-revolutionary activities which are the main end in themselves, utilizing foreign policy only as a means! Here is the root of the great difficulty that faces anyone who wants to have a real understanding of the motives of Soviet behavior.

It would be rash to assert that the revolutionary goal has definitely been transformed into an instrument subordinated to the Soviet

4 *Vtoroi kongress kommunisticheskogo internatsionala, stenografcheskii otchët* (Petrograd, 1921), p. 647.

5 Em. Yaroslavskii, ed., *Vos'moi s'ezd RKP(b), 18–23 Marta 1919 g.* Institut Marksa-Engel'sa-Lenina pri TsK VKP(b) (Partizdat, Moscow, 1933), p. 392.

raison d'état. The first steps toward the development of a foreign policy, taken at Brest-Litovsk, were meant to be no more than a temporary expedient designed to secure a breathing space during which the headquarters of the revolution could carry on while the world proletariat prepared to come to its aid. This theory of the "breathing space" (*peredyshka*) was an opportunistic resolve to adjust policy to momentary circumstances. This type of concept does not provide the rulers with a policy, but with a justification; instead of prescribing any specific course of action it merely justifies *not* doing certain things, that is, not pursuing an active and unbending world-revolutionary policy. The net effect was that the Kremlin developed two lines of policy that had little to do with each other in aim and execution. When Lenin told the Eleventh Party Congress on March 27, 1922, that "we are going to Genoa not as Communists but as traders," [6] the implication was that a sharp line could be drawn between the two courses of action, and that the trading hand of the Kremlin need not know what the revolutionary hand was doing.

As the revolutionary storm unleashed by the war began to abate, the concept of the "breathing space" turned into that of the "transitional period." Karl Radek roundly asserted that the situation had been changed completely. The world revolution would not come as a sudden explosion, but would take the form of corrosion, that is, a long process; "and because it will be a long process with which we have to reckon, Soviet Russia will not be spared the problem of seeking and finding a *modus vivendi* with the states that are still capitalistic." [7] Some months earlier Lenin had stated the same thing in much more positive terms; he proudly claimed that "we have won ourselves conditions under which we may exist side by side with capitalist states who are now forced to enter into trade relations with us . . . we have won ourselves the right to an independent existence. Thus . . . we see that we have . . . not only a breathing space but something much more substantial . . . we have a phase when our basic international existence has been fought for and attained within the framework of capitalist states." [8] From this to

---

[6] V. I. Lenin, *Sochineniya,* 2nd ed., XXVII, 226.

[7] Karl Radek, *Die auswärtige Politik Sowjet-Russlands,* Bibliothek der Kommunistischen Internationale (Hamburg, 1921), pp. 37–38.

[8] Lenin, *op. cit.,* XXV, 401.

Stalin's demand to build Socialism in Russia alone is only one step.

But even when Stalin, sensing that the stability and prosperity of the mid-twenties would last for a number of years in the capitalist world, proclaimed the feasibility and necessity of building Socialism in a single country, the world-revolutionary goals of the Soviet regime were by no means forgotten. Even if some of the Bolshevik leaders were ready to devote all their efforts to the strengthening of their domestic regime, the cause of continued world revolution was squarely represented in the Comintern as well as in the Russian Communist party; and the Soviet *raison d'état* had to be on the defensive much of the time. Thus, at the Fourth Congress of the Third International Bukharin had to assure the foreign comrades that it was perfectly proper for a proletarian state to form alliances with capitalist governments or accept loans from them, and he exhorted the foreign parties to be loyal to such alliances and to support them.[9] Such assurances and exhortations had to be repeated again and again.

Eight years after the proclamation of the NEP, eleven years after Brest-Litovsk, the world depression once again provided fertile ground for revolutionary discontent, and the left-wing internationalists within the Communist movement were heartened by a new intensification of the Comintern's revolutionary activities. A new revolutionary situation seemed to be in the making. Yet it is interesting to compare Stalin's reaction to this new rise of the tide with Lenin's customary reaction. At the peak of world prosperity, on December 5, 1927, Stalin spoke before the Fifteenth Party Congress. We live, he said, on the eve of a new revolutionary period. Imperialism is rotten to the core; but, in its agony, it is preparing desperate moves. A new anti-Bolshevik crusade is being planned. How should the party meet this threat? Stalin's proposed policy is remarkable: The task, he said, is to postpone and avoid war. Soviet Russia should pay ransom to the capitalist world and try to maintain peaceful relations with it. The slogan should be, *"Do ut des";* I shall make concessions if you make concessions.

Before Brest-Litovsk, if not afterward as well, Lenin would have drawn the entirely opposite conclusion from Stalin's first sentence. A new revolutionary tide is rising? A crisis is ripening? How wonderful! The party's task will be to further this development and speed

---

[9] *IV. Vsemirnyi Kongress Kommunisticheskogo Internatsionala, Izbrannye Doklady, Rechi i Rezoliutsii* (Moscow-Petrograd, 1923), pp. 195–196.

it up, to deepen the crisis and sharpen the class war so as to bring it to a revolutionary clash.

Now we see how much the strategy of world Communism was being subordinated to the national policy of the Soviet state.

Official Soviet ideology has never admitted the existence of such a problem and denies that ideals be subordinated to power politics or intraparty machinations. For that purpose it must proclaim the absolute identity of the interests of the world proletariat with the aims of the Soviet government and the activities of the Russian Communist party. But this is at best a highly doubtful proposition. In the past, at least, these two interests have often been in conflict, and only now, as Soviet Russia has grown to the strength of a real world power, and revolution is spread on the bayonets of the Red Army, world revolution and Soviet security considerations appear to merge. But in the past the world-revolutionary activity of the Comintern and the foreign policy of the Soviet state have handicapped and frustrated each other. Moscow's lead in the Communist International and Moscow's endeavors to co-ordinate Comintern policy with purely Russian policy have utterly wrecked a number of good chances for successful revolution and have in other ways damaged non-Russian Communist movements. Conversely, Moscow's association with the Comintern has often been a source of serious embarrassment and a dangerous obstacle to the Soviet state. Marxian Socialist though he was, Chicherin often felt the Communist ideological heritage to be a very undesirable impediment to the free pursuit of Soviet foreign policy. A colleague of mine once asked him (in December, 1925) why the Soviet Union would not consider entering the League of Nations. Chicherin's reply was: "If we were in the League, we should have to take a stand on every question that comes up; as it is, we have a free hand to act as we see fit. Moreover, in the League we should have to play the same role as the KPD does in your Reichstag; but we have not the slightest intention of playing that role." In short, Chicherin was aware that the world expected Communists to behave like Communists, and the world should not be let down; hence his desire to avoid all situations in which it would be necessary to behave according to this pattern.

Little incidents sometimes illustrate the relationship between Communist ideals and the Soviet *raison d'état* more strikingly than large political developments. In 1923 the Third International was

running sailors' homes in Odessa, Murmansk, and other ports, and its agents successfully persuaded a number of foreign sailors to jump ship and stay in the homeland of all proletarians. But the GPU would regularly deport the sailors as suspicious foreigners who had entered the country illegally; it was far more concerned with the task of national domestic security than with the problem of recruiting new members for the cause of world Communism.

The foreign Communist and the internationalist dissenter within the Russian party who felt his ideals betrayed by a selfish Soviet national policy or by personality clashes within the Russian party hierarchy naturally stressed the evils of Moscow's influence over the revolutionary cause. As early as 1924 a then prominent German Communist, Karl Korsch, dared to shout the epithet "Soviet imperialism" before the assembled Fifth Comintern Congress in Moscow. Karl Korsch, Ruth Fischer, Leon Trotsky, Ignazio Silone, Tito, and similar heretics are, or have been, divided by many important issues; but the complaint they all make, or have made, is that the Communist International and the Communist movements all over the world have become tools of Soviet national policy and the Russian Communist party.

It was equally natural, however, that my diplomatic colleagues and I, who were trying to conduct diplomatic business with the Soviet state, were perturbed over the affiliation of Moscow with the Comintern for the exactly opposite reason. We did not mind if considerations of narrow national interest wrecked movements of proletarian revolt in Germany, England, China, or anywhere else; we worried, instead, over the lingering influence of world Communism on Soviet foreign policy. Count Rantzau, in particular, fretted constantly over the influence of the Comintern, which, he said, burdened the structure of German-Soviet relations like an excessive mortgage, and he was among those who constantly urged the Soviet foreign commissar to clarify the precise influence of the Comintern over the Soviet state. Under this insistent prodding, Chicherin from the very beginning made a strenuous effort to dissociate Soviet foreign policy from revolutionary Communism, and the Soviet state in general from the Communist party, at least in the eyes of foreign diplomats. And the acceptance of this myth became one of the conditions of maintaining tenable relations with the Soviet state. As a *Pravda* editorial of March 18, 1930, put it, "If the German government . . . wants to

allege the 'identity of the Comintern with the Soviet government,' such a step would not be interpreted otherwise than as Germany's stepping into a position of open hostility against the USSR and as a resolve to join the anti-Soviet campaign which has no scruples against any sort of reactionary inventions for the purpose of creating a moral atmosphere for military intervention."

This myth was an all too transparent device to save the face not only of the Foreign Commissariat but also of the foreign governments dealing with Moscow. Great as was the insistence with which Moscow asserted it, it was swallowed only with the greatest difficulty. When Chicherin said at a Soviet Congress in Tiflis, in March, 1925, "We are forced to declare once more before the German government that our government is not responsible for the activities of the Comintern and has nothing at all to do with it" (*i ne imeet s nim nichego obshchego*), his audience responded with resounding guffaws, much to the blushing commissar's confusion. Foreign Communists in particular had great difficulty keeping the myth in mind, since they were also told to regard Soviet Russia as the fatherland of the world's proletariat. When Chicherin was in Berlin during November and December of 1925, he was extremely embarrassed when a delegation of about a hundred German workers made a pilgrimage to the Soviet Embassy to greet him. Upon their insistent demand for a speech, Chicherin gave them a lecture about the "Leninist principle" of non-interference by Soviet Russia in the domestic affairs of other states. Immediately after he had dismissed his unwelcome visitors, he rushed to the German Foreign Ministry to report about the incident, apologized for it, and made sure the press would not report it. In May of the previous year a German Communist, fleeing from the custody of two policemen, sought refuge in the premises of the Soviet Trade Delegation in Berlin, a rash action which led to a sharp conflict between Berlin and Moscow when two hours later German police made a thorough search of the Soviet offices. The point is that ever since then Communist writers have denounced their hapless German comrade, Bozenhardt, as a "provocator" out to make trouble for the Soviet Union. There is not the slightest reason to believe this explanation; but in the eyes of Moscow it was unpardonable for a foreign Communist to involve an official Soviet agency in the affairs of his local party.

To conduct foreign policy with this millstone around his neck re-

quired heroic efforts on the part of the ailing Chicherin, and only a man with his fanatical, self-immolating devotion to his job could have carried on for almost twelve years, as he did. Moreover, he had enemies in influential places; as a matter of fact, one of his bitterest antagonists, with whom he led a running battle of minds and influence, was his first deputy commissar, Maxim M. Litvinov. It is possible that the antagonism between the latter and Chicherin dated back from the early days of their exile in England, where both of them spent a good portion of the years before the Revolution of 1917. They could not have helped knowing each other then, and it is unlikely that there was any sympathy or agreement between the cultured, sensitive Menshevik and the ruthless, intriguing, and coldly rational Bolshevik who was to become his deputy. Moreover, on one issue they must have clashed head on: At the Sixth Congress of the Russian Social Democratic Labor Party, held at Stockholm in 1906 by Menshevik and Bolshevik factions together, Chicherin was elected chairman of an *ad hoc* commission to inquire into the highway robberies through which Lenin's Bolsheviks had begun to fill their party treasury. It so happened that Litvinov was deeply involved in these high-jacking ventures, and it would be astonishing if no personal resentment against Chicherin had remained from the inquiry. It is well known how important petty personal antagonisms are to the lonely circles of fanatical exiles, and how long the memory of past rivalries lingers in their minds.

Altogether, the antagonism between Chicherin and his first assistant was based both on personality differences and on conflicts over policy. The clash of personalities resulted in part from the profound difference in the two men's origins. Without being fully aware of it himself, Chicherin, the product of high social circles of Old Russia, had retained certain prejudices and inclinations for which Litvinov could not have the slightest understanding. Even within the circle of his Bolshevik comrades, Chicherin could not forget the manners and mores of noble society. Once, at a dinner given him by a fellow Bolshevik, he could not understand why his host asked, "And what kind of wine would you like with your meal, Comrade People's Commissar?" "Just as it should properly be," he answered. "First the white, and then the red wine." He was a very emotional man, whose views and thoughts were strongly influenced by feelings. And he was extremely touchy. Litvinov's quiet assurance and determina-

tion constantly irritated him, and he once complained about him in the Kremlin with the characteristic words: "My assistant is utterly unbearable. He treats me as Xanthippe treated Socrates." Yet Litvinov probably was not deliberately rude to him; it was only that he was a sober, rational thinker who would not allow sympathies or antipathies to influence him. His policy, his attitude to people and things, were to be determined only by considerations of expedience.

Litvinov had no friends. There was one member of the *kollegia* of the Foreign Commissariat with whom I had established a relationship of mutual confidence. I asked him once how he got along with Litvinov, and received the significant answer, "You don't *get along* with Litvinov; you only work with him—if you have no other choice!"

The sharp difference in their daily routine further contributed to make collaboration between them difficult and steadily cooled their relationship. Chicherin worked through the nights, and often he could not be reached in the daytime. He was a poor administrator and spent himself on minutiae. Mountains of dusty files were heaped on desks and tables in his office, so that at times he was hard put to find a spot where he could scribble a note to one of his subordinates or draft an important diplomatic communication. In contrast, Litvinov would receive his visitors behind an empty desk which attested to his systematic method. He would not bother with details; he did not waste any time, and he was very skillful in distributing the burden of work among his collaborators.

The fact that, in addition, the two men did not see eye to eye in questions of long-range policy led to an unhealthy rivalry and caused the prestige of the Foreign Commissariat to go down considerably, since it had to turn to higher authorities for a decision even in unimportant matters over which Chicherin and Litvinov could not come to an agreement.

For Chicherin, Rapallo was one of the main pillars of Soviet foreign policy. The nocturnal discussions with Rantzau about the meaning and aims of Rapallo were, for him, a spiritual need, and the concept of *Schicksalsgemeinschaft* was no empty phrase for him. In Litvinov's eyes, however, Rapallo was a political expedient just as any other measure was. He defended it with his mind, not with his heart. He was by no means blind to the benefits which Rapallo had brought to the Soviet Union; hence he fought consistently to maintain this relationship and carry it further, but only to the extent in which the policy

of Rapallo fitted in the far broader framework of Soviet foreign policy as a whole.

He had scant understanding of the burning interest with which Chicherin dealt with the political problems of the Near and Far East. His political attention was centered on the West, which he knew from the long years of his exile, and with whose problems he was familiar. And so, while Chicherin argued that in China the Kremlin's policy ought to be to further and deepen the revolution, Litvinov advocated caution and argued that the Soviet government should play the Chinese trump only for the purpose of putting pressure on England with the aim of reaching an understanding with her. I was told that in a conference on this problem Chicherin with great agitation accused Litvinov of wanting to sell China down the river, whereupon Litvinov coolly and contemptuously replied with an obscene remark to the effect that it would be better to sell China than to miss the bus on concrete political opportunities.[10]

In many respects it was easier and more profitable to deal with Litvinov than with his chief. The latter was not only a funny and irritable old man; he was also extremely unsure of himself and his superiors. Hence he was extremely hesitant to make even minor decisions and unimportant concessions, whereas his assistant readily undertook responsibilities with the air of self-assurance and even showed a certain largesse in many controversial questions. He was always extremely factual and to the point, and he combined a quick grasp of essentials with the ability of getting much work done.

He gave repeated signs of great personal courage. Thus, during a stay in Lausanne in 1932, he received a delegation of European Socialists who pointed out the dangers of letting the Nazis in Germany grow strong, and who tried to convince him of the need for common action of all states against Germany. Litvinov replied that he was by no means in agreement with his government's attitude toward National Socialism, but that he was in no position to exert his influence in the suggested direction. Today it would be unthinkable for a Soviet diplomat to say that he did not agree with the policies of his government. The same thing applies to a remark he dropped in Paris in 1937, when he was asked about the meaning of the great

---

10 His remark is untranslatable also because it is a play on words: *"Luchshe segodnia prodat' chem zavtra prosrat'."*

Georgi V. Chicherin

Karl Radek

purges that were then under way in Moscow, the wholesale shooting of marshals and generals, and the public trials of the Bolshevik old guard. Litvinov shrugged his shoulders and said that he too could not understand everything his government was doing.

Another example of his typical frankness is a conversation he had with Léon Blum in September, 1938, immediately before the Munich Conference. Blum asked him whether France could expect Soviet Russia to come to her assistance in case the Czech crisis led to a conflict with Germany. According to a very reliable source, Litvinov is said to have replied, "If I remain Foreign Commissar, yes; otherwise, no." In the light of all these examples I am quite prepared to believe the recent report of the American correspondent Richard C. Hottelet about an interview Litvinov supposedly gave him in the summer of 1946. I should not be surprised if Litvinov was somewhat more cautious in formulating his views on the intentions of the Soviet government and on the inevitability of a conflict between the Communist and capitalist worlds; but even then the interview would furnish a valuable addition to our knowledge of Litvinov as a man and as a statesman.

In view of all these qualities, the Moscow diplomatic corps was disposed to overlook Litvinov's negative character traits, the seamy aspects of his personal style of life, and his family problems, even though most of us sympathized thoroughly with Mrs. Litvinov, an intelligent and unproblematic woman whom everyone seemed to like. Ivy Low was born in England. Her uncle, Sir Sidney Low, was a well known expert in international law whose books had been translated even into Russian before the revolution. The carefree frankness with which Mrs. Litvinov used to talk to members of the diplomatic corps was also quite exceptional in Moscow. Perhaps this was one of the reasons why she was given the advice, in the thirties, to move to Sverdlovsk for a while and teach English there. But not even this experience prevented Mrs. Litvinov, after her return, from describing life in a Soviet provincial town to me in such blunt terms that I worried considerably about her personal safety.

The Litvinovs had two children, whom I watched grow up in the thirties. The boy in particular showed signs of great intelligence. Once I played a game of chess with his father and was beaten in a very short time. But when I complimented him for his skill, the

proud father pointed out that his boy was a far better chess player than he.

With all their differences of background, personality, and policy orientation, Litvinov, Chicherin, and most of their collaborators in the Foreign Commissariat belonged to the same type of Bolshevik intellectual who had spent years of exile in Europe. On the average these men and women were well educated, highly cultured and sensitive people; many of them were Jews, and a few came from the highest strata of the old society. One of the latter was Radek's beautiful and enchanting mistress, Larissa Reissner, whose premature death was felt as a most cruel blow of fate by this satyr-like man. As a rule, these people possessed initiative, imagination, cleverness, and negotiating skill. Many of them had mastered several foreign languages and had learned to adapt themselves to the Western mentality. Thus they were invaluable as diplomats and trade representatives, and contact with them was a rewarding experience, even though the non-Communist could never overcome the feeling that, fundamentally, these Marxist intellectuals looked down with a certain condescending pity on us poor blundering representatives of the doomed bourgeois class.

In the earliest years of my stay in Moscow, the material misery of the country was so great that not even the members of the government nor I myself could escape its effects. This precluded any form of social life. How could I, for instance, have given a party of any sort as long as I lived in just one very modest room? Yet there was ample opportunity for me to learn about people and affairs in Moscow. The Cheka did not yet consider every foreigner as a dangerous spy. Nor was it considered to be an act of treason if Soviet officials who could manage to get away from their duties entered into an exchange of ideas with foreigners. Scientists and professors were not in danger of arrest when they tried to re-establish contacts with the outside world after the many years of isolation through war and revolution. The entrance to the Kremlin was not yet so hermetically sealed as it is today, so that officials like Radek, Bukharin, and many others felt free to invite foreigners. This changed, however, as early as the mid twenties, when the protocol office of the Foreign Commissariat, and through it the GPU, increasingly regulated the contact of Soviet officials with foreigners. Thus we had, on certain occasions to deal with obvious agents of the secret police, if we wanted to maintain informal out-of-channel contacts with otherwise inaccessible Soviet officials.

3. *A YEAR OF CRISIS*

We of the German Embassy often tried to impress on our colleagues in Berlin the comparative insignificance of the Foreign Commissariat. Much to Chicherin's acute discomfort, he was often reduced to the rule of spokesman and whipping boy for the Central Committee or even the GPU. His Commissariat fulfilled the role of public relations office and complaint department where foreign governments could turn to seek redress against the Kremlin's offensive actions. It would have liked to engage in ambitious and clever world politics, but was reduced to be the voice which announced and defended, but seldom made, foreign policy. The real decisions were made by the Central Committee of the Communist party, or by the Politburo. Only at this level could attempts be made to co-ordinate Soviet policy as a whole and let a unified line emerge from party feuds, international considerations, domestic issues, and world-revolutionary aspirations.

This struggle between the major forces in Soviet society, and the way in which it robbed the NKID of policy-making functions, became very obvious to us in 1923, perhaps the most exciting and critical period in German-Soviet relations. This was the last year of the postwar aftermath, the period when the shooting had ended and the peace treaties were signed, but the war was still being fought with great bitterness on the political front, with the problem of reparations as the outstanding issue between Germany and France. Equally, the Russian Revolution was still causing some of its initial chain reactions, though we can say in retrospect that the tide of proletarian revolution was gradually receding after 1918. Europe, in this period, was paying heavily for the war, and violent class struggles raged to decide how the burden of sacrifice was to be distributed. A state of near war continued in Central Europe and elsewhere, even after the peace treaties had been signed, and a state of near revolution or near civil war prevailed within a number of countries. This situation reached the breaking point in January of 1923, when French and Belgian troops occupied the vital Ruhr basin, heart of industrial Germany, and isolated it from the rest of the country. The difficulties, hardships, and humiliations that fell on the shoulders of the nation brought the economic and political crisis in Germany to

a fever pitch. It looked as if the war might break out anew, this time to deliver a death blow to the German Republic; and for the first time since the spring of 1921 the Kremlin appeared to believe in the real possibility of a Bolshevik revolution in Germany.

Moscow's relations to Germany had been characterized by the Rapallo Treaty, an agreement made with a bourgeois government, and directed against the victor powers, on the assumption that, as Chicherin once put it, Soviet Russia could maintain friendly relations much more easily with oppressed nations than with the victors. "The government of the oppressed class"—he had said—"has, of course, far fewer quarrels with the governments of oppressed nations. And it is only natural that we should want to have good-neighborly relations with a state that wishes neither to subject nor to exploit Soviet Russia." But, until the end of 1923, Germany was equally the center of hope and focus of interest for the Communist International and its revolutionary aspirations. The greatest expectations of the Russian Communists for a supporting revolution had been concentrated there. By the time of the Ruhr occupation, these expectations had, it is true, been severely disappointed; but they had not yet been killed. The revolution of November, 1918, had not wrought any substantial changes in the class structure of Germany, and the short-lived Bavarian Soviet Republic had proved to be a pitiful adventure. Somehow, the German proletariat had not come up to the traditional expectations the Communists had of it. Lenin's frame of ideas prevented him, however, from acknowledging the disappointing fact squarely. Instead of blaming the German proletariat as a class for being disinclined toward revolution, the Russian Communists blamed its leadership, the Social Democratic party. They could do so more easily since the two outstanding revolutionary leaders in Germany, Karl Liebknecht and Rosa Luxemburg, had been murdered after the abortive Spartacus uprising of January, 1919. In a political sense Lenin and his friends were quite right if they attributed the failure of Communism in Germany to the Social Democrats. For, from the very beginning of the disintegration of the Kaiser's regime, the Socialists had shirked no means to combat the danger from the Left; if Communism was defeated in Germany, this was largely to the credit of Ebert, Noske, Scheidemann, and the other right-wing Socialist leaders. Of course, these men did not fail to meet stiff resistance against their *ad hoc* alliances with the old ruling classes;

and for a while Moscow sought vigorously to exploit the resistance on the part of large sections of the working class. In the summer of 1920 the Independent Socialist party was invited to participate at the Second Comintern Congress, and four of its chiefs appeared in Moscow, giving me a chance to meet them. During their stay I tried my best to acquaint them with the real situation in Russia as I saw it and to enlighten them about the waning popularity of the Communist regime even among the Russian working population. Together with Dittmann, Crispien, Däumig, and Koenen, I took a trip to the town of Kolomna, eighty miles southeast of Moscow, to visit a large machine works, where the shortcomings of the Bolshevik experiment in the field of industry could be visibly demonstrated. I found the first two men predisposed to share my views, but failed to convince the others. (Koenen later joined the German Communist party and is today a member of the SED [Socialist Unity Party].) Later that year, at its Halle Congress, the Independent Socialist party split; the left wing joined the Comintern, and the right wing gradually found its way back into the Social-Democratic party. The Comintern had sent its eloquent head, Zinovyev, to the congress to ply his art of persuasion. One of his chief antagonists at Halle turned out to be Dittmann, who threw the experiences and observations he had gathered in Moscow into the scales and thus prevented some of the Independents from merging with the Communists. In connection with his performance at Halle, Zinovyev, together with Lozovsky, was expelled from Germany. (He had entered with Berlin's express approval, granted on the theory that it might be best to let the Russians have their say. Apparently the German authorities changed their mind after witnessing his dazzling performance on the speaker's platform.) Shortly afterward I heard and watched him deliver a four-hour speech about his experiences, in which he angrily denounced Dittman and his ilk as traitors to the cause of the German and international proletariat.

Zinovyev was one of the most brilliant speakers the party had in Russia. His passionate delivery, his vivid descriptions, and his dazzling oratory not only caught the momentary attention of his audience but gripped them for hours on end. The heart and faith of the masses were not with him, however, because basically he was no more than an ambitious and selfish demagogue. Nor were the people slow in finding out that his style of life was anything but proletarian. Zinovyev's bearing could at times be actually provocative. I remember,

for example, an incident in the summer of 1921 when the departure of a train in which I was going from Petrograd to Moscow was delayed two hours at the order of Zinovyev just because the schedule was inconvenient for him, and two coaches crammed full with passengers were disconnected because Zinovyev insisted that his heavy parlor car be attached to the train. He obviously did not mind the fact that, after we arrived in Moscow, his car blocked the rails for a considerable time because he had not finished his morning toilet and showed no intention of getting out. The brash manner in which he showed himself at the open window in flashy pajamas could not be anything but extremely provocative in those years.

The Russian Communists' hatred of right-wing Socialists, and of the German Social-Democratic party in particular, is one of the most important factors that shaped the relationship between Soviet Russia and bourgeois Germany. This hatred was much deeper and bitterer than their feelings toward the bourgeoisie or the feudal reaction; that was more like a healthy, normal antagonism. Communism had foreseen and expected it as the inevitable class antagonism of the capitalist mode of production; hence it was so much taken for granted that relations that were almost cordial could arise, as between natural enemies who yet respect each other and at times conclude and keep agreements. It was much more difficult for the Communists to have any dealings with right-wing Socialists, and they felt it utterly impossible to have respect for them. The Socialists' aversion from a preoccupation with revolutionary action was seen as a deviation from the expected norm, a dirty and despicable perversion. The enmity of capitalists was "normal" and could be explained; that of the Socialists could only be condemned in moral terms. Reactionaries and bourgeois parties could be used as partners in temporary alliances, Social Democrats could only be destroyed as a political force.

This feeling was mutual; hence, even though the right-wing parties in Germany claimed to have a virtual monopoly on patriotism and anti-Communism, no political group was more consistent in its opposition to Moscow than the SPD. This opposition expressed itself not only in domestic affairs, where alliances with the Communists were almost inevitably shunned, but also in an equally strong preference for the West in foreign policy. No wonder, then, that the Kremlin worked hard to prevent the establishment of a Socialist government in Germany, an effort which was watched with satisfac-

tion by some of the embassy personnel. In retrospect it seems really remarkable that Chicherin and Litvinov could openly discuss with German diplomats the desirability of keeping the SPD out of office. Only Soviet attacks on Friedrich Ebert, who after all was the President, would elicit protests from the embassy.

If the Kremlin's attitude toward the German Socialists was negative, its appraisal of the right-wing parties was quite ambivalent. On the one hand, they preferred men like Rantzau, von Seeckt, and Hoetzsch to the Socialists because the former worked for a German alliance with Soviet Russia. But they were also representatives of the ruling classes; they did not conceal their hatred of Socialism in any form; and ultimately they had to be feared as counter-revolutionaries. For that reason the Kremlin's readiness to make a pact with the Conservatives would, every once in a while, give way to the exact opposite, an intense fear of reaction. At such times the Communists would push their profound revulsion against Social Democracy into the background and would seek an alliance with it.

For instance, the pitiful failure of the Communist uprisings that had broken out in Central Germany early in 1921 had demonstrated the weak hold the German Communist party had on the German workers and the strength of the ruling classes. Moderates within the party had used the moment of disgust and disappointment to wrest control from the radical wing; and though the Communist International loudly blamed the German Socialists for having helped the bourgeoisie and the generals back into power it proclaimed the need for a broad front of the entire proletariat against the threat from the right. For the sake of saving the republic, the Bolsheviks sought the co-operation of all working-class elements and declared themselves willing to make compromise with the right-wing Socialists. And when the latter showed tendencies, in turn, to make compromises with the bourgeois parties, the Comintern Executive Committee screamed, "German workers: Do not permit the United Front to collapse!" [11] Yet less than five months later, Karl Radek, writing in *Pravda*, on November 24, 1922, asserted that the German bourgeoisie was readying itself for a "white dictatorship," and exhorted the German workers to wage open revolutionary battle. This rapid change of tune is indicative of the dilemma Communist Russia was facing as the crisis in Germany sharpened.

[11] *Pravda*, July 9, 1922.

In Moscow we became aware of the dilemma when a Russian-language paper in Reval, *Zhizn'*, reported on September 1, 1922, that the Soviet Council of Peoples' Commissars, a week before, had debated what to do in case of a French seizure of the Ruhr, which had been expected ever since the middle of the year. Radek and Karakhan were alleged to have advanced the proposal that Soviet Russia should prepare to come to Germany's help if the Ruhr were occupied by France. The famous head of the GPU, Dzerzhinsky, and the commissar of justice, Kursky, according to the paper, had opposed the proposition on the basis of arguing that a French occupation would produce such upheavals as would unleash a Communist revolution. Moscow, they allegedly argued, should wait until the Communists were in power in Germany; only then should the Red Army cross through Lithuania and Poland and attack the French in Germany. At this point, the paper continued, Trotsky spoke up to support Radek and Karakhan; Russia could not afford to wait for a Communist revolution in Germany; instead it would be in her interest to support the existing German government. For, by threatening Germany, France constituted an immediate threat against the Soviet state. "The opinion of Trotsky and Radek prevailed," the paper concluded.

I have no way of determining to what extent this report was based on fact. Nevertheless, whether the conference took place or not, it is true that in the last months of 1922 Moscow made great efforts to assure us of its support in the event of a Ruhr occupation. Trotsky himself came to Count Rantzau on December 22nd and promised that Russia would interfere if, in the event of a Ruhr invasion, Poland should simultaneously try to occupy Silesia. After French and Belgian troops had actually moved into the Ruhr basin, the Soviet government immediately made open protests against the act, and many leading Soviet statesmen assured us of their country's support. "The main plank in our foreign-policy platform," said Chicherin to Rantzau at that time, "is to cultivate more cordial relations with Germany than with any other country." Yet there were indications that Moscow did not unequivocally take the German side in the conflict. An editorial in the official government organ *Izvestiya* of March 14, 1923, asserted that Russia was eager to establish normal relations with France. As for the events in the Ruhr, the paper took an attitude of detachment: All this, it said, was an episode in the

disintegration of capitalism going on before Soviet eyes; and it did not force Russia to take sides. More disturbing than the flirting with France was the news received from Germany that Russian Communist agents were steadily intensifying their activities there. Was the Kremlin pursuing a two-faced policy of openly supporting the bourgeois government and secretly fanning a proletarian revolution?

For our part, isolated from events in the home country, dependent on dispatches from Berlin, we were at that time fully convinced of the Janus-headed policy of the Kremlin. But it was not a simple proletarian Communist revolution that was being prepared. Instead, Moscow's emissaries were at that time planning a "national Bolshevik" uprising that was directed as much against the French occupation as against the German bourgeoisie. The plan was an ingenious attempt to link proletarian socialism with the national sentiments that had been aroused in Germany, and by the same token it sought to combine the interests of Soviet security with those of world Communism.

It seems that Moscow in the beginning regarded the Ruhr events primarily as a threat to its own security. "The Ruhr adventure," Chicherin wrote with obvious annoyance, "has administered a shock to the political and economic life of all Europe, and thus brought great harm upon the Soviet republics which require economic relations with other countries." [12]

Karl Radek was even more specific. In an article published in *Izvestiya* on August 31st under the title "Hands off Germany," he wrote: "If the capitalists of the Entente should succeed in tearing Germany in pieces and erecting their rule at the expense of the defeated working people, that would constitute the greatest danger for Soviet Russia." Indeed, the total occupation of Germany by French troops would have posed an immediate threat to Soviet Russia's Western border. That, before all, had to be prevented. As long as a right-wing bourgeois government in Berlin stood up to France, Moscow would give it its support. Only when the cabinet of Wilhelm Cuno was replaced by the Stresemann cabinet, an indication that Berlin's resistance was weakening, did the Kremlin begin looking for other ways. Some leaders seem to have pressed for preparing a proletarian revolution. But the prevailing opinion in Moscow seemed to be, during the

[12] *Ibid.*, Feb. 15, 1923.

summer months, that a Communist uprising in Germany, even if feasible, would only invite disaster because Poincaré would immediately use it as a pretext for further repressive measures against Germany. As Radek put it in a confidential chat with one of my colleagues: "In case of radical upheavals in Germany, Russia will have to expect to see French troops on the shores of the Berezina. Hence we Communists are interested in Germany's political and economic stability. Theoretically, a German Communist regime would be highly desirable, but it would at once be crushed by France. I have told my comrades in Germany," Radek concluded, "that they would commit the greatest blunder if they let themselves be beaten in case of an attack, and that they must defend their country to the last breath." And he spoke moving words about the common destiny of Germany and Russia.

But if Radek was so pessimistic about the chances of a German proletarian revolution, and given Stresemann's efforts at a conciliatory policy of "fulfillment," what could be done to keep the French out of Germany? Radek's solution was a plan to enlist the broadest sections of the German population in a national Bolshevik revolt directed simultaneously against the French invasion and the German bourgeoisie that seemed ready to come to terms with the West. He wanted to utilize not only the grievances of the proletariat but also the outraged patriotic sentiments of the farmer, the student, the small businessman, in short, of all the petty-bourgeois elements who could be aroused by slogans of nationalism. He meant to make an alliance with all the extreme right-wing enemies of the republic, that "fascist scum" against which the rank and file of the party were waging bloody guerrilla warfare. For that purpose he wanted to persuade the extreme right that Germany's national struggle of revenge against Versailles could never be waged successfully without the enthusiastic participation of the proletariat. Thus in late summer, while Chicherin, Kamenev, and Rykov were apparently still advocating that Moscow stick by the government of Stresemann, Radek held that a national Communist revolution was approaching and should be supported.[13] The facts that Count Rantzau none the less

[13] In late September the embassy received an anonymous report about a conference held by Trotsky, in which Radek, Kamenev, Rykov, Molotov, Chicherin, Dzerzhinsky, and Krasin were said to have participated. Rykov, Kamenev, and Chicherin, it said, had expressed no confidence in a German revolution and had

continued to cultivate his contacts with Radek and that my relationship with him remained undisturbed are typical of the whole nature of German-Soviet relations in those years, and of Radek's special position.

By October, 1923, many indications pointed to a change in Soviet policy. Moscow appeared now to work for an exclusively Communist revolution in Germany, abandoning its efforts at a nationalist Bolshevik front against the bourgeoisie. The secret flow of Russian emissaries to Germany intensified; Berlin was anxiously asking the embassy to keep a check on it. Particularly Radek's whereabouts were worrying the German police; as early as May they had asked us not to give him another visa.

On October 10th two German *Länder* formed left-wing coalition governments in which Social Democrats and Communists divided the cabinet posts between them. On that day the Berlin organ of the Communist party, *Rote Fahne,* printed a letter written by Stalin to one of the German Communist leaders. "Dear Comrade Thalheimer," the letter began, "the coming revolution in Germany is the most important event of our days. The victory of the revolution in Germany will have greater importance for the proletariat in Europe and America than the victory of the Russian revolution six years ago. The victory of the German proletarian will without doubt transfer the center of world revolution from Moscow to Berlin. . . ." But the Socialist governments of Saxony and Thuringia, although established in strictly constitutional ways, were crushed a few days later when President Ebert sent Army units into Central Germany to establish a temporary military government. The last isolated attempt to revive the proletarian revolution, the Hamburg uprising which began on October 22nd, was suppressed within a few days.

More than any other event, the failure of the "German October Revolution" determined the subsequent history of world Communism and the strategy of the Third International. Within the Russian Communist party it caused severe disagreements over policy and sharp personality clashes to break into the open; it was one of the immediate

pointed out the economic advantages of continuing to support the Stresemann government. Trotsky, Dzerzhinsky, and Krasin, the report alleged, had taken a middle position by supporting Radek's thesis that a revolution was imminent, but arguing that Russia could not contribute much help to the German revolution. Again I have no indication concerning the reliability of this report; but it fits a pattern that has been sketched by others.

reasons for the outbreak of the Stalin-Trotsky feud, and it gave
Stalin occasion to develop his theory of "Socialism in a single country." In Moscow's relations with Germany, it resulted in a determined
return to the Rapallo policy of friendship with the bourgeois government in Berlin. In this sense the policy of Chicherin had won a
complete victory. None the less a strain had been introduced into the
German-Soviet "common destiny." Toward the end of December
some documents published by Ruth Fischer gave a glimpse into the
extent to which Russian emissaries had participated in the attempts
at Communist revolt. Fifteen months later one of the principal
Russian organizers of the Communist military apparatus, Skoblevsky, was publicly tried before the Supreme Court in Leipzig.[14] In
addition, in December, 1923, Berlin asked the Soviet government to
recall a member of its embassy, because he had been found to be a
military agent. This man, who went under the name Petrov, was
actually a French Communist, who had very successfully wormed
himself into the confidence of high military circles in Berlin. According to police reports, he had bought weapons and ammunition
on a large scale in preparation for revolutionary barricade fighting,
paying with dollar drafts on the Soviet Embassy. Count Rantzau,
boiling with indignation, confronted Trotsky with these reports;
his rage knew no bounds when Trotsky calmly admitted that he had
personally attached Petrov to the Soviet Embassy because he had
counted on the imminence of revolution in Germany. Had not the
German cabinet itself declared that it was, perhaps, the last bourgeois government in Germany? In any event, he as a Communist had
felt it his duty to be prepared for such an eventuality. In the event
of a French occupation of all of Germany, he said, it would have
been Petrov's mission to subvert the discipline of the French troops
and to convert them to Communism. Early in the next year Petrov
was recalled from Berlin.

Chicherin obviously regarded the affair as a terrible personal embarrassment. As a matter of fact, he would have loved to eradicate the
memory of the German October days entirely from our minds, and
to remind us instead of the fact that his government had been the
first to protest against the Ruhr occupation. He would never let us
forget that Soviet-Russian declarations had prevented the Poles from
invading Germany's eastern provinces. Early in December of 1923

[14] Cf. Chapter V, pp. 140–41.

he gave a luncheon for the German ambassador at which the entire *kollegia* of the Foreign Commissariat was present, together with Krestinsky and Radek. Afterward Chicherin, Rantzau, and Radek had an intimate talk in which the ambassador led off by urging that the Soviet government openly sever its connections with the policies of the Third International. The count emphasized the danger threatening German-Soviet relations if during Germany's most trying times Russian emissaries were busy preparing world revolution. Besides, he flatly stated, the German Communist party was unfit to govern the country; it would only wreck everything and deliver Germany to the French. Had not Radek himself declared a year ago that the time was not yet ripe for world revolution? Annoyed at the challenge, Radek cockily said that he thought that the German Communists' unfitness to govern had yet to be proved, whereas the bourgeois parties had already demonstrated their political bankruptcy. As for the declaration suggested by Rantzau, he intimated that the Comintern was not run by the Soviet government, and that, in case of a conflict of policies, he himself would go with the International and resign his post in the Central Executive Committee. At this point Chicherin tried to introduce a conciliatory tone by suggesting that, really, it was by pure chance that the Third International had its seat in Moscow. After all, he smiled, no one had been so foolish as to make King Leopold of Belgium responsible for the Second International just because it had its headquarters in Brussels. By this time Radek had calmed down and was trying to appease Rantzau. The Soviet state, he said, would always know how to collaborate with a reactionary government in Germany. He reminded the ambassador of the words of General von Seeckt: "We have to keep our fingers tight on the gullet of the Communists, but go together with Soviet Russia." We are prepared to go with him, Radek said; and Chicherin injected, "Mussolini, you know very well, is our best friend." What frantic efforts to mend the cracks in the German-Soviet common destiny! Yet the scars made by the events of October, 1923, could never be removed.

V THE RAPALLO ERA

1. TOWARD LOCARNO

With the settlement of the Ruhr conflict and the acceptance by Germany of the Dawes Plan of reparation payments, the history of Europe entered a new stage which had important repercussions in the political relations between Germany and Soviet Russia.

The years 1919–1923 had been a continuation of World War I, as it were. The armies of the Central Powers had capitulated; but the bitterness of political, economic, and ideological warfare lingered until the end of 1923. Versailles, the snub at Genoa, the Ruhr occupation, and the disastrous inflation—these were only the major milestones on the bitter road of defeat the German people had to travel.

Rantzau's mission to Moscow had stood under the aspect of this aftermath of Germany's defeat; that was both its weakness and its strength. In the "common destiny" linking the two pariah nations, the count had seen a means toward breaking the oppressive predominance of the "imperialists" in the West through a firm Soviet-German friendship.

The year 1924 marked the end of the five-year aftermath that had followed the First World War and the beginning of Germany's recuperation from the violent convulsions she had undergone in the preceding period. The London Conference and the Dawes Plan gave the victor powers a stake in her economic revival. Moreover, the Western World once more sought to engage Germany in international politics as a partner, not merely as an object of negotiations. In London the German delegates had begun to feel that, in spite of all political differences, it would be easier to represent German interests in personal negotiations with Allied politicians than in dealing with Soviet representatives, because all mutual faith and confidence were

126

lacking in dealing with the Russians. Both sides constantly suspected the other of wanting to play the partner out against his enemies. The Russians, moreover, acted as if it were a crime if Germany allowed herself to be exploited by the victor states, but only just and proper if Soviet Russia did the exploiting. Many German diplomats had begun to be very tired of dealing with the Soviet state and to feel our relations to Russia as a burden in our domestic and foreign policy.

In Russia, meanwhile, the failure of the German Communist uprising of 1923 and, in January, 1924, the death of Lenin ushered in a period during which the international politics of the regime underwent some noticeable changes, which were dramatized by the legal recognition of the Soviet state by most governments of the West. Moreover, the reconstruction of the national economy to prewar levels, which was being achieved toward the second half of the twenties, brought the NEP to a point of crisis and marked the beginning of the bitter factional disputes within the party over the tasks ahead. As a consequence, there was in Russia a marked preoccupation with domestic matters which contributed toward easing her relations with the bourgeois world as a whole.

Thus both Russia and Germany had ceased to be the pariahs of international politics; and with this, German-Russian relations were inevitably taken out of the realm of political romanticism. The two powers were no longer so dependent on each other. Instead, both tried to gain a maximum of advantages from the improved situation, even if it were at the expense of the old *Schicksalsgemeinschaft*. German-Soviet relations thus assumed the nature of a sober political chess game.

Very similar to the "Old Bolsheviks" who looked back to the turbulent years of War Communism with romantic nostalgia, Count Rantzau had some difficulty adjusting to the subtle change. "All the old *charme* is gone out of our relations with Russia," he would often remark wistfully. And, in a certain sense, many of his activities during the last years of his life must be interpreted as a futile but stubborn struggle against the change.

Rantzau used to talk about a two-front war he had to wage constantly. One of the obstacles he had to overcome in his attempts to maintain and revive the German-Soviet "common destiny" was the affiliation of the Moscow regime with the international Communist

movement. This affiliation (not to say identity) of the Soviet government with the Comintern produced continual tension in the cordial relations Rantzau sought to foster; and much of his energy was expended in the struggle against the doctrinaires within the Soviet government. Allied with this was an even more tedious and unrewarding fight against Soviet bureaucratic red tape and the clumsiness and stubbornness it injected into all dealings with the Kremlin. The other "front" on which Rantzau fought was the policy of "fulfillment" adopted by the Wilhelmstrasse, which to him was a constant threat to the Rapallo relationship.

A conscientious ambassador who aims to cultivate good relations between his home country and the state to which he is accredited inevitably becomes a double representative. Not only does he represent his own country at the foreign government but he will also often be called to be the spokesman of the latter for their point of view before his own people and policy makers. Not only will his foreign minister ask him about the opinions, intentions, and reactions of his host; if the ambassador feels the need, he will call such opinions and reactions to the attention of his chiefs without being asked. And he will struggle against all those who disturb friendly relations between the two states, not only in the country to which he is accredited but even more so in his own homeland.

It is only natural that, in view of this, Rantzau and his entourage, including myself, were in certain German and Western European circles regarded as spokesmen for the interests of the Soviet Union, or even of international Bolshevism; and we became targets for bitter attacks from these quarters.

There were not many in the higher ranks of Germany's policy makers who stood by Rantzau in his struggle against the Western orientation of the Wilhelmstrasse during the mid-twenties. To be sure, one man had not only shared his views but had also brought similar fine diplomatic skills and administrative experience into his high office. Baron Ago von Maltzan, as permanent undersecretary, had been Rantzau's *alter ego* in Berlin during the turbulent years between Rapallo and the Dawes Plan. When in 1924 Maltzan exchanged the office of *Staatssekretär* for that of German ambassador in Washington, Rantzau felt that his position had lost much of its foundation. The new undersecretary, Herr von Schubert, never concealed his profound dislike of the Russians. His political disagree-

ment with Rantzau inevitably caused the latter to develop a sharp personal antipathy toward Schubert. And his relations with the foreign minister were similarly strained. But however great Rantzau's unconcealed personal dislike of Stresemann and von Schubert, we must not forget that both these men appreciated the importance of Rapallo and did their best to further German-Soviet relations. Stresemann was fully aware of the value of Russia as a trump to be played out against the West.

Rantzau's war against two fronts thus stemmed mostly from the count's very particular sensitivity, which was not only inherent in his own character but which also reflected the even greater sensitivity of the revolutionary regime in Moscow. Only this morbid fear and suspicion on the part of the Kremlin could, after all, explain Rantzau's eternal warnings to avoid—in and out of office—everything that might nourish Moscow's deeply rooted distrust of the bourgeois world anew. I remember driving to the Foreign Commissariat with him one day, to discuss a case of alleged espionage by German nationals, when a platoon of Red Army soldiers marched by. "Look the other way, Hilger," he said jokingly; "I don't want them to accuse *us* of espionage." Again and again he emphasized in his reports to Berlin that the Russian people must be actively convinced of Germany's good intentions. And particularly, the German policy makers should never let themselves be abused by the Western powers for the purpose of anti-Soviet campaigns or deals.

We should not let Rantzau's sensitivity obscure the fact that his policy was in principle identical with that of the Reich government: he certainly was no spokesman for the Kremlin. The difference between his policy and that of Stresemann was, therefore, quantitative, not qualitative. In Rantzau's view the German government tended to go too far in its attempts at a rapprochement with the West and the policy of fulfillment; it showed itself too eager, and by doing so threatened that German-Soviet friendship which even the Wilhelmstrasse recognized as necessary. Hence the struggle between Rantzau and his superiors was often over details of execution; no one, after all, is so much concerned over slight nuances in behavior as the professional diplomat.

Nevertheless, there were larger issues over which Berlin and Moscow wrangled, with the embassy trying to mediate between the two. All these problems derived from Germany's gradual swing toward

the West and the suspicions this aroused in the Kremlin. One of the problems was the attitude of the two Rapallo powers to England. In the Kremlin, England was, during the twenties, regarded as the chief representative of the capitalist world, and as the principal enemy, therefore, of the October Revolution. London, not Wall Street, was the one symbol which, during these years, epitomized the capitalist system. The reasons for this opinion were partly ideological, since England was traditionally regarded as the home of classical capitalism. More immediate and concrete reasons for the Soviet attitude dated back to the Civil War, during which English troops had occupied sizable parts of northern Russia, and Admiral Kolchak had ruled Siberia mostly by the grace of England. The hate and fear concentrated on England had found an individual focus, among others, in the person of Winston Churchill, who, for a while, had advocated with his characteristic vigor an international crusade of the bourgeois world against Russian Communism. His stand made him one of the chief personal symbols for the capitalist encirclement threatening the Soviet regime.

The antagonism between Britain and the Soviet Union must, of course, be seen in the larger perspective of history; specifically, in the fact that England and Russia had throughout the nineteenth century been rivals on the Asiatic continent. From Istanbul to Mukden there were a number of tension areas, all along the southern border of the Russian Empire, in which the two nations were poised against each other in watchful hostility; and the Bolshevik Revolution did not do anything to relieve the tension. For England's political leaders either had to regard it as a threat no less dangerous than tsarist imperialism, or as a welcome opportunity to mend political fences while Russia was weakened and torn by civil war, and pre-occupied with domestic problems. The resulting aggressive attitude of the British has never been forgotten in the Soviet Union.

The German Foreign Office could never identify itself with this attitude. There, too, England was regarded as the kingpin of world politics. And Germany, like the Soviet state, was, for a while, in the position of outcast within the concert of nations. But Russia's attitude of defiance put her into irreconcilable antagonism to the nation that seemed to play the first fiddle; whereas Germany, "bourgeois" in character and aspirations, wanted to stage a comeback, and could not, therefore, afford to spoil it by her relations with England. This

The Rapallo Era 131

fundamental difference of attitudes constituted the prime obstacle to a real Soviet-German friendship. In this lay the reason why the *Schicksalsgemeinschaft* of which both Rantzau and Chicherin dreamed never became more than a *Zweckgemeinschaft* (community of purpose).

No such loose alliance could, however, satisfy the Soviets. The Communist principle that "those who are not for us are against us" was transferred from the area of class warfare into the realm of international politics; and all our assertions that our policy was neither pro-Russian nor pro-British, but simply pro-German, were of no avail. Every act and every semblance of an act of reconciliation with England evoked indignation, accusations, *démarches*—all implying that Germany was joining the anti-Soviet bourgeois coalition. Similar nervous irritation resulted from any such dealings Berlin had with other Western nations. The slightest gesture of good will toward the West, the least indication that Germany wanted to negotiate with the Versailles powers, was regarded as a symbol of the deterioration of German-Soviet relations.[1]

Undeniably, the drift of German foreign policy under Stresemann's guidance was toward reconciliation with the victor powers. Six weeks after the Dawes Plan had been accepted, Germany declared its willingness to accept membership in the League of Nations, and immediately not only the Moscow Embassy but also the foreign minister had to go to great lengths to assure the Russians that no fundamental change in German foreign policy was intended.

Chicherin had a difficult time defending his protest against the German move. He could not, of course, tell us outright that his chief aim was to keep Germany at odds with the Versailles nations. He could only argue that the League was a victors' club usurping privileges which the Soviet Union, as champion of international justice, would never condone. And he scored a hit in Rantzau's Achilles' heel when he asserted that, by entering the League, Germany would be recognizing Versailles and the shameful boundary decision in Upper Silesia. "In the present international situation, orientation toward the West means for Germany simply an acknowledgment of her present subjugation and promises her absolutely nothing positive," Yuri Steklov wrote in *Izvestiya* of May 24, 1925.

[1] Typical of the countless comments was, for instance, Karl Radek's bitter denunciation of the replacement of Maltzan by von Schubert (*Pravda*, Dec. 18, 1924).

Litvinov warned us that Germany could play a much stronger role if she remained outside the League than if she entered. These points were exactly those made by the German right-wing foes of the policy of fulfillment. To refute them, Stresemann referred to Article 19 of the League Covenant providing for the possibility of adjusting the peace settlement in the face of changing conditions.

When the Russians, in their first sharp reactions against Stresemann's policies, argued that Germany's entry into the League would be irreconcilable with the "spirit of Rapallo," they thereby implied that, in their view, Rapallo was meant to be a league against the League. But this view was precisely what the foreign minister wished to dispel. In his instructions to the embassy he insisted that Rapallo could be given a wider and vaguer interpretation making the treaty applicable even when the peculiar conditions of the early twenties disappeared.

The Russians scored a more telling point when, instead of warning Germany against her doom, they spelled out the fears for their own security which Germany's policy switch occasioned. By entering the League and underwriting the Covenant, they argued, Germany would automatically be obliged, under the provisions of Articles 16 and 17, to participate in League sanctions against Soviet Russia and even to give the right of passage to Western troops embarking on an anti-Soviet crusade. If Germany were to insist on joining the League, Moscow demanded that she at least demand to be freed from the provisions of these articles. Thus the struggle between Moscow and Berlin turned from the question over Germany's intention to join to the question whether Russia could allow her to enter the League unconditionally. As the editors of *Izvestiya* put it: [2] "The harmful and unacceptable aspect of the League of Nations consists just in the fact that during an international conflict it can force weaker states to comply with its sovereign will in the interests of a bandit or a group of bandits." Germany's good will toward Soviet Russia would be measured by the degree of sincere resistance Berlin put up against Article 16, the editorial continued.

Now, even though Chicherin and his subordinates constantly complained about Germany's lukewarm efforts in this direction, no one in Berlin wanted to see French and British troops march through Germany on their way to battle with Communist Russia. But for

[2] Nov. 27, 1925.

Stresemann the task of associating his country with the League without incurring obligations that might spoil the Rapallo relationship was a ticklish one. Some of Germany's leading diplomats, particularly Leopold Hoesch, the ambassador in Paris, warned that any attempts to relieve Germany of the provisions of Article 16 would smack of duplicity. Moreover, any reassuring declaration Berlin might give to Russia could provoke the League powers to issue, even at this late date, a very stringent interpretation of the article. It speaks for the eagerness of the Western powers to accept Germany as a sovereign partner that, shortly before the end of the Locarno negotiations, they declared in a collective note that Germany, were she to enter the League, would be obliged to participate in sanctions only to the extent commensurate with her military and geographic situation.

To a considerable extent this took the ground from under the Soviet fears; but it never removed these fears completely, and every once in a while they cropped up to disturb German-Soviet relations. As late as March, 1927, the Soviet press featured an interview von Schubert was alleged to have given the Geneva correspondent of the Paris *Excelsior*. Von Schubert, the Soviet papers maintained, had spoken about the right of French troops to march through Germany in order to come to the aid of Poland and Czechoslovakia. There had indeed been a private conversation between the two men, but no mention had been made of the delicate subject. When Rantzau lodged a sharp protest against the vicious press campaign this "news" unleashed in Soviet Russia, Litvinov replied that he did not really care whether or not such statements had been made by von Schubert. His government was, however, very much concerned to find out whether or not Germany had already at Locarno declared herself ready to give French troops the right of passage in case of necessity. Whereupon Stresemann told the Russians that he resented their voicing doubts concerning his truthfulness. Despite such protests, *Izvestiya* continued its campaign. "Soviet public opinion," the paper said in its March 17, 1927, number, "still has not been given a reply concerning the obligations Germany incurred at Locarno with regard to the right of French troops to pass through Germany." The polemics continued well into the following month, even though, from Stresemann on down, we did our utmost to dispel the unwarranted fears Litvinov kept voicing. To this day I still wonder what real purpose was hidden behind the *Excelsior* affair.

In early April, 1925, the ambassador was asked by Stresemann to inform the Soviet government of the negotiations between Germany and the Entente powers about the conclusion of a guarantee pact which was actually signed later at Locarno. Chicherin and Litvinov became excited to the point of bitterness. They asserted that Germany, with malicious duplicity, had already made up her mind and was confronting the Soviet government with a *fait accompli*. Assured that the negotiations were still going on, they roundly asserted that Germany's entry into the League would mean the end of the Rapallo relationship. Germany may have all good will toward Soviet Russia, Chicherin said at the Soviet Congress on May 16, 1925, but once she has joined her former enemies at Geneva she will be prevented from continuing her present relations with Russia. "The logic of things is stronger than any subjective intentions, and there can be no doubt that after entering the League of Nations, that is, after submitting to the command of the Western imperialist powers, Germany will sooner or later—probably sooner—become a helpless plaything in their hands and will be forced to execute their wishes even when these wishes are directly contrary to Germany's urgent interests. It goes without saying that for the Soviet Union Germany's choice of a definitely Western orientation and entry into the League of Nations can objectively lead only to the deterioration of relations between Germany and the Soviet Republic." [3] These words sound as if Chicherin had dictated them to the *Izvestiya* editor.

In his dispatches to Berlin, Rantzau echoed or even anticipated this reaction. German entry into the League, he wrote, would be an unbearable burden to the Rapallo relationship and would completely frustrate its further development. Moreover, any attempt to convince the Russians to the contrary would be hopeless from the beginning.

Stresemann's reply dismissed this point of view. Instead of saying either West or East, Germany should do her utmost to avoid such an alternative. And if Chicherin remained adamant, he wrote to Rantzau, that would only show his intention to isolate Germany and increase the tensions in her relationship with the Western powers. Germany, by negotiating with the League, wants nothing more than to find a formula which would prevent the possibility of a conflict with Soviet Russia; if anything was going to make continued good

[3] Yuri Steklov in *Izvestiya*, May 24, 1925.

relations between the two nations impossible, he concluded, it would only be the Kremlin's suspicions and distrust.

Anticipating this reaction, Rantzau had bombarded the foreign minister with urgent requests to postpone any discussion of the delicate topic with the Russians for the time being. Overruled, he made an honest effort to shake them out of their intransigence, and many days were spent in acrimonious debate. As was often the case, he entered the debate halfheartedly, himself unconvinced of his arguments. The reason that he talked to the Russians at all was not to convince them—that, he thought, would be impossible—but only to avoid a sudden rupture of relations and to find out whether the Soviet Union still thought it possible to make counter-proposals.

On April 10, 1925, Rantzau departed for Berlin to argue his point of view personally. He stayed for almost three months; this incidentally led to a further disturbance of his relationship to von Schubert, who was said to have made critical remarks to others about Rantzau's long absence from his post. When the count returned to Moscow at the end of June, he was accompanied by Herbert von Dirksen, the then head of the Eastern Department in the German Foreign Office, who was to revive the negotiations about the important economic treaty, which had come to a dead stop. (We shall discuss the treaty in the next chapter.) But German-Soviet relations were once again at a very low ebb, and the Rapallo relationship was shaken to its very foundations. Moscow's suspicions had never been so aroused, and consequently Soviet stubbornness was at an unprecedented high. In July von Dirksen returned to Berlin without having reached any further agreement on the economic treaty. Rantzau had wanted to pursue negotiations concerning a political pact designed to elaborate and confirm the Treaty of Rapallo. Discussions of such a pact had begun in great secrecy in December, 1924. Now these too bogged down hopelessly. Relations were further aggravated by the show trial the Russians staged against two German students, during which the Soviet prosecutor accused me—and by implication the embassy—of having taken part in an alleged plot to poison Stalin and Trotsky.

Toward the end of September Chicherin departed for a lengthy stay in German health resorts. His departure became the occasion for a grand ceremony at the railroad station, where a large honor guard of troops and the entire diplomatic corps had come to bid him farewell.

On such trips Chicherin always used to combine business with the care of his health. This time he would, upon his arrival in Berlin, exert the whole pressure of his personality to swing the German government away from its Western orientation. As a matter of fact, the very travel route he had chosen acquired diplomatic significance: Instead of going straight to Berlin, as was his custom, Chicherin stopped over in Warsaw, with the obvious intention of playing out the French-Polish card against Germany. The world press reacted with a stir; but we in the embassy were not unduly alarmed. We thought—and, I believe, correctly—that Chicherin was bluffing. Particularly Rantzau was convinced of Chicherin's loyalty; and, in his dispatches to Berlin, he urged that Chicherin be given a most spectacular and cordial welcome.

While the foreign commissar was nursing his health in Wiesbaden, the last disagreements over the economic treaty were ironed out by mutual concessions, and the voluminous and complex document was signed on October 12, 1925. At this time the German government was already actively engaged in negotiations at Locarno; and soon afterward the Locarno Pact, guaranteeing Germany's Western boundaries adjoining Belgium and France, was signed. In January, 1926, Germany made formal application for admission to the League of Nations.

In the Soviet Union, Locarno was seen as a pact of European capitalism directed against Russia, because no guarantees had been made for the maintenance of the border settlement in the East, thus giving Germany a free hand there, at least by default. Austen Chamberlain's words that "Locarno was only a beginning" were quoted in the Soviet press and given ominous interpretations. Whether the deductions were correct or not, it is easy to understand the apprehension the pact produced in Moscow. No one, however, reacted with greater sharpness than the German ambassador. He had not often made use of the privilege of reporting directly to the Reich President, which he had obtained as one of the conditions for accepting his post, but this time he took advantage of it. Early in November he wrote a memorandum to von Hindenburg—a carbon copy going to Stresemann—in which he summed up his views on the latter's policies. Our relations to Russia, he warned, were going to be changed fundamentally. Whatever our real intentions, he said, Moscow interpreted our policy as being a rapprochement with the West. By thus antagon-

izing Soviet Russia, Germany was throwing away the last trump card she held against the Allies. He, Rantzau, could not identify himself with such a policy, and was therefore very seriously considering resigning from his post. Later that month the count went to Germany and requested an interview with the President. During the interview he complained very bitterly that he had not been consulted properly during the negotiations leading to Locarno. Now that the pact had been approved by the Reichstag, the conditions under which he had accepted his post in Moscow had vanished; and he formally tended his resignation. The old field marshal persuaded him to stay. If you go now, he argued (most probably briefed by Stresemann), you will give the Russians additional indications of fundamental changes in Germany's policy. After all, the task now is to reassure them; and nothing would accomplish this more than your return to Moscow. The two men also discussed Rantzau's privilege of out-of-channel communication with the President. Stresemann had complained that the count was trying to sabotage the cabinet's policies by the use of this unconstitutional right. The foreign minister and his ambassador were now fighting it out through the person of the head of the state. Von Hindenburg tried to conciliate by suggesting that Rantzau at least let the foreign minister know when he was going over his head. In any event, no further use was made of the privilege. But the relations between Stresemann and Rantzau became rather strained. The ambassador never overcame the feeling that he had been insufficiently consulted and informed during the crucial negotiations, and Stresemann could not help resenting Rantzau's special position.

2. THE CASE AGAINST KINDERMANN AND WOLSCHT

Whether or not it was due to Rantzau's complaints, Berlin now decided that a political act was desirable which would balance out Germany's commitments in the West and simultaneously reaffirm and redefine her relations to Soviet Russia. Such an act should not so much be a gesture of independence from the West as, rather, a token of continued good will toward the big neighbor in the East. This decision coincided with an oft-voiced suggestion of Moscow, or at least met it halfway.

As early as December, 1924, the Russians had made attempts to

renew the Treaty of Rapallo in all its original significance, or, if that was not possible, at least to neutralize Stresemann's policy of fulfillment. Chicherin had at that time proposed to conclude a formal treaty of neutrality, or at least to sign a declaration of neutrality in the form of a protocol. Such a treaty or declaration should contain the mutual obligation to refrain from joining any economic, political, or military combination directed against the other partner.[4] The dangers from which Chicherin wished to protect his country were not only the threat contained in Articles 16 and 17 of the League Covenant but also the oft-debated formation of an international creditors' association to press the question of the old tsarist debts and organize other economic campaigns—specters which continually haunted his imagination.

Berlin was very hesitant to sign such a declaration, mainly because Stresemann did not wish to let any semblance of duplicity jeopardize his policy of fulfillment. The Russians were told that loyal co-operation within the League on the part of Germany was by no means irreconcilable with continued German-Soviet friendship. Article 16 and the obligation to participate in sanctions were played down as much as possible. Finally, to provide a concrete alternative for Chicherin's neutrality treaty, Germany made a counter-proposal in the form of a preamble to a treaty. This draft preamble demanded that Germany and Soviet Russia should remain in "continued friendly consultation" and should "strive for mutual agreement" on all political questions. Those vague words, in the opinion of the Wilhelmstrasse, constituted the most to which Germany could commit herself; but Berlin affirmed that they ought to give complete satisfaction to the Soviet desire for security.

Before negotiations to iron out these two widely diverging conceptions could get very far, the German-Soviet association was seriously strained by an incident which illustrates many critical problems of their relationship.

In the night from October 26 to 27, 1924, agents of the GPU had entered a Soviet student home in Moscow and arrested two German students, recently arrived, under alleged suspicion of espionage. Their names were Karl Kindermann and Theodor Wolscht. In any other country the little incident would have been investigated

---

[4] "You keep away from England, and we'll keep away from France," he said to Stresemann.

quickly by the German consular staff in co-operation with the other country's police, and, after a brief interlude, it would have ended to mutual satisfaction by the deportation of the men arrested. Not so in Soviet Russia. First of all, none of our efforts to find out something about the further fate of Kindermann and Wolscht were successful. But on June 19, 1925, almost eight months after the arrest, a virtual bombshell exploded: The entire Soviet press published a state prosecutor's accusation against the two, alleging that they had been sent to Soviet Russia by the underground fascist terror organization whose members had plotted the murder of Walther Rathenau; one of their plans, the prosecutor's brief went on, had been to poison Stalin and Trotsky with cyanide of potassium. The appearance of the students in Soviet Russia had been accomplished with the connivance of German government circles, or persons formerly connected with the government. More specifically, I was accused of having given assistance and advice to Kindermann and Wolscht. All of this was a fabric of lies.

I had, indeed, met the two young men on my return trip to Moscow after a furlough in Germany. At that time, in October, 1924, the number of foreigners traveling to Moscow was still so small that the only means of transportation available was the official Soviet courier car which went from Riga to Moscow three times a week to accommodate diplomatic couriers and other officials. The two Germans told me that they intended to travel through the Soviet Union as far as Central Asia and Cape Chelyuskin. To finance their trip they had engaged themselves as traveling agents for a German machine factory. Their entire plan was fantastic and impossible to carry out. I called their attention to the fact that Central Asia was forbidden territory for foreigners; that a trip to Cape Chelyuskin, situated beyond the Arctic Circle, would be an extremely difficult and costly expedition; and that Soviet laws concerning the foreign-trade monopoly provided stiff penalties for anyone representing the interests of foreign firms without proper permission.

The young men would not let me convince them. With a frivolous devil-may-care attitude and puerile stubbornness they persisted in their claim that everything had been carefully planned and prepared. In actual fact, their preparations could not have been more miserable—nor more harmless. This was shown by the state of their luggage alone, into which I looked during the customs inspection. I

made them promise to report to me at the embassy soon after their arrival in Moscow, and I resolved to warn them sharply against careless actions. For this purpose I handed them my calling card, and wrote my address and phone number down on it.

As soon as I learned about their arrest, I got in touch with the Foreign Commissariat in order to get them released and deported. Victor Kopp, who had meanwhile been made a member of the *kollegia* of the commissariat, proved to be a reasonable partner in negotiations; he was obviously ready to believe my story and he promised to exert his influence with the GPU. In time, however, the attitude of the Foreign Commissariat stiffened markedly, although I was unable to recognize the cause. When in December, 1924, Count Brockdorff-Rantzau personally appealed to Chicherin on the ground that I had found Kindermann and Wolscht to be puerile but harmless adventurers, the foreign commissar replied that my judgment of people must in this case have deserted me, since it had been found meanwhile that the two students were not innocuous youths, but hardened criminals who had entered the Soviet Union in order to do it serious harm.

Chicherin's words mystified us. We were unaware that a trial was being prepared in Germany, in which a dangerous emissary of the Comintern was to be brought to judgment. The trial began in February, 1925, before the State Court for the Protection of the Republic, one of the chambers of the German Supreme Court, in Leipzig. The "Cheka case," as it was colloquially called, revealed the existence in Germany of a terrorist organization sponsored by Comintern headquarters. Its leader, and the principal defendant in the trial, was a Russian named Skoblevsky. Pëtr Aleksandrovich Skoblevsky, born on June 16, 1890, in Tambov, had been assigned to the German Communist party in 1923 to help prepare the armed uprising planned for October of that year. As "military" advisor to the KPD, he gave orders, in November, 1923, to set up a German "Cheka" for the purpose of liquidating stool pigeons and other dangerous persons. This "Cheka" was nothing more nor less than a murder gang. It actually killed one alleged spy (a hairdresser named Rauch); five other assassinations never got beyond the planning stage. The list of intended victims included not only a renegade Communist but also General von Seeckt and the industrial tycoons Conrad von Borsig and Hugo Stinnes. Both in Russia and Germany the trial

created excitement, even though the German Foreign Ministry repeatedly tried to exert its influence on the press so as to tone down their comments and avoid a serious cooling of German-Soviet relations. After all, Skoblevsky's activities were a thing of the past; and the Wilhelmstrasse did not believe that stirring up the memory of 1923 would benefit the conduct of Germany's foreign policy.

To the Kremlin's great indignation, the trial revealed some relations between Skoblevsky's group and the Soviet Embassy in Berlin. At least the Soviet counselor of embassy, Bratman-Brodovsky, appears to have been informed about their activities. When this was brought out during the trial, Litvinov approached us with the proposition that any mention of the Soviet Embassy be deleted from the verdict. He was seeking to safeguard Russia's international prestige and to preserve the myth that the international Communist movement had nothing whatsoever to do with the Soviet state. As it happened, the German Foreign Ministry in 1925 had no constitutional means of influencing the judiciary, quite apart from the question whether they would have heeded the Soviet request. In any event, the verdict handed down on April 22nd clearly implicated the Soviet Embassy. Skoblevsky was sentenced to death.

The Kindermann-Wolscht affair was artificially constructed for the purpose of creating a direct counterpart to the Cheka case. This was shown particularly by the fact that I, as well as the German Embassy, was implicated and compromised, so that the score would now be even. The two hapless Germans were clearly intended to serve as objects of exchange for Skoblevsky and his aides.

The reasons for which the Soviet Union created such a scandalous affair were thus not hard to find; and yet it is difficult to understand why they were considered important enough to jeopardize long-range German-Soviet relations. My own consternation over the way in which I had been made the object of Soviet vengeance was all the greater since nothing had until then indicated that I was to be victimized in such fashion. Just one day before the bill of indictment was published, the Foreign Commissariat had remembered that exactly five years had passed since I had begun my activity in Moscow; and the chief of the German Division, Boris Stein, had visited me to bring his own and Chicherin's personal felicitations. As token of his government's appreciation, he handed me a large volume on the history of the Soviet Republic during the first five years of its exist-

ence. Yet it is beyond doubt that the NKID was not only well informed about the accusations to be published on the following day but had also taken a very active part in elaborating the plans for the trial.

The proceedings were opened on the 25th of June, and the play they were given, as well as the rank of the persons conducting them, indicated the importance which the Soviet government attributed to Skoblevsky and hence to the Kindermann-Wolscht affair. The presiding judge was the same man who some ten years later was to preside over the show trials of the most prominent Old Bolsheviks. N. V. Krylenko acted as prosecutor. Endowed with unusual oratorical gifts and filled with venom against the bourgeois order, he had been an obscure cadet in 1917 when Lenin appointed him to be the first Bolshevik commander in chief of Russia's armed forces. In 1922 he became deputy people's commissar of justice. Now, as public prosecutor, he rode roughshod over my diplomatic immunity in a manner unprecedented in diplomatic history. The accusation containing my name was scattered throughout the country in millions of copies; and during the trial the prosecutor made the accused repeat orally all the false confessions and allegations that had been squeezed out of them during the pretrial investigation, so that my name once more appeared in the press.

In order to clear me of the accusations, the German Embassy immediately demanded that I be called to the witness stand to present my own version of the story; but the Soviet government declined and continued to publish the damaging allegations about me. Only when Rantzau, after his return from Germany, lodged a sharp *démarche* with Chicherin and threatened to leave Moscow, did my name cease to be mentioned in the press. Before that, I had withstood the temptation of watching the trial, in order to avoid unnecessary complications. Now I took one of the admission tickets given to the embassy for the duration of the trial, and entered the courtroom.[5]

I have never been able to overcome all the bitterness and indignation these weeks caused me. I have always thought that the state ought not to abuse judicial proceedings for political purposes; and I could never draw the line between personal and political relationships. In this I differed from the Soviet politicians for whom it was still very

[5] The GPU called my appearance at the trial a "provocation," and requested the Foreign Commissariat to protest sharply to the German ambassador.

easy at the time to make the separation. Shortly after the start of the trial, I saw Boris Stein again. We had both gone to the railroad station to greet Count Rantzau, arriving from Berlin. With all his customary cordiality, Stein, who had paid me such a pleasant visit a few days before, came up to greet me, and he was quite obviously taken aback when I studiously turned away to avoid him. At that moment, he later confided in me, he had felt like rushing to meet me and to shake both of my hands, had I not so obviously cold-shouldered him. This confession was made in the course of a friendly conversation we had about the trial, during which I tried in vain to show him the dastardly breach of faith his government had committed in accusing me. But he insisted that the entire affair had been a matter a sheer political expediency, with no personal insult intended. The same idea was expressed more cynically by Radek, to whom Louis Fischer voiced his astonishment over the Soviet attitude toward me. "What of it?" he grinned. "When we do filthy political things like that, it's always things that matter, not persons. Doesn't Hilger know that?"

What Chicherin himself really thought is not quite so easy to determine. After his return to Moscow, Rantzau asked him why the Soviet government picked me as a scapegoat, even though they ought to be fully aware of my positive attitude toward German-Soviet friendship. "Well," said Chicherin, wagging his head, "the GPU is of the opinion that Mr. Hilger is especially dangerous because he has learned how to win the good faith of our men by hiding under the mask of a really honest man." Perhaps this reply only expressed the power of the GPU over the Foreign Commissariat.

Apart from the personal shock it dealt me, the crudeness of the grotesque affair might have been cause for laughter had it not led to some ominous political conclusions. We had to ask ourselves whether the influence of the GPU over the conduct of foreign affairs was really so strong as to jeopardize Soviet foreign policy. In that case serious negotiations with the Soviet state were from the very start condemned to failure. If, however, the Kindermann-Wolscht maneuver represented Soviet policy as a whole, and not just GPU interference, then the same conclusion was even more obvious; for how could one deal profitably with a state that shamelessly used extortion to avenge an embarrassment? We asked Chicherin these questions but received only evasive replies. What kind of trump card was the

alliance with a government which indulged in such unsavory practices? Could German prestige allow political relations with that country to continue?

Even while he weighed these ominous considerations, the German ambassador attempted to bring the affair to a satisfactory conclusion, not only to rescue and revive Soviet-German relations but also to allay the clamor of criticism at home, which was the most vociferous among the moderate Leftist parties, who were attacking the government for taking such insults from Moscow. Rantzau resolved to be extremely sharp and indignant in his talks with Chicherin, and to demand the immediate cessation of the accusations against me. Should his step be unsuccessful, he was resolved to carry the conflict into the open, and in that case the serious considerations discussed above would enter; a diplomatic break would loom on the horizon. His determined stand showed some results. We had feared that two German witnesses involved in the case might be arrested at any moment; when Rantzau warned that this would lead to a break, Moscow had them deported instead of thrown into jail. More important, the verdict handed down on July 3, 1925, did not mention my name. Kindermann and Wolscht, however, were condemned to death.[6]

That ended the matter for the Russians. They thought German indignation would now simmer down, and expected that our political and economic negotiations would be resumed. Skoblevsky and his men would, in due time, be exchanged for the German students, and the mutual embarrassments would cancel each other. Hence Chicherin was full of good spirit and expectancy when he received the German ambassador three days after the end of the trial. He was painfully surprised when Rantzau began the conversation with a sharp demand that the sentence be abrogated and that the Soviet government openly exonerate the embassy and myself. Otherwise all negotiations would be broken off. At that point Chicherin frankly revealed the real reason behind the Kindermann-Wolscht trial. "After all," he said with irritation and truculence, "your government never fulfilled our request to exonerate the Soviet Embassy in a press communiqué" (a request, by the way, which the Russians had never made). He

---

[6] The sentence was never carried out. Instead, Kindermann, Wolscht, and a number of other Germans who had been arrested on trumped-up charges were exchanged, in 1926, against Skoblevsky, whose death sentence had also been commuted.

Litvinov and Count Brockdorff-Rantzau shaking hands after the signing of the German-Soviet commercial treaty, October 12, 1925

The distance between von Seeckt and Chicherin during their luncheon meeting

"According to the Entente press: barely two inches."

"Actually: fifteen feet . . . at least!"

From the German satirical periodical Kladderadatsch

called Rantzau's statement an ultimatum which it was a matter of Soviet prestige to refuse, but finally promised to clear up the matter if Germany would continue with the economic and political treaty discussions.

The form in which I was to be exonerated was discussed in long and bitter negotiations, during which Chicherin tried to link his concessions with some we should make in economic matters. Berlin countered with threats of recalling the ambassador, and also seriously considered requesting Krestinsky's recall from Berlin. Rantzau himself was more than once ready to pack up and go. A compromise was finally reached. Since the NKID categorically refused to take the initiative of publishing a denial of all the accusations against me, *Izvestiya,* on August 8, 1925, printed a German declaration to the Foreign Commissariat in which my story was told in its essentials. A short paragraph followed:

In publishing the declaration of the German Embassy, the NKID notes that Counselor of Legation Hilger was not mentioned in the verdict. On the basis of negotiations held since, both governments regard the matter as closed.

3. THE TREATY OF BERLIN

After the communiqué in *Izvestiya* had cleared my name to the satisfaction of both governments, the negotiations concerning a political treaty could be resumed. On July 18th Chicherin gave to Brockdorff-Rantzau a new preamble he had drafted. It amounted to a formal declaration of neutrality and included a sentence which would have prevented Germany from joining the League without Soviet consent. All this was unacceptable to Berlin. At that time Germany had not yet been freed from the provisions of Article 16, so that she could not have signed a declaration of neutrality; nor could she allow her way into the League to be blocked by a Soviet veto. The impression was that Russia was less interested in Germany's good will to collaborate than in compromising Germany in the West. Chicherin insisted that the new preamble be published, which would have created the impression that Germany really did not want to join the League at all. Clearly, the Russians aimed to retain a monopoly on friendly relations with Germany, while Stresemann already thought that the mere fact that negotiations with Moscow

were running parallel with the talks at Locarno was a great concession. He had no desire to opt for one or the other partner, and
he was very disappointed that Moscow would not understand his
position.

Locarno finally convinced the Russians that they had lost their
game. Germany would never exclusively rely on her friendship with
the Soviet Union in her attempts at recovery. At the same time the
pact intensified their efforts to balance out the settlement in the
West with a treaty of neutrality, thus taking the eastward sting out
of Locarno. What type of treaty they had in mind became clear in
December when during his stay in Paris Chicherin signed a treaty with
the Turkish ambassador (December 12, 1925) providing for neutrality
in case of military action, and incorporating a non-aggression promise.
Both countries also agreed not to participate in any political, economic, or financial combinations, military or naval conventions, or
hostile acts of any kind directed against the other partner. In a
protocol appended to the treaty both partners reserved their freedom
of action in every other respect.

A few days later Chicherin arrived in Berlin, where he stayed for
about two weeks for intensive discussions with leading political
personalities, but without achieving any real agreement. The matter
had by now boiled down to this: Chicherin insisted that his government needed the guarantee furnished by a formal treaty of neutrality,
and held that the freedom from Article 16 which the Allies had
granted Germany automatically permitted her to conclude such a
treaty, whereas Stresemann wanted to know why a formal declaration
of neutrality was still necessary after the note from the League
powers. Thus the differences had been reduced mainly to formal
considerations, Stresemann being wary of a spectacular document
with all its international repercussions. But the Foreign Ministry
now felt pressure not only from the Soviet side but also from the
Reichstag, where the opinion was expressed overwhelmingly that
Locarno must by no means lead to a disturbance of Germany's relations with Russia.

Toward the end of February, 1926, the cabinet ended its hesitation
and decided to propose a formal treaty to the Soviet Union. The
draft Berlin sent us consisted of four short paragraphs and an appended protocol. According to Article 1, the Treaty of Rapallo would

remain the basis of German-Soviet relations; both governments were to remain in friendly contact concerning all problems touching their relationship. Article 2 called for neutrality in case of unprovoked aggression on one of the partners by a third power. In Article 3 the partners promised not to join any sort of coalition or economic campaign directed against the other partner. The last Article concerned ratification and duration of the treaty.

The appended protocol took the form of a German note to the Soviet government in which it was stated that both governments considered the treaty to be an essential contribution to world peace. Both governments, the note continued, had discussed Germany's plan to join the League of Nations; and the German government expressed its conviction that to do so would not jeopardize good relations between itself and Soviet Russia. Should the League develop tendencies toward an anti-Soviet policy, then Germany would use her influence to counteract them. This, the note concluded, would not contradict the provisions of Articles 16 and 17, since these provided for sanctions against Soviet Russia only in the event of Soviet aggression; and in deciding whether or not the Soviet Union was an aggressor Germany would have veto power, so that she could not be forced against her will to participate in sanctions.

As formulated, the proposed treaty constituted a major concession to the Soviet demands. Heretofore, Berlin had steadfastly rejected the idea of a formal treaty; the present version corresponded much more to Chicherin's initial suggestions. In presenting the draft to the Foreign Commissariat, we made clear that Germany would sign the treaty only after the next session in Geneva should have decided the question of Germany's admission to the League. To conclude the treaty before that time would create the impression that Germany considered her admission an accomplished fact, which in turn would deprive her of a strong means with which to press her fight for a Council seat in the League.

Early in 1926, quite contrary to Stresemann's expectations, the League rejected Germany's application for membership. It has been argued by competent writers, among them Lord D'Abernon, that this grave rebuff "caused German public opinion and the leaders of the German nation to turn their gaze once more eastward," and that "M. Tchitcherin and the Soviet Foreign Office should once more

seize upon German disappointment . . . to insinuate the benefits of increased and more intimate Russo-German co-operation." [7] It ought to be clear to the reader that this explanation of the Berlin Treaty (as it came to be called) is not correct. The treaty was no spontaneous reaction to Stresemann's disappointment in the West; on the contrary, it had been intended as a device to balance out the successes of German foreign policy in the West, both those achieved and those still being expected. Of course, after the League powers had shut the door in the face of the Germans, it was inevitable that the treaty which was concluded a few weeks afterward should be given a more ominous interpretation than it deserved.

Shortly before the treaty was actually concluded, a number of disturbing incidents once more poisoned the atmosphere of German-Soviet relations and delayed the final treaty negotiations by another few weeks. Throughout the early months of 1926, arrests of German citizens in the Soviet Union had mounted sufficiently to alarm the Foreign Ministry in Berlin. Moreover, in January, Soviet officials had opened a package addressed to the embassy and mailed in Tiflis by a German citizen; they had removed a number of documents from the package and replaced them by a Bible, in an obvious attempt to make fun of the embassy.

This rifling of mail from Tiflis was probably connected with an even more serious incident that had occurred on December 13, 1925. "Consular agents" of the Reich in three Caucasian cities, Baku, Poti, and Batum, were arrested by the Cheka and accused of espionage. The Baku office, which also served as the agent's residence, was sealed and put under guard. All three men were taken to the Cheka jail in Tiflis. Their official mail was confiscated; their official seals were broken.

These gentlemen, Schmitz, Cornehlsen, and Eck, were German businessmen who had been living in Transcaucasia for quite a number of years, and who had for a long time carried out the functions of honorary consular officials. As such, they had been duly reported to the Soviet government by the embassy in 1923, but Moscow had never officially recognized them. Nor had the consular treaty of October 12, 1925, provided for "consular agents." Because the Soviet

7 Lord D'Abernon, *An Ambassador of Peace* (Hodder & Stoughton, Ltd., London, 1929–1930), III, 245.

government wanted to get rid of them, all three were arrested under the customary suspicion of espionage.

The usual rounds of protests and denials followed. Finally Chicherin asserted that conclusive evidence existed against the alleged spies, and he declared his willingness to give Rantzau access to the GPU dossiers on them. "Let's go together," the ambassador urged me. "I can't read that crap by myself, anyway." So we both went to the Foreign Commissariat, and Chicherin gave us GPU files in which the places concerning the "consular agents" had been marked for our convenience. The material contained allegations that the men now under arrest had conducted espionage work of all kinds and made reports concerning their activities to the consulate general in Tiflis. As I read the statements bit by bit, Rantzau soon became bored and started a political conversation with Chicherin. I used the opportunity for the purpose of leafing through the entire file; on several of the documents I saw my own name, and made the surprising discovery that the GPU suspected me, too, and other members of the embassy, of having engaged in espionage work in Transcaucasia. For instance, I read that as early as 1921 I had sent an emissary to Tiflis to gather information about a strategically important bridge over the Kura River. These and all the other statements were ridiculous lies. I did not know anything about such a bridge, nor had I ever given such an order. The official whom I had sent to Transcaucasia had gone on the perfectly legal mission of caring for the German prisoners of war still in captivity there. Suddenly Chicherin looked up and saw me leafing through the GPU files. Hurriedly, he requested them back.

Cornehlsen, Schmitz, and Eck were later deported to Germany, which ended the matter. But while the affair was in its acute stages, it had a curious effect on the embassy. On the one hand, our indignation was aroused, and our sense of national prestige violated. In an effort to force the Russians to make amends, our negotiators stopped all talks about the political treaty we had planned to conclude, saying that negotiations would be resumed only after the incident was settled to the satisfaction of the Reich government. On the other hand, some of the same officials who made threatening gestures toward the Soviet side were in almost panicky fear that the treaty talks might actually founder on the rock of such disturbances.

Rantzau, who once again talked about packing his bags, at the same time made an almost inhuman effort to avoid an open clash.

One difficulty still remained to be overcome before the treaty could be concluded. Early in April the Foreign Commissariat, which in general was satisfied with the draft, raised strong objections to one word in Article 2, which provided for neutrality in case of *unprovoked* aggression on one of the partners by a third power. The Russians objected to the insinuation, implied in the word "unprovoked," that they might provoke a third power to attack them. Actually, the wording of this clause was by no means unusual in neutrality treaties; it occurred even in the French-Polish treaty of alliance. Consequently, the alleged insinuation would be clear only to a government as sensitive and touchy in questions of international prestige as the Soviet state. After lengthy and arduous bickering we finally proposed to replace the objectionable word by the phrase "in spite of a peaceful attitude," declaring that no greater compromise could be made. A few days later, on April 24, 1926, the treaty was signed, not, as Rantzau had hoped, by Chicherin and himself in Moscow, but in Berlin, by Stresemann and Krestinsky. What he thought would be called the Rantzau Treaty therefore came to be known as the Berlin Treaty. In spite of this disappointment, its conclusion marked the high point of the ambassador's career, for Germany's friendly relations to Russia had been maintained and even strengthened in spite of the policy of fulfillment. Now the count was only too glad to admit that it would have been a mistake to resign after Locarno.

4. COUNT RANTZAU'S "OTHER FRONT"

The conclusion of the Berlin Treaty marks the culmination of a period of remarkable friendship and collaboration between two countries very different in their history and aspirations. The friendship was all the more remarkable because no love was lost between the policy makers of the two states; it was a purely pragmatic arrangement between two governments sharing a few problems and a few enemies in common. And yet, the Rapallo era—if we may thus call the years from 1922 to 1928—witnessed the extension of friendly relations into a variety of non-political and non-economic pursuits. Vivid intellectual curiosity and cosmopolitan grasp of cultural affairs had not yet been stamped out in the higher reaches of the party, and

Germany was regarded by many of the men in the Kremlin as an important cultural center with which it would be advantageous for the new Soviet state to have dealings. It was not that the Communist regime thought bourgeois Germany could offer any lessons or experiences in running society as a whole; but in the field of applied sciences the Soviet rulers had a high respect for German achievements. Hence, during those years it was primarily Germans to whom they turned when they were in need of technical advice unobtainable in their own country, whether the problem was in the field of ordnance, heavy construction, or forestry. On a personal level this attitude was particularly striking in the field of medicine. Chicherin went to Rantzau's physician at Wiesbaden for treatment of his ailments; Trotsky went to a clinic in Berlin to find relief from his stomach troubles in the spring of 1926 (going incognito, by a special arrangement with the German authorities which was very secretively handled by the embassy); and in his last months Lenin, too, had been treated by many eminent German physicians and surgeons. Today, the presumptuous pride with which Soviet science announces its superiority over that of the West would make such visits quite impossible.

Though in the twenties personal relations between members of the German Embassy and Soviet officials were not only correct but even cordial, there was, of course, an inner core of party personnel completely inaccessible to foreigners; and the Soviet government gradually narrowed the number of officials authorized to deal with us to a very small number. In the area of high political relations, there were a great number of tensions and conflicts; we have mentioned some of them and we shall deal with many more. However, the important thing to realize is that these conflicts were ironed out, even though in long-dragged-out negotiations in which both parties drove stiff bargains. In spite of these tactics of mutual extortion, there prevailed an astonishing degree of trust and faithful collaboration behind the scenes. In demanding mutual consultation on all matters of common concern, the Treaty of Berlin did little more than state the actual habits of Berlin and Moscow. During the entire Rapallo period close mutual consultation and exchange of information were practiced without any serious breaches of faith on the part of either government. It has been said that Lord D'Abernon, the British ambassador in Berlin during those years, was in such close touch with Stresemann and von Schubert that he might well be called an un-

official permanent consultant to the Foreign Ministry. What is not
so well known is the fact that Chicherin, as well as Litvinov and
Krestinsky, occupied a very similar status in the Wilhelmstrasse;
very frequently the foreign minister and his permanent undersecretary would indulge in the frankest discussions about international
politics with them. But neither Chicherin's nor Lord D'Abernon's
position in Berlin could compare with that of Rantzau in Moscow,
whose close personal friendship with the foreign commissar found
its political expression in the frequent political discussions they would
have deep into the night.

One might say that the Treaty of Berlin marks the culmination
point of the Brockdorff-Rantzau era in German-Soviet relations. It
was a decisive victory on one of the two fronts on which the count had
been struggling all the time, for it meant the neutralization of all
efforts in Berlin to guide German policy into a predominantly Western orientation. The treaty made sure that Berlin and Moscow would
continue to hold hands even while Stresemann pursued the policy of
fulfillment. Henceforth, it was the other front which required the
ambassador's attention in an increasing measure.

When I speak of the second front of battle, I refer in part to the
atmosphere created by the ideological orientation of the Soviet regime. But beyond that, Rantzau and the policy makers in Berlin were
perturbed by something which had nothing to do with the Communist ideas of Moscow. There was a general lack of faith in the
Kremlin, a belief that, whatever their revolutionary aspirations and
plans, the Soviet rulers were basically untrustworthy, plebeian usurpers whom an honest diplomat should not touch with a ten-foot pole,
if he could help it. The specific fear which haunted the ambassador
was that Soviet Russia might become dependent on the Entente
powers. This fear had been one of the reasons for concluding the
Treaty of Rapallo; and it remained ever present among the German
diplomats around Rantzau who, among themselves, would plaintively
moralize about the latent ingratitude and disloyalty of the Soviet
regime. Since Moscow harbored equally strong suspicions of German
duplicity, the diplomats of both countries were constantly on the
alert for signs of disloyalty, constantly asking themselves who would
be the first to sell the partner down the river by making a deal with
Poland, England, or France. In the spring of 1923 Rantzau had been
very nervous about the possibility of a Soviet-French deal at Ger-

many's expense, and he was extremely annoyed over the splendid reception Moscow gave in the summer of the same year to the French Senator de Monzie, who later embarked on his crusade for *de jure* recognition of the Soviet government by France.

The year in which the principal European countries entered into full diplomatic relations with the Bolshevik regime was 1924. The MacDonald government started the round in February, with Mussolini following a few days later. Last to resume diplomatic relations was the French government, which waited until October. When the Soviet press commented by talking about a new era of peace and understanding, Rantzau's suspicions were aroused once again. The new French ambassador, Jean Herbette, arrived in Moscow in mid-January, 1925. A well known financier, he had been connected with the conservative daily *Le Temps,* which had supported Poincaré in his Ruhr policies. Two days after he was formally accredited to the Kremlin, Herbette paid a courtesy visit to the count; but Rantzau met his conciliatory phrases with unconcealed hostility and bitter references to the editorial policy of *Le Temps.* Rantzau's personal antagonism toward Herbette was later extended to the Polish ambassador Stanislaw Patek, and the Italian Gaetano Manzoni.

The emotional attitude Rantzau nursed against France made it impossible for him to respond to Chicherin's repeated proposals to attempt forming a continental bloc of the three great powers, Germany, France, and Russia, in which the Soviet regime would undertake to mediate between the two old antagonists. Besides, any such scheme, which would have antagonized England, was out of the question for the German ambassador. Nevertheless, he did not openly refuse to play along with the foreign commissar's scheme; it seemed to him a nice bit of diplomatic intrigue which might serve to neutralize France and at the same time raise the value of Germany's friendship in the eyes of London.

Late in 1925 Chicherin had been in Berlin, trying to dissuade Stresemann from entanglements that might be prepared for him at Locarno. He had left Berlin very worried about the course of Stresemann's policy of fulfillment, and his next stop was Paris. In Berlin he had made it plain that he wanted to improve Soviet relations with France; obviously he feared that Locarno might tie Germany together with his own arch-antagonist, England. The trip to Paris must have been an attempt to place another iron in the fire.

The foreign commissar also made a stopover in Warsaw, no doubt as a warning to Berlin that the antagonism between Poland and the Soviet Union was not unbridgeable. Yet there was little possibility of a Soviet-Polish rapprochement in those years. Too many burning issues that had remained unsolved had created a well established tradition of hostility between the two countries, so that any German fears that the Kremlin might sell out to Warsaw were little less than hysterical.[8] On the contrary, one might say that a common sharp hostility to the new Polish state was one of the most potent bonds between Berlin and Moscow, and another partition of Poland the silent maximal aim of both governments throughout the interwar period. (The phrase that was used was, "To push Poland back to her ethnographic frontiers.") This maximal aim, was, however, seldom mentioned, and it was not actively pursued between 1920 and 1939. It was the less ambitious aim of neutralizing the Polish state on which Berlin and Moscow were in agreement throughout the Rantzau era.

In this connection both governments were concerned with maintaining the independence and integrity of Lithuania as a pawn that might be played out against Poland. On September 28, 1926, the Soviet Union concluded a neutrality treaty with Lithuania which was modeled on the Soviet-Turkish Treaty of December 12, 1925, but which contained an additional note in which the Soviet government refused to recognize the Polish occupation of Vilna. Over the Vilna question a near war between the two buffer states erupted in early 1927, and the constant consultation over the conflict between Berlin and Moscow demonstrates the close community of interests of the two countries in this regard. But on June 7, 1927, the Soviet ambassador in Warsaw, Voikov, was assassinated by a white-guardist émigré named Koverda, and in its demands for retribution against the assassin and his accomplices Moscow made most excessive demands.

[8] In the early days of March, 1926, Chicherin told Count Rantzau that his government would be ready to recognize Poland's eastern boundary, as drawn in the Treaty of Riga, as a price to be paid for the normalization of Polish-Soviet relations. Such a normalization would have been an inauspicious prelude to the conclusion of the Berlin Treaty. To our great relief the Russo-Polish talks came to nought, but not until after Rantzau had made clear that the conclusion of the German-Soviet treaty and the maintenance of good relations between Berlin and Moscow depended on the abandonment of any intentions the Kremlin might have had to guarantee Poland's boundaries.

The German Foreign Ministry seems to have regarded a sharpening of the Soviet-Polish conflict at that time as highly undesirable; according to the *Vossische Zeitung* of June 16th Chicherin was told that his ultimatums were making a very bad impression in Berlin. Later that month the Foreign Commissariat was buzzing with indignation over a speech Stresemann was alleged to have made in Geneva, in which he had declared himself ready to intervene on behalf of Poland in an effort to tone down Moscow's demands. This, Chicherin exclaimed to Rantzau, meant that he had sided with the Poles in the eyes of world opinion. Thus the fear of duplicity was by no means restricted to the German side.

But there was another aspect of the "other front" which gave much greater concern to the Germans than to their Soviet partners. I have in mind the never ending tendency of the Soviet regime to interfere in the internal affairs of the German state.

After the abortive uprising of October and November, 1923, the German Communist party (KPD) spontaneously rid itself of its hesitant and cautious leaders, whom it blamed for the failure of the revolt, and took a decided step to the Left, a swing toward radicalism which raised Ruth Fischer to the position of party secretary. Even though this radicalization of the KPD was somewhat out of tune with the seemingly evolutionary course of development in Russia at that time, a number of influential Soviet personalities endorsed it with more or less enthusiasm and indulged in most inflammatory revolutionary talks. Some of this reached the ears of the embassy personnel by way of rumor or informal reports. We had indications that a number of prominent Comintern leaders were going to Germany every once in a while. Karl Radek was one on whom our attention was naturally focused because he had been involved in previous revolutionary disturbances in Germany. There was, of course, little we could do to prevent these trips, which were always made incognito; we could not even protest, because we lacked definite proof.

I once devised an easy way of finding out whether Radek had recently been in Germany or not. All that was necessary was to invite him for lunch. If he came wearing his characteristic beard, we could be sure that he had not gone on an illegal trip abroad; but if he came clean-shaved or with stubbles there could be only one reason why he had taken off his beard. Without suspecting that he was being

investigated, Radek cleared himself this time by showing up in all the exotic splendor of his bushy beard.

Protests could be lodged, however, when Soviet officials openly came out, in speech or print, with revolutionary messages directed specifically to the German workers, or when they made remarks that might offend the German state or damage German prestige. Thus, on the eve of general elections, in its November 27, 1924, number, the Communist *Rote Fahne,* official organ of the KPD, published a proclamation by Stalin in which the German government was called a chain-gang regime, and the coming elections chain-gang elections (*Zuchthauswahlen*). "The German proletariat," the proclamation read, "will not speak its last word in the election"—a clear call for revolt. One month previously the same paper had published a manifesto of the ECCI (Executive Committee of the Communist International) signed by Zinovyev and Manuilsky which closed with the words, "Long live the German revolution!" Zinovyev had come out with similar inflammatory exhortations several times in the same year. Each of these pronouncements elicited extremely sharp protests from the Germans, which the Foreign Commissariat inevitably dismissed with the remark that the Soviet state was not responsible for the pronouncements of the Communist party and the Communist International. But, after all, Zinovyev, as mayor of Leningrad, and Stalin, as member of the Presidium of the Central Executive Committee, were officials of the Soviet government.

The years 1925 and 1926 were years of retrenchment in the Communist International, or at least in the German Communist party; and there was a decided lull in this type of incident, if we forget the indignation that was caused by Voroshilov in February of 1926 when in his speech on Red Army Day he hinted that Germany was once again rearming. The offensive passage was quietly removed from the record by the Soviet authorities. But in the following year Bukharin openly accused Germany of conniving in the Lithuanian fascist coup and other acts of duplicity; and Rantzau was particularly annoyed by an *Izvestiya* editorial of March 25, 1927, in which Germany was held primarily responsible for the First World War. In November of that year Trotsky declared that the "Russian Communists must rush to aid their Western brothers in the struggle against their oppressors, even if such a step might spoil Russia's relations with one or the other bourgeois government." We knew, of course, that

Trotsky's influence had sunk to nothing in the Soviet government by this time; and yet even after Trotsky had been sent into his Central Asian exile Rantzau was still quoting his statement in his dispatches to Berlin.

No incident, however, aroused more indignation and bitter wranglings than the following: In November, 1927, the Soviet Union and world Communism celebrated the tenth anniversary of the October Revolution. Among the many organizations who met for the jubilee celebrations was the International Congress of the Friends of the Soviet Union. At this congress, held in Moscow on the 12th, Voroshilov said that "the October Revolution is only the introduction to the greatest drama that has ever been enacted in the human arena. But we know," he continued, "that the following acts of this drama are going to start soon." Afterward Budënny, speaking in the name of the Revolutionary War Council, pinned the order of the Red Banner on a number of prominent French, German, and Hungarian Communists, expressing the hope that "the blows of the proletariat will soon make the chains fall from our brothers languishing in capitalist prisons." This was a broad reference to Max Hölz, a German Communist at that time in jail in his home country. He was awarded the medal *in absentia,* and this honor, given to a man whom the German authorities regarded as a convicted felon, could not but be interpreted as a hostile demonstration against our government. Count Rantzau declared to Chicherin that he regarded it as a vicious provocation, and threatened to leave for Berlin if he were not given a satisfactory explanation. The case was finally settled when Krestinsky gave the Foreign Ministry a statement declaring that the Red Army had awarded the order without consulting the government or the Foreign Commissariat, and that Max Hölz had been honored only for his services against the French at the time of the intervention in Russia, so that no hostile demonstration against the German government had been intended. The Foreign Minister acquiesced, but his ambassador in Moscow remained dissatisfied and blamed Stresemann for excessive softness in taking such an insult. The latter and von Schubert argued that a strengthened and consolidated German Republic could well afford to shut an eye to Communist interference that only irritated, but presented no danger to, the existing political order, as long as really dangerous propaganda from Moscow was kept in check. But Rantzau maintained a much

more alarmist position, and felt himself betrayed by his superiors.

On January 30, 1924, Kamenev had said in a speech before the Soviet Congress that the Soviet government could not look at the recent revolutionary events in Germany as a detached observer because the proletarian Soviet state was immediately affected by every struggle of the workers for liberty; moreover, a victory of German fascism and a resultant French invasion of Germany would also have led to profound changes in the international situation. Given the ideological orientation of the Soviet regime, this was certainly a reasonable statement, and the German government might have been wise to acknowledge the fact that Soviet Russia would always be interested in proletarian revolution everywhere. This would not have prevented the German police authorities from being as ruthless in their fight against domestic Communism as they wanted, and it would have obviated the silly and transparent pretenses in which both Berlin and Moscow indulged. But age-old conceptions of diplomatic etiquette and national sovereignty, as well as the anti-Communist conscience of German government officials, militated against such frankness. As we have seen, the insistence on keeping Communist ideology out of Soviet foreign politics forced the Kremlin to pretend that there was no official connection at all between the Soviet state and the Comintern or the Soviet government and the Russian Communist party, which enabled them to claim that the Soviet government could not be held responsible for the acts and statements of party members.

At the same time Soviet officials were always insisting that other countries had no right to interfere in Russia's domestic affairs. In effect, they told the outside world that it would only be good sense to acknowledge the Communist orientation of the regime, and that it would be interference in Russia's internal affairs not to acknowledge and accept this orientation. Moreover, there were occasions when political realism and common sense broke through the ideological rigidity of men like Chicherin and Litvinov, which aided the settlement of disputes of this kind. But the customary attitude in international relations was an insistence on separating Communism from the Soviet government. And just because the bourgeois governments in their relations with Moscow went through the motions of accepting this pretense in all seriousness, great indignation was aroused when the ideological nature of the regime expressed itself.

There were, in spite of these considerations, good reasons for taking occasional outbursts seriously. Difficulties arising out of them were not only a matter of prestige and of keeping up a pretense; they were at times quite useful as a means of extorting advantages in all sorts of negotiations. Political capital could be made of indiscretions committed by the other side. The difficulty, however, was that the Soviet negotiators showed themselves smarter in the game of blackmail than the German diplomats, and more ruthless in fabricating suitable incidents, although they did not always have to resort to fabrication, as the police raid on their trade delegation in Berlin shows.

In addition, indiscretions and outbursts, even when they were unauthorized and a source of embarrassment to the Foreign Commissariat, were nevertheless a useful barometer of opinion in the party, which, after all, was guiding the affairs of the Soviet state. For that reason, the excuse that the state apparatus had no influence over opinions in the party, though formally correct, was insufficient; as a matter of fact, more attention should have been paid, perhaps, to statements of policy coming from the party than to similar statements coming from Soviet officials. In this we have ample justification for the close attention the embassy paid to the Soviet press. Even though in the early years of this period the radical opposition within the party still had some opportunities to voice its opinions in the press, the more important papers were already carefully managed, and expressed nothing but official party opinion; and when an editorial in the official party paper, *Pravda,* poured venom on German capitalism, everyone knew that it was the party that was in control of the state which tried to do business with the German bourgeoisie. In this sense the Germans had much greater justification in being indignant about unfavorable press comments than the Russians. The German Foreign Ministry had no influence over most of the press; as a matter of fact, newspapers were the first place in which anti-Soviet sentiments not voiced by the Wilhelmstrasse could be freely expressed. Nevertheless, the Soviet government, perhaps mistaking the influence of the government over the press, unceasingly protested, and was so insistent about it that at one point Berlin asked the embassy to collect unfavorable comments in the Soviet press so that the Foreign Ministry might have material for counter-protests.

It must be admitted that the bulk of the German press was not

very well acquainted with Soviet affairs. To be sure, German social scientists led the Western world in East-European and Soviet studies; anyone who reads Professor Otto Hoetzsch's monthly reports on Soviet political developments in the journal *Osteuropa* must be struck by the validity his keen and lucid essays still possess today. But the audience of these reports was restricted to narrow academic circles. The common man received scant and quite one-sided views of Soviet Russia. If he was a worker, he read the indignant and gleeful exposés in the Social Democratic press. If he read the large bourgeois dailies, he was dependent on the alarmist reports of Alfred Hugenberg's extremely reactionary *Tele-Union,* which got its news about Russia from a highly spurious propaganda organization in Kovno. Lacking a proper intelligence department to deal with Communist activities, the minister for the maintenance of public order for a long time obtained most of his "information" about Soviet developments from an anti-Communist propaganda organization run by a Russian émigré named Orlov, who specialized in forging documents which he then transmitted to the police. He was tried and convicted early in 1929; but because the defense pleaded that he had committed his forgeries for lofty political motives his only punishment was deportation. Even the Foreign Ministry fell for many wild rumors about the Soviet Union, which the embassy had to dispel. Such occasions arose again and again. Some of these "confidential" reports to the Foreign Ministry contained fantastic inventions; thus in January of 1926 Berlin asked the embassy whether it was true that the recent Fourteenth Party Congress had resulted in the end of the Communist dictatorship, the democratization of the regime, its transformation into a parliamentary government, and the growth of an opposition party.

At that, there was always at least one German press correspondent in Moscow whose reports were carefully weighed and were based on a thorough acquaintance with Soviet developments. From November, 1921, to September, 1929, the liberal *Berliner Tageblatt* received clear, realistic, and unsentimental reports from its correspondent Paul Scheffer.[9] In the fall of 1921 the *Berliner Tageblatt* had begun to try to obtain a visa for Scheffer. These attempts had at first been in vain because the Foreign Commissariat refused to give its Berlin

---

[9] A representative selection was later published under the title *Sieben Jahre Sowjet-Union* (Bibliographisches Institut, Leipzig, 1930).

representative permission to grant such a visa. I was then asked to make representations in Scheffer's behalf with a high official of the Foreign Commissariat, and I decided to talk to Litvinov. But on the day when I had planned to approach him personally in this matter he was just about to take a trip to Petrograd. I therefore went to the station and caught Litvinov in his parlor car. He first maintained that the Soviet government had no interest whatsoever in permitting a representative of the bourgeois *Berliner Tageblatt* to come to the Soviet Republic, a paper which, he said, was consistently unfriendly toward the Soviet government. I countered by saying that his government could scarcely expect a different attitude from the newspaper if it refused admission to one of its most prominent correspondents. Further, I said that an immediate view into Soviet conditions was the precondition of objective reporting; and I finally persuaded him to give the orders I had requested. Soon afterward Scheffer arrived in Moscow, and, for the time being, I obtained quarters for him in the house in which we lived ourselves. Our relationship rapidly developed into a warm friendship which was nourished by a never ending exchange of views. Scheffer shared the political opinions of the Rantzau circle in their general outlines. He was always in close touch with the embassy, often echoing our views in his dispatches. In his articles he tried to create an atmosphere of good will and understanding, but, as we shall see later, like so many who started out not unfavorably disposed toward German-Soviet collaboration, he too underwent his "Kronstadt." Even his most favorable reports were not, however, quite what the Russians would have liked him to write, and just because he combined an open mind and sober observation with a growing personal knowledge of the regime and its personalities his presence in Moscow became more and more obnoxious to the Soviet bureaucracy. An old trick was tried with success: Instead of directly accusing him, the GPU centered its attacks on his wife, a member of the oldest Russian nobility, whom he had married in Moscow. She was alleged to exert an evil influence over him and to confirm him in his anti-Soviet tendencies.

At this point it might be well to go into yet another, and perhaps the most annoying, aspect of the "other front" against which Rantzau and his embassy staff were struggling: the Soviet police state, the domination of the political police over all other institutions of the Soviet state, the slow-moving, ponderous manner in which the bureau-

cratic machinery turned, and the coercive policies of the state, which went contrary to all Western principles of judicial procedure.

In its attitude toward the diplomatic corps, the Soviet government naturally sought to keep within the bounds of prescribed behavior; particularly it wanted to prevent any violation of the foreign diplomat's immunity. None the less it permitted the GPU, and later the NKVD, to spy on foreign missions with methods which aroused our disgust and anger. For instance, in the mid-1920's, I came into my office one morning and noticed that a broken-off key was sticking in my desk, an unmistakable sign that someone had tried during the night to open the drawer, probably under the delusion that it might contain secret political documents. Another typical incident that occurred in 1929 gave us proof that the GPU possessed forged facsimiles of the official seals used by the German consulates in the Soviet Union. One day we received a parcel from the German consul in Novosibirsk which had been sealed with the seal of the Kiev consulate. Obviously the GPU had looked into the official consular mail and then mixed up the seals in closing the package.

One of the methods used by the GPU for the purpose of exploring the political views of individual embassy members was to manufacture letters in which alleged counter-revolutionaries turned to us, promising important information. As a compensation for such favors, the letters said, they counted on the embassy to support their efforts at overthrowing the Soviet regime. The recipients were asked to signify their agreement by placing a burning candle behind a designated window of the embassy during a certain night.

For purposes of provocation the GPU usually made use of pretty women who sought to compromise younger members of the foreign missions. Afterward the way would be open for the GPU to blackmail the young men for information. In 1932 an attempt at assassinating the German ambassador was used by the GPU as a pretext for having two or three of its agents accompany members of the diplomatic corps, particularly the chiefs of missions, wherever they went, in order to "protect" them. In their vigilance some of these agents went so far as to go in the water with the object of their protection when the latter was going for a swim.

Every once in a while, the GPU's rule over the country broke through the thin coat of politeness and decency and violated international law or custom. By rights, the embassy could act only when

German interests were affected by such incidents, as in the case of Kindermann and Wolscht or the "consular agents." Our right to lodge protests was already challenged by the NKID when the embassy supported private German concessionaires in their fight against arbitrary or unfavorable decisions. In this the Soviet Foreign Commissariat was quite unjustified; but at times our right to take action against arbitrary acts of the Soviet state was at least doubtful. For the embassy did not restrict its actions to the protection of German rights; it also attempted to interfere in purely domestic cases when world opinion had been aroused and the German press clamored for such action. Thus in March, 1923, Rantzau saw himself obliged to intervene with Chicherin on behalf of the Catholic Archbishop Cepljak, to the great resentment of Moscow. A new outburst of oppression and violence against churches and priests occurred in the early months of 1930, and again the German ambassador intervened with the foreign commissar, this time on behalf of the Protestant ministers who had been arrested. Here we were on very shaky ground, and our protests were repudiated. The same thing occurred in the summer of 1927, when we tried to intervene on behalf of Soviet citizens of German origin who had fallen victim to the wave of terror sweeping the country at that time, producing mass arrests and wholesale death sentences. Again, in the winter of 1929–1930 many peasants of German origin were affected by the merciless drive against the kulaks, and were driven off their farms in the middle of the winter months. Rumors spread among these Germans that they would be permitted to emigrate to the New World, and about thirteen thousand Mennonite farmers left Siberia to gather near Moscow in makeshift camps and press for their release. They were visited by the then agricultural attaché of the German Embassy, Professor Otto Auhagen, who openly reported their plight and aroused German public opinion to mass support of their desire to emigrate. Had he not been a member of the embassy, the Soviet government would most probably have arrested him; as it was, he enjoyed the privilege of extraterritoriality, and all the Russians could do was to designate him *persona non grata* and demand his recall. After much pressure Moscow agreed to release the German farmers for emigration overseas. The German cabinet voted funds for their care in transit and pleaded with the Canadian authorities to accept the emigrants. At this point Moscow became impatient to get rid of the German peasants

and threatened to send them back to Siberia if they were not taken over presently. Some were actually shipped back; the majority, however, succeeded in going to Canada. The case is significant not so much because of the ruthlessness of Soviet actions, but because, for this one time, both Berlin and Moscow tacitly accepted the principle that the embassy could assume protection not only over German citizens but also over Soviet citizens of German origin. Moscow relented because of the overwhelming pressure of public opinion in Germany.

As in the case of Soviet interference in German internal affairs, our diplomats were often in disagreement over the importance that should be given to incidents of this sort, and over the proper action to be taken. Some of us felt that, in the very beginning years of German-Soviet relations, Berlin had been too soft and had taken Soviet insults too lightly. As it was, a truly enormous amount of labor, worry, and paper was wasted on incidents of this kind. The proportion of official dispatches filled with problems arising from them must be seen to be believed. Difficulties of this sort took up so much of our time that, to me, they have often appeared to be the essence of our entire work in Moscow, and one of the chief reasons why there can be no lasting relations between the Soviet Union and the capitalist world. Perhaps this view is somewhat exaggerated. But surely the constant irritation and annoyance of such incidents, the burden they put on all embassy personnel, the strain they put upon all serious negotiations, were less alarming in themselves than as symptoms of grave ills within Soviet society. As symptoms, therefore, these incidents should, and did, cause concern as to whether collaboration with the Soviet was really fruitful in the long run. For the power of the GPU over Soviet foreign affairs was, among other things, a reflection of serious weaknesses of the regime; and the intensification of this GPU rule, as well as the multiplication of serious disturbances it produced in German-Soviet relations toward the turn of the 1920's, was a symptom of a serious crisis which the Soviet state was undergoing at that time. Before we discuss the ramifications of this crisis, let us turn to the economic and military aspects of German-Soviet relations.

VI GERMAN-SOVIET
ECONOMIC RELATIONS
1921-1928

1. CONCESSIONS

I had officially joined the staff of the German Embassy in January, 1923. The President of the Reich, upon Rantzau's request, had appointed me a counselor of legation, and a letter to me from the ambassador outlined the duties awaiting me. I was to devote myself to political as well as economic affairs. According to rank I was immediately below the counselor of embassy provided for in the table of organization; but I would take orders only from the ambassador directly. With this, Count Rantzau consciously waived all well established diplomatic notions and created a delicate problem of personal and official relationships that might easily have led to frictions. But the then counselor of embassy was characteristically unperturbed by questions of rank and chain of command, and I always did my best to use a proper amount of discretion in our relationship.

My chief job in the embassy was to be that of the head of the economic department, even though I was also to be the ambassador's constant adviser in all important political affairs. When I entered the embassy, however, someone else still headed the economic department, and a few months passed before he was transferred to Kharkov as consul general. In the meantime I was given the task of organizing a department for cultural relations in the embassy; I went about this at once and remained in charge of this department to the very end, even though the economic department claimed the main share of my time and effort. In any event, maintenance of a cultural department made sense only as long as the Soviet government was still

interested in cultural relations with foreign countries and was not merely using them for its own propaganda purposes.

In many respects the economic department was a logical assignment for me. I was familiar with the Russian economy since prewar times and, in the years 1910 to 1914, I had broadened and perfected my knowledge in frequent travels throughout the entire country. My technical knowledge, too, proved valuable, since the bulk of German deliveries to Soviet Russia always consisted of machinery; hence, I was in a position to give technical advice to the representatives of German firms who came to Russia in great numbers to negotiate and close deals with the Soviet authorities.

Early in May, 1923, I submitted a memorandum to the ambassador in which I reviewed the status of German-Soviet economic relations and discussed the possibility of concluding an economic treaty with Soviet Russia. In this memorandum I pointed out that, after concluding the treaty of May 6, 1921, Germany had had excellent opportunities to do business with Russia on a grand scale, but these opportunities had been missed irretrievably. At that time the Soviet government had still been in doubt whether it might have sufficient economic strength to reconstruct its most important industries and restore the railroads to operating conditions in the foreseeable future. Guided by these doubts in its own capacity, the Soviet government in the fall of 1921 had promised substantial concessions to German industrial and financial circles if they would help it in tasks of reconstruction. For instance, in talks with Schlesinger held in Moscow, the Russians had declared their willingness to grant extraterritorial rights to a German business association to engage in trade within the area fed by an important railroad trunk line going East, if the association would undertake the reconstruction of the line. The project remained on paper because the German business corporations that might have taken up the proposition were not interested, partly because they had no faith in the Soviet government, and perhaps because in those days of the great German inflation they could not gather the necessary capital.

There were further proofs that in 1921 and 1922 conditions were very propitious for economic relations between Germany and the Soviet Republic. At that time the Soviet government, in my opinion, had not yet become fully aware of the great political and economic advantages that could be derived from an aggressive use of the foreign-

trade monopoly. Otherwise they would scarcely have suggested (as they did in conversations with me) that the German government establish a central agency to handle all matters concerning German-Soviet trade relations. I transmitted the suggestion to Berlin, but the Foreign Ministry refused to "obstruct the development of private initiative" in our trade with Soviet Russia. Thus the opportunity of meeting the Soviet foreign-trade monopoly with an effective central organization of German business was missed because of the tenacity with which the predominantly Socialist government of Germany stuck to the principles of private enterprise. With this, the Germans also missed the chance of creating an important precedent. In later years the Soviet government was extremely anxious to retain its advantage and fought with great tenacity against the so-called "Russia Committee of the German Economy" (Russlandausschuss der Deutschen Wirtschaft), an organization founded for the purpose of providing orientation, information, and advice to German firms interested in trading with Russia.

The policy of the German Embassy was to safeguard the interests of all German firms and individual business persons negotiating with the Soviet government or doing business in Russia on the basis of government contracts. We regarded this not only as our natural duty but also as a clear right; and this right seemed guaranteed by a provision contained in the provisional treaty of May 6, 1921, which granted the commercial representative attached to the German Mission direct access to all Soviet economic agencies, circumventing diplomatic channels. On the basis of this provision, and in my capacity as head of the embassy's economic department, I maintained frequent contact with the leading officials of the Main Concessions Committee for a number of years. In the beginning I encountered a surprising amount of understanding and accommodation, and I found some of the committee members to be men with a great sense of responsibility, who did not in principle avoid dealing with foreign representatives. There were open and cultured persons like Matvei Skobelev, a former minister of labor in Kerensky's cabinet; Adolf Yoffe, the former Soviet ambassador in Berlin, and others. They had had a Western education and corresponding manners; more important, they still felt that even a non-Communist foreigner could be a trustworthy partner in negotiations. Devoted Bolsheviks though they were, they did not lack a certain ability of detachment, of seeing the other man's

point of view, and of recognizing weaknesses in their own position. Hence an atmosphere of mutual accommodation was not entirely stifled, and the Soviet negotiators themselves would at times tone down excessive demands or remove needless chicaneries. I had many fruitful discussions with these men, and together we conquered many difficult hurdles.

Gradually, the Soviet authorities began to restrict and prevent contacts with the Main Concessions Committee by various methods. When the embassy protested against this interference in our duties, we were told that negotiations concerning concessions contracts were sovereign acts in which the Soviet government could tolerate no interference from outside, least of all from diplomatic agencies. We countered with the claim that my contacts with the Main Concessions Committee served to safeguard German economic interests and were therefore an inalienable part of my functions as head of the embassy's economic department, and we appealed to the provisional treaty of 1921. Legally we were on somewhat shaky grounds because the treaty had granted the right of out-of-channels communication to a "commercial representative attached to the German Mission" but not to an organic official of the embassy in charge of its economic department. However, the agreement of May, 1921, was void after the treaty of October 12, 1925, had been concluded, and it did not help matters that the latter document in a vague fashion obliged the Soviet government to "take an accommodating attitude" toward German applicants in granting concessions. Our disagreement over the problem grew sharper as the years went by and the Soviet attitude stiffened. The question was not resolved until December, 1928, when it was discussed in the course of German-Soviet talks in Moscow. At that time we had to admit the impossibility of making the Soviet government abandon its views. One of the reasons was probably their conviction that the difficulties and disappointments in the field of concessions, about which we shall talk below, were bound to increase; and by preventing diplomatic intervention in concessions matters they obviously sought to escape the blame for future failures in this field. But when the entire negotiations threatened to break up over the question of our direct access to the Main Concessions Committee, the Soviet delegation proposed a compromise: If we would abandon our demand, they would be willing to give the head of the economic department of the embassy the right to deal directly (in economic

matters) not only with the People's Commissariats for Foreign Affairs and Foreign Trade but also with all other central authorities of the USSR, *except* the Main Concessions Committee. The Germans resisted for a long time but finally accepted the compromise, even though they doubted the good faith of the Soviet government from the very beginning. In this they proved quite justified. As it turned our later, the different central authorities, doubtless instructed from above, disregarded their obligation to deal with us, sabotaged direct negotiations right and left, and went out of their way to avoid any contact with the embassy. Economic information which was essential to me if I was to give expert advice to German firms and their representatives was not given by the commissariats even though I appealed to the assurances their government had given. Written inquiries were either left unanswered or yielded less information than could be gathered from Soviet newspapers. Frequently I was referred to the Foreign Commissariat, even though the very aim of the agreement had been to circumvent the Foreign Commissariat and thus to facilitate and speed up direct communications with the competent organizations. And when we complained to the Foreign Commissariat that the agreement was being sabotaged, we received evasive and unsatisfactory replies.

Later, in recalling these years, I have often thought that my original belief in the valuable opportunities open to Germany in 1921–1922 was far too optimistic. The brutality with which the Soviet government defied the concessions made to their own people and to foreign business when the NEP was introduced made me believe that the seeds planted in the seemingly fertile soil of 1921–1922 would not have come to full fruition. I was convinced that the Kremlin's readiness to cede portions of Russia's sovereignty as a price for the help of foreign capitalists would not have lasted long. Moreover, I traced a good deal of this readiness for sacrifice to the influence of bourgeois specialists, who at that time still had an appreciable influence in Soviet economic agencies. They were very eager in working out projects that would have linked the Soviet economy to the entire world economy, and, in private conversations with me, they frankly admitted that they regarded such policies and projects as a means by which the Soviet regime might be steered on a course of slow and gradual evolution.

But there are strong indications that the NEP, and with it a

grandiose policy of concessions to foreign capital, was meant very seriously at first. After all, the terror and the miseries of War Communism were still very much alive in every Communist leader. It was not only Lenin who announced the NEP "in earnest and for a long time"; it was not only bourgeois specialists who were ready to make astonishing concessions in order to attract foreign capital; even the most radical left-wing oppositionists within the party recognized at the time that their dreams of a speedy realization of Socialism had to be given up. Virtually every leading Communist at first accepted the NEP and its integral part, the concessions policy, as a large-scale strategic retreat that would have to be undertaken "in earnest and for a long time." The initial resistance against the retreat came not from the leading circles of the party, but from its lower levels, local Soviet organs, individuals within the bureaucracy; and there were widespread efforts in these lower levels of the Soviet state machine to sabotage the policy of retreat. Particularly the Cheka and GPU seem to have had difficulty in reconciling themselves with the intrusion of capitalistic elements into Soviet life. At first the reason was primarily ideological; the Cheka was the watchdog of revolutionary consciousness, the zealous guardian of proletarian orthodoxy. Later the GPU's hostility to the NEP was probably due more to fears that the concessions granted by the policy might undermine the powers of the secret police.

In the case of the highest Soviet leaders, we can speak of duplicity only in the long run. It is true that they meant to carry out the NEP in all seriousness; but it was never more than a retreat. Once the remaining terrain had been fortified, the party might try once more to attack. The general purpose of the foreign-trade commissar, Leonid Krasin, was to attract foreign concessionaires on a large scale. He seems to have believed that foreign capital should be allowed to build up the Soviet economy, and that then, instead of repaying its debts, the proletariat should do away with world capital by revolution. There is another sense in which one might speak of duplicity: Even while retreating, the Communist party meant to retain possession of the "commanding heights" in Russia's economy. And to the extent that the concessions policy threatened the hold of the party on these commanding heights, every Communist could not help regarding it as a thorn in the flesh of the Soviet organism.

This picture must be rounded out by viewing it from yet another

angle: Let us assume that Lenin and his comrades had grandiose ideas concerning the scope of the concessions policy. Whatever possibilities were opened, the capitalist world failed to make use of them. German business could not, in those years, muster sufficient capital for large-scale projects of reconstruction. Further West there was still too much open hostility against the Soviet regime to consider concessions very seriously, and the few ventures that were made did not show satisfactory results. W. A. Harriman, of the famous American family, had little reason to be pleased with the results of his manganese-ore concession at Chiatura in the Transcaucasus, and English attempts to run their former property, the Lena Goldfields Company, on a concessions basis turned out to be a failure. Thus the concessions policy developed only on a disappointingly small scale, and one might say that it was never really tried out. This forced the Russians to learn to stand on their own feet, and after they had tried their own strength they began to think that they could afford to give up the old plans of large-scale collaboration with the capitalist West. Trying to strengthen the foreign-trade monopoly, they sought by all means to prevent direct contacts between foreign firms and Soviet purchasers of their goods. The same Leonid Krasin who had endeavored to cater to concessionaires became one of the main defendants of the foreign-trade monopoly.

Thus the helpful attitude of Soviet officials in 1921–1922 was more than a bait guilefully thrown out. For such games the situation of the state was much too desperate in those early years. If the Soviet attitude stiffened, a great share of the blame falls on the inability of the bourgeois world to exploit Russia's weakness, or on its unwillingness to do business with Moscow. Perhaps it was mainly this failure of the West which virtually forced the Russians to return to sharper measures. In this sense never returning opportunities may indeed have been missed, opportunities, that is, of driving a permanent wedge into the doctrinaire isolationism of Soviet foreign economic policy and of thus steering the Soviet economy into a more moderate course. In retrospect it seems that the Russians were never serious and honest with their concessions propositions; but this may be a deceptive impression in which effects are taken for causes.

The first German firm to try the concessions game was the Krupp Corporation of Essen. Forced to convert its plants to peacetime demands, the firm was looking for means to prepare the way for large-

scale sales of its products in Soviet Russia. With this in mind, it concluded a concessions contract with the Soviet government in the fall of 1922, providing for the exploitation of agricultural land on the Manych River in the North Caucasus. The intention was to familiarize the Soviet government with German production methods in growing grain and to demonstrate the advantages of German agricultural implements. The project failed in the end, partly because the land given to the Krupp concession by the Soviet government was unsuitable for growing grain. It could, indeed, be utilized for raising sheep; and the managers of the concession successfully adapted themselves to the change. But they were confronted by so many material and administrative difficulties that after protracted and unpleasant negotiations, the contract was dissolved.[1]

The next step in German-Russian economic relations was taken toward the end of 1922 when an association of German business concerns led by the well known steel corporation Otto Wolff, of Cologne, jointly with the People's Commissariat for Foreign Trade, founded a mixed German-Soviet trading corporation which was given the name "Rusgertorg." [2] The structure of Rusgertorg became the model for similar contracts that were subsequently concluded in greater numbers between the Soviet government and foreign partners. These agreements were founded on the principle that the foreign partner was to furnish the capital and the necessary credits, whereas the contribution of the Soviet government consisted, as a rule, of no more than the granting of a concession to do business in the Soviet Union. The shares put forth by the newly founded corporation were, in the case of Rusgertorg, distributed equally between the two partners. In subsequent enterprises of this kind, however, the Soviet Government usually secured a majority of at least 51 per cent of the original capital stock. The problem of control turned into a continual source of friction and discussions and, in most of the cases, led to the premature dissolution of the contracts.

Rusgertorg, too, did not survive very long; but in its initial stages it was extremely profitable for both parties. Otto Wolff made a great

---

[1] The name Krupp sufficed to arouse the suspicion in other countries that the Manych concession was hiding secret German-Soviet collaboration in the military field. Nor was Manych a mining concession, as Ruth Fischer asserts.

[2] Russian abbreviation for "Russo-German Trade."

deal of money on sales to Russia, whereas the Soviet government obtained sorely needed credits and also profited from the fact that the example of Otto Wolff stimulated the interest of other firms, particularly in Germany and Austria, to conclude similar contracts with the Russians. Most of these subsequent contracts were concluded under conditions still more favorable for the Soviet government. On the other hand, the contract between Otto Wolff and the Foreign Trade Commissariat was abrogated by Wolff as early as January, 1924, after a sharp difference of opinion had developed between him and his Soviet partner in the question of credits. The wording of the contract had been ambiguous regarding the duration and extent of credits to be furnished; and the demands made by the Soviet government were rejected by Otto Wolff as unjustified. Thereupon the Russians accused him of breach of contract and began to throw difficulties in the path of Rusgertorg, thus provoking Wolff into canceling the contract. It seems to me that this was exactly what the Soviet government wanted; for Rusgertorg had succeeded in a very short time in attaining such an important place in the Soviet domestic trade that the government regarded its continued existence as a threat to its interests and to its own governmental trade organizations.

The case of Rusgertorg was a typical example of the way in which the Soviet government made use of its foreign partners as long as it derived benefit from such contracts, and dropped them as soon as the conditions under which the contracts were concluded had changed. One thing that aided them in this was the insufficient attention most Western businessmen paid to the formulation of agreements. Instead of working out the precise wording of agreements, and instead of insisting that they be fixed in writing, many of these men relied firmly on vague promises made orally and put their faith in general principles and customs of international trade. Inevitably differences of opinion would arise over the application of various points in the contract; and when these differences were to be ironed out in discussions the foreign entrepreneurs would usually be faced with Soviet government functionaries with whom they had had no dealings before, and who could quite properly refuse to talk about oral promises made by others. Inevitably the Soviet side would insist on the strict fulfillment of the letter of the contract, rejecting any liberal interpretation. Consequently, any agreement with Soviet economic or-

ganizations, even contracts of very minor importance, came to require difficult and time-consuming negotiations which taxed the patience and negotiating skill of the foreign partners quite heavily.

If we look back to the year 1922, we see how hesitatingly Germany approached the intensification of its political and economic relations with Soviet Russia even after Rapallo. Almost seven months went by, as the reader will recall, until Count Brockdorff-Rantzau assumed his duties as the first German ambassador. It took the Germans even longer to try to give an economic support to the new political relationship by the acquisition of a major lumber concession.

Negotiations, which began in late March, 1923, and ended in October of that year with the conclusion of a concessions contract, were conducted by a German delegation set up and sent to Moscow by the Rhine-Elbe-Union cartel and the Himmelsbach wholesale lumber company of Freiburg, Baden. The leader of the delegation was the former German Chancellor Dr. Josef Wirth. The personal interest he showed in the concessions contract favorably affected the spirit in which the negotiations were conducted, because Wirth had been one of the fathers of the Rapallo Treaty and enjoyed the good will of the Soviet government. Later he became the chairman of the board of directors in the German corporation that obtained the concessions, and evil tongues asserted that the whole concession was his reward for Rapallo. How far from the mark this bolt hit was subsequently proved by the lack of understanding the Soviet authorities showed for the needs of the concession and by the tenacity with which they stood up for their own interests in the enterprise.

At the start of the negotiations the Soviet government proposed to grant the concession to a mixed corporation, to be founded by itself and the German partner. The Germans, however, refused because they correctly feared that such an arrangement would jeopardize their freedom of action excessively. The Russians relented and declared themselves willing to recognize a purely German joint-stock corporation as carrier of the concession.

In the choice of the object of concession, sober economic considerations played a much smaller role on both sides than the idea of making the concession as large as possible, by all means, in order to make it an effective advertisement for Rapallo. Consequently, they agreed on a timber area comprising no less than 800,000 hectares (about 2,000,000 acres). We shall talk about the burdens which this

enormous area placed upon the shoulders of the concessionaire in a moment—burdens which were all the more unbearable because the entire enterprise seems to have been born under an unlucky star. While the negotiations went on, Germany's economic and financial situation went from bad to worse under the impact of the galloping inflation. Soon after the contract had been concluded, it became apparent that the entire capital originally furnished by the concessionaires had been swallowed by the inflation, and the project had to be shored up by loans. This, together with some other adversities, resulted in the failure of all attempts to keep the enterprise going, and in the spring of 1927 it had to be liquidated.

As we shall see, the German concessionaire bore part of the responsibility for the failure of this particular enterprise. But its unfavorable development was decisively influenced and deepened by the inability and unwillingness of the Soviet government to create conditions under which foreign capital might have worked successfully in the Soviet Union. The very atmosphere in which the concessions contracts were shaped was in most cases ill suited to create healthy preconditions for mutually beneficial collaboration. The Soviet negotiators usually had one-sided and exaggerated notions of the alleged greed for profit and cunning of their capitalist partners; hence their attitude of extreme distrust. They had, moreover, an intense fear of responsibility, particularly when it came to granting benefits or acceding to unforeseen demands. Since the would-be concessionaires usually lacked the necessary experience and knowledge, the Soviet negotiators often succeeded in carrying through demands which later turned out to be incapable of fulfillment and thus sapped the life out of the concessions.

The attitude of the foreign negotiators was often based on limited faith in the staying power of the Soviet system, an attitude that prompted them to invest a minimum of capital with the purpose of recovering it as fast as possible by making a maximum of profits from the very beginning, so that they could withdraw, if necessary, after a short time. This criticism, by the way, does not apply to those Germans who founded "Mologales," [3] for they had the honest intention of founding an enterprise useful for both partners and effective for a long period; and they believed that the Soviet government was

---

[3] Mologa is the name of a tributary of the Volga, on the banks of which the timber area of the concession was situated. *Les* is Russian for "wood."

motivated by the same good will. Nevertheless, they share the guilt in the failure of the concession because they approached their task with insufficient knowledge of Russian conditions and without the necessary financial backing. Even during the negotiations over the concessions contract they committed grave mistakes by not recognizing that the demands put to them by the Soviet side were impossible to fulfill. Later they failed to see the danger inherent in the disproportion between capital stock and borrowed capital which burdened the enterprise with unbearable interest payments. In spite of these difficulties, they continued to manage their affairs on the grandiose style which they thought the long-range aims of the undertaking demanded.

Nevertheless it might have been possible to weather the crisis and to save the business, since the German government, for political motives, was willing, in principle, to make financial contributions to keep the concession alive. But at this point the Soviet government refused to make any sacrifices of their own for the sake of reconstructing Mologales by freeing it of some of the unbearable obligations of the concessions contract. These obligations called, among other things, for the construction of a railroad line through the timber area, the erection of numerous workers' dwellings, and the financing of welfare institutions to an extent amounting to not less than 40 per cent of the wages. An additional burden was the fact that the concession could not compete with the Soviet lumber trusts because the latter paid 30 per cent lower rail freight and were favored in all other aspects by the government.

When the balance sheet of the concession was drawn in the summer of 1926, it became apparent that it had lost 20,000,000 reichsmarks in the course of two and a half years; of this loss 3,000,000 fell on the capital stock, and 17,000,000 on the German creditors. The German government faced the alternative of lending a helping hand or watching the advertising sign for Rapallo being pulled in. The decision was very difficult for the cabinet, particularly because Germany had no economic interest in maintaining the concession, which was working exclusively for the Russian market. Only political motives favored the reconstruction of the enterprise. The Foreign Ministry feared that the Soviet government would regard the abandonment of the concession as a sign that Germany's attitude to Soviet Russia was

cooling. Berlin thought it necessary to make sacrifices for the sake of maintaining friendly relations with the Soviet state. As a consequence, the Reich Credit Corporation (Reichskreditgesellschaft) decided to advance 15 million marks for the reconstruction of Mologales under the conditions that the Soviet government participate in the reconstruction by discounting the concession's bills of exchange, and that the enterprise be freed from some of the most unbearable obligations. By refuting all these conditions, the Soviet government condemned all German efforts to keep the concession alive to failure and made its liquidation inevitable.

Among the other enterprises founded in the Soviet Union after 1923 with German capital were three transport companies, two agricultural concessions, and four small industrial undertakings. The three transport companies were organized as mixed German-Russian joint-stock corporations. Their management was partly in German and partly in Soviet hands, which often led to friction; on the other hand, the mixed-company type offered advantages even for the German partners in that it gave them a certain backing in their dealings with Soviet authorities. The German partners in mixed companies usually had an easier time than concessionaires because the latter were completely on their own in dealings with Soviet officialdom, except for the support given them in some cases by the embassy.

The first of the transport companies to be founded was "Derutra," a German-Russian transport company created by the Foreign Trade Commissariat and the Hamburg-American Line. In its attempt to work with its Soviet partner, the Hamburg-American Line from the beginning met great difficulties which were due to the clumsiness of the Soviet economic system and the distrustful attitude of Soviet agencies. Things were made more difficult for the Germans by virtue of the fact that Derutra obtained a virtual monopoly in the transportation business connected wth German-Soviet trade. This netted them the enmity of all those German transportation firms which were also interested in the German-Soviet freight business. In 1926 Derutra ceased its activities after the partnership had been dissolved by the Soviet government. The Russians never gave their German partners a plausible explanation for their step; but the obvious reason was that the Hamburg-American Line, through its participa-

tion in the mixed enterprise, had had a closer view of Soviet economic conditions than Moscow desired.

Very early, the joint interest of Germany and Soviet Russia in regular air communications between Berlin and Moscow led to the creation of "Deruluft," a mixed German-Soviet air transport company which survived because its existence corresponded to a mutual necessity.

"Rustransit," on the other hand, created by a German association and the Foreign Trade Commissariat for transit traffic to Persia, had to fight against constant difficulties because the Soviet government had granted transit rights to the East only very grudgingly, and sought to restrict their use as much as possible.

Of the two agricultural concessions only "Drusag" (Deutsch-Russische Saatbau-Aktiengesellschaft) survived for a long time, and that only because the Reich in the end granted financial assistance to keep the concession above water. What finally spelled the doom of Drusag was the fact that, owing to expert management, it developed into a model agricultural enterprise, the prosperity of which stood in sharp contrast to the misery of the North Caucasian villages surrounding it. For the Soviet government this was reason enough to turn against the concession with customary ruthlessness. It harassed the managers of Drusag through the arrest of key employees and the institution of a criminal trial against them, as well as discriminatory taxation; finally its liquidation became inevitable.

The four industrial concessions were plants producing commodities which were of only minor importance for the Soviet economy. Moreover, the capacity of these works did not by any means reach the proportions of which the Soviet government had dreamed when it decided to give foreign capital the opportunity of participating in the reconstruction of the Soviet economy. The insecure profits which the German entrepreneurs gained from the concessions were utterly inadequate in relation to the pain and sacrifices expended to keep the enterprises operating. On the other hand, the benefits the concessions offered to the Soviet economy were not sufficient to justify the dent which their existence made in the planned economy of the Socialist state. Thus, in the long run, the four concessions, engaged in the manufacture of printer's ink, buttons, enamelware, and toothpaste, respectively, caused more annoyance and vexation than practical benefits, and neither party regretted the inevitable consequences.

2. THE ECONOMIC TREATIES OF OCTOBER 12, 1925

In my memorandum of May, 1923, I had suggested that it was time to begin regulating the legal bases of German-Soviet trade relations by a comprehensive treaty, even though Germany was then in a state of extreme economic weakness owing to the occupation of the Ruhr Basin. I mentioned several reasons why negotiations for such a treaty should be started now: Russia's relations to England had cooled markedly; possibilities for an understanding with France had still not become apparent; negotiations with Sweden had been broken off without result; the ratification of a treaty concluded with Denmark was being delayed; and the possibility of a rapprochement with Poland was far off. All of these factors would dispose the Soviet government to make concessions, particularly since she was vitally interested in exporting her agricultural produce. In a report to Berlin the ambassador endorsed my views and added his own comments, reflecting the impression which the events in the Ruhr had made on him. The road to the West, he asserted, could lead Germany only to a slave status. The only way to get Germany out of her misery lay, not in unconditional surrender to Moscow, but in planned and purposive collaboration with the Russians economically and politically.

The negotiations which began in Berlin in June, 1923, lasted altogether for more than two years. Interrupted several times, they ended on October 12, 1925, with the conclusion of a voluminous cluster of treaties laying down a network of rules and regulations governing the economic relations between the two countries. An incident that occurred on May 3, 1924, in Berlin, rudely interrupted these talks about a German-Russian trade treaty and also interrupted active trade relations. The occurrence played a role transcending the framework of German-Soviet relations, and turned into a precedent-setting affair. For the Soviet government succeeded in having the incident settled under conditions which decidedly favored their long-standing attempts to obtain extraterritorial privileges for their trade representations abroad.

A German Communist, under arrest, was being escorted through the streets of Berlin by two officers of the criminal police who were

strangers in the city. Taking advantage of their ignorance, the Communist led them to the building of the Soviet trade representation,
freed himself, and disappeared in the building. Two hours later a
squad of German police broke into the premises of the trade representation and, under the pretext of searching for the escaped prisoner,
made a thorough search of the rooms, including desks and file cabinets. It is alleged that Communist propaganda literature in the German language was discovered in the course of the search, though
naturally the Soviet version denies this part of the story. In any
event, it is of no great importance in this case. The Soviet protests
were based on the claim that the police search of the offices constituted a breach of international law inasmuch as the trade representation enjoyed the privilege of extraterritoriality on the bases of
existing agreements. The agreement referred to was the provisional
treaty of May 6, 1921; but this granted extraterritorial rights only
to the head and seven members of the trade representation. Whatever the legality of the search, however, it was clear that the police
had gone further than the most liberal interpretation of existing
agreements would have permitted, for an escaped prisoner is not
found in desk drawers and file cabinets. For once, therefore, the burden of settling the incident rested squarely on our shoulders.

The Soviet government from the beginning made an attempt to
use the incident for the purpose of having the trade representation
recognized as an integral part of the embassy, and hence as extraterritorial without limitations. It immediately resorted to reprisals
by breaking off all economic relations with Germany, regardless of
the fact that the measure at that time was a severe blow to their own
interests. Obviously, they were ready to incur even these disadvantages
and losses as a price that had to be paid. The break placed the German government in a very uncomfortable position because German
business circles interested in trade with the Soviet Union felt the
rupture of relations as a detrimental blow, and they immediately applied pressure for a speedy settlement of the conflict. Count Rantzau
suggested creating a joint court of arbitration to decide the issue.
The German police, however, through the Ministry of the Interior,
categorically refused his proposal, for they could not bear the thought
that the justice of their measures against the trade representation
should be challenged and judged by an *ad hoc* organization whose
legitimacy they refused to acknowledge. How curiously similar—at

least in this respect—were the relations of the German police and the GPU to their respective Foreign Offices! Negotiations to settle the conflict dragged on for almost three months, particularly since the Russians demanded in addition that the German government apologize and punish the guilty police officials. Nor did it desist from its demands when the ambassador once again threatened to leave Moscow and even asked for exit visas for himself and the closest members of his entourage.

I participated in all the negotiations between Rantzau and the Russians over the settlement of the conflict; and the more they were drawn out, and the more the situation sharpened, the greater grew my worries over the future of German-Soviet relations. I finally decided, therefore, to resort to means I had already used with success on similar occasions: an appeal to Radek, for whom the maintenance of German-Russian relations meant more than a useful means to an end, and who always reacted positively when these relations were in danger. After the death of Lenin he had lost some of his political importance, but in the summer of 1924 he was still able to influence personalities and politics in the Kremlin. When I invited him to my house, he came at once, and in the ensuing tête-à-tête I first of all convinced myself that he was fully aware of the seriousness of the situation. On the condition that Rantzau would retract his threat to leave Moscow, Radek offered to influence the Soviet government sufficiently to avoid a rupture in our negotiations. Upon this I telephoned the ambassador. Although it was very late at night, he hurried to my place immediately, and we three continued our talk. The sun was already in the sky when we parted. We all felt that the situation was not at all so hopeless as it had seemed a day earlier; with the help of such additional channels as Karl Radek could open for us it would be possible to settle the conflict. The final result of the talks was that the Russians obtained most of what they wanted and thus scored a decisive gain, which we had to concede as the lesser evil under the circumstances. A protocol, which was signed on July 29, 1924, in Berlin, recognized three-fifths of the premises of the trade representation as being extraterritorial and thus created a situation from which it was only one more step to recognize the full extraterritoriality of the entire trade representation. An agreement to that effect was incorporated in the trade treaty of October 12, 1925; and this in turn subsequently served the Russians as an important

precedent for getting other states to grant extraterritorial privileges to Soviet trade representations. In this way the Russians once again made Germany the involuntary pacemaker in shaping their relations with the outside world.

The settlement of the conflict opened the way toward a renewal of the trade-treaty negotiations that had begun in Berlin. The talks were resumed in Moscow in November, 1924.

The Moscow negotiations were characterized by the fact that, in working for a broad treaty regulating the economic relations between the two countries, the Germans were mainly interested in material results, whereas the Russians had their eye principally on the tactical advantages that might be gained. Moscow was primarily interested in demonstrating that an understanding of, and economic interchange with, the Soviet regime was possible, whatever the differences in social systems. In this manner the Russians wanted to arouse the competitive spirit of the capitalist world and open the way for corresponding agreements with other countries. They were by no means willing, however, to make concessions on the subject of the foreign-trade monopoly. In his opening speech Krasin left no doubt that the Soviet government would under no circumstances let anyone prevent it from realizing the plans for industrialization which were already then being envisaged, and that it was firmly resolved to enter no agreements tending to restrict the foreign-trade monopoly, which he characterized as one of the main pillars of the Soviet structure. He indicated that he would strive for the untrammeled recognition of this monopoly as well as of the extraterritorial privileges of the Soviet trade representations, and the Russians wanted this recognition incorporated in the treaty permanently.

The Germans, on the other hand, tried to lessen the effect of the monopoly by demanding that German firms be given the right of acquisition in the Soviet Union, that German sales in Soviet Russia be guaranteed by fixing quotas, and that the most-favored-nation treatment provided for in the Rapallo Treaty remain unrestricted. Even tsarist Russia had traditionally made significant exceptions in the application of most-favored-nation clauses, pleading that owing to certain peculiarities in her relations with China and the Middle East she had to grant these neighbors a number of favorable conditions which could not be granted to Western nations. The Soviet negotiators demanded that this practice be recognized; but because recogni-

tion would have meant a serious qualification of the most-favored-nation treatment Germany had been granted in the Rapallo Treaty the German delegation fought against it with great vigor, though without success. In general the Russians had their way on most important issues, and if the voluminous treaty was nevertheless concluded it was because for political reasons Germany at that time could ill afford to let the negotiations fail. In a memorandum which Stresemann submitted to the Reich cabinet on July 13, 1925, he wrote that the German delegation had suggested postponing all further negotiations until the fall because they were taking such an unsatisfactory course, but its proposal was rejected by him. Moscow, he said, had become so suspicious of German dealings with the Western powers that it would have regarded the mere move to adjourn as a sign that German foreign policy was definitely turning away from Soviet Russia; and in view of the unfortunate course of recent economic negotiations with the French and the Poles, Germany's foreign trade, the minister concluded, was in need of the Soviet business.

The German government, therefore, abandoned its original demands and had to be satisfied that at least the form of the treaties, the juridical formulation of the specific agreements, and a number of detailed provisions corresponded to its ideas. The treaty that was signed was a cluster of agreements codifying in considerable detail consular relations, customs, inspection, residence and property regulations, and other problems arising in various types of economic dealings.

From the Soviet point of view, the treaty was, on the whole, a great success. True, some clauses that were inserted for the protection of various German economic interests, particularly the farmers, tended to restrict Soviet exports to Germany. But the foreign-trade monopoly and the extraterritoriality of trade representations had been given additional treaty recognition and were being firmly anchored in international custom. The great expectations which German business circles had in the treaty at the time of its conclusion were hardly realized. The hope that Russia's gradual integration into the world economy would render the foreign-trade monopoly more flexible and accommodating in application was not fulfilled. Neither did the careful codification of economic relations help to adjust the economic and legal systems of the two countries to each other, as some had predicted. Contrary to German expectations, moreover, the

proportion of exports into Soviet Russia to the total German exports did not rise appreciably. From 1925 to 1928 the proportion rose only from 2.9 per cent to 3.3 per cent, and in 1928 the Soviet Union ranked twelfth as a customer for German goods.

3. CREDITS

German-Soviet trade relations were from the very beginning characterized by Russia's constant great need for large, long-term credits. But Germany's own financial strength was limited in the early 1920's, and German as well as foreign banking circles had little faith in the Bolshevik regime's ability or willingness to repay any advances. In addition, the German government had to take into consideration the attitude of the Western powers with whom it was bargaining over reparations payments; it could hardly afford to prejudice the reduction of the reparations load by granting credits to the Soviet Union.

None the less, mutual German-Soviet interest clearly called for generous credit arrangements. The first modest attempt to further German trade with Soviet Russia by a credit transaction was made in 1923 when the so-called "grain agreement" was concluded. This agreement was based on German willingness to advance 50 per cent of the value of twenty million poods [4] of grain to be delivered by Russia. In turn, the Soviet trade representation agreed to use the advance for the purpose of placing additional orders with German industrial firms.

Fully two more years passed before the Germans took another step in the same direction. In the negotiations that led to the conclusion of the treaty of October 12, 1925, the Soviet delegation had repeatedly and emphatically pointed out that credits were the essential precondition for the development of German-Soviet trade. The government in Berlin was not in principle opposed to a discussion of pertinent Soviet proposals, but it roundly declined to grant a credit of several hundred million reichsmarks demanded by the Russians. On October 6, 1925, an agreement was signed by which an initial credit of 75 million reichsmarks was granted, an amount which was later raised to 100 million. The funds were raised by a group of leading German banks and secured by two drafts made out by the Soviet State Bank and accepted by the Soviet trade representation in Berlin. The notes

[4] About 328,000 tons.

were payable in New York, one half of the loan on January 29th, the remainder on February 28, 1926, with 8½ per cent interest added.

Neither the amount of the credit nor its very short term corresponded to the wishes and expectations of the Soviet government; but the transaction none the less turned out to be a precedent of great importance to them, and one from which it derived great benefit in the development of trade relations with other countries. Little immediate boost, however, was given to German-Soviet trade itself, since individual German firms had meanwhile given the Soviet government credits of greater duration; hence the very short-term bank credit provided no stimulus to place additional orders with German industry. If we wished to put our trade with the Soviet Union on a healthier and broader basis, we had to take the Russians' need for greater and long-term credits into consideration; moreover, we had to be aware that the majority of German business corporations interested in trading with the Soviet Union were in no position to assume the whole risk of such credits.

Opinions in Germany were sharply divided at that time over the question whether trade with Soviet Russia on the basis of long-term credits would constitute an undue risk for the seller. Wide circles asserted that the financial collapse of the Soviet economy would only be a question of time, and that business relations with Moscow should be undertaken only with the greatest caution. I, together with many others, held the contrary opinion. My continuous observation of Soviet reality had taught me, among other things, that the Soviet government regarded the prompt fulfillment of its international obligations as a factor on which its very economic existence would depend. The Russians were aware that if only one Soviet note were dishonored, all foreign sources of credit would dry up at once. For that reason they lacked neither consistency nor ruthlessness when they felt the need to squeeze the last remnants of gold and *valuta* from their own harassed population by methods that need not be discussed in detail here. If we want to assess the possibilities open to a dictatorially governed state, we cannot overlook the decisive fact that the financial collapse of the Soviet economy, so often predicted throughout the 1920's, failed to occur; on the contrary, then and later all international obligations were punctually met, and the subsequent years of the world depression became a period of stupendous economic advance in Soviet Russia.

Theoretical considerations of this sort were not, however, sufficient to make long-term credits in sizable amounts available to the Soviet economy. In order to attain this end, and for the purpose of enabling German firms to grant credits to their Soviet customer, the German government at long last decided on a novel measure, which was applied for the first time in February, 1926, when German business made a credit of 300 million reichsmarks available to the Soviet government. This credit was made possible by a decision of the German government to diminish the risk by backing the creditors with a 35 per cent guarantee in case of default. In other words, should the Soviet government fail to honor its debt the German Reich would reimburse the German creditors 35 per cent of their loss. In addition, the creditors were assured that in actual fact 60 per cent of their risk was taken off their own shoulders, since the Reich government had requested the various German *Länder* to participate in the transaction with a further 25 per cent.

Such "Reich Default Guarantees" subsequently became a standard feature of German-Soviet trade relations. And yet the remaining clauses of this first agreement show how very carefully Berlin was still approaching credit deals with the Soviet Union. For instance, half of the 300 million had to be paid back by the end of 1928, that is, after little more than two years, and the use of this part of the sum was restricted to the purchase of commodities which demonstrably constituted export beyond and above normal deliveries. The remaining half became due at the end of 1930 and could be used only for machinery destined to equip precisely defined Soviet industries. As we shall see in a later chapter, trade relations with the Soviet Union did not become vitally important to the German economy until after the world economic crisis had set in.

VII MILITARY
COLLABORATION 1919-1930

1. THE BEGINNINGS

In the last days of 1925 the German press reported that the Soviet foreign commissar had been the luncheon guest of none other than Colonel General Hans von Seeckt, chief of the army's high command. The reader will recall that at this time Chicherin was spending a few weeks in Berlin on his return from German and French health resorts. The source of the news concerning his visit with von Seeckt immediately became a subject for speculation. *Germania,* the organ of the Center party, alleged that Count Brockdorff-Rantzau had deliberately let the news leak out in an attempt to sabotage Germany's rapprochement with the Western powers. The count was said to be seriously at odds with the Foreign Ministry, particularly with Herr von Schubert, its permanent undersecretary. I have no indication that this story is correct; but, given Rantzau's bitter feelings over the Locarno settlement and Stresemann's efforts to join the League, it is not entirely impossible that it was he who released the story. In the Social Democratic press the reaction was sharp and indignant. Friendly relations of the Reichswehr chief with the Soviet Union behind the backs of the Reichstag and, presumably, the foreign minister were considered to be an arbitrary act contrary to the Reich's policy, and one which called for von Seeckt's dismissal. The Social Democratic papers featured exaggerated reports about unfavorable reaction to the "secret talks" in France and England. The Communist *Rote Fahne,* on the other hand, wrote on December 31, 1925: "A man would have to be very stupid indeed to believe in actual fact that the Reich government would negotiate about a military alliance with Soviet Russia just after the conclusion of the Locarno

187

Treaty; he would have to be even dumber to suppose that the Soviet government would enter into such secret negotiations."

Even at that time no attempt was made by the German government to deny that the two gentlemen had met. Instead, the Foreign Ministry tried to put the luncheon meeting into a harmless light. Upon the suggestion of the Wilhelmstrasse, *Kreuz-Zeitung* declared the meeting to have been a courtesy visit, purely a matter of form, at which, moreover, two officials from the Foreign Office had been present to prevent any unauthorized "deals." The rumors concerning Rantzau's poor relations with the Foreign Ministry were dismissed as without foundation. Similar attempts to minimize the significance of the luncheon were made by TASS a few days later.

Eleven months later, on December 3, 1926, the *Manchester Guardian* published a sensational article asserting that the German armed forces, in blatant violation of the Versailles Peace Treaty, were closely collaborating with the Red Army. The German aircraft firm of Junkers, the *Guardian* stated, was operating a branch factory near Moscow; Germans had established poison-gas factories in the Soviet Union; frequent trips were being made by officers of the German Army to the Soviet Union; and finally, the *Guardian* claimed to have knowledge about large shipments of ammunition from Leningrad to Germany. These shipments had allegedly been observed in transit in the harbor of Stettin.

The British Liberal paper severely castigated German military circles for the secret dealings of which the above information was an indication, but it emphatically absolved the Foreign Ministry and the German government as a whole from any responsibility for the dealings; indeed, it expressed the belief that the German government would "terminate forthwith" such illegal doings now that they had been exposed, "so that, sensational as the facts may seem, it will soon be possible to regard them as belonging to the past."

The *Manchester Guardian* article, as well as subsequent, more specific, charges, were reprinted in full by the Berlin Social Democratic paper *Vorwärts* two days later. Though the serious political storm unleashed led to the fall of the cabinet, it did not have any appreciable lasting effects on Soviet or German policy, nor did it elicit any additional information from any source concerning the precise nature and extent of German-Soviet military collaboration, except for a vague declaration from the ministries concerned that the col-

laboration, which had, admittedly, taken place, had already been terminated. A short history of German-Soviet military collaboration will show that this was only half of the truth.[1]

On February 12, 1919, the German police arrested Karl Radek, who had been one of the Soviet emissaries participating in the

[1] Disagreements between Socialist and Communist stevedores in Stettin at the time three steamships carrying Soviet ammunition were being unloaded had put the Social Democratic party on the trail of some of the evidence in October, 1926, and further revelations were made in February, 1927, by the French news agency Havas and by the Social Democratic paper *Leipziger Volkszeitung*. Later, in November, 1929, the Soviet counselor of embassy at Paris, Besedovsky, who had refused to return to Moscow when he was recalled, made similar revelations.

Rumors about a secret German-Soviet military alliance had, however, been spread ever since Rapallo, and would be aired in the press every once in a while. Typical of these vague accusations was an article in the *Morning Post* of Aug. 16, 1923, entitled "German Influence in Russia: A Military Monopoly." These rumors were given credence even in the highest political circles in Germany; von Hindenburg still believed them after he had been sworn in as Reich President in 1925. Stresemann's papers relate the old field marshal's great relief when he was informed to the contrary by his foreign minister (Stresemann, *Vermächtnis*, II, 60). Few people, it seems, were convinced by the intermittent denials issued in Berlin and Moscow (for instance, Trotsky's attempt to ridicule the rumors in *Izvestiya*, Aug. 27, 1922, and a TASS denial in *Izvestiya*, Oct. 6, 1923).

German-Soviet military co-operation became the subject of much speculation and indignant exposés written by scholars and journalists with axes to grind. The most thorough utilization of all available scraps of information is C. F. Melville's *The Russian Face of Germany* (London, Wishart & Company, 1932). Other important references are Erich Wollenberg's *The Red Army* (London, Secker & Warburg, 1941), and two recent articles, George W. F. Hallgarten's "General Hans von Seeckt and Russia, 1920-1922" (*Journal of Modern History*, Vol. XXI, No. 1, pp. 28-34), and G. Strohm's "Vierzehn Jahre deutsch-sowjetische Militärallianz" (*Stuttgarter Rundschau*, III, 11, 12). Further bits of information are revealed in the November, 1948, issue of *Der Monat* under the title "Der Seeckt-Plan," by Julius Epstein; in Graf Heinrich Einsiedel's *Tagebuch der Versuchung* (Berlin-Stuttgart, Pontes-Verlag), and in Jesco von Puttkamer's *Irrtum und Schuld*. Besides Wollenberg, Ruth Fischer (*Stalin and German Communism*) and Franz Borkenau (*World Communism*) are among the former German Communists who refer to the subject.

None of the references cited go very far beyond the material revealed in the beginning of 1926, except by guesswork, unproven allegations, and at times wild speculation not based on any sound evidence. Strohm implicitly makes the agreement of May 6, 1921, into a military agreement negotiated by Krasin and General von Seeckt; both Borkenau and Melville are certain that the Treaty of Rapallo included a secret military agreement; Hallgarten converts the Krupp agricultural concession into a sinister military business.

What almost all these sources have in common—and what has been the reason for many of their factual errors—is the tone of righteous indignation over the sinister dealings between Prussian generals and Red dictators, an attitude that belongs quite properly in political pamphlets, but is not always conducive to correct historical scholarship.

abortive Communist uprising known as the Spartacus Rebellion. Radek was thrown in jail in Berlin and treated very roughly at first, according to the story he told some years later. Gradually, however, his jailers became more polite. His manacles were removed, he was given a better cell and better food, and he was even permitted to obtain German and foreign newspapers. One day, Radek continues his story, his guard handed him a rather fancy chamber pot, a strange present which caused him some wonder:

I immediately came to the conclusion that the affair was a strange reflection of some kind of changes in world politics. In fact, from the London *Times* I found out that the Soviet government of the Ukraine had appointed me ambassador in Berlin and had demanded that I be freed and installed in the embassy. . . . Since diplomatic relations had been severed with the Soviet government of Russia, but not the Ukraine, my dear friend Christian Georgievich Rakovsky had resolved to try getting me out of jail by appointing me to a diplomatic post. The German Ministry of Foreign Affairs, headed by the Social Democrat August Müller, did not agree with Rakovsky, but decided nevertheless to show a little concern for the situation of the unrecognized diplomat sitting in jail. It asked the Ministry of Justice about my circumstances. Justice asked the prison, and the head of the prison decided to show politeness by a present of prime necessity. "Small causes frequently have great consequences," said some ancient who amused himself in the old days by formulating human experience in pretty aphorisms. Here great causes led to tiny consequences.[2]

This little story and Radek's comment on it are significant only because Radek was correct in sensing a change in the attitude of his jailers. Upon his arrest he had calmed down an angry colonel, who was hurling abusive threats at him, with the question, "Now that the Entente is disarming you, why do you Germans want to make yourselves yet another enemy, Soviet Russia?" Clearly, the German military thought of Communism as a menace; but Russia would remain a possible ally of great potential strength.

Radek was soon transferred to a comfortable room in the prison; and after he was given permission to receive visitors (permits to see him were obtained in the War Ministry) his quarters turned into a

[2] Karl Radek, "November," in *Krasnaia nov'*, No. 10, pp. 139–175 (October, 1926). Prof. E. H. Carr, to whom the present chapter was shown in manuscript, subsequently translated Radek's article and published excerpts from it in *Soviet Studies*, Vol. III, No. 4.

political salon, where young Communist leaders came for advice, statesmen to air their views—and officers to establish contact and talk about possible military collaboration, particularly against Poland. After his release from prison, Radek lived for a while in the apartment of one of these officers, a Baron Eugen von Reibnitz, who many years later revealed that definite arrangements for a new division of Poland were made by him and Radek. The capture of Warsaw by the Red Army was to have been the signal for the German Freikorps to move across the new boundaries.

It seems that von Reibnitz and another of Radek's visitors, Colonel Max Bauer, were both connected closely with General Ludendorff. Like their chief, they were not typical of German military opinion in these days. In the first months after the revolution, the prevailing attitude among the German generals seems to have been the hope that they could make themselves indispensable to England and France by fighting Bolshevism. The hope may have been coupled with long-standing ambitions of Eastward expansion, of which a memorandum penned by General von Seeckt, probably in 1915, is one of the most radical expressions.[3] The combination of the two

---

[3] General Hans von Seeckt, it seems, was not always in favor of military cooperation between Germany and Russia. His policy of collaboration was the consequence of Germany's defeat and the irreconcilable attitude of the Western Allies at Versailles. Before that time, the general seems to have had somewhat different ideas.

Among the voluminous papers of General von Seeckt, now in the United States National Archives, there is a memorandum written unmistakably in the general's own hand. According to a penciled notation (most probably added by General von Rabenau, von Seeckt's official biographer), the memorandum was probably written in 1915. It is here printed for the first time.

Whether the war aims expressed in the memorandum are those he himself advocated in 1915, or whether he merely copied someone else's ideas, cannot be ascertained. It is certain that von Seeckt was at least not unsympathetic to them, even though he might have put them in a less radical form. Even so, they deserve to be published as a typical expression of traditional aspirations gone wild during wartime. It reads as follows:

Separate peace with France and Belgium, on the basis of status quo ante. Then all land forces against Russia. Conquest of ten thousand square miles, expelling the population, except, of course, Germans. Russia has a lot of room for them, particularly in magnificent Southern Siberia.

The German people needs great tasks. But we must not diffuse ourselves all over the world, but must concentrate our efforts in Europe. Form: Kingdom of Ostmark under Eitel Friedrich. Free distribution of vastest lands to a million or more veterans who want to become colonizers, the size growing with the rank. Faced with the greed this stimulates, all resistance on the part of Social Democracy and Center will collapse at once. Once there are 200 millions of healthy and

ambitions led to the Baltic adventure, in which German irregulars, with the tacit connivance of the War Ministry, fought side by side with Allied troops and domestic anti-Communists to expel the Red forces from the Baltic provinces. Once their mission was completed, the German units were forced by the Allies to dissolve. The maneuver had failed; the Baltic adventure had been nothing more than an important breeding ground for German fascism. And Versailles proved conclusively that the West did not think a well armed Germany indispensable.

But even before Versailles more influential sections of the military turned toward collaboration with Soviet Russia. The first attempt of General von Seeckt to make contact with the Russians seems to have been made in April of 1919. At that time the general aided his good friend Enver Pasha to cross the *cordon sanitaire* and reach Soviet territory. A Turkish revolutionary, nationalist, officer, and an ardent foe of British imperialism, Enver had become acquainted with the general during the war; after the defeat of Turkey he had fled to Germany and remained in close contact with his friend von Seeckt;

---

mostly German people on 200 thousand square miles of soil, say in the year 2000, we shall be at least somewhat secure against this immense Russia that might one day give birth to another Peter the Great. Skobelev already was dangerous.

This war will probably cost us a million men, among them the best. (In the beginning of January we had a total of 150,000 dead, 550,000 wounded, 225,000 of them serious, 325,000 light, and 150,000 missing.) Against this what does it mean to expel 20 million men, among them a lot of riffraff of Jews, Poles, Masurians, Lithuanians, Letts, Esthonians, etc.?

We have the power to do it; and we have been plunged into conditions which in terms of blood and destruction leave the age of migration far behind; hence, let us behave according to the customs of the age of migration.

Our ally can get his share of the spoils in Volhynia and Podolia if he wants.

Russia with her 400 thousand square miles will come to accept the loss of land, particularly if we cover her rear for further expansion in Asia.

In any event it seems to me to be easier to expel 20 million Russians than to digest 7½ million Belgians.

Were she to win the war, Russia would take from us at least East Prussia, and West Prussia on the right bank of the Vistula, i.e., about one tenth of the area and one twentieth of the population of the German Reich.

If thus the entire German surplus of energy is for three generations concentrated on colonization in the East, then peace with England on the basis of the status quo also becomes possible; for we shall then have no conflicting interests in the foreseeable future. But if England wants it differently, then our navy is strong enough to continue the war ad infinitum.

Should we need more colonies later, we could conquer them. But in the year 2000 the issue will hardly be between Germany and England, but between Europe, Asia, and America.

and now he was given an airplane with which he set out to fly to Soviet Russia.[4] He was captured by British troops, however, when he had to make a forced landing in Lithuania. By a miracle a friend of General von Seeckt, Major Fritz Tschunke, who was leading a Freikorps unit in Lithuania, recognized Enver before the British had seen through his disguise, and he helped him to escape.[5] I saw Enver Pasha in Moscow several times in the early 1920's. About the nature of his mission on behalf of General von Seeckt or his accomplishments I have no knowledge. There are no indications, however, that the German feeler had any appreciable results.

New attempts at military collaboration were made after the end of the civil war in Russia. In the fall of 1921, a Junkers director came to Berlin to sound out officials of the Foreign and War ministries about any aid the Reich might give his firm in establishing an airplane motors works in the Soviet Union. To participate in these talks, the War Ministry detailed officers from "Special Group R." Special Group R had been established some months earlier within the army organization for the specific purpose of conducting any collaboration that might be arranged with the Red Army. There are indications that Major Tschunke belonged to it and that it might have been headed by a Major (later Colonel) Fischer. In the talks between the Junkers representative and the Foreign Ministry, Special Group R took an active hand by guaranteeing the airplane firm that it would take over all political risks that might be involved in the transactions planned. It further guaranteed to furnish Junkers a working capital of 600 million marks. At that time this sum represented roughly $3,000,000; but the inflation of the German mark took such rapid strides that a few months later, in March, 1922, the sum was worth no more than $250,000.[6] In spite of such financial difficulties, agreements made in 1922 and 1923 led to the conclusion of a contract by which the Soviet government granted the Junkers corporation concessions for the manufacture of airplane motors in a plant at Fili, eight miles outside Moscow. In the same months a

---

[4] The actual arrangements were made by von Seeckt's aide, Köstring, who many years later became the German military attaché in Moscow.

[5] This story is based on Tschunke's reminiscences contained in the von Seeckt Archives. Tschunke, with whom I was personally acquainted, later became managing director of the Russia Committee of the German Economy.

[6] For further details about the contract, cf. Melville, *op. cit.*, p. 69. I have no way of judging the reliability of the data given by Melville.

German-Soviet joint-stock company, "Bersol," was founded for the purpose of manufacturing poison gases at Trotsk, in Samara Province. The manager of the enterprise was a Dr. Hugo Stolzenberg. Contracts were also concluded under which the Soviet government was to receive technical assistance from Germany in the manufacture of ammunition in Zlatoust, Tula, and Petrograd. The Reich War Ministry was to receive a certain share of the production of these works. This last arrangement was drafted in Berlin in the summer of 1923, with a Soviet delegation headed by Arkady Pavlovich Rozengolts, at that time a member of the Revolutionary Military Council and chief of the central board of the Soviet air force.

In order to cover up its financial backing of these enterprises, the German War Ministry launched a sort of holding corporation with the innocuous name Gesellschaft zur Förderung gewerblicher Unternehmungen (GEFU),[7] with head offices in Berlin and Moscow. GEFU's working capital in 1923, after the end of the German inflation, amounted to 75,000,000 reichsmarks (approximately $18,000,-000). But the company did not last very long. Perhaps the army did not know how to pick efficient business managers; in any event GEFU engaged in dubious financial maneuvers abroad, and by the mid-1920's it had speculated itself out of existence. Its functions were taken over by a similar organization called Wirtschaftskontor (WIKO).[8]

Special Group R conducted its business not only in Berlin, but simultaneously established a branch office in the Soviet capital named Zentrale Moskau. In the summer of 1921, a certain Herr Neumann arrived in Moscow, as the representative of the War Ministry, to study possibilities of military collaboration and to establish the necessary connections. The pseudonym "Neumann" hid the identity of the then Major Oskar Ritter von Niedermayer, who was born in Bavaria in 1885. A career officer, he had acquired fame during World War I as the head of a German military expedition to Afghanistan, and by his adventurous escape from this enterprise. Von Seeckt's interest in him was natural, since he himself had been interested in the Near East ever since his service as chief of staff of an Austrian Army group in Turkey. Von Seeckt's private papers, now in the United States Archives, contain a lengthy typewritten article

[7] Company for the Development of Trade Enterprises.
[8] Economic Office.

by von Niedermayer, probably written around 1920, on geopolitical problems of that area, with particular attention given to Pan Islamic and Pan Turanian currents. Von Niedermayer always loved to hear himself called the "German Lawrence" in view of his adventures in Afghanistan and his studies of the Iranian Basin.

I first became acquainted with him upon his arrival in Moscow in the summer of 1921. One of his tasks at that time was the inspection of armament factories and shipyards in Petrograd which the Soviet authorities had told the German War Ministry might serve as a suitable basis for German-Soviet collaboration in the field of war industry. The Soviet government suggested that Germany should give technical and financial assistance in the restoration of the most important armament works of Petrograd; in consideration of such assistance Germany would be given a proportion of the products. Although I had, even in advance, the impression that Soviet plans went far beyond the limit of possibilities open to a beaten and impoverished Germany, I was ready to participate in the inspection of the works, especially since I expected thereby to obtain invaluable insight into the state of Soviet industry. That the Soviet government had great hopes of the outcome of this inspection was clear from the fact that the vice commissar for foreign affairs, Karakhan, as well as the Soviet representative in Berlin, Victor Kopp, were ordered to accompany us on our trip to Petrograd.

The impression von Niedermayer and I received from the inspections was devastating. Most of the factories and shipyards were not in operation because raw materials were non-existent and because a large part of the workers had taken refuge in the villages in order to escape starvation in the city. Roofs everywhere were damaged, so that the machinery was exposed to the destructive effects of rain and snow; and for the most part the machines were in an unspeakable condition. It was clear to us that any German participation in the reconstruction of Petrograd's industry was, under these circumstances, out of the question, since it would have demanded more than Germany at that time could afford. All the more remarkable is the fact that the Soviet government did succeed in subsequent years in restoring Petrograd's industries to running condition without foreign assistance. Obviously, it had underestimated its own strength in the summer of 1921; otherwise it would hardly have thought of asking German capital to participate in the reconstruction of Petrograd's

armament industry and of thus offering Germany a good look into a branch of the economy which constituted such a vital part of Russia's military capacity. Or was the attitude of the Soviet government based on the conviction that the days of capitalism in Germany were numbered and that, therefore, her economic possibilities and technical capacities could be used for the benefit of the Soviet Republic without any danger?

Von Niedermayer's report on the results of his trip had the consequence that the Reich War Ministry dropped the idea of German participation in the restoration of Petrograd's industry. The subsequent agreement with Junkers, the founding of Bersol, and the arrangement for German technical assistance in the manufacture of ammunition were somewhat less ambitious but safer means toward such restoration.

In addition, the War Ministry concluded an agreement with the Red Army by which German pilots and tank experts were given the opportunity of acquainting themselves with the construction and use of aircraft and tanks in Russia; the construction of these weapons was forbidden the Reich by the Versailles Peace Treaty. The Red Army created a flying school near the town of Lipetsk, in Tambov Province, where hundreds of German experts who came and went in a steady flow were trained. Although the school was financed by the German Army, participation in it of German personnel was camouflaged. German mechanics and former air officers on the permanent staff were employed as private persons. But even officers on active service who were sent to Lipetsk on temporary duty were formally separated from the service for the duration of their courses. The arrangements that had been made for a tank school near Kazan were identical. Tanks used there were bought in England, and both Soviet and German personnel used them in their studies.

From its establishment until about 1932, Oskar von Niedermayer was head of Zentrale Moskau, which had administrative, economic, and financial control over these affairs and which, furthermore, acted as administrative center for all German personnel in Russia connected with them. In addition, he fulfilled the functions of an unofficial German military attaché by making regular reports about his impressions and observations. In this he was more important than the official military attaché, whose contacts with the Red Army were

much more restricted than those of Zentrale Moskau. Moreover, for security reasons, the official military attaché was not allowed to have any contacts with von Niedermayer and his group, so that he had no opportunity to talk to the constant stream of German Army personnel passing through Zentrale Moskau on their way to or from different places within the Soviet Union.[9]

After being relieved from his duties with Zentrale Moskau, von Niedermayer returned to Germany and took a position as professor at the Berlin University for Geography and Geopolitics. When World War II broke out, he placed himself at the disposal of the armed forces, and later was made the commanding general of a volunteer division composed of soldiers from Soviet Central Asia. In the beginning of the Hitler regime, von Niedermayer had had no unfriendly feelings toward National Socialism; he had even joined the party at a relatively early date. During the war, however, he developed a sharp antagonism toward Nazi policies in occupied Soviet territories. Since he did not hide his opinions, he found himself, some months before the collapse of Germany, in a concentration camp, from which the American troops liberated him. Soon afterward he moved into the Soviet zone of occupation because he fancied that the Soviet government would receive him with open arms, in recognition of his services on behalf of German-Soviet understanding. But, instead of being cordially welcomed, he was arrested under the customary suspicion of espionage and transported to Russia. There Hans Fritzsche saw him in the notorious Butyrka Jail in Moscow, in a state that makes one fear the worst for his subsequent fate. It seems logical to assume that the Soviet authorities have meanwhile done away with him as a living witness of an uncomfortable past.

Von Niedermayer was replaced as head of Zentrale Moskau by a Colonel von der Lieth-Thomsen, who had been the senior airforce officer during World War I. Retained in the Reichswehr, even though Germany was forbidden the re-establishment of an air force, he was an important link in German-Soviet military co-operation, especially as it involved air-force affairs. He participated in the Junkers agreements and assisted in the establishment of the Lipetsk school.

Some of those who have written on this subject have wondered about the motives of the German generals in this close collaboration

[9] Köstring's letter to von Seeckt, Aug. 27, 1931, von Seeckt Archives.

with the Red Army. Implying that the two armies were plotting a joint war against the West for the revision of the peace settlement, Melville wrote, "The Reichswehr chiefs who are conducting the *Abmachungen* delude themselves that they can use Bolshevist Russia to help them in their hoped-for war of revenge against Europe, and then, in the hour of victory, hold the bolshevists at bay and keep them in their place." [10] In actual fact the short-range aims of both armies were much more restricted. Germany (or her military leaders) wanted to rearm, maintain cadres from its technical arms well in training, and develop up-to-date methods of warfare. This could be accomplished only in violation of Versailles; and Soviet Russia was the logical place to hide such activities. The Red Army, of course, could not but benefit from this relationship; but as long as the Russian trump card was still to be retained, that by-product was quite desirable.

For the Red Army, contact with the Reichswehr provided sorely needed training in staff work and organization. Many high-ranking Soviet officers profited from centuries of Prussian military experience in courses taken at the War Academy in Berlin. Moreover, German technical assistance helped speed the construction of a Soviet war industry. The fact that Soviet Russia was thereby simultaneously aiding German rearmament was a price paid willingly. Perhaps the Russians reckoned that German ingenuity would in any event have found ways of circumventing the provisions of Versailles; in that case it might as well be the Red Army that would profit from it by improving its own methods, obtaining information about the Reichswehr, and helping the Germans to sabotage Versailles.

Moreover, the collaboration of the two armies never stopped the Communist International from vigorous attempts to subvert the German armed forces.[11] Wollenberg even claims that some of the funds obtained from the Reichswehr were turned over to the German Communist party for antimilitarist campaigns and efforts to create Communist cells among the rank-and-file soldiers. In turn, von Seeckt's eternal fight against Communist activities in the army went hand in hand with his policy of co-operation. In view of all this, it is perhaps surprising that military affairs were the one field of Soviet-German relations not disturbed by any serious incidents. On the con-

[10] *Op. cit.*, p. 6.
[11] Wollenberg, *op. cit.*, p. 237.

trary, personal relations between the two armies were excellent and rapidly developed into cordial friendship.

2. *GENERALS AND DIPLOMATS*

In its article of "revelations" of December, 1926, the *Manchester Guardian* had graciously absolved the Reich government of all guilt in connection with the secret dealings revealed, and had placed the blame squarely and exclusively on the shoulders of the military. Melville correctly questioned this by asking: "Can it be reasonably supposed that residing in the Chancellor's palace Dr. Wirth was entirely ignorant of the happenings in the palace in the Bendlerstrasse, the headquarters of the Ministry of the Reichswehr?" [12] From the preceding pages it should be clear that Melville was on the right track: The contract between Soviet Russia and the Junkers works had been concluded with the co-operation of the Foreign Ministry.

Much had nevertheless been accomplished by Special Group R and its Zentrale Moskau without any liaison with other departments of the government. The policy of direct negotiations between the two armies had been advocated by von Seeckt as early as 1922. In the memorandum he had submitted to the Chancellor in reply to Brockdorff-Rantzau's *pro memoria*, he had said that such direct dealings would obviate the necessity of involving the non-military agencies of the Reich, and thus would save the political and civil service branches of the administration all possible embarrassment. "That these [military agencies] should not make any agreements binding the Reich without the knowledge of the policy-making agencies should be assumed as a matter of course," he had added. In fact, he had gone beyond this proposal by stating that it was not up to the Reichswehr, but to German business to create a Russian war industry able to help Germany in case of necessity, provided that business were to follow the directions laid down by the War Ministry.

As a consequence, the government appears to have lost not only control over German-Soviet military collaboration, but seems to have had only the sketchiest knowledge of the activities and deals of von Seeckt and his officers. This appears to be the most logical explanation of the many misconceptions concerning a German-Soviet military alliance that were the basis of von Hindenburg's fears and the

[12] *Op. cit.*, p. 54.

warnings expressed in Rantzau's *pro memoria*. After the latter's appointment as ambassador, he convinced himself that no such alliance had been contemplated, much less concluded; but he never ceased complaining about the lack of liaison between the military and other branches of the executive. Military missions came to Soviet Russia either without the knowledge of the ambassador, or, if they did report to the embassy, they paid no heed to the rules laid down by Rantzau for their negotiations. German officers in Russia made wholly irresponsible statements and proposed fantastic deals which the Russians seem to have taken for bare coin only for a while; later these proposals were nothing but a source of embarrassment for the political representative of the Reich.

In February, 1923, a group of six high-ranking officers, including General Hasse, Major Tschunke, and the then Major Fischer spent some time in Moscow; and Count Rantzau complained sharply to the foreign minister over General Hasse's wild talk about a great war of liberation to be launched in three to five years, and his bland promise to send a regular military attaché to Moscow soon, a policy which the ambassador rejected categorically. Other missions engaged in financial transactions or negotiations the magnitude of which, in the count's opinion, far transcended the competency of the military and which were to be regarded as primarily political. Hence his repeated demands that the political and military authorities should establish close liaison and come to terms about Soviet-German military co-operation. Nor did the independent initiative given to private business work to everyone's satisfaction, for in the final analysis it was based on self-deception. Berlin was always well aware that these dealings had a decidedly political character. Once business had been given the go-ahead sign, however, the Foreign Ministry could do no more than offer unsolicited advice. The Russians, in turn, were also aware that the dealings transcended the realm of private business; but they made the contrary mistake of regarding business too much as a semiofficial exponent of the German state. Consequently, they gave talks with private businessmen an openly political tone.

The ambassador's chief complaint was focused on his suspicion that Soviet Russia continually got the better part of the deal in military agreements. I remember a conversation with Rozengolts, in the

summer of 1923, in which Rantzau bluntly asserted that German orders for war material should really be regarded as an outright subvention of the Soviet armament industry, particularly in view of the exorbitant prices Germany had to pay. Rantzau would have insisted on concrete political advantages to be derived from the military agreements. While von Seeckt either was satisfied with the military benefits of obtaining weapons, ammunition, and maintaining the instruction of his personnel, or believed that political advantages would be a natural and automatic consequence of close military co-operation, the ambassador continually demanded that the negotiators request of the Soviet government at least an explicit guarantee against Poland.

The ambassador continuously bombarded his superiors in Berlin with all of these complaints. Although the causes for them were never removed to his complete satisfaction, he succeeded at least in compelling the cabinet to assume a certain amount of control over the matter of military collaboration. As early as November, 1922, Dr. Wirth took pains to reassure him that the generals would henceforth be made to co-operate. More active support was given him in the summer of 1923 by Chancellor Cuno. The latter and some of his cabinet ministers decided to assist Rantzau by removing some of the negotiations to Berlin, which eliminated von Niedermayer, who had particularly antagonized the ambassador by his high-handed, irresponsible actions. Another reason that the count wanted the Russians to go to Berlin was to prevent the possibility that, in the event of a leak, Germany alone might be made responsible for politically explosive negotiations. When, therefore, in July, 1923, Chicherin told us that his government would send Arkady Rosengolts to Berlin for direct negotiations with the cabinet, Rantzau had won a tactical victory, which was made into a triumph when in one of the first conferences in Berlin it was decided that the embassy in Moscow should henceforth be in control of military agreements.

By the end of 1926, when the *Manchester Guardian* came out with its "revelations," the purely military co-operation in the aircraft and tank schools was in full swing. German financial participation and technical advice in the enlargement and improvement of Soviet ammunition plants had ceased, although the German Army was still receiving shipments of ammunition from these factories. The Soviet-

German chemical company Bersol had been liquidated a few years after its founding; but early in 1926 Unshlikht, the vice commissar of war, traveled to Berlin in greatest secrecy [13] and made ambitious proposals to Stresemann, von Seeckt, and other political leaders in the cabinet. He outlined plans for building plants for the manufacture of heavy artillery, chemical-warfare stuffs, precision instruments, and other material which the Versailles Treaty prohibited Germany from owning or using. He proposed that officer-training schools be connected with these industrial enterprises. In return he asked for financial backing and for guarantees that Germany would buy a certain proportion of the products, since the Red Army would not be able to absorb enough of them to make the construction of the plants pay.

I do not know whether Unshlikht's proposals ever materialized in full. In any event, German technical and medical experts were still in the Soviet Union at the end of 1926 to assist in experiments with new chemicals. In addition, general staff officers from both countries were continually participating in maneuvers of the other's army and were exchanging military information and experience.

The Junkers plant at Fili had closed by the time of the *Manchester Guardian*'s "revelations." The contract between Junkers and the Soviet Union had been terminated prematurely, and each side blamed the other for the failure. The general concessions regulations, and particularly the Soviet labor law under which plants had to operate, constituted such difficulties that Junkers had repeatedly attempted to have them set aside. The Soviet authorities, however, had shown themselves absolutely unwilling to do so; and perhaps it was politically and economically impossible for them to give exceptional status to a foreign concessionaire in violation of their own laws. Unsuccessful in surmounting this hurdle, the Junkers people accused the Soviet authorities of bad faith in making the operations agreed upon by the contract impossible to carry out. The latter countered with the justified accusation that Junkers had committed outright breaches of contract by failing to start with the manufacture of airplane motors by the agreed-upon date; nor had the company imported some of the necessary raw materials or shown any effort to organize their production in the Soviet Union.[14]

13 Under the name "Mr. Untermann."
14 *Pravda*, March 24, 1926.

3. THE REVELATIONS AND THEIR AFTERMATH

The *Manchester Guardian* article came as a political bombshell at a time when War Minister Otto Gessler was under sustained fire from the Social Democrats for his alleged collusion with anti-Republican circles on the extreme right. The new revelations, which during the next ten days were substantiated by new bits of evidence, came as the final blow. On December 16, 1926, the Social Democratic deputy Scheidemann, in a militant and angry speech on the floor of the Reichstag, moved that that body withdraw its confidence from the cabinet; when the motion was voted the cabinet of Chancellor Wilhelm Marx was defeated by a crushing majority. The Social Democrats were determined to probe deeply into the matter and to bring the military to account.

In the Foreign Ministry, among the military, and in the embassy in Moscow, the mood was mainly one of sadness and anger over the fact that the Socialists could let considerations of partisan politics override what many of my colleagues thought was the national interest. They thought of foreign policy as "bipartisan," believing that no loyal German would jeopardize the fragile fabric of foreign relations which the expert officials of the Foreign and War ministries had so carefully spun for the nation's benefit. Their sentiments were bluntly expressed on the floor of the Reichstag by the representatives of the conservative parties who hurled the epithet "traitor" at Scheidemann and his party comrades. For, in the opinion of the solid, respectable citizen, the military affairs of the Reich were beyond public discussion, particularly when they not only violated routine security considerations but also created serious political embarrassment.[15] The publication of the *Manchester Guardian* and *Vorwärts* articles was viewed with such alarm by the Foreign Ministry because it threatened, on the one hand, to heighten the suspicion

---

[15] The German judiciary also co-operated to keep the critics and tattlers quiet. When the *Münchener Post,* on Jan. 19, 1927, published the names of Reichswehr officers on temporary duty in Russia, its editor was indicted for treason. In the summer of 1930 a Captain Amlinger crashed while testing a fighter plane in Russia, and his widow published the customary death notice with the remark that her husband had died "for his German fatherland in far-away Russia while practicing his flying profession." Here too the authorities quickly moved in to suppress the story.

of the Western powers whose friendship Stresemann was then most carefully seeking. But it was an even greater threat to the policy of keeping the door to Russia open by friendly relations.

The exposure of German-Soviet military collaboration had put the German Communist party into the most serious embarrassment, a fact that was eagerly exploited by the Social Democratic press. *Vorwärts* gleefully speculated that the bullets with which Reichswehr troops had bloodily suppressed the 1923 Communist uprisings in Central Germany had probably been manufactured in the "fatherland of the proletariat." On the floor of the Reichstag, the representatives of the bourgeoisie could enjoy the even more diverting spectacle of three mutually hostile Communist factions bitterly fighting and insulting each other. (The Reichstag had been elected in 1924, and some of its Communist members had meanwhile gone into opposition to the Stalinist "center," but had refused to relinquish their seats.) All through the weeks during which this political storm was raging, the official Communist paper *Rote Fahne* either issued point-blank denials of the charges or protected itself by discreet and embarrassed silence. Nevertheless, bitter disputes must have been raging within the Comintern over the revelations, and it seemed likely that the parties of the Comintern, ideologically pledged to unrelenting struggle against militarism and rearmament, would force the government of the Soviet Union to break off its military co-operation with the Reich.

Meanwhile the Soviet authorities, both in Moscow and in Berlin, urgently requested that nothing be revealed to the public or even to the Reichstag. But the moderate parties, and particularly the Social Democrats, insistently demanded explanations from the war minister. Asked by the Appropriations Committee to comment on the revelations, War Minister Gessler stalled by promising to make a satisfactory explanation to the Foreign Affairs Committee. Even this promise, which was reported in the German press, was interpreted by the Soviet leaders as an indiscretion, and as usual Rantzau, in Moscow, had somber visions of the entire German-Soviet collaboration collapsing.

Upon the angry insistence of the Social Democratic leaders, a session of the Foreign Affairs Committee of the Reichstag was called together hastily, and after an unsuccessful plea to the Chancellor made by Herr von Schubert and General Heye to have the session

canceled, the cabinet finally agreed to have the Ministries of War and Foreign Affairs prepare a joint statement to the committee. Because Herr von Dirksen and Colonel Fischer, who prepared the statement, were resigned to the fact that no point-blank denial of the charges could be made, they tried to reveal as little as possible. Their chief consideration was the fear of being disloyal to the Russians. Before the meeting of the committee, the two men submitted their prepared statement to the Soviet Embassy, and the latter declared itself satisfied. The cabinet admitted no more than what the articles had revealed, pointing out that the contracts had been economic, and not primarily military in nature. Moreover, the gentlemen could truthfully tell the Reichstag committee that the agreements had already been liquidated in full. They finally urged the members to regard the information as confidential in loyalty to the Soviet Union.

The statement began a lively discussion in which Communists, Social Democrats, and Dr. Wirth, of the Center party, took an active part. The attack on the secret deals was led by Rudolf Hilferding. It was repudiated by Dr. Wirth, who admitted, to Colonel Fischer's pleasant surprise, that the deals had not been made by the War Ministry without the cabinet's knowledge, but that he, Wirth, had "stood at the cradle of relations with Russia," together with General von Seeckt. He vigorously came out in favor of *Ostpolitik*, holding that in 1922 and 1923 it had been the greatest achievement of German foreign policy. His speech encouraged even the Social Democrat Hermann Müller to admit that "he, too, had helped to rock the Russian cradle." The session ended with a few words by von Schubert advocating a policy of balance of power between East and West, which would leave Germany freedom of action in every direction by leaving all doors open. The Reichstag seems to have acquiesced.

In spite of Brockdorff-Rantzau's gloomy prediction that military co-operation would now be at an end, the German authorities never for a moment thought of abandoning their policies. For one thing, limited relations were perfectly legal: therefore there need be no radical rupture. But even a partial rupture would not only mean a severe loss of prestige but would also damage Germany's political situation considerably. "If we break off," the generals asserted bluntly, "the Russians will go to the French." Finally, it was clear to us that the military would openly or secretly continue its military

co-operation even if the political leadership were to break off all such relationships. Thus, the Foreign Office capitulated to the generals with the greatest of pleasure. All concerned, from Stresemann on down, were resolved not only to continue as before with military co-operation, but to intensify it, though with the greatest caution.

Nevertheless, something was changed: The Russians had become extremely cautious. On the one hand, Chicherin, Litvinov, Voroshilov, and Unshlikht took the opportunity to press for much wider and closer collaboration, which should also extend to the problem of disarmament. On the other hand, they made any further collaboration dependent on firm German guarantees that no further "revelations" would trouble them in the future. After one of his conversations with Lunev, the Soviet military attaché in Berlin, Fischer wrote to von Seeckt, "This time, strangely enough, it is the other side which has voiced misgivings, whereas our Foreign Office has declared its agreement with the way in which our work is being carried on." [16]

In the early months of 1927 General von Seeckt, then without official position, was vacationing in Italy. Before returning home to Germany, he planned to take a trip to Turkey, where he had fought his World War battles, and from there make a visit to Russia. In the light of the recent "revelations" his projected visit suddenly threatened to bring with it more political difficulties than the Russians were then prepared to shoulder. In line with their cautious, suspicious attitude, they intimated to the Foreign Ministry, through Brockdorff-Rantzau, that it might be wise to postpone the visit until the storm had abated. Although Colonel Fischer urged the general to disregard the warnings for caution, the Foreign Ministry succeeded in persuading him to postpone his trip. Von Seeckt never went to Russia. Even though he occupied no official position, he must have realized that after Berlin's intervention the entire political responsibility for the visit would have fallen on the Soviet authorities; and he had no wish to cause them any additional embarrassment.[17]

In the end Soviet suspicions were allayed, and instead of being broken off military co-operation between Germany and the Soviet

[16] Fischer to von Seeckt, March 12, 1927, von Seeckt Archives.
[17] *Ibid.*

Union was intensified. Stresemann gave his approval to the continued operation of the schools at Lipetsk and Kazan. German scientists were sent to Orenburg to assist in chemical-warfare experiments. For a short while the German Army ceased sending its own active officers to Russian schools, but it was not long before more German officers were coming through Zentrale Moskau than ever before, although much greater care was taken to camouflage them as civilians. On the other hand, German officers participating in Red Army maneuvers were now permitted to wear uniforms, a concession which the German authorities had refused as late as 1926. German officers of the highest rank visited the Soviet Union, among them the then Colonel Werner von Blomberg, and even General Kurt von Hammerstein, then chief of the army command. The German military attaché, Colonel (later General) Köstring, was taken on a 7,000-mile inspection tour of Red Army units in the summer of 1931 and upon his return reported to his former chief, General von Seeckt, that the effects of German military influence could be seen in all aspects of the Soviet Army. "Our views and methods go through theirs like a red thread," he wrote.[18]

A similar intensification of good relations occurred in the economic aspect of German-Soviet military collaboration. In 1928 Krupp concluded an agreement by which they were to give technical assistance in the manufacture of high-grade steels both for military and for civilian uses. Further negotiations took place in the spring of 1930 between War Commissar Voroshilov, Vice Commissar Unshlikht, and the Soviet chief of ordnance General Uborevich, on the

[18] It was about this time that Colonel James Marshall Cornwall, the British military attaché in Berlin, handed his ambassador, Sir Horace Rumbold, a report on German Army affairs which contained the following passage:

"The relations between the German and Soviet Russian military authorities remain somewhat of a mystery. Such cooperation as exists is purely on the basis of reciprocal benefit, but it appears that relations have been less cordial of late, and there have certainly been fewer exchanges of visits between senior staff officers of the two countries. The practice of seconding German officers in order to practice flying in Russia, prevalent from 1927 to 1930, seems to have recently ceased. There are certainly no German officer instructors attached to the Soviet army. A new German unofficial military representative, Colonel Koestring, has been sent to Moscow. The cooling off of German-Soviet relations may be in part attributed to the violent propaganda campaign directed against the Reichswehr by the Communist party."—Ernest Woodward and R. Butler, eds., *Documents on British Foreign Policy 1919–1939* (London, 1947), Second Series, II (1931), 520–521.

one hand, and German corporations, such as Krupp and Rheinmetall-Borsig, on the other.

We still have to talk about the effect of Hitler's coming to power on the friendship between the Reichswehr and the Red Army. But first the larger outlines of Soviet-German relations in the late 1920's and early 1930's have to be discussed.

VIII FROM THE TREATY OF BERLIN TO THE RISE OF NATIONAL SOCIALISM

1. THE CRISIS OF THE NEP AND THE REVOLUTION FROM ABOVE

The era of the New Economic Policy was drawing to a close. A strategic retreat before the rebellious forces inside Russia, the NEP had been designed to pacify the peasantry, stimulate agricultural production, and uncover all the economic reserves hidden within the Russian population so that the stagnating economy could be revived. The primary necessity was to set the existing forces of production going again after years of inaction. The existing reserves of capital equipment were in a most miserable condition after seven years of international and civil war; none the less they existed, and were now supposed to be put to use.

Quite clearly this was a retreat from previous dreams of the speedy establishment of Socialism. But instead of abandoning this "maximal aim" for the duration of the NEP, Lenin and some of his comrades combined the policy of retreat with expressions of hope that the new course would, however slowly, lead to the same end. In his political report to the Eleventh Party Congress (1922), Lenin cried: "Link up with the peasant masses . . . and begin to move forward, immeasurably, infinitely more slowly than we dreamed, but so that the whole mass will actually move forward with us. If we do that we shall in time get an acceleration of this movement such as we cannot dream of now." After Lenin passed from the political scene, the vague hope was taken up by Bukharin and the entire right wing of

209

the Russian Communist party. In his economic writings Bukharin expounded the idea that, by slow evolution, the Socialist sector of the economy would, through open competition, gradually absorb the capitalist sector, so that, "by using the economic initiative of peasants, small producers, and even the bourgeoisie, by tolerating . . . private accumulation, we are putting them objectively to the service of the socialist state industry and of the economy as a whole! This is what the meaning of the NEP consists of." [1]

The problem which such optimistic expectations obscured was the fact that these plans would work only if the peasant and the small businessman were given some real incentives in addition to the new economic freedom provided by the NEP. If the peasants were to produce the foodstuffs and raw materials required for reconstructing the national economy, they would have to be offered material inducements—not just money, but, much more important, a chance to spend the money. But the low level of industrial production and the low credit of the Soviet Union abroad made this virtually impossible, except by devoting a considerable part of the national production effort to satisfying the consumers' demands of the peasantry, a course which would, from the very beginning, have doomed even the least ambitious plans for the gradual creation of industrial socialism in Russia. Moreover, the existing capital equipment, already in an unspeakable condition, was rapidly being used up, and at first no provisions were made even for its replacement, not to speak of any increase. After 1924 a certain proportion of the national income was used for the purpose of replacing worn-out machinery; but the day when the existing facilities for production would be completely exhausted loomed in the not too distant future.

The fundamental economic difficulty of the regime was at the same time a political impasse: The Communist regime could maintain itself in a predominantly agrarian country only by making concessions to the vast agrarian population; but, by doing so, it alienated not only the intellectuals making up the core of the party's old guard but also the urban proletariat, the class with which it primarily identified itself. Concessions made to the peasantry would strengthen that class more and more and endanger the power monopoly of the

[1] "O novoi economicheskoi politike i nashikh zadachakh," Pt. I, *Bol'shevik,* 1925, No. 8, p. 8.

Communist party; on the other hand, the leaders did not believe that they could afford to antagonize the peasantry.

The bitter struggles fought within the party during the 1920's were, in part, a naked struggle for power, a struggle that was intimately linked, however, with very real controversies over the policies that might lead the regime out of its impasse. Stressing the dangers to the cause of the revolution arising out of a policy of coddling the peasantry, the Left, popularly identified with the person of Leon Trotsky, demanded a turn toward rapid industrialization, a policy of "primitive accumulation" which would tax the endurance, labor, power, and resources of the Russian population to the utmost, and which would place the main burden upon the peasantry. The Russian Revolution, they warned, was in danger of becoming bourgeois; and only a frank return to the dictatorship of the industrial proletariat would preserve the revolutionary heritage. The fate of Soviet Russia, however, was not the only concern of the Left. The Russian Revolution made sense to them only as part of the major world revolution they desired. In this connection they warned that the interests of the world revolution should not be subordinated to the narrower interests of the Soviet state. The Kremlin's *raison d'état* should not interfere with revolutionary developments abroad; on the contrary, the Soviet regime should openly identify itself with the world proletariat and support its revolutionary activities. In one of his monthly essays on political developments in the Soviet Union, Professor Hoetzsch asked the rhetorical question. "What, after all, did Trotsky expect for Russia from his radical, extreme, and consistent Bolshevism?" The answer would be that, in Trotsky's opinion, nothing could have been expected "for Russia" if the old course were pursued further, and that Trotsky was not exclusively interested in knowing what might be expected "for Russia." He was also an internationalist and a world revolutionary.

Thus the Left was thinking about problems of revolution, problems concerning the transition from one social order to another. Against this, the so-called Center, controlled by Stalin, stressed the necessity for maintaining a working alliance with the peasantry. Trotsky discussed what the regime should do with its power (industrialization) and how it should be distributed (dictatorship of industry over agriculture); Stalin was preoccupied with the problem

of keeping the party apparatus in power. "If we antagonize the peasantry," he said, "industrialization and the development of Socialism will be impossible from the very beginning," thus justifying his program in the name of Trotsky's aims.

Stalin's program was based on three principles: (1) appeasement of the peasantry; (2) appeasement of the capitalist world; and (3) industrialization. As we have seen, the last plank of this platform was irreconcilable with the first; and, for a number of years, it remained a promise to which scant lip service was paid. A sharp economic crisis in 1923, expressing itself in a rapidly growing disparity between rising industrial prices and falling prices for agricultural produce, had opened up discussions of the problem. In an effort to keep the support of the peasantry, the government forced industrial prices down and ordered a number of stringent measures designed to increase the efficiency of industry. Since none of these measures attacked the deep roots of the difficulty, the inflation of industrial prices reappeared two years later, in hidden form, as an acute scarcity of commodities, the so-called "goods famine." The steady fall in the value of the currency was only another symbol of the crisis.

The second plank in Stalin's platform, a foreign policy designed to keep his country out of war, was based, first, on the realization that the proletariat in the Western countries was not yet ready to come to power, and, second, on the assumption, made somewhat glibly, that the Soviet regime could reconstruct its economy and "build Socialism" without the help of the world proletariat. While it would be useful to have friendly Communist parties in every country, the main task in the international scene would be to keep the outside world in check. Against this the Left asserted that, because the Soviet economy was dependent on the world economy of capitalism, "Socialist construction" could succeed only with the help of further revolutions in the West. Denouncing these warnings as "defeatism," Stalin in a sense built his policy on the continued existence of the bourgeois governments, even though he lived in constant fear that the bourgeois world might band together against the Soviet state in an anti-Bolshevik crusade.

It is an easy fallacy to underestimate in retrospect the influence of the Left opposition, because it was so completely and hopelessly liquidated after 1927. But in the mid-1920's the end of the Trotsky opposition was by no means so obvious to the outside observer. In-

deed, the spectacular radical slogans of the opposition and the noise of their campaign obscured their growing isolation within the party. In addition, the opposition not only contained most of the illustrious names of the Old Bolshevik leadership (while Stalin was relatively unknown at first), but for a long time the Center paid lip service to many of its orthodox tenets. Yet the development of the Stalin-Trotsky controversy took place openly enough so that the outside world could follow its main steps. In and around the German Embassy there were some disagreements over the interpretation these developments should be given, and over the future course they were bound to take. Together with the ambassador, I tended to regard the Trotsky faction as radical dreamers who offered nothing constructive to Soviet Russia. Moreover, as representatives of the German Reich, we felt that the coming to power of the faction demanding world revolution would seriously endanger the working of the Rapallo relationship which we sought to promote. Ever since the end of 1923, when Trotsky had lent support to Petrov, the Comintern agent who had been involved in the preparations for the abortive Communist Revolution of October–November, Count Rantzau was deeply suspicious of the opposition leader; and Chicherin did his best to confirm Rantzau's attitude by pointing out the dangers to Rapallo should Trotsky come to power. The ambassador, in a report to Berlin, stressed that the elimination of Trotsky and Zinovyev would be a tremendous gain for Germany, and that it would be a great mistake to side with the opposition out of humanitarian considerations. The tragedy of Trotsky's fate was something he did not deny; but it would be very shortsighted, he thought, if the German press were to emphasize that aspect of the story and thus create sympathy for the fallen leader among the German public.

Rantzau's dispatch to the Foreign Ministry was prompted by the fact that Paul Scheffer had for a long time been writing fair and balanced reports on the intraparty struggles for the *Berliner Tageblatt,* reports in which he did not conceal his warm sympathy with the human qualities of some of the leading oppositionists. When Trotsky and about thirty other prominent Old Bolsheviks were sent into their Siberian or Asiatic exile, Scheffer's article was full of the anger and pity he felt as these veterans of revolution were subjected to traditional tsarist methods by the state they themselves had created. Since with these reports Scheffer jeopardized his own person and position,

they attest to his courage in the face of Soviet efforts to silence him. In Germany his articles created a minor sensation, particularly because the Soviet press kept strict silence about such affairs; our own reports to the Foreign Ministry were not, of course, revealed to the public. Rantzau was obliged to discuss the effect of Scheffer's articles with him, but Scheffer quite rightly insisted that he had by no means intended to support the opposition against the government; he had merely done fair and sober reporting. Moscow, however, never forgave Scheffer for his reports.

While eliminating his left-wing critics from the political scene, Stalin saw himself more and more obliged to resort to the very policies they had advocated. In 1928 a five-year plan for the industrialization of Russia at a forced pace was adopted. Simultaneously, repressive measures against the peasantry were taken to ensure the food supply, and the last remnants of the NEP were abolished. Stalin later called the period of transformation which now began a second revolution, a revolution which this time came from above. Indeed, around 1928 a new period of violent social upheavel was gradually inaugurated by the regime, a period in which the former policies of domestic and international appeasement were abandoned for the sake of renewed warfare of unprecedented ruthlessness. It was war against all elements of the peasantry who had improved their lot during the NEP; war against the trader, the small entrepreneur, against the bourgeois specialist, and against anything or anybody from the old ruling classes; last but not least, the war was directed against the remnants of influence the trade unions had had in the management of the economy. The "revolution from above" was a gigantic effort to marshal all the material and human resources of the country for a forced march toward industrialization. For this march, made at breakneck speed, all opposition had to be crushed. More than that: everyone who lagged behind in his efforts, his enthusiasm, or his unquestioning obedience to the central command was silenced and eliminated. Not a voice of criticism should impede the mighty effort of the country to lift itself out of an economic and political impasse by its own bootstraps.

The immediate result of the revolution from above was a deepening of the political and economic crisis. As a consequence of the peasants' active resistance against the collectivization drive, agriculture was brought to the very edge of utter ruin; grain exports, and

with them Soviet exports as a whole, fell to such a low that the government, in search of hard currency, was forced to export commodities sorely required by the urban population. With this, bitterness spread to the cities, and the loyalty of the proletariat, even of the Red Army, seemed in jeopardy. Meanwhile, a Right opposition to Stalin's radical experiments raised its head, and the regime began to fear that the Right and Left oppositions might join forces on the basis of their common enmity to the official policy.

The profound upheavals of these years of internal stress and transformation coincided with a sharp crisis in the international situation of the Soviet Union. In 1927 official circles in Moscow experienced an acute war scare that brought them to the verge of panic. The immediate signal for the wave of hysteria was the raid on the premises of ARCOS in London, on May 12, 1927, which led to the rupture of all British-Soviet relations two weeks later. Throughout the following months Soviet officials played up the danger of an immediate Anglo-imperialist intervention. England, they maintained, was inciting its Eastern-European and Asiatic satellites to aggression against Soviet Russia. Poland, where the Soviet ambassador was murdered in June, and China, where relations with the Kuomintang had been severed bloodily, were particular foci of Soviet worries.

In retrospect, the danger of war was certainly overestimated by Moscow partly because of the primitive thinking with which the Bolsheviks indulged in these matters, and partly because the war scare was a quite convenient weapon in the intraparty conflict. The Stalinist Center could wag a moralizing finger in the faces of the Trotsky opposition and say, "Look at the acute danger in which the Soviet state is today. Do you want to sow dissension at such a time?" Another element contributing to the war scare may have been the familiar scapegoat reaction of the Kremlin, that is, a conscious or unconscious attempt to distract public attention from the serious domestic difficulties by blaming them on evil disturbances from the outside. There were no indications, however, that Soviet Russia, pressed by economic and political problems, was about to run amuck by preparing a military adventure in a desperate effort to solve her domestic troubles. Actually, Moscow was too busy with its internal difficulties; as earlier, she wanted peace and foreign economic aid. The hypothesis that domestic problems were precisely what would

cause the Soviet regime to undertake foreign aggression was always being discussed; but certainly in those years it had been too often discredited. On the contrary, the sharp break with England and the generally poor position of the Soviet Union in world politics caused the Kremlin, in September, 1927, to propose a non-aggression treaty to the French government. The Quai d'Orsay made only one condition: Poland and Romania should be included in such a pact. But Poland, in turn, would go into treaty relations with the USSR only on a collective basis together with the Baltic States and Finland, and she made some other conditions which the Kremlin thought unacceptable. In addition, the negotiations with France also miscarried because of a sharp conflict which disrupted good relations between Paris and Moscow for a while.

The conflict between France and Russia, which arose over Communist interference in French domestic affairs, shows that there was at least some connection between the international and domestic difficulties of the Soviet regime. The Soviet ambassador in Paris, Christian Rakovsky, one of the outstanding leaders of the Left opposition, had signed a declaration of August 8, 1927, in which the opposition asked all honest workers in capitalist countries to help overthrow their governments. All soldiers, the declaration said, should join the Red Army. Much to Chicherin's dismay, Rakovsky's act was given broad publicity by the right-wing parties in France, who wanted to make political capital of it because of imminent elections. Attempts were made to settle the incident and in the negotiations the French government introduced the issue of the old Russian debts. At that point Rakovsky committed another affront when he published appeals to French investors in the French press, advising them to oppose the settlement proposed by their government. In mid-October, Rakovsky had to be recalled.

Earlier that year, in July, a sudden workers' revolt in Vienna, quickly suppressed, came as a complete surprise to the Comintern; but it was received as the first harbinger of new revolutionary rumblings in Europe, and one that was particularly welcome in view of the miserable collapse of Chinese Communism. For the next few years Comintern activities in Europe intensified considerably, particularly after the Great Depression had begun its work of social and political dislocation. The depression came as a godsend to Stalin, not only because it gave a boost to the European Communist parties

but also because he could use it as a potent argument against the Right opposition in Russia who had warned against any policies designed to antagonize Western capitalism, the source of material and financial aid in the construction of Socialism. At the same time the Great Depression also gave a boost to right-wing elements in Europe, and by this token served to increase Moscow's fears and Moscow's determination to become self-sufficient and powerful. In this sense the world depression and its political consequences in the Western World must be seen as an essential background to the seemingly autonomous development of Stalin's "revolution from above."

In the early weeks of 1929 the regime decided to expel Trotsky, the figurehead and symbol of all intraparty oppositions, from Soviet territory. When asked whether he might be given refuge in Turkey, the government in Ankara at once gave a positive reply. But on January 30th Litvinov asked the German ambassador to grant Trotsky permission to live in Germany. The opposition leader, he revealed, had categorically refused to go to Turkey. In conveying Litvinov's request to the Foreign Ministry, Ambassador Dirksen endorsed it by suggesting that Trotsky's presence in Germany would seriously weaken the German Communist party because he would no doubt make vigorous propaganda for his views of the Soviet government. After all, he wrote, our entire policy toward the Soviet Union was based on our own domestic strength and immunity against Bolshevik methods. But both the Chancellor and the Reich President, hesitant to play with fire, argued against his views; the German government's refusal to admit Trotsky was finally made on the pretext that his presence in Germany might burden Soviet-German relations.

Even before the expulsion of Trotsky, Stalin's need for a scapegoat on whom he could blame the troubles of the regime had produced an affair which caused much concern to the German Embassy and placed relations between Berlin and Moscow under a great strain. On March 7, 1928, when Count Rantzau came to see Chicherin, the foreign commissar opened the conversation by saying that he and the ambassador must co-operate in an effort to prevent an extremely disagreeable affair, which was about to break, from having any untoward effect on German-Soviet relations. He said he was referring to a public trial in which certain employees of AEG, the German General Electric Corporation, would be involved. The GPU, he said,

was just now arresting the Germans. Some time later a message reached the embassy from Kharkov, from whence our consulate general reported that on the previous day a number of engineers and technicians, employees of AEG, had been arrested while delivering some turbines to Soviet coal-mining corporations. Simultaneously a large number of Soviet-Russian engineers had been arrested. All those arrested were alleged to have engaged in sabotage, industrial espionage, and attempts to establish contact with the former owners of the mines, now in emigration. Two days later the Soviet press broke the story by asserting that there had been a counter-revolutionary organization in the Donets coal-mine area, the guiding center of which consisted of former owners and shareholders of the mines who were in close touch with individual agents of German industrial firms and the Polish counter-espionage service. *Pravda,* on March 10th, elaborated on the story; the arrested individuals, it wrote, had received money from their former employers. They had allegedly been instructed to wage systematic sabotage so that the mines would be paralyzed during the coming war of intervention.

Two of the Germans were released ten days after their arrest. One of them made a detailed report of the way he had been treated which would have a familiar ring to anyone who had read accounts of life in Soviet jails. Three other Germans remained among the fifty-three accused. In the trial that was staged, sixteen attorneys argued against a battery of five public prosecutors. But in the main it was Chief Prosecutor Krylenko's show. From the first day of the trial he ruthlessly revealed the nature and purpose of his case. What was enacted was not an attempt to bring culprits before the bar of justice. If ever a public trial meant to make open mockery of judicial procedure, it was the Shakhty case. The purpose of the show—and it was basically a show, a drama—was that of demonstrating to the Soviet workers the idea of industrialization, to gather them around the task in spite of all the well known difficulties, bottlenecks, and grievances, and, most important, to blame all such troubles on bourgeois specialists and foreign capitalists, thus distracting the workers' attention from the serious blunders of Soviet policy.

Among the three Germans standing trial, our interest was concentrated on the engineer Otto and the technician Mayer; the third, a technician named Badstieber, had shown himself demonstrably

weak in the pretrial investigation, making all the confessions that were asked of him. I attended all the proceedings of the trial, and the observations I made at the time have contributed considerably to the formation of my judgment concerning Soviet justice, which presented itself in this and all the show trials in its most abominable and contemptible light. I shall never forget Mayer's strong and highly indignant reaction to the court's allegation that he had sabotaged the turbines delivered by his firm. At that point the presiding judge, Andrei Vyshinsky, who would at critical moments take the lead in the proceedings, presented to Mayer a confession he had signed. Mayer admitted that it was indeed his personal signature; but he added that he had signed the document only because he had had enough of the prolonged nightly interrogations. Furthermore, he had had no idea at all of what he was signing, since the paper was in Russian, a language he did not know.

Vyshinsky tried to get out of his uncomfortable predicament by asking Mayer to confirm that, if not he, then at least the Russian co-defendant, Bashkin, had been engaged in sabotaging the turbine. Had not Bashkin inquired about the most suitable means of accomplishing that sort of sabotage? Mayer, not knowing enough Russian, had not understood Bashkin when he had confessed; but now he became excited once more and, with raised voice and in great firmness, declared that not one word of it was true. Bashkin, he cried, was the most conscientious engineer he had ever met in Russia; and it had been Bashkin who had constantly been concerned about the fate of the turbines. That was why he had continually inquired how he could take the best possible care of them.

When Bashkin, sitting on the defendants' bench, heard Mayer speak, his nerves snapped. He sprang from his seat and, tears streaming from his eyes, shouted to the large room that Mayer's statement was true, and that his own confession was false. Vyshinsky at once announced a recess.

About forty minutes later, when the trial was reopened, Bashkin stood before the court with a pale face in which the wrinkles had in the meantime become deeper, and accused himself of being a coward and a liar. All of the statements he had made in the pretrial investigation and in the trial itself, he said, had been true; only his last assertions had been despicable lies. Thus the court had saved its

face; but the audience—at least that part of it that had not yet fallen completely into a state of psychosis—was richer by an amazing experience.

For forty-two days the court was in session. In his final speech Krylenko demanded the death sentence for nineteen of the accused. Of the eleven death sentences actually handed down, only five were carried out. Of the Germans Badstieber was given a suspended jail sentence; Otto and Mayer were acquitted. Four years later, when I was making a trip through the newly built industrial areas of Siberia, I learned by chance that the same Bashkin who had been given a long prison sentence at the Shakhty trial was working in one of the plants I visited. I was told that he was one of the best and most reliable engineers in the factory.

Domestically, this first of the great show trials of the Stalin era probably had the desired effect. But for the purpose of discrediting specialists and foreigners in the eyes of the Russian people, Moscow had seriously jeopardized relations with Germany; she had put a glaring spotlight on serious political and economic problems, and had thus undermined the credit of the regime. Chicherin and the other officials of the Foreign Commissariat realized this very well, and from the very beginning they were extremely worried over the arrest of the German engineers and the subsequent trial. As a matter of fact, Boris Stein attempted to allay our indignation and perturbation by pointing to the choice of Vyshinsky as presiding judge. Vyshinsky, Stein assured us, could surely be expected to show sufficient wisdom and moderation not to jeopardize German-Soviet relations. And it is a fact that, at least as far as the German defendants were concerned, Vyshinsky did his work with great skill and tact, obviously well aware that the German ambassador personally was witnessing the trial of the Germans and that the latter would not hesitate to adopt severe measures if necessary.

I must explain my own and the German Embassy's reaction to the Shakhty trial. When Count Brockdorff-Rantzau first reported the arrest of the German technicians to Berlin, he was careful to add that Chicherin and the entire NKID were extremely embarrassed by the new GPU move, and that they sympathized with the German position but were powerless against the political police. But his tolerant interpretation of the affair was mixed with great bitterness and indignation. The ambassador's reaction to the trial was in-

fluenced by the curious dilemma that, on the one hand, we wanted to do our utmost to preserve the Rapallo relationship, while we were determined, on the other hand, to take no insults from the Russians. We were against destroying the bridges to Moscow, but we were also very angry with the elements in the Soviet state who, by their actions, again and again added to the arguments of those who maintained that any attempt to do business with Russia was futile. The defeatist view was increasingly being accepted in the Foreign Ministry. Much as I fought against it emotionally, it forced itself on me also.

The embassy's efforts to define the proper course of action in the case was made unnecessarily difficult by the firm that employed the accused Germans. The directors of the AEG in the first flush of indignation had initially declared that they would immediately withdraw all their engineers who were in Russia mounting machinery, regardless of existing contracts. A few days later, however, they seem to have regretted their impetuosity; they withdrew their initial declaration, obviously afraid of the losses that would occur because of the non-fulfillment of contractual agreements.

The trial of Kindermann and Wolscht, during which my personal integrity had been publicly questioned in the Soviet press, had shaken me in my belief that the outside world could fruitfully enter into lasting relations with Soviet Russia. Even though the wound healed after the conclusion of the Treaty of Berlin, a scar remained. The Shakhty trial became a turning point in my attitude toward Soviet Russia because it opened the wound anew and deepened my disappointment. The atmosphere of the entire trial impressed me as being profoundly and disgustingly pathological; that impression, and the uncertainty into which it had once again thrown German-Soviet relations, produced in me a leaden melancholy that lasted through the summer of 1928. I avoided my Soviet acquaintances, my friends, because I did not want to embarrass them; I avoided those with whom I disagreed because I should only have heaped bitter and futile reproach on them.

Two years later a trial was staged against an alleged counter-revolutionary organization of saboteurs and wreckers, the so-called Industrial party (Prompartia). The accused technicians, led by the head of the Thermo-Technical Institute in Moscow, Professor Ramzin, were alleged to have engaged in systematic sabotage with the purpose

of bringing about an economic crisis and a war of foreign intervention. Plans for such intervention, it was asserted, had been worked out by them in collaboration with former Russian industrialists and the French general staff. The purpose of the trial was to "uncover" the causes for the crisis of the first Five-Year Plan. If the Shakhty trial had been staged to "explain" the crisis in coal production, the Prompartia case was to do the same for the crisis in total production and the stoppage of supplies of consumers' goods.

It is quite probable that there were some tenuous connections between former Russian capitalists and their erstwhile employees, even though these connections could scarcely have had political significance; doubtless, also, the French intelligence service was actively interested in data on Soviet industrialization. As in the Shakhty trial, the accusations were based on minute shreds of actual facts which were enlarged by pure fabrication. Nevertheless, the Prompartia trial was managed far better than the previous one. The implication of foreigners in the Shakhty case had been a mistake because the methods of the GPU had not been successful with them, and the defense had riddled the case the government tried to make. At the Prompartia affair no foreigners sat on the defendants' bench, and the trial was much more successful. The accused not only confessed everything but also tried to outdo one another in self-accusations, so that little remained for the prosecutor to do.

2. THE DIRKSEN ERA

POLITICAL BICKERING

In the summer of 1928 Count Brockdorff-Rantzau was a very ill man; he had for a long time contemplated a lengthy furlough, which his physician had said was essential to prolong his life. Urged on him for years, the furlough had been postponed again and again because one problem after another held the ambassador in Moscow; or at least Rantzau believed his presence there to be indispensable. In December, 1923, just after the settlement of the Ruhr conflict, he had gone so far as to stay at his post while his mother lay dying in Germany. Now the Shakhty case once more made him postpone his departure. When at last he departed for Germany at the end of the summer, he went home not to recuperate but to die.

Rantzau's death caused Soviet officialdom to break one of its most rigid rules, the prohibition against participating in religious ceremonies. On the ground of the strict separation between church and state in the Soviet Union, and because of their personal atheism, Soviet diplomats had refused to attend the funeral masses for the Italian Dowager Queen and the Lithuanian President. When in August, 1927, the Berlin diplomatic corps had congratulated President Hindenburg on his eightieth birthday, Krestinsky and his staff had been absent because Nunzio Pacelli, the dean of the diplomatic corps, in his message of congratulation had proposed to make reference to the "Highest One who guides the fate of mankind." All this was forgotten one year later when the Soviet chargé d'affaires, Bratman-Brodovsky, attended Rantzau's funeral.

After the ceremonies Brodovsky took me aside and remarked that it would be a good idea, from the Kremlin's point of view, if Herbert von Dirksen were to be appointed Germany's next ambassador in Moscow. For Dirksen, he said, "was trained in the school of von Maltzan and represents the spirit of Rantzau." Indeed, von Dirksen belonged to the very small circle around Count Rantzau which comprised, in addition, only Baron von Maltzan, Hencke, Schlesinger, myself, and perhaps Paul Scheffer.

After von Maltzan's appointment as ambassador in Washington, von Dirksen had been the chief representative of Rantzau's policy ideas in the Foreign Ministry, occupying Maltzan's former position as chief of the Ministry's Eastern Division, though for a while only as deputy chief. Until May, 1928, his immediate superior had been a man who was little interested in Soviet Russia as a political partner, an attitude that was annoying to the Rantzau circle. W. T. E. Wallroth, chief of the Eastern Division until his appointment as minister to Norway, was one of those who tended to think that the Soviet regime could not last much longer and was therefore a negligible factor in world politics. His transfer to Oslo and von Dirksen's simultaneous promotion were a source of great satisfaction for Rantzau and his entourage.

When I told von Dirksen about Bratman-Brodovsky's remark at Rantzau's funeral, he was visibly pleased, for he already had his eye on the vacant post in Moscow, considering himself, not unjustly, a very suitable candidate for it. In view of his ambition, it was, of course, good to know that the Soviet government would welcome

his appointment. That I was pleased when he was actually given the post need not be emphasized. The hopes I placed in him were never disappointed. He possessed human qualities which greatly contributed to an especially pleasant atmosphere in the Moscow Embassy in those years. The fact that he demanded more from himself than from his subordinates would in itself have been sufficient to earn him their loyalty and respect; but in addition he impressed his collaborators by the selflessness which motivated him, the steadiness and coolness with which he held to the official business at hand, and his exemplary devotion to his work. He approached the many complex political and economic problems that came up day after day with such objectivity and such scrupulous attention to detail that the honesty of his aims was recognized even by the chronically suspicious men in the Kremlin. Without doubt, therefore, he was the most suitable man to represent German interests in Moscow at a time when the maintenance of German-Soviet relations demanded not only consistency and dogged persistence but also wise moderation in striving for realistic aims.

The period during which Herbert von Dirksen served as German ambassador in Moscow was, in Russia, the period of the first Five-Year Plan; in Germany it coincided, though not completely, with the Great Depression. During the first year of his service as ambassador, Germany was still at the peak of prosperity. With this exception in mind, it can nevertheless be asserted that, while von Dirksen was in Moscow, both countries were shaken by economic distress, and both were in the throes of acute political crisis. In Russia Stalin could implement his revolution from above only by the most ruthless means of coercion and terror, paying for it with acute economic disorders. In Germany, after the world crisis had begun to affect her, the burden of insecurity, bankruptcies, and mass unemployment produced political unrest which strengthened the radical parties of the Right and the Left to such an extent that the middle-of-the-road forces of constitutionalism were crushed, and the Weimar Republic was wrecked.

Intensely preoccupied with their internal troubles, Germany and the Soviet Union for a number of years somewhat neglected problems of foreign policy. It was not that foreign problems were completely disregarded; but they receded in relative importance behind acute domestic issues and increasingly became the shuttlecocks of

domestic political struggles. Recurrent problems of foreign policy facing the two countries came to be used for purposes that had little to do with international politics. Thus Russia concealed an iron-clad isolationism behind a façade of intensified Comintern activity which was designed in part to detract attention from her acute internal troubles. In Germany the continued challenge of the reparations problem kept foreign policy more in the foreground, particularly after the depression made the problem more pressing. But there, too, it was the growing crisis in the domestic political scene which gave a semblance of urgency to foreign problems. The revival of the spirit of revisionism was directed not only against the Western powers as the authors of Versailles and the reparations settlement, but equally, if not primarily, against the forces of moderation at home, the advocates of the policy of fulfillment. The growing anti-Western resentment, however, was matched by a feeling of disappointment over the fruits of Rapallo. There was a tendency to complain of the cabinet's foreign policy as insufficiently aggressive.

Our diplomatic circles, in turn, were weary of the stupid and irksome problems posed by Moscow's ruthlessness and clumsiness. Trade relations were indeed developing; but in 1929, before the beginning of the economic crisis in Germany, our business circles tended to view Russia's efforts at industrialization with considerable alarm. As a purchaser of finished industrial products and supplier of raw materials and foodstuffs, Russia could have been an ideal business partner for Germany because the two economies complemented each other. But a more self-sufficient industrial Russia, a country producing its own industrial commodities, might turn into a competitor; and even if the Soviet Union should remain a ready market for German industrial products, the new plans for industrialization nevertheless were forcing German business to adjust itself to the new type of demand. Hence there was dissatisfaction and grumbling. The Russians, in turn, reacted to the slightest expression of such moods with the greatest sensitivity; they were ideologically predisposed to expect them, and interpreted them as imperialist desires to keep Russia an economically backward, underdeveloped, "semicolonial" country for ever.

In my opinion the Kremlin's touchiness was just as unjustified as the occasional German comments on which it was based. Even an industrialized Russia, I thought, would not be able to manage with-

out close economic relations with Germany, and the advantages of an intensive commodity exchange with the vast neighbor in the East would surely outweigh the inconvenience of adjusting to that neighbor's changed demands. Russia's industrialization would not, in the long run, restrict the market for German commodities; on the contrary, it would create new and increased wants and would inevitably lead to the expansion of foreign trade. After all, England was traditionally the greatest customer for German industrial products even though—or perhaps because—its industries were highly developed. Of course, when I thought that an industrialized Russia would continue to be dependent on Germany, I took it for granted that technologically Germany would always be ahead of the Soviet Union.

Observing the anger with which the Russians reacted to German expressions of dissatisfaction over her industrialization plans, I thought that an authoritative statement by a high-ranking policy maker, dispelling their worries, was very much needed. The opportunity came early in 1929. On January 9th a "German Technology Week" was to be opened with official ceremonies in an attempt to bridge the cultural boundaries between the two countries by acquainting the Moscow public with our technological achievements and current research. It had been arranged in collaboration with German scientists, and a number of famous men in German science had come to Moscow to give lectures about their fields of specialization. The commissar for heavy industry, Kuibyshev, was going to speak at the opening of the event, and the new German ambassador, too, was invited to participate.

Von Dirksen had arrived in Moscow only two days before. As he wanted to be duly accredited before his first public appearance he went at once through the customary proceedings, while I set out to draft a speech for him. He was to dispel, once for all, Soviet suspicion that Germany was opposed to their industrialization plans and would sabotage them. Instead of wanting to keep Russia a semi-colonial agricultural nation, he told his audience, we were watching her industrialization efforts with sympathetic interest and would give wholehearted aid to them by granting credits and rendering technical advice. The example of German-English trade relations showed that Russia's industrialization would serve to intensify

German-Soviet commodity exchange, and the speaker promised that he would propagate this view politically and personally. The speech cleared the atmosphere, politically, of much uneasy suspicion, at least for a while; personally it was the best introduction the new ambassador could have given himself in the Moscow of 1929. It must be realized that a certain amount of courage was required to adopt and defend ideas that were not shared by significant parts of the German business world, and von Dirksen has my respect for showing such courage. Of course, the scientists who participated in German Technology Week were already in full agreement with his speech.

Such diplomatic adroitness, whatever its ephemeral successes, could not go deeper than the surface. Basically, German-Soviet relations around 1930 had neither improved nor cooled. They had simply become a matter of routine, and were taken for granted. As far as the two Foreign Offices were concerned, German-Soviet relations were fixed, and fixed to mutual satisfaction, by existing political, economic, and military agreements. Everyone was aware of the mental reservations with which both partners had entered into their relationship, and neither side desired to have the relationship seriously disturbed. Thus the matter seemed settled and hardly worth discussing.

In this situation the embassy had no opportunity to display great statesmanship in high-level negotiations. There was nothing important to negotiate about. After the break of relations between Soviet Russia and China, Berlin had undertaken to represent Soviet interests in China and Chinese interests in the Soviet Union, which caused both sides to accuse us of duplicity. But there were no really grave issues that came up between ourselves and Russia. As a curious result, little problems were blown up to undue importance, mutual criticism and complaints filled the press in both countries at the slightest provocation, and much of the diplomats' time was wasted on the most insignificant difficulties. Both countries were so intensely preoccupied with their internal affairs that they gave little constructive thought to foreign relations. Hence the maintenance of friendly relations with other countries was neglected. The recklessness with which international issues were used by demagogues in one country boosted the same kind of adventurism in the other; and while the Soviet rulers sought to divert their people's attention from internal difficulties by dangling the prospects of impending world revolution

before their eyes, professional anti-Communism had a field day in Germany. The presses of the two countries were blasting broadsides of invective against each other.

One incident was that of the 1929 May Day celebration. Because the police chief of Berlin, Zörgiebel, had forbidden any demonstrations on that day, Moscow apparently thought that it must speak for the German workers who were thus silenced. The parade that rolled past the Soviet leaders and the foreign diplomats in Red Square featured a float depicting a pocket battleship of the type then being built in Germany. The ship was identified by the flags of imperial and republican Germany, and large banners told the crowd that Germany was letting its workers starve while pouring millions into rearmament. Ugly caricatures depicting German cabinet ministers and the police chief stood on top of the float. In a militant speech to the parading crowd, Voroshilov made reference to the political repression under which the working class smarted in other countries, and singled the Social Democratic police chief out for attack. But, he continued, the workers would demonstrate in spite of all repression. There are indications that Comintern circles were in actual fact expecting a general strike in Germany at that time.

Voroshilov's harangues and the mockery made of the German flag were not the only insults dealt out. A week after May Day large crowds came out for a hostile demonstration in front of our consulate general in Leningrad, and protest meetings were staged in numerous factories all over the country to voice Russian sympathy with the German working class. As usual, the Foreign Commissariat went through the motions of apologizing. Karakhan promised to study Voroshilov's speech, and when the official text was published in *Izvestiya* the offensive passages had been deleted. As for the demonstration, Karakhan thought that it was in the nature of a popular carnival which could not be controlled easily, and he suggested that it should not be taken too seriously by us since, after all, such demonstrations had by now become a tradition in Soviet Russia. Similarly, he called the demonstration in Leningrad a spontaneous expression of public opinion. None the less, he assured us that insults of the German flag would not be tolerated again on Soviet territory.

Later that summer leading German Communists were received in Russia with conspicuous honors. German "barricade fighters of the 1st of May" made a trip through the country, and Young Pioneers

from Germany, who had come for a youth rally, were told in an official pamphlet that the demonstration in which they were about to participate was to serve the cause of world revolution. In January, 1930, a number of German Red Front militia men traveled to the Soviet Far East and were officially received by Marshal Blücher. At an official welcome given them, one of the Germans assured the Red Army men that the German proletariat would fall on the back of its own bourgeoisie if ever Soviet Russia were attacked.

Early in 1930 we learned that Soviet trade unions were trying to extend "Socialist competition" to German workers. Individuals participating in such "competition" were pledged to resistance against imperialist wars and to the defense of the Soviet Union, to form Communist cells in their factories, fight against the Social Democrats, subvert the Reichswehr, and participate in May Day demonstrations. International seamen's clubs were spreading Communist propaganda among German sailors, arranging meetings, giving lectures, distributing literature, and inciting the sailors against their officers and captains. Radio Moscow, meanwhile, sharply increased its German-language broadcasting activity.

The tone of the entire Soviet press was taking a turn toward insolence. Every German step designed to improve our relations with the Western powers aroused angry comments; every German failure evoked gleeful derision. Prominent political leaders were dragged through the mud without discrimination. The number and variety of pinpricks that were dealt us by Moscow could be described in much greater detail, from anti-German films and dramas to calculated provocations, such as having the Soviet steamers *Thälmann* and *Max Hölz* run into German ports, where their names would have an obviously subversive significance.

In turn every political movement in Germany seemed to have some reason for anger and resentment toward the Soviet Union. The nationalist Right seized upon the treatment of the German-speaking population, the antireligious campaign, and the open sympathy of Moscow with civil war and revolt in Germany; the moderate Left was indignant over the venom poured out over the government parties by the Soviet press. A general press campaign against Soviet politics set in throughout Germany, in which every single "incident" was given sensational treatment. The Russians were extremely annoyed by our reaction. In his last years as foreign commissar, Chi-

cherin worried much about it and saw in it one of the chief reasons for the deterioration of German-Soviet relations. He thought, for instance, that the sharp German reaction to the Shakhty trial had been unjustified. Similarly, the Foreign Commissariat deplored the way in which our press treated collectivization and the campaign against the kulaks, the systematic efforts to stamp out religion, the terror directed against technicians, intellectuals, and political dissenters, the sharp rate of taxation adopted under the Five-Year Plan, and the activities of the Comintern. Boris Stein's irritated comments in *Izvestiya* on January 21, 1930, and February 4, 1930, written under the pseudonym "Sovremennik" (The Contemporary), were typical reactions. The Russians scored the increasing frequency with which official and non-official dignitaries, from cabinet ministers to cardinals, were making anti-Soviet pronouncements. *Izvestiya* of November 18, 1930, referred to a mass rally of the League for the Protection of Western Culture as a "cannibals' meeting."

Certain legal decisions irked Moscow intensely. There was the case against the well known Berlin art dealer Lepke in November, 1928. Lepke had undertaken to auction off a number of art objects for the Soviet government. Among them were some that had originally been in possession of individual Russians, and had been nationalized by the Soviet government. Some Russian émigrés obtained injunctions against the action, successfully pleading that Lepke was attempting to sell stolen property. More serious was the acquittal of a gang of counterfeiters in February, 1930, who had circulated large quantities of forged chervonets notes. The chervonets was the gold-based currency which the Soviet government had created in 1922 to stop the running inflation of the preceding years. During the trial, which took place in Berlin between January 6th and February 8, 1930, an unhappy atmosphere was created by the aura of politics which the case immediately assumed. The defendants, a number of German citizens and two stateless persons of Georgian origin, pleaded that their counterfeiting activities had been guided exclusively by the lofty political motives of weakening the Soviet Union and furthering the cause of Georgian independence, and that base motives of gain had not been involved. In turn, *Izvestiya*, on February 7, 1930, denounced the defendants as tools in the hands of political adventurers bent on a new war of intervention against the Soviet state, and demanded that the court impose a stiff penalty lest the belief be

created that all crimes against the Soviet Union would go unpunished. In his dispatches to Berlin, the German ambassador seconded the idea, and we were almost as shocked as Litvinov when the defendants were roundly acquitted. The foreign commissar called the decision a catastrophe for the relationship between our two countries; since the raid on the Soviet trade delegation's premises in May, 1924, he said, nothing had happened that boded such ill.

In addition the Foreign Commissariat had occasion to complain about minor economic discriminations, about difficulties Soviet students had encountered in Germany, and small violations of agreements in various matters. One matter that incited them very much illustrates the maddening lack of reciprocity in our dealing with Soviet Russia, a phenomenon which constantly irritated us. For instance, the Soviet government thought it quite natural that German businessmen and representatives applying for a visa to enter the Soviet Union were thoroughly investigated by the embassy in Berlin and interrogated about the purpose of their trip. As a rule only such people would receive visas who had been expressly asked to come by Soviet economic agencies. But when I began to ask Soviet economists for whom a German visa was requested to come into my office and tell me about the purpose of their trip to Germany, the Soviet government lodged such emphatic protests against the practice that we had to abandon it. In such cases Moscow always had more leverage because it could threaten and apply repressive measures, which we could not so easily do. Thus the Soviet government began to restrict the issuance of visas to German business representatives when the German Embassy began interrogations of Soviet economists, which led to protests on the part of the German firms affected which we could not disregard.

Finally, there were a few violations of Soviet extraterritorial privileges; early in February, 1930, the offices of the trade delegation in Munich were raided on a warrant alleging that its chief had violated German laws by trying to sell explosives, and in August, 1932, an officer of the criminal police forced his way into the Soviet Consulate General at Königsberg, an act for which we had to apologize. On the occasion of the fourth anniversary of the Treaty of Berlin, *Izvestiya* complained that the "angry anti-Soviet campaign that has been reigning in Germany in the last months, fed by legal decisions and demonstrations of all sorts, has considerably shaken the

structure for which the foundation was laid in Genoa in 1922," and added pointedly that the German government had not moved a finger to end the press campaign. "The tactics of the German government give the impression that it approves." In conversations with us, Litvinov expressed fears that the anti-Soviet current in German public opinion could get so much out of hand that Berlin might see itself obliged to change the course of its foreign policies. Boris Stein, too, complained bitterly about the attitude of the German press. Outside the NKID, he said, no one still believes in Germany's good will toward Soviet Russia. Stresemann's death was made the occasion for plaintive comments in Soviet circles. He had been roundly distrusted at first, but the NKID had gradually become convinced that he would not abandon the policy of friendship with East and West alike. They were not so sure about Dr. Julius Curtius, his successor.

In reporting such conversations, Ambassador von Dirksen urged the new foreign minister to make a show of good will. Disturbing incidents, he pointed out, had always occurred to mar the good relations between Germany and Soviet Russia, but they had never stood in the way of positive collaboration if both parties wanted it. Von Dirksen suggested that the maintenance of friendly international relations was something on which two governments would have to work continually, and he thought Berlin might have shown a little more eagerness to maintain Moscow's friendship. One thing the Soviet statesmen could not fail to notice was that not a single German foreign minister or undersecretary of foreign affairs had ever visited the Soviet Union, quite in contrast to the practice of other countries. Moreover, recent suggestions by Moscow that German business leaders come for a visit had remained completely without an echo in Germany. Nor had the German press taken notice of Litvinov's friendly and understanding remarks about Germany in a speech he had made before the Central Executive Committee in December, 1929. Dirksen thought that Berlin should take the initiative. He suggested that Soviet fears be allayed by a public declaration which the foreign minister should make before the Reichstag, denying that Germany had changed her attitude toward Russia. Moreover, leading German personalities should visit Moscow in a show of cordiality.

At the time the ambassador made these proposals, mutual complaints, some of them over rather petty grievances, had come to be

virtually the only business that was transacted in the two embassies, except for important economic transactions. Ever since the end of 1929, when the German cabinet had authorized the foreign minister to clear the slate of mutual complaints with Moscow, Krestinsky in Berlin and von Dirksen in Moscow spent much time with the foreign ministers of their guest countries, complaining about untoward incidents, questioning each other's motives, and criticizing each other's system of government. All the bitterness that had gathered in recent years was spilled in an amazing and unprecedented catharsis, of which one of the most surprising features was the frankness with which Germans and Russians discussed their mutual shortcomings. The discussions between Krestinsky and von Schubert were marked by flares of temper and an entirely "undiplomatic" candidness. Both embassies and foreign ministries were busy preparing exhaustive briefs of complaint, and an untold number of hours was spent by ambassadors and their aides over arduous bargaining, in which one insult was weighed against another, and formal denials were traded like rare commodities, with the most amazing concern for detail. The purpose of the discussions was to make a clean slate of all the grievances that had mounted, and each side demanded that the other give firm assurances and indications of its good will. The Germans wanted an open declaration from the Soviet government dissociating itself from international, and particularly German, Communism. The Russians in turn demanded no more than a public affirmation that Germany continue to conduct its foreign policy in the spirit of Rapallo.

However, even these modest demands were more than either partner was willing to concede. Eager as Krestinsky was in von Schubert's office to deny all ties between the Kremlin and the Comintern, Moscow found it utterly impossible to make such a denial in public. And though the German foreign minister, prodded by his ambassador, might have thought it reasonable to swear once more by the spirit of Rapallo, he anxiously sought to avoid giving the West even the slightest suspicion of a new German turn toward Soviet Russia. Both countries thus avoided any public commitments.

By the beginning of May both parties had agreed to transfer the entire discussion to a joint arbitration commission that was to meet in Moscow at once. A German-Soviet communiqué, still to be drafted,

was to announce the first meeting of the commission. Here too Curtius and Chancellor Heinrich Brüning were determined to avoid giving any impression that Germany was, even in the most cautious manner, opting for the East. Other problems came up when the communiqué was to be written. Negotiations about it, conducted by Litvinov and von Dirksen, lasted literally for weeks. Every word, every shade of meaning became the cause of disagreements. A German draft contained references to mutual guarantee of non-interference. The reason that this phrase had been inserted was not only to have Moscow's promise not to interfere in German internal affairs but also to give German public opinion a certain guarantee and thus to make the continuation of friendly German-Soviet relations politically palatable. Without such a phrase, Curtius thought, he would have a difficult time before the Reichstag. But the Russians rejected the wording on the ground that they could be interpreted by the world as a Soviet admission that there had been interference before. The Russian draft, in turn, contained the sentence, "Both governments are agreed that no attempts to influence the internal affairs of the other country actively must be made, just as heretofore." The German ambassador objected to the last three words, for they seemed to give the impression that there had *not* been any Soviet interference before. The Soviet draft in its preamble contained the statement that in the relations between Germany and the Soviet Union a number of problems had "naturally" come up in the course of time which required to be dispersed in the interest of continued good relations. Von Dirksen objected to the word "naturally," and the discussions over it seemed never to end. A compromise was finally reached: the words "naturally" and "just as heretofore" were omitted, and more emphasis was given to the Treaty of Rapallo. The full text read like this:

In the relations between Germany and the Soviet Union a number of questions have arisen in the course of time which need to be cleared up in the interest of carrying on mutual friendly relations. The two governments have therefore made the totality of these questions the subject of comprehensive diplomatic discussions which have taken place in Moscow and Berlin during the past weeks and have now reached a certain conclusion. A part of the mutual individual grievances has already been cleared up satisfactorily in these conversations; the remaining questions are to be submitted to an arbitration commission as provided for in the agreement of

January 25, 1929, which shall gather once yearly about the middle of the year, and which will this year meet on June 16th in Moscow for its ordinary session.

In dealing with the existing individual problems, both governments agree in beginning with the desire to overcome the difficulties that have arisen in the spirit of the Rapallo Treaty and the other treaties in existence between them, and thus to continue the policy they have for long years conducted on the basis of these treaties even under new international developments. In open discussions they have once again become clearly aware that the principal difference of the two governmental systems need be no obstacle to the fruitful development of their friendly relations. At the same time both governments begin with the acknowledgment that no attempts to influence the internal affairs of the other country actively must be made. Both governments are resolved to cultivate mutual relations on this basis and to grapple with tasks that will come up in the future, whether these tasks concern the immediate relationship between the two countries or other questions touching their interests. They are convinced that they will in this manner further not only the benefit of their own countries but also the security of world peace.

ECONOMIC RELATIONS

The period of von Dirksen's service as ambassador in Moscow was the time of the most intensive economic collaboration between the two countries. It began very auspiciously with the signing of a so-called "arbitration agreement" on January 25, 1929, in Moscow. Such an agreement had been discussed ever since the beginning of the previous year, when the President of the Soviet State Bank, Aaron Sheinman, had gone to Berlin for broad discussions of various economic problems. These discussions were broken off in March, 1928, because of the Shakhty trial, and were resumed only after Count Rantzau's death. According to a joint protocol signed in Moscow on December 21, 1928, the newly resumed talks had the preliminary aim of giving precision and clarity to moot points in the treaties of October 12, 1925.

In the course of these discussions the German delegation expressed the desire for a permanent arbitration machinery to settle any subsequent differences of opinion over existing treaties and agreements, and the Russians agreed forthwith. On the basis of these proposals, an agreement was signed by Litvinov and von Dirksen which pro-

vided that any disputes which would not be settled by routine diplomatic negotiation be submitted to a mediation commission that would be composed of an equal number of German and Soviet delegates, two from each country. This commission was not to be a court of arbitration that could make binding decisions, but one that would merely work out compromises which could then be submitted to the two governments for ratification. The Germans had hoped that provisions could be made for a neutral arbiter to be designated as chairman, which would have given the commission more the character of a real arbitration court; but the Soviet government refused to discuss such an appointment because it did not believe anyone could be really neutral in relation to Soviet Russia. In the protocol accompanying the agreement, this was phrased in more diplomatic language: "The Soviet government," the protocol read, "considers the appointment of a neutral chairman unnecessary in view of its good relations with Germany." At the same time the way was left open for a neutral arbiter in special cases.

The German-Soviet mediation commission created in this agreement was to meet once a year, alternately in the German and the Soviet capital, and the first meeting took place in Moscow in June and July of 1930, to discuss political and economic grievances between the two countries. Much had been lost by default in the preceding years, and little had been accomplished since the 300-million credit transaction of 1926. During the years of prosperity, German business had tended to regard trade with Soviet Russia as a risky undertaking made difficult by petty formalism, tiresome bargaining, and an annoying fear of responsibility on the part of the Soviet negotiators. Hence, as German exports rose to the value of 14 billion reichsmarks annually, no more than 3 per cent of the total exports went to the Soviet Union. Little Denmark purchased more goods from Germany than Russia, and our trade balance with the Soviet Union changed little in 1929. The German share of Soviet imports was barely half of what it had been before the war, even though Article 1 of the economic treaty of 1925 had stipulated that the proportion of Russian purchases in Germany should approximate those of prewar times.

Our firms were incensed at the discriminatory manner in which the Russians placed orders so as to play country against country and firm against firm, making purchases in other countries for political

reasons. The benefits Moscow derived from the foreign-trade monopoly and the privileges of its trade representation had become quite obvious. We became painfully aware that German business was virtually being eliminated from all middle-man positions in German-Soviet trade; Derutra and Sowtorgflot had a monopoly on shipping; Gosstrakh on the insurance business; and so on. The trade representation itself engaged in direct sales of Soviet foodstuffs. At the same time Moscow directed sharp attacks against all and any attempts on our part to co-ordinate German business dealings with the Soviet Union through a central agency. On the whole, it had become clear that the principle of most-favored-nation treatment, coupled with these special privileges for Soviet agencies, offered far greater advantages to the Russians than to us, so that there was a fundamental imparity.

The question of alleged Soviet dumping played a great role after the beginning of the first Five-Year Plan. It was asserted in the West that Russia sold goods below cost in order to ruin the foreign trade of other countries; and on the basis of this accusation sharp economic warfare set in between Soviet Russia and the West. Moscow answered these claims by indignant protests against the new "bourgeois conspiracy" and roundly denied that its prices were below cost. If they were below world-market prices, wrote the commissar of foreign trade, Rosengolts, the reason was that all middle men were excluded in the Soviet economy.[2] Actually, it was extremely difficult to determine the actual cost of Soviet commodities. But the foreign-trade monopoly enabled the Soviet government to let political considerations help determine its export policies, the placing of orders, and the fixing of a price. Nor could the Russians deny that they were actually doing these things; and were doing them suddenly so that there was an additional factor of surprise which was even more effective in times of crisis. Hence there were grounds for complaints, particularly among the agrarian countries of Eastern Europe, which suffered most under Soviet competition. On the other hand, the volume of Soviet exports was never large enough to affect world-market conditions by whatever practices were adopted, so that the clamor of the antidumping campaign was not fully justified. Moreover, no one who mentions the subject should forget that Soviet export prices were to a considerable extent determined also by the

[2] *Izvestiya,* Oct. 22, 1930.

purchasers of Russian goods. The Western importer knew very well how desperately Moscow was seeking gold or hard currency, and if they could get away with it they offered prices so low that they were often less than the cost of production. If such offers were accepted by the Russians, it was because the Soviet government did not mind the loss. None the less, there is no reason to disbelieve the former Soviet trade representative who writes that "the prime task of the foreign-trade delegates abroad was to try to get better prices, fighting for every dollar of gold that could be squeezed out." [3]

Another issue clouding the atmosphere of German-Soviet trade relations at the time of von Dirksen's arrival in Moscow was that of the Russian prewar debts. Though the Rapallo Treaty had in effect canceled all claims between the two countries arising out of the war or out of prewar obligations, some fears were now voiced that by the treaty Germany might have thrown away some valuable trump cards. There were a number of German concerns that could never forget how much they had lost in Russia through nationalization; outstanding among them were the mining firms who had once owned valuable manganese deposits in the Caucasus. A few weeks after the death of Count Brockdorff-Rantzau, some of these old creditor firms participated in establishing an international committee for the protection of Russian bond owners, against the sharp protest of the Foreign Ministry, which desperately tried to prevent such participation on the part of German firms.

From the beginning of his term as ambassador, von Dirksen sought to revive and extend German trade relations with Soviet Russia by encouraging long-term credit transactions, technical aid, and close cultural interchange. In his advocacy of further generous credits he was at first handicapped by the external reparations problem; during 1929 Berlin was discussing the Young plan of determining the reparations burden, and the Reich government was unwilling to make any promises before the weighty question was decided. What aided von Dirksen's efforts was, however, the beginning of world economic crisis, coinciding as it did with the Soviet first Five-Year Plan. Intensive Russian demands for machines and other industrial products were created at the very moment when under the impact of the

[3] Alexander Barmine, *One Who Survived* (New York, G. P. Putnam's Sons, 1945), p. 175.

depression Germany's foreign trade began to shrink rapidly and her industry was more desperate than ever for customers.

At the close of 1929 Moscow still owed roughly one tenth of the 300-million credit it had obtained in 1926. But further credits had been granted in subsequent years to finance orders placed in Germany, and these debts, too, had not yet been fully liquidated. From all these transactions the Soviet government still owed almost 80 million reichsmarks. In view of Germany's economic difficulties, the Ministry of Finance seemed very disquieted by this figure. Some leading officials were haunted by the fear that the Russians might stop paying even for a short time, which might have had disastrous consequences. These fears were not shared, however, by those who made economic policy in the Foreign Ministry. As a matter of fact, through the efforts of Schlesinger, the 300-million credit had already been made into a revolving credit. In other words, the installments paid by the Russians were plowed back into the credit for further purchases. As a consequence, the actual Soviet debt was still around 300 million reichsmarks. This revolving of the credit had been done quietly and without publicity; all official discussions had been avoided not only to forestall the ifs and buts of the German doubters but also to prevent the Soviet negotiators from using pressure to obtain even better conditions. Moreover, Schlesinger would have been loath to give the Russians the political victory of open credit negotiations, which would once again have demonstrated to the world the close ties binding the two countries together. For a while he tried to organize a credit deal in co-operation with American financial interests, but the project failed over the objections of Karl Ritter, the then chief of the Economic Division in the Foreign Ministry. Late in January, 1930, after an intensive exchange of views with Schlesinger, the ambassador dispatched a lengthy memorandum to his superiors pleading for German initiative in getting a new credit transaction going. He pointed out that previous negotiations had been interrupted in the spring of 1929 with the promise that they would be resumed after the settlement of the reparations problem. This promise, he wrote, should not be left unfulfilled. Bringing up all the old arguments in favor of generous credits, he pleaded for a grant of no less than 300 million, and demanded that it be made revolving. Such a long-term investment, he argued, would be re-

garded as a token of good will and would yield corresponding political benefits. He even insisted on dramatizing the new credit by sending an official delegation to Russia and organizing appropriate public ceremonies.

Von Dirksen's views were seconded in Berlin by Hans von Raumer, the head of the German arbitration commission, who had returned from Moscow with rather positive impressions, and in this way his memorandum actually initiated a new credit transaction of the type he had suggested. Within a year after the new credit had been granted, German exports to the Soviet Union rose very sharply, with imports from Russia lagging behind, to Moscow's great disappointment. The total value of Soviet orders placed in Germany during 1931 reached the record sum of 919.2 million reichsmarks. If several important German manufacturing firms, particularly in the field of tool machinery, weathered the depression and could be put to work by Hitler in his rearmament efforts after 1933, it was due exclusively to the Soviet orders which kept them in business. Thus in the first half of 1932, Soviet Russia purchased 50 per cent of all the cast iron and nickel exported by Germany, 60 per cent of all earth-moving equipment and dynamos sold abroad, 70 per cent of all metal-working machines, 80 per cent of cranes and sheet metals, and as much as 90 per cent of all steam and gas turbines and steam presses Germany exported. There were German firms, in those years, who were creditors of the Soviet Union in amounts up to 100 per cent of their capital stock, and who could do business with Russia only with the help of Reich default guarantees. Of course, this was not a healthy state, and it used to worry everyone concerned. But these German firms were certainly aware that they owed their survival to the big customer in the East, and the German government clearly realized that without the Soviet market unemployment in Germany would be even more serious than it already was.

The Soviet Five-Year Plan helped to relieve German unemployment in still another way: Hundreds or even thousands of German technicians and engineers who were unemployed or facing unemployment were engaged by the Soviet government as specialists to aid in the industrialization of the country. Their number was so great that the German Embassy had to organize a school for their children in Moscow and was forced to deal with various special problems,

like those created by mixed marriages of German technical personnel with Soviet women.

In consequence of this intensified exchange of commodities and skills, interest in the Soviet Union was very high at that time. In 1930 and 1931 German business circles turned to the Foreign Ministry with requests for information about the general situation in Soviet Russia, and Berlin requested me to go on a tour through Germany to give public talks and private consultation about possibilities of further increases in German exports to the Soviet Union. Inevitably I faced packed lecture halls and keenly interested industrialists, indicating a widespread inclination, in those years, to do business with the Russians. In Berlin alone, in the course of about ten days I received more than two hundred business leaders who were interested in Soviet trade.

It was this attitude which prompted a number of leading German industrialists to make a visit to Soviet Russia in the spring of 1931. A trip like that had often been discussed, and less important groups of business representatives had made occasional trips to Russia. But in January, 1931, Grigori Konstantinovich Ordzhonikidze, the chairman of the Supreme Economic Council, invited an impressive list of prominent industrial leaders to discuss with him to what extent German industry might assist the Five-Year Plan by supplying machinery and other essential products. The Foreign Ministry was kept informed of the negotiations for the visit but it was not directly involved, which was very much to its satisfaction, since the phobia against showing any particular intimacy with the Russians had by then become well ingrained. Moreover, Schlesinger feared that the main purpose of the invitation was to bait American industrial firms to do greater business with Russia.

The group that left Berlin on February 26, 1931, for a two weeks' trip to Russia included some of the most illustrious names of Germany's heavy industry. World-famous producers of steel, machinery, and electrical equipment, like Krupp, Borsig, Klöckner, AEG, MAN, Demag, and Vereinigte Stahlwerke, were sending their top executives to Moscow for exploratory talks. They wanted orders, and the Kremlin wanted credits. At first the Russians seemed to believe that they could have the capitalists in their pockets by merely making their mouths water at the prospect of huge sales. For they immediately

dangled big deals before their eyes, talking vaguely about orders amounting to over a billion reichsmarks. At the same time they demanded commensurate credits. They were greatly disappointed when the delegation declared that they had come in order to look around and not to close business deals. This, in turn, was no more than a device which gave the Germans a tactical advantage. Before the delegation left the Soviet Union, an agreement had been reached that an additional 300 million reichsmarks' worth of orders would be accepted. This led at once to discussions as to how the new orders should be financed. The suggestion was even made to adjust all German-Soviet economic relations to the Soviet Five-Year Plan, but it was not pursued very far. On March 24, 1931, the Reich cabinet agreed to give default guarantees for the additional 300-million credit, and two weeks later Grigori Pyatakov came to Berlin to discuss and sign the so-called Pyatakov Agreement, which specified the precise conditions of the transaction.

MY INFORMATION TRIP THROUGH THE SOVIET UNION

"The first Five-Year Plan must be fulfilled and will be fulfilled in four years." Under this slogan the Soviet government raised to the very limit the demands for output and self-sacrifice which it put to the population. The beginning of the plan, originally set for October 1, 1928, was later moved to January 1, 1929, when the fiscal year was made to coincide with the calendar year. But after three years had passed, it was announced that the production goals of the Five-Year Plan must be fulfilled by the end of 1932, that is, within four years, and that this required one last heroic effort. From the preceding pages it appears obvious that German business circles were extremely keen on determining whether the astounding Soviet claims concerning their successes in industrializing their country were true, and to what extent the gigantic effort connected with the industrialization affected the solvency of the Soviet government and the morale of the population. Moreover, the German firms who had sold machinery to the Soviet Union were vitally interested in finding out what was being done with their products, whether they were being utilized efficiently, and whether there was anything to the rumors that much precious industrial equipment was being left to spoil because of faulty handling or negligent treatment.

The information we obtained from the numerous German experts working in the Soviet Union was insufficient and did not enable us to form a reliable and exhaustive impression of the situation because it was of a sporadic nature and, in many instances, was strongly distorted by the bias of the informants. Only a personal inspection could give a somewhat correct estimate of what actually went on in the great many new industrial enterprises of the Ural Mountains and Siberia.

On the basis of these considerations, and because of the initiative of Moritz Schlesinger, a plan for an information trip through the new industrial areas of the Soviet Union was conceived, a trip in which he and I were to be accompanied by Otto Mossdorf of the Soviet Union desk in the Reich Ministry of the Economy.

At first Moscow had grave doubt about such a trip. But we made it clear that further German credits would become available only if we were convinced that the money was being invested intelligently. Finally, the Soviet government gave its agreement, but only on the condition that we should not go alone, but should be accompanied by an official of the Foreign Commissariat who would allegedly facilitate our contact with local officials and factory managers. We had no choice except to agree, though we were fully convinced that our companion's main task would be to curb our curiosity, if necessary. These fears proved to be partly unjustified. Our companion manifested a very agreeable reticence, and many of the factory managers were extremely proud and eager to demonstrate their achievements to us as fully as possible; as a consequence we were shown far more than we had ever hoped to see. In general, the mania for secrecy in the Soviet Union had not yet reached the excesses with which it is being practiced today.

We started our trip in the second half of August, 1932, and returned to Moscow in the middle of October. Our route was about as follows: Moscow, Saratov, Stalingrad, Rostov, Northern Caucasus (for a visit to the German agricultural concession Drusag), Baku, Tiflis, Batum, Crimea, Kharkov, Moscow, Magnitogorsk, Chelyabinsk, Sverdlovsk, Novosibirsk, Kuznetsk (Stalinsk), Prokopevsk, Moscow. Although twenty years have passed since I took the trip, I still have a very vivid recollection of its different stages. There were a number of outstanding impressions that I brought home with me: first, the grandiose scale of the industrial enterprises and the bold-

ness of their planning; second, the unspeakable demands which the
Soviet government made on the population's ability to suffer and
do without; third, the striking discrepancy between the ultramodern
technical equipment of the factories and the primitive nature of the
methods used in accomplishing the necessary auxiliary tasks; fourth,
the tenacity and the hope and the courage shown by the technical
personnel, even though the difficulties often seemed insuperable;
fifth, the enthusiasm that had taken hold of some of the young workers; and finally, the rapid speed with which even members of primitive tribes learned how to handle the most modern technical devices.

Just a year before I had visited the Stalingrad tractor plant and
made an exhaustive inspection of it, so that I did not learn anything
new about it this time. But I was struck by the fact that a single
year had been enough to put the valuable foreign-made tool machinery, most of it made in the United States and Germany, in a state of
wear and tear that ten or fifteen years could hardly have done in the
West. And when we saw a great many other Soviet industrial enterprises, among them the great ball-bearing works in Moscow, we became convinced that the Stalingrad tractor plant was no exception
in this respect. Wherever we went in the Soviet Union, we saw a depreciation of machinery and a decay of buildings only recently
erected which was more rapid than a Westerner could imagine. I
am told that not much has changed in this respect since the war, so
that anyone who wants to estimate the present Soviet industrial potential will have to calculate a much higher depreciation rate than
that customary in the West.

On the other hand, my trip did not confirm the widespread rumors
that a large proportion of machinery purchased abroad by the Soviet
government was left to rot under the open sky because the buildings
that were to house it had not been finished and because the technical
personnel required for expert mounting was lacking. On the contrary, I noted that even young and inexperienced Soviet technicians
showed surprising skill and ingenuity in mounting industrial equipment. With the most primitive means, and lacking some of the devices which are considered utterly essential in the West, things were
done in the Soviet Union that often would amaze foreigners. Yet
all this was accomplished with such an enormous expenditure of
capital and with such tremendous demands on the energies of all

concerned that I asked myself how long the population could stand the pressure.

Owing to the ruthlessness with which agricultural enterprises were being collectivized, there was no lack of labor force wherever industrial establishments were being set up. But the construction of dwellings for the laborers was far, far behind the minimal requirements. Hence the factory workers, men and women, who wished to find shelter around Stalingrad, Magnitogorsk, or Kuznetsk, had to live in caves which they dug in the nearby hills. If people could exist and accomplish useful work under such living conditions and with the great shortage of foodstuffs and consumer goods, it could be explained only by the proverbial fact that the Russian population was not used to much else except suffering and want. This applied particularly to the Eastern nationalities from among whom a substantial part of the workers in the new industrial establishments was recruited.

In contrast to the conditions we found in the Ural area and in Siberia, Transcaucasia offered a much friendlier picture. Particularly in Baku, which I had known well before the First World War, I was surprised by the progress that had been made in building dwellings for the workers. Cities like Tiflis and Batum, too, did not seem to share the extremely low living standard of the population in other parts of the Soviet Union.

Sverdlovsk, in the Ural Mountains, had turned from a picturesque provincial town of Old Russia into a vast and bleak industrial center. We were put up in a hotel which had been built two years before; yet owing to the use of third-rate building materials and to neglect it already showed the most pitiful signs of decay. Moreover, its washrooms and privies were in a state that defied description, which substantially lessened our feeling of comfort. All the more surprising, and typical of the contrasts that have always been characteristic of Russia, was the fact that Sverdlovsk could boast of two theaters whose operatic and dramatic productions could easily have stood comparison with the achievements of the best Moscow stages.

One of the sights I saw while staying in Sverdlovsk was the house in which, on July 17, 1918, the last tsar and his family were killed by the bullets of Bolshevik hangmen so that they would not fall into the hands of the Whites and become symbols of counter-revolution-

ary resistance. The modest dwelling in which the family of the tsar had spent their last months had belonged to a railroad engineer named Ipatyev, and the Bolsheviks had made it into some sort of national monument. An official guide led me to the dark cellar and showed me the bullet marks in the wall. He called my attention to the fact that they were only knee-high, and said, in explanation:

"The people who received their just deserts here at the hands of revolutionary justice had millions of human lives on their conscience. They themselves, however, did not have courage enough to face death standing up, but sank to their knees like cowards."

The idea that some people might kneel down to call to their God in the presence of death seemed to be beyond the man's mental horizon.

In Magnitogorsk I was greatly impressed by the giant blast furnaces, built after the newest American models, with a capacity of a thousand metric tons each, and I marveled at the nearby "magnet mountain" with its inexhaustible stores of high-grade iron ore which can be dug from the surface and which forms the basis of an annual production of 2.4 million metric tons of pig iron.

An iron and steel works of equal size was just being built in Kuznetsk (today called Stalinsk). It is based on the rich coal seams of Prokopevsk, where I went down into the pits and spent several hours underground. There too the contrasts of Soviet industrialization were manifested by the co-existence of the most modern technical equipment with the use of some of the most primitive methods of work.

I have already indicated the eagerness with which most plant managers fulfilled our wishes and answered our questions. Of course, there were exceptions. A young engineer in a Batum oil refinery refused to give me some information which I could have found in every pertinent textbook. I had to complain about this needless secrecy-mongering to the director of the refinery and to our Soviet companion until I finally elicited the harmless bit of information. In Stalingrad the manager pleaded ignorance when I asked about the purpose of a large building that was just being erected immediately in front of his office windows. I later discovered that it was the beginnings of a tank factory that was to be connected with the nearby tractor works.

It was at a factory in Chelyabinsk that I found the engineer Bash-

kin about whose behavior during the Shakhty trial, in the summer of 1928, I have already told. The man who told me about his presence made much of the excellent services which Bashkin had meanwhile rendered during the construction of the plant. I took this incident as one of the many examples of the wanton and capricious brutality with which the Soviet regime makes everyone serve its purposes.

ONCE MORE, A SOVIET TRIAL

The chancery of the German Embassy stood in a narrow lane which was, in von Dirksen's time, still called Leontyevski Pereulok. In 1938 it was renamed Ulitsa Stanisslavskogo, in honor of the famous Russian theater director who had died shortly before. At the end of this narrow lane, where it meets with Ulitsa Gertsena, five shots were fired on Saturday, March 5, 1932, at one thirty in the afternoon. They were aimed at a car belonging to the German Embassy, and in which my good friend and colleague, Counselor of Embassy Fritz von Twardowski, was sitting. The first bullet grazed his neck, very close to the artery. The second smashed a few bones of his left hand, which he had lifted in an immediate reflex movement. Two other bullets missed, and the last one lodged in the back rest of the seat. In view of the proximity of the embassy, there was never a lack of Soviet secret police in Leontyevski Pereulok, and the would-be assassin was seized at once and taken away. Von Twardowski had sufficient presence of mind to order the driver to take him at once to the nearby Kremlin Hospital. There medical aid was administered.

From the beginning there was no doubt that the plot had been aimed against the ambassador himself. Von Dirksen was saved only by chance circumstances. Contrary to his custom, he had not gone home at one twenty by the usual route, but had left the embassy a few minutes earlier in the opposite direction, for he wanted to do an errand in town. Had von Dirksen been in the car instead of von Twardowski, the assassination would probably have succeeded, for the much larger body of the ambassador would have presented a much better target for the bullets than that of his assistant.

A curious concatenation of circumstances also saved me the experience of being in front of a murderer's weapon. Von Twardowski and I usually rode to lunch together because our residences were in the same direction. On this day too he had called me before leaving

and asked whether I wanted to join him as usual. But I had just returned from a meeting in the Commissariat of Finance, and I wanted to write a report about the talks before the week end. Five minutes later the shots rang out. There is no doubt that one of us would have been killed if we had gone together.

For the Soviet government it was an extremely disagreeable incident. The political and economic situation in Russia at that time was marked by the consequences of forced collectivization and the suffering deprivation which the execution of the first Five-Year Plan demanded of the Soviet population. The Kremlin would have done anything to prevent its relations with Germany from getting worse, particularly since the anti-Soviet tendencies of National Socialism were becoming more and more active. A frantic attempt, therefore, was made by the Soviet government to prove its good will to Berlin. Within the shortest possible time a trial was staged in which, besides the assassin, Yuda Mironovich Stern, a second defendant named Vasilyev faced the court. It was obvious that Vasilyev was a pliable tool in the hands of the judge as well as of Krylenko, the prosecutor. At the latter's prompting, he testified that he had persuaded Stern to execute the plot against the German Embassy in order to ruin the relations between Germany and the Soviet Union. Vasilyev said he had been requested to do so by the Polish Embassy.

We never could find out anything about Vasilyev, his life, or the reasons that caused him to make his testimony. But as far as Stern was concerned, I had no doubts. I attended the trial from beginning to end and received the very strong impression that the twenty-eight-year-old student was a pathologically unbalanced person, an utter failure in life, who was forced by an irresistible compulsion to do something to catch the attention of the world. Whether Vasilyev had been involved in the plot at all, or to what extent he had participated in organizing it, remained obscure or at least questionable.[4]

The court's main purpose was to prove that Stern's plot was not the incidental deed of a single individual but the well considered act of a conspiratorial group whose wires were being pulled by the Polish Embassy. In order to prove the great political importance

[4] One author's claim that Stern and Vasilyev committed their deed at the behest of the GPU itself appears extremely dubious. The details in his story which are subject to verification show great inaccuracies, and the entire book in which it appears, Karl I. Albrecht's *Der verratene Sozialismus* (Berlin-Leipzig, Volksansgabe 1943), pp. 338–341, is of very doubtful value as a source.

inherent in the assassin's intent, Krylenko tried with particular stubbornness to extract the confession from Stern that he had noted down the numbers of several cars belonging to the German Embassy and that he had lain in wait for the cars systematically. Krylenko finally got Stern to name two license numbers, which the court then identified as those of the cars used by von Dirksen and von Twardowski. Apparently, however, that was not sufficient in the eyes of the Foreign Commissariat. Immediately after Stern had named the two numbers, the Assistant Commissar for Foreign Affairs Nikolai Krestinsky, who had been sitting among the audience, came up to me and asked me the license number of my own car. Without thinking much about it, I willingly gave him the information. Shortly afterward the trial was adjourned for a short time. When it was resumed, Krylenko once more began to insist that the accused Stern had not told the full truth, but had kept something concerning the license numbers from the court. Thereupon Stern with halting voice produced the number of my car, and Krylenko moved another adjournment so that an investigation could be made to discover whose number it might be. After a fifteen-minute break, the session was re-opened with a statement by Krylenko. Clear proof, he said, had finally been established that Stern had intended to "hit the very heart" of the German Embassy with his plot, for the three license numbers he had memorized were those of the ambassador himself and his two most immediate collaborators.

Even from my long observation of Soviet show trials I can hardly recall another example in which the collaboration between public prosecutor, court, and a governmental agency interested in the result of the trial was manifested in such blatant form as in this case of an assistant foreign commissar's interference.

IX GERMANY AND
RUSSIA 1933-1938

1. HITLER'S ACCESSION TO POWER

As the political crisis deepened in Germany, the voices which warned
against all dealings with Soviet Russia grew louder and stronger. On
the extreme right wing of the political spectrum, dreams of German
expansion toward the East were revived; Chapter XIV of Hitler's
Mein Kampf openly proclaimed the fertile lands of Russia to be
the destined *Lebensraum* for Germany's expanding Nordic population. Hitler's propaganda made skillful use of the discontent created
by the depression and unemployment and the fears aroused by the
growing Communist vote. Representatives of business, politicians
and civil servants, alarmed by the growing strength and virulence of
the Communist International, more and more regarded the Soviet
government exclusively as the headquarters of world revolution.
With the awareness of the difficulties and hardships connected with
the first Five-Year Plan, moreover, the tendency grew in the Foreign
Ministry to write Russia off as a negligible factor in world politics,
and as a state whose friendship was more of a burden than an asset.
In 1931 Dr. Curtius resigned from the cabinet and Heinrich Brüning,
the Chancellor, took over the Foreign Ministry. Both he and his
permanent undersecretary, Bernhard von Bülow, were very skeptical
about the usefulness of good relations with Soviet Russia. While
they were not ready to make any sudden turns away from Moscow,
they certainly sought to keep German-Soviet dealings on a cool and
noncommittal level. Franz von Papen, who became Chancellor in
June, 1932, embarked on a much more decided attempt at a rapprochement with France; evidence of this, embellished by much rumor, created serious concern in Moscow.
250

But even during the reign of the von Papen and Kurt von Schleicher cabinets, German-Soviet relations on the surface remained as friendly as ever. Shortly after von Papen took over the government, a large delegation of Soviet officers, led by Tukhachevsky, attended the Reichswehr summer maneuvers and were even received by von Hindenburg; in Moscow, meanwhile, von Dirksen and his staff strove to reassure the Kremlin that German policy toward Soviet Russia had not changed. Underneath this façade of politeness, however, German policy was straining away from Rapallo. Nothing illustrates this so well as the difficulties encountered in renewing the Treaty of Berlin. The treaty would have expired on June 24, 1931, and several months before the date von Dirksen and Litvinov, discussing the matter, agreed that it should be renewed. At once it became clear that Berlin wanted to avoid all discussions or questions about it in the Reichstag, where the "national opposition" would certainly have seized the opportunity of making nasty attacks on the government's foreign policy. In order to tread as cautiously as possible, the Foreign Ministry proposed to renew the treaty for an indefinite period but reserve the right to terminate it at any time on one year's notice. Moscow, on the other hand, wanted to extend it for five years. The protocol which was finally drafted provided that the treaty be renewed for an indefinite time, but one year's notice of cancellation could be given any time after June 30, 1933. This protocol was signed just before the treaty expired, and still required ratification by the Reichstag. In the last minute Brüning made an unsuccessful attempt to keep the news of the renewal out of the press, lest French nationalist opinion be aroused. Moreover, he was very reluctant to submit the protocol to the Reichstag. A year after it had been signed, the protocol had not yet been ratified, and a quick succession of Reichstag dissolutions kept it from coming up for action. It had to wait until early May, 1933, three months after Hitler came to power, before a National Socialist Reichstag stamped its approval on it.

The fall of the Brüning cabinet in February, 1932, caused the Soviet press to comment that German politics had taken a decided turn toward fascist dictatorship. The Russians' attitude toward this rise of fascism was quite ambivalent. There were, first of all, expressions of confidence that the reign of fascism would soon give way to the dictatorship of the proletariat. Until Hitler's actual accession to

power, Moscow could point out with satisfaction that the German Communist party was gaining strength in step with the National Socialists, and every change of cabinet, every tightening of the right-wing dictatorship was hailed as a sure indication that the revolutionary crisis was being accelerated. One day after Hitler assumed the office of Reich Chancellor, *Izvestiya* wrote that the moment was near where the struggle for power among the capitalist factions could turn into open class war; and as late as March, 1933, Radek assured the readers of the same paper that the National Socialists had won only an illusory victory. On the basis of such considerations certain circles within the Soviet government actually gave silent welcome to Hitler's accession to power because they believed that he could not last very long, and that his fall would speed the development of a proletarian revolution in Germany.

But side by side with confidence in the inevitable victory of the proletariat came creeping fears and premonitions. Even while the depression and its political consequences were hailed as the harbingers of proletarian revolution, the very fact that the outside world was racked by crises at a time when the Soviet Union more than ever wished to be left alone to deal with its own problems was cause for worry. Nor could Communist Moscow remain unconcerned about the growth of anti-Communist sentiments in Germany, even though it sought valiantly to see only the progress of revolutionary crisis. None the less, official Soviet Russia did not cease to express its firm willingness to maintain its good relations even with a Germany ruled by the Hitler party, and its diplomats never tired of pointing out how well Moscow got along with Italy and Turkey, even though the Communist parties there were completely outlawed. The official Soviet line on that subject was summed up when Litvinov said, "We don't care if you shoot your German Communists." In any event, Moscow did not know how to prevent Hitler's rise to power. After all, it could not recommend to the German Communist party an alliance with the Social Democrats, or other parties that might have saved the republic, at a time when the Russian party was loudly condemning the right-wing opposition.

What Litvinov and his government did very much care about was the foreign policy of a possible Hitler regime. In their conversations with us the Russians made it quite clear that they had read *Mein Kampf* either in the original or in a Russian translation. Fif-

teen years earlier, ideas similar to those of Hitler had inspired the Treaty of Brest-Litovsk, and the thought that the spirit of Brest might supersede the spirit of Rapallo in German-Soviet relations gave Soviet policy makers acute discomfort. In order to forestall such a change of Germany policy, the Russians made every effort to show their own good will even before the National Socialists came to power. A conversation I had with the manager of TASS, Doletsky, in July, 1932, was typical. Doletsky voiced all the worries that were bothering Moscow, but in the same breath he expressed his conviction that healthy political common sense would win out in a National Socialist government; even the Nazis would be sensible and continue a policy toward Russia that, in his opinion, was consonant with the long-range interests of Germany. Doletsky assured me in all confidence that the Soviet press had been instructed to avoid all appearances of interfering in Germany's political crisis and even to refrain from criticism of German policy. All he feared was that the accession of Hitler might be followed by a rather disturbing period of transition before normal relations could again be achieved. The general impression in the German Embassy was that the Soviet government would have liked to establish contact with the National Socialists for the purpose of preventing such temporary difficulties.

Doletsky's tempered optimism was shared by many German diplomats both in Berlin and in Moscow. We too could not help being aware of the decidedly anti-Soviet tendency of National Socialist statements; for more than ten years Hitler's party had consistently criticized Rapallo as a treacherous deal, and had castigated all those who believed in cultivating even the slightest diplomatic relations with the Soviet state. One of Hitler's chief spokesmen in ideological matters, Alfred Rosenberg, was obviously motivated by a truly pathological hatred of everything Russian; and all National Socialists consistently refused to regard the Soviet state and Soviet representatives as anything but thinly veiled agents of a "Jewish-Bolshevik" international. Yet few of us were prepared to regard these never ending outbursts as serious statements of future policy. Shocked as most of us were by the accession of the loud-mouthed demagogue and his brown-shirted militia who so utterly lacked all attributes of respectability, we were convinced that no responsible cabinet chief, once in office, could fail to consider the advantages of Germany's continued

relations with Soviet Russia. For the time being, Ambassador von Dirksen bombarded the foreign minister with emphatic pleas that the old policy be continued, urging him to persuade Hitler to make statements that might reassure the Russians; and there are indications that the Foreign Ministry in Berlin supported von Dirksen in these pleas, pointing out that the murky international situation argued against any sudden adventures in foreign policy.

For many weeks in the spring of 1933 the actual policy of the Hitler regime toward the Soviet Union was vague, hesitating, and quite ambiguous. Together with terrorist measures against the German Communist party and agents of the Communist International, a few similar steps were taken against Soviet citizens and Soviet installations. Some of the incidents were acts of hooliganism organized, encouraged, or tolerated by local storm-troop leaders. Brown shirts raided a Soviet clubhouse in Hamburg, looting and wrecking the place; Soviet citizens, particularly Jews, were molested, so that Soviet officials who had so willingly come to Germany in previous years now avoided being sent there. In July three prominent political leaders, Krestinsky, Yenukidze, and Surits encountered great difficulties when they tried to obtain hotel reservations for a vacation in Germany. In the German press Soviet leaders, particularly Litvinov, began to be exposed to unbridled ridicule and defamation.

Other measures had a more official character. Four weeks after the accession of Hitler the Berlin correspondent of *Izvestiya,* Mrs. Lilly Keith, was arrested on the grounds of anti-German bias in her reports.[1] Police raided the Soviet trade delegations in Hamburg and Leipzig; the premises of the mixed oil firm, Derop, were occupied, and its German employees arrested as being Communists. All activities of the trade delegations were seriously hampered when attorneys, notaries, and other agents of Jewish faith employed by Soviet agencies were no longer recognized by German tax and customs authorities, while non-Jewish German attorneys refused to do further work for their Soviet clients, in view of the political risk involved in this activity.

Several times during the spring of 1933 Hitler made public declarations in which he affirmed that German policy toward the Soviet Union remained unchanged. In Nazi party circles, and in the party

---

[1] Since Mrs. Keith was a German citizen this could not, of course, be cause for any Soviet protest.

press, such statements were rationalized by the argument that healthy political relations between Germany and the Soviet state had become possible only now after the complete elimination of the Communist movement from German politics.[2] The actual reason for Hitler's attempt to soothe the Kremlin's mind was that a clear line toward Soviet Russia had not yet been developed. In Germany's Eastern policies, the initial sharp tension with Poland seemed much more acute. Hence the ratification of the renewal of the Treaty of Berlin voted by the Reichstag in April was not very much more than a routine act which recognized that there were as yet no intentions to make a sudden break with Moscow. Foreign Minister von Neurath assured the Soviet representative in Berlin, Khinchuk, that Hitler's constant anti-Communist statements were not directed against the Soviet Union but only against the German Communist party. On April 28th the Soviet plenipotentiary was actually received by Göring and later by Hitler himself. On this occasion, too, the Chancellor replied to Khinchuk's complaints and demands with reassurances that no changes would occur in the good relations between their two countries, which were bound together by economic ties and by having common enemies.

Soviet faith in these pronouncements was shaky, as they were contradicted by the increasing terror directed not only against German Communism but also against Soviet installations. After the Reichstag fire, the KPD was virtually liquidated, its members hounded, imprisoned, and killed. This stunning blow to world Communism, with its headquarters in Moscow, led to some soul-searching analysis of the mistakes that had been made, and to the belated realization that National Socialism was Enemy No. 1 of the German Communist movement. The Moscow funeral services for Klara Zetkin, a veteran leader of the KPD, on June 22, 1933, were turned into a mass demonstration against National Socialism and its leaders, now governing Germany; we assigned political significance to the rally because such important personalities as Stalin and Molotov participated in it. And yet, during the first five or six months of Hitler's rule we noted marked efforts at restraint in the Soviet press. While Hitler was rooting out the entire KPD apparatus which Moscow had spent so much care and money to build up, considerations of Soviet foreign policy retained paramount importance in the minds of Russia's lead-

2 Cf. *Völkischer Beobachter,* May 6, 1933.

ers to such an extent that willingness to go on with Germany as before was expressed again and again. Such persons as Krestinsky, Litvinov, and Molotov went out of their way to assure us that their government had no desire to reorient its foreign policy. The chief of the German Division in the Foreign Commissariat, Stern, went so far as to tell us that the French had more than once asked Moscow to join the free world in its condemnation of the new government of Germany, and still the Soviet press had, in the main, refrained from unfavorable comments. Dirksen felt confident that German-Soviet relations would be straightened out to mutual satisfaction. In May he was in Berlin to talk to his chiefs, and on his return he told us that the German government was going to "stabilize its relations to Moscow, although on a low level."

Instead, relations went from bad to worse, as Hitler showed not the slightest intentions to restrain his subordinates in their open hostility to the Soviet Union. In 1933 a sharp famine broke out in Russia. It was our impression then that the authorities deliberately refrained from aiding the stricken population, except those organized in collective farms, in order to demonstrate to the recalcitrant peasant that death by starvation was the only alternative to collectivization. Among the areas affected were the German-speaking regions on the Volga, and the propaganda mill of Dr. Goebbels eagerly seized upon their plight for its own purposes. An *ad hoc* committee, "Brothers in Need," was formed, and much resented in Moscow. But a very factual article by our expert agricultural attaché, Otto Schiller, was also received with great indignation. Various other factors aggravated the tension. In September six German employees of the Berlin trade delegation were arrested on the grounds of Communist activity. German imports during the first half of 1933 dropped to 56 per cent of the previous six months.

In the first half of May a group of high-ranking German officers led by a General von Bockelberg came to Moscow for conferences with the Red Army general staff. Their visit took place in the old spirit of complete harmony and good will. At a dinner given by von Dirksen for the von Bockelberg group everyone, Germans and Russians, was in excellent spirits. Every member of the Soviet War Council was present, and Voroshilov loudly stressed his intention to maintain the ties between the two armies intact. Von Bockelberg left with the good wishes of his Soviet friends, but before he and his

party had reached Berlin the Red Army suddenly demanded that the Reichswehr liquidate every one of its enterprises in Russia. Shortly afterward the Russians brusquely declined to attend any further courses at the German War Academy.

Soviet officials later claimed they had received reliable information that the German Vice Chancellor, von Papen, had told the French ambassador in Berlin, André François-Poncet, every detail of German-Soviet military co-operation. Von Papen later vigorously denied it when confronted with the allegation by von Neurath; and to the best of my knowledge the report was false. But the readiness with which it was believed in Moscow and the promptness with which the Kremlin took such decisive action are good indications of the very great strain under which the German-Soviet friendship had come to labor. Thus ended a significant chapter in German-Soviet relations. At once good will was replaced by chicanery. Less than two months after General von Bockelberg's visit, a German Army detachment that was to help liquidate some of the Reichswehr installations on Soviet soil met with difficulties in obtaining the necessary visas.

In June, 1933, an international economic conference met in London to discuss problems arising from the world depression. One of the German delegates to the conference was Dr. Alfred Hugenberg, industrial tycoon, movie magnate, and king of a news empire. As leader of the German National party's right wing he had been an important instrument in Hitler's rise to power, and in the first National Socialist cabinet he occupied the dual post of minister of economics and agriculture. At the conference he came forth with a memorandum in which Eastern Europe, including the Ukraine, was clearly marked as Germany's sphere of economic expansion. The memorandum sounded like an open call to conquer and colonize Soviet territory; it caused acute excitement, bitterness, and worry in Moscow, sentiments which were hardly allayed when Hitler disavowed his minister and took the welcome opportunity to drop him from his cabinet.[3]

Toward the end of summer the trial of the alleged Reichstag in-

---

[3] Hugenberg had tried to persuade the German delegation to bring his opinion to the attention of the conference. He was soundly rebuffed by the German delegation, whereupon he distributed copies of his memorandum among the press reporters. The German government ordered his return to Germany.

cendiaries began before the German supreme court in Leipzig. More clearly than any other event, the course of the trial, particularly Göring's testimony, threw a significant light on the course which the Nazis intended to follow toward the Soviet Union, and Moscow gradually reacted to the new political configuration. One of the Kremlin's acts was in retaliation against a specific matter of minor importance: Pointing out that Soviet reporters, and Soviet reporters alone, had been debarred from covering the trial, Litvinov answered with a new weapon of his own invention; he announced that Soviet Russia was severing its press relations with the German Reich. This meant that the three German correspondents then in the Soviet Union were ordered out of the country on short notice. Our protest against this act for the first time made clear to us in the Moscow Embassy to what extent Hitler's rise and his initial policies had antagonized public opinion in the West, for it turned out to be the first occasion on which the diplomatic corps of Moscow did not back up a German protest. Later in the same year, when the United States government at last gave *de jure* recognition to the Soviet government, we became more aware that the Western democracies and the Soviet state were gradually becoming allied on the basis of their common antagonism to Hitler's Germany.

Most readers will be familiar with the ideological reflections of this in Soviet politics of the middle and later 1930's. This was the era of the Popular Front, a strategy designed to combat the enemy on the extreme right by means of broad alliances with right-wing Socialists and left-of-center liberals of every shade, as long as they were prepared to fight against fascism, a policy which adopted liberal and patriotic slogans with the aim of making the antifascist crusade attractive to as many as possible everywhere. Diplomatically, this was the Litvinov era, the years in which the Soviet Union occupied its seat in the League of Nations. From this world rostrum Litvinov proclaimed the principles of peace indivisible and collective security, agitating against both Hitler and those who sought to appease him.

One of the first pieces of evidence which made the German Embassy aware of this swing was a new attitude official Moscow adopted toward the Versailles peace settlement. A sharp antagonism toward Versailles had been an ideological cornerstone of Soviet foreign policy. The Russians had always felt that the treaty was directed just as much against them as against Germany. Hence they denounced

the entire Versailles system as irresponsible, harmful, and untenable imperialist policy which was bound to lead to a second world war. Official interpretation at times held bourgeois Germany to be a victim of imperialist vengeance. Thus Bukharin wrote in March, 1927, that Germany's struggle against France at the time of the Ruhr occupation had turned into a war of liberation; and Communist Russia, he added, supports such wars. Apart from Bukharin's scholastic differentiations between bourgeois and bourgeois-imperialist nations, the unequivocal stand the Kremlin took against Versailles was dictated by the desire to play off one part of the capitalist world against another; and it seemed logical to seek alliances with the defeated, weakened, and resentful nations against the ruling powers of the imperialist world. As Lenin put it in December, 1920, the untenable provisions of Versailles were naturally pushing Germany into an alliance with Bolshevik Russia. Not that the Germans were turning into Communists, for "the German bourgeois government madly hates the Bolsheviks, but the interests of its international position drive it toward peace with Soviet Russia against its own will. This, comrades, is the second pillar of our international and foreign policy: To prove to those peoples, conscious of the bourgeois yoke, that there is no salvation for them outside the Soviet Republic. Our policy," he summed up, "is to gather around the Soviet Republic capitalist countries that are being oppressed by imperialism." [4] And so it came about that German anger and German self-pity over the Versailles settlement had always found a very sympathetic echo in Moscow. The senselessness of the Polish Corridor, the untenable position of Danzig, the wanton injustice of the division of Upper Silesia, the distribution of Germany's oversea possessions as League of Nations Mandates, all these points were denounced by Soviet spokesmen with almost as much vehemence as by the average German.

Some months after Hitler's accession to power, this tune changed markedly. "Why should I toot into Hitler's horn?" asked Radek when I wanted to know what kept him so silent of late about the Corridor. "Why should I make propaganda for the Germans after so many things have changed?" What had actually changed was that German resentment against Versailles for the first time seemed about to be turned into action by the National Socialist government. And,

---

[4] From Lenin's speech on concessions, Dec. 21, 1920, to the Communist party faction at the Eighth Congress of Soviets, *Sochineniya*, XXVI, 14–16.

useful though that resentment had been to Soviet foreign policy, Moscow now became apprehensive about the action that might be taken. The prospect of a second world war for the redistribution of the world, in which a strengthened Germany might even defeat the Western democracies, was by no means cherished. Russia was in no way ready for another great conflict. Even less agreeable was the specter of a German attempt to revise Versailles "by peaceful means," that is, at the expense of Soviet Russia, and with the connivance of the Western powers. A new Brest-Litovsk was not the method by which Moscow had thought Germany would revise Versailles. And even if the fear was without real foundation at that time, the Soviet leaders were so suspicious of Hitler's motives and attached so much significance to incidental intelligence supporting their fears that they rather abruptly abandoned their stand against Versailles altogether. For a while the new "line" was that a real revision and abolition of the entire Versailles system could be accomplished only by a proletarian revolution. Later, when the struggle against the fascist danger was uppermost in the Kremlin's minds, the theme was dropped altogether.

Meanwhile, both sides continued to go through the reflex motions of attempting to patch up the shredded fabric of German-Soviet relations, though with increasing fatigue and pessimism. The Russians trusted less and less to the honeyed words von Dirksen was still giving them, though a number of prominent Soviet leaders continued discussions with us in a moderately hopeful spirit. Early in August, von Dirksen was transferred to the post of ambassador in Tokyo. He was realistic enough to end his last report from Moscow with the statement, "The Rapallo chapter is closed." And yet he left for Berlin confident that a positive relationship between the two countries was still possible. But the closer he came to the office of the Reich Chancellor, the more he met with a firm determination not to renew good relations with Soviet Russia in any form. At a cabinet meeting held on September 26, 1933, the undersecretary in the Foreign Ministry, von Bülow, still stressed that Germany had nothing to gain from breaking with Russia and would only lose decided economic and military advantages. But Hitler, now pleading the ideological incompatibility of the two regimes, would only make token concessions; it took much persuasion before he grudgingly declared himself ready to receive Krestinsky, who was scheduled

to pass through Berlin en route from a vacation. Krestinsky, however, changed his route to avoid Berlin, perhaps because he thought that Hitler and he had nothing more to say to each other. Ten days later Litvinov passed through the German capital on his way to Washington. His visit with the foreign minister was spent in weary arguments.

Von Dirksen's successor as ambassador in Moscow was Rudolf Nadolny. Born in East Prussia in 1873, Nadolny was surprisingly un-Prussian in his physical appearance. His ancestors had come from Salzburg with the 20,000-odd Austrian Protestants whom Archbishop Count Firmian had forced to leave the country in 1731 and 1732. Most of these "Salzburg émigrés" had been taken in by the Prussian king, Frederick William I, and settled in East Prussia. Nadolny's father still used to ride a bicycle when he was already over ninety; from him, Nadolny seems to have inherited his extraordinary robust and rugged vitality. At seventy the former ambassador looked about fifteen years younger.

The transfer to Moscow meant the fulfillment of a wish Nadolny had nursed for many years. The special interest he had always shown for Russia and for German-Soviet relations may have been awakened around 1905, when he had worked as a young vice consul in St. Petersburg. In these early years he had acquired such a thorough knowledge of the Russian language that, many years later, as ambassador in Moscow, he could employ it without effort in his meetings with members of the Soviet government. The history of relations between Germans and Slavs had for a long time been his hobby. In 1928 he published a book directed against expansionist aspirations of both the Slavic and the Germanic worlds, in which he pleaded that the two peoples be encouraged to melt into a new unit between the Elbe and Vistula rivers.[5]

As a young man he had entered the consular service, which at that time had been separate from the diplomatic career. I met him for the first time in 1921, when he occupied a leading position in the office of Reich President Ebert. Soon afterward he was appointed minister in Stockholm, and afterward ambassador in Ankara. In Ankara he established friendly personal relations with his Soviet colleague Surits, who was sent to Berlin in October, 1934.

For reasons I cannot quite understand, Nadolny was not very well

[5] *Germanisierung oder Slavisierung?* (Berlin, Otto Stollberg Verlag, 1928).

liked in the Foreign Ministry. Some said he was an intriguer; others appeared not to take him very seriously and, behind his back, called him the "Podunk County Judge" (*Amtsrichter aus Pillkallen*). They disliked him as being overeager and too bourgeois. I was warned against him, but I had only good experiences with him as my superior as well as a human being. Among other things, I was told that Nadolny not only thought himself to be an outstanding diplomat but also a first-class economic expert, and that he would restrict my independence and want to interfere with every detail of my job. Nothing like that ever happened. Nadolny turned out to be reasonable and quite ready to take the counsel of others. His "bourgeois" traits came out very pleasantly, among other things, in a charming relationship with his simple and winning wife and his two daughters, who would have been the pride of any ambassador.

Nadolny came to Moscow with the firm resolve to leave no stone unturned in order to create the necessary conditions for the maintenance and further development of German-Soviet relations, whatever the conflicts between National Socialism and Bolshevism. Into the task he threw all the vitality of his rugged personality, particularly since he was confident he would persuade Hitler that Germany could not afford to waste its good relations with the Soviet Union. That a man with these opinions should have been chosen to succeed von Dirksen may in part have been due to the malice of his superiors. "He has always wanted to go to Moscow; well, let him have his fun now!" they may well have said with secret glee.

The latest official policy statement on which the foreign minister could base his instructions to the new ambassador, written in November, 1933, had to be taken from a speech Hitler delivered eight months before, on March 23rd, where he had said:

> Vis-à-vis the Soviet Union, the Reich government is willing to cultivate friendly relations benefiting both partners. The government of the National Revolution is able more than anyone else to conduct such a positive policy toward Soviet Russia. The fight against Communism in Germany is our internal affair, in which we shall never tolerate interference from outside. The international political relations with other countries to whom important common interests tie us are not affected by it.

Consequently, Nadolny could be sent to Moscow with instructions that were still well in the tradition of the 1920's and were character-

ized by an obvious desire to overlook certain stubborn facts; thus the new ambassador was enjoined to cultivate friendly relations between the Reichswehr and the Red Army five months after their relationship had collapsed completely! Germany's good relations with Soviet Russia, the instructions maintained, must once again become a valuable asset of her foreign policy, and an effort should be made to guide the Kremlin's political orientation into a corresponding direction, if an opportunity should arise. On the basis of these considerations, the ambassador's first task would be to create a better atmosphere by eliminating grievances and preventing further disturbing incidents, without, however, using the slightest pressure of any sort.

We know now that these instructions were in basic contradiction with the spirit which had already taken hold of Hitler's policy toward the Soviet Union. But this spirit was not so readily discernible at that time. The relationship between the two countries was threatened, but nothing definite had happened. Hitler had not yet divulged his real intentions, even to the Foreign Office, apart from his well known political writings. Hence the Wilhelmstrasse was able to continue in the old course, and Undersecretary von Bülow could assert his influence and his spirit of independence.

Nadolny arrived in Moscow in the second half of November and immediately began vigorous diplomatic activity designed to sound out the Foreign Commissariat about Moscow's policy, her grievances against the Reich, and what might be done by the Germans to improve relations. These efforts were from the very beginning doomed to failure. They fell on fallow ground in Moscow, and did not have the support of Berlin.

The Russians had already made up their minds that the Nazi danger had to be stopped. Over their common fear of Germany, France and the Soviet Union had been coming together ever since Herriot's visit to Moscow in September, 1933. The reciprocal good will that was being established between the two countries gradually spread to other nations in the West. Italy signed a treaty of friendship. The Roosevelt government accorded its recognition. Soviet Russia was invited to international conferences. And, later, in September, 1934, the Soviet Union entered the League of Nations. The Litvinov era was beginning. Quite fittingly, it was ushered in with an important speech by the foreign commissar himself. On

December 29, 1933, he spoke before the Central Executive Committee, and his wrath was directed primarily against Hitler's foreign policy. The era of bourgeois pacifism was over, he said, because of the saber rattling of Germany and Japan. His government was not opposed to revision of the peace treaties; after all, it had not even signed them. But it was against unilateral revision, and against revision at the expense of smaller states in the East. Such "Aryan" justice could not be tolerated. Despite all his concern, and his acceptance of traditionally French notions of collective security, Litvinov still made clear that it was Hitler's foreign policy, not the nature of the Nazi regime, which guided the actions of the Soviet government. Alluding to the destruction of the German Communist party, he said:

> We certainly have our own opinion about the German regime. We certainly are sympathetic toward the suffering of our German comrades; but you can reproach us Marxists least of all for permitting our sympathies to rule our policy. All the world knows that we can and do maintain good relations with capitalist governments of any regime including Fascist. We do not interfere in the internal affairs of Germany or of any other countries, and our relations with her are determined not by her domestic but by her foreign policy.[6]

This speech confronted the new German ambassador a few weeks after his arrival. Nadolny's first reaction was one of surprise: he had not expected the Russians to be so determined in their new course. His second thought concerned his instructions: Could he make Moscow change its attitude once more?

The very first gambit with which Nadolny and the Soviet foreign commissar opened their game was typical of the futility of the effort. Litvinov had proposed that the German government guarantee it would never attack the Baltic States. Nadolny pointed out that such a proposal was unacceptable because there had never been any intention on the part of Germany to make such an attack. Litvinov insisted; and Berlin naturally rejected the proposal.

The German ambassador now proposed to Litvinov that the two countries conclude a general treaty broadening the Treaty of Berlin, which might contain guarantee clauses such as the foreign commissar desired. Litvinov assented, but asked for concrete German proposals which he might examine in detail.

[6] Litvinov, *Vneshniaia Politika SSSR*, p. 70.

In relaying the request to Berlin, Nadolny tried to explain to his foreign minister the reasons for the Soviet apprehensions. "The fear of a German *Drang nach Osten*," he wrote, "is a very real fear in Moscow, and it has now become a nightmare." He was convinced that the new line still had not been adopted by the Politburo, but if Litvinov's known anti-German resentment were given further material with which to impress his superiors his policy would surely win.

In searching for ways to convince Litvinov that Germany had no aggressive designs against Soviet Russia, Nadolny did not hesitate to subject the ideas of Hitler and Rosenberg to fundamental criticism. In their printed utterances, he pointed out, both men demanded a policy leading to the collapse of the Soviet regime, and Russia's conflict with Japan was already being utilized toward that end. Against this he argued that Germany had no interest in the collapse of the Soviet Union and no claims against her. Furthermore, Nadolny thought that any co-operation with Poland to satisfy German needs for expansion at the expense of Russia would be foolish; on the contrary, Poland should be kept in check, and should by all means be prevented from rapprochement with the Soviet Union. Hence friendly relations with Moscow were imperative, and Germany, he argued, should avoid even the semblance of harboring aggressive plans. The ambassador urged that positive assurances to that effect be given to Soviet diplomats; moreover, he had the temerity of demanding that the Reich government dissociate itself from the statements made in *Mein Kampf* and from the activities of Alfred Rosenberg. He further suggested that the anti-Soviet press campaign be called off and that Litvinov be treated with great politeness at his next visit in Berlin. All these thoughts and suggestions were contained in a long brief sent to the foreign minister in January, 1934.

Von Neurath's reply, probably written by von Bülow, put all the onus of maintaining relations on a friendly level upon the Soviet government. The German cabinet, he asserted, had never changed its policy since Hitler's speech of March 23, 1933; it was only the Russians, offended by the successes of National Socialism, who had broken away from Germany. The foreign minister recommended an attitude of "cool, self-assured reserve" toward the Kremlin. Germany, he thought, could afford to wait until Moscow made the first move, and would only lose face from the ambassador's attempts to influence them. Nadolny was ordered to take no initiative in talking

to leading Soviet personalities about German-Russian relations. This order clearly prevented him from carrying out the mission on which he had been sent. Again and again he pleaded in vain that Litvinov's thesis about the German danger had not yet been accepted by the Politburo. Stalin, Molotov, and many others, he thought, were only too willing to continue doing business with National Socialist Germany and were only waiting for tokens of good intentions. In order to press his points, Nadolny left Moscow on May 12, 1934, to discuss his views with the foreign minister personally. In Berlin, von Neurath listened to his pleas and told him he was in full agreement with them. But Hitler would doubtless make difficulties. "In that case you will have to help me," Nadolny told him. Some time later he was ordered to see Chancellor Hitler, who had learned about his stay in Berlin, probably from the war minister, von Blomberg, whom Nadolny had seen in matters pertaining to the Disarmament Conference. During his conference with Hitler, the ambassador again voiced his views. Hitler listened to him quietly, admitted that they were sound, but insisted that he wanted to have nothing to do with the Bolsheviks. Nadolny urged him to read his latest memoranda and left them with him. About ten days later, he was again asked to see the Chancellor. Let us hear, in Nadolny's own words, translated rather freely and taken from a recent letter of his, how the conference went:

Hitler gave me the memoranda back and repeated what he had said before; namely, that he did not want to have anything to do with these people. Meanwhile the Foreign Minister came in. He said he did not know the memoranda, that he had nothing to offer the Russians—in short he took Hitler's side completely and fully repudiated me. I did not want to take that and kept on fighting until Hitler told me to hand in my proposals in writing, within three days, and through the Foreign Minister. I went home, put down my proposals, and gave them to Bülow. The latter added a memorandum made by the Foreign Office which went even further than my proposals, and gave both documents to Neurath. But Neurath put the Foreign Office memorandum in his drawer, saying that it contained the same things as my proposals, had someone write a negative report, and with this went to the Chancellor. Hitler gave his approval to the report, and it was given to me, together with the order to go back to Moscow. Thereupon I refused to go back and demanded that the report be changed. "And what if the report is not changed?" asked Neurath. "In that case," I said, "I should have to hand you my job, which I am doing herewith."

The next day he told me the report would not be changed, that he had no other post for me, and I was therefore suspended.

Upon this, Nadolny left the foreign service altogether.[7]

Nadolny's assertion that Litvinov's policy of collective security against Germany had not yet been fully accepted in the Kremlin was quite realistic. Of course, I have never had direct knowledge about the deliberations of the Politburo, but there were many indications that influential government and party officials had by no means decided to endorse the policies of the foreign commissar. Or, rather, they endorsed them only with the greatest reluctance, and with constant expressions of regret. We found among many Soviet leaders a deep and lasting nostalgia for the old days of German-Soviet collaboration, and some of them were frank enough to voice this nostalgia before their German friends. Radek, for instance, repeatedly emphasized in private conversations that nothing would forever block Russia's road toward friendship with Germany. But Stalin, he continued, was tough and careful and suspicious, and he was uncertain about the attitude of Berlin. How could he be expected to trust the author of *Mein Kampf*, which he had read in its Russian translation? In spite of Germany's aggressive designs, Radek insisted upon his friendly feelings toward the German people. In August, 1934, he had a meeting with Professor Oberländer and the German press attaché Baum in his *dacha* near Moscow. The initiative in arranging the conversation was probably Oberländer's, but Radek seems to have con-

---

[7] In time Nadolny turned into an open enemy of the Nazi regime. During the war we saw each other frequently, and I still see him step into my office and hear him say, "Hilger, the Nazis are ruining Germany; those guys have to go, and we count on your help in getting rid of them." How he wanted to accomplish this aim he never revealed, however.

The end of the war found him in a small town near Berlin. The Russians arrested him at first, but released him after three days and did not even touch his property. On Dec. 30, 1950, he wrote me from his new residence, a pretty little town in the Rhine Valley. According to that letter he had had frequent discussions with high Soviet administrators. For a while these talks seemed to take a course quite to his satisfaction, but in the end he became convinced that he could not comply with what they requested of him, and the relationship dissolved itself.

After moving to the Western zone, Nadolny became one of the co-founders of the highly controversial Society for the Reunification of Germany and for a while belonged to its directorate. He resigned from this quite a while ago, for reasons with which I am not familiar. By the time of his death in the spring of 1953 he had ceased to be the center of controversies.

268 — The Incompatible Allies

sented readily. Oberländer was a young National Socialist professor at the University of Königsberg, and a trusted friend of the East Prussian gauleiter Erich Koch. During World War II Koch turned out to be one of the most ruthless advocates of a policy of annexation and extermination in occupied Soviet territory. But at the time of the Radek-Oberländer meeting he was generally considered one of the few high-ranking Nazi leaders who believed in furthering friendly German-Soviet relations, and Oberländer shared these ideas. Moreover, he did not abandon them to the extent his gauleiter friend later did; and during the Second World War he got into trouble because of his courageous critique of German occupation policies in the East.

Baum later told me about some of Radek's startling statements at the meeting. In the presence of his friend Bukharin, he allegedly voiced great admiration for the organizing talent of the National Socialists, the power of their movement, and the devoted enthusiasm of its youth. "In the faces of brown-shirted German students," he exclaimed, "we see the same dedication and inspiration that once brightened the faces of Red Army officer candidates and the volunteers of 1813." [8] Baum further related that both Radek and Bukharin had expressed their deep confidence in the "wonderful German people." "There are magnificent lads in the SA and SS," Radek said. "You'll see, the day will come when they'll be throwing hand grenades for us." And at the same time both men expressed their firm conviction that the Nazi regime would collapse in economic and social crises.

This conversation was later used against Radek when he was tried for treason in January, 1937. But if the Soviet government was thereby disavowing the sentiments he had voiced and castigating such ideas as treasonable, many more leading personalities, who voiced them even more openly, should have been equally punished, among them some of Stalin's closest associates. Lazar Kaganovich, for instance, speaking at a regional party conference on January 17, 1934, publicly expressed his regret that Hitler's policies were compelling the Soviet government to discontinue its dealings with Germany. As late as January 28, 1935, Litvinov's immediate superior, Molotov, said in a speech before the Seventh Congress of Soviets that even the Nazi doctrine of a German master race constituted no

---

[8] Radek was here referring to the Prussian volunteers in the war of liberation against Napoleon.

obstacle to mutually fruitful relations. Quite obviously, the chair-man of the Council of People's Commissars was still very reluctant to burn the bridges between his government and that in Berlin.

Similar sentiments were expressed in party circles below this high level and even among the rank and file of the Soviet population. I was given a significant demonstration of this attitude during a trip to the Ukraine I made in the late spring of 1935. While I was staying in Kiev, the German consul there gave a reception in my honor, and a number of high Soviet functionaries accepted the invitation. Among them was Bredenko, a local liaison officer from the Foreign Commissariat; Vasilenko, the chairman of the Kiev Regional Executive Committee; Kattel, the Ukrainian people's commissar for foreign trade; Pevzner, the president of the Ukrainian state bank; Palladin, the secretary of the Ukrainian Academy of Sciences; and Grushevsky, the vice commissar of agriculture. During a conversation I had with Vasilenko and Pevzner, both officials called the state of German-Soviet relations highly unnatural. Did not Germany realize that Russia had no evil intentions against her? And, on the other hand, did not Germany enjoy the highest esteem among all sections of the Soviet population? Vasilenko told me that some workers had come to him not long ago to tell him that they could not understand the current party line concerning Germany. After all, Germany was only trying to liberate herself from the oppressive fetters of Versailles. But instead of aiding her to do so, the Soviet government was making a pact with Germany's oppressors. In short, said Vasilenko, Litvinov's policy does not convince the masses, and history will soon pass over Litvinov. How absurd of Soviet Russia to ally herself with a "degenerate" state like France! Peace would be secure only through friendship with Germany. Who cares about the racial concepts of National Socialism? (This remark was made even though Pevzner was a Jew himself.) The two officials closed by making disparaging remarks about Anthony Eden, who had just been in Moscow, and compared him with Schacht, "who knew how to do business." In mentioning Schacht, Pevzner was referring to certain credit transactions that had recently been concluded successfully between the two governments. Schacht had handled the negotiations for the German side; his Soviet partner had been the head of the Soviet trade delegation in Berlin, Kandelaki.

There were slight indications that even Stalin himself still thought

about the possibility of improving relations with Hitler. Kandelaki was rumored to be one of the few persons who enjoyed Stalin's confidence. For that reason the Foreign Ministry and the Moscow Embassy attached great significance to the report that in one of his conversations with Schacht in July, 1935, Kandelaki suddenly stopped talking about credits and commodity exchange and, without further ado, asked whether political relations between the two countries could not be improved. Whereupon Schacht replied only that intensive business relations between the two economies would be the best possible beginning of a general improvement in their relations and that that was as far as his competence went. If Kandelaki thought the subject should be pursued on a political plane, had not the Soviet Embassy better get in touch with the foreign minister? Naturally, Schacht reported the conversation to von Neurath, and the latter took the matter up with Hitler. The latter is said to have rejected the idea that an understanding with the Russians was possible at the time. Talks about it would only be used by the Kremlin to press the French for a firmer military alliance and perhaps also to achieve a rapprochement with the British. Nor would it help if the Soviet government disassociated itself from the Communist International by mere declarations. The matter would be different, however, if actual developments in Russia were to indicate a move away from International Communism and in the direction of an absolute despotism, perhaps supported mainly by the military. Should this occur, Hitler warned, Germany must not miss the proper opportunity for the re-establishment of good relations with Moscow. This was the first indication that Hitler was at last considering the possibility of renewed collaboration if he could feel convinced that ideological motives no longer guided Soviet foreign policy and that the ties between the Soviet state and the Comintern were actually being severed.

Nowhere, perhaps, was the nostalgia for the good old days of cordiality greater than among the officers of the two armies. In October, 1933, five months after the Red Army had abruptly called off all collaboration with the Germans, Tukhachevsky, in a long conversation with the then chargé d'affaires, Counselor von Twardowski, deplored the recent political developments and stressed that sympathy and good will toward the Reichswehr had not diminished among his fellow officers, and that the German Army's valuable aid

in building up Russia's forces would always be remembered. "Don't forget," he said when he was about to leave, "it is politics, your politics, which separates us, not our Red Army's sympathetic attitude toward the Reichswehr." As late as October, 1935, at a reception given by the German Embassy in honor of von Twardowski, who was being transferred to Berlin, Tukhachevsky expressed his deep regrets over the break. If Germany and Soviet Russia were to march together, he said, they could dictate peace to all the world; but if they were to clash, the Germans would find out that the Red Army had learned a lot in the meantime. Similar statements were made by the Soviet Chief of Staff Yegorov and a number of other prominent Red Army commanders. Nor was this the dissident opinion of oppositionists within the Red Army who later paid with their lives for such "treachery." Voroshilov himself more than once expressed the same sentiments. Early in 1934, for instance, he urged Nadolny to influence his government to adopt a less anti-Soviet policy. Just a few reassuring words from Hitler, he said, would be enough to show the Kremlin that *Mein Kampf* was no longer his basic policy statement. He too had nostalgic words for the former smooth collaboration between the two armies. It is therefore absurd to suggest that the great wave of liquidations which removed virtually the entire high command of the Red Army in 1937 was belated punishment for undercover dealings with Nazi Germany. The generals' feelers had the obvious approval of the highest chiefs of the Soviet state; moreover, Tukhachevsky was one of the first to warn against the German danger and to endorse the Litvinov policy. His *Pravda* article of March 31, 1935, in which he discussed German war plans, caused great indignation in Germany for its blunt analysis of Hitler's aggressive designs. And when the German ambassador protested against its publication, Litvinov explained frankly that Tukhachevsky had intended to inform and warn the Western powers.

2. THE LOWEST EBB OF GERMAN-SOVIET RELATIONS

THE MOSCOW ATMOSPHERE IN THE MID-1930'S

This work would not be complete without a few words about my attitude toward the National Socialist regime under which I con-

tinued to serve from 1933 to 1945. The reader should not expect me to offer the apologies and self-justifications which have become the custom in the postwar writings of former German statesmen, diplomats, and officers. I feel no need to defend my actions or opinions; nothing urges me to make emphatic avowals or denials of my past life.

I was neither an ardent follower of National Socialism nor an underground oppositionist. I belonged neither to the party nor to any sort of resistance movement. As a matter of fact, I have never belonged to any party. Being in Moscow most of my life, I had no opportunity to participate in German domestic politics or even to vote in an election. Nor was Moscow a good vantage point from which to survey the events and developments in Germany, and my annual summer vacations were insufficient to give me a thorough impression of what was going on, particularly since I spent most of my vacations in Mediterranean countries.

My feelings about the Hitler regime were therefore based on quite insufficient evidence; and these feelings were quite mixed. Even before 1933, the sight of brown-shirted hoodlums marching through the streets of Germany had disgusted me. The accession of their chief as Reich Chancellor had made me very uneasy. The first eighteen months of his rule were a time of open terrorism and political oppression, a reign of organized violence against dissenters, trade unions, churches, Jews, and, finally, against the highest storm-troop leaders themselves. I still remember the gloomy comments with which some of my colleagues and I discussed the bloody assassination of Röhm, von Schleicher, and others on June 30, 1934.

My Jewish friends dropped from my sight. Schlesinger was one of the first to emigrate to the United States. Some of my Jewish friends in Moscow began to avoid having contacts with Germans.

In Germany the outward signs of terror soon disappeared. To the summer tourist—and I was little more than that—the general appearance became one of neatness, order, and unprecedented prosperity. Added to this were the great successes of Hitler's foreign policy. I could not help being impressed by the new position of strength which Germany had assumed among the nations since his accession to power. And even though creeping doubts about the final outcome of these daring coups never ceased to disturb me deeply, there seemed no reason why I should refuse to serve a government with

Count von der Schulenburg, leaving the Chancery of the German Embassy
in Moscow

Molotov is greeted in Berlin by von Ribbentrop, on November 11, 1940.
Mr. Hilger is interpreting.

which all the Western democracies continued to maintain diplomatic relations. There were no visible signs that any foreign government was willing to give support to forces of resistance within Germany. On the contrary, Hitler was given such encouragement as the British-German naval agreement of 1935 and the universal participation of all nations in the Olympic Games of 1936, not to speak of the Munich pact two years later.

Within the embassy the coming of the Third Reich had only very slight effects. There were no changes in personnel whatever. The only outward sign of the new era was the party-membership buttons which could soon be seen on the lapels of everyone except myself and one or two lower-ranking subordinates. One of our senior officials became the representative of the party within the embassy. The first man to hold the post openly flaunted his National Socialist views. He was highly unpopular with his colleagues and hated by the entire diplomatic corps of Moscow. In his presence all conversation about political matters would stop. His successor was a mild-mannered man, very correct in his bearing, who inspired little fear, particularly since his own allegiance to National Socialist doctrines was of such recent vintage that he himself was somewhat vulnerable. I, for one, could never understand why he, who had once been the Moscow correspondent for a German democratic newspaper, let the party use him as its agent in the embassy; on the other hand, he was generally praised for the loyalty with which he stood up for his Polish wife and her relatives.

Altogether, the embassy succeeded in keeping the party out of its house as much as possible. A local party cell (*Ortsgruppe*) was never established, though the presence of a designated party informer was, of course, sufficient to make everyone careful in choosing partners for political conversations. Fortunately, neither Nadolny nor his successor, Count Schulenburg, were died-in-the-wool National Socialists; hence they were far from demanding any particular signs of loyalty from their personnel. Schulenburg did not even trouble to compose the speeches which he had to make on official occasions, like the Führer's birthday. He would have the party representative write a suitable text and then read it off in a bored monotone. But let us now resume the narrative of German-Soviet relations.

When in May, 1934, Nadolny left Moscow to hand his lengthy

memorandum on German-Soviet relations to Chancellor Hitler, he breathed so much blithe confidence in the sure success of his mission that I could not help being affected by his optimism. Once the preparations for his trip to Berlin were made, I saw no reason why I should not take my customary summer vacation and leave Moscow together with the ambassador and his family. For that reason I was completely surprised by his sudden dismissal. When I read the news in Swiss papers, I decided to cut my furlough short; for the change of ambassadors in Moscow, and even more the reasons behind it, filled me with considerable anxiety. I considered Nadolny's dismissal as a further indication that Hitler was going to persist in his hostile attitude toward the Soviet Union. Moreover, I very much regretted Nadolny's departure from Moscow on purely personal grounds, for it had been a pleasure to work under him.

Soon afterward the news that Count Friedrich Werner von der Schulenburg had been appointed to the vacant post gave me a feeling of relief. I knew Count Schulenburg from the years in which he had served as minister in Persia, for on his trips between Teheran and Berlin he used to stop over in Moscow. He had the reputation of having only friends and no enemies; and indeed, Schulenburg possessed quite extraordinary charm which netted him the affection of superiors and subordinates alike and enabled him to gain the trust and friendship of foreign diplomats and statesmen. An experienced career diplomat, he had gathered vast knowledge with the aid of an amazing memory, and this too gave anyone's dealings with him a particular charm of their own.

On the other hand, Schulenburg possessed none of the specific traits or abilities that had seemed to predestine each one of his three predecessors for the Moscow post, one way or another. This caused one Swiss paper to write a somewhat paradoxical comment about his appointment. The transfer of Schulenburg to Moscow, it said, indicated a political program precisely because he lacked any political program. The implication was obvious: Hitler, the paper thought, was purposely sending a man to Moscow who had no decided views concerning German-Soviet relations and would therefore be a pliable messenger, but no more. In the course of the following seven years which Schulenburg served in Moscow, it became apparent, however, that any other man could scarcely have represented Germany's interests in the Soviet Union with so much skill and dignity in that

difficult period as he. Schulenburg quite consciously renounced all political initiative of his own and followed the adage that politics is the art of making the best of what is possible; by his cautious course he rendered the German interests a service that must not be underestimated. In view of the constant danger in which German-Soviet relations were tenuously carried on in those years, another would have given up in despair or reacted to the continual barrage of mutual recriminations in a manner which would have made it impossible for him to stay in Moscow. Schulenburg allowed nothing to deter him. He treated even the most unpleasant matters with unshakable calmness and met even the NKVD agents who shadowed him with inimitable graciousness. Thus he made the nasty realities of daily life in Moscow rebound from him without effect. As a result, German-Soviet relations weathered the crisis and could, in August, 1939, be put to use for the sake of an aim which Schulenburg believed would serve not only the interests of Germany but also the cause of world peace.

For him as well as for myself it was a sore disappointment that developments later took a completely opposite course. During the war between Germany and the Soviet Union, we both did our very best to oppose Hitler's criminal policies in the occupied territories of the East and the inhuman treatment of Soviet prisoners of war. If our efforts were without success, the fault was not ours. And when the opposition group in Germany approached Schulenburg with the aim of winning him for their purposes, he declared himself ready to take over the office of foreign minister in a new national government should the revolt succeed. After the abortive attempt to kill Hitler on July 20, 1944, his connections with the plotters were revealed; he was arrested, and on November 10th executed by a firing squad. All who knew him and appreciated his personal traits will forever treasure their memory of an upright and conscientious man.

The arrival of the new ambassador in Moscow almost coincided with the entry of the Soviet Union into the League of Nations. Only two weeks had passed since Russia had taken her seat in the Council of the League when on October 3, 1934, Count von der Schulenburg handed his letter of accreditation to Mikhail Kalinin, chairman of the Presidium of the Supreme Soviet of the USSR. Later, in the customary private audience with Kalinin, the usual phrases of good will were exchanged; similarly, Hitler felt the urge of exchanging

some noncommittal words of reconciliation with Surits, the new Soviet ambassador, who presented his papers to him on the 27th of the same month. But Litvinov and his deputies, Krestinsky, and Stomonyakov, whom Schulenburg visited a few days later, studiously avoided political discussions altogether.

It cannot be my task, here, to write a full history of Soviet foreign policy in the Litvinov era. All I hope to do is to give some glimpses of how this policy, and German attitudes toward Soviet Russia, were felt by us in the embassy and found their reflection in the business we had to do in those years, in the documents that crossed our desks, and the incidents we reported in our dispatches.

There is not the slightest doubt that a deep fear of Hitler's Germany was the essential guide to all Soviet foreign policy in the mid-1930's. It led Moscow to enter the League of Nations and conduct a painfully futile struggle for active collective security against the Axis. At the same time it made the Kremlin bend every effort and strain every muscle to render the country strong politically, economically, ideologically, and militarily. A desperate race against time ensued which was carried on in a spirit of hysterical urgency. Enemies were seen everywhere around and inside Soviet society. The assassination of Kirov on December 1, 1934, became the prelude to several years of terror that was unprecedented in its direction as well as its intensity. The first reaction to Kirov's death was an official spy scare and xenophobia which more than ever made Soviet citizens go out of their way to avoid contact with foreigners, for the NKVD was ruthless in eliminating anyone who was even suspected of having contacts abroad or with people from abroad. For four years the Communist party was shaken by the great purges during which Stalin eliminated everyone from among the Old Bolshevik leadership who might inject even the slightest note of hesitation, doubt, or dissent at a time when every ounce of force was to be marshaled in a concerted effort to stave off the German danger. Born in revolution and established in radical criticism of other social systems, the Soviet regime, trying desperately to maintain itself in the face of external danger, was becoming strangely conservative. Ideas of rebellion and equality were now openly and officially branded as sentimental nonsense, while authoritarian and traditional features, previously scorned, were resurrected and put to the service of a newly stratified bureaucratic state. Abroad, Soviet Russia stood for the defense

of the status quo; and that meant not only the maintenance of the boundaries established at Versailles: the Kremlin also turned away from proletarian revolution for the time being. Under the slogan of the Popular Front, Communist parties everywhere enjoined their followers to ally themselves with all forces to the left of fascism, in defense of democracy and national independence.

Underneath this, however, there remained a deep-seated distrust against the middle-of-the-road parties, a distrust which grew as the record of appeasement piled up. In retrospect one may assume that Litvinov's insistence on measures of collective security was at least in part motivated by Moscow's silent conviction that the Western democracies would continue to appease Hitler; for that reason Soviet proposals to stop German aggression were at least in part propaganda designed to show the extent to which the West was in willing or unwilling collusion with Nazi Germany. Though Litvinov himself may have been desperately serious in his battle for sanctions and other measures to stop the Axis, every failure of his policy raised voices in Moscow that pointed out the unreliability of England, France, and other "bourgeois democracies." On the other hand, the Kremlin itself did not hesitate to violate its own demands for action against the aggressors. During Mussolini's Ethiopian venture, for instance, Moscow continued to ship vital strategic materials to Italy even while its representatives in the League were clamoring for rigid sanctions. At least two reasons were behind this double play: In the first place it would have been hard for Moscow to pass up an opportunity of doing profitable export business; but in addition we in the embassy felt that the Kremlin anticipated serious social disturbances in Italy if Mussolini should lose his war. But revolutionary outbreaks were something Moscow did not in the least desire at that time. Preoccupied as the Russians were with their own security problems, they would have been extremely loath to divert their forces in support of an Italian proletarian revolution.

In view of such conflicting motives and policies underneath the seemingly unambiguous front of Litvinov's foreign policy, it is only natural that constant and never ceasing efforts were made by Soviet representatives to improve their country's relations with the Third Reich. Usually this amounted to nothing more than verbal prodding, feeble attempts to sound the Germans out and to manifest the Soviet desire to re-establish a tenable relationship. In early 1935, while the

Soviet press and Soviet dignitaries were baiting the Hitler regime in speech and in print, linking it to every failure and to every oppositional force in Russia, officials of the Foreign Commissariat itself pressed Berlin to join a mutual assistance pact of all Eastern European states. Only such a pact, they pleaded, would bring greater stability to the countries concerned. As Krestinsky said in all frankness to the German ambassador, Hitler's words and actions so far had created such deep distrust that words alone could not re-establish confidence. Nor could any bilateral treaty between Germany and the Soviet Union suffice to give Russia the security she needed, hence the Kremlin's pressure for a multilateral pact providing for mutual assistance. Such a pact would offer Germany all the security she wanted and would thus relieve the pressing need for rearmament. The reply we were instructed to give to such overtures was that Germany preferred to take care of her own protection. The mutual assistance pact was rejected as a measure from which only the Soviet Union and France could benefit. Hitler had no fears for Germany's security; on the contrary, he felt strong and confident and had not the slightest intention of reducing his armament program. None the less, the Russians continued to suggest the pact through the early months of 1935. Late in March, at the height of an extremely violent anti-German campaign which made even the NKID officials avoid political conversations with us, Karl Radek publicly advocated a pact, in a gesture of conciliation.

The proposed *Ostpakt,* as the embassy called it, was only the most ambitious Soviet attempt to establish a *modus vivendi* with National Socialist Germany. Less systematic feelers were made constantly, not only in confidential conversation but also in occasional public utterances. But every act of Hitler's foreign policy sharpened the political tension between the two countries. His Reichstag speeches of March 8, 1936, and January 30, 1937, were virtual declarations of cold war against Bolshevism; and in his speech of September 12, 1936, at the Nuremberg Party Congress, he went so far as to say how wonderful it would be if Germany had the riches of the Urals, Siberia, and the Ukraine at her disposal. Four days later Voroshilov answered by declaring that his country was ready for war.

The year 1936 saw the beginning of the Spanish civil war, the European prelude to the general armed conflict. It was also the year in which Germany and Japan sealed their partnership in a formal

treaty implicitly directed against the Soviet Union, the so-called Anti-Comintern pact. Yet even after 1936 feelers for a rapprochement were continually being extended by the Russians both in Berlin and in Moscow.

Strangely enough, the diplomatic corps in Moscow seemed to have a feeling that a German-Soviet rapprochement was in the air. We were repeatedly asked to confirm or deny current rumors to that effect. Similar rumors cropped up even in the British press; and some time in the spring of 1937 a question was asked in Parliament in connection with these rumors. Some of my friends, I believe, had the distinct impression that the Soviet press had toned down its anti-German tirades at that time, though I do not recall sharing their opinion. But even if a careful "content analysis" of *Pravda* and other papers should reveal a decrease in the intensity of bitterness, it may have been the expression of an even greater cooling off. Such a decrease may have indicated that the Soviet Union had finally overcome the shock of its alienation from Germany and was ready to adopt the part of an implacable adversary.

These conditions were sharply reflected in the change which the official duties and personal life of the embassy personnel in Moscow gradually underwent. We had to give up all social contacts with Soviet citizens if we did not want to endanger their lives. The entire diplomatic corps isolated itself in this fashion because the NKVD did not differentiate greatly between the representatives of different bourgeois nations. As a consequence, the Moscow diplomatic corps, which at that time was not yet familiar with the phenomenon of "satellite" diplomats, came to form one great family, whose members led a very active social life among themselves and engaged in intensive exchange of opinions. On this basis relationships and friendships were formed which rested on such strong personal sympathy and so much mutual trust that they lasted even beyond the war and its aftermath.

In official business the center of gravity in the embassy had until then been its political and economic affairs. With the low ebb in German-Soviet relations, the bulk of our activities was concentrated in the consular department,[9] which had to care for German nationals

---

[9] Another reason that this department had more to do than ever was that the entire net of German consulates in the USSR was dissolved in 1937 after months of bitter negotiations. The Soviet Union, in turn, closed its consulates in Germany.

who had fallen into the clutches of the NKVD or the internal revenue office, or who had to be freed from jails or supported there to whatever extent possible under the circumstances. A wearing and usually unsuccessful duty of the department was to represent the interests of married couples of mixed nationality. Soviet citizens who were the wives of German nationals were only rarely permitted to leave the Soviet Union.

Until the early 1930's German business circles as well as the Foreign Office had constantly pressed the embassy for more and more information about the economic situation in the Soviet Union. The volume of trade had constantly risen; no less than a thousand German experts had entered Soviet service; and there was always a large number of German business representatives who came to the embassy for advice and support in closing deals. In all these activities a marked lull now set in. My office was no longer crowded with German businessmen, to whom I had in previous years given most of my time, for the Soviet government began to concentrate its purchases on larger objects, and often preferred to negotiate the deals in Germany rather than in Moscow. The Soviet government sent most of the German specialists home because it did not trust them any longer; and the experts themselves now felt the urge to return to Germany because Hitler's rearmament program offered them new job opportunities.

In Germany a general anti-Soviet attitude had become widely accepted, for Hitler's propaganda machine had a monopoly on opinion-forming. Moreover, the rearmament program had succeeded in doing away with unemployment, the Soviet Union had become a relatively negligible purchaser, and the individual citizen could only gain by manifesting as much anti-Soviet sentiment as possible. Many German technicians who had meanwhile returned to Germany disgusted and disillusioned participated in Hitler's propaganda campaign with the greatest enthusiasm. Some of them undoubtedly felt that they had to rehabilitate themselves after having served the Russians. In short, it was a period of growing isolation and relative inactivity, and the only advantage that I personally derived from it was the possibility of devoting much time to the classics of world literature and to the study of broad historical problems, something that I had had no time to do in the preceding years.

The NKVD's activities concerning the German Embassy were intensified, particularly during the great purge trials. In 1937 an especially blatant attempt was made to gain access to our most secret political files. But the key which was used in the effort to open one of the safes broke off and remained stuck in the keyhole. There could be no doubt that at least one of the embassy's night watchmen was a traitor who was in the services of the NKVD or who had been coerced by them. The Foreign Ministry sent a ranking member of its personnel office to Moscow for a strict investigation; but with all his soul-searching interrogations he did not find the culprit. As a result, no less than eight employees of the embassies were dismissed as suspect, either because they were Soviet citizens or because they had Russian wives. As a further precautionary measure the embassy constructed a vault for its records which was henceforth guarded day and night by a reliable official.

Four years later the secret was cleared up when, shortly after the beginning of the war, I had an opportunity to talk to a former NKVD official, Zhigunov, who had fallen into German hands. He had been recommended to me by the military as "politically interesting," since he had worked in Moscow for the NKVD agency in charge of observing the foreign diplomatic missions. Indeed, my conversation with him turned out to be quite revealing, as Zhigunov, who did not know that I was a former member of the embassy, and who had never seen me before, was well informed about the break into the German Embassy in 1937. I learned from him that one embassy employee had several times earlier handed over to the NKVD documents from our secret safe; the police had then photographed them and returned them the same night so that they would be back in the safe before the next morning. Only the last attempt had failed. Zhigunov's story clearly showed that the embassy employee who had been their accomplice had been among those who were fired in 1937.

Zhigunov himself had been in charge of watching the Hungarian Mission in Moscow. Indeed, he showed himself surprisingly well informed about the political reports of the Hungarian minister, which was due to the fact that the minister usually threw the drafts of his reports in the wastepaper basket, from whence they were promptly delivered to the NKVD because the charwoman of the Hungarian Mission was in their services. Zhigunov gave me an ex-

cellent characterization of the Hungarian minister, whom I had personally known very well, and presented a very correct picture of the internal conditions of the mission.

I readily believed his statement that the interest of the NKVD and of his own colleagues was concentrated mainly on the German Embassy. I asked him whether he had known the ranking members. He had not met them but he was familiar with their names. When I asked him what he knew about Counselor of Embassy Hilger, he said, "We all thought Hilger to be the most dangerous antagonist of the NKVD." Beriya himself, he explained, had told his men on August 20, 1940, that they should especially watch this man Hilger because "he knows the Soviet Union better than most of us." [10]

After all has been said about the isolation and supervision of the diplomatic corps in the Moscow of fifteen years ago, it would be a mistake to believe that we were subjected to limitations which even approach those which the representatives of friendly states have to suffer in the Soviet Union today. Thus up to the beginning of the war in 1941 we not only enjoyed the right to move with complete freedom in and around the Moscow area; we could even undertake trips into distant areas of the Soviet Union. And in 1937 the Soviet authorities made no difficulties when I wanted to return to Moscow by car after a vacation in Germany and France. I had made a similar motor trip to Moscow six years earlier after buying my first car in Germany. Both were somewhat grueling experiences because of the abominable state of repair of the roads, the suspicions of the population, and the difficulties of obtaining gasoline. On the second trip I had to drive the last fifty miles in first gear because the only fuel I had been able to purchase was high-octane aviation gasoline for which my eight-cylinder Horch was hardly built.

[10] Zhigunov did not agree with me when I pointed out that Hilger was probably just as isolated from his environment as everyone else in the diplomatic corps, and that he could not therefore be dangerous. I then talked about Krestinsky, because I wanted to show that many erroneous ideas had arisen in the Soviet Union about many people, among them Krestinsky. The latter had testified at his own trial that he had worked as a German spy for ten years, and I told Zhigunov that he had never spied for Germany, but that he had always been a faithful servant of the Soviet state. This only made him smile indulgently and say with conviction, *"Of course* Krestinsky was a German spy." Thus even Zhigunov, a man of above-average talents and excellent political training, was blinded as soon as he talked about things that fell in the NKVD's jurisdiction.

GERMAN-SOVIET TRADE UNDER HITLER

All this while Soviet-German trade relations continued without serious interruptions and, in some respects, with unprecedented smoothness. German agrarian interests that in the days of the Weimar Republic had been able to restrict German imports from Russia were now given far less opportunity to influence purchasing policies. Paradoxically, too, the political enmity of the two countries was so much taken for granted that trade relations were now removed from the realm of controversy and could be discussed with an amount of detachment that made for far greater efficiency. In some respects the two economies had become more complementary than ever before. Hitler's four-year plans of rearmament created acute shortages of certain food staples and raw materials which Russia had to offer, particularly timber, oil, feed grains, oil cake, and manganese ore. Finally, the chronic shortage of hard currency made it essential to obtain Soviet gold. In short, Germany was quite dependent on Russian business.

After the tight money shortage of the depression, Hitler's economic policies gradually created inflationary trends which facilitated the conclusion of credit agreements; but even before these trends became apparent credit negotiations were resumed. At the time Hitler came to power, Soviet Russia's debts to German creditors had grown to the substantial sum of 1.2 billion reichsmarks, of which more than 700 million were due during 1933. Shortly before Hitler's accession refinancing negotiations had been initiated which the Nazi government did not break off. In March, 1933, a refinancing credit of 140 million reichsmarks was granted against collateral put up by the Russians; in this manner the Soviet government obtained its first important financial credit from the National Socialists. Such money credits became almost a routine in the following years, and the amounts showed a tendency to increase. An agreement signed on April 9, 1935, granted Moscow a five-year financial credit of 200 million, on which the Soviet trade representative could draw any time until June 30, 1937. By the end of 1935, Dr. Schacht told Kandelaki that Berlin was ready to grant a ten-year financial credit of 500 million reichsmarks to be used for Soviet purchases in Germany. A

number of conditions attached to the offer were accepted by the Russians, and in December, 1935, Kandelaki handed the minister of the economy an impressive list of commodities desired by his government. Among the items in the list were warships, and particularly submarines. In addition, the Russians requested the closest scientific and economic exchange with I. G. Farben and Zeiss.

Schacht's offer led to some sharp discussions in Berlin. Representatives both of the Finance and of the Foreign ministries warned that Germany would lose money on such long-term credits. Moreover, Germany would once again be setting a dangerous precedent by such an agreement, and since other countries would be able to offer better terms, a competition for the Russian business would ensue in which Moscow could not lose. Since these views were expressed after Schacht had virtually closed the deal, they placed him in a somewhat embarrassing situation. Without knowing it, however, Molotov saved him. In a public speech before the Central Executive Committee, on January 18, 1936, he alluded to the offer and thus committed an indiscretion, allowing Schacht to break off further discussions with Kandelaki by saying that Molotov had apparently taken the matter in his own hands.

By this time the German government had introduced rigid *valuta*-control legislation which severely restricted the disposition which foreign creditors could make of their money holdings in Germany. To circumvent them, short-term clearing treaties were devised to regulate the exchange of commodities and payments between Germany and Soviet Russia. The first agreement of this sort was signed on April 29, 1936, and in December of that year it was extended until December 31, 1937. On the German side nothing stood in the way of another renewal. But the last months of 1937 went by without the Soviet government designating a negotiator empowered to sign the agreement. Consequently, our trade relations came to a general halt in the first months of 1938, and business resumed only after March 1st, when the treaty of December 24, 1936, was renewed until the end of 1938. The further renewal through 1939, which was signed on December 19, 1938, was almost a routine matter. But the German and Soviet presses played it up, and it created quite a stir in the West because it had generally been taken for granted that the two countries had separated so far as to preclude agreements of any sort.

Unknown to the outside world, there were, moreover, other indications that both sides wished to end the state of tension between them. As early as March, 1938, when the clearing agreement for 1938 had been signed, there had been discussions of a new commodity credit. Nine months later, on December 22nd, Dr. Karl Schnurre, the German negotiator, approached Skosyrev, the Soviet trade representative, with the offer to resume the talks. The Reich, he said, was ready to grant a six-year credit of 200 million reichsmarks on the condition that three-quarters of the amount would be repaid in the form of strategic raw materials. Three weeks later, on January 11, 1939, Soviet Ambassador Merekalov himself accompanied Skosyrev to the Foreign Ministry to declare that his government was ready to discuss credit terms on those conditions. But he asked that the negotiations be held in Moscow; and the Reich's interest in Soviet raw materials was so great that Wiehl, the chief of the economic division of the Foreign Ministry, gave strong support to Merekalov's wish. It was decided that the dispatch of a large delegation to Moscow was not warranted, but that Dr. Schnurre, of the Eastern European desk in the Economic Department of the Foreign Ministry, should go alone to negotiate the credit. Earlier, Schnurre had distinguished himself as a young secretary of legation in Budapest during economic negotiations with the Hungarian governments, and he had since advanced rapidly. He was extremely capable and efficient, and very ambitious. Moreover, he had great zeal, perseverance, and a real understanding for economic problems and the whole complex economic system. Thus the Russians would face an intelligent and purposeful negotiator who combined strong personal ambitions with great expertness.

The Moscow talks were to start on January 31, 1939. Schnurre had gone to Warsaw earlier that month to participate in negotiations with the Polish government about German-Polish trade. Afterward he was to continue his trip to Moscow to arrange for the new credit with Commissar for Foreign Trade Mikoyan.[11] I went to meet

11 Born in 1895, Mikoyan was thirty-one years old when he was appointed people's commissar for trade of the USSR. One year later he told me very proudly that he was the youngest cabinet minister in the whole world. Ever since November, 1926, he had been a candidate member of the Politburo, and in 1939 he became a regular member of that highest decision-making body in the Soviet Union. Being a man of exceptional intelligence, who had profited greatly from his long experience, Mikoyan was one of the most agreeable partners in negotiations I met in these years. Of course, the nature of the regime under which he

Schnurre in the Polish capital to inform him about my preparatory talks with the commissar and to describe to him the general mood in Moscow. Together, in Warsaw, we mapped out our plans for the impending negotiations.

In the meantime the *Daily Mail* and some French and Polish papers published news, in rather sensational form, about a large German trade delegation allegedly on its way to Moscow for economic talks on a grand scale. Von Ribbentrop interpreted the report as a deliberate attempt to wreck his attempts for an understanding with Poland, through which he still sought to solve the problems of Danzig and the Corridor by means short of war. His immediate reaction was to cancel Schnurre's trip to Moscow and order him back to Berlin.

Schnurre's abrupt recall was taken by the Russians as a slap in the face which strengthened their old suspicion that the Germans were playing a political game at their expense in order to gain advantages elsewhere. Several times later we were made to feel the ill will that had thus been created in January, 1939. None the less, it would be misleading to claim that our economic relations were abruptly severed by the insult. On the contrary, both sides were still vitally interested in the transaction, though some points still had to be clarified. Berlin now wanted at least 200 million reichsmarks' worth of strategic raw materials, while the Russians were asking for tool machinery, industrial equipment, and similar capital goods. Both sides were eager to get as much, and part with as little, as possible; both were as anxious to come to terms as they were prepared to drive a hard bargain. By the end of February, 1939, Mikoyan handed me his draft of an agreement indicating the conditions under which his government would be prepared to deliver additional strategic materials, and from then until June I remained in constant touch with the foreign-trade commissar. The actual negotiations were conducted

---

operated severely restricted his adaptability, his initiative, and his readiness to shoulder responsibility. I often noted that even he could not make real decisions without consulting the Politburo as a whole or Stalin. It was also typical that he never received me alone. The terror which the purge trials of 1936–1938 had created in the survivors was still so strong that not even a Politburo member dared to deal with a foreigner without witnesses. Consequently, his pleasant manners became really effective only in social contact with him. He knew how to make interesting and witty conversation about a great variety of subjects even though he seemed to take a real interest only in his own work.

in Berlin, while my talks with Mikoyan had the purpose of removing the difficulties that had arisen in Berlin and of working out compromise solutions. This explains why the final treaty was signed in Berlin, and not in Moscow.

The signature took place on August 19, 1939. According to the agreement, the USSR purchased machinery and equipment worth 200 million reichsmarks and promised to sell the Reich 180 million reichsmarks' worth of goods. Repayment was due after seven years, and the interest rate of 5 per cent was almost as reasonable as Mikoyan had initially demanded.

Begun as one in a long series of economic agreements between Nazi Germany and Soviet Russia which were concluded in spite of the prevailing political enmity between the two regimes, the treaty of August 19, 1939, would perhaps not have been signed if a political rapprochement had not paralleled it. The Schnurre incident of January, 1939, had convinced the Russians that economic relations could not be separated too rigidly from political relations. In the spring the talks in Berlin had begun to drag, and on May 20th Molotov could say that they had virtually faded out. Eager as the Kremlin was to come to terms on trade deals with Germany, the Russians had come to the conclusion that a resumption of economic negotiations would be agreeable only if a political basis of some sort could be created for them.

X NAZI-SOVIET COLLABORATION

1. THE HITLER-STALIN TREATIES

The political rapprochement between the two countries was the result of a curious give-and-take in which it is very difficult to assess the importance of the diplomats' contribution at any given time. Nor could one determine the precise moment at which either of the dictators made up his mind to work for a full understanding. Both in Berlin and in Moscow the idea appears to have ripened gradually as evidence of the other partner's readiness to talk business accumulated. Both governments had enormous doubts, suspicions, and ideological scruples to overcome, but once the many counter-arguments had been disposed of both went ahead with surprising enthusiasm and a certain feeling of release; hence a protracted period during which both felt out the terrain with great caution and restraint was followed by a very brief span of time during which events followed each other with dramatic speed.

The first weak signs that the tension was easing could be noticed in the summer of 1938. At that time the atmosphere created by the mutual recriminations had become intolerable, and both sides expressed the desire for a let-up. The German Embassy was the first to suggest that measures should be taken, as a token of mutual good will, to end the mud-slinging aimed at the two heads of state. The idea was Schulenburg's; but he discussed it with the first counselor of the embassy and myself before taking it up with Litvinov. The suggestion fell on fertile soil; it was discussed in various meetings, both in Moscow and in Berlin, and an agreement was finally reached. A further step in the same direction was taken in October, 1938, when Litvinov and Schulenburg came to an oral understanding that

288

the press and radio of both states should henceforth restrain themselves and cease attacking the other country. The consequences of the agreement were the first visible indication that a change in the relations between the Soviet Union and Germany was in the offing.

Stalin's willingness to enter into agreements of this sort was primarily a consequence of the Munich conference. From the course the conference had taken, and from the fact that the Soviet Union was kept out of it, Stalin drew the conclusions that the Western powers had no intention of showing Hitler serious resistance, and that they would even support him if he turned upon the Soviet Union. But Hitler, too, was pushed, by the events of Munich, in the direction of a settlement with the Soviet Union. Particularly, the remarks which Neville Chamberlain had made on his return to London confirmed Hitler in the opinion that he had to create additional safeguards if he wanted to gain further successes with his old methods.

Once again the world took notice when, in late December, 1938, news came from Berlin that a German-Soviet trade agreement had been signed in the German capital. True, it was a routine affair, since the continuation of German-Soviet trade depended on the annual renewal of such business transactions; but the fact that on this occasion the agreement had been signed in time, and not with the great delay of the previous year, was regarded as symptomatic. The conclusion of the agreement served as the prologue to further German-Soviet talks that had been suggested by the trade representation of the USSR. In these discussions, carried on by the Soviet trade representative and Karl Schnurre, both sides expressed great interest in the creation of broader bases for commodity exchange; they also made arrangements for Schnurre's trip from Warsaw to Moscow in the second half of January, which was canceled so abruptly.

In spite of the ill feelings and suspicion created by this slap to the face of the Soviet government, the thread that was being spun between Moscow and Berlin did not break again, and the behavior of the Kremlin's representatives in Berlin obviously showed that they had been ordered to continue spinning it upon every suitable occasion. If there were still any doubts concerning the Soviet motives in these overtures, they should have been removed by Stalin's speech of March 10th, at the Eighteenth Party Congress, in which he clearly stated that there were no unsurpassable differences between the two countries apart from their ideological disagreements. But, said Stalin,

other powers seem to be at work to deepen the existing conflicts:
"Look at the hullabaloo made over the Soviet Ukraine in the
English, French, and North American press. . . . It looks very much
as if this suspicious noise is designed to incense the Soviet Union
against Germany, to poison the atmosphere, and to provoke a conflict with Germany without any visible grounds. . . . The Soviet
Union is not willing to pull chestnuts out of the fire for anyone else."

In the long run, his declaration contributed substantially to preparation of the soil for a German-Soviet understanding. An immediate reaction from Berlin was not forthcoming, however; and Stalin
must have realized that a more dramatic show of a change in policy
was necessary: Maxim Litvinov had to be removed. The change of
personnel came with surprising abruptness. At the May Day parade
he was seen on the reviewing stand in Stalin's closest entourage; on
May 2nd and 3rd he negotiated with the British ambassador Sir
William Seeds. One day later the Moscow press announced that his
post had been assumed by Chairman of the Council of People's
Commissars Vyacheslav Mikhailovich Molotov.

Molotov is a highly efficient administrator, a capable executive of
policies that are handed down to him, and an experienced bureaucrat. In contrast to his predecessor in the Foreign Commissariat,
however, he has no creative mind. In negotiations which I witnessed
or in which I took part, he never showed any personal initiative, but
seemed to keep strictly to the rules laid down by Stalin. When problems came up, he would regularly say that he had to consult his
"government." A typical example was Molotov's behavior in an
important meeting with the German ambassador on August 19, 1939.
Count Schulenburg called on him to transmit a communication to
the effect that, if a non-aggression pact was concluded between the
two powers, Ribbentrop would be in a position to sign a special
protocol on the settlement of spheres of interest in the Baltic area.
Although such a declaration was precisely what the Soviet government wanted, Molotov did not dare make a proper response by himself. The ambassador left without obtaining an answer; but he had
not been back in the nearby embassy for ten minutes when the
phone rang and he was asked to return to the Kremlin at once. He
hurried back, and Molotov announced that he had meanwhile consulted his "government" (which could only mean Stalin), which had
authorized him to hand the ambassador a draft of the non-aggres-

sion pact and which would be expecting the arrival of the German foreign minister at an early date for the conclusion of the pact.

I am sure that Molotov's lack of adaptability and his fear of responsibility have harmed the Soviet government in its dealings with the Western Allies; but it apparently was more important to Stalin to have a man who had no other ambition than to play the role of a willing tool in his hands. Besides his unquestionable loyalty, he has other traits which make him extremely valuable, for instance, an unflagging energy and exemplary devotion to his work. His amazing memory enables him to master a vast and manifold complex of problems. One thing which demonstrates his tenacity is the fact that even at an advanced age he succeeded in overcoming a stutter which used to bother him very much.

Whenever I observed Molotov at social occasions or official receptions, I always had the impression that, basically, he felt very insecure and needed to remind himself of his own importance in order to manage an attitude of assurance. After the first meeting between him and Hitler, on November 12, 1940, I accompanied Molotov to Bellevue Castle, where he had been lodged. When I asked him what impression the Führer had made on him, he replied spontaneously, and with obvious sincerity, "You know, he is not nearly so stern as I had imagined him!" I thought his reply was indicative of the inner insecurity he must have felt when he first stepped before Hitler.[1]

His insecurity must have made him quite uncomfortable among the brilliant and imaginative minds still remaining in the Foreign Commissariat, an agency that had always had a very special attraction for the cultured, educated, and widely traveled élite of the Old Bolsheviks because it offered welcome opportunities to keep in touch with developments outside the Chinese walls enclosing Stalin's Russia. But there, too, the purge finally caught up with them.

The kind of understanding which the cultured type of official had for Western ways of life and thought had become rather suspect in the late 1930's. In addition, Molotov personally seems to have all the inferiority feelings of a provincial Russian bureaucrat, for which he compensates by a narrow nationalism and a deep-rooted suspicion against foreigners and "cosmopolitans." But whatever the reason, he

---

[1] Molotov's discovery that Hitler was not, after all, "so stern" as he had expected may have contributed to the stiffness and intransigence he showed on the second day of negotiations.

wasted little time in undertaking a thorough house cleaning in the Foreign Commissariat, and soon surrounded himself almost entirely with Great Russians of the newly trained generation of Soviet civil servants.

With this, Molotov completed the process of replacing amateurs in the Foreign Commissariat with professional administrators. At the beginning of Communist rule the notion had been that Bolshevik conviction or special meritorious service in the cause of the revolution guaranteed an individual's effectiveness in high administrative and executive positions, though Lenin had already recognized the fallacy of the idea. But it took many years before a system of selection and training could be created to ensure the education of a new generation of competent civil service personnel. Partly because the foreign service required men with "cosmopolitan" backgrounds, and partly because of a party habit of transferring opposition leaders to foreign-service posts, the Old Bolsheviks had retained leading positions longer in the Foreign Commissariat than in most other governmental agencies. The great purge trials of 1936–1938 therefore put a large number of former Soviet diplomats in the defendants' box, yet only Molotov's accession marks the final triumph of the new generation of Soviet civil servants in the Foreign Commissariat. One should not forget, however, that several of the old and experienced officials who survived the purges, but were swept out by Molotov's broom, were put to use in training the new generation. Among them were Litvinov and Maisky, the former ambassador in London; Rothstein, a former press chief in the NKID; and Boris Stein, a proven collaborator of Chicherin and Litvinov, under whose guidance Gromyko in 1946 made his first steps as representative of the Soviet government in the United Nations.[2]

Thus the fundamental turn in Soviet foreign policy which is marked by the Stalin-Hitler Pact was prepared by the great purges of the preceding years. Viewed in the light of this sensational diplo-

----

[2] It might be of interest to compare the effect of Molotov's accession with those of von Ribbentrop's appointment as foreign minister on Feb. 4, 1938. Whereas in the Soviet civil service the old party men were replaced by a new generation of professional bureaucrats, Hitler placed his party cronies in positions of control over professional civil service men of the old type. At the same time both shifts in personnel have in common that men of a certain intellectual integrity, be it as professional administrators wedded to their jobs or as convinced Communists, were replaced by men whose outstanding trait was their *loyalty* to the leader.

matic act (and only in this light), the great purges can be regarded as a necessary preparation for the German-Soviet alliance. For only a Communist party purged of the Bukharins, Krestinskys, Radeks, and so forth, could tolerate the treaty signed by Molotov and Ribbentrop in August, 1939; therefore, to claim that the purges meant the elimination of a "pro-German" faction within the party appears utterly ridiculous.

Litvinov's abrupt dismissal did not fail to impress Hitler. Two days after the German government had learned the news, I received orders from Berlin to come to Germany immediately and report to the foreign minister for consultation. Until that time I had not met von Ribbentrop. According to what I had heard about him, I looked forward to the meeting with rather mixed feelings; and the task assigned to me would surely have fallen on someone else's shoulder if Count Schulenburg had not been in Teheran at the moment to represent the German government at the Iranian crown prince's wedding, while General Köstring was traveling somewhere in eastern Siberia.

When I arrived in Berlin, I learned that von Ribbentrop was in Munich, since Hitler was staying on his Bavarian property on the Obersalzberg mountain, and von Ribbentrop always strove to be in his close neighborhood. My first meeting with the foreign minister took place in Munich on May 9th. The impression he made on me at the time was confirmed by later observations when I became more closely acquainted with him. He was a man who occupied a responsible position for which he had neither talent, knowledge, nor experience, and he himself knew or sensed this very well. As a consequence, he made himself abjectly dependent on a vast staff of expert and not so expert advisers who had to be at his beck and call every minute. At the same time he sought to hide his feelings of inferiority by an arrogance that often seemed unbearable. That a minister should shout at a gray-haired counselor until his voice snapped was unheard-of until von Ribbentrop introduced the language and the brutal tone of voice of a drill sergeant in the Foreign Office. Moreover, he was under a morbid compulsion to put his own person in the foreground all the time and to live in the grandest possible style. The amount of time he wasted on bitter jurisdictional wrangles with his fellow cabinet members is hard to believe. He felt himself to be utterly dependent on Hitler's favor and graces, and strove with

frantic efforts to keep them. One of the devices he used was that he asked the liaison man he kept around Hitler to tell him what the Führer had said in the circle of his closest confidants. From statements of this kind he drew conclusions about Hitler's intentions and ideas and, at suitable opportunities, would present them to him as his own thoughts. People who knew assured me that Hitler more than once fell for the trick and praised the "phenomenal intuition and long-range thinking of his foreign minister."

One of the many attributes which von Ribbentrop thought he owed to his position was a special train for which he asked after the beginning of the war, and in which he followed Hitler everywhere in order to be close to him at all times. The special train included a parlor car for the minister himself, two dining cars, and no less than eight sleeping cars housing a crew of aides, male and female secretaries, counselors and expert consultants, and a numerous bodyguard responsible for von Ribbentrop's personal safety. The whole thing was very much like a circus which put up its tents here or there just as required, or just as the foreign minister's whims dictated.

From the questions von Ribbentrop asked me in Munich, and from the attention with which he listened to my report about the general situation in the Soviet Union, I recognized that he wanted information to give to Hitler, who, after the news of Litvinov's dismissal, had manifested a renewed interest in the problem of whether an understanding with Stalin might be possible. Apparently my statements fitted von Ribbentrop's purposes. He concluded the meeting by telling me that he would visit Hitler on the Obersalzberg mountain that afternoon and that I should go to nearby Berchtesgaden and hold myself in readiness in case Hitler desired to see me personally.

Nothing like that occurred, however, and I spent the following night in a hotel at Salzburg, where von Ribbentrop, too, arrived late at night. Shortly before noon the next day we received a message that Hitler was expecting us in his house at one o'clock. Von Ribbentrop was still in bed, as he had the habit of sleeping until noon. He got ready in frantic haste, during which he completely lost his temper, and our departure was considerably delayed. After a mad trip over the curving road leading up the Obersalzberg mountain, we were very late in arriving at Hitler's home. Nervously fidgeting aides were

running to and fro. The Führer, they whispered to us, had already shown signs of impatience.

A few seconds later I stood before Hitler, who approached us slowly, gazing at us with strangely shifty, cunning eyes. Neither then nor during later meetings with Hitler did I feel anything of the hypnotizing effect that has been attributed to him. At the sight of his small stature, the funny forelock that hung in his face, and the ridiculous little mustache, I felt only indifference, which in the following hour changed into physical revulsion produced by the fact that he was constantly chewing his fingernails. After a short greeting, during which hardly a word was exchanged, we followed Hitler into a large room, the narrow side of which was entirely taken up by a huge window offering a gorgeous alpine view. It was the only thing that made the room remarkable. We sat down at a round table; I faced Hitler, while von Ribbentrop sat at his right. Three other people were present during the conversation: Colonel General Wilhelm Keitel, the chief of the high command of the armed forces; Karl Schnurre, and Walter Hewel, von Ribbentrop's liaison man in Hitler's personal entourage. An old personal friend of Hitler's, who had been in Landsberg Prison with him, Hewel was an exception among those in the Führer's closest circle, for he possessed not only very many pleasant human traits but also the open outlook of a man who has traveled abroad a good deal. In this respect he was quite a contrast to Hitler, who had neither of these virtues—something, by the way, which Hewel never denied when talking with me.

On the previous evening I had discussed the impending meeting with Hewel, and I had wondered whether I, who lived in a completely different ideological world, could ever succeed in finding a common language with Hitler concerning Russian problems. But Hewel assured me there would be no difficulties. "Don't worry about it at all," he said. "I bet he won't let you get a word in edgewise; instead, he himself will do the talking, and then he'll end the session before you'll have had an opportunity to make any comments." It turned out to be quite different. Hitler opened the discussion by asking for the reasons which might have caused Stalin to dismiss Litvinov. I answered that, according to my firm belief, he had done so because Litvinov had pressed for an understanding with England and France while Stalin thought the Western powers were aiming to

have the Soviet Union pull the chestnuts out of the fire for them in the event of war. Though Hitler said nothing, he gave von Ribbentrop a glance indicating that my explanation made sense to him. His second question pursued the topic further: Did I believe that Stalin might, under certain circumstances, be ready for an understanding with Germany? I was tempted to give Hitler a résumé of German-Soviet relations since 1933, and to remind him how often the Soviet government, during the first years of his rule, had expressed the desire of maintaining the old friendly relationship; but I did no more than mention Stalin's speech of March 10th, in which the Soviet leader had declared that there were no visible grounds for a conflict between Germany and the Soviet Union. I was quite surprised when neither Hitler nor von Ribbentrop could remember what Stalin had said in the speech, though the Moscow Embassy had given a detailed report on it at the time. At von Ribbentrop's request, I quoted the pertinent passage once more.

Hitler gave no indication of his own views concerning an understanding with the Soviet Union. Instead, he asked me to tell him "how things looked in Russia." After Hewel's prognosis I had expected that least of all, so I had to take a very deep breath before deciding where to begin and where to end. I began by outlining my honest belief that Bolshevism constituted a great danger, but that it would be possible to neutralize it by engaging it in reasonable economic and political ties. I emphasized the undeniable successes of Soviet industrialization and the growing strength of the Soviet regime, but I pointed out at the same time that the great purges of 1936–1938, to which about 80 per cent of the Red Army's high-ranking officer corps had fallen victim, had seriously weakened the military power and administrative structure of the Soviet state. Elaborating on the significance of the power struggle between Stalin and the oppositions, I pointed out how much ideological ballast had been thrown overboard after Stalin realized that a healthy and strong political structure could not be erected on the basis of Communist doctrines. In place of revolutionary enthusiasm, Stalin was trying to foster a new Soviet patriotism. I alluded to the condemnation of "equality-mongering" and to the resurrection of tsarist Russia's old military heroes; I told Hitler about the renewed strengthening of parental authority and school discipline, about the fight against experiments in music, theater, the arts, and other cultural areas.

Hitler had bent forward and was listening with eager attention. Once, when I had made a short pause, he emphatically requested me to go on speaking. When I had finished at last, I thought Hitler would now reveal his views about the future relations between Germany and Russia. Instead, he dismissed me with a few formal words of thanks. As I was told later, he afterward expressed to von Ribbentrop his displeasure over my tale about the successes of Soviet industrialization and the strengthening of national consciousness in the population. "One possibility," he said to von Ribbentrop, "is that Hilger has fallen victim to Soviet propaganda. In that case his description of conditions in the Soviet Union is worthless. But if he is right, then we have no time to lose in taking measures to prevent any further consolidation of Soviet power."

Ten days after my visit to the Berghof, the embassy was ordered to tell the Russians that we were now ready to resume discussions about a new trade agreement and would now be willing to send Dr. Schnurre to Moscow to come to terms with Mikoyan. To the ambassador's surprise, Molotov replied that the past months, and particularly the cancellation of Schnurre's trip in January, had given the impression that the German government was not really serious about negotiations, but was pursuing them only as a game with which to obtain political advantages elsewhere; hence he could agree to a resumption of the trade talks only after the necessary political basis for them had been created. In vain Count Schulenburg tried to make the foreign commissar explain what he meant by "political basis."

In Berlin the ambassador's report created the impression that Molotov had given a veiled rebuff to the German advances. Von Ribbentrop and Hitler thereupon decided to retire, sulking, into a corner and make no further advances. In the Moscow Embassy, on the other hand, we tended to regard Molotov's words as an implicit invitation to come to a political understanding, since he did not think good economic relations could develop, in the long run, except in a politically tolerable atmosphere. But this raised the question whether such an overture could be taken at face value. Had the Russians actually decided to come to terms with Nazi Germany, or was their offer no more than a device by which Britain and France might be put under pressure? On the other hand, we saw Molotov's intransigence toward England, his insistence on conditions which the

Western powers could hardly be expected to grant. Did he really want an alliance with them? Whom was Stalin out to double-cross? Though we reported all these doubts to Berlin, in general we adopted a note of optimism; it would be interesting to watch how Moscow would develop the matter further.

Whatever the mental reservations both sides still had, the possibility of a rapprochement had evoked keen interest in the two capitals. In the beginning of June the Foreign Ministry began to look into the Treaty of Berlin. Formally, it was still in force because it had been renewed indefinitely in 1931 and had never been canceled. Yet it had lost every trace of meaning. The question was whether it could be revived. Or had it, perhaps, been violated or canceled by the so-called Anti-Comintern Pact? Would a Soviet-British alliance violate it? On June 28th Count Schulenburg had a conversation with Molotov in which some of these questions were brought up. By the middle of the month, the trade talks really got a good start when Mikoyan's proposal for a credit agreement was accepted. For the first time in years, a Soviet officer appeared at a cocktail party which General Köstring gave in the early days of July.

Toward the end of July, Hitler apparently decided to take the initiative in working for a settlement with the Russians. In the private room of an exclusive Berlin restaurant, Schnurre had a long conversation with the Soviet chargé d'affaires and the Soviet trade representative on July 26th. On this occasion both Russians explicitly described a rapprochement between Germany and the Soviet Union as corresponding to the vital interests of both countries. On August 3rd Count Schulenburg and I talked with Molotov for over an hour, gaining the impression that the Kremlin was indeed ready to improve its relations with Germany, but that the old suspicions against the Third Reich and its anti-Soviet policies had not yet been allayed. It would take much persuasion and patience to remove their ingrained fear of German duplicity. Nor did the ambassador believe they would be swept off their feet by intensive wooing. "I still think," he wrote on August 14th, "that we ought to avoid any stormy advances concerning our relations with the Soviet Union; it would almost inevitably have a bad effect."

But three days before, the British and French military missions had arrived in Moscow. At that point Hitler seems to have become fully convinced of the need to secure Soviet Russia's neutrality if

he wanted to start a war with Poland before the end of summer. In the early morning hours of August 15th, the ambassador received an urgent telegram from von Ribbentrop instructing him to tell Molotov that the German foreign minister would be willing to come to Moscow to discuss the possibility of a treaty of friendship. "There is no doubt," the note read in part, "that German-Soviet policy has come to a historic turning point. . . . On the decisions which have to be taken will depend whether the two peoples will some day again, and without any compelling reason, take up arms against each other or pass into a friendly relationship. It has gone well with both countries when they were friendly and badly when they were enemies."

After such frank overtures, Molotov could afford to stall and to bargain. Visibly impressed by the ambassador's message, he cautioned that a trip of such an "eminent diplomat and statesman" as von Ribbentrop required most careful preparations. Moreover, he wished to have a few questions cleared up first: Would Germany be willing to conclude a non-aggression pact with Soviet Russia? Would she use her influence on Japan to improve Russia's relations with that country? And would the Baltic States be a topic in the discussions to be held?

When, two days later, Schulenburg gave affirmative replies to all of these questions, Molotov stated that he considered the prior conclusion of a trade treaty to be a further precondition for any talks about a political treaty.[3] He suggested the following procedure: A commercial agreement should be followed by a non-aggression pact; and the latter should be complemented by a protocol in which certain important questions of foreign policy should be settled.

To this statement of Molotov's von Ribbentrop responded by a telegram directing Count Schulenburg to tell Molotov that if the Soviet government would agree to von Ribbentrop's proposal concerning his immediate departure to Moscow he would be in a position to sign there a special protocol settling the spheres of interests in the Baltic area.

Although von Ribbentrop's message clearly indicated that Hitler was willing to yield the Baltic States to the Soviet Union, Molotov still hesitated and demanded a "more precise" statement by the

---

[3] With this he reversed his stand of May 20th. Then he had demanded that negotiations about a trade treaty be based on a political settlement; now the political settlement was made dependent on the success of the trade talks.

German government. Stalin, on the other hand, grasped at once what was being offered to him. Less than half an hour after Molotov had dismissed us, we were recalled to the Kremlin, where the foreign commissar told us that he had meanwhile consulted his "government" (Stalin) and had been asked to hand us a draft of a non-aggression pact and to tell us that the Soviet government was ready to receive von Ribbentrop in Moscow one week after the signing of the commercial treaty, that is, around August 27th.

Still the development in Moscow seemed not to be progressing fast enough for Hitler, who had planned operations against Poland for the beginning of September and who wanted to have the Russian situation settled beforehand. He therefore directed Count Schulenburg to transmit a personal telegram from him to Stalin in which he insisted that Stalin should receive von Ribbentrop not later than August 23rd. Hitler's telegram further said that with the signing of the commercial treaty on the previous day (August 19th), the way for the conclusion of a non-aggression pact was now open, and the problem of the supplementary protocol desired by the Soviet government could be settled in the shortest time if a responsible German statesman could come to Moscow.

The mentioning of the secret protocol by Hitler himself and the latter's statement that "the tension between Germany and Poland has become intolerable and a crisis may arise any day" convinced Stalin that now it was time for him to act. Thus, he let Hitler know his agreement for von Ribbentrop's arrival in Moscow on August 23rd.

I later learned from Hewel that Hitler received the message of von Ribbentrop's invitation to Moscow with exultant joy, and that he exclaimed, drumming with both fists against the wall, "Now I have the world in my pocket!" In the embassy, we too were seized with great excitement.

Von Ribbentrop arrived by plane about noon on August 23rd. The first discussion in the Kremlin began at three thirty; it lasted for three hours and was continued in the evening. Long after midnight the talks culminated in the signing of the non-aggression pact and the secret protocol, both of which carry the 23rd of August as the dateline. The German foreign minister left the Soviet capital twenty-four hours after his arrival there.

It was the first time Stalin personally negotiated with the rep-

resentative of a foreign government about international relations. Until then he had avoided contact with foreigners on principle, except for a few meetings with prominent persons like United States Ambassador William C. Bullitt or some foreign journalists. Whenever foreign diplomats had sought to get in touch with him, the Foreign Commissariat had objected on the grounds that Stalin was purely a party man and did not deal with foreign affairs. Strictly legally, this status ended only in May, 1941, when Stalin took over Molotov's job as chairman of the Council of People's Commissars.

When von Ribbentrop, accompanied by Count Schulenburg and myself, entered the Kremlin for the first time on August 23rd, he was convinced that he would first deal with Molotov alone, and that Stalin's presence could be expected in a later stage of negotiations. Therefore his surprise was very great when Stalin stood next to Molotov as we entered the room. It was a move that was calculated to put the foreign minister off balance; it was also meant as a hint that the treaty would be concluded now or never.

Stalin's behavior was simple and unpretentious, an attitude that was just as much a part of his discussion tactics as the paternal benevolence with which he knew how to win his opponents and make them less vigilant. But it was interesting to observe the swiftness with which the jovial friendliness of Stalin's attitude toward von Ribbentrop or the jocular and kind manner in which he dealt with one of his junior assistants turned into icy coldness when he rapped out short orders or asked some pertinent question.

I have seen with my own eyes the submissive attitude of the Red Army's chief of staff, General Boris Shaposhnikov, when Stalin would converse with him. I remember the officious and obedient manner in which people's commissars like Tevosyan would rise from their seats like schoolboys when Stalin would deign to ask them a question. In all the conferences at which I saw Stalin, Molotov was the only subordinate who would talk to his chief as one comrade to another. Yet one could clearly sense how he looked up to him, and how lucky he felt to be privileged to serve him. In subsequent meetings Stalin would often ask Molotov, at the beginning of a session, to chair the discussions. Perhaps that was because officially Stalin did not yet occupy a government post. But it obviously was one of the rules of the game that Molotov would refuse to take over as chairman; and from then on Stalin alone would speak for the Soviet government.

Once, when Stalin tried to make Molotov conduct the negotiation, the latter argued: "No, Joe, you do the talking; I'm sure you'll do a better job than I." Then Stalin outlined the Soviet point of view in his concise and clear manner, and Molotov turned to the German delegation with a smile of satisfaction, saying: "Didn't I tell you that he would do a better job than I?"

Every other Politburo member's behavior toward Stalin seemed to reflect a particular personal relationship with him. The tone of his conversation with Voroshilov was cordial, as between comrades; with Beriya and Mikoyan he was friendly, and with Kaganovich matter-of-fact and somewhat reserved. I never heard Stalin say anything to Malenkov; but at public occasions I attended, as for instance the sessions of the Supreme Soviet of the Soviet Union, he would usually sit down next to Malenkov and eagerly converse with him, demonstrating a particularly close relationship between them.

In meetings with Stalin he frequently surprised us by the extent of his knowledge in technical questions that were being debated, and by the assurance with which he made decisions. Even in matters of style, when the problem was to find the correct words for a diplomatic document or an official communiqué, he would act with assurance and display great judgment and tact. I remember handing him the draft of the joint communiqué explaining the Soviet move into Poland, which I had translated into Russian. Stalin glanced at it quickly, then took a pencil and asked the ambassador's permission to make a few changes in the text. He did so in a matter of minutes, without once consulting Molotov, who sat beside him; then he handed me the amended text, asking me to translate it into German for the ambassador. I whispered to Count Schulenburg, "He has improved it tremendously." Indeed, Stalin's text was a much more "diplomatic" announcement of the move we intended to bring to public knowledge. "The old Romans," Stalin said, turning to me, "did not go into battle naked, but covered themselves with shields. Today correctly worded political communiqués play the role of such shields." The original draft had been transmitted to us from Berlin; hence, even though the ambassador shared my opinion of the amended text, he had to get Berlin's consent to let the changes stand. The permission was granted at once. Later I was told that both texts had been submitted to Hitler for comparison, and he had immediately chosen the one drafted by Stalin, saying, "This one, of

course. Don't you see that it is much better? By the way, who wrote it?"

I was similarly impressed by Stalin's technical knowledge when, for instance, he chaired a meeting of German and Russian experts discussing the ordnance specifications of the turrets for a cruiser which Germany was to deliver to the Soviet Union, or when the German trade delegation discussed with Stalin the volume and character of deliveries to be made by both countries. Without Stalin's express permission it was impossible to obtain any Soviet agreement to sell us certain raw materials; but once his permission had been given it was tantamount to an order which was faithfully executed.

The negotiations of August 23rd proved to be easy. Von Ribbentrop brought no new proposals but repeated himself in the ideas which had been discussed at great length in the preparatory talks between Molotov and Schulenburg, and which were also contained in Hitler's telegram to Stalin. Von Ribbentrop indulged in overwhelming declarations of friendship, to which Stalin gave dry, factual, and brief acknowledgment. The wording of the pact proved no difficulty since Hitler had accepted the Soviet draft in principle. The final draft contained two important additions, Article 3, in which the two parties agreed to consult and inform each other continuously on all diplomatic steps to be taken in matters of interest to the other party, and Article 4, providing that neither partner could participate in any power bloc directly or indirectly aimed against the other power. The duration of the pact was changed from the five years originally proposed to ten years; and Article 7 stated that the pact would be valid after signing, not after its ratification as originally proposed.

The Russians put greatest emphasis on the secret protocol that was to be appended to the pact. According to the protocol the line of demarcation between the spheres of influence of Germany and the Soviet Union in the Baltic area ran along the northern boundary of Lithuania, whereas in Poland it was to follow the Narev, Vistula, and San rivers.[4] The secret protocol further contained a German recognition of Soviet claims for Bessarabia.

---

[4] Upon Stalin's suggestion, the line was amended in the treaty of friendship signed five weeks later, on Sept. 28, 1939. Lithuania became part of the Soviet sphere of interest. For this, Germany was recompensed by the Polish territories situated between the Vistula and Bug rivers.

After the final text of the pact and the protocol was agreed upon, von Ribbentrop submitted a draft for a joint communiqué to be published by both governments on the following day. The text praised the newly formed German-Soviet friendship in flowery and bombastic terms. Stalin read it and smiled indulgently. "Don't you think," he said, turning to the foreign minister, "that we have to pay a little more attention to public opinion in our countries? For many years now we have been pouring buckets of slop over each other's heads, and our propaganda boys could never do enough in that direction; and now all of a sudden are we to make our peoples believe that all is forgotten and forgiven? Things don't work so fast. Public opinion in our country, and probably in Germany too, will have to be prepared slowly for the change in our relations this treaty is to bring about, and will have to be made familiar with it." With these words he suggested a more moderately worded communiqué which was readily accepted. Apart from this little lecture on diplomatic finesse, Stalin was very polite throughout the discussions, and his initial reserve gradually turned into a certain jovial friendliness that was very characteristic of him. At the end of the discussions champagne was served, and Stalin even proposed a toast to Hitler.

After the conclusion of the treaty of August 23rd, and especially of the treaty of September 28th, the German negotiators were fêted lavishly by Stalin. Upon these occasions he voiced some opinions which may have been attuned to the need of the moment, but which may yet permit certain conclusions as to his thinking. Thus the tone in which he talked about Hitler, and the manner in which he toasted him, led to the conclusion that he was visibly impressed by certain traits and actions of Hitler; but I could not help feeling that they were precisely the traits and acts which would be most sharply rejected by Germans opposed to the Nazi regime. The admiration, by the way, seems to have been mutual, with the difference, however, that Hitler remained an admirer of Stalin's until the last moment, whereas Stalin's attitude toward Hitler after the attack on the Soviet Union is said to have turned first into burning hatred and later into contempt.

Stalin did not seek to hide his dislike and distrust of England. In his eyes Britain was past her prime and had lost her ability to make great political decisions. However, he spoke with unconcealed re-

Von Ribbentrop, signing the German-Soviet treaty of friendship. *Standing, right to left:* Stalin, Molotov, Shkvartsev (Soviet Ambassador to Germany), General Shaposhnikov, Hilger

At the conclusion of the German-Soviet treaty of friendship, von Ribbentrop
and Stalin pose, all smiles

spect of the United States and particularly her economic achievements.

Stalin was quite frank about his view of Japan as a dangerous adversary. He boasted of the lesson which Soviet troops had dealt the Japanese during a border incident and mentioned with almost sadistic glee that twenty thousand Japanese had been killed on that occasion. "That is the only language these Asiatics understand," he said. "After all, I am an Asiatic too, so I ought to know."

How could the German-Soviet Non-Aggression Pact be signed by two governments who had for years been on the verge of a complete break? How, particularly, could the Kremlin make such a dramatic turn from its previous policies?

Throughout the years we have called the Litvinov era, the possibility of an alternative to the policy of collective security was never quite absent, even though conditions for it became ripe only in 1939. Like the policy of the mid-1930's, the possible alternative would have been based on the fear of Germany. There was common agreement in Russia that Hitler's Germany presented a great and immediate danger to the continued existence of the Soviet regime. But there were, at least in theory, two ways to meet the threat: a friendly one and a hostile one. In the first months of Hitler's rule, Litvinov himself had been among those who tried to convince the Germans that the change of governments in Berlin need not be an obstacle to the maintenance of friendly relations. To be sure, the foreign commissar had been less optimistic in his attempts than some of his assistants, or the military leaders, had. In any event, their futility had soon become apparent, and the Soviet Union accepted the consequences by joining the League (November 18, 1934) and concluding mutual assistance pacts with France (May 2, 1935) and Czechoslovakia (May 16, 1935). Its entire foreign policy now moved in the direction of isolating Germany even while avoiding an open clash; to this end close and determined co-operation among all countries threatened by the Axis was promoted.

There is nothing to indicate that Litvinov did not have the Kremlin's full support in the pursuit of such policy. It would be rash indeed to imagine that the repeated advances made by men outside diplomatic channels, like Tukhachevsky or Kandelaki, represented views opposing the official foreign policy. It can well be imagined

that Litvinov himself believed it necessary to extend such feelers again and again, if only to sound out Hitler's intentions and moods.

As Hitler took step after step in his program of attaining mastery over Central Europe and tearing up the Versailles settlement, arguments both for and against the current Soviet policy toward Germany gained in strength. On the one hand, Hitler's successes increased the Kremlin's determination to stop him; the stronger Germany grew, the more Moscow labored for collective security, for with every new stroke of the Third Reich Russia's security became more dependent on England and France. But the longer they struggled for a united front against the Axis, the more the Russians became aware of the West's irresolution in stopping Hitler; and the Munich Conference, of September, 1938, led them to the conclusion that the Western powers not only were unwilling to resist Hitler but might possibly welcome German action against the Soviet Union. The policy of collective security had become an impossibility, if this were true. Stalin's suspicions were heightened by the behavior of the English and French during their Moscow negotiations in the spring and summer of 1939. Their unwillingness to make sacrifices, their inability to persuade Poland and Romania to do so, confirmed Moscow in the view that the Western powers would, indeed, like to engage the Soviet Union in a war with Nazi Germany, but that they would not be willing to pay the price.

Ever since Munich, Stalin must have thought about an understanding with Germany, though it is highly unlikely that he had such thoroughgoing agreements in mind as were made in August and September of 1939. Almost until the last days before von Ribbentrop's visit to Moscow, the Soviet government continued to consider the other alternative—a firm alliance with England and France. The unfavorable development of the talks with the British and French, and the broad perspectives offered by a grand settlement with Germany, made Stalin decide for a pact with Hitler. It had always been the Kremlin's firm conviction that, sooner or later, war would break out between the capitalist powers. If the Soviet Union could be kept out of such an armed conflict, she could be expected to reap great benefits from it, since the capitalist powers would be weakened, and the balance of power would be shifted in favor of Soviet Russia. The declarations given by the Germans a few days before signing the pact convinced Stalin that Hitler would invade

Poland as soon as the Soviet Union would back him up. Moreover, because Stalin had no doubt that England and France would honor their obligations toward Poland, a war between the Western powers and Germany could be considered a certainty; and, according to Stalin's calculations, it would be a long war which would exhaust all the countries involved in it.

Moreover, in Stalin's eyes the conclusion of a non-aggression pact with Hitler meant the removal of the danger of a German attack on the Soviet Union. This danger had weighed on the Soviet government and people like an evil nightmare ever since 1933, particularly after the events of 1937–1938 had substantially weakened the Red Army. Stalin had little fear of Germany's turning against her Soviet ally after a victory over Poland because he was convinced that the bulk of Hitler's war machinery would be engaged in the West for a long time to come. Thus he hoped to gain valuable time to push the Soviet armaments program at an accelerated pace. And then he would watch further developments. At a propitious moment, when the warring nations would be weakened sufficiently, he would be in a position to throw the power of the Soviet Union into the scales of world politics.

The delimitation of interest spheres, finally, which was agreed upon in the secret protocol appended to the non-aggression pact, gave the Soviet Union possession of some most important strategic positions in the Baltic area. Two hundred and fifty years earlier Peter the Great had spent two decades in bloody warfare for the same positions, while the pact with Hitler made them fall into Stalin's lap without fighting. The agreement with Germany would also mean a diminution of Japanese pressure on Russia's eastern frontier.

In brief, Stalin had all reason to be satisfied with the agreements he had made with Hitler. This was quite clear in the satisfaction he showed when the treaty was signed, and in the attentiveness with which he looked after its execution.

As for Hitler, I can say the following: Both when the treaties with the Soviet Union were concluded and in the subsequent few months, he appears to have believed firmly that the German-Russian agreements not only fulfilled their immediate purpose but would for a long time to come form the basis for a relationship that could benefit both partners. I have reliable information to the effect that Hitler repeatedly voiced this opinion before his closest entourage in the

fall of 1939. Upon such occasions he would declare his rapprochement with the Soviet Union to have been a great political stroke, and he would emphasize how each country complemented the other very favorably. The circumstances under which Hitler made such remarks left no doubt that he really believed what he said.

Apparently Hitler was not at that time worried by the idea that Stalin might put a Germany weakened by the war under pressure. On the contrary, he seemed to be convinced that Germany's military superiority was secured for a long time and that, for that reason alone, Stalin would feel obliged to adhere to the existing treaties. We shall speak afterward of the change in Hitler's attitude to Stalin and the Soviet Union which took place later.

Apparently some persons in the Foreign Ministry were against the pact. Ernst von Weizsäcker, von Ribbentrop's permanent undersecretary at that time, claims to have been opposed to it, or at least to have hoped for a great delay in its conclusion. He says he argued that Hitler would attack Poland, and plunge Europe into a second World War only after securing Moscow's neutrality. A delay in the Kremlin might thus save the peace for another few months.

Neither Count Schulenburg nor I shared these views; on the contrary, we desired nothing so much as the normalization of German-Soviet relations because we considered the existing situation to be untenable and feared that it might, in the end, lead to an armed conflict. If we cautioned von Ribbentrop to go slow, it was because we thought we knew the semi-Asiatic temperament of the Russians, who would not let themselves be rushed; excessive haste, we reasoned, might spoil everything. But, despite some forebodings that haunted me on August 23rd—I shall speak about them in a moment—the signing of the pact meant the crowning of many long years of my efforts on behalf of good German-Soviet relations. Both Count Schulenburg and I, moreover, thought for a long time that the pact would, far from unleashing a war, serve as an instrument of peace. In retrospect this may sound naïve or even unbelievable. None the less, we both actually hoped that the new constellation of forces resulting from the treaty would cause the Western powers to caution Poland and persuade her to seek a compromise with Germany. Our hope originated from the assumption that Hitler, in turn, would be satisfied with Danzig and a "corridor through the corridor," and make no further territorial demands. Hence, we saw in the pact not

only a brilliant coup that would settle the German-Polish problem but also the only solution to prevent a second World War. An era of peace seemed to be dawning, and in contrast to the Treaty of Versailles it seemed to be a peace that would secure Germany a powerful position on the European continent.

In the later stages of the negotiations, when we became aware of Hitler's war plans against Poland, we consoled ourselves that such a conflict would still be preferable to a German-Soviet clash; yet the feelings with which the ambassador and I executed Berlin's orders in the last stages of the discussions were mixed.

My worries grew as the further course of developments became more and more discernible; I voiced them even to von Ribbentrop, though in somewhat veiled fashion. On August 23rd as von Ribbentrop, Schulenburg, and I were just about to depart for the Kremlin for the foreign minister's first meeting with the Soviet government, the minister suddenly took me aside and asked in an unexpected rush of humane concern: "You look so worried. Is there any reason?"

I replied: "That is correct, Herr Reichsminister. I am indeed quite worried, for I believe that what you are about to do in the Kremlin will go well only as long as Germany remains strong." With this I wanted to say that I now thought a war with the Western powers unavoidable in the event of a German attack on Poland, and that I doubted whether Germany would, in the long run, be a match for the West. Von Ribbentrop seemed to have understood me, but he did not take up the idea.

"If that is all," he said lightly, "then I can only tell you that Germany will be able to deal with any situation that comes up."

The mass of the Soviet population received the news of the treaty, on the whole, with relief and satisfaction. For them a German-Soviet understanding meant the removal of the war scare which had weighed on them like a nightmare since 1933. I myself heard several remarks in this direction from Russians. It became apparent that the propaganda campaign which the Soviet state had for years waged against Nazi Germany had not been too successful in inculcating a lasting hatred of Germany in the population. Instead, the majority readily followed the turn in official Soviet policy and registered with satisfaction all indications to the effect that the Soviet government was serious about the new settlement. The population seemed surprisingly receptive for official Soviet explanations in which the West-

ern powers were designated as warmongers and accused of having wished to use the Soviet Union for their own selfish purposes. A two-line ditty which made the rounds of Moscow at the time mirrored the widespread opinion that the pact would greatly benefit Soviet Russia's international position. Parodying a popular saying about Peter the Great, the verse thanked Ribbentrop for having opened "a window on Europe" for the Russian people by giving them access to the Baltic shore. (*Spasibo Iashe Ribbentropu, chto on otkryl okno v Evropu.*)

At no time were there any signs that the Politburo was not unanimously backing Stalin's decision to make the treaties with Germany. On the contrary, everything indicated that the Politburo members shared Stalin's view concerning the usefulness of an understanding with Hitler. At the same time, I frequently had the impression, during the negotiations, that the Soviet side could make decisions so quickly only because Stalin often did not think it necessary to consult the members of the Politburo. Molotov, as foreign commissar, seemed to be the only one at that time who functioned as Stalin's permanent adviser.

Here and there it became apparent that the sudden change of course created some consternation and insecurity among ordinary party members who were not initiated in the mysteries of high policy. Many comrades seemed to have a hard time getting used to the idea that overnight Germany had turned from Enemy No. 1 into a friend. Some voiced fear of war: Would not Germany turn against Soviet Russia after swallowing Poland? No one, of course, dared to voice open and sharp criticism, and no crisis rocked the party. The purges of 1936–1938 insured Stalin against that. Yet because the leaders felt the necessity of paying respect to such sentiments within the party, in closed meetings, at which only party functionaries and so-called "activists" participated, the slogan was promulgated that the understanding with Germany was no love match, but only a marriage of convenience which could at any time be adjusted to changed conditions. Moreover, it was emphasized again and again that the first duty of a party comrade was to have unbounded confidence in Stalin, who knew exactly what he was doing, and why. At the same time the entire vast propaganda machinery of the party began to churn out explanations of the shift for every citizen who might have felt puzzled and perturbed. In Moscow's Park of Culture

and Rest, information booths were set up where "agitators," so called, patiently explained the new policy to all those who queued up for enlightenment.

Outward manifestations of the shift were many. Immediately after the conclusion of the pact, all criticism of Germany and the Nazi regime disappeared from the Soviet press, stage, and screen. Formerly there had been outbursts against Germany's policy toward the Soviet state and the old tsarist state; now one could read about the importance of German-Russian friendship and the pioneering work of Germans in Russia's cultural developments. The well known historian Eugene Tarlé, who after 1933 had always tried to show the disastrous influence which Germans had had on the policy of the Russian Empire, discovered overnight that the Germans had for a long time played a positive role in Russia. In order to honor von Bismarck's memory, and to familiarize the Soviet public with his policies, the State Publishing House of the USSR undertook to publish his *Gedanken und Erinnerungen*. The operas of Richard Wagner were once again given on the stage of the Bolshoi Theater in Moscow, and proved very popular. The official German war communiqués were printed conspicuously by all Soviet newspapers. The Soviet government furnished many other concrete indications of its good will; for instance, it established supply depots for German submarines on the shores of the Kola Peninsula; and a number of officers from the German battleship *Graf Spee*, who had managed to escape to the Far East, were given permission to travel through the Soviet Union and were treated with courtesy and friendliness.

On September 1st, in the early hours of the morning, German troops crossed the Polish border and began advancing into the country with amazing rapidity. World War II had begun. Two days later Count Schulenburg suggested to Molotov that the Soviet government, in turn, draw the consequences of the secret protocol signed on August 23rd, and move its troops into its sphere of influence in eastern Poland.

Noted for his caution and patience, Stalin refused to let himself be pushed into unpremeditated action. For two weeks he remained calm, watching the advance of Hitler's armies. Even when German troops, pursuing beaten Polish units across the Vistula River, entered the Soviet sphere of influence, he desisted from occupying his part

of Poland, despite our urging, expressing confidence that temporary disregard of the line of division between the two zones would not prevent the final division of Poland from being carried out as planned. There were two reasons for his inaction: Conscious of world opinion, and loath to antagonize it more than necessary, Stalin was resolved to act only after a suitable pretext could be found to justify his move. In addition, the Kremlin had overlooked Germany's military superiority over the Polish armies and had therefore counted on a much longer campaign. On September 10th Molotov had to admit to Count Schulenburg that the Red Army would require another two or three weeks for its preparations; but during the next few days it became clear that the definite collapse of Poland was imminent, and on the 14th Molotov told us that Soviet troops would be able to march earlier than expected. Even so, he still proposed to wait until a good pretext had been found.

Such a pretext offered itself two days later, when the Polish government fled abroad and found refuge in Romania. None the less, Stalin was not satisfied to justify the occupation of eastern Poland by the collapse of the Polish state alone, but inserted in the communiqués issued by the Soviet government the statement that the fall of Poland had obliged the Soviet Union to protect the interests of the Ukrainian and Byelorussian populations in the eastern parts of that country. The question remained open, against whom these populations required protection, which gave rise to angry German comments. But Stalin apparently thought the carefully worded announcement of the reasons for his invasion of Poland so important that he took some ill feelings on the part of his German ally in the bargain.

A similar lack of consideration was shown when the Russians actually announced to us the exact time their troops would move. At two o'clock in the morning of September 17th, Count Schulenburg, General Köstring, and I were called to Stalin, who had Molotov and Voroshilov with him. "At 6:00 A.M., four hours from now," Stalin announced, "the Red Army will cross into Poland all along the border, and the Red Air Force will begin bombarding the area east of Lvov." He asked us to notify German armed forces immediately so that incidents could be avoided. General Köstring became excited at such short notice and almost desperately pleaded that the time was not enough to notify the troops in the field. Clashes be-

tween German and Soviet troops would be unavoidable. All his objections, however, were brushed aside by Voroshilov, who said, with unmistakable admiration of German military achievements, that the organizational genius of the German Army would surely find time, even on such short notice, to relay the message. In fact, when the armies joined hands in the center of Poland no incident occurred to mar relations between the two countries.

Two days later Stalin called the ambassador to propose to him a revised delimitation of spheres of influence which would give the USSR control over Lithuania while extending the German-controlled territory up to the old Curzon Line, thus eliminating a rump Poland that might otherwise have remained. Von Ribbentrop wired his agreement and announced that he would come to Moscow to conduct the negotiations himself.

At 5:00 P.M. on September 27th he arrived in the Soviet capital for the second time. A number of high functionaries and Red Army officers greeted him, and there was an honor guard. The first discussion with Stalin and Molotov took place late that evening; the talks were continued the following afternoon and ended in the early hours of the 29th with the signing of a border-and-friendship treaty which carried September 28, 1939, as its dateline. Its main point was that the two governments agreed on the division of spheres of influence as proposed by Stalin. Some additional agreements were reached concerning the beginning of trade discussions, Soviet oil deliveries, and the resettlement of the German national minorities from the Baltic area. In talking about the war in the West, von Ribbentrop showed great optimism, and he repeated several times that Germany did not need any military assistance from the Soviet Union, though he expected the Russians to support the Reich with certain crucial raw materials.

In the late afternoon of September 28th, Molotov gave a banquet in honor of von Ribbentrop. Stalin, as well as many high Soviet functionaries, such as Mikoyan, Kaganovich, and Voroshilov, participated. Stalin was in a very cheerful mood, and von Ribbentrop later remarked to friends that he had felt as at ease in the Kremlin as he had among his old Nazi cronies. Stalin contributed to the life of the party by encouraging Molotov to propose toasts, drawing his neighbors into conversation, and emphatically urging everyone to drink. He himself, however, drank almost nothing that evening. (It is well known that

in former years he was very fond of parties, and drank quite heavily; but he later became very careful upon his doctors' advice.) I was sitting diagonally opposite him. Beriya, who was sitting on my right, was trying to make me drink more than I wished. Stalin soon noticed that Beriya and I were in dispute about something, and asked across the table: "What's the argument about?" When I told him, he replied, "Well, if you don't want to drink, no one can force you."

"Not even the chief of the NKVD himself?" I joked.

Whereupon he answered, "Here, at this table, even the chief of the NKVD has no more to say than anyone else."

2. THE CURTAIN FALLS

Poland was destroyed and divided. Stalin, in our presence, had drawn a thick blue pencil line on the map that ran from the German-Lithuanian border on the Baltic shores all the way south to the Slovakian boundary, and had staked out his claims to the Baltic States and Bessarabia. Two exciting months had passed, and now the time had come to survey the prospects for the future.

To me it seemed certain that the new German-Soviet friendship, sealed by two solemn treaties, would be of advantage to both partners, and that it would be of long duration. All the familiar arguments favoring close relations between the two countries went through my mind again, and I noted with satisfaction that there seemed to be no dissent from any quarter. For many months there were neither documents nor hearsay evidence that Hitler intended to break the pact at an opportune moment and attack the Soviet Union. Not till the Nürnberg war-crimes trial did the world learn that a veiled reference to a future German-Soviet conflict was made as early as November 23, 1939, when Hitler spoke as follows to the chiefs of staff of his armed forces:

"At the present time Russia presents no danger. She is now weakened through a number of internal events. Besides, we have the pact with Russia. But treaties are kept only as long as they are expedient. Russia too will stick to them only as long as she herself believes that this is to her advantage. Bismarck, too, thought that way. Now Russia still has far-reaching aims, particularly the strengthening of her position on the shores of the Baltic Sea. We can oppose her only if we are free in the West. In addition, Russia strives to strengthen

her influence on the Balkan peninsula and aims toward the Persian Gulf. But those are also aims of our own foreign policy." [5] Even this document shows that Hitler then had no ideas of a reckoning with Soviet Russia in the near future.

On the whole, the first year after the signing of the Moscow treaties appeared to all but a handful of initiated as a honeymoon during which the partners outdid each other in demonstrations of good will and co-operation. As a consequence, the embassy once again came into the limelight as an important link between the two countries. Its personnel increased rapidly, and a number of its old members were promoted. Some of the new personnel brought functions with them that had not been performed in the embassy before; thus the German Forestry Office sent a forestry attaché. The Propaganda Ministry became quite interested in the activities of our press department. Moreover, a number of consular offices closed since 1937 were reopened. All this activity pointed to the conviction current in Berlin that the political ties with Russia could only grow firmer, and that a close relationship of collaboration would soon develop between all fields of endeavor in the two countries.

Similarly, there is every indication that the Kremlin believed firmly in the new political constellation. Stalin thought he had gained a breathing spell for a long time to come. Granted that the war in the West would drag out into a long struggle of attrition, he could derive great advantages at little cost from a continuation of peaceful German-Soviet relations. And he often went out of his way to demonstrate his good will.

True enough, there were misunderstandings and frictions from the very beginning to mar the new friendship. Shells flew, as a matter of fact, toward the end of 1939 when Soviet batteries fired on German ships off the Finnish coast, and one German freighter was sunk by a Soviet submarine. Moreover, in the early months of 1940 there was a period during which Soviet friendliness cooled off markedly, and their officials began to make all sorts of difficulties. Instead of showing a benevolent attitude, the official organs of the Soviet state during those weeks insisted on showing the strictest neutrality. After the occupation of Denmark and Norway, however, a sudden return to friendliness could be noted. All difficulties ceased, and apologies were

[5] Quoted in Heinz Georg Holldack, *Was wirklich geschah* (Nymphenburger Verlagshandlung, München, 1949), p. 460.

offered that "excessive eagerness in subordinate organizations" had led to the temporary stoppage of grain and oil deliveries. (The "subordinate organization" had been none other than the foreign-trade commissar and Politburo member Mikoyan.) There seems no doubt that the Kremlin had watched developments in northern Europe with increasing worry, and had reckoned with a British occupation of the countries controlling the exit from the Baltic Sea; hence derived its anxiousness to show itself completely neutral, which was relieved only by the German action of April 9, 1940.

Two months previously, on February 11, 1940, trade negotiations begun in October, 1939, ended with the conclusion of an extensive barter agreement, in which the Soviet government agreed to deliver certain critical raw materials in exchange for German industrial products. In principle it was agreed that the deliveries should balance each other in value. Upon German insistence, however, the Soviet Union agreed to deliver certain raw materials in advance, since they were available immediately, while the production of machinery and other German deliveries required more time. The point was settled after hard and seemingly fruitless bargaining by a personal letter from von Ribbentrop to Stalin. As a compromise, the Germans agreed to balance deliveries every six months.

The list of items promised by the Russians was impressive, particularly if we add deliveries still outstanding from the credit agreement of August 19, 1939. In the first twelve months the Soviet government was to ship one million metric tons of feed grains, 900,000 metric tons of oil, 100,000 tons of cotton, 500,000 tons of phosphates, 100,000 tons of chromium ore, 500,000 tons of iron ore, 300,000 tons of scrap and pig iron, 2.4 metric tons of platinum, and a number of other items, valued altogether at 600 million reichsmarks. The German deliveries were to comprise industrial products, machinery, and armaments, goods that were considered scarce in Germany, too. The quantities for which Moscow had originally asked were considered exorbitant by the German negotiators, and they were scaled down considerably after Molotov admitted, in December, that he had never expected to receive everything for which he had asked. Thus instead of three battle cruisers, the Russians had to be satisfied with one.

One great difficulty, from the German point of view, was the fact that almost everything the Russians asked for contained iron or steel, a critical raw material in the months shortly before the battle

of France. In order to get even a fraction of their initial orders, the Russians finally declared themselves ready to ship more raw materials to Germany than even we thought they could afford. At this stage of the negotiations Stalin himself had to be consulted; we were told that he was the only one who could override a Soviet embargo on certain materials in which Germany was particularly interested. Here too Stalin was revealed to have not only the supreme power of making decisions but also a surprising amount of expert knowledge. He surprised us by explaining that Soviet-German economic relations were a matter of mutual aid, in which both sides were to make sacrifices; his government, he continued, showed its willingness by going down in its prices and by not insisting on hard-currency payments.

On the whole the negotiations were marked by the chronic suspicion of the Soviet negotiators and by the fear of responsibility even on the part of a Politburo member like Mikoyan; this in part explains the fact that it took four months of active discussions to come to terms. On the other hand, the Russians manifested their intention of helping Germany so that the political relationship might be fortified economically. For the German war effort the result of the negotiations was, naturally, a tremendous success. A door to the East had been opened wide, and British efforts at an economic blockade of Germany had been weakened considerably.

Why, then, did Hitler attack Soviet Russia less than two years after making high-sounding treaties with her? What made him exchange the advantages of German-Soviet collaboration for the gamble of total war against a mighty empire? The answers to these questions can be gleaned only from the changing situation, the changing hopes, the shifting calculations, and the errors in judgment of both sides in the course of the thirteen months from May, 1940, to June, 1941. It is a story with which I am especially familiar because I personally participated in every one of the most important meetings and discussions that took place.

One reason for Count Schulenburg's numerous visits to the Kremlin was furnished by Article 3 of the non-aggression pact, which provided for mutual consultation on questions touching the interests of both partners. For a while each government faithfully informed the other of important actions it intended to take. Thus on May 7, 1940, three days before the German invasion of Holland and Belgium, the ambassador called on Molotov to inform him of Hitler's inten-

tions. The manner in which Molotov reacted to the information showed that the Soviet government wholeheartedly welcomed the German step. Molotov said that his government fully understood Germany's need to protect herself against an Anglo-French attack, and he added that he had not the slightest doubts about a German success. What the Kremlin expected from the German advance into Belgium and Holland was clear: a stiffening of English and French resistance, a prolongation of the war, and an even more serious weakening of Germany as well as her adversaries.

But in assessing the strength of the various armies and judging the presumable development of military operations in France, Stalin had made the great mistake of overestimating the importance of the Maginot Line and of counting on a long period of trench warfare between Germany and the Western powers. Instead, the Soviet government saw itself obliged to congratulate the German ambassador on the victory in France as early as June 18, 1940.[6] At the same time Molotov notified Count Schulenburg that his government had sent emissaries into the Baltic States in order to secure the formation of new governments who would be more agreeable to the Kremlin. Five days later Molotov told us that the Soviet government had decided to carry out the restoration of Bessarabia to Russian territory, if necessary by force, and to stake out claims for Bukovina.

Shortly afterward the Baltic States, Bessarabia, and the northern part of Bukovina were incorporated into the Soviet Union. It was obvious that the Soviet government, worried over the lightning successes of the German armies in France, had decided to build up its own positions at an accelerated pace and to make the most of its agreements with Germany concerning spheres of interest. In doing so Stalin was careless enough to include Bukovina in his expansionist activities, though nothing had been said about the territory in the talks between the two governments. Therefore the incorporation of Bukovina constituted a violation of the agreements made in 1939. When we lodged a protest with Molotov against the annexation of the northern part of Bukovina, he not only tried to vindicate the step but even went so far as to state that if the Soviet government

---

[6] Two months later, in August, 1940, *Pravda* took the opportunity to make comments about the sale of fifty American destroyers to Britain. The transaction was taken by the Soviet paper as an indication that the war would still last a long time, in spite of Hitler's spectacular victory in France.

should one day also seek to obtain the southern part of Bukovina it would expect Germany to support its claims.

In the preceding fall Finland had refused to meet Soviet demands for the cession of strategic bases on the Baltic shore, a refusal that was used as a pretext to start a war with Finland in November, 1939. German sympathies clearly were with Finland in the struggle, but the German government not only kept neutral but supported the Soviet point of view in the German press since, in accordance with the secret protocol of August 23rd, Finland belonged to Moscow's sphere of interest. None the less, in the long run the Finnish question did throw a shadow on German-Soviet relations.

Another disturbance was added when Lithuania was occupied by Soviet troops. The treaty of September 28, 1939, had provided that a small portion in the southwest corner of Lithuania was to go to Germany. Nevertheless, the Red Army occupied it and treated it as part of the new Soviet Republic of Lithuania. When the Germans protested, Molotov replied to the German ambassador, on September 13, 1940, that Stalin had examined the problem, and that the German claim for the piece of land was certainly justified. None the less, his government felt that it would be extremely difficult to fulfill our request, and they would appreciate it very much if Germany, in the true spirit of friendship and collaboration, would try to find a way to permit the territory to remain with Lithuania. Discussions on the subject lasted for several months, and a solution was found only much later in connection with talks about a second barter agreement. On January 10, 1941, Schulenburg and Molotov signed a secret protocol in which the Soviet Union agreed to pay 31.5 million reichsmarks in compensation for the territory. (In gold dollars, the sum was greater than that which the United States paid for Alaska.) The time required to arrive at this rather insignificant agreement shows clearly to what extent the relations between the two countries had deteriorated.

The timing of Moscow's actions was much more significant for further developments than the actions themselves. The Soviet government began to strengthen its positions at a time when Hitler's successes in the West had put him in a mental state bordering on megalomania. At that time statements of his became known in which he expressed the view that there was no limit to his possibilities. More and more he talked himself into the idea that destiny had called him

to make an end of Bolshevism, and that he must not rest until he had conquered for the German people that *Lebensraum* which was its due. From now on he observed Stalin's actions with growing suspicion and drew the conclusion that Stalin was systematically strengthening his position so as to be able to put pressure on Germany when the time was ripe. It was in this mental state that Hitler, for the first time, around August 4, 1940, gave clear indications to responsible military leaders that sooner or later they would have to reckon with a military clash with the Soviet Union.

On its part, the Soviet government, too, had reason to be critical of Hitler's behavior. They were particularly worried about Germany's expansionist designs in the Balkan countries. Thus Molotov expressed great annoyance over the so-called Vienna arbitration of August, 1940, by which Germany and Italy decided a territorial dispute between Romania and Hungary without consulting Moscow; he claimed that the decision was in violation of Article 3 of the non-aggression pact, which provided for mutual consultation. If the German government now denied its obligation to give prior information of acts affecting Soviet interests, he warned moodily, the question came up whether the clause was in force at all. Three weeks later he lodged a sharp protest against the unilateral act following the Vienna arbitration, by which Italy and Germany had guaranteed Romania's territorial integrity, and in early October he reacted wryly when Hitler dispatched German troop contingents to Romania. He gave a sour smile when, following Berlin's instructions, Count Schulenburg argued that Romania's oil fields had to be protected against British threats, and that most of the troops were only instruction personnel which the Romanian government had specifically requested.

Trade relations between Germany and the Soviet Union also developed unsatisfactorily, since Germany had very seriously fallen behind with its deliveries by the fall of 1940. Moscow announced that it would take advantage of its treaty right to stop its own shipments until Germany caught up on its obligations. There were indications that the Soviet government had begun to doubt Germany's ability to fulfill its delivery obligations. For instance, the Soviet government no longer placed long-term orders in Germany; instead, it limited its orders to articles which could be delivered in eight to ten months, and which served the short-range ends of Soviet military preparedness.

Thus German-Soviet relations, in the course of one year, had taken

on a character quite detrimental to the German interest. Hitler was well aware of the fact, and therefore resolved, in the fall of 1940, to enter into negotiations with the Soviet government, to probe into their intentions, and to draw the necessary conclusions from whatever the result might be.

Upon instructions by the German government, I notified Foreign Trade Commissar Mikoyan, on October 7, 1940, that my government had decided to resume immediately the recently interrupted trade negotiations and to send a competent German delegation to Moscow for that purpose.

On October 13, 1940, von Ribbentrop wrote a personal letter to Stalin which seemingly aimed to restore the friendly atmosphere of a year before. In nineteen pages he gave a detailed résumé of German foreign policy in the last months, together with reasons and justifications for every step that had been taken. He pointed out how important it would be to intensify the political and economic collaboration between Germany and Russia and assured Stalin that the Three-Power Pact between Germany, Italy, and Japan, concluded on September 27, 1940, did not in any way violate German-Soviet agreements. He concluded by inviting Molotov to visit Berlin so that further development of the relationship between the two countries could be discussed. The letter had a sincere ring, and the German Embassy, including Count Schulenburg himself, regarded it as a sure sign that the recent irritations had left no scar; on the contrary, an even friendlier atmosphere could now be expected. In fact, however, the kind invitation that had been tendered the foreign commissar was Hitler's device to feel out Soviet intentions. But, for the time being, the embassy was completely in the dark about his plans.

In his short reply of October 21, 1940, Stalin, with hidden sarcasm, thanked the German foreign minister for his "very instructive analysis of the latest events." He agreed with von Ribbentrop that a further improvement of the relations between the two states was absolutely possible on the durable basis of a long-range delineation of mutual interests. The invitation for Molotov was accepted. The style of the letter left no doubt that Stalin wrote it personally.

Four weeks later Molotov took off for Berlin where he arrived on November 12, 1940, and stayed for forty-eight hours. For the first time in history a chairman of the Council of People's Commissars traveled abroad on official business. He was accompanied by more

than sixty persons, including sixteen security guards, a physician, and three personal servants. In Berlin the Soviet officials were extraordinarily impressed by the pomp and glitter of the reception and by the splendid quarters they were given, something the proud and prestige-conscious Russians seldom admitted.

The German ambassador and I went to Berlin at the same time as Molotov and returned to Moscow together with him. Among the high functionaries in the Soviet party were Dekanozov, later the Soviet ambassador to Berlin, and Merkulov, vice commissar of the interior, who later was promoted to minister for state security, and who was responsible for Molotov's personal safety. Typical of Merkulov's mentality, and the consequences to which excessive secrecy and stupid subordination lead in the Soviet Union, was the following occurrence which happened during the trip to Berlin. Shortly before we were to cross the German-Soviet border, I asked Merkulov at what place we would change trains, as I had forgotten the name of the station at which the Soviet broad gauge stopped and the German normal gauge began.[7] Merkulov replied, "We shall change trains at such a place as will be designated by the chairman of the Council of People's Commissars." In vain I argued that I could not be satisfied with his answer, since the place at which we had to change trains did not depend on Mr. Molotov's decision, but exclusively on where one gauge ended and the other began. He stuck to his position, and I could do no more than have patience for a couple of hours and read the name of the station from the signs that were affixed to the building.

It was eleven o'clock in the morning, November 12, 1940, when Molotov arrived in Berlin, and he left the German capital exactly forty-eight hours later. In those two days the following meetings took place: a relatively brief discussion with von Ribbentrop at noon, a three-hour session with Hitler in the afternoon, and a dinner at the foreign minister's in the evening of the first day; brief visits with Göring and Hess the next morning,[8] lunch with Hitler, followed by

[7] After annexing the eastern part of Poland, the Soviet government had extended broad gauge up to the new boundaries.

[8] In his meeting with Hess, Molotov was interested primarily in the organizational structure of the Nazi state. He wanted to know what the precise functions of the Deputy Führer's office were, and the two men talked at length about the relations between party and state in their respective countries. The conversation with Göring dealt exclusively with German-Soviet trade relations. Göring ex-

another three-hour session with him; then, after a dinner given in the Soviet Embassy, a final meeting of two hours in von Ribbentrop's air raid shelter during which Molotov held final discussions with the foreign minister. I attended every one of these meetings from beginning to end; but, since the pertinent reports have all been published by the Department of State,[9] I shall forego a detailed description of everything that was said and merely give my personal impressions of the meetings.

When greeting Molotov on November 12th, Hitler was surprisingly gracious and friendly. After a few words of welcome he launched into a long-winded speech, full of repetitions, in which he outlined grandiose but vague plans for the division of the world between the remaining great powers (England was written off, on the assumption that her definite collapse was assured). He recognized Russia's need for safe warm-water ports, indicated that Germany would gladly co-operate with the Soviet Union in attaining that aim, and assured Molotov that he was not interested in any eastward expansion. He brushed aside any existent or latent territorial conflicts as meaningless, and his entire behavior showed that he was eager to win Molotov personally and wanted him to share his views. And he seemed to succeed in this at first. Molotov listened to Hitler's lengthy and redundant explanations with great attention and replied that he agreed in principle, though certain terms would still have to be cleared up. When I accompanied him to his quarters afterward, he seemed relieved at Hitler's amiability.

On the following day, however, the conflict of the aims of the partners in negotiation became so obvious that it was clear even then that there was little hope left for the possibility of reaching an understanding. Molotov wanted to clear up questions connected with

---

plained the difficulties and setbacks in Germany's deliveries by the fact that the Soviet orders were too much concentrated in a very narrow sector; namely, tool machinery and armament material, commodities that were in unusually great demand in Germany itself. Molotov thought, however, that Germany, after occupying extensive foreign territories, now controlled increased resources, so that his government could still not understand why Germany had difficulty in filling Soviet orders. In addition Göring complained about the extent to which the Soviet Union had asked for technical aid; some of its demands, he said, amounted to a request for manufacturing secrets. On the whole the tone of the conversation was quite friendly, and Göring revealed all the jovial character traits with which he impressed so many Western statesmen.

[9] *Nazi-Soviet Relations, 1939–1941* (Washington, 1948).

German-Soviet relations in general, and with the treaties of 1939 in particular. He emphasized that Germany, in violation of the treaties, was keeping troops in Finland, and demanded that they be withdrawn. He called the German action in Vienna and the guarantee given by the Axis powers to the Romanian borders violations of the agreement concerning mutual consultation. He voiced desires concerning the creation of security points for the Soviet Union in Bulgaria, on the Bosporus, and in the Dardanelles. But not one of his questions was satisfactorily answered by Hitler. Instead, Hitler kept indulging in general speeches about the postwar division of the world. Two things became clear in the discussions: Hitler's intention to push the Soviet Union in the direction of the Persian Gulf, and his unwillingness to acknowledge any Soviet interests in Europe. How Molotov himself thought about these questions became apparent that same evening during the conversation with von Ribbentrop, in which Molotov emphasized Soviet interest not only in the Balkans but also in free passage out of the Baltic Sea. The remainder of the talk with von Ribbentrop was devoted to the conditions under which the Soviet government would be ready to join the Three-Power Pact between Germany, Japan, and Italy.

After Molotov's return to Moscow the Soviet government took the question up once more, in the form of a memorandum which Molotov handed to the German ambassador on November 25, 1940. The gist of the memorandum was contained in the conditions on which the Soviet government made its joining the pact dependent. They corresponded, in the main, to the wishes which Molotov had voiced to Hitler; namely, withdrawal of the German troops from Finland, conclusion of a mutual-aid treaty between the Soviet Union and Bulgaria, creation of strongholds at the Straits, and recognition of Soviet aspirations in the direction of the Persian Gulf. To this memorandum the Soviet government never received a reply. Hitler considered it as proof that the Soviet government had decided to push its own desires and to resist the German aspirations. He was not slow to draw conclusions from the Soviet government's arguments. On December 18, 1940, five weeks after Molotov's visit in Berlin, Hitler issued the famous order known by the code name Operation Barbarossa; it began with the following words: "The German armed forces must be prepared . . . to crush Soviet Russia in a swift campaign." In Moscow, at the same time, several persons who had spread rumors

about an impending German-Soviet war were sentenced to long terms of forced labor.

Despite the tension which had entered into German-Soviet relations after Molotov's visit in Berlin, the trade negotiations resumed in October were carried on in the following three months. They ended on January 10, 1941, when a treaty was signed in which the Soviet government, on the basis of reciprocity, undertook not only to continue its deliveries of grain, crude oil, cotton, and so forth, to Germany, but even promised some substantial increases. At the same time the conflict over the southwest corner of Lithuania was settled. None the less, the German side retained some resentment over the treaty violation committed by the Soviet government.

In the first half of January, 1941, German-Soviet relations were sharpened further because the German government had sent strong contingents of troops into Romania, on the pretext that it had to take preventive measures in the face of operations allegedly planned by the English in Greece, thus openly revealing German intentions to march into Bulgaria, which disturbed the Soviet government very much. On January 17, 1941, Molotov expressed anxiety to the German ambassador by pointing out that the Soviet government had repeatedly referred to Bulgaria and the Straits as security zones of the USSR, and that it would have to consider the appearance of German troops in those areas as a violation of its security interests. At the same time Molotov voiced his government's astonishment that the German government had not yet taken a definite stand on the questions that had been raised in the Berlin talks of November 12–14, 1940, and that the Soviet memorandum of November 25th, dealing with the questions, had remained without an answer. This and similar *démarches* which followed received no more than evasive answers from Berlin, which made the Soviet government increasingly suspicious of German intentions.

Tension was further heightened when Bulgaria joined the Three-Power Pact on March 1, 1941, and German troops marched into Bulgaria. These acts led to talks between the German ambassador and Molotov, during which the latter emphasized the worry which the German step was causing his government, declaring again and again that Bulgaria was within the Soviet Union's security zone.

During the time when the German advances on the Balkan Peninsula had worsened political ties between Germany and the Soviet

Union, the Soviet government indicated by its attitude in economic questions that it wanted to prevent as much as possible any further deterioration of their relations. In place of a certain reticence with which the Soviet government had fulfilled its delivery obligations toward Germany in January and February, 1941, March brought a surprising change. Soviet deliveries suddenly jumped to a peak, in spite of the fact that Germany had fallen far behind with her deliveries and that there were no indications that the situation might change to the benefit of the Soviet Union in the foreseeable future. It was obvious that the Soviet government at that time wanted to avoid anything that might have contributed toward angering Germany.

In contrast, the Soviet government consciously ran the risk of a further deterioration of its relations with Germany when it concluded a treaty of friendship and non-aggression with the new Yugoslav government on the night of August 5 to 6, 1941.[10] Stalin obviously hoped to strengthen its will to resist, thus causing the war on the Balkan Peninsula to spread, and turning the immediate German danger away from the Soviet Union. In this manner he would gain additional time for the purpose of pushing the Soviet armament program with the greatest vigor.

Within a few days after hostilities between Germany and Yugoslavia had broken out, it appeared that in weighing the advantages which a German campaign on the Balkan Peninsula would bring the Soviet Union Stalin had proceeded from faulty premises. Before the start of Balkan war operations, he is said to have stated that the Germans were in error if they believed that they could advance as fast in the mountains of Yugoslavia and Greece as on the asphalt roads of France. The Serbs, he argued, would give the Germans a hard nut to crack, for you could not compare the Serbs, so full of resistance, so used to hardships, with the French; hence the Balkan campaign would last a long time and would test German strength to the utmost. But Stalin had made as big a mistake in judging the probable course of the Balkan campaign as he had made in the case of Poland and France.

Nothing the Russians did between 1939 and 1941 made Hitler more genuinely angry than the treaty with Yugoslavia; nothing contributed

---

[10] The government had just replaced its predecessor, which had fallen because it had joined the Three-Power Pact.

more directly to the final break; and Stalin must have sensed it. Ever since the collapse of Yugoslavia and Greece cast its shadow, he left no stone unturned to appease Germany. The first step was taken as early as April 13th, that is, a week after hostilities had broken out in the Balkans. On that day Stalin appeared at the railroad station for Japanese Foreign Minister Matsuoka's departure from Moscow, and he used the opportunity to pat the German ambassador on the shoulder, asking him to see that Germany and the Soviet Union would remain friends. He then turned to a German officer standing close to the ambassador (it was Colonel Krebs, the assistant military attaché), made certain that he was a German, and virtually insisted that he give confirmation of the lasting friendship between the two countries. The colonel could only say, "Yes, sir!" The demonstration was made in the presence of numerous witnesses, including almost the entire diplomatic corps. During the next weeks and months it was followed by further proofs that the Soviet government was trying to keep the German government in a good mood and not to give it any reason for doubting Moscow's loyalty. Thus the Russians faithfully continued to fulfill their delivery obligations promptly, even though Germany lagged behind with her deliveries to the Soviet Union as before. The Soviet government went so far as to break diplomatic relations with Norway, Belgium, Yugoslavia, and Greece, in May, 1941, under the pretext that they had lost their sovereignty by virtue of the fact that they were under German occupation.

The appeasement policy of the Soviet government did not, however, make the impression on Hitler which Stalin had wished and expected. On the contrary, Hitler saw in the constant efforts of the Russians to prevent a conflict proof that the Kremlin was afraid of a military conflict with Germany because the Red Army was not ready for it, which increasingly confirmed him in his opinion that he would never again have such a good opportunity to crush the Soviet Union, destroy the Soviet regime, and provide the German people with the *Lebensraum* it allegedly needed through the conquest of Russian and Ukrainian territories.

Rumors about German troops concentrations at the Soviet border and an impending surprise attack meanwhile reached their peak. They came to us from officials and occasional businessmen who had recently been in Germany. Yet we had no concrete indication that Hitler actually contemplated an invasion of Soviet Russia. On the

contrary, we evaluated the rumors as bluff; we thought the stories were being circulated deliberately, to exert pressure upon the Soviet Union. Even if it were true that German troops had been concentrated near the Soviet border, we thought that Hitler wanted merely to extort some concessions from the Kremlin. It could be assumed that such pressure would be of an economic nature, since Germany had a large backlog of goods that should have been delivered to the Russians, thus enabling the latter to hold back an equivalent amount of shipments to Germany.

In mid-April the ambassador went to Germany to obtain reliable information about the situation and to make clear to Hitler the dangers of a campaign against the Soviet Union. For this purpose the ambassador, aided by his immediate collaborators, wrote a suitable memorandum which he took with him to Germany and transmitted to Hitler after his arrival.

The composition of this memorandum was a collective undertaking. The ambassador, his minister-counselor, von Tippelskirch, his military attaché General Köstring, and I drafted various portions and discussed them together. Tippelskirch, by the way, should be characterized as a dutiful and careful official who, in the crucial years 1939–1941 loyally carried out his orders but developed little initiative of his own. Yet he had a keen eye for political developments, a sharp judgment, and a good deal of assurance.

A personal meeting between Hitler and Count Schulenburg did not take place until April 28th. On that occasion the memorandum was lying on Hitler's desk; but he did not indicate by a single word whether or not he had read it in the meantime; instead, he limited himself to general and meaningless political statements. The ambassador took this to indicate that Hitler did not agree with the opinions contained or thought by him to be contained in the memorandum. Yet, as he took leave, Hitler, quite out of context, dropped the remark: "Oh, one more thing: I do not intend a war against Russia!"

When the ambassador returned to Moscow on April 30th, and I greeted him at the airport, he took me aside and whispered: "The die has been cast. War against Russia has been decided!" Only when we continued the conversation while riding to the embassy, did he tell me what Hitler had said to him. When I asked Count Schulenburg how this fitted with his remark that Hitler had decided on war, he

shrugged his shoulders in resignation and answered, "Well, he deliberately lied to me."

On May 6, 1941, Stalin took over from Molotov the chairmanship in the Council of People's Commissars of the USSR and thus officially became the head of the government of the Soviet Union, thereby documenting his resolution to carry, from then on, the constitutional responsibility for the fate of the state. To me it was additional proof that he was determined to keep the Soviet Union out of a conflict with Germany, and to use all the authority of his person and his official position to that end, if necessary. The ambassador reported our impression to Berlin.

Without doubt Stalin had hoped that his action would make a suitable impression on Hitler and cause him to show some moderation. It was a hope in vain, however, because Stalin had overestimated Hitler's political horizon as well as his sense of realism.

Hitler was just as little influenced by the reports of the embassy which pointed out the faultless tone of the Soviet press and the punctilious fulfillment of economic agreements on the part of the Soviet government, seeing in them further proof that the Soviet government above all aimed to avoid a conflict with Germany.

Some time in May Colonel Krebs returned to Moscow after an absence of several weeks. When he paid a visit to my office, I sounded him out about the rumors of war that were going from mouth to mouth. If there were anything true about the rumors, I said, it would be his duty to enlighten Hitler that a war against the Soviet Union would be the final ruin of Germany. I appealed to Krebs' knowledge of Russian history, repeating the old saying, "Often beaten, but never defeated"; I alluded to the strength of the Red Army, the resilience of the Russian people, the vastness of the country, and its inexhaustible reserves. "I know all that perfectly well," Krebs replied; "but I can't use it in conversation with Hitler. He doesn't listen to us General Staff officers any longer after we warned him against the campaign against France and called the Maginot Line an unsurmountable obstacle. He did it against all odds, and we have to shut up if we don't want to risk our heads." [11]

For the German Embassy in Moscow the last weeks before the German invasion of the Soviet Union were a tragic experience. After

[11] On April 30, 1945, Krebs died in the Führer's air-raid shelter as Hitler's last chief of general staff.

the abortive efforts to influence Hitler with the memorandum of April, the embassy had no more means at its disposal by which the course of events might be averted. Moreover, in view of the character which German-Russian relations had assumed, the ambassador for weeks hardly had an opportunity to talk to Molotov, especially since Molotov in his turn wrapped himself in silence.

The more time progressed, and the longer I observed the behavior of the Russians, the more I became convinced that Stalin was unaware how immediately he was threatened by a German attack. Everything indicated that he thought Hitler was preparing for a game of extortion in which threatening military moves would be followed by sudden demands for economic or even territorial concessions. He seems to have believed that he would be able to negotiate with Hitler over such demands when they were presented.

On May 5, 1941, a grand banquet was given in the Kremlin for the graduates of sixteen military academies of the Red Army. No foreigners were present, but a German correspondent named Schüle was tipped off about the proceedings by an informant who seemed reliable. According to this underground source, Stalin gave a speech in which he made a careful and sober comparison between the striking power of the German and Soviet armed forces, and came to the conclusion that the Red Army, so far, was no match for the *Wehrmacht*. Schüle's informant interpreted the speech by saying that Stalin had obviously wished to prepare his audience for new concessions he would make to Germany. The report and the interpretation fitted very well into the picture I had formed of Stalin's thoughts and intentions.[12]

---

[12] During the war, informal conversations I had with officers who had participated at the banquet yielded a completely different story and make the gyrations of Stalin's mind appear more complex than I had imagined. According to these witnesses, whose stories agreed with each other to a remarkable degree, a high-ranking general proposed a toast to the peace policy of the Soviet Union. The toast, they said, elicited the following reply from Stalin: "The slogan, 'Long live the peace policy of the Soviet Union,' is now outdated. It's about time to end this old nonsense. It is true, with our defensive policy we have succeeded in extending our borders in the north and the west and in increasing the Soviet population by 13 million. But this is now over. With this slogan we won't be able to win another foot of territory. Instead, we'll have to get used to the idea that *offensive* action is necessary. The era of peaceful policies is over; the era of spreading the Socialist front by force of arms has begun. Anyone who does not understand this is a petty-bourgeois fool." Someone else was said to have toasted the friendship with Germany, and Stalin allegedly replied that the Soviet people should stop praising the German Army to the skies.

I came to the conclusion that peace could perhaps still be saved if the Soviet government could be made to take the diplomatic initiative and involve Hitler in negotiations which would rob him, for the time being, of all pretexts for military action against the Soviet Union. I thought that the Soviet government ought to be enlightened about the seriousness of the situation. The Kremlin had to be persuaded by all means to do something to avert the danger of a German attack. It so happened that the Soviet ambassador in Berlin, Dekanozov, was in Moscow just then, and I decided that we had to get in touch with him and open his eyes about the game that was up. To lend the action some added weight, it would be necessary for Count Schulenburg to participate in it. But it was extremely difficult to persuade him. He said, quite correctly, that the German government would try him and me for treason if it leaked out that we were about to warn the Russians. I argued, however, that too much was at stake, and that we should not let any concern about our own existence deter us from such a desperate step. I finally allayed his misgivings and obtained his permission to arrange the secret meeting. Dekanozov, invited to come to a confidential meeting at the ambassador's residence, agreed to have lunch with us there. The only other person present was the then chief of the German section in the Foreign Commissariat and Molotov's permanent interpreter, V. N. Pavlov.

Count Schulenburg and I talked and talked, trying to show the Russians how serious the situation had become. Again and again we urged that his government must by all means get in touch with Berlin before Hitler decided to strike. Our efforts proved to be a complete failure. From the very beginning we had told Dekanozov that we were acting on our own responsibility and without the knowledge of our superiors; yet he kept asking us with maddening stubbornness whether we were speaking at the request of the German government; otherwise, he said, he would not be able to transmit our statements to his superiors. "You'll have to speak to the foreign minister," he kept repeating. Obviously, he could not imagine that we were knowingly and deliberately incurring the greatest danger for the purpose of making a last effort to save the peace. He must have believed that we were acting on Hitler's behalf and that we were trying to make the Kremlin take a step that would damage its prestige and its concrete interests. The more we talked to him, the more it became clear that he had no comprehension of the good will

that moved us. Perhaps it was the logical and obvious thing for him
to think we were playing Hitler's game; if that is correct then my
entire undertaking was not only doomed to failure from the start but
would actually confirm the Russians in their reasoning. If I am
correct in assuming that Stalin believed Hitler was bluffing, we have
a plausible explanation as to why he disregarded the many warnings
he was given. The very fact that several sources predicted the German
invasion for the same date must have confirmed his suspicion that
the story had been planted by the Germans. In any event, Dekanozov
acted strictly according to Stalin's directives, who, true enough,
wanted to appease Germany, but wished to do nothing that might
betray his anxieties, because that might make Hitler even more in-
transigent in his demands. In short, Stalin had to act as if nothing
was wrong with the German-Soviet relationship.

This tendency came out with particular clarity in the treatment
which the Soviet government at that time gave the British ambassador,
Sir Stafford Cripps, and in the TASS report of June 13, 1941, in which
the Soviet government denied all rumors about an alleged deterioration of relations between Germany and the Soviet Union, calling them
a lie and a provocation, and attesting that Germany was unceasingly
fulfilling the provisions of the non-aggression pact.

But all efforts were in vain. For Hitler was so inebriated by his
successes and so crazed with the idea that he would now or never
attain his life's dreams, that nothing could any longer change his
resolve to give the Soviet Union the *coup de grâce*.

During the last weeks preceding the German attack against the
Soviet Union, we lived under a very severe strain of apprehensions
and gloomy forebodings. Since the embassy was no longer in a position to perform any useful work and Berlin quite obviously was no
more interested in our reporting, I could indulge in reading, as well
as in prolonged discussions with the ambassador and those of my
colleagues whom I could trust.

Among the books which I read at that time with special interest
were the memoirs of the Marquis de Caulaincourt, the famous French
diplomat and statesman who served in the French Revolutionary and
Napoleonic wars and was the French Ambassador to Russia from
1807 to 1811. These memoirs were first published in France between
1837 and 1840 and republished shortly before the outbreak of the

Second World War. In their main part they contained Caulaincourt's recital of his conversations with Napoleon when he served with the French Emperor during the invasion of Russia in 1812 and accompanied his defeated master on his flight from Russia back to France.

The contents of these conversations fascinated me particularly because they gave evidence of the fact that the role which Caulaincourt had played with Napoleon was very similar to that which fate had assigned to Count Schulenburg in his relations with Hitler.

Both the Marquis de Caulaincourt and Count Schulenburg were ardent advocates of friendly relations between their countries and Russia. Both had warned against the dangers involved in a war against the Eastern colossus; and both had failed in their efforts to persuade their masters to abstain from attacking Russia.

In reading Caulaincourt's reminiscences, I was especially impressed by a passage in which the author described how he tried to bring home to Napoleon his opinions on Russia and the necessity to maintain good Franco-Russian relations. This passage reminded me so vividly of the point of view which Schulenburg voiced whenever he had an opportunity to speak to Hitler about the Soviet Union, that I decided to use this coincidence for a practical joke.

One day, when the ambassador was visiting me, I told him that I had quite recently received a confidential letter from a friend in Berlin containing a very interesting report on the contents of the ambassador's last conversation with Hitler. Count Schulenburg voiced surprise, since he had reason to believe that the course of the above conversation was known in Berlin only to a very few persons. "Anyhow," I replied, "here is the text." With these words, I began to read to him a passage from Caulaincourt's book which I had carefully concealed from the ambassador's view in a letter folder.

While reading, I neither omitted nor added a single word to the original text. I only changed the names of the persons involved, substituting Hitler for Napoleon and Schulenburg for Caulaincourt. The ambassador's surprise was genuine and great. "Though this seems not to be the original memorandum which I wrote myself after the meeting with Hitler," he exclaimed, "nevertheless, the text corresponds almost verbatim to what I said to Hitler on that occasion. These were exactly the words which I used in talking to him. Please, show me where the paper comes from."

When I handed the ambassador the hidden volume of Caulain-court's memoirs, his astonishment had no limits since the coincidence was really striking. We both regarded this as a very bad omen.[13]

Until immediately before the outbreak of hostilities, the German Embassy in Moscow was not clearly aware whether Hitler had actually and definitely decided to attack the Soviet Union, and what date he had fixed for the beginning of operations. In order to end the uncertainty, the ambassador, in early June, sent one of his trusted collaborators to Berlin with the order to pry out all the information he could get and report to him orally. The man returned to Moscow on June 14th with the news that the decision had been made and that the attack would be made some time around June 22nd. Almost at the same time the Foreign Ministry ordered the embassy to make provisions for the security of the secret archives; moreover, the embassy was told that Berlin had no objection to the inconspicuous departure of women and children. All dependents of the embassy's personnel thereupon made use of the opportunity to leave Moscow, so that my wife was the only non-official member of the embassy who was still in town when the conflict broke out. With typical consistency the Soviet government until the last moment followed its policy of appeasement toward Germany. For instance, the Soviet officials gave full co-operation in going through all the exit formalities for the numerous German citizens leaving the country, and the frontier officials were even more polite to the German travelers than they had ever been.

[13] Another example of how strangely history sometimes repeats itself, is the following fact.

According to Caulaincourt, Napoleon, while staying in the Kremlin in the fall of 1812, was quite surprised by the quite unseasonable warm weather which in that year prevailed in Moscow at the end of September. His observations on this theme culminated in the following statement: "My ambassador to Russia provided me with quite false information on the rigors of the Russian climate. Why, the fall weather here in Moscow is even milder than in Fontainebleau!" When some time later, strong frosts helped the Russians to harass the invaders and to destroy the retreating French Army, Napoleon must have remembered how right Caulaincourt was in warning him against the inclemency of the climate in Russia.

One hundred and twenty-nine years later, when Hitler's army began to suffer from the harshness of the Russian winter, Hitler exclaimed: "The reports of my embassy in Moscow on the Russian climate were as false as its other statements. Otherwise, our troops would have been better equipped against these dreadful Russian frosts!"

Thus, both Napoleon and Hitler used almost identical words in trying to blame others for their own failures.

Meetings between Count Schulenburg and Molotov, which had been so frequent for twenty months preceding, were no longer taking place. Current matters were dealt with at lower levels or were handled by Molotov's assistant, Vyshinsky. But on Saturday, June 21st, Molotov quite unexpectedly requested the German ambassador to call on him in the Kremlin at 9:30 P.M. It was the next to the last of the numerous trips to the Kremlin I made.

Molotov began the conversation by stating that German airplanes had for some time, and in increasing numbers, violated the Soviet border. In the last two months alone, no less than two hundred cases of such border violations had been noted. Hence his government, he said, had asked its ambassador in Berlin to point out to the German government that the situation was untenable. He asked the German ambassador to transmit the same message to his government. For Molotov, the declaration was only a pretext for starting a conversation with Schulenburg about the general character of German-Russian relations. Various indications, he said, gave the impression that "the German government is dissatisfied with the Soviet government." As a matter of fact, rumors were going around to the effect that a war between Germany and the Soviet Union was in preparation. One thing that was nourishing these rumors was the fact that the German side had in no way reacted to the TASS news item of June 13th; indeed, it had not even been published in Germany. The Soviet government, he continued, did not know how to explain this dissatisfaction. If it was caused by the Yugoslav question, he believed to have resolved it satisfactorily by his previous explanations; hence he would be grateful if the ambassador could enlighten him about the reasons that had caused the present state of affairs.

Count Schulenburg, who was an honest and open man, was put into an unhappy and embarrassing situation by the question. He could only reply that he had no information whatsoever that might throw a light on the matter. But Molotov was not satisfied, and he continued to wonder whether there was not something to the rumors. He had received news, he said, that not only all German business people had departed from the Soviet Union, but that the dependent women and children of the embassy, too, had left the country. The ambassador could not conceal the embarrassment into which Molotov's remark had placed him. He tried to justify the departures by saying that they were only the customary vacation trips to Germany

which were a natural consequence of the rigors of the Moscow climate. He also alluded to the fact that "not *all* women" had left Moscow, since my wife was still in town. Thereupon Molotov gave up his efforts with a resigned shrug of his shoulders. At the moment none of us knew that within another six hours we would stand before a *fait accompli.*

On June 22nd, at three o'clock in the morning, a telegram was received from Berlin in which the ambassador was ordered to go to Molotov at once and give him the following declaration: Soviet troop concentrations near the German border have reached dimensions which the German government feels it cannot tolerate. It has therefore decided to take appropriate counter-measures. The telegram concluded with the order to let no further discussions with Molotov develop.

Shortly after four in the morning we were once more entering the Kremlin, where Molotov received us at once. He wore a tired and worn-out expression. After the ambassador delivered his message, there were several seconds of deep silence. Molotov was visibly struggling with deep inner excitement. Then he asked: "Is this supposed to be a declaration of war?" The ambassador reacted in silence with a gesture characteristic of him, that of drawing up his shoulders and making a helpless motion with his arms. Then Molotov said, with slightly raised voice, that the message he had just been given could not, of course, mean anything but a declaration of war, since German troops had already crossed the Soviet border, and Soviet cities, like Odessa, Kiev, and Minsk, had been bombarded by German airplanes for an hour and a half. And then Molotov gave free reign to his indignation. He called the German action a breach of confidence unprecedented in history. Germany without any reason had attacked a country with which it had concluded a pact of non-aggression and friendship. The reason given by Germany was an empty pretext, since it was sheer nonsense to speak of Soviet troop concentrations at the German border. If any Soviet troops were there, it was for the purpose of the usual summer maneuvers. If the German government thought it necessary to take offense, then a note to the Soviet government would have sufficed to cause it to withdraw its troops. Instead, the German government was unleashing a war with all its consequences. "Surely we have not deserved that." With these words Molotov closed his declaration.

The ambassador replied that he could add nothing to what he had just said at the order of his government. He only wished to add the request that the members of the embassy be allowed to leave the Soviet Union in conformity with the rules of international law. Molotov tersely replied that the German Embassy would be treated strictly on the basis of reciprocity. With this we took leave of him in silence, but with the customary handshake.

As we drove out of the Kremlin, we met a number of cars in which high-ranking generals could be recognized. One proof that the German attack in the early morning of June 22nd came as a complete surprise was the fact, established later, that on that Sunday morning a number of leading military personalities were not available at once because they were spending the week end outside Moscow in their *dachas*.

In the evening of June 22nd the NKVD requested all members of the German Embassy to leave their private residences and to assemble in the embassy chancellery. Since our party contained well over a hundred persons, the building was far too small for us. I had to negotiate for a very long time with the Soviet officials in charge until some of us were permitted to move to another building belonging to the embassy. On June 24th we were all taken to Kostroma-on-Volga where we were billeted in a workers' rest home for five days. Then we were taken clear across Russia to Leninakan, near the Armenian-Turkish border, and kept there while the exact procedure for the exchange of personnel was being worked out by the protecting powers and Turkey, the country of transit.

Before our detention I had twelve or fourteen hours during which I still had occasion to talk with a few Russians. In these conversations my partners unanimously expressed their conviction that the Soviet government must have provoked the German action by some gross mistake. They could not otherwise explain the German attack, after the Soviet government had asserted to the last moment that the relation between Germany and the Soviet Union continued to be friendly, and that Germany was correctly fulfilling all its treaty obligations. Thus the population was not at first ready to pin the blame for the war on the Germans. This was also shown during the eight-day trip to Leninakan. The stations where our transport stopped were crowded with people. The windows of the train were open, because of the summer temperature, so that there could be no doubt as to the

identity of the passengers. None the less, during the whole trip I heard not a single unfriendly word and saw not a single unfriendly gesture. The people who looked at us seemed perturbed, puzzled, and embarrassed, as if they were searching in vain for an answer to the question of who really was to blame for the catastrophe. The lack of the slightest psychological preparation of the Russian people for the possibility of a war with Germany was one of the reasons for the lack of fighting spirit shown by the Red Army and the people in the first stage of the war.

I never worried about the treatment which the Soviet government would give the German Embassy, for I knew that about three times as many Soviet citizens were in Germany at that time as there were Germans in the Soviet Union. Among the Soviet citizens were many Soviet engineers and other technical experts who were in Germany as receiving officers, and the Soviet government could not be anything but very eager to have them return to the Soviet Union.

The trip from Kostroma to Leninakan was much less tiring than the subsequent stay at the border, where the train stood in the burning sun for seven days, and the sanitary conditions were so bad that the majority of the passengers were attacked by intestinal infections. Meanwhile, the Soviet citizens from Germany traveled through Bulgaria and arrived at the other end of Turkey, at Svilengrad. When this group crossed into Turkey, on July 13, 1941, our transport was permitted to leave the Soviet Union.

After our return to Germany I became a member of a small group of experts on Russia headed by the former ambassador, the so-called *Russland-Gremium,* which was made part of von Ribbentrop's immediate advisory staff. It must be realized that the Moscow negotiations of 1939 had been the high point of von Ribbentrop's career; and since I, as a competent interpreter, had done my share to make the meetings a success, my person became an integral part of the foreign minister's Moscow memories.[14] Thus, having me in his entourage offered him the opportunity to recapture something of his

---

[14] Hitler, too, seemed to have been impressed with my services during Molotov's stay in Berlin. Late in 1943, von Ribbentrop took me with him to the railroad station where Mussolini was to arrive having been liberated from captivity. Before the train rolled in, Hitler strutted in front of the assembled dignitaries and suddenly stopped to speak to me. "Well, Hilger, you don't have much of a chance to use your Russian these days, do you?" he said. "Yes," I replied, "it's a great pity." Hitler gave me a startled glance and turned away.

moments of glory. Besides, he never ceased dreaming about another chance to talk with Stalin. And, being basically ignorant and hardly capable of independent thought, he constantly surrounded himself with experts and idea-men whose brains he could pick whenever it suited his whim. He seemed to think that I would be indispensable for him should any future dealings with the Soviet government materialize. In the meantime, he kept asking me the most inconsequential and disconnected questions about Russia and her rulers, showing me by this that he often thought about them.

Working in the *Russland-Gremium,* I spent the war years in Berlin watching with dismay and horror the muddle of German occupation policies in the conquered territories of the East. The conflict of policies, the bitter struggles over jurisdiction fought by the highest leaders around Hitler, and the Führer's own ruthless policy of exploitation, destruction, and colonization are too long and complicated a story for this book. Suffice it to say that German rule in the occupied territories succeeded in a very short time in alienating a population many of whom had greeted Hitler's armies as liberators from Soviet terror.[15]

I had never believed that Russia could be defeated, hence I had always considered a war a disaster for Germany. Now my apprehensions turned into more concrete visions of utter defeat and destruction owing to our own mistakes. It was dangerous to have such thoughts; it was even more dangerous to express them. On January 30, 1942, I handed the foreign minister a memorandum in which I maintained that German occupation policies and the treatment of Soviet prisoners of war must be changed fundamentally if disastrous results were to be avoided. Von Ribbentrop read it and completely lost his temper. "What do you think you are doing?" he screamed at me. "If the Führer finds out what you wrote in this memorandum he'll have you shot at once. And rightly so. You should have gone to a concentration camp long ago, anyway." Count Schulenburg, who witnessed the outburst in silence, later apologized to me. "What could I have done?" he said. "If I had interfered he would have gone even madder, and it would not have done any good at all."

As the Allied and Soviet armies closed in on Germany, von Ribben-

---

[15] Many Ukrainians, even those who had openly welcomed the German Army, were now saying, "If we are to be governed by scoundrels, then we prefer our own, whose language we understand at least."

trop's moves and thoughts betrayed greater and greater hopelessness. As late as March, 1945, he seriously suggested that I go to Stockholm and try to get in touch with the Soviet Mission there in order to sound them out about a possible separate peace. It was with great difficulty that I talked him out of his wild scheme. Early in April he called me to his bedside one day. "Hilger," he said, "I want to ask you something, and I want you to be perfectly honest with me in answering. Do you think Stalin will ever be ready to negotiate with us again?"

"Herr Reichsminister," I replied, "I don't know whether you really want me to answer you; because, if I were to tell you what I honestly think, you won't like the answer at all. As a matter of fact, you might become quite upset." He brushed my reply aside with some impatience.

"I have always wanted you to be perfectly frank with me," he sputtered in an attempted show of righteous indignation.

"All right," I said, "since you insist, here is my reply: As long as Germany is ruled by the present government, there is not the slightest chance that Stalin will even think of negotiating with it again."

My remarks seemed more than the foreign minister was ready to swallow. His face flushed, his eyes popped, and he seemed to choke on the words he wanted to say. At that moment his wife stuck her head in at the door. "Get up, Joachim," she called, "and down to the shelter with you. Mass air attack coming over Berlin."

That was the last I ever saw of von Ribbentrop. A few days later, on April 14th, the remainder of the Foreign Office staff still in Berlin was evacuated to a place near Salzburg, which it took us three days to reach. There we spent another two and a half weeks in enforced idleness, most of the time following the collapse of Germany over the radio. On May 5, 1945, units of the United States Army reached our place. The inevitable end had become living reality for me.

XI CONCLUSION

Somewhere along the Georgian Military Highway, which begins in the European part of Russia, crosses the high mountains of the Caucasus, and leads into Transcaucasia, there is a place where a huge rock juts out of the mighty mountain range along the road and hangs over the highway in such a threatening manner that it gives the impression that it may tumble down at any moment and bury the hapless passerby beneath its weight. For that reason the population has given the rock the name *"Pronesi, Gospodi!"* which, translated freely, means, "Good Lord, please let me get out from under this thing!"

Today the rock is still in the same position in which it was one hundred and fifty years ago, when the tsarist government began constructing the road. It is propped up and made safe by artificial supports, but it has never been blasted away.

I have traveled down the Georgian Highway quite a few times, and whenever I passed by the rock I too would look at it with the same sense of apprehension. And every time the feeling of dread came over me, I was reminded of the very similar anxiety which was part of the traditional attitude of the German people toward its great neighbor to the east. Even at earlier times, when the very best relationship prevailed between the two countries, and when no insuperable ideological conflict made their collaboration difficult, even then Germany was never free from the dread of the colossus in the east, whose impenetrable political plans and intentions she always suspected.

The Germany of William II could have found the proper political means by which to secure herself against Russian surprise moves. Instead, she chose war; and both states were ruined by it.

After the War of 1914–1918, a German republic and a Communist Russia found each other under completely different circumstances. Rapallo, the "agreement between a blind man and a lame man," was

a natural solution which corresponded to the vital interests of both powers without being directed against third states, or without harming them.

In the two decades following Rapallo, it was shown that collaboration with the Soviet Union was a painful job, full of mishaps and disappointments, but a paying proposition nevertheless, which rested on the principle, *Do ut des*. Neither of the two states felt itself to be stronger than the other; neither therefore dared force its will upon the other. And so German-Soviet relations, as they developed in the years from 1922 to 1941, gave proof that a bourgeois state can maintain relations with the Soviet Union which are useful and not immediately dangerous as long as it is at least as strong, or at most as weak, as the Soviet Union.

Once, however, the equilibrium of forces is disturbed or shifted through domestic or international developments, the other partner will constantly be aware that he is helplessly exposed to the pressure and blackmail methods of Soviet foreign policy. The only thing that can save a weak state in this situation—apart from its geographical position—is an alliance with stronger states which are willing and able to resist the expansionist aspirations, "imperialistic" or ideological, of the Soviet Union. The only alternative is the course taken by the satellites, whose fate has been sealed, for a long time if not forever, by their alliance with the USSR.

World War II has wrought fundamental changes in the power pattern of Europe. Foremost among them are the destruction of Hitler's "Greater Germany" and the emergence of the Soviet Union as the second greatest power in the world. With these changes the possibilities open to Germany at the time of Rapallo have disappeared, and only two alternatives are open to her. She can either seek security against the Soviet threat by an alliance with the Western powers, or else she can ally herself with the Soviet Union. But in the event of the latter, Western Germany, and probably the rest of Europe, would doubtless share the fate of the East European satellites.

INDEX

NEE

POLITICS AND IDEOLOGY
IN THE AGE OF THE CIVIL WAR

--·✦{ O N E }✦·--

Introduction

For historians of the American Civil War, the 1970s was a troubled decade. The success of *Roots* on television and in bookstores appeared to reflect an enormous popular interest in slavery and emancipation, the issues central to the sectional conflict. But within the discipline of history itself, the situation could not have been bleaker. At a time when the experiences of "ordinary" people became the central concern of historians, the fundamental reference point in the lives of nineteenth-century Americans was all but ignored.

Traditionally, the Civil War framed and provided unity to the inquiries of American historians. Works on slavery and abolition, on intellectual life and economic change, were pursued not simply for their own sake, but to shed light on the causes and consequences of the Civil War. To some extent, these subjects remained vital concerns in the 1970s; indeed, the outstanding body of new literature on the American past probably was that reexamining the South's "peculiar institution." But with few exceptions, it was the social or cultural aspects of slavery which now commanded attention, rather than slavery as a source of political and economic power and a fundamental cause of the Civil War.

The decline of Civil War studies was to some extent self-inflicted, for the subject had by the end of the 1950s reached a conceptual impasse. Discussions of the war's causes had too often resolved into a fruitless metaphysical debate over the problem of inevitability, while their single-minded focus on the sectional conflict had led nineteenth-century historians to ignore other aspects of the period—immigration and the history of women, for example—that bore little apparent relation to the slavery controversy. Those who viewed the Civil War as a great divide in American life often disregarded social and intellectual continuities spanning the decades of the nineteenth century. The study of the Civil War, in other words, was in need of a vigorous infusion of new ideas and approaches. Instead, the Civil War, once at the center stage of historical debate, had, by the end of the 1970s, been relegated to the wings. By 1980, a 500-page volume on historical writing in this country could leave this central concern of earlier generations of historians virtually unmentioned.[1]

The predicament of Civil War historians was more than a reflection of the overall crisis of academic history in the 1970s. It derived from an unprecedented redefinition of historical studies in which a traditional emphasis on institutions and events, politics and ideas, was superseded by a host of "social" concerns. To a large extent, this transformation was a by-product of the ferment of the sixties. Blacks—followed by women, "ethnics," and other groups—looked to history for a "usable past," while traditional political narratives—especially those of the then-dominant "consensus" school—proved unable to explain the reemergence of deep divisions in American life. At the same time, a new technology—the computer—made possible the analysis of vast amounts of quantitative data concerning those Americans who had not produced letters, diaries, speeches, and the other sources historians were accustomed to examining.

New methods, such as quantification, oral history, and demography, and a new purpose—recovering the history of ordinary Americans rather than the elite—defined what came to be called the "new social history." In place of conventional narratives of political and intellectual development, American historians now produced an abundance of works in the various subfields of social investigation: family history, ethnic history, labor history, the histories of sexuality, criminality, and childhood. There were community studies, urban studies, and social mobility studies. Many of these works were inspired not by traditional historical models, but by theories borrowed from allied social sciences. Frequently, they appeared in new journals devoted exclusively to the subdisciplines of social history. As historians intruded into the intimate lives of past generations of Americans, public events and institutions receded into the background. No alternative theory of politics emerged from the ferment within and outside the historical profession. If "the personal is political" was a slogan of the 1960s, "the historical is personal" described much of the historical writing of the seventies.

What was new about the new social history was not simply its innovations in methodology and subject matter, but its high standing within the profession and the insistence with which some of its practitioners pressed its claims. Until the 1960s, social history had been a catch-all for those subjects passed over by more conventional approaches. Often, it was yoked together with intellectual history in the single college course offering departing from a focus on politics. Then, in the seventies, political historians suddenly felt themselves beleaguered, their narrative works never referred to without the mildly patronizing adjective "traditional," their sources deprecated as "impressionistic," their concern with national public issues branded "elitist."

That the new history has broadened—indeed, revolutionized—our understanding of the American experience cannot be doubted. It has delved into realms hitherto all but ignored, and forced all historians to adopt a more critical posture toward their evidence, calling into question broad generalizations based on fragmentary data or the experience of a few eminent individuals. It has reintroduced a sense of complexity to the study of the American past, and destroyed the old "presidential synthesis" in which historical study was organized around the terms of office of elected leaders. American history has been revitalized by an infusion of the new perspectives of blacks, women, labor, and others.

Somehow, however, these advances did not add up to a coherent new vision of the American past. Indeed, what was most striking in the 1970s was the fragmentation of historical scholarship and the larger notion of social process. The broadening of historians' concerns went hand in hand with a narrowing of their vision and the result was often specialized, even trivial, inquiries. American society was divided and subdivided so completely that the ideal of re-creating history as a lived experience seemed more remote than ever. A few books did appear—one thinks of Anthony Wallace's reconstruction of the experience of Rockdale, Pennsylvania, during the industrial revolution—which transcended divisions between the public and private, political and social realms of experience, and saw social classes not in isolation from one another but enmeshed in a complex series of interrelationships. But E. J. Hobsbawm's call, at the beginning of the decade, for a shift from social history to a "history of society" remained largely unfulfilled.[2] One reason for the retreat from Civil War studies may be that events like the Civil War, which affected every facet of American life, are unintelligible if divided into the various subcategories of contemporary historical inquiry.

Older coherent visions of American history, ranging from Turner's frontier thesis to the consensus view of the 1950s, have been shattered, but no new synthesis has emerged to fill the void. Indeed, only a small number of historians continue to believe that a comprehensive view of the American past is possible. Those who do have generally looked beyond American historiography to European Marxist and *Annales* models for an integrated vision. (On the other hand, modernization theory, a home-grown approach, seems, after a brief vogue, to have fallen by the wayside, a victim of its own vagueness and determinism.) Most American historians, however, continue to mistrust theoretical formulations. For many, the need to integrate so many different "histories" has led to a retreat from notions of historical causation altogether. In her study of recent American history textbooks, Frances FitzGerald noted a pervasive confusion as to the causes of historical events. "Problems" appeared and disappeared, events simply happened, with no sense of systematic relationships or underlying causes. Moreover, individual actors seemed to have no discernible effect on the historical process. "There are no human agencies left," wrote FitzGerald, "only abstractions and passive verbs."[3]

The flight from theories of causation underscores the deep strain of empiricism so rooted in American culture, and reinforced among historians by the current vogue of quantification. Indispensable as a tool of historical inquiry, quantitative analysis of statistical data often gained the upper hand in the 1970s, determining the questions to be asked and inspiring an obsession with method at the expense of any larger purpose. Equally significant was the authority of the French *Annales* school. Its emphasis on persistent inherited structures as forces determining historical development rendered the actions of individual men and women all but superfluous.

The influence of the *Annales* school in shaping the agenda of social history could also be detected in the precipitous decline of politics as a subject of inquiry (although this was less pronounced in twentieth-century studies, where the rise of the Presidency remained a central concern and manuscript census data, the raw material of the social historian, are as yet unavailable). When dealt with at all, politics was reduced to a branch of social history—as in the "new political history," which pointedly ignored national issues and explained voting behavior on the basis of ethnocultural affiliations. The British historian G. M. Trevelyan once described social history as "history with the politics left out." Such a definition could hardly encompass the diverse approaches and findings, to say nothing of intentions, of social historians in the 1970s. But it remained apropos in one respect: politics was, indeed, excluded.

So, too, was the history of ideas, especially political ideas. Intellectual history has always occupied a curious status in a society skeptical of non-utilitarian motives and general theorizing. Even in the 1950s and early 1960s, the heyday of intellectual history, many of the genre's most prominent practitioners devoted their works to chronicling the "absence" of ideas in America. Daniel Boorstin celebrated the triumph of indigenous pragmatism over imported theory; Louis Hartz lamented that Americans had never produced an original political idea worthy of note; and Richard Hofstadter perceived anti-intellectualism as a far more potent force than the life of the mind in American culture. In the 1960s, pathbreaking works on American political ideology did appear, especially for the period of the American Revolution. But the dominance of social history in the seventies led to a renewed quest for the social roots of ideas. A salutary counterpoint to an earlier search for a disembodied national character, this strategy was extremely vulnerable to intellectual reductionism. Rather than taking ideas seriously in their own right, many historians sought to study them as either direct reflections of underlying social processes or as inferences from statistically ascertainable data about human behavior. Customs, values, and psychological motivations took the place of ideas in many accounts. Ironically, as a new generation of American Marxist historians was abandoning the mechanistic base-superstructure model for a more dialectical view of the relationship between ideas and social reality, many social historians, when they considered ideas at all, adopted this outmoded framework.

The divorce of social from political and intellectual history had unfortunate consequences for all concerned. For one thing, it remained impossible to fit the findings of social historians into the traditional narrative framework of American history. The failure to consider politics—by which I mean not simply voting returns and legislative alignments, but the ways in which power in civil society is ordered and exercised—and the retreat from the analysis of political ideas deprived social history of the larger context which alone could have imparted to it a broader meaning.

In a sense, the foregoing is by way of explaining why the major concerns of the essays in this collection are subjects eclipsed in recent years: politics and ideology. As my former teacher Richard Hofstadter observed, the best argument for such collections may be the simple one of accessibility—drawing together articles originally published in obscure corners of the academic world into a more readily available and permanent format. But, he went on, such a book also possesses value in illustrating a common cast of mind, for whatever their subject matter, the essays "are at least in their style of thought and their concerns, unified by some underlying intellectual intent . . . a set of related concerns and methods."[4] These essays, written between 1965 and 1980, reflect not simply a common interest in the causes and consequences of the American Civil War, but my ongoing desire to reintegrate the political, social, and intellectual history of that period. Obviously, no single essay or group of essays can fully do this. But I do believe the essays at least illustrate the value of bringing to bear on one another, and on the overall historical process, the insights of the now fragmented disciplines of social, political, economic, and intellectual history. The concerns of the "new" histories have much to contribute to an understanding of American political development in these years. One theme running through several of these essays, in fact, is the interplay of race, class, and political ideology in a society undergoing both a sectional confrontation and an economic revolution. My argument, however, is that the Civil War era cannot be understood unless the way in which power was wielded and conceptualized stands at the forefront of analysis.

American political culture, until well into the nineteenth century, was framed by an ideology of republicanism, a lasting
legacy of the American Revolution. The present dissolution of
the links between the distinctive realms of public and private
experience would have been inconceivable to men and women
reared in the republican tradition, for that ideology was
grounded in a belief in the interdependence of polity, economy, and society. Republican government, it was thought,
could exist only with a certain type of citizenry (virtuous and
independent) and a certain kind of society (one characterized
by economic equality). Several of the following essays examine
a central theme of nineteenth-century development: the contradiction between republican thought and the expansion of
capitalist production and market relations which transformed
every aspect of American life. The recurrent tension between
"virtue and commerce," as J. G. A. Pocock has put it,[5] bore a
direct relation to the political debate over slavery and emancipation, posing ideological problems for abolitionism (essay
III), and shaping debates over land and labor after the Civil
War (essays V–VII). The republican concept of economic independence as the key to personal freedom informed a radical
tradition which stretched from Tom Paine and other ideologues of the American Revolution through the labor movement of the 1830s, to the opposition to industrial capitalism
expressed so violently during the Gilded Age. The confrontation between this tradition and the complex, interrelated issues
of race, class, and ethnicity in American life, and the forging of
a comprehensive definition of freedom in a society profoundly
divided by slavery, are themes of the essays in this collection.
Several trace the historical evolution of the "free labor" ideology which dominated northern society in the Civil War era, a
particular expression of republican thought which has been a
continuing concern of mine.

Over and above these themes, however, these essays reassert
the centrality of the Civil War to the experience of nineteenth-
century Americans. For at least half the century, the sectional

conflict and its aftermath, or, to put it another way, the institution of slavery and its implications and legacy, dominated
American life. This does not mean that it affected every American in the same way, or that issues like immigration and the
family were unimportant. It simply means that it increasingly
became impossible to think seriously about American society
without somehow coming to grips with slavery and the Union.
From the standpoint of physical destruction, loss of life, structural changes in the economy, the introduction of new ideas,
and the diffusion of enduring sectional passions, the Civil War
shaped and altered the lives and consciousness of several historical generations. The sectional controversy spawned the
greatest reform movement of the nineteenth century, anti-
slavery, whose legacy affected virtually every subsequent effort
to recast American society, even as its triumph—emancipation—strengthened a middle-class culture which saw the end of
slavery as a preeminent vindication of its own values. The
equivocal legacy of abolition—a theme of several essays—
reflects the larger ambiguity of the Civil War and its heritage;
the war stood as both a "new birth of freedom" and the
wellspring of much that was wrong in Gilded Age America.
The "massive, inconvenient reality" of the Civil War, Hofstadter once wrote, posed a serious challenge for earlier consensus historians, for it belied their vision of America as "a land
without serious disagreements over fundamental issues."[6] It
remains equally true today that a satisfactory portrait of the
American experience cannot emerge from an attempt to read
the Civil War out of American history.

The age of the Civil War, finally, is the period of our past
most relevant to the contemporary concerns of American society. I use the much-abused word "relevant" advisedly. I do not
mean by it a one-to-one correlation between our time and the
past, nor do I suggest that direct answers to the issues of the
present will emerge from the study of the nineteenth century. I
mean simply that it is possible to connect history with the
present without succumbing to present-mindedness, to respect

the integrity, the pastness, of the past while confronting a set of issues as yet unresolved in American life.

The Civil War, after all, raised the decisive questions of our national existence—war and peace, relations between the states and the federal government, the balance between force and consent in generating obedience to authority, and, of course, the pervasive problem of race which still bedevils American society, challenging it to live up to its lofty professed ideals. The themes of race and class, the debates over the meaning of freedom and disadvantage in America, remain controversial. The failure of the first Reconstruction on the rock of intractable racial prejudices and economic inequalities has its parallel in the dissipating of the second in the face of analogous barriers.

Like any political crisis, the Civil War raised timeless moral questions concerning the uses of power and the consequences of human choices—questions of "why," rather than "how," which gave traditional historical studies much of their vitality and which never appear in "social science" history. History teaches few easy lessons, but it should assist us to think creatively about ourselves. By looking again at the age of the Civil War, we may gain insight into the choices facing our own time, and enable history to become, in place of a collection of assorted facts, once again a mode of collective self-education.

ORIGINS
OF THE
CIVIL WAR

The Causes
of the
American Civil War:
Recent Interpretations
and New Directions

In 1960, as Americans prepared to observe the centennial of the Civil War, one of the foremost historians of that conflict published a brief article entitled, "American Historians and the Causes of the Civil War."[1] Most readers probably expected another survey of the changing course of Civil War interpretation. Instead the author announced that as a subject of serious historical analysis, Civil War causation was "dead."

Looking back over the decade and a half since David Donald wrote, it would appear that he somewhat exaggerated the death of this field of inquiry. In the 1950s, historians were concerned with investigating periods of consensus in America's past. But in the 1960s, as the issues of race and war came to the forefront of national life, earlier times of civil strife in American history attracted renewed attention.

The 1960s, for example, witnessed a renascence of the study of slavery. It is now no longer possible to view the peculiar institution as some kind of accident or aberration, existing out-

Originally published in *Civil War History*, XX (Sept. 1974), 197–214. Reprinted by permission of Kent State University Press.

side the mainstream of national development. Rather, slavery
was absolutely central to the American experience, intimately
bound up with the settlement of the western hemisphere, the
American Revolution, and industrial expansion. It was what
defined the Old South and drew southern society along a path
of development which set it increasingly apart from the rest of
the nation.[2]

At the same time, a striking reversal of interpretations of the
abolitionists took place.[3] In fact, there was a paradoxical double
reversal. On the one hand the abolitionists, previously castigated as fanatics and agitators, suddenly emerged as the conscience of a sinning nation—much as the Garrisons and Welds
had portrayed themselves a century earlier. But simultaneously, a number of writers argued that not only were the
friends of the slave not immune from racism, but, far from
being truly "radical," they seemed to accept the middle-class
values of northern society.[4]

The flood of studies of slavery, abolitionism, and the race
issue does not seem, however, to have brought historians much
closer to a generally accepted interpretation of the coming of
the Civil War than they were in 1960. As the late David Potter
pointed out, the irony is that disagreements of interpretation
persist in the face of a greatly increased body of historical
knowledge.[5] This is partially because the Civil War raised so
many still unresolved issues. Perhaps, however, there is another
reason. Historians' methodologies and value judgments have
changed considerably, but the questions historians have asked
of their data have remained relatively static. Like the debate
over slavery before the appearance of Stanley Elkins's pathbreaking study in 1959, discussion of the causes of the Civil
War continues to be locked into an antiquated interpretive
framework. Historians of the Civil War era seem to be in
greater need of new models of interpretation and new questions than an additional accumulation of data.

A number of works have appeared, however, in the past fifteen years which have attempted to develop entirely new ways

of looking at ante-bellum America and the origins of the Civil War. One of the most striking developments of these years has been the emergence of the "new political historians," who have attempted to recast our understanding of ante-bellum political alignments. They have deemphasized "national" issues like slavery and the tariff, and substituted ethnocultural conflicts between Protestants and Catholics, or between pietistic and ritualistic religious groups, as the major determinants of voting behavior. These works have broadened our understanding of ante-bellum political culture, and demonstrated the inevitable failure of any "monistic interpretation" of political conflict. And they should force historians to abandon whatever economic determinism still persists in the writing of political history. Perhaps most important, they have demonstrated the virtues of viewing voters not as isolated individuals, but as men and women embedded in a complex network of social and cultural relationships.[6]

The "new political history" involves both a new methodology—the statistical analysis of quantitative data—and a distinctive model of historical explanation. The broadening of the methodological tools available to historians can only be applauded, although some writers may at times be guilty of mistaking correlations for causes, and inducing the behavior of individuals from aggregate data. It sometimes seems that the very sophistication of the new methodology has unfortunate effects on these writers' approach to historical data. Not only is undue weight often assigned to historical variables such as ethnicity for which quantifiable data happens to be available, but the definition of basic concepts is reduced to the most easily quantifiable elements. Thus, class is measured by data on occupation and assessed property holdings, culture is reduced to a mixture of ethnicity and religion, and religion is measured purely by church affiliation.[7]

It is in the realm of explanation, and as a contribution to our understanding of the coming of the Civil War, that the "new political history" is most open to criticism. First, while rightly rejecting the economic determinism of progressive historians, the new political historians seem to be in danger of substituting a religious or cultural determinism of their own. Indeed, the interpretive framework of the new school is strikingly similar to that of the progressives. Both pose a sharp distinction between "real" and "unreal" issues, both put thousands of persons in the quasi-conspiratorial position of concealing their real intentions, and both take an extremely limited view of individual motivation. For the "economic man" of the progressives, the new political history has substituted an equally one-dimensional "religious man."

Most important, this new mode of explanation is fundamentally ahistorical; its key variables exist independently of historical context. Religion and ethnicity are generally treated as "unidimensional concepts, without reference to time, place, rate of acculturation, or individual personality." The point is that all historical variables are interrelated, and change as society develops. To take one key variable—religious belief in this case, or an oversimplified version of class for the progressives—and abstract it from its social context and the processes of historical change, is to distort and fracture historical reality.[8]

The arguments of the "new political historians" have profound implications for the question of Civil War causation. Their basic outlook was announced in 1964, in Joel Silbey's influential article, "The Civil War Synthesis," which chided historians for writing the history of the 1850s solely from the vantage point of the slavery issue, ignoring questions, like nativism, which seemed to have little to do with the coming of war. Subsequent writers have agreed with Silbey that a split existed between northern political elites and the mass of voters. The former were, for a variety of reasons, increasingly anti-southern, the latter were "basically unmoved" by the issues of slavery and sectional conflict and were more concerned with so-called "cultural" questions like immigration and temperance.[9]

While often criticizing traditional historians for using such "elite sources" as newspapers, speeches, and letters, this new interpretation of ante-bellum politics has its own elitist bias. It assumes that "large portions of the electorate do not have meaningful beliefs,"[10] that only elites are truly issue-oriented. This kind of reasoning, however, can never illuminate the relationship between political leaders and voters in a democratic political culture. Nor can it explain under what circumstances local issues will dominate politics and when national issues will come to the fore, or tell us why Republicans in the late 1850s were constantly trying to play down the issues of temperance and nativism which had supposedly created their party in the first place.[11] The view of the Republican party as the political expression of pietistic Protestantism can hardly encompass a figure like Lincoln, who was southern-born and whose religious beliefs were akin to the deism of that infidel Thomas Paine, whom Lincoln greatly admired.[12] According to the aggregate data, Lincoln should have been a pro-slavery Democrat. At best, he was a historical accident, an ecological fallacy.

But what of the Civil War? Supposedly, when the scientist Laplace described the Newtonian system to Napoleon, the emperor asked, "But where is God in your system?" To which Laplace replied, "I have no need for that hypothesis." Similarly, the "system" of the new political history has no need for the Civil War. Unfortunately, the Civil War did take place. But the new interpretation leaves a yawning gap between political processes and the outbreak of war. Recently, Lee Benson has tried to bridge this gap by arguing that a "small group" of southern conspirators, taking advantage of the "irresponsible character" of the political system, caused the war.[13] To pursue our Enlightenment analogy and paraphrase Voltaire, if Benson's explanation did not exist, we would have to invent it. If only elites cared about the slavery question, we are logically driven back to a neo-revisionist conspiracy theory of the coming of the war. One does not have to assume that great events always have great causes to believe that conspiracy theories are rarely satisfactory as historical explanations.

A second school of historical writing places the coming of the

Civil War within the process political scientists have termed "modernization." This is as yet an imprecisely defined concept, but it involves such basic changes in the structure of a society as rapid economic development, urbanization, industrialization, the creation of an integrated national economic and political structure, and generally, the spread of market-oriented capitalist economic relations and of mental attitudes viewing continuous social change as natural and desirable.[14] Within this context, the Civil War becomes the process by which the "modern" or "modernizing" North integrated the "pre-modern" South into a national political and economic system. As Raimondo Luraghi explains, "So, in the nineteenth century, as the industrial revolution was expanding on a worldwide scale, the days of wrath were coming for a series of agrarian, pre-capitalistic, 'backward' societies throughout the world, from the Italian and American South down to India."[15] Aside from Luraghi's work, the modernization framework has not yet been systematically applied to the coming of the Civil War, although in many respects it is compatible with the work of Eugene Genovese on the South and with my own discussion of the Republican party in the 1850s.[16]

As Robert Kelley demonstrates, the ethnocultural and modernization interpretations are not necessarily incompatible. In his book, *The Transatlantic Persuasion,* the Republicans in America and the Tories in England become the nationalists, homogenizers, and cosmopolitans. Intolerant of any social diversity within their societies, they attempted to impose their values on dissident groups—temperance legislation on the Irish immigrants, anti-slavery on the South—while the party of the regional and ethnic minorities (Democrats in America, Liberals in Britain), called for cultural pluralism and local autonomy.[17]

The problem with this analysis is that it views the sectional conflict primarily as a struggle between local and national institutions. It is significant that in Kelley's stimulating book, the institution of slavery is conspicuous by its absence. But slavery was what made the South distinct—it was central to the moral, economic, and political antagonisms between the sections.

Nonetheless, this framework has much to offer toward an understanding of the politics of the 1850s. Lincoln's House Divided speech, as J. R. Pole has written, can be viewed as the outlook of a man "who had grasped the essentials of the process of nationalisation that was overtaking the main institutions of American life." Conversely, Stephen A. Douglas's objection to what he termed Lincoln's belief that "there must be uniformity in the local laws and domestic institutions of each and all states of the Union," and his plea for recognition of "diversity and dissimilarity" within the nation, can be read as the cry of all the out-groups and backward areas confronted by the process of modernization in the nineteenth century.[18]

Having said this, I hasten to add that there are certain problems in applying this model to the causes of the Civil War. First, there is the imprecision of the term "modernization." At times, it seems to be used more or less interchangeably with "industrialization," and, in effect, becomes a restatement of the Beardian view of the Civil War as a conflict between industrial and agrarian economies. In this form, the model exaggerates the extent to which northern society itself was as yet fully modernized in the ante-bellum years. Historians, indeed, have not yet produced the studies which will enable us to state with assurance what the class structure of the North was, or how far industrialization had advanced by 1860. Before we can assess the effects of modernization, in other words, we need to know exactly what kind of society was undergoing that process. Antebellum northern society may well have been "modern" in some respects. Certainly capitalist economic relations and democratic political procedures prevailed, and according to Richard Brown, the "modern personality" had been dominant since colonial days. But the economy was almost certainly pre-industrial, and the ideals of the yeoman farmer and independent artisan, their belief in the natural right of each individual to the fruits of his labor (which became in the hands of Lincoln so damning an indictment of slavery), still permeated society.[19]

Nevertheless, the modernization model does have two great virtues. First, it enables us to see that what happened in nineteenth-century America was not a unique or local occurrence, but a process which had deep affinities with events in many other areas of the world. Secondly, it demands that political historians place their work in the largest context of the development of American society, for, as Albert Soboul writes, "all studies of political history entail a study of social history."[20] To me, moreover, it suggests a framework for beginning to answer the crucial question raised by David Brion Davis in *The Problem of Slavery in Western Culture*. Why does slavery, which for centuries had been considered a normal part of the social order, suddenly come to be viewed by large numbers of men and women as a totally unacceptable form of labor and social organization? Why, that is, does an anti-slavery movement emerge?

To answer this question, we must place the Civil War in the context of the general abolition of unfree labor systems in the nineteenth century, from slavery in the western hemisphere, to serfdom in Russia and *robot* in the Austrian Empire. Within this context, we need to relate the emergence of the modern anti-slavery movement to two related processes—changes in attitudes toward labor and the condition of laboring classes,[21] and the enormous economic and social transformations of the nineteenth century. Of course, American anti-slavery thought did not emerge full-blown in the 1830s. As C. Vann Woodward has pointed out, patterns of derogatory sectional imagery stretch back into the colonial era. Many New England Federalists employed anti-southern and anti-slavery rhetoric highly suggestive of the Republican assaults of the 1850s. They not only condemned the three-fifths clause of the Constitution and southern domination of the national government, but spoke of the superiority of free labor, the economic stagnation of the South, and the differences in "manners, habits, customs, principles and ways of thinking" between the sections.[22]

The elements of an anti-slavery ideology, therefore, had long been present in America, but a coherent critique of slavery had not. Why could the Federalists not develop one? For one thing, until 1800 they had powerful allies in the South, and after then, the dream of a reunited and triumphant Federalist party never entirely disappeared. Moreover, as several recent writers have emphasized, the Federalist world view centered on a society of order, harmony, and organic unity, one composed of stable and distinctly separated ranks and orders.[23] It was not until this older organic conception of society broke down that a complete anti-slavery ideology could emerge.

We know of course that in the 1820s and 1830s this older vision was thoroughly disrupted, and replaced by one of a society of competing individuals, a vision more in keeping with the requirements of an expanding, market-oriented capitalist society. Why this ideological transformation occurred is not yet, in my opinion, entirely clear. The transportation revolution was a major determinant, but we know too little about the nature of economic change in the ante-bellum era to be able to place this ideological development in its proper social setting. We do know that the ideological transformation had profound effects on the nature of anti-slavery thought. As Rowland Berthoff has observed, "if classes supposedly did not exist, they could not be accepted as constituent institutions of American society; rank or degree was no longer an admissible principle for organizing or even thinking about the social order." That abolitionist thought was utterly individualistic and atomistic has by now become an axiom of historical writing. Historians as diverse in their ideological preconceptions as Stanley Elkins and William Appleman Williams severely chide the abolitionists for viewing slavery not as a functioning institution, embedded in a distinct society, but as a personal sin of the individual master against the individual slave.[24] But it may be that it was only when the ideas of an organic society, and the permanent subordination of any class of men, had been overthrown, that anti-slavery thought could develop in a consistent form. Only a movement that viewed society as a collection of individuals, that viewed freedom as the property of every man, that believed every individual had the right to seek advancement as a unit in competitive society, could condemn slavery as utterly and completely as, in their own ways, abolitionists and Republicans did.[25]

Anti-slavery thus fed on the anti-monopoly, anti-corporate, egalitarian ethos of Jacksonian America. At the same time, as a vision of labor, anti-slavery was curiously ambiguous. Anti-slavery men exalted "free labor," meaning labor working because of incentive instead of coercion, labor with education, skill, the desire for advancement, and also the freedom to move from job to job according to the changing demands of the marketplace.[26] On the other hand, many anti-slavery men were also opponents of union activity, and were closely involved in other reforms—such as the creation of prisons and asylums, temperance, and poor relief (with the ever-present distinction between the deserving and undeserving poor) which to a certain extent can be interpreted as attempts to transform the life style and work habits of labor in an industrializing society.

One could argue that the anti-slavery movement, by glorifying northern society and by isolating slavery as an unacceptable form of labor exploitation, while refusing to condemn the exploitative aspects of "free" labor relations, served to justify the emerging capitalist order of the North. In fact, it is possible that the growing ideological conflict between the sections had the effect of undermining a tradition of radical criticism within northern society.[27] Men like Horace Greeley, highly critical of certain aspects of their society in the 1840s, became more and more uncritical when faced with the need to defend the North against southern assaults. The choices for America came to be defined as free society versus slave society—the idea of alternatives within free society was increasingly lost sight of.[28]

To develop this point further, many anti-slavery men believed in an ideal of human character which emphasized an internalized self-discipline. They condemned slavery as a lack of control over one's own destiny and the fruits of one's labor, but defined freedom as more than a simple lack of restraint. The truly free man, in the eyes of ante-bellum reformers, was one who imposed restraints upon himself. This was also the ideal, as David Rothman shows, of the reformers who constructed the prisons and asylums of this era—to transform the human personality so that the poor, insane, and criminal would internalize a sense of discipline, order, and restraint.[29]

There are parallels between this aim and Lincoln's condemnation in his famous lyceum speech of 1838 of "the increasing disregard for law which pervades the country," of vigilanteeism, mob violence, and those who hoped for the "total annihilation of government." For Lincoln, law, order, and union, commonly accepted and internalized, allowed civilization and progress to exist in America, especially given the highly competitive nature of the society. Or, to quote Theodore Weld, "restraints are the web of civilized society, warp and woof." Of course, on one level, slavery, as some pro-slavery writers argued, solved the problem of disciplining the labor force, but the ideal of the reformers was a society of free (self-governing) individuals. Slavery may have been like an asylum or a school in some respects, but it lacked one essential element of those institutions—release, or graduation. Moreover, it allowed full rein to the very passions which so many northerners desired to see repressed—it encouraged greed, self-indulgence, and all sorts of illicit personal and sexual activities on the part of the masters. When Lincoln in 1861 declared, "plainly, the central idea of secession, is the essence of anarchy," he could have chosen no more damning description.[30]

Thus the anti-slavery movement exalted the character traits demanded by a "modernizing" society while it condemned an institution which impeded that "modernization." Interpreted in this way, the modernization thesis can assimilate some of the insights of the new political history. For example, the ethnoculturalists never deal directly with the relationship between ethnocultural identity and class relations in the setting of a modernizing society. We know how closely related certain ethnic and class patterns were—how, in urban areas, Irish immigrants were overwhelmingly lower-class unskilled laborers, and how, to quote Ronald Formisano, "prosperity and evangelical political character often went together." It is also well known that class and ethnic prejudices were inextricably linked in nativist attacks on Irish immigrants.[31]

If we do expand our notion of culture beyond a relatively narrow definition of ethnicity and religious belief, we may find that "pietists" were much more hospitable to the Protestant work ethic and the economic demands of a modernizing society than were "ritualists" and Catholic immigrants.[32] Is it possible that the resistance of the Irish to "Americanization," rather than simply a desire to maintain cultural identity, was the attempt of a pre-industrial people to resist the hegemony of a modernizing culture, with all that that implied for character structure, work patterns, and life styles? May we view the Democratic party as the representative of the great pre-modern cultures within American society—the white South and the Irish immigrants—and perhaps then better understand why the nativist image of the Irish and the anti-slavery critique of the southern slaveholder stressed the same "undesirable" traits of lack of economic enterprise and self-discipline, and the attack on the Slave Power and Catholic Church denounced corporate monoliths which restricted individual freedom? Was the northern Democratic machine at the local level attuned to the communal, traditionalist behavior of the peasant immigrants, while the intense individualism of the Republicans had little to offer them?

Before we attempt to locate the crusade against slavery within the social history of ante-bellum America, there is a more basic historical question to answer. We still do not understand the social composition of that movement. We do have information about the abolitionist leadership, but also disagreement as to whether abolitionists were a declining elite, using reform as an effort to regain a waning status,[33] or a rising group, challenging older elites, North and South, for social dominance. This latter would seem to be the implication of Leonard Richards's recent study of anti-abolitionist mobs, which concludes that in Utica and Cincinnati, the mobs were composed of members of the pre-industrial upper class of commercial and professional men, while abolitionist membership drew much more heavily on artisans, manufacturers, and tradesmen.[34] Generally, however, to quote David Brion Davis, "little is known of the rank and file members, to say nothing of the passive supporters, of a single reform movement."[35] Historians of reform over the past fifteen years have been much more successful in explicating ideologies than in giving us a clear picture of the movements' social roots.

Without such studies, we have been guilty of accepting an oversimplified version of reform, e.g., the temperance movement was an effort of middle-class Yankees to exert their cultural dominance over immigrant Catholics and the unruly poor. That for many supporters the movement did have his character cannot be doubted, but we need only to read Brian Harrison's study of the English temperance movement to see that our studies have been noticeably one dimensional. Harrison showed that temperance was a cross-class movement which had deep roots in the working class, appealing to aspirations for self-help and social betterment. It was not simply an attempt "to impose middle-class manners on the working class."[36] The same, I suspect, can be said for temperance in this country, and for other reforms, such as the movement for expanded public education, that have been interpreted through the eyes of their middle-class proponents. Historians have often ignored the very different aims of workingmen who supported these reforms. But at present, we know far too little of the extent to which workers, skilled or unskilled, were sympathetic to one phase or another of the anti-slavery movement, or whether anti-slavery workingmen viewed slavery differently than did its middle-class foes. Thus, while Garrison drew a sharp distinction between slavery and the northern system of free labor, how many workingmen were impressed by the *simi-larities* between the chattel slavery of the South and the "wage slavery" of the North?

Many labor spokesmen were initially hostile to the abolitionists precisely because they believed the Garrisons and Welds were diverting attention from the pressing social problems of the industrializing North. But in the late 1840s and 1850s many workingmen were attracted to free-soilism and the Republican party by the issues of land reform and opposition to the expansion of slavery.[37] To what extent did workingmen oppose the extension of slavery to preserve the safety-valve which, they believed, guaranteed the independence of the northern laborer, and prevented him from being subjected to the degrading discipline of the factory or from being permanently trapped in the status of wage earner? In other words, antislavery could have served as an ideological vehicle for both the proponents of modernization and for those whose objective was to preserve the pre-modern status of the independent artisan.

In a similar vein, many questions remain about the social history of the ante-bellum South. Several recent studies emphasize the "obsession" of the secessionist leadership with internal unity, their fear that slavery was weak and declining in the border area and that the loyalty of the non-slaveholding whites was questionable. The secession of the South on the election of Lincoln, these works argue, was motivated not by paranoia or hysterical fear, but by a realistic assessment that the unity of their society could not survive the open debate on the future of slavery which Republicans seemed determined to stimulate within the slave states.[38]

Before we can assess this interpretation, we must take a new look at the social and economic structure of the Old South. The non-slaveholding whites are probably the least studied of all our social classes. Of course, such an investigation may indeed reveal that the hegemony of the planter class was complete.[39] Or we may find that the loyalty of the non-slaveholders, while real, was unstable; that, especially in the backwoods areas outside direct planter control, there had developed a culture which was in many ways hostile to planter rule while, at the same time, cut off from both the market economy and from effective political power.

Fear of internal disunity can explain the belief of Edmund Ruffin that a Republican government could accomplish "the ruin of the South" without a direct assault upon slavery.[40]* Ruffin was convinced that in the event of civil war, a Southern victory would ensue, a belief he predicated on the continued loyalty of the slaves. But if we are to look at the question of internal disunity and its relation to secession, the slaves themselves cannot be ignored. Southerners knew that to exist as a regional institution within a larger free society, slavery required a community consensus, voluntary or enforced. Division among the whites had always been disastrous for discipline of the slaves. This was why the South had suppressed its own anti-slavery movement and continually demanded the silencing of northern abolitionists. Once a Republican administration was inaugurated, who knew what ideas would circulate in the slave quarters? Before we can answer these questions, we need to know more about how the slaves themselves were affected by, and perceived, the vast changes which took place in the South in the fifty years preceding secession—the ending of the slave trade, the rise of the Cotton Kingdom, and the expansion of slavery southward and westward.

In this connection, one of the most intriguing findings of Robert Fogel and Stanley Engerman's controversial study of the economics of slavery is the extent to which the lower level of the slave system was in the hands of blacks—how slaves were becoming a larger proportion of the drivers and managers on

---

*Published in the fall of 1860, Ruffin's *Anticipations of the Future* might be considered the first contribution to Civil War historiography. It details the administrations of Presidents Abraham Lincoln and William Seward, and the course of a war in 1867 in which the South wins a glorious military victory, New York City is destroyed by a mob, and Washington becomes the capital of a new southern republic.

plantations. This is precisely the class which, in the British West
Indies, during the agitation of the years 1816–33, was most
strongly influenced by humanitarian anti-slavery ideas and
which developed a campaign of non-violent resistance which
undermined West Indian slavery in the years immediately preceding emancipation. Of course, the situation in the United
States was vastly different from that in the islands, but the experience there, and similar events in the 1880s in Brazil, should
remind us again of the dangers of subversive ideas among the
slave population, and the reality of southern fears that the very
existence of a hostile central government was a threat to the
stability of their peculiar institution.[41]

Having previously called on political historians to pay more
attention to social history, I would like to conclude by reversing
this equation. Of course, our knowledge of the social history of
ante-bellum America is still in some ways in its infancy. One of
the striking features of the writing of the past fifteen years is
the curious disjunction between a growing body of knowledge
about nineteenth-century American society, and the reluctance
or inability of social historians to relate this information either
to the politics of the period or the question of Civil War causation.[42] As one of our most creative social historians, Rowland
Berthoff, reminds us, "any basic interpretation of American
history will have to account for . . . the coming of the Civil
War." And no such interpretation can be complete which does
not encompass the course of American political development.
"Politics bears critical importance to the history of society, for
politics affects the social structure, the economy, and the life of
a people."[43]

In other words, the social cleavages that existed in ante-
bellum America were bound to be reflected in politics. This was
an era when the mass political party galvanized voter participation to an unprecedented degree, and in which politics
formed an essential component of American mass culture. Politics became the stage on which the sectional conflict was played
out.[44]

Lawrence Stone has identified as an essential prerequisite to any revolution the "polarization into two coherent groups or alliances of what are naturally and normally a series of fractional and shifting tensions and conflicts within a society."[45] For most of the ante-bellum period, the political system served to prevent such a polarization. The existence of national political parties necessitated both the creation of linkages and alliances between elites in various parts of the country, and the conscious suppression of disruptive sectional issues. We can, in fact, view the political history of the coming of the Civil War as an accelerating struggle between the demands of party and those of sectional ideology, in which the latter slowly gained the upper hand. But the triumph was late and never complete. As late as 1860, major political leaders like Stephen A. Douglas hoped to curtail sectional controversy by restoring the political system to its traditional basis, with slavery carefully excluded from partisan debate.

Changes in the political system itself, changes related in ways still obscure to changes in the structure of American society, doomed the old basis of sectional political balance. If the anti-slavery crusade could not have emerged without the transformation of northern society, it could not have entered politics until the instruments of mass democracy had developed. It was no accident that the same decade witnessed the rise of the anti-slavery movement and the height of "Jacksonian democracy." The same institutions which created mass participation in politics also made possible the emergence of the sectional agitator—the radical, North and South, who consciously strove to influence public opinion through speeches, newspapers, lectures, and postal campaigns. This was now an efficacious way both to affect political decision-making and, if Richards is right, to challenge the social and political dominance of older entrenched elites.

Just as the abolitionist assault emerged in the 1830s, so too, spurred by it, did the coherent southern defense of slavery. The process of ideological response and counterresponse, once

set in motion, proved extremely difficult to curtail. In the next
two decades, these sectional ideologies became more and more
sophisticated. As each came to focus on its lowest common de-
nominator, with the widest possible base of support in its society, the political system proved incapable of preventing first the
intrusion, then the triumph of sectional ideology as the organizing principle of political combat.

The Civil War was, at base, a struggle for the future of the
nation. Within the context of modernization, one can agree
with Luraghi that it became part of the process of "building a
modern, centralized nation-state based on a national market,
totally and unopposedly controlled by an industrial capitalistic
class."[46] But is not there a danger here of transposing consequences and causes? It might be more accurate to say that each
side fought to preserve a society it believed was threatened.
Southerners fought to perserve the world the slaveholders
made. As for the North, Lincoln expressed the hopes of his
section, when he defined the Union cause as a struggle to preserve a system in which every man, whatever his station at
birth, could achieve social advancement and economic independence. Lincoln's Union was one of self-made men. The society
he was attempting to preserve was, in this respect, also pre-
modern—the world of the small shop, the independent farm,
and the village artisan. Republicans certainly condemned slavery as an obstacle to national economic development and as a
"relic of barbarism" out of touch with the modern spirit of the
nineteenth century. They exalted the virtues of economic
growth, but only within the context of a familar social order. If
modernization means the growth of large-scale industry, large
cities, and the leviathan state, northerners were no more fighting to create it than were southerners.

Yet modern, total war, against the intentions of those who
fought, was a powerful modernizing force.[47] In the South, the
war experience not only destroyed slavery, but created the opportunity for the two subordinate pre-modern classes, the poor
whites and the slaves, to organize and express their resentment

of planter control. In the North, the war gave a tremendous impetus to the rationalization of capitalist enterprise, the centralization of national institutions, and, in certain industries, mechanization and factory production. The foundations of the industrial capitalist state of the late nineteenth century, so similar in individualist rhetoric yet so different in social reality from Lincoln's America, were to a large extent laid during the Civil War. Here, indeed, is the tragic irony of that conflict. Each side fought to defend a distinct vision of the good society, but each vision was destroyed by the very struggle to preserve it.

--⊰ T H R E E ⊱--

Politics, Ideology,
and the
Origins of the American
Civil War

It has long been an axiom of political science that political parties help to hold together diverse, heterogeneous societies like our own. Since most major parties in American history have tried, in Seymour Lipset's phrase, to "appear as plausible representatives of the whole society," they have been broad coalitions cutting across lines of class, race, religion, and section. And although party competition requires that there be differences between the major parties, these differences usually have not been along sharp ideological lines. In fact, the very diversity of American society has inhibited the formation of ideological parties, for such parties assume the existence of a single line of social division along which a majority of the electorate can be mobilized. In a large, heterogeneous society, such a line rarely exists. There are, therefore, strong reasons why, in a two-party system, a major party—or a party aspiring to become "major"—will eschew ideology, for the statement of a co-

Originally published in *A Nation Divided: Problems and Issues of the Civil War and Reconstruction*, ed., George M. Fredrickson (Minneapolis, 1975), 15–34. Reprinted by permission of Burgess Publishing Company.

herent ideology will set limits to the groups in the electorate to which the party can hope to appeal. Under most circumstances, in other words, the party's role as a carrier of a coherent ideology will conflict with its role as an electoral machine bent on winning the largest possible number of votes.[1]

For much of the seventy years preceding the Civil War, the American political system functioned as a mechanism for relieving social tensions, ordering group conflict, and integrating the society. The existence of national political parties, increasingly focused on the contest for the Presidency, necessitated alliances between political elites in various sections of the country. A recent study of early American politics notes that "political nationalization was far ahead of economic, cultural, and social nationalization"—that is, that the national political system was itself a major bond of union in a diverse, growing society.[2] But as North and South increasingly took different paths of economic and social development and as, from the 1830s onward, antagonistic value systems and ideologies grounded in the question of slavery emerged in these sections, the political system inevitably came under severe disruptive pressures. Because they brought into play basic values and moral judgments, the competing sectional ideologies could not be defused by the normal processes of political compromise, nor could they be contained within the existing inter-sectional political system. Once parties began to reorient themselves on sectional lines, a fundamental necessity of democratic politics— that each party look upon the other as a legitimate alternative government—was destroyed.

When we consider the causes of the sectional conflict, we must ask ourselves not only why civil war came when it did, but why it did not come sooner. How did a divided nation manage to hold itself together for as long as it did? In part, the answer lies in the unifying effects of inter-sectional political parties. On the level of politics, the coming of the Civil War is the story of the intrusion of sectional ideology into the political system, despite the efforts of political leaders of both parties to keep it

out. Once this happened, political competition worked to ex-
acerbate, rather than to solve, social and sectional conflicts. For
as Frank Sorauf has explained: [3]

> The party of extensive ideology develops in and reflects the soci-
> ety in which little consensus prevails on basic social values and in-
> stitutions. It betokens deep social disagreements and conflicts. In-
> deed, the party of ideology that is also a major, competitive party
> accompanies a politics of almost total concern. Since its ideology
> defines political issues as including almost every facet of life, it
> brings to the political system almost every division, every dif-
> ference, every conflict of any importance in society.

"Parties in this country," wrote a conservative northern Whig
in 1855, "heretofore have helped, not delayed, the slow and
difficult growth of a consummated nationality." Rufus Choate
was lamenting the passing of a bygone era, a time when "our
allies were everywhere . . . there were no Alleghenies nor Mississippi rivers in our politics."[4] Party organization and the nature of political conflict had taken on new and unprecedented
forms in the 1850s. It is no accident that the breakup of the last
major inter-sectional party preceded by less than a year the
breakup of the Union or that the final crisis was precipitated
not by any "overt act," but by a presidential election.

From the beginning of national government, of course, differences of opinion over slavery constituted an important obstacle to the formation of a national community. "The great
danger to our general government," as Madison remarked at
the Constitutional Convention, "is the great southern and
northern interests of the continent, being opposed to each
other." "The institution of slavery and its consequences," according to him, was the main "line of discrimination" in convention disputes. As far as slavery was concerned, the Constitution amply fulfilled Lord Acton's dictum that it was an effort to
avoid settling basic questions. Aside from the Atlantic slave
trade, Congress was given no power to regulate slavery in any
way—the framers' main intention seems to have been to place

slavery completely outside the national political arena. The only basis on which a national politics could exist—the avoidance of sectional issues—was thus defined at the outset.[5]

Although the slavery question was never completely excluded from political debate in the 1790s, and there was considerable Federalist grumbling about the three-fifths clause of the Constitution after 1800, the first full demonstration of the political possibilities inherent in a sectional attack on slavery occurred in the Missouri controversy of 1819–21. These debates established a number of precedents which forecast the future course of the slavery extension issue in Congress. Most important was the fact that the issue was able for a time to completely obliterate party lines. In the first votes on slavery in Missouri, virtually every northerner, regardless of party, voted against expansion. It was not surprising, of course, that northern Federalists would try to make political capital out of the issue. What was unexpected was that northern Republicans, many of whom were aggrieved by Virginia's long dominance of the Presidency and by the Monroe administration's tariff and internal improvements policies, would unite with the Federalists. As John Quincy Adams observed, the debate "disclosed a secret: it revealed the basis for a new organization of parties. . . . Here was a new party really formed . . . terrible to the whole Union, but portentously terrible to the South." But the final compromise set another important precedent: enough northern Republicans became convinced that the Federalists were making political gains from the debates and that the Union was seriously endangered to break with the sectional bloc and support a compromise which a majority of northern Congressmen—Republicans and Federalists—opposed. As for the Monroe administration, its semiofficial spokesman, the *National Intelligencer,* pleaded for a return to the policy of avoiding sectional issues, even to the extent of refusing to publish letters which dealt in any way with the subject of slavery.[6]

The Missouri controversy and the election of 1824, in which four candidates contested the Presidency, largely drawing support from their home sections, revealed that in the absence of two-party competition, sectional loyalties would constitute the lines of political division. No one recognized this more clearly than the architect of the second party system, Martin Van Buren. In his well-known letter to Thomas Ritchie of Virginia, Van Buren explained the need for a revival of national two-party politics on precisely this ground: "Party attachment in former times furnished a complete antidote for sectional prejudices by producing counteracting feelings. It was not until that defense had been broken down that the clamor against Southern Influence and African Slavery could be made effectual in the North." Van Buren and many of his generation of politicians had been genuinely frightened by the threats of disunion which echoed through Congress in 1820; they saw national two-party competition as the alternative to sectional conflict and eventual disunion. Ironically, as Richard McCormick has made clear, the creation of the second party system owed as much to sectionalism as to national loyalties. The South, for example, only developed an organized, competitive Whig party in 1835 and 1836 when it became apparent that Jackson, the southern President, had chosen Van Buren, a northerner, as his successor. Once party divisions had emerged, however, they stuck, and by 1840, for one of the very few times in American history, two truly inter-sectional parties, each united behind a single candidate, competed for the Presidency.[7]

The 1830s witnessed a vast expansion of political loyalties and awareness and the creation of party mechanisms to channel voter participation in politics. But the new mass sense of identification with politics had ominous implications for the sectional antagonisms which the party system sought to suppress. The historian of the Missouri Compromise has observed that "if there had been a civil war in 1819–1821 it would have been between the members of Congress, with the rest of the country looking on in amazement." This is only one example of the intellectual and political isolation of Washington from the general populace which James Young has described in *The*

Washington Community.[8] The mass, non-ideological politics of the Jackson era created the desperately needed link between governors and governed. But this very link made possible the emergence of two kinds of sectional agitators: the abolitionists, who stood outside of politics and hoped to force public opinion—and through it, politicians—to confront the slavery issue, and political agitators, who used politics as a way of heightening sectional self-consciousness and antagonism in the populace at large.

Because of the rise of mass politics and the emergence of these sectional agitators, the 1830s was the decade in which long-standing, latent sectional divisions were suddenly activated, and previously unrelated patterns of derogatory sectional imagery began to emerge into full-blown sectional ideology. Many of the anti-slavery arguments which gained wide currency in the 1830s had roots stretching back into the eighteenth century. The idea that slavery degraded white labor and retarded economic development, for example, had been voiced by Benjamin Franklin. After 1800, the Federalists, increasingly localized in New England, had developed a fairly coherent critique, not only of the social and economic effects of slavery, but of what Harrison Gray Otis called the divergence of "manners, habits, customs, principles, and ways of thinking" which separated northerners and southerners. And, during the Missouri debates, almost every economic, political, and moral argument against slavery that would be used in the later sectional debate was voiced. In fact, one recurring argument was not picked up later—the warning of northern Congressmen that the South faced the danger of slave rebellion if steps were not taken toward abolition. (As far as I know, only Thaddeus Stevens of Republican spokesmen in the 1850s would explicitly use this line of argument.)[9]

The similarity between Federalist attacks on the South and later abolitionist and Republican arguments, coupled with the fact that many abolitionists—including Garrison, Phillips, the Tappans, and others—came from Federalist backgrounds, has

led James Banner to describe abolitionism as "the Massachusetts Federalist ideology come back to life." Yet there was
a long road to be traveled from Harrison Gray Otis to William
H. Seward, just as there was from Thomas Jefferson to George
Fitzhugh. For one thing, the Federalist distrust of democracy,
social competition, and the Jeffersonian cry of "equal rights,"
their commitment to social inequality, hierarchy, tradition, and
order prevented them from pushing their anti-slavery views to
their logical conclusion. And New England Federalists were
inhibited by the requirements of national party organization
and competition from voicing anti-slavery views. In the 1790s,
they maintained close ties with southern Federalists, and after
1800 hope of reviving their strength in the South never completely died. Only a party which embraced social mobility and
competitive individualism, rejected the permanent subordination of any "rank" in society, and was unburdened by a southern wing could develop a fully coherent anti-slavery ideology.[10]

An equally important reason why the Federalists did not develop a consistent sectional ideology was that the South in the
early part of the nineteenth century shared many of the Federalists' reservations about slavery. The growth of an anti-slavery
ideology, in other words, depended in large measure on the
growth of pro-slavery thought, and, by the same token, it was
the abolitionist assault which brought into being the coherent
defense of slavery. The opening years of the 1830s, of course,
were ones of crisis for the South. The emergence of militant
abolitionism, Nat Turner's rebellion, the Virginia debates on
slavery, and the nullification crisis suddenly presented assaults
to the institution of slavery from within and outside the South.
The reaction was the closing of southern society in defense of
slavery, "the most thorough-going repression of free thought,
free speech, and a free press ever witnessed in an American
community." At the same time, southerners increasingly abandoned their previous, highly qualified defenses of slavery and
embarked on the formulation of the pro-slavery argument. By

1837, as is well known, John C. Calhoun could thank the abolitionists on precisely this ground:[11]

> This agitation has produced one happy effect at least; it has com-
> pelled us at the South to look into the nature and character of this
> great institution, and to correct many false impressions that even
> we had entertained in relation to it. Many in the South once be-
> lieved that it was a moral and political evil; that folly and delusion
> are gone; we see it now in its true light, and regard it as the most
> safe and stable basis for free institutions in the world.

The South, of course, was hardly as united as Calhoun asserted. But the progressive rejection of the Jeffersonian tradition, the suppression of civil liberties, and the increasing stri-
dency of the defense of slavery all pushed the South further
and further out of the inter-sectional mainstream, setting it increasingly apart from the rest of the country. Coupled with the
Gag Rule and the mobs which broke up abolitionist presses and
meetings, the growth of pro-slavery thought was vital to a new
anti-slavery formulation which emerged in the late 1830s and
which had been absent from both the Federalist attacks on slavery and the Missouri debates—the idea of the Slave Power. The
Slave Power replaced the three-fifths clause as the symbol of
southern power, and it was a far more sophisticated and complex formulation. Abolitionists could now argue that slavery
was not only morally repugnant, it was incompatible with the
basic democratic values and liberties of white Americans. As
one abolitionist declared, "We commenced the present struggle
to obtain the freedom of the slave; we are compelled to continue it to preserve our own." In other words, a process of
ideological expansion had begun, fed in large measure by the
sequence of response and counterresponse between the competing sectional outlooks.[12] Once this process had begun, it had
an internal dynamic which made it extremely difficult to stop.
This was especially true because of the emergence of agitators
whose avowed purpose was to sharpen sectional conflict, polar-

ize public opinion, and develop sectional ideologies to their logical extremes.

As the 1840s opened, most political leaders still clung to the traditional basis of politics, but the sectional, ideological political agitators formed growing minorities in each section. In the South, there was a small group of outright secessionists and a larger group, led by Calhoun, who were firmly committed to the Union but who viewed sectional organization and self-defense, not the traditional reliance on inter-sectional political parties, as the surest means of protecting southern interests within the Union. In the North, a small radical group gathered in Congress around John Quincy Adams and Congressmen like Joshua Giddings, William Slade, and Seth Gates—men who represented areas of the most intense abolitionist agitation and whose presence confirmed Garrison's belief that, once public opinion was aroused on the slavery issue, politicians would have to follow step. These radicals were determined to force slavery into every congressional debate. They were continually frustrated but never suppressed, and the reelection of Giddings in 1842 after his censure and resignation from the House proved that in some districts party discipline was no longer able to control the slavery issue.[13]

The northern political agitators, both Congressmen and Liberty party leaders, also performed the function of developing and popularizing a political rhetoric, especially focused on fear of the Slave Power, which could be seized upon by traditional politicians and large masses of voters if slavery ever entered the center of political conflict.

In the 1840s, this is precisely what happened. As one politician later recalled, "Slavery upon which by common consent no party issue had been made was then obtruded upon the field of party action." It is significant that John Tyler and John C. Calhoun, the two men most responsible for this intrusion, were political outsiders, men without places in the national party structure. Both of their careers were blocked by the major parties but might be advanced if tied to the slavery question in the form of Texas annexation. Once introduced into politics, slavery was there to stay. The Wilmot Proviso, introduced in 1846, had precisely the same effect as the proposal two decades earlier to restrict slavery in Missouri—it completely fractured the major parties along sectional lines. As in 1820, opposition to the expansion of slavery became the way in which a diverse group of northerners expressed their various resentments against a southern-dominated administration. And, as in 1821, a small group of northern Democrats eventually broke with their section, reaffirmed their primary loyalty to the party, and joined with the South to kill the Proviso in 1847. In the same year, enough southerners rejected Calhoun's call for united sectional action to doom his personal and sectional ambitions.[14]

But the slavery extension debates of the 1840s had far greater effects on the political system than the Missouri controversy had had. Within each party, they created a significant group of sectional politicians—men whose careers were linked to the slavery question and who would therefore resist its exclusion from future politics. And in the North, the 1840s witnessed the expansion of sectional political rhetoric—as more and more northerners became familiar with the "aggressions" of the Slave Power and the need to resist them. At the same time, as anti-slavery ideas expanded, unpopular and divisive elements were weeded out, especially the old alliance of anti-slavery with demands for the rights of free blacks. Opposition to slavery was already coming to focus on its lowest common denominators—free soil, opposition to the Slave Power, and the union.[15]

The political system reacted to the intrusion of the slavery question in the traditional ways. At first, it tried to suppress it. This is the meaning of the famous letters opposing the immediate annexation of Texas issued by Clay and Van Buren on the same spring day in 1844, probably after consultation on the subject. It was an agreement that slavery was too explosive a question for either party to try to take partisan advantage of it. The agreement, of course, was torpedoed by the defeat of Van

Buren for the Democratic nomination, a defeat caused in part
by the willingness of his Democratic opponents to use the
Texas and slavery questions to discredit Van Buren—thereby
violating the previously established rules of political conduct.
In the North from 1844 onward, both parties, particularly the
Whigs, tried to defuse the slavery issue and minimize defection
to the Liberty party by adopting anti-southern rhetoric. This
tended to prevent defections to third parties, but it had the effect of nurturing and legitimating anti-southern sentiment
within the ranks of the major parties themselves. After the
1848 election in which northern Whigs and Democrats vied for
title of "free soil" to minimize the impact of the Free Soil party,
William H. Seward commented, "Antislavery is at length a respectable element in politics."[16]

Both parties also attempted to devise formulas for compromising the divisive issue. For the Whigs, it was "no territory"—
an end to expansion would end the question of the spread of
slavery. The Democratic answer, first announced by Vice President Dallas in 1847 and picked up by Lewis Cass, was popular
sovereignty or non-intervention: giving to the people of each
territory the right to decide on slavery. As has often been
pointed out, popular sovereignty was an exceedingly vague and
ambiguous doctrine. It was never precisely clear what the powers of a territorial legislature were to be or at what point the
question of slavery was to be decided.[17] But politically such ambiguity was essential (and intentional) if popular sovereignty
were to serve as a means of settling the slavery issue on the
traditional basis—by removing it from national politics and
transferring the battleground from Congress to the territories.[18] Popular sovereignty formed one basis of the compromise of 1850, the last attempt of the political system to expel
the disease of sectional ideology by finally settling all the points
at which slavery and national politics intersected.

That compromise was possible in 1850 was testimony to the
resiliency of the political system and the continuing ability of
party loyalty to compete with sectional commitments. But the

very method of passage revealed how deeply sectional divisions
were embedded in party politics. Because only a small group of
Congressmen—mostly northwestern Democrats and southern
Whigs—were committed to compromise on every issue, the
"omnibus" compromise measure could not pass. The compromise had to be enacted serially with the small compromise bloc,
led by Stephen A. Douglas of Illinois, aligned with first one sectional bloc, then the other, to pass the individual measures.[19]

His role in the passage of the compromise announced the
emergence of Douglas as the last of the great Unionist, compromising politicians, the heir of Clay, Webster, and other
spokesmen for the center. And his career, like Webster's,
showed that it was no longer possible to win the confidence of
both sections with a combination of extreme nationalism and
the calculated suppression of the slavery issue in national politics. Like his predecessors, Douglas called for a policy of "entire
silence on the slavery question," and throughout the 1850s, as
Robert Johannsen has written, his aim was to restore "order
and stability to American politics through the agency of a national, conservative Democratic party." Ultimately, Douglas
failed—a traditional career for the Union was simply not possible in the 1850s—but it is equally true that in 1860 he was the
only presidential candidate to draw significant support in all
parts of the country.[20]

It is, of course, highly ironic that it was Douglas's attempt to
extend the principle of popular sovereignty to territory already
guaranteed to free labor by the Missouri Compromise which finally shattered the second party system. We can date exactly
the final collapse of that system—February 15, 1854—the day a
caucus of southern Whig Congressmen and Senators decided
to support Douglas's Nebraska bill, despite the fact that they
could have united with northern Whigs in opposition both to
the repeal of the Missouri Compromise and the revival of sectional agitation.[21] But in spite of the sectionalization of politics
which occurred after 1854, Douglas continued his attempt to
maintain a national basis of party competition. In fact, from

one angle of vision, whether politics was to be national or sectional was the basic issue of the Lincoln-Douglas debates of 1858. The Little Giant presented local autonomy—popular sovereignty for states and territories—as the only "national" solution to the slavery question, while Lincoln attempted to destroy this middle ground and force a single, sectional solution on the entire Union. There is a common critique of Douglas's politics, expressed perhaps most persuasively by Allan Nevins, which argues that, as a man with no moral feelings about slavery, Douglas was incapable of recognizing that this moral issue affected millions of northern voters.[22] This, in my opinion, is a serious misunderstanding of Douglas's politics. What he insisted was not that there was no moral question involved in slavery but that it was not the function of the politician to deal in moral judgments. To Lincoln's prediction that the nation could not exist half slave and half free, Douglas replied that it had so existed for seventy years and could continue to do so if northerners stopped trying to impose their own brand of morality upon the South.

Douglas's insistence on the separation of politics and morality was expressed in his oft-quoted statement that—in his role as a politician—he did not care if the people of a territory voted slavery "up or down." As he explained in his Chicago speech of July 1858, just before the opening of the great debates:

> I deny the right of Congress to force a slave-holding state upon an unwilling people. I deny their right to force a free state upon an unwilling people. I deny their right to force a good thing upon a people who are unwilling to receive it. . . . It is no answer to this argument to say that slavery is an evil and hence should not be tolerated. You must allow the people to decide for themselves whether it is a good or an evil.

When Lincoln, therefore, said the real purpose of popular sovereignty was "to educate and mould public opinion, at least northern public opinion, to not care whether slavery is voted down or up," he was, of course, right. For Douglas recognized

that moral categories, being essentially uncompr
unassimilable in politics. The only solution to the sla
was local autonomy. Whatever a majority of a state or ter
wished to do about slavery was right—or at least should not b
tampered with by politicians from other areas. To this, Lincoln's only possible reply was the one formulated in the debates—the will of the majority must be tempered by considerations of morality. Slavery was not, he declared, an "*ordinary*
matter of domestic concern in the states and territories." Because of its essential immorality, it tainted the entire nation, and its disposition in the territories, and eventually in the entire nation, was a matter of national concern to be decided by a national, not a local, majority. As the debates continued, Lincoln increasingly moved to this moral level of the slavery argument: "Everything that emanates from [Douglas] or his coadjutors, carefully excludes the thought that there is anything wrong with slavery. All their arguments, if you will consider them, will be seen to exclude the thought. . . . If you do admit that it is wrong, Judge Douglas can't logically say that he don't care whether a wrong is voted up or down."[23]

In order to press home the moral argument, moreover, Lincoln had to insist throughout the debates on the basic humanity of the black; while Douglas, by the same token, logically had to define blacks as subhuman, or at least, as the Dred Scott decision had insisted, not part of the American "people" included in the Declaration of Independence and the Constitution. Douglas's view of the black, Lincoln declared, conveyed "no vivid impression that the Negro is a human, and consequently has no idea that there can be any moral question in legislating about him."[24] Of course, the standard of morality which Lincoln felt the nation should adopt regarding slavery and the black was the sectional morality of the Republican party.

By 1860, Douglas's local majoritarianism was no more acceptable to southern political leaders than Lincoln's national and moral majoritarianism. The principle of state rights and minority self-determination had always been the first line of defense

interference, but southerners now
d that Congress intervene to establish
. the territories. The Lecompton fight
d that southerners would no longer be
,uglas hoped the territories would be-
.ic states. And the refusal of the Douglas
ιo southern demands was the culmination
:esentment on the part of northern Demo-
crats, ꞏ   .k into the 1840s, at the impossible political
dilemma of ᴜᴄ. caught between increasingly anti-southern
constituency pressure and loyalty to an increasingly pro-
southern national party. For their part, southern Democrats
viewed their northern allies as too weak at home and too
tainted with anti-southernism after the Lecompton battle to be
relied on to protect southern interests any longer.[25]

As for the Republicans, by the late 1850s they had succeeded
in developing a coherent ideology which, despite internal ambiguities and contradictions, incorporated the fundamental values, hopes, and fears of a majority of northerners. As I have
argued elsewhere, it rested on a commitment to the northern
social order, founded on the dignity and opportunities of free
labor, and to social mobility, enterprise, and "progress." It
gloried in the same qualities of northern life—materialism, social fluidity, and the dominance of the self-made man—which
twenty years earlier had been the source of widespread anxiety
and fear in Jacksonian America. And it defined the South as a
backward, stagnant, aristocratic society, totally alien in values
and social order to the middle-class capitalism of the North.[26]

Some elements of the Republican ideology had roots stretching back into the eighteenth century. Others, especially the
Republican emphasis on the threat of the Slave Power, were
relatively new. Northern politics and thought were permeated
by the Slave Power idea in the 1850s. The effect can perhaps
be gauged by a brief look at the career of the leading Republican spokesman of the 1850s, William H. Seward. As a political
child of upstate New York's burned-over district and anti-

masonic crusade, Seward had long believed that the Whig party's main political liability was its image as the spokeman of the wealthy and aristocratic. Firmly committed to egalitarian democracy, Seward had attempted to reorient the New York State Whigs into a reformist, egalitarian party, friendly to immigrants and embracing political and economic democracy, but he was always defeated by the party's downstate conservative wing. In the 1840s, he became convinced that the only way for the party to counteract the Democrats' monopoly of the rhetoric of democracy and equality was for the Whigs to embrace anti-slavery as a party platform.[27]

The Slave Power idea gave the Republicans the anti-aristocratic appeal with which men like Seward had long wished to be associated politically. By fusing older anti-slavery arguments with the idea that slavery posed a threat to northern free labor and democratic values, it enabled the Republicans to tap the egalitarian outlook which lay at the heart of northern society. At the same time, it enabled Republicans to present anti-slavery as an essentially conservative reform, an attempt to reestablish the anti-slavery principles of the founding fathers and rescue the federal government from southern usurpation. And, of course, the Slave Power idea had a far greater appeal to northern self-interest than arguments based on the plight of black slaves in the South. As the black abolitionist Frederick Douglass noted, "The cry of Free Men was raised, not for the extension of liberty to the black man, but for the protection of the liberty of the white."[28]

By the late 1850s, it had become a standard part of Republican rhetoric to accuse the Slave Power of a long series of transgressions against northern rights and liberties and to predict that, unless halted by effective political action, the ultimate aim of the conspiracy—the complete subordination of the national government to slavery and the suppression of northern liberties—would be accomplished. Like other conspiracy theories, the Slave Power idea was a way of ordering and interpreting history, assigning clear causes to otherwise inexplicable events, from the Gag Rule to Bleeding Kansas and the Dred Scott decision. It also provided a convenient symbol through which a host of anxieties about the future could be expressed. At the same time, the notion of a black Republican conspiracy to overthrow slavery and southern society had taken hold in the South. These competing conspiratorial outlooks were reflections, not merely of sectional "paranoia," but of the fact that the nation was every day growing apart and into two societies whose ultimate interests were diametrically opposed. The South's fear of black Republicans, despite its exaggerated rhetoric, was based on the realistic assessment that at the heart of Republican aspirations for the nation's future was the restriction and eventual eradication of slavery. And the Slave Power expressed northerners' conviction, not only that slavery was incompatible with basic democratic values, but that to protect slavery, southerners were determined to control the federal government and use it to foster the expansion of slavery. In summary, the Slave Power idea was the ideological glue of the Republican party—it enabled them to elect in 1860 a man conservative enough to sweep to victory in every northern state, yet radical enough to trigger the secession crisis.

Did the election of Lincoln pose any real danger to the institution of slavery? In my view, it is only possible to argue that it did not if one takes a completely static—and therefore ahistorical—view of the slavery issue. The expansion of slavery was not simply an issue; it was a fact. By 1860, over half the slaves lived in areas outside the original slave states. At the same time, however, the South had become a permanent and shrinking minority within the nation. And in the majority section, antislavery sentiment had expanded at a phenomenal rate. Within one generation, it had moved from the commitment of a small minority of northerners to the motive force behind a victorious party. That sentiment now demanded the exclusion of slavery from the territories. Who could tell what its demands would be in ten or twenty years? The incoming President had often declared his commitment to the "ultimate extinction" of slavery.

In Alton, Illinois, in the heart of the most pro-slavery area of the North, he had condemned Douglas because "he looks to no end of the institution of slavery."[29] A Lincoln administration seemed likely to be only the beginning of a prolonged period of Republican hegemony. And the succession of generally weak, one-term Presidents between 1836 and 1860 did not obscure the great expansion in the potential power of the Presidency which had taken place during the administration of Andrew Jackson. Old Hickory had clearly shown that a strong-willed President, backed by a united political party, had tremendous power to shape the affairs of government and to transform into policy his version of majority will.

What was at stake in 1860, as in the entire sectional conflict, was the character of the nation's future. This was one reason Republicans had placed so much stress on the question of the expansion of slavery. Not only was this the most available issue concerning slavery constitutionally open to them, but it involved the nation's future in the most direct way. In the West, the future was tabula rasa, and the future course of western development would gravely affect the direction of the entire nation. Now that the territorial issue was settled by Lincoln's election, it seemed likely that the slavery controversy would be transferred back into the southern states themselves. Secessionists, as William Freehling has argued, feared that slavery was weak and vulnerable in the border states, even in Virginia.[30] They feared Republican efforts to encourage the formation of Republican organizations in these areas and the renewal of the long-suppressed internal debate on slavery in the South itself. And, lurking behind these anxieties, may have been fear of anti-slavery debate reaching the slave quarters, of an undermining of the masters' authority, and, ultimately, of slave rebellion itself. The slaveholders knew, despite the great economic strength of King Cotton, that the existence of slavery as a local institution in a larger free economy demanded an inter-sectional community consensus, real or enforced. It was this consensus which Lincoln's election seemed to undermine, which is why the secession convention of South Carolina declared, "Experience has proved that slaveholding states cannot be safe in subjection to non-slaveholding states."[31]

More than seventy years before the secession crisis, James Madison had laid down the principles by which a central government and individual and minority liberties could coexist in a large and heterogeneous Union. The very diversity of interests in the nation, he argued in the Federalist papers, was the security for the rights of minorities, for it ensured that no one interest would ever gain control of the government.[32] In the 1830s, John C. Calhoun recognized the danger which abolitionism posed to the South—it threatened to rally the North in the way Madison had said would not happen—in terms of one commitment hostile to the interests of the minority South. Moreover, Calhoun recognized, when a majority interest is organized into an effective political party, it can seize control of all the branches of government, overturning the system of constitutional checks and balances which supposedly protected minority rights. Only the principle of the concurrent majority—a veto which each major interest could exercise over policies directly affecting it—could reestablish this constitutional balance.

At the outset of the abolitionist crusade, Calhoun had been convinced that, while emancipation must be "resisted at all costs," the South should avoid hasty action until it was "certain that it is the real object, not by a few, but by a very large portion of the non-slaveholding states." By 1850, Calhoun was convinced that "Every portion of the North entertains views more or less hostile to slavery." And by 1860, the election returns demonstrated that this anti-slavery sentiment, contrary to Madison's expectations, had united in an interest capable of electing a President, despite the fact that it had not the slightest support from the sectional minority. The character of Lincoln's election, in other words, completely overturned the ground rules which were supposed to govern American politics. The South Carolina secession convention expressed secessionists' reaction when it declared that once the sectional Republican

party, founded on hostility to sou(´
took over control of the federal gove,
of the Constitution will then no longer e.

Thus the South came face to face with a
loyalty to the nation and loyalty to the Soutʰ.
ery, which, more than anything else, made the
David Potter has pointed out that the principle of ,
implies the existence of a coherent, clearly recogniza∟
which more than half may be legitimately considered ∟
jority of the whole. For the South to accept majority ɪ∖
1860, in other words, would have been an affirmation ⊂
common nationality with the North. Certainly, it is true that ɪ∖
terms of ethnicity, language, religion—many of the usual com-
ponents of nationality—Americans, North and South, were still
quite close. On the other hand, one important element, community of interest, was not present. And perhaps most important, the preceding decades had witnessed an escalation of distrust—an erosion of the reciprocal currents of good will so
essential for national harmony. "We are not one people," declared the New York *Tribune* in 1855. "We are two peoples. We
are a people for Freedom and a people for Slavery. Between
the two, conflict is inevitable."[34] We can paraphrase John
Adams's famous comment on the American Revolution and
apply it to the coming of the Civil War—the separation was
complete, in the minds of the people, before the war began. In
a sense, the Constitution and national political system had
failed in the difficult task of creating a nation—only the Civil
War itself would accomplish it.

AMBIGUITIES
OF
ANTI-SLAVERY

FOUR

Abolitionism
and the
Labor Movement
in Ante-bellum America

Among the more ironic conjunctures of ante-bellum American history is the fact that the expansion of capitalist labor relations evoked severe criticism from two very different quarters: the pro-slavery ideologues of the South and the labor movement of the North. Standing outside the emerging capitalist economy of the free states (although also providing the raw material essential for its early development), the South gave birth to a group of thinkers who developed a striking critique of northern labor relations. The liberty of the northern wage earner, according to George Fitzhugh, John C. Calhoun, and the others, amounted to little more than the freedom to sell his labor for a fraction of its true value, or to starve. In contrast to the southern slave, who was ostensibly provided for in sickness and old age, and regardless of the vicissitudes of prices and production, the free laborer was the slave of the marketplace, and his condition exceeded in degradation and cruelty that of the chattel

Originally published in *Anti-Slavery, Religion, and Reform: Essays in Memory of Roger Anstey*, eds. Christine Bolt and Seymour Drescher (Folkestone, 1980). Reprinted by permission of William Dawson and Sons, Ltd.

slave. The prevailing ethos of northern society—free competition—inevitably resulted in poverty for the many and riches for the few.

The somewhat bizarre spectacle of defenders of slavery justifying the peculiar institution in language redolent of a Marxian class struggle has long fascinated historians, as has the response of anti-slavery spokesmen to the southern charges.[1] Less attention has been paid to the role of a third participant in the complex debate over the relative status of labor in North and South: the northern labor movement. It is well known that relations between abolitionists and the radical labor leaders of the North were by no means cordial during the 1830s and 1840s. But the reasons remain elusive. Nonetheless, the not-too-close encounter between abolitionism and the labor movement not only raises important questions about the constituencies and ideological assumptions underpinning each movement, but also illuminates in a new way that historical perennial, the relationship between capitalism and slavery.

The emergence of the nation's first labor movement in the late 1820s and 1830s was, of course, a response to fundamental changes taking place in the work patterns and authority relationships within traditional artisan production. Labor historians have made the elements of this transformation familiar: the emergence of the factory system, the dilution of craft skill, the imposition of a new labor discipline in traditional craft production, the growing gap between masters and journeymen, and the increasing stratification of the social order, especially in the large eastern cities. Workingmen responded to these developments within the context of an ideology dating back to the Paineite republicanism of the American Revolution. The central ingredients in this ideology were a passionate attachment to equality (defined not as a leveling of all distinctions, but as the absence of large inequalities of wealth and influence), belief that independence—the ability to resist personal or economic coercion—was an essential attribute of the republican citizenry, and a commitment to the labor theory of value, along with its corollary, that labor should receive the full value of its product. The economic changes of the early nineteenth century posed a direct challenge to these traditional ideals. "You are the real producers of all the wealth of the community," declared New York's *Workingman's Advocate*. "Without your labors no class could live. How is it then you are so poor while those who labor not are rich?"[2]

The search for an answer to this question led labor leaders to a wide variety of programs, ranging from Thomas Skidmore's attack on the inheritance of property, to the more typical denunciation of banks, merchants, and "non-producers" in general, for robbing labor of a portion of its product. Whatever the specific programs advocated, however, labor spokesmen agreed that workingmen were faced with a loss of their status both within the crafts and in the republican polity. Conditions of labor both in the new factories of New England and in the artisan workshops of New York and Philadelphia symbolized the decline of the "dignity of labor." The phrase which entered the language of politics in the 1830s to describe the plight and grievances of the labor movement was "wage slavery." A comparison between the status of the northern worker and the southern slave—usually to the detriment of the former— became a standard component of labor rhetoric in these years. In language remarkably similar to the southern critique of northern labor conditions, Seth Luther declared that northern mill workers labored longer each day than southern slaves, and in worse conditions. A New Hampshire labor newspaper asked, "A great cry is raised in the northern states against southern slavery. The sin of slavery may be abominable there, but is it not equally so here? If they have black slaves, have we not white ones? Or how much better is the condition of some of our laborers here at the North, than the slaves of the South?" The famous Coffin handbill distributed in New York City after striking journeyman tailors were convicted of conspiracy declared, "The Freemen of the North are now on a level with the slaves of the South." And the militant female textile workers of

Lowell, Massachusetts, referred to themselves during one strike as the "white slaves" of New England, and their newspaper, the *Voice of Industry,* claimed the women operatives were "in fact nothing more nor less than slaves in every sense of the word."[3]

There is no point in further multiplying quotations to demonstrate that the idea of "wage slavery" played a central role in the rhetoric of the labor movement. Sometimes, "wage slavery" was used more or less as an equivalent for long working hours or for poverty. But the meaning of the metaphor was far broader than this. The phrase evoked the fears so prevalent in the labor movement of the 1830s and 1840s of the erosion of respect for labor, the loss of independence by the craftsman, and the emergence of "European" social conditions and class stratification in republican America. Most importantly, working for wages itself was often perceived as a form of "slavery," an affront to the traditional artisanal ideal of economic and personal independence. As Orestes Brownson explained in his remarkable and influential essay, "The Laboring Classes," it was not simply low wages, but the wage system itself which lay at the root of labor's probelms. The wage system, said Brownson, enabled employers to "retain all the advantages of the slave system without the expense, trouble, and odium of being slaveholders. . . . There must be no class of our fellow men doomed to toil through life as mere workmen at wages." The emergence of a permanent wage-earning class challenged the traditional definition of the social order of republican America.[4]

What was the attitude of those who raised the cry of "wage slavery" toward slavery in the South? It has often been argued that northern workingmen were indifferent or hostile to the anti-slavery crusade, or even pro-slavery. White laborers, it is argued, feared emancipation would unleash a flood of freedmen to compete for northern jobs and further degrade the dignity of labor.[5] Yet it is important to distinguish the labor movement's response to abolitionism, and, indeed, to black competition, from its attitude toward slavery. After all, inherent in the notion of "wage slavery," in the comparison of the status of the northern laborer with the southern slave, was a critique of the peculiar institution as an extreme form of oppression (unless one agreed with Fitzhugh that northern labor should be enslaved for its own benefit, a position not likely to find many adherents in the labor movement). The entire ideology of the labor movement was implicitly hostile to slavery: slavery contradicted the central ideas and values of artisan radicalism—liberty, democracy, equality, independence. The ideological fathers of the movement, Thomas Paine and Robert Owen, were both strongly anti-slavery.

Recent research, moreover, moving away from an earlier definition of abolitionists as representatives of a declining traditional elite, has underscored the central role played by artisans in the urban abolitionist constituency (although not the leadership of the movement). In Lynn, Massachusetts, according to Alan Dawley, shoemakers equated slaveowners with the city's factory magnates as "a set of lordly tyrants." In Utica and Cincinnati, writes Leonard Richards, artisans were represented far more heavily among the abolitionist constituency than in the mobs which broke up abolitionist meetings. And the careful analysis of New York City anti-slavery petitions between 1829 and 1837 by John Jentz reveals that in most cases, artisans were the largest occupational group among the signers. In New York, the only newspaper publicly to defend Nat Turner's rebellion was not an anti-slavery journal, but the *Daily Sentinel,* edited for the Workingman's party by the immigrant English radical George Henry Evans. The radical artisans who met each year in New York to celebrate Tom Paine's birthday often included a toast to the liberators of Haiti in their celebrations, and Evans's *Workingman's Advocate* went so far as to claim, rather implausibly, that "the Government of Haiti approaches nearer to pure Republicanism than any other now in use or on record." Evans did acknowledge in 1831 that the labor movement sometimes neglected the cause of the slave because of its preoccupation with the grievances of northern workers. But he added that he remained committed to the total eradication of slavery in the South.[6]

The year 1831, of course, was also the one in which William Lloyd Garrison commenced publication of *The Liberator*, the point from which historians usually date the emergence of a new, militant, immediatist abolitionist crusade. As is well known, Garrison addressed the condition of northern labor, and the activities of the labor movement, in his very first issue:[7]

> An attempt has been made—it is still making—we regret to say, with considerable success—to inflame the minds of our working classes against the more opulent, and to persuade men that they are contemned and oppressed by a wealthy aristocracy. . . . It is in the highest degree criminal . . . to exasperate our mechanics to deeds of violence, or to array them under a party banner, for it is not true that, at any time, they have been the objects of reproach. Labour is not dishonourable. The industrious artisan, in a government like ours, will always be held in better estimation than the wealthy idler. . . . We are the friends of reform; but this is not reform, which in curing one evil, threatens to inflict a thousand others.

Of course, Garrison's point about the high regard in which labor was held was precisely what the labor movement contended was no longer true. Four weeks after the editorial appeared, Garrison published a response by the labor reformer William West, arguing that there was, in fact, a "very intimate connexion" between abolition and the labor movement, since each was striving to secure "the fruits of their toil" to a class of workingmen. To which Garrison responded with another denunciation, phrased in the extreme language so characteristic of all his writing:[8]

> In a republican government . . . where hereditary distinctions are obsolete . . . where the avenues of wealth, distinction and supremacy are open to all; [society] must, in the nature of things, be full of inequalities. But these can exist without an assumption of rights—without even a semblance of oppression. There is a prevalent opinion, that wealth and aristocracy are indissolubly allied;

and the poor and vulgar are taught to consider the opulent as their natural enemies. Those who inculcate this pernicious doctrine are the worst enemies of the people, and, in grain, the real nobility. . . . It is a miserable characteristic of human nature to look with an envious eye upon those who are more fortunate in their pursuits, or more exalted in their station.

Thus, from the very outset, a failure of communication characterized relations between the two movements. Fifteen years later, the utopian socialist Albert Brisbane called on abolitionists to "include in their movement, a reform of the present wretched organization of labor, called the wage system. It would add to their power by interesting the producing classes . . . and would prepare a better state for the slaves when emancipated, than the servitude to capital, to which they now seem destined."[9] The proposed alliance never did take place, and Garrison's early editorials suggest some of the reasons. It is not precisely that the abolitionists were complacently "middle class" in outlook, a characterization found quite frequently in the recent historical literature. Abolitionists—both Garrisonians and their opponents within the movement—threw themselves with enthusiasm into all sorts of other movements to reform American society, from the abolition of capital punishment to women's rights, temperance, peace, etc. They often criticized the spirit of competition, individualism, and greed so visible in northern life, as the antithesis of Christian brotherhood and love.[10] It will not do to defang the abolitionist crusade: it was indeed a radical impulse, challenging fundamental aspects of American life (and none so deeply embedded as racism). But in its view of economic relations it did speak the language of northern society. Perhaps this is why the movement, so feared at the outset, eventually could become respectable.

In contrast to the labor movement, most abolitionists—as Garrison's early editorials made clear—accepted social inequality as a natural reflection of individual differences in talent, ambition, and diligence, and perceived the interests of capital and labor as existing in harmony rather than conflict. As a result, they were unable to understand, much less sympathize with, the aims of the labor movement or the concept of "wage slavery." Their attitude toward labor was graphicly revealed in a pamphlet published by the New York abolitionist William Jay in the mid-1830s. In the course of a discussion of the benefits of immediate emancipation, Jay sought to answer the perennial question, what would happen to the slave when free:[11]

> He is free, and his own master, and can ask for no more. Yet he is, in fact, for a time, absolutely dependent on his late owner. He can look to no other person for food to eat, clothes to put on, or house to shelter him. . . . [He is required to work], but labor is no longer the badge of his servitude and the consummation of his misery, for it is *voluntary*. For the first time in his life, he is a party to a contract. . . . In the course of time, the value of negro labor, like all other vendible commodities, will be regulated by the supply and demand.

What is particularly noteworthy in this extraordinary argument is, first, Jay's ready acceptance of the condition which caused so much complaint among the labor movement—the treatment of human labor as a "vendible commodity," and second, the rather loose use of the word "voluntary" to describe the labor of an individual who owns nothing and is "absolutely dependent" on his employer. To the labor movement, Jay's description of emancipation would qualify as a classic instance of "wage slavery"; to Jay, it was an economic definition of freedom.

The labor movement, articulating an ideal stretching back to the republican tradition of the American Revolution, equated freedom with ownership of productive property. To the abolitionists, expressing a newer, liberal definition, freedom meant self-ownership—that is, simply not being a slave. It is one of the more tragic ironies of this complex debate that, in the process of attempting to liberate the slave, the abolitionists did so much to promote a new and severely truncated definition of freedom for both blacks and whites. As many historians have observed, the abolitionist conception of both slavery and freedom was profoundly individualistic. Abolitionism understood slavery not as a class relationship, but as a system of arbitrary and illegitimate power exercised by one individual over another. The slaves and, to some extent, northern workers, were not downtrodden classes but suffering individuals, and it was this liberal, individualist definition of personal freedom which not only cut abolitionists off from the labor movement, but, as Gilbert Osofsky argued, prevented them from making a meaningful response to the economic condition of the Irish, despite a principled effort to overcome nativism and reach out for Irish-American support in the 1840s.[12]

The intense individualism of the abolitionists, historians are agreed, derived from the great revivals of the Second Great Awakening, which identified moral progress with each individual's capacity to act as an instrument of God and opened the possibility of conversion for all as the prelude to eliminating sin from society and paving the way for the Second Coming. Religious benevolence was, it seems clear, the primary root of ante-bellum reform.[13] But it was not the only root, and historians' single-minded emphasis on revivalist Protestantism as the origin of immediate abolitionism has tended to obscure the equally sincere anti-slavery convictions of the radical artisans, so many of whom were influenced by Enlightenment deism. Indeed, the tensions between the labor movement and evangelical abolitionism were part of a larger confrontation during the 1830s between evangelicism and the powerful opposition it generated within northern society. As Jentz has shown, the New York Workingman's leaders were intensely hostile to the evangelical campaign, viewing it as an attempt to unite church and state in a campaign for special privileges incompatible with the principles of republicanism. The campaign against the Sunday mails, led by Lewis and Arthur Tappan shortly before their involvement in abolitionism, aroused considerable opposition among free-thinking artisans, and these same radical artisans were estranged from the anti-slavery movement because of the presence of evangelicals like the Tappans in leadership positions. Nonetheless, when New York's anti-abolitionist riot occurred in 1834, George Henry Evans defended the right of the Tappan brothers to freedom of speech. Later, he again praised abolition as a "just and good cause," although he could not resist the opportunity to add, "many of the Abolitionists are actuated by a species of fanaticism, and are desirous of freeing the slaves, more for the purpose of adding them to a religious sect, than for a love of liberty and justice."[14]

In the eyes of Evans and the radical workingmen for whom he spoke, moreover, Tappan the intolerant Sabbatarian was not unrelated to Tappan the wealthy merchant who was one of the very men helping to transform labor relations at the expense of the laborer. Certainly, the Tappan brothers were not averse to using their economic power to coerce artisans into supporting their various causes. In January 1830, a tailor complained that Lewis Tappan approached him with a petition against the Sunday mails and, when refused, threatened that the tailor would get no more of the trade of his brother Arthur's mercantile firm. To the tailor, Tappan was a "redoubtable champion of Calvinism, illiberalism, etc." To the Tappans, the "infidelity" of men like Robert Owen and George Henry Evans was as offensive as their economic views. Indeed, before leaders of the benevolent empire like the Tappans took control of New York City's abolition movement, anti-slavery had a reputation for being "largely composed of irreligious men, some of infidel sentiments."[15] The great revival of the 1830s changed that, identifying abolitionism with evangelicism and, one presumes, alienating anti-slavery men like Evans from organized abolitionism. But, given the large number of artisans who signed abolitionist petitions, we should not let the evangelicism of the abolitionist leaders obscure that portion of the anti-slavery constituency whose roots lay in Enlightenment rationalism and republican notions of equality and liberty, rather than in Christian benevolence.

For most of the 1830s and 1840s, relations between the abolition and labor movements remained strained. Open attacks on labor organizations, such as that in the first issue of *The Liberator*, were not, however, typical of abolitionist literature. By the end of the 1830s, abolitionists were making an attempt to appeal to workingmen for support. But, whereas labor leaders tended to see abolition as a diversion from the grievances of northern labor and slavery as simply one example of more pervasive problems in American life, abolitionists considered the labor issue as artificial or secondary. Whatever problems northern labor might have, whatever legitimate grievances it might articulate, were all rooted in the peculiar institution. Slavery, said abolitionist literature, made all labor disreputable and was the cause of the degradation of labor in the North. "American slavery," as one abolitionist resolution put it, "is an evil of such gigantic magnitude, that it must be uprooted and overthrown, before the elevation sought by the laboring classes can be effected." Both abolitionists and labor leaders spoke of the alliance between the Lords of the Loom and Lords of the Lash—the textile manufacturers of New England and slaveowners of the South—but each drew from it a different conclusion. To the labor movement, factory owner and slaveowner were both nonproducers who fattened on the fruits of the labor of others; to the abolitionists what was objectionable in the factory owners was precisely their pro-slavery political stance, not their treatment of their employees.[16]

During the 1840s, a handful of abolitionist spokesmen did attempt to forge an alliance with the labor leaders, moving toward a critique of labor relations in the North. John A. Collins became convinced on an abolitionist trip to England that the condition of the working classes deserved attention from opponents of slavery. Slavery, he concluded, was but a symptom of a deeper problem. "The cause of all causes," the deep underlying root of poverty, war, intemperance, and slavery was private property, "the admitted right of individual ownership in the soil and its products." In 1843, Collins joined the communistic society at Skaneateles in western New York State and the next year began publishing *The Communist*. Still later, this peripatetic reformer returned to the Whig party, convinced that only governmental power could effect social reform. His mercurial career did not exactly generate enthusiasm among his erstwhile abolitionist colleagues. Garrison condemned the Owenite environmentalism which lay behind Collins's utopian experiment, interpreting it to mean that men were not individually responsible for their sins. And Frederick Douglass accused Collins, not without plausibility, of "imposing an additional burden of unpopularity on our cause" when Collins attempted to introduce socialist ideas at abolitionist meetings.[17]

Probably the most prominent abolitionist who attempted to rethink the relation between northern and southern labor conditions was Nathaniel P. Rogers, editor of the *Herald of Freedom,* published in Concord, New Hampshire. (I leave aside here John Brown who was, in this as in everything else, *sui generis* among abolitionists. Brown's career of business failures in the 1830s and 1840s, usually taken by historians as evidence of maladjustment, may have made him rather more skeptical of the virtues of the northern economic order than other abolitionists. Interestingly, the Provisional Constitution Brown drafted to apply to territory he planned to "liberate" in the South included a provision that all property captured from the enemy or produced by the labor of his associates would be held "as the property of the whole" and used "for the common benefit.")[18] Rogers proposed a grand alliance of the producing classes North and South, free and slave, against all exploiters of labor. Living amidst the burgeoning factory system of New Hampshire, Rogers concluded that the abolitionist movement had not only been blind to social conditions in the North, but had directed its appeals to the wrong constituency. "We have got to look to the working people of the North, to sustain and carry on the Anti-Slavery Movement," he announced in 1843. "The people who work and are disrespected here, and who disrespect labor themselves, and disrespect themselves because they labor—have got to abolish slavery. And in order to do this, they must be emancipated themselves first." Rogers soon took to organizing anti-slavery meetings at which the condition of northern workingmen received more attention than the plight of the slave. "Very little time was wasted in talk about floggings and starvings, etc.," he said of one such meeting. "Tyranny here at the North; northern servitude and lack of liberty were our main topics. The working people were admonished of their own bondage and degradation." It is easy to understand why veteran abolitionists might find such meetings disquieting. At one New Hampshire gathering, the *Herald of Freedom* was denounced as an "infidel paper" and members of "the Priesthood," as Rogers called the local clergy, attempted to break up the meeting.

Rogers was unique among abolitionist leaders in his complete rejection of the ethos of technological progress and his acceptance of the idea of conflict between capital and labor. Many abolitonists condemned an excessive spirit of greed in northern society, but most were fascinated by technological change, viewing it, indeed, as yet another evidence of the superiority of the northern social system to that of the slave South. Rogers, however, could write: "The money-built Railroad, like all other labor-saving machinery, makes the rich, richer, and the poor, poorer. . . . Monopoly and capital seize on the labor-saving machine, and wield it to the poor man's destruction." Northern labor, "the slave of Capital," was bought and sold "at auction" as in the South, and the abolitionist movement, Rogers insisted, should demand "Liberty for the New Hampshire day-laborers" as well as for the southern bondsman.[19]

Rogers's position was, to say the least, atypical of the abolition leadership. This was made abundantly clear in a lengthy series of letters and editorials which appeared in *The Liberator* in 1846 and 1847. The issue of September 4, 1846, contained a letter Wendell Phillips had addressed to George Henry Evans, whose quest for a solution to the problems of poverty and inequality had come to focus on land policy. Along with the emigrant Irish radical Thomas Devyr, Horace Greeley, and a few

others, Evans now identified land monopoly as the root cause
of poverty and demanded the free distribution of homesteads
to settlers on the public lands, and a limitation on the amount
of land any individual could own. Land monopoly, which
caused low wages and poverty in the eastern cities, was the underlying reason for the "wages slavery" which, Evans still believed, was "even more destructive of the life, health and happiness than chattel slavery as it exists in our Southern States."
(Moreover, insisted the land reformers in a striking antici-
pation of the debates of the Reconstruction years, the emancipated slave would simply "be subject to the slavery of wages,
to be ground down by the competition in the labor market"—a
view of the post-emancipation situation quite different from
that of William Jay quoted above.) Phillips, while admitting the
validity of some of Evans's criticisms of the concentration of
land ownership, was forced to take exception to the equation
of "wages slavery" with slavery in the South, proposing once
again the abolitionist definition of freedom as self-ownership.
Whereupon Evans responded, "the men robbed of their land
are robbed of themselves most effectually."[20]

This exchange touched off a series of editorials and letters
lasting well into the following year. William West rushed to
Evans's defense, insisting land reformers did not ignore the
plight of the slave. "They do not hate chattel slavery less, but
they hate wages slavery more. Their rallying cry is, 'Down with
all slavery, both chattel and wages.' " Some months later, Garrison accused land reformers of "magnifying mole-hills into
mountains, and reducing mountains to the size of mole-hills" in
comparing labor conditions in the North with slavery. "To say
that it is worse for a man to be free, than to be a slave, worse to
work for whom he pleases, when he pleases, and where he
pleases," was simply ridiculous, Garrison insisted. Moreover, it
was "an abuse of language to talk of the slavery of wages. . . .
The evil in society is not that labor receives wages, but that the
wages given are not generally in proportion to the value of the
labor performed. We cannot see that it is wrong to give or re-

ceive wages." Nothing could have made more clear the gap which separated the social outlook of the abolitionists from that of the labor movement. Garrison, defending capitalist labor relations, viewed the ability to contract for wages as a mark of liberty, and he was wholly unable to appreciate the coercions implicit in the marketplace for labor and the wage relation itself. As the indefatigable William West responded, it seemed "surpassing strange" that Garrison had "lived forty years" and still could believe that the northern laborer possessed complete freedom to work when and for whom he desired.[21]

The debate continued in the pages of *The Liberator* until October 1847, when Edmund Quincy closed it with yet another abolitionist defense of northern labor relations. But, apart from a slight diversion in which one correspondent explained that the rule of Christ on earth required a shift to communal ownership of property, the most revealing contribution came from the pen of Wendell Phillips. Once again denying the applicability of the concept "wage slavery" to northern conditions, Phillips perceptively observed that "many of the errors on this point seem to me to proceed from looking at American questions through European spectacles, and transplanting the eloquent complaints against capital and monopoly, which are well-grounded and well-applied there, to a state of society here, where they have little meaning or application." Phillips was certainly correct that many labor leaders viewed American conditions "through European spectacles." The ferocious attack on the evangelical movement in the 1830s, for example, was seemingly more relevant to the situation in the Old World, where the established churches were bulwarks of the status quo, than the very different religious environment of the United States. But Phillips perhaps failed to appreciate fully the central importance of fear of "Europeanization" as an ideological inspiration of the labor movement. Later in his career, of course, Phillips would himself emerge as an eloquent defender of the rights of labor. But in 1847, his prescription for the grievances of the workingman left little room for social reform or institutional change: "to economy, self-denial, temperance, education and moral and religious character, the laboring class, and every other class in this country, must owe its elevation and improvement."[22]

Perhaps the differences in perception which characterized relations between abolitionists and labor leaders down to the late 1840s are symbolized by the fact that when *The Liberator* in 1847 reprinted an article identifying the condition of northern workers as "white slavery," it did so in its column, "Refuge of Oppression"—a portion of the newspaper reserved for items from the pro-slavery press.[23] Garrison could not free himself from the conviction that, by diverting attention from slavery in the South, the labor movement was, in effect, playing into the hands of the defenders of slavery. Yet at this very moment, changes were taking place within both movements which would transform the relations between labor leaders and anti-slavery. One set of changes involved the emergence of opposition to the expansion of slavery as the central political question of the late 1840s, and the vehicle by which anti-slavery became, for the first time, a truly mass movement in the North. Increasingly, the abolitionists were pushed to the side, while free-soilism took center stage as the most available mode of anti-slavery and anti-southern protest. Evangelical abolitionism, it may be suggested, had done its main work in the 1830s. It had succeeded in shattering the conspiracy of silence surrounding the question of slavery. But because it also generated a powerful opposition within northern society—not only from pro-slavery forces, but from those who could not accept the impulse toward "moral stewardship" which was so integral a part of benevolent reform—evangelicism could not make of abolition a majority sentiment. The more secular, rational, and moderate free-soil position could succeed in a way abolitionism could not.

At the same time, the labor movement, devastated by the depression of 1837–42, was turning toward more individualist and self-help-oriented solutions to the problems of northern workingmen.[24] Evans's own emphasis on the land question, which linked social justice so closely to individual ownership of private property, while seemingly abandoning the cooperative thrust of the labor movement of the 1830s, reflected the change. Evans, as we have seen, still insisted that true freedom required economic independence, but he appeared to be abandoning his critique of the wage system itself. Land reform, not a change in the system of production and labor relations, would solve the problem of urban poverty and offer every workingman the opportunity to achieve economic independence, in the form of a homestead.[25]

Free-soilism was not only the means by which anti-slavery rose to political dominance in the 1850s, but the meeting ground for the two strands of anti-slavery thought which had remained estranged in the 1830s and 1840s. The ideological debate between labor and abolition was solved, in a sense, by the early Republican party, for whom the difference between the condition of labor North and South became a potent political rallying cry. The Republican ideology has been analyzed in detail elsewhere[26]; here I want only to suggest that while the Republicans absorbed much of the moral fervor of the abolitionists—while at the same time making that fervor politically respectable and abandoning the abolitionist demand for equal rights for free blacks—their conception of labor and their definition of freedom had much in common with the themes articulated by the labor movement. In the hands of Abraham Lincoln, the workingman's right to the fruits of his own labor became a devastating critique of the peculiar institution. The Republicans accepted the labor leaders' definition of freedom as resting on economic independence rather than, as the abolitionists had insisted, on self-ownership. To Lincoln, the man who worked for wages all his life was indeed almost as unfree as the southern slave. The anti-slavery of a man like Lincoln (who was personally something of a deist) seemed to connect more directly with the artisan anti-slavery tradition than with evangelical abolition. But like the abolitionists, Lincoln and the Republicans located the threat to the independence of the northern workingman outside northern society. It was not the wage system, but the expansion of slavery, which threatened to destroy the independence of the northern worker, his opportunity to escape from the wage-earning class and own a small farm or shop. For if slavery were allowed to expand into the western territories, the safety-valve of free land for the northern worker and farmer would be eliminated, and northern social conditions would soon come to resemble those of Europe. The Republicans therefore identified themselves with the aspirations of northern labor in a way abolitionists never did, but at the same time, helped turn those aspirations into a critique of the South, not an attack on the northern social order.[27]

It has recently been argued, in quite brilliant fashion, that the abolitionist movement in England helped to crystallize middle-class values and identify them with the interests of society at large. By isolating slavery as an unacceptable form of labor exploitation, abolition implicitly (though usually unintentionally) diverted attention from the exploitation of labor taking place within the emergent factory system. "The anti-slavery movement," in other words, "reflected the needs and values of the emerging capitalist order."[28]

Professor David Brion Davis, who is, of course, responsible for this interpretation, does note, almost in passing, that in the 1790s anti-slavery maintained strong links to the radical artisan societies, who were anything but defenders of "the emerging capitalist order." Yet he gives the impression, perhaps inadvertently, that labor anti-slavery either died out, or was subsumed within an evangelical abolitionism which represented the hegemony of middle-class values in nineteenth-century England. A somewhat similar point has recently been made by Alan Dawley regarding the United States. In his study of the transformation of work in Lynn, Dawley argues that the crusade against slavery diverted attention from the evils of the factory system, stunted the growth of ideas critical of the regime of the factory owners, and, in general, crowded labor radicalism "off the center stage" of political debate. Had it not been for the dominance of the slavery issue in the 1850s and 1860s, Dawley suggests—rather implausibly, I might add—an independent labor party might have emerged in the North. As it was, the Lynn shoemakers joined hands with their employers in a crusade against the South, instead of directing their assault against targets at home. "It is difficult to avoid the conclusion that an entire generation was side-tracked in the 1860s because of the Civil War."[29]

Did the crusade against slavery foreclose the possibility of radical criticism within northern society? Toward the end of the nineteenth century, the great reformer Edward Bellamy made a similar point about Horace Greeley. Greeley, who had been attracted to communitarianism in the 1840s and had authored stinging condemnations of northern labor conditions, by the next decade, as spokesman for the Republican party, was glorifying northern labor relations in contrast to those of the South. "Horace Greeley," wrote Bellamy, "would very possibly have devoted himself to some kind of socialistic agitation had not the slavery agitation come on." Bellamy considered Greeley's change of heart inevitable and necessary: "slavery had to be done away with" before social reform could commence in the North. But others were not so certain. Even during the 1830s and 1840s some labor leaders had accused the abolitionists of being the stalking horses for northern capitalists, seeking to divert attention from the labor issue in the North. One anti-abolitionist pamphlet charged that abolitionists themselves were employers who "bask in the sunshine of wealth obtained by pilfering the mechanic's labor." More typical was the perception of an alliance of abolitionists and capitalists, expressed, for instance, in a poem originally published in England and reprinted in an American labor journal, describing the death of a factory girl from starvation:[30]

That night a chariot passed her
While on the ground she lay,
The daughters of her master
An evening visit pay.
Their tender hearts are sighing
As Negroes' woes are told
While the white slave was dying,
Who earned her father's gold.

Unfortunately, this is not only bad poetry, but bad history. The Lords of the Loom were not interested in hearing about "Negroes' woes." Far from being in some kind of tacit alliance with abolitionists, they were among the most pro-slavery and anti-abolitionist group in the North. This fact, it seems to me, casts a certain doubt on the Davis thesis—at least if one wanted to apply it to America—and the arguments of Dawley. Or, perhaps, it simply points up again the ambiguity of the abolitionist heritage. In the hands of a Garrison, anti-slavery did, indeed, promote the acceptance of the free labor market and the capitalist order of the North. So too did the glorification of the northern social order by the Republicans in the 1850s. But that fact should not lead us to forget the other anti-slavery tradition, that of the early labor movement. Eclipsed by the rise of evangelical reform, sidetracked, perhaps, by the free-labor ethos of the Republican party, the labor-oriented critique which linked slavery to labor conditions in the North rose like a phoenix from the ashes of the Civil War, to inspire the great crusades of the National Labor Union, the Knights of Labor, and even the Irish-American Land League.[31] If anti-slavery promoted the hegemony of middle-class values, it also provided a language of politics, a training in organization, for critics of the emerging order. The anti-slavery crusade was a central terminus, from which tracks ran leading to every significant attempt to reform American society after the Civil War. And the notion of "wage slavery," and the traditional republican definition of freedom it embodied, lived on to help frame the social conflicts of late nineteenth-century America.[32]

--<f F I V E f>--

Racial Attitudes
of the
New York Free Soilers

In the United States of the mid-nineteenth century, racial prejudice was all but universal. Belief in black inferiority formed a central tenet of the southern defense of slavery, and in the North too, many who were undecided on the merits of the peculiar institution, and even those who disapproved of it, believed that the Negro was by nature destined to occupy a subordinate position in society. After all, until 1780 slavery had existed throughout the country, and it was only in 1818 that provision had been made for its abolition in every northern state. And even after slavery had been banished from the North, that section continued to subject free Negroes to legal and extra-legal discrimination in almost every phase of their lives. Though these restrictions were less severe than in the South, most of the free states denied blacks the right of suffrage, subjected them to segregation in transportation, excluded them from all but menial employment, and barred their children from the public schools. In the decade of the 1850s,

Originally published in *New York History*, XLVI (Oct. 1965), 311–29. Reprinted by permission of the New York State Historical Association.

four northern states—Indiana, Iowa, Illinois, and Oregon
—went so far as to pass legislation prohibiting Negroes from
entering their territory. One contemporary black writer could
well complain of the "bitterness, malignity, and cruelty of the
American prejudice against colour." The Free Soiler from Indiana George W. Julian put it more bluntly. "The American
people," he wrote, "are emphatically a *Negro-hating* people."[1]

With anti-black feeling so deep-seated and widespread, it
was inevitable that all political parties would have to cope with
the problem of racial prejudice. From its beginning, the anti-
slavery movement had included social and political equality for
northern Negroes as an essential aspect of its program. But
even the abolitionist Liberty party found that its efforts were
hampered by prejudice within its ranks. In one celebrated incident, a Michigan convention denied two Negro delegates the
right to participate in the nomination of candidates on the
ground that they were not legal voters. And in 1844, the party
nominated for the Vice-Presidency ex-Senator Thomas Morris,
a staunch foe of Negro suffrage. Nonetheless, the party constantly avowed its commitment to "the principles of Equal
Rights," and urged its supporters to combat "any inequality of
rights and privileges . . . on account of color." Almost without
exception, the state and national Liberty platforms included
such resolutions, and throughout the North, the party was an
ardent opponent of political and social discrimination against
the free Negro.[2]

During the decade of the 1840s, great numbers of northerners became opponents of slavery, moved either by the moral
appeals of the abolitionists, fear of the southern Slave Power,
or apprehension that the extension of slavery into the newly
acquired territories would exclude free northern settlers. But
astute observers recognized that many who held these views
had been prevented from embracing anti-slavery because of
the Liberty party's adoption of political and social equality for
blacks as one of its major goals. In order for the political
anti-slavery movement to attract a wide following it would have

to adopt a platform so broad that both the prejudiced and the advocates of equal rights could support it. In other words, it would have to divorce itself from the ideal of equality.

That the Free Soil party would achieve this divorce was perhaps to be expected. For although it was established in 1848 as a coalition of anti-slavery Democrats, Whigs, and Liberty party men, united by their opposition to the extension of slavery, the leading organizers of the party came from the Democracy of New York State, which had long opposed the granting of political rights to black citizens. In New York, where Negro suffrage had been almost wholly a party issue, first the Federalists and then the Whigs had endorsed political equality, while the Democratic-Republicans and later the Jacksonian Democrats, with their close ties to the South, had taken the opposite position. Since Negroes, who until 1821 enjoyed full suffrage rights, tended to vote Federalist, and since the Democratic-Republicans and the Democrats were chiefly supported by those elements of the population that feared Negro competition and wished to make the state unattractive for black immigration, the Democrats had both political and economic reasons for wishing to restrict Negro suffrage. At the Constitutional Convention of 1821, the Democrats, even as they were striving to remove all property qualifications for white voters, succeeded in instituting a $250 property requirement for blacks.[3]

In 1846, when another Constitutional Convention was held, friends and opponents of the Negro again divided along party lines. The Whig party did not formally endorse equal suffrage, doubtless because of the prevailing prejudice, but its views were made known through unofficial sources. The leading Whig journal, Horace Greeley's New York *Tribune,* listed elimination of the property qualification for Negroes among its proposals for constitutional reform, and bewailed the "Colorphobia which prevails so extensively in the ranks of our modern 'Democracy.' "[4] The Liberty party took the same position.[5]

The Democratic press, on the other hand, staunchly opposed

any reduction in the property requirement. The *Morning News,* which espoused the views of the party's loco-foco wing, from which many of the Free Soilers would come, had, in 1845, argued that the annexation of Texas would rid the nation of Negroes by providing a "safety-valve" for their migration to Latin America. Now, it bluntly asserted that the Negro race was inferior to the white, insisted that free Negroes should be allowed no political rights at all, and defended Samuel J. Tilden against the "base charge" of favoring Negro suffrage. William Cullen Bryant's *Evening Post,* soon to become the state's chief Free Soil organ, completely avoided the issue of Negro suffrage in its discussions of constitutional reform, but seemed to agree with other Democratic papers that equal suffrage would dangerously increase Whig power in the state. Though Bryant insisted that free Negroes should be considered citizens, he pointed out that New York's white voters had the right to place limits on that citizenship, if they chose. When the election of delegates to the Convention took place, the Democrats appealed so blatantly to racial prejudice that Greeley later recalled, "we should, in all probability, have carried two-thirds of the Constitutional Convention but for the cries of 'Nigger Party,' 'Amalgamation,' and 'Fried Wool,' etc., which were raised against us."[6]

For some years, the New York Democracy had been divided into two wings, differing on matters of economic policy and federal patronage. At the Convention of 1846, however, both Hunkers and Barnburners stood together to block any extension of Negro suffrage. Thirteen of the Democratic delegates later became prominent Free Soilers, yet none voted in favor of a motion granting equal suffrage to the state's black citizens.[7] Indeed, a majority of these delegates, including Samuel J. Tilden, also opposed a proposal to reduce the property qualification to $100. And when equal suffrage was voted upon as a separate issue in November, it was defeated by a resounding margin: 223,845 to 85,306. St. Lawrence County, in 1848 termed the "banner county" of the Free Soil party, opposed equal suffrage by a two-to-one margin. Years later, Horace Greeley would tell a New York audience how he had stood at a polling place on that rainy election day, peddling ballots for equal suffrage. "I got many Whigs to take them," he recalled, "but not one Democrat."[8]

But the Democracy's unity on the question of Negro rights could not offset its internal divisions on other issues. The party which had enjoyed political hegemony for so many years in the Empire State was disrupted and driven from power by the issue of the Wilmot Proviso. In September 1847, when the State Democratic Convention, controlled by the Hunker faction, tabled a resolution demanding that slavery be excluded from the territory acquired from Mexico, and then denied renomination to the Barnburner Comptroller Azariah C. Flagg, the Barnburners walked out. A month later they met at Herkimer, endorsed the Proviso, and repudiated the Hunker nominees, who were decisively defeated at the polls by the Whigs. The most prominent members of the New York Democracy— John Van Buren, Preston King, Samuel J. Tilden, C. C. Cambreleng, and Flagg—remained aloof from their party in 1848, and organized the Free Soil party.[9]

Although the question of the extension of slavery was the immediate cause of the Barnburner revolt, the bolters did not alter their attitude toward the Negro as a result of their adherence to the Proviso. On the contrary, they made it clear that their support of the Proviso was based as much on repugnance to the prospect of a Negro population, free or slave, in the territories, as on an opposition to the spread of the institution of slavery. Theirs was no moral opposition to the slave system; ex-Congressman Michael Hoffman, for example, a leading Barnburner until his death early in 1848, had sneered at John P. Hale's anti-slavery campaign a few years earlier as "that *Negroism* that shakes the granite hills of New Hampshire." The Barnburners were concerned for the fate of the free white laborer of the North. They had been ardent expansionists and were now determined to prevent the new territories from being

swallowed up by slavery. Free white laborers would never mi-
grate to an area of slavery, both because of their animosity to
the Negro, and because they could not compete with slave
labor.[10]

Over and over the Barnburners reiterated that their interest
was not in the Negro, free or slave, but in the free white laborer. As one Barnburner Congressman put it in 1848:

> I speak not of the condition of the slave. I do not pretend to
> know, nor is it necessary that I should express an opinion in this
> place, whether the effect of slavery is beneficial or injurious to
> him. I am looking to its effect upon the white man, the free white
> man of this territory.[11]

Moreover, when they enumerated the degrading effects of
slavery on the free white worker, the Barnburners invariably
listed association with Negro slaves as most important. They
were worried by the assertions of some southerners, that the
territories provided a "natural outlet" for some of the South's
Negro population, and in order to safeguard the rights of
white labor in the territories, they insisted that slavery, and
therefore the Negro, be excluded. The Barnburners made no
real distinction between the free Negro and the slave, and believed that white labor would be degraded by association with
"the labor of the black race." For them, the terms "free labor"
and "white labor" were interchangeable, as were "black labor"
and "slave labor." Often, the seemingly unnecessary adjective
"black" before the word "slave" testified to an aversion to the
presence of any black men in the territories. "We deem it indispensable," wrote Martin Van Buren (who, in 1821, had been
one of the few Democrats at the Constitutional Convention to
support Negro suffrage) "that black slaves shall be excluded
from the territories." On other occasions, the structure of a
sentence indicated that, in Barnburner rhetoric, white and
slave, and black and free, were perfect antonyms. One pamphlet, for example, spoke of a West settled "exclusively by
white yeomen," as contrasted with the vision of "the same

region given up . . . to a slave population." Thus, the Negro,
free or slave, had no place in the Barnburners' image of life in
the territories. The Wilmot Proviso, as they saw it, was emphatically "the Laboring White Man's Proviso." [12]

The spokesmen of the Barnburners in Congress reiterated
this position. Senator John A. Dix, the Free Soil gubernatorial
candidate in 1848, who had made frequent assertions of his
belief in Negro inferiority, declared in the Senate that North
America was destined to be populated by the white race. In a
much publicized speech, he declared that the Negro race was
doomed "by the unalterable law of its destiny," to die out
within a few generations. The extension of slavery would only
diffuse the black race, and prolong its existence. The territories, Dix continued, should be reserved for "the multiplication of the white race . . . the highest in the order of intellectual and physical endowments." Dix's speech was widely
circulated and one Barnburner wrote him enthusiastically that
it was "the great speech of the present age." Dix also indicated
that he opposed the abolition of slavery in the District of Columbia, even though the Free Soil platform called for emancipation there.[13] His attitude toward the Negro and slavery was
strikingly different from that of his running mate, the veteran
anti-slavery Whig Seth M. Gates, who had voted for James G.
Birney, the Liberty party candidate, in 1844. Gates's name was
revered by Negroes in both northern and border states as one
who hid fugitive slaves in his upstate New York home, and
helped them reach Canada.[14]

Even Preston King, the Congressman from St. Lawrence
County, who represented the most radical wing of the Barnburners, and who had been denied the Free Soil nomination
for governor because of his extreme anti-slavery views, insisted
that white labor must not be excluded from the territories, nor
subjected to association with "the black labor of slaves." The
Northwest Ordinance, he declared, had saved the Northwest
from "the evils of slavery and a black population," and any man
who opposed a similar proscription for the newly acquired ter-

ritories, he termed "false and recreant to his race." This did
not, of course, alter his hatred of slavery, but surely President
Polk's Secretary of War, William L. Marcy, was right when he
wrote of John Van Buren and King that, though they would
"break up the union" over the Wilmot Proviso, "yet neither
. . . care for negroes."[15]

These prejudices were shared by the man whose name had
become a symbol of resistance to the extension of slavery,
David Wilmot, the Democrat who became leader of the Free
Soil party of Pennsylvania. Wilmot, like the Barnburners, did
not regard slavery as a moral issue. Although he viewed the institution as a political, economic, and social evil, he was particularly outraged by its degradation of the white race. The Proviso, he explained in Congress, was not motivated by any
"squeamish sensitiveness upon the subject of slavery, [or] morbid sympathy for the slave," and he objected strenuously when,
as he put it, an attempt was made "to bring odium upon this
movement, as one designed especially for the benefit of the
black race." Instead, he insisted, "I plead the cause and rights
of the free white man." The question was simple—should the
territories be reserved for the white laborer, "or shall [they] be
given up to the African and his descendants?" Wilmot's answer
was emphatic—white labor must not be degraded by association
with "the servile labor of the black." Besides, he declared, "the
negro race already occupy enough of this fair continent."
Speaking at the Herkimer Convention, the Pennsylvanian accepted the phrase "White Man's Proviso" as an accurate description of the measure which bore his name.[16]

Indeed, when Wilmot, a life-long opponent of abolitionism,
cautiously held out the hope that in the remote future, the
South might voluntarily emancipate its slaves, he stressed that
coupled with this should be the "great work . . . [of] the separation of the two races." In addition, Wilmot consistently opposed the granting of political rights to northern Negroes.
When a southern Congressman charged that he favored political and social equality between the races, the Pennsylvanian

cried out indignantly, "my vote shows no such thing." And
when Joshua Giddings proposed that *all* the residents of the
District of Columbia vote in a referendum to determine the
fate of slavery in the nation's capital, Wilmot was incensed. He
found it "highly objectionable," he wrote, "to admit the blacks,
bond and free, to vote upon the question."[17]

This blatant prejudice did not go unnoticed in Wilmot's own
state. A month after the election of 1848, the *Pennsylvania Freeman*, the Keystone State's abolitionist journal, lashed out at Wilmot after a speech in which he repeated his contrast between
"black labor" and "free labor" as if, wrote the *Freeman*, "it were
the negro and not slavery which degraded labor." The anti-
slavery organ continued:

> A man of Mr. Wilmot's intelligence and observation ought to
> know that it matters very little for the honor of labor what is the
> color of the laborers. Enslaved, his labor is degraded, free, it
> becomes honorable. Let slavery be abolished and the colored peo-
> ple of the North no longer be identified with an *enslaved* race, and
> this truth will be seen.

Wilmot's attitude, the *Freeman* conjectured, "seemed the result
of an old and unconscious prejudice in his mind."[18]

II

It is not surprising that Negroes and many white anti-slavery
men were aware of, and distressed by, these expressions of race
bias, even during the organizational period of the Free Soil
party. Many looked forward to the party's first national assembly, the Buffalo Convention of August 1848, to determine
how widespread prejudice would be in the new party. The fact
that Negroes were in attendance at Buffalo, and addressed the
Convention, led some to hope that the party would not be
marred by anti-Negro feeling. One abolitionist wrote enthusiastically to the Liberty party leader Gerrit Smith, that "men of
all political and religious complexions and of all *colors* were

called to the platform to address the Convention."[19] Yet the
harmony which seemed to prevail at Buffalo was, at best, delu-
sive. Abolitionists did not know that it was only after a bitter
argument among the Barnburners, and at the insistence of
Martin Van Buren, that they had been invited to the gathering
at all. Nor were they cognizant of the behind-the-scenes maneuvering which had been necessary to secure the nomination of
the ex-President.[20]

And even in the atmosphere of enthusiasm which animated
the delegates, racial prejudice did not subside. Francis W. Bird
of Massachusetts was presiding officer of one of the sessions.
Years later he told how Barnburner delegates surrounded him,
urging him not to give the floor to the black abolitionist Frederick Douglass. "They didn't want a 'nigger' to talk to them," he
recalled. "I told them," Bird continued, "we came there for
free soil, free speech and free men; and I gave a hint to Mr.
Douglass that if he would claim the floor when the gentleman
who was then speaking gave it up, he should certainly have
it."[21] It is true that Douglass was warmly applauded, and that
when he indicated that he did not intend to speak, the delegates seemed disappointed. Yet the Negroes who did speak did
not receive a completely cordial reception. One Ohio delegate,
for example, complained that he resented "taking his cue from
a 'nigger.' "[22]

The platform adopted at Buffalo, written by Salmon P.
Chase, the Liberty party leader from Ohio, and the Barnburner Benjamin F. Butler, met with the almost unanimous approval of the Liberty men present.[23] In order to secure the
nomination of Van Buren, the Barnburners had had to accept
a more radical program than they themselves would have written. Thus, the Buffalo platform not only opposed the extension of slavery, but also advocated homestead legislation, and
called upon the federal government to disassociate itself from
the institution of slavery. Though it acknowledged that slavery
in the states was outside the province of federal power, it did
call for abolition in the District of Columbia. "The Liberty plat-

form," exclaimed the Chicago *Western Citizen*, "has been adopted by the Free Soil party and its nominee," and almost without exception, the Liberty press of the country flocked to the new standard. Joshua Leavitt, Liberty party leader from Massachusetts, in a widely publicized remark asserted at Buffalo, "the Liberty party is not dead, but translated," and he later wrote an open letter to the supporters of the Liberty party, urging them to vote for Van Buren. The Liberty presidential candidate, John P. Hale, quickly withdrew his candidacy, and one of his abolitionist constituents wrote him that he could "stand very comfortably" on the Buffalo platform.[24]

But one basic plank of the Liberty platform had been sacrificed. Leavitt could ask rhetorically, "what have we lost? Not one of our principles, not one of our aims, not one of our men," but many Liberty men and many Negroes remembered that James G. Birney had written that "the grant of the Elective Franchise to the colored people" was a primary goal of his party.[25] The "translation" of the Liberty party had only been achieved at the expense of the ideal of equality.

To many black leaders, and to the radical wing of the Liberty party, led by Gerrit Smith, this change could not go unnoticed. When a small Negro newspaper, the *Ram's Horn* of New York City, endorsed Van Buren, Smith wrote a sharp letter of protest. He had thought, he wrote, that it would be unnecessary to explain to black men why they should not support the Free Soilers. It was obvious that Van Buren was making no efforts either to deliver the Negro race from slavery, or to combat racial prejudice. The Free Soil candidate, Smith insisted, differed in no essential respect from the vast majority of his fellow Americans in his "views and treatment of the colored race." In view of these facts, Smith contended, black citizens could not expect any better treatment from a Free Soil government than a Democratic or Whig administration. Negroes, he concluded, should not vote for Free Soilers, who "acquiesce, and even take part, in the proscription and crushing of your race," but should give their suffrage to Smith himself. Smith was running as a Liberty party candidate, and espoused equal rights for all men.[26]

Samuel R. Ward, a black abolitionist who had been present at Buffalo, offered the same advice to the Negro community. The absence of a plank advocating equal rights in the Buffalo platform might seem an oversight, he wrote, but actually, "it has the appearance of studied and deliberate design." Ward pointed out that the Barnburners had always opposed Negro suffrage, and argued that the equal rights plank had been intentionally left out of the platform, in order not to conflict with the "words, deeds and character of the leading men of the Free Soil party in this state." The Free Soilers of New York, wrote Ward, were "as ready to rob black men of their rights now as ever they were . . . Mr. Dix and Mr. Butler we know to be approvers and fosterers of the bitterest prejudices against us."[27]

Not all Negro leaders, however, agreed with Ward. Frederick Douglass, for example, though he himself was a non-voting, or Garrisonian, abolitionist in 1848, urged those friends of the slave who did vote to support Van Buren. Many Free Soilers, he insisted, had changed their attitude toward the Negro, and the party as a whole should be judged by its deeds, not its words. Besides, few abolitionists had completely freed themselves from prejudice, and bias in the Free Soil party might be combatted by Negroes working within the new organization. Douglass realized that men like Gerrit Smith, who had close personal relationships with free Negroes, were much more likely to be egalitarian in their views than men like the upstate New York Barnburners, who rarely saw a Negro. Another Negro, in a letter to Douglass's newspaper, the *North Star*, though admitting that it was "well known" that nine-tenths of the Barnburners had opposed equal suffrage, and would in all probability do so again, argued that the absence of an equal rights plank in the Buffalo platform should not prevent Negroes in other states from supporting the party. This, he continued, was a local, not a national issue, and would therefore be out of place in a national platform. New York Negroes, however, were advised to think twice before supporting Dix and the other Barnburners, who had openly proclaimed the white race's superiority.[28]

Apparently, most of the free Negroes of the North adopted this line of thinking, for outside New York, where Free Soil leaders were mostly former Liberty men or Whigs, more favorable to Negro rights than the New York Free Soilers, black citizens overwhelmingly supported the new party. In the Empire State, however, many remembered that the Liberty party, as late as 1847, had included the "local issue" of equal rights in its national resolutions, and followed the advice of Ward: vote "for Smith and Equal Rights."[29]

By 1850, the New York Democracy had been reunited, and many of the Free Soil leaders, including C. C. Cambreleng, John Van Buren, and Samuel J. Tilden, remained with their party through the Civil War. Even those who, like King, were destined to join the Republican party within a few years, accepted the Compromise of 1850 and expressed the hope that agitation of the slavery question was at an end.[30] Many of the Barnburners had joined the Free Soil party with the primary purpose of restoring the balance of power between the sections in the Democratic party by demonstrating that General Lewis Cass could not be elected without the votes of northern Democrats, and some desired to defeat Cass solely to "revenge" the denial of the Democratic nomination to Van Buren four years earlier. With Cass defeated, they were ready to regard the Hunkers, as John Van Buren said, as "enemies in war—in peace, friends."[31] Those New York Negroes who had supported the ex-President in 1848 resumed their attitude of hostility to the Democratic party. Just before the election of 1849, a meeting of black citizens in New York City announced its determination to work for the defeat of the "union" Democratic ticket. Commenting on this, the *National Era*, the only national journal of the Free Soil party, indicated that it was "not much surprised at the conduct of the colored people." "We trust," the

Era continued, "that the reunited Democracy of New York henceforth will show that it no longer measures out justice according to complexion."[32]

The New York *Evening Post*, however, rejected this advice. In the campaign of 1848, Bryant's journal, like the rest of the Barnburner organs, had opposed the introduction of "negro labor" into the territories. After the election, the *Post* continued to object to the introduction of slavery into the territories, either "under the form of well subdued slaves, or hoardes of free negroes," and it protested vigorously when a southern paper proposed that some of the "dense free black population" of the South be sent to New Mexico and California. Bryant did favor the repeal of some discriminatory laws in the North, but he argued that the free states were an "uncongenial clime" for Negroes, and hoped that the races might be permanently separated. Though the *Post* opposed compulsory colonization, it praised the Colonization Society and the Anti-Slavery Society for "contemplating, in different ways, the good of the African race," and said it hoped that both would achieve their objectives.[33]

In addition, the *Post*, which, even after the reunion of the New York Democracy, continued to consider itself a "free soil" journal, bluntly asserted that the white race was superior to the Negro. In urging black citizens to emigrate to some tropical region, it argued that "unequal laws and inveterate social prejudices" made the elevation of the free Negro impossible in this country. Yet it was sure to suggest that the inveterate prejudices were not entirely unfounded. The Negro was, to be sure, unequal to the white man, for in his new home he would have to "take those primary lessons in civilization which his race has never yet mastered." The two races, associate editor John Bigelow (one of the few Barnburners to support equal suffrage in 1846) wrote, could not prosper together, for "the superior intelligence and advantages of the whites" would prevent the Negroes from acquiring self-reliance and independence. Finally, in 1853, the *Post* published a series of articles which perhaps best characterized its position on race and slavery. The series, a "scientific" study of the Negro race, concluded that although the Negro was by nature indolent, mentally inferior, and "hardly capable of elevating himself to the height of civilization," he was a man, and slavery was "an abuse of superior mental endowment." In this manner, the *Post* was able to combine an unrelenting racial prejudice with an anti-slavery position.[34]

III

In assessing the racial attitudes of the Free Soil party of New York, it must be remembered that the Barnburners were less prejudiced in their outlook than their Hunker opponents. Thus, although the New York counties which Van Buren carried in 1848 had, two years earlier, opposed equal suffrage by 16,668 to 10,166, this ratio (1.6 to 1) was much smaller than the state-wide margin of 2.7 to 1. On the other hand, the counties carried by Cass voted against removing the property qualification for black citizens by 8,597 to 2,540, or 3.6 to 1, far greater than the overall margin. After all, the Barnburners, despite their reservations, were able to participate in the Buffalo Convention alongside Negro delegates, while the prospect of an integrated convention filled the Hunkers with horror. As a Boston Free Soil newspaper put it, "there is no hatred so infernal as the hatred of a Northern Hunker towards the blacks."[35]

Moreover, the rather blatant prejudice of the Free Soilers of Democratic extraction was by no means representative of the views of the entire party. Indeed, the *National Era*, in June 1848, sharply criticized the Barnburners' prejudice. "Studiously placing their opposition to the extension of slavery on the ground of abhorrence of 'black slaves,' rather than the despotism that imbrutes them" it charged, many Barnburners were "apparently fearful of having their Anti-Slavery position attributed to generous convictions of the brotherhood of the

Human Race." "We distrust these men," the *Era* added. And in
Pennsylvania, the leading Free Soil newspaper, the Philadelphia *Republic,* openly differed with the views of David Wilmot
by denouncing racial prejudice and calling the restriction of
suffrage to white citizens a disgrace to the state.[36]

It is thus an oversimplification to equate Free Soil with an
aversion to the presence of Negroes in the territories, as some
historians have done.[37] The Free Soil party, or, as it was later
called, the Free Democracy, was a political party with no truly
national organization, only one national newspaper (the *National Era*), and only a handful of recognized spokesmen in
Washington. Most of its work was done by the various state
parties, some of which died out soon after the election of 1848,
some of which survived until 1854, and all of which were completely autonomous. In most of the states outside New York,
the Free Soilers came from a tradition of support for Negro
rights, and the party, though by no means free from prejudice,
sincerely strove to combat discrimination.[38]

But the main organizational impulse in 1848 had come from
the Barnburners of New York, and it was inevitable that the
Buffalo Free Soil platform would reflect their views. And so for
the first time, an anti-slavery political party disregarded the
issue of equal rights for free Negroes in its national platform.
"The old negro-hating colonizationist of '33 would almost have
accepted the present Free Soil platform," complained the *Pennsylvania Freeman,* and it was right.[39] The party's platform was so
broad that it could gain the support of those who opposed slavery in order to prevent Negroes from fleeing North and those
who desired to keep the territories free from the presence of
the Negro slave, as well as the veteran anti-slavery men with
their moral abhorrence of the institution, and northerners
worried by the great influence of the Slave Power in the federal
government. The Free Soil party numbered in its ranks the
most vulgar racists and the most determined supporters of
Negro rights, as well as all shades of opinion between these extremes. It was the only anti-slavery position that could ac-

complish this because the question of Negro rights, potentially such a divisive issue, was simply avoided in its national platform.

In this sense, the Free Soil party marked a vital turning point in the development of the anti-slavery crusade. It represented anti-slavery in its least radical form, and its platform gained a popularity which no other could have achieved. Southerners realized that the very fact that the sage old politician from Kinderhook had agreed to run as the party's standard-bearer was proof of its wide support. "Such a man," Calhoun recognized, "would never have consented to be placed in that position unless he was convinced that the North had determined to rally on this great question. . . ." Indeed, some observers believed that Van Buren would have carried the North, had not the free state Whigs and Democrats claimed free soil as their own cause. By the end of 1849, every northern legislature except Iowa's had endorsed the Proviso, and some had even called for abolition in the nation's capital. The effect was summed up by New York's William H. Seward; "Anti-slavery is at length a respectable element in politics."[40]

Even in 1852, when the Barnburners were no longer in the Free Soil party, the ex-Whigs and Liberty men realized that it would be politically inadvisable to call for political and social equality for free Negroes in their national platform.[41] Samuel R. Ward may have been right when he suggested in 1848 that this plank was omitted at Buffalo so as not to offend the Barnburners. But the bulk of the Liberty party and the Free Soilers of Whig background had reacted enthusiastically to the Buffalo platform, even without an equal rights plank, and Free Soil leaders after 1848 realized that to reintroduce a call for equality for the free Negro would cost the party far more support than it would gain. In their short association with the anti-slavery movement the Barnburners thus changed that movement's course decisively. Once the commitment to equal rights had been deleted from the platform of political anti-slavery, it would never again be reinstated.

LAND AND LABOR
AFTER THE
CIVIL WAR

Reconstruction and the Crisis of Free Labor

No period of American history has been the subject of a more thoroughgoing transformation in historical interpretation than Reconstruction, the turbulent era which followed the Civil War. The successive transitions from traditional to revisionist to post-revisionist views of Reconstruction have often been chronicled.[1] More striking, if less frequently noted, is the fact that while an older view of these years as a time of "black supremacy" and rampant misgovernment has long been discredited, no coherent vision of the totality of political and social life has emerged to replace it. Historians have been unable to construct a modern synthesis from the vastly increased body of knowledge and the sensitivity to the politics of race which have been the hallmarks of recent scholarship.

Among the ironies of writing on Reconstruction is that in the desire to jettison the racism of William Dunning and his students—who inaugurated the scholarly study of the period at the turn of this century—their insights have also been abandoned. For, apart from racism, if anything characterized the Dunningites, it was a recognition that Reconstruction was a na-

ld only be understood within a na-
10 less than the South, was recon-

ruction, North and South, stood a
ations and the emergence of wide-
ital and labor as the principal eco-
m of the period. The change was
it involved not the overthrow of an
the spread of new forms of indus-
r discipline, and a crisis of the free
labor ideology inherited from the pre-war years and based
upon the idea of harmony between diverse economic groups.
In the South, the abolition of slavery posed the question of
labor in a starker form. There, the crucial problem became the
one which, over forty years ago, W. E. B. Du Bois identified as
the key to Reconstruction: the new status of black labor in the
aftermath of emancipation. As William H. Trescot, an unusually far-sighted South Carolina planter, explained to his
state's governor late in 1865, "You will find that this question of
the control of labor underlies every other question of state interest."[2]

That the transition from slave to free labor involved a revolution in social and racial relations in the South, few contemporaries doubted. "Society has been completely changed by the
war," observed former Confederate General Richard Taylor.
"The revolution of [1789] did not produce a greater change in
the 'Ancien Regime' than has this in our social life." A striking
example of the pervasive experience of revolutionary change is
afforded in the account of a visit by the great rice planter Louis
Manigault to his Savannah River plantation in 1867:

> I imagined myself, for the moment a Planter once more, followed
> by Overseer and Driver. . . . These were only passing momentary
> thoughts . . . soon dispelled by the sad reality of affairs. . . . In
> my conversation with these Negroes, now free, and in beholding
> them my thoughts turned to other Countries, and I almost
> imagined myself with Chinese, Malays, or even the Indians in the

interior of the Philippine islands. That mutual and pleasant feeling of Master toward Slave and vice versa is now as a dream of the
past.

Manigault, of course, may have been entirely mistaken as to
how extensively that "mutual and pleasant feeling" had been
shared by his slaves. But it is clear that he perceived himself to
be living in a new and alien world.[3]

The confused early years of Reconstruction become more
comprehensible when we consider the difficulty planters had in
adjusting to their new status as employers, and freedmen in
becoming free laborers. "The former relation has to be un-
learnt by both parties," was how a South Carolina planter put
it. For many planters, the unlearning process was a painful
one. The normal give and take of employer and employee was
difficult to accept; "it seems humiliating," wrote one Georgian,
"to be compelled to bargain and haggle with our servants about
wages." One North Carolina farmer employed a freedman in
the spring of 1865, promising to give him "whatever was right"
when the crop was gathered. Another said he would pay wages
"where I thought them earned, but this must be left to me."
Behavior completely normal in the North, such as a freedman
informing a Georgia farmer he was leaving because "he
thought he could do better," provoked cries of outrage and
charges of ingratitude.[4]

Among white southerners, the all-absorbing question of 1865
and 1866 was, "Will the free Negro work?" For it was an article
of faith among white southerners that the freedmen were in-
herently indolent and would work only under supervision and
coercion by whites. The papers of planters, as well as newspapers and magazines, were filled with complaints of black labor
having become "disorganized and repugnant to work or direction." As one group of Mississippi blacks observed, "Our faults
are daily published by the editors, not a statement will you ever
see in our favor. There is surely some among us that is honest,
truthful and industrious." But to whites, the problem was clear-

cut: as a member of South Carolina's Middleton family put it, "there is no power to make the negroes work and we know that without that they will not work."[5]

In the years following the Civil War, a complex triangular debate was played out among freedmen, northern whites, and southern planters, over the nature of the South's new free labor system. For northerners, the meaning of "free labor" derived from the anti-slavery crusade, at the heart of which stood a critique of slavery dating back at least as far as Adam Smith. Slavery, Smith had insisted (more as an ideological article of faith than on the basis of empirical investigation) was the least efficient, most expensive method of making people work. The reason lay in unalterable facts of human nature. Labor was distasteful, and the only reason men worked productively was to acquire property and satisfy their material wants. Since the slave had no vested interest in the results of his labor, he worked as little as possible. Smith's message had been hammered home by the anti-slavery movement in the years before the Civil War: slavery was costly, inefficient, and unproductive; freedom meant prosperity, efficiency, and material progress.

An elaborate ideology defending the northern system of "free labor" had developed in the two decades before the Civil War. To men like Abraham Lincoln the salient quality of northern society was the ability of the laborer to escape the status of wage earner and rise to petty entrepreneurship and economic independence. Speaking within a republican tradition which defined freedom as resting on ownership of productive property, Lincoln used the term "free labor" to embrace small farmers and petty producers as well as wage laborers. But within this definition a question persisted: why should the independent artisan or farmer work at all, except to satisfy his immediate wants? The answer, once again, derived from the classical paradigm of Adam Smith, as elaborated by his American descendants Henry Carey, E. Pershine Smith, and others. The ever-increasing variety of human wants, desires, and ambitions was, for these writers, the greatest spur to economic progress. It was these "wants" which led northern farmers to produce for the market; indeed, from the northern point of view, participation in the marketplace honed those very qualities that distinguished northern labor from that of the slave—efficiency, productivity, industriousness.[6]

Thus, there was no contradiction, in northern eyes, between the freedom of the laborer and unrelenting personal effort in the marketplace. As General O. O. Howard, head of the Freedmen's Bureau, told a group of blacks in 1865, "he would promise them nothing but their freedom, and freedom means work." Such statements, as well as the coercive labor policies adopted by the Bureau in many localities, have convinced recent scholars that an identity of interests existed between the Bureau and southern planters. Certainly, many Bureau practices seemed designed to serve the needs of the planters, especially the stringent orders of 1865 restricting blacks' freedom of movement and requiring them to sign labor contracts, while withholding relief rations from those who refused. On the other hand, it is difficult to reconcile this recent view of the Bureau with the unrelenting hostility of southern whites to its presence in the South.[7]

The Freedmen's Bureau was not, in reality, the agent of the planters, nor was it precisely the agent of the former slaves. It can best be understood as the agent of the northern free labor ideology itself; its main concern was to put into operation a viable free labor system in the South. To the extent that this meant putting freedmen back to work on plantations, the Bureau's interests coincided with those of the planters. To the extent that the Bureau demanded for the freedmen the rights to which northern laborers were accustomed, it meant an alliance with the blacks. The issue was how the freedmen should be induced to work. Northerners looked to the market itself to provide the incentive, for it was participation in the marketplace which would make self-disciplined free laborers of the blacks, as well as generating a harmony of interests between capital and labor and allowing for social mobility, as, ostensibly, existed in the North. The northern preference for a system in which skilled and educated men worked voluntarily to satisfy ever-expanding wants, generating an endless spiral of prosperity for both capital and labor, was strikingly articulated by the Maine-born Georgia Bureau agent, John E. Bryant:[8]

> Formerly, you were obliged to work or submit to punishment, now you must be induced to work, not compelled to do it. . . . You will be better laborers if educated. Men do not naturally love work, they are induced to work from necessity or interest. That man who has the most wants will usually labor with the greatest industry unless those wants are supplied without labor. The more intelligent men are the more wants they have, hence it is for the interest of all that the laborers shall be educated.

Although Bryant, like so many other Army and Bureau agents in 1865, issued stringent regulations against black "idleness and vagrancy," he essentially viewed the problem of southern economic readjustment through the lens of labor, rather than race. The same psychology that governed white labor, applied to blacks: "*No* man loves work naturally. . . . Why does the *white man* labor? That he may acquire property and the means of purchasing the comforts and luxuries of life. The *colored man* will labor for the same reason."[9]

Spokesmen for the free labor ideology like Bryant viewed the contract system inaugurated by the Freedmen's Bureau in 1865 not as a permanent framework for the southern economy, but as a transitional arrangement, a way of reestablishing agricultural production until cash became readily available and a bona fide free labor system could emerge. General Robert K. Scott, head of the Bureau in South Carolina, explained rather cavalierly to Governor James L. Orr that the state could not hope to escape "the fixed principles which govern [free labor] all over the world." "To the establishment of these principles," he added, "the Bureau is committed." Even Wager Swayne, considered one of the most pro-planter state Bureau chiefs, believed the contract system was "only excusable as a transient." Eventually, as in the North, the natural internal mechanisms of the labor market would regulate employment: "This is more and better than all laws."[10]

Men like Swayne and Scott, however, quickly became convinced that the planters did not comprehend the first principles of free labor. Scott found in 1866 that their idea of a contract was one "that would give the land owner an absolute control over the freedman as though he was his slave." Northern visitors to the South reached the same conclusion. Whitelaw Reid found planters "have no sort of conception of free labor. They do not comprehend any law for controlling laborers, save the law of force." Carl Schurz, one of the most articulate spokesmen for the free labor ideology before the war, concluded that white southerners were unable to accept the cardinal principles that "the only incentive to faithful labor is self-interest," and that a labor contract must be "a free transaction in which neither coercion nor protection is necessary."[11]

Northern and southern perceptions of "free labor" did indeed differ. Planters did not believe that freedmen could ever achieve the internal self-discipline necessary for self-directed labor. The free labor ideology, they insisted, ignored "the characteristic indolence of the negro, which will ever be manifested and indulged in a condition of freedom." It was pointless, therefore, to speak of white and black labor in the same breath: the black was *sui generis,* and you must argue for him upon his own characteristics." Only legal and physical compulsion could maintain the discipline and availability of plantation labor, in the face of the collapse of the planters' authority and the "indolence" of the laborers. "Our little sovereignties and Feudal arrangements are all levelled to the ground," bemoaned one South Carolina planter. As a result, planters turned to the state to provide the labor discipline which they could no longer command as individuals. "A new labor system," declared a New Orleans newspaper in 1865, must be "prescribed and enforced by the state." Hence, the southern legislatures of 1865–66 enacted a series of vagrancy laws, apprenticeship systems, criminal penalties for breach of contract, and all the other coercive measures of the Black Codes, in an effort to control the black labor force. As one Georgian explained, despite the general conviction that "the negro will not work. . . . we can control by wise laws."[12]

The differences in outlook which divided northern and southern whites were strikingly expressed by a southern planter who told a northern visitor, "all we want, is that our Yankee rulers should give us the same privileges with regard to the control of labor which they themselves have." When informed that northern workers were not legally obligated to sign yearly contracts, and that there were no criminal penalties for leaving one's employment, he was incredulous: "How can you get work out of a man unless you *compel* him in some way?" This very question as Joyce Appleby has observed, haunted seventeenth- and eighteenth-century English economic theorists: how could individual freedom and the need for labor be reconciled, especially if it were assumed that men naturally desired to avoid labor? The answer was to posit a labor force imbued with economic rationality, that is, the willingness to subordinate itself to the incentives of the marketplace. "The acceptance of the idea of universal economic rationality," according to Appleby, "was the key step in the triumph of modern liberalism."[13]

"Modern liberalism," however, had implications the leaders of southern society could not accept. The ideological underpinning of economic liberalism is freedom of choice among equals, however much free contract and equality may in fact diverge. By the time of the Civil War, the symbiotic relationship between political and economic liberty had become an article of faith in the North. "Everything which secures freedom and equality of rights at the South," a Republican newspaper stated in 1865, "tends directly to the benefit of trade."[14] And, it might have added, vice versa. As Smith had argued, the market was egalitarian. It freed men from dependent relationships and paternalist obligations, and threatened traditional ruling classes with its guarantee of perpetual social and economic change. By breaking down traditional economic privileges, it fostered the idea of equality.[15]

Yet planter spokesmen did not want a laboring force, black or white, with such ideas. The central premise of the free labor ideology—the opportunity for social mobility for the laborer—was anathema to planters, who could not conceive of either a plantation economy or their own social privileges surviving if freedmen were able to move up the social scale. "You must begin at the bottom of the ladder and climb up," General Howard informed a black New Orleans audience in 1865, but at least he offered the opportunity to climb. A Natchez newspaper at the same time was informing its readers, "the true station of the negro is that of a servant. The wants and state of our country demand that he should remain a servant." A delegate to the Texas Constitutional Convention of 1866 agreed: the freedmen must remain "hewers of wood and drawers of water." As for white labor, there was a concerted, though unsuccessful effort to attract immigrants to the South during Reconstruction. Pamphlets appeared singing the praises of "the thrifty German, the versatile Italian, the sober Englishman, the sturdy sons of Erin," in contrast to blacks who did not understand "the moral obligations of a contract." Yet others noted that such immigrants might bring with them unwanted ideas. "Servants of this description may please some tastes," said a southern newspaper in 1867, "but the majority of our people would probably prefer the sort we have, who neither feel nor profess equality with their employer."[16]

Nor could white southerners accept the other half of the free labor equation—market-oriented rationality on the part of their laborers. In the recent work of "cliometricians" investigating post-bellum southern history, the freedmen emerge from slavery as, to use their terminology, rational, market-oriented profit-maximizers.[17] It is difficult, however, to accept the idea that slavery produced workers socialized to the discipline of capitalist wage labor. The slave's standard of consumption, and his experience with the marketplace, was, of necessity, very limited. The logic of ever-greater effort to meet ever-expanding needs (what capitalist society calls "ambition") had no meaning for him. As one planter complained, freedmen did not respond to the marketplace incentives to steady labor: "released from the discipline of slavery, unappreciative of the value of money, and but little desirous of comfort, his efforts are capricious."[18]

Here, indeed, lies the ultimate meaning of the innumerable complaints about the freedman's work habits—so reminiscent, it might be noted, of labor "problems" in the Third World today. Why did so many whites constantly claim that blacks were lazy and idle? The tendency of historians has been to deny the accuracy of such complaints, attributing them to simple racism. Doubtless, there is justification for this response, but it does not go to the heart of the matter. Consider two examples of such complaints. The first is from a Maryland newspaper in 1864, just after emancipation in that state: "The ambition of the negro, as a race, when left to his own volition, does not rise above the meagre necessaries of life. . . . One fruitful source of idleness has been the ability to possess themselves of a hut and a few acres of land, thereby enabling them to preserve the semblance of a means of living." The second is a remark by the North Carolina planter and political leader Kemp P. Battle in 1866: "Want of ambition will be the devil of the race, I think. Some of my most sensible men say they have no other desire than to cultivate their own land in grain and raise bacon."[19]

On the face of it, a desire to cultivate one's own land in food crops does not appear to warrant the charge of "want of ambition." The term "indolence," it appears, encompassed not simply blacks unwilling to work at all, but those who preferred to work for themselves. The same plantation blacks arraigned for idleness spent considerable time and effort on their own garden plots and, as is well known, it was the universal desire of the freedmen to own their own plots of land. What one Mississippi white called the freedman's "wild notions of right and freedom" were actually very traditional in republican America. Blacks believed, according to another Mississippi planter, "that if they are hirelings they will still be slaves." Whether in withdrawing from churches dominated by whites, refusing to work under drivers and overseers, or in their ubiquitous desire for forty acres and a mule, blacks made clear that, for them, freedom meant independence from white control. "Their great desire," wrote a Georgia planter, "seems to be to get away from all overseers, to hire or purchase land, and work for themselves." From the freedmen's point of view, an Alabama Bureau agent reported, this would "complete their emancipation."[20]

The vast majority of freedmen, of course, were compelled by necessity to labor on the plantations, but they too appeared to respond only imperfectly to the incentives and demands of the marketplace. Many freedmen did seek the highest wages available, whether this meant moving to states like Texas and Arkansas where labor was scarce and wages high, or seeking employment in railroad construction crews, turpentine mills, and lumber companies. Others, however, seemed to value things like freedom of movement off the plantations and personal autonomy more than pecuniary rewards. "Let any man offer them some little thing of no real benefit to them, but which looks like a little more freedom," Georgia's Howell Cobb observed, "and they catch at it with alacrity." And a Mississippi Bureau agent reported, "many have said to me they cared not for the pay if they were only treated with kindness and not over worked."[21]

Instead of working harder than they had as slaves, as Adam Smith would have predicted, the freedmen desired to work less, and black women sought to withdraw from field labor altogether. "The women say that they never mean to do any more outdoor work," said a report from Alabama. "White men support their wives and they mean that their husbands shall support them." Those women who did remain in the fields were sometimes even more "undisciplined" than the men. One

rice plantation worker told her employer in 1866 on being ordered to complete a task, "she did not know if she would . . .
and could 'not work herself to death before her time came.' "[22]

Most distressing of all, many freedmen evinced a strong resistance to growing the "slave crop" cotton. As one Georgia
freedman said, "If ole massa want to grow cotton, let him plant
it himself." On the Sea Islands, they refused to repair broken
cotton gins and displayed more interest in subsisting on garden
plots, fishing, and hunting than producing a crop for the marketplace. Freedom, for Sea Island blacks, seemed to mean "no
more driver, no more cotton." The South Carolina planter Edward B. Heyward noted the irony of the situation:[23]

> It seems the belief among planters, that negroes *will not plant cot-
> ton* but are interested only in *food*. Wouldn't it be curious if by the
> voluntary act of the emancipated blacks, the New England manu-
> facturers should fail. . . . They are going to worry somebody,
> and I think it will be their friends the Yankees. They say we can't
> *eat cotton* and there they stop.

As Heyward suggested, on the question of cotton a community of interest did indeed exist between northern and southern whites interested in the revitalization of the plantation
economy. Their great fear was that the freedmen might retreat
into self-sufficiency. "The products of these islands are absolutely necessary to supply the wants of the commercial world,"
wrote a northern investor from St. Helena, South Carolina, in
1865. Two years later another northerner with an eye to southern investments commented on the absolute necessity of reviving an export cotton crop to "pay our debts and get the balance
of trade in our favor." To such men, and many others who
looked to the post-war South for the investment of war-
generated surplus capital, the idea of granting subsistence plots
to the freedmen was disastrous. As Willie Lee Rose has shown,
the arguments between land reform and cotton production
were articulated during the war itself, in the conflict on the Sea
Islands between the freedmen and moral reformers like Laura

Towne on the one hand, and representatives of northeastern business like Edward Atkinson and Edward Philbrick, who envisioned a post-war economy in which blacks worked cotton plantations for reasonable wages.

To Atkinson and Philbrick, the Port Royal experiment provided a golden opportunity to prove "that the abandonment of slavery did not mean the abandonment of cotton," that free blacks could raise the crop more efficiently and profitably than as slaves. Cotton was the measure of freedom, for as Philbrick put it, "as a general thing, the amount of cotton planted will always be a pretty sure index to the state of industry of the people." In order to "multiply their simple wants" as a means of stimulating interest in cotton among blacks, Philbrick established plantation stores, placing a variety of new products within the freedmen's reach. His great fear was that they might retreat into self-sufficiency, removing themselves from the disciplines of the marketplace, eliminating them as consumers of northern goods, and enabling them to resist the exploitation of their labor (except by themselves).[24]

Of course, complete self-sufficiency was rarely possible in nineteenth-century America. But the Sea Island experience—where many blacks did acquire small plots of land—as well as scattered evidence from other states, suggests that black landowners and renters preferred to farm much in the manner of ante-bellum upcountry white yeomen, concentrating on food crops as a first priority, and only to a lesser extent on cotton, for ready cash.[25] The pattern persisted into the 1870s, except where rental contracts specifically required, in the words of one, that "all of said land is to be cultivated in cotton." The ambition of the freedmen to own or rent land, therefore, cannot be understood as simply a quest for material accumulation and social mobility; it reflected above all a desire for autonomy from both individual whites, and the impersonal marketplace. And it was this ambition which frightened both southern planters and the Atkinsons and Philbricks.[26]

The experience of labor in other post-emancipation situations was hardly reassuring to such men. Southerners were well aware of the aftermath of emancipation in the West Indies, which appeared to demonstrate that the end of slavery spelled the end of plantation agriculture. Plantations could not be maintained with free labor, wrote a prominent Charlestonian, "the experiments made in Hayti and Jamaica settled that question long ago." On those islands the freedmen had been able to drift off the plantations and take up small farming, and the result had been a catastrophic decline in sugar production. "See what ruin emancipation brought on that paradise of the tropics," observed one southern writer.[27] Comparative studies of emancipation in the West Indies and South America reveal that nearly every plantation society enacted vagrancy, contract, and debt peonage laws in an attempt to keep freedmen on the plantations. But only where land was not available—or another source of unfree labor was—did the plantation survive. Trinidad, with little free land, was a success: "land . . . is owned by the white man and the negro is unable to get possession of a foot of it." So was Guyana, where imported East Indian coolies replaced the blacks on sugar plantations. But not Jamaica, where uninhabited land was available for the freedmen.[28]

The lesson of the West Indies seemed clear: without "some well regulated system of labor . . . devised by the white man . . . the South would soon become a second Haiti." Basically, the problem seemed to be that free people do not like to work on plantations. This was why slavery had been "necessary" in the first place, and why the chimera of white immigration was bound to fail. As a Georgia newspaper observed in 1866, "everybody must know that no white man is going to work as a negro on a large estate, to rise at the sound of a horn and return when the dews are heavy." But the myth that they would persisted for years, as did the reluctance of white immigrants to move South. The Selma *Southern Argus*, one of the most perceptive spokesmen for the planter class, explained the problem: "Our people . . . have vainly expected an impossibility—white immigrants to take the place of the negro as hewers of wood and drawers of water. . . . They want . . . labor to occupy the social position of negroes and to be treated like negroes." Others looked to the Chinese immigrant, who, it was believed, was more manageable than the black. "He is not likely to covet ownership of the soil, and . . . he is not likely to become a politician," commented a Mississippi planter.[29]

In the end, if the plantations were to continue, it would have to be with black labor. This was why white southerners absolutely insisted that blacks not be allowed access to land. Unlike the West Indies, the "availability" of land in the South was a political issue, not a matter determined by geography, for there was an abundance of uncultivated land. Less than a tenth of Louisiana's thirty million acres, for example, were being tilled at the end of Reconstruction.[30] The fear that access to land for blacks would lead to the disintegration of staple production was graphically expressed by an Alabama newspaper, commenting on the Southern Homestead Act of 1866, which offered public land to black farmers:

> The negroes will become possessed of a small freehold, will raise their corn, squashes, pigs and chickens, and will work no more in the cotton, rice and sugar fields. In other words, their labor will become unavailable for those products which the world especially needs. . . . The title of this law ought to have been, "A bill to get rid of the laboring class of the South and make Cuffee a self-supporting nuisance."

Even if relatively few independent black farmers succeeded economically, the result would be disastrous. As a Mississippi planter put it, in that case, "all the others will be dissatisfied with their wages no matter how good they may be and thus our whole labor system is bound to be upset."[31]

Thus, the problem of adjustment from slave to free labor was compounded by racial and class assumptions, ideas about the nature of labor itself, which dictated to white southerners that blacks not be allowed to escape the plantations, and led many northerners to agree that the road to black landownership should lie through patient wage labor—while market values and responses were learned—rather than a sudden "gift" of land.[32] To complicate matters further, the transition to a free labor system took place within the context of an economic transformation which profoundly affected the status of white farmers in the South as well as blacks.

As is well known, the southern states emerged from the war into a pattern of economic underdevelopment and dependency. Whether one views the ante-bellum South as capitalist (Fogel and Engerman), pre-capitalist (Genovese), or capitalist but not bourgeois—whatever that means—(Barrington Moore),[33] it is certain that the Civil War unleashed an expansion of market relations, reflected in both the emancipation of the slaves and the transformation of the status of the white farmer. The extension of transportation into the predominantly white upcountry, the increased use of commercial fertilizer, and the spread of country stores made possible the absorption of the previously subsistence-oriented upcountry into the Cotton Kingdom during and after Reconstruction. A recent article by Grady McWhiney delineates the change in Alabama from a relatively self-sufficient late ante-bellum society in which 70 per cent of white farmers owned their own land, to a colonial economy, forced into a one-crop mould, and a region that could not feed itself. The most significant aspects of the transformation were first, the fastening of endemic poverty upon the entire South and second, the loss of what McWhiney describes as an independent and leisured, if not indeed "lazy" way of life, based on the free ranging of livestock in the ante-bellum years. The debate over fencing laws in the South after the Civil War reflects the controversy engendered by the change from an almost communal view of land, in which all unenclosed property was deemed open to neighbors' livestock, to a more capitalist and individualist conception. Certainly, economic changes were rapidly undermining the traditional idea that ownership of land was a guarantee of personal autonomy.[34]

The transformation of the status of the white farmer pro-

vides an indispensable angle of vision on one of the least understood aspects of Reconstruction, southern white Republicanism. For a time, scalawags, as they were called, controlled
the politics of Tennessee, Missouri, Arkansas, North Carolina,
and to a lesser degree, Georgia and Alabama. Studies of individual states in recent years have moved beyond earlier debates
over whether scalawags were pre-war Democrats or Whigs, to
an emphasis on ante-bellum hostility to the planter regime, and
Unionist disaffection during the Civil War, as the roots of white
Republicanism, especially in the mountain areas stretching
from West Virginia down into northern Georgia, Alabama, and
Mississippi.[35]

But second only to Unionism as an issue in these areas was
the question of debt, the vehicle by which thousands of white
farmers were trapped into the cycle of tenancy and cotton production in the post-war decades. The mountain and piedmont
areas of Mississippi, Alabama, Georgia, and other states had
been devastated by a civil war within the Civil War. Property,
tools, and livestock had been destroyed, and the result was
severe destitution in 1865–67. "Scenes of the Irish famine"
were reported in northern Alabama. As small farmers went
bankrupt, large numbers fell into tenancy and lost their lands.
Others were forced to grow cotton to obtain needed credit.
Governor James L. Alcorn reported in 1871 that tenant farming among Mississippi whites had doubled in the previous decade, and by 1880 one-third of the white farmers in the cotton
states were tenants.[36]

The issue of debtor relief pervades the early years of Reconstruction; debates over stay laws and homestead exemptions
were as intense as those concerning civil rights for blacks. One
correspondent of the North Carolina railroad promoter and
banker George Swepson reported in 1867, "everything is so demoralized that men have lost all sight of paying debts," adding
that the people would surely "defeat the constitution if repudi-
ation is not in." In Georgia, the homestead and debtor relief
provisions of the Constitution of 1868 were the "strong card"

of the Republican party, "the most serious obstacle" to Democratic attempts to unite the white vote against Reconstruction. In our preoccupation with the racial politics of Reconstruction we may have overlooked the first stirring of class politics within the white community, a politics as yet inchoate and inhibited by racial divisions, but which foreshadowed the great agrarian upheaval two decades later.[37]

Like the Black Codes of 1865–66, the issue of debtor relief illustrates how economics and politics were intertwined during Reconstruction. For blacks, having lost the struggle for land distribution immediately after the Civil War, the political arena offered an opportunity to compensate for their economic weakness. In many respects, of course, the Reconstruction governments betrayed black dreams. Except in South Carolina, and to a lesser extent, Mississippi, Republican regimes did little to fulfill the shattered dream of forty acres and a mule.[38] In less dramatic ways, however, blacks and their white allies used political power to provide a modicum of protection for black laborers. From the beginning of Radical rule, black legislators pressed for laws granting agricultural laborers a first lien on crops, and such measures were enacted by most of the southern states during Reconstruction. The Black Codes were repealed, along with legislation like that enacted by North Carolina Democrats on the eve of Military Reconstruction, granting a double settlement to landlords in legal disputes with tenants and awarding them the right to appropriate a portion of a tenant's crop on suspicion of an intent to leave for other employment. New tax laws shifted the burden of taxation in a progressive direction, reversing the Presidential Reconstruction policy of high poll taxes and low rates on landed property. And legislation made it illegal to discharge plantation workers for political reasons or, at the end of the year, until they had been paid. "Under the laws of most of the Southern States," a planter complained in 1872, "ample protection is afforded to tenants and very little to landlords."[39]

Perhaps even more significant was the emergence during

Reconstruction of local officials, black and white, who actively sympathized with the economic plight of the black laborer. A recent study criticizes South Carolina's black legislators for not using their power "for the social and economic advancement of the black masses." At the local level, however, that was precisely what many Republican officials tried to do. Contract disputes, during Reconstruction, were heard by locally elected trial justices, and planters were bitter in their complaints over the partiality of these officials toward their black constituents. One leading rice planter observed in 1869, "the planter must have entire control of the crop," but that this was impossible in a situation where "the negro magistrate or majesty as they call him tells them that no rice is to be shipped until it is all got out and divided 'according to law.' " Another Carolinian informed Governor Daniel H. Chamberlain that the state's game laws "would be of great benefit . . . but with such trial justices as we now have, they are not enforced," enabling blacks to hunt on white-owned land.[40]

Similar protests were heard in other states. In Mississippi, it was a standing complaint of whites that they could not prevent the theft of seed cotton and livestock on account of the leniency of black magistrates. Alabama's vagrancy law, still on the books in 1870, was "a dead letter, because those who are charged with its enforcement are indebted to the vagrant vote for their offices and emoluments." In Georgia too, black sheriffs refused to enforce vagrancy statutes and at Darien, where the Rev. Tunis G. Campbell had established an enclave of black political power, a plantation agent found himself "powerless to enforce his orders," fearing the local sheriff would arrest him if he attempted to coerce his black laborers.[41]

An understanding of the class constituency of the southern Republican party not only helps us appreciate the intense opposition it generated, but to reconsider the whole question of the "extravagant" taxation and state expenditures during Reconstruction. That there was corruption and misappropriation of funds is undeniable. But, as Howard K. Beale observed forty years ago, "was not a part of the offense of the Radical leaders that they sought to serve the interests of *poor* men?" As Beale suggested, it was not simply the amount of state expenditure, but that it was "money lavishly spent by men who pay no taxes"—as a Mississippi Democrat put it—which aroused hostility. Property-holders blamed the increasing tax burden on the fact that blacks had no vested interest in government economy, since "nine-tenths of the members of the Legislature own no property and pay no taxes." But there was more here than simply a desire of the propertyless to despoil the propertied. State expenditures during Reconstruction reflected an activism common enough in the North in these years, and should perhaps be viewed as a kind of unarticulated Keynesianism, in which deficit spending financed the promotion of economic growth and the creation of an economic and social infrastructure (railroads and schools) while tax policy promoted a modest redistribution of wealth.[42]

"The Republican party is emphatically the poor man's party of the State," declared a black political leader in South Carolina in 1870. "We favor laws to foster and elevate labor . . . we denounce all attempts of capital to control labor by legislation," a Georgia Republican meeting echoed.[43] In terms of its constituency, the Republicans were indeed "the poor man's party" of the South, but in policy, the situation was more ambiguous. The dominant theme in the policies of state Republican leadership was not precisely the elevation of the poor, but economic modernization. A subsidiary theme, articulated primarily by black leaders (although by no means all of them) looked to a more class-conscious program of economic redistribution. The division was analogous to the Civil War debate on the Sea Islands between humanitarian reformers favoring land distribution and northern investors like Atkinson and Philbrick who feared such a policy would prevent the revitalization of staple agriculture. It had also surfaced in the debates in 1867 over whether southern Republicans should endorse the idea of the confiscation of planter lands.

At stake were competing visions of the role of the state in the post-Civil War South. The "modernizers" saw the task of the Radical governments as moving the South as quickly as possible along the economic road marked out by the North, through aid to railroads, industry, and agricultural diversification. They were willing to protect the essential political and economic rights of southern laborers, and harass the planters with heavy taxation, but would generally go no further, although the assumption of their free labor outlook was that their policies would produce a prosperity in which blacks would share. The "redistributionists" were not opposed to economic diversification, but had little interest in grandiose schemes of economic development. Their aim was to use the power of the state to promote land distribution and in other ways directly assist the black and white poor. Generally, party discipline led most Republicans to support such modernizing programs as aid to railroad development, but there were exceptions. The South Carolina Labor Convention of 1869, headed by the state's most prominent black politicians, urged the legislature to withhold the state's credit from railroads, using the money instead to secure land for agricultural laborers. There were also disputes over the exemption of manufacturing corporations from taxation and the repeal of usury laws, measures modernizers believed necessary to attract outside investment, but which others feared would simply raise the tax bill and credit prices for the poor. As for fence laws, demanded by those seeking a more diversified and modern agricultural system, it was widely assumed that "the negroes will defeat any measures" for such legislation, which would deprive landless blacks of the right to graze their livestock on the land of others.[44]

Control of the state, therefore, played a critical role in labor relations during Reconstruction. The point is not that Reconstruction revolutionized the southern economic order—recent research has demonstrated convincingly that it did not.[45] But in seeking seismic changes, historians may have overlooked ones more subtle but significant nonetheless. In some areas, Reconstruction did serve as a shield, protecting black labor from the most exploitative implications of economic relationships, and preventing planters from using the state to bolster their own position. The class conflict between planters and freedmen in this period should be viewed as an anomalous struggle between two weak economic classes, each of which sought to use political power to obtain economic objectives. The result was a stalemate, in which neither side obtained what it wanted. "Capital is powerless and labor demoralized," complained the South Carolina agricultural reformer D. Wyatt Aiken in 1871. What he meant was that, in the absence of Black Codes and vagrancy laws, blacks, though generally landless, were able to utilize the "labor shortage" to improve their economic standing. Like the land question, the labor shortage was a question not simply of numbers, but of power. Labor was scarce, Aiken explained, not primarily because there were fewer workers, but because those who did work were unmanageable: "Though abundant, this labor is virtually scarce because not available, and almost wholly unreliable." "The power to control [black labor]," the *Southern Argus* agreed, "is gone."[46]

Complaints about labor being "perfectly worthless," so prominent in 1865, persisted throughout Reconstruction. "We are the capital," a Mississippi planter declared in 1871, "then let us dictate terms." But virtually every effort to control wages and prevent the "enticement" of workers by others failed, because they were not backed up by the long arm of the law. And although the data are scattered, it does seem that blacks were able to use the "labor shortage" to effect real material gains, especially between 1867 and 1873, when reports from throughout the South spoke of rising wages for agricultural laborers, increasing numbers of blacks able to become renters, and large numbers squatting on uncultivated land, farming "on their own hook." "The struggle," a Texas planter commented, "seems to be who will get the negro at any price."[47]

Southern proponents of agricultural reform were particularly frustrated at their inability to make labor more manageable, for their plans for a more diversified agriculture required a disciplined labor force. They viewed sharecropping—which had developed as a compromise between black desire for autonomy and planter determination not to abandon plantation agriculture—as a particularly inefficient mode of economic organization. A wage system, Ralph I. Middleton believed, was the only way to control plantation labor, but his employees insisted on a share of the crop, and he was compelled to agree. Middleton envied what he considered the labor discipline enjoyed by northern capitalists. "Rice planting cannot be profitable until the plantations are worked up like factories—on *wages*," he insisted. Aiken agreed: "As soon would I think the Lowell manufacturer should share his manufactured calicoes with his operatives, as to approve giving my labour part of the crop." But like Middleton, he had to agree to this "nefarious practice": "I had to yield or lose my labor."[48]

Some agricultural reformers, indeed, advocated the introduction of machinery and a shift to livestock and less labor-intensive crops like hay, corn, and wheat, precisely because they would eliminate the labor shortage. Unlike human beings, the steam plow was "perfectly manageable." Moreover, said a South Carolina newspaper, "machinery . . . cannot vote." From throughout the South came reports that, beginning in 1867, politics was exacerbating the unreliability of labor. Blacks would simply leave plantations without permission to attend political rallies. Once a week, during the summer of 1867, "the negroes from the entire county" quit work and flocked to Waco, Texas, for political rallies. In Alabama, "they stop at any time and go off to Greensboro" for the same purpose.[49]

Obviously, the economic gains achieved by blacks during Reconstruction were more modest than their striking advances in political and civil rights and education. The failure of land distribution ensured that this would be the case. Moreover, another signal failing of the Reconstruction governments, their inability to protect blacks against violence, often had disastrous economic consequences. While Klan violence was most com-

monly intended to intimidate Republican local leaders and
voters, it had economic motivations and consequences as well.
Victims were often those blacks who had succeeded economically, or simply resisted white control of their labor. In De-
mopolis, Alabama, the Klan acted to prevent black renters from
gathering their crops. In Georgia, according to a black legisla-
tor, "whenever a colored man acquires property and becomes
in a measure independent, they take it from him." In South
Carolina, a "posse" illegally harassed a plantation, "because it is
rented by colored men, and their desire is that such a thing
ought not to be."[50]

Even in the absence of violence, the depression that began in
1873 led to a fall in agricultural wages and drove many black
renters back into the ranks of sharecroppers and laborers. And
planters increasingly learned to use blacks' indebtedness to
limit the freedmen's economic leverage. Even in the best of circumstances, Reconstruction would have been an uphill
struggle. Every advantage of education, wealth, and prestige
were arrayed against these governments. As a freedman told a
northern teacher in 1871, "we've no chance—the white people's arms are longer than ours." But as long as Reconstruction
survived, so too did the gains blacks did achieve, as well as the
possibility of more radical change, a potential which was only
closed off completely with Redemption.[51]

In his classic study *Black Reconstruction,* W. E. B. Du Bois referred to the Reconstruction regimes as the rule of the "black
proletariat." The terminology is exaggerated, but Du Bois did
have a point, for this was how these governments were viewed
by their Conservative opponents. Despite all the complaints
about corruption, it was the disjunction between property-hold-
ing and political power which most alarmed them. The situation in the South, claimed one "Tax-Payers Convention," was
entirely "anomalous; it is perhaps without a parallel in the history of civilized communities." The problem, put simply, was
the inability of the upper class to exert its traditional influence
on state and local government. Reconstruction, this address

continued, presented "the unprecedented spectacle of a state in which the Government is arrayed against property."[52]

The complaints of Democratic politicians and Tax-Payers Conventions present a curious amalgam of simple racism, planter elitism, and traditional Jeffersonian country-party ideology, in which corruption, indebtedness, and the decline of republicanism were the inevitable fate of governments controlled by men lacking the virtue and intelligence derived from possession of property. Generally, the racist element was in the ascendant, but at the same time, opposition to Reconstruction generated an elitist rejection of democracy in any form. This was most striking in states like North Carolina, where a large population of white yeomen had long demanded political and social reforms from the state's Whig elite. "Mere numbers," ignoring "virtue and property and intelligence," was no proper basis for government, according to Jonathan Worth, the state's Presidential Reconstruction Governor, for it would produce only "agrarianism and anarchy." Universal suffrage, Worth wrote in 1868, "I regard as undermining civilization," and civilization he defined as "the possession and protection of property." It was clear that such remarks did not apply to blacks alone. In 1867, when General Daniel E. Sickles ordered that all taxpayers—instead of only freeholders—be eligible for jury duty, Worth protested to President Johnson: "to say nothing of negroes, juries drawn from the whites only under this order, would not be fit to pass on the rights of their fellow men."[53]

The idea that republican citizenship should rest on the possession of property was, of course, hardly new. Radical carpetbaggers like the Rev. S. S. Ashley, a religious missionary and later superintendent of education in North Carolina, also accepted the idea that "a great landless class will *per force* be lawless and vicious." Like Thaddeus Stevens and George Julian, Ashley believed the solution was to break up the plantations and "secure homesteads to the landless." Southerners, confronting the challenge emancipation posed to traditional republicanism, favored a different approach—keep the freedmen landless and control their votes or exclude them from the political nation. Allen S. Izard, a South Carolina rice planter, agreed with Ashley that landholding would create a feeling of autonomy among blacks, but his conclusion was far different: "that feeling of security and independence has to be eradicated." Men like Izard wanted the best of both worlds: a free labor system which, however, denied the right of the laborers to a free choice in politics. The requirements of the plantation society demanded a revolutionary rethinking of the definition of freedom in republican America. As a Mississippi planter wrote in December 1865:[54]

> Our negroes have a fall, a tall fall ahead of them, in my humble opinion. They will have to learn that freedom and independence are different things. A man may be free and yet not independent.

In South Carolina, where black political power was most pronounced, so too was the assertion by the white upper class that men of property had a right to rule, and willingness to threaten economic reprisals against those who disagreed. Thus, a Democratic address to black citizens, written by Civil War General James Conner, put the issue with admirable candor:

> We have the capital and give employment. We own the lands and require labor to make them productive. . . . You desire to be employed. . . . We know we can do without you. We think you will find it very difficult to do without us. . . . We have the wealth. The houses in which you live are ours; the lands upon which you must labor or starve are ours.

This address, the wife of a planter observed, was "clear and to the point." The problem was that blacks did not respond to such threats. Unexpectedly, perhaps, while the freedmen did not achieve economic autonomy, they did exhibit a remarkable political independence. As Trescot complained, the result of the Civil War and Reconstruction was to destroy utterly "the natural influence of capital on labor, of employer on employee," with the result that "negroes who will trust their white employers in all their personal affairs . . . are entirely beyond advice on all political issues." (Trescot's interchangeable use of the terminology of race and class was not uncommon during Reconstruction—an Alabama opponent of that state's 1867 Constitution asked, "Shall the white man be subordinated to the negro? Shall the property classes be robbed by the no property herd?") It was the remarkable tenacity of black voters in loyalty to the Republican party, despite economic intimidation, which led Democrats increasingly to resort to violence to destroy their political rights. But whatever the method, "the first thing to be done," as Georgia's Democratic leader Benjamin H. Hill explained, "is to secure Home Government for Home Affairs . . . . We must get control of our own labor."[55]

Only with Redemption could the full force of the state's legislative, executive, and judicial authority be mobilized toward the goal of labor control. As C. Vann Woodward has shown, the Redeemers did not immediately disfranchise black voters or impose a legal system of racial segregation. But in the realm of labor relations, there was no delay. "We may hold inviolate every law of the United States," Georgia's Redeemer Governor James M. Smith explained, "and still legislate upon our labor system as to retain our old plantation system." To this end, Redeemer legislatures during the 1870s enacted a series of measures "for the protection of the cotton planters."[56] Some, like severe punishments for burglary and criminal penalties against laborers (but not employers) violating contracts, harked back to the Black Codes of 1865–66. Others, such as the prohibition of the sale of seed cotton between sundown and sunrise and a change in tax laws to benefit planters, had been demanded for years but rejected by Republican lawmakers. Landlords in several states were guaranteed a first lien on crops, and laws and court decisions now defined the sharecropper as a mere employee, with no property right in his share of the crop until division by the landlord.[57]

At the same time, Redeemer legislatures moved to exert control over the all-important local courts which, in the black belt, could still be controlled by black voters. Throughout the South, as an Alabamian explained in 1876, the proper personnel in local courts, "which deal with the practical rights of the people . . . our 'business and lives' " was essential for "confidence . . . in commercial dealing." Or, as a North Carolinian echoed, "it is absolutely necessary . . . that the county funds shall be placed beyond the reach of the large negro majorities" in the eastern part of that state. Responding to such appeals, Alabama and North Carolina Redeemers adopted new constitutions transferring the power to elect justices of the peace from voters to the state legislature. Moreover, local officials like Georgia's Tunis G. Campbell, who had used their authority to protect the rights of black laborers, were driven from office. Campbell himself was jailed on a flimsy charge of illegally arresting a white man. The consequence of Redemption was summed up by a New York business journal at the end of 1877: "This year . . . labor is under control for the first season since the war, and the next year will be more entirely so."[58]

In 1875, as the struggle over Reconstruction entered its final years, John E. Bryant penned an article for the New York *Times,* explaining political alignments in Georgia and the South. After his retirement from the Freedmen's Bureau, Bryant had enjoyed a prominent political career, although he had alienated many Georgia Republicans by aligning himself on occasion with the state's Democrats. But in 1875, his analysis was fully within the free labor tradition. The actions of Georgia's Redeemers, Bryant argued, demonstrated that at the heart of Reconstruction lay the same issue which had caused the Civil War—the struggle between "two systems of labor," one slave and one free. Northerners believed "that the laboring man should be as independent as the capitalist." Southern whites still, in their heart of hearts, felt workers "ought to be slaves."

Although perhaps overstated, Bryant's analysis did underscore once again the centrality of the labor question to the politics of Reconstruction. But on one point, he was out of date. Was it still an article of faith in the North that the laborer should be "as independent as the capitalist?" As one of Bryant's northern friends informed him, while the *Times* article "shows clearly the views of the old ruling class at the South with regard to the labor question," there was "reason to fear that their general view of society and government was substantially shared by a large class in the North."[59]

From his southern vantage point, Bryant was perhaps unaware of the decline of the Radical impulse in the northern Republican party, its shift, as a recent student has noted, toward "a more distinctly antilabor and procorporate stance." Here, in the increasingly divergent social and ideological bases of northern and southern Republicanism, lay a crucial weakness of the Reconstruction governments. They depended for their existence on the support of the federal government and northern public opinion, but their northern allies were now emerging as the party of respectability, the Union, and business. And northern businessmen, especially those interested in investment in the South had, even in the late 1860s, concluded that the policies of Reconstruction governments were inimical to business enterprise. "No one," a New Yorker wrote Governor Orr, "will invest or emigrate, so long as . . . stay laws are made to prevent the collection of debts." Others insisted that so long as ignorant blacks had a dominant voice in southern public affairs, capital would boycott the South. The conclusion was heightened by the effects of the Panic of 1873, for, as Bryant's northern correspondent informed him, "there is a pretty general impression in the country that the financial crisis of 1873 was owing in great part to the paralysis of the South."[60] But there was more to the erosion of support for Reconstruction than a simple matter of dollars and cents, more, too, than the racism which remained so pervasive in northern life. The change in northern attitudes reflected a crisis of the free labor ideology itself. The rapid expansion of industrial capitalism in the post-war years, reflected in the spread of factory production, the beginnings of modern managerial institutions, the expansion of the mining and farming frontiers, the emergence of a powerful trade unionism, and the devastating depression of the 1870s, posed issues which that ideology, with its emphasis on a harmony of interests between capital and labor, proved unable to answer. For one thing, it seemed increasingly difficult to contend that wage labor was simply a temporary stopping point on the road to economic independence. During Reconstruction the coalition which had fought the Civil War dissolved into its component elements, and strands of the free labor ideology were adopted by contending social classes, each for its own purposes. For the middle class, free labor became a stolid liberal orthodoxy, in which individualism, laissez-faire, the defense of private property, and the rule of the "Best Men" defined good government. At the same time, the labor movement, especially after 1873, adopted the free labor outlook as an affirmation of the primacy of the producing classes and a critique of the emerging capitalist order, rather than as a testament to the harmony of all interests in society.[61]

The irony here is indeed striking. With emancipation, the South came face to face with the problem which, according to Edmund Morgan, had generated slavery in the first place—how to preserve social order in the face of a large, propertyless class of laborers. Yet at the same time, the North was also having to face up to this question. After all, 1877 was not only the year of the end of Reconstruction, but of the great railroad strike, the first national strike in American history, and the first to be suppressed by the massive intervention of federal troops. The same administration which withdrew the last federal troops from the South, within a few months sent them against strikers in the North, while the city of Baltimore, which had rioted against the entrance of federal troops on their way to Washington early in 1861, frantically requested the army to restrain the strikers in 1877. "The Southern question," a Charleston newspaper declared, was "dead"—the railroad strike had propelled to the forefront of politics "the question of labor and capital, work and wages."[62]

Sometimes, historical coincidences are revealing, and 1877 is one of those occasions. For if the Civil War proved that America was not unique politically—that it could not always solve its problems by reasoned disputation—the railroad strike shattered an even greater myth, that Americans could have industrialization without the dark satanic mills of Europe and a permanent wage-earning class, could have capitalism without class conflict. So, in the end, Reconstruction came full circle. It began with southerners trying to adjust to the northern system of free labor. It ended with northerners having to accept the reality of conflict between capital and labor—a reality that southerners, white and black alike, had understood all along.

--◄{ S E V E N }►--

Thaddeus Stevens, Confiscation, and Reconstruction

In the history of American politics, Thaddeus Stevens is something of an anomaly. As a self-proclaimed radical, he seemed out of place at the center of a political system which—with the glaring exception of the Civil War—has perennially prided itself on its ability to resolve disputes without resort to extreme measures. Historians have found Stevens a baffling figure, whose unusual complexity of motivations and unique blend of idealism with political opportunism made him almost impossible to categorize. The most perceptive of his contemporaries described him simply as a revolutionary—or at least the closest thing to one imaginable in American politics. To a British observer, he was "the Robespierre, Danton, and Marat of America, all rolled into one." And a leading American newspaper attributed his influence in the 1860s to the nation's having undergone a political and social revolution which "demanded

Originally published in *The Hofstadter Aegis: A Memorial,* eds. Stanley Elkins and Eric McKitrick (New York, 1974). Reprinted by permission of Alfred A. Knopf, Inc.

revolutionary qualities" of its leaders—qualities Stevens seemed to have in abundance.[1]

Only an unparalleled crisis like the Civil War could have brought a man like Stevens to the fore. His personal characteristics—cynicism, courage, imperviousness to criticism or flattery, brutal honesty, and willingness to use daring and even outrageous means to achieve his ends—were as necessary in wartime as they seemed inappropriate in peace.[2] And Stevens's combination of genuine idealism with a pragmatism learned in the school of Pennsylvania politics enabled him to recognize and articulate the policies which Union victory required. While Lincoln declared his conviction that the war must not degenerate into "a violent and remorseless revolutionary struggle," Stevens saw that this was precisely what it must become. From the outset he insisted that only the seemingly draconian measures of freeing and arming the slaves and seizing the property of the leading rebels could produce victory. In Congress, as chairman of the House Committee on Ways and Means, Stevens became "the master-spirit of every aggressive movement . . . to overthrow the Rebellion and slavery." By the end of the war he had acquired a national reputation as the radical of radicals, and at an age when most men have retired from active pursuits—he was seventy-three in 1865—Stevens embarked on the most important phase of his career.[3]

Any attempt to analyze Stevens's role in Reconstruction is immediately confronted with a paradox. Many historians of the period have depicted him as the dictator of the House and the major architect of Reconstruction. Even such hard-headed contemporary political leaders as James G. Blaine and Justin Morrill viewed him as "the animating spirit and unquestioned leader" of the House of Representatives. Stevens was certainly a master of parliamentary tactics. More than once he bullied the House into passing measures by choosing just the right moment to call the previous question, cutting off debate and forcing a vote. His quick tongue and sarcastic wit, moreover, made his colleagues of both parties consciously avoid tangling with him in debate. As one of them remarked, "I would sooner get into difficulty with a porcupine."[4]

And yet if Stevens was a political "dictator," his power was strangely limited. In Pennsylvania he was never able to challenge the Republican kingpins, Simon Cameron and Andrew Curtin, for control of the party machinery; and even in the House, as one puzzled newspaper observed, "no man was oftener outvoted." In addition, as recent research has made clear, the major Reconstruction legislation was the work of no one man or faction but the result of a complex series of legislative compromises and maneuvers in which moderate Senators and Congressmen had as much influence as radicals like Stevens.[5]

Stevens was in fact not a dictator, but neither was he just another Republican politician. In a period of intense political and ideological crisis, his function was to outline a radical position toward which events would force the party to move, and to project the conditions under which change would occur. At a time when every Congress witnessed a high turnover of Representatives, Stevens had a career of service stretching back into the 1850s. He could remind younger colleagues that he had been through the revolution from the beginning, and could speak of the times when southerners like "the mighty Toombs, with his shaggy locks, headed a gang who, with shouts of defiance, rendered this a hell of legislation." Throughout the Civil War, Stevens would stake out a position, confidently predicting that the nation would move leftward and adopt it within a year or two, and usually he was right. As a newspaper in his home district in Pennsylvania declared, "In all the leading questions of the late war, Mr. Stevens has been in advance of his compeers, but the Government has eventually seen the necessity of giving practical effect to his views of the national policy."[6]

Stevens, then, was "a man absolutely convinced, and in a sense rightly, that he and history were for the moment in perfect step." His record of having been proved right by events helps explain why, when Stevens rose to speak, the House fell uncommonly quiet, the galleries quickly filled, Senators often dropped their work to attend, and, as a freshman Congress-man commented, "everyone expects something worth hear-ing."[7] And yet by the very nature of his leadership Stevens was most effective in providing his party with means, rather than ends. During the Civil War, Republicans eventually came to agree with Stevens that freeing and arming the slaves was the only way to achieve the unquestioned goal of Union victory. And during Reconstruction, Stevens would be most successful when his proposals seemed to provide ways of moving toward the party's commonly held goals of Republican ascendancy in the national government, protection of the basic rights of the freedmen, and reorganization of southern governments under the control of genuinely loyal men. Thus as events convinced Republicans that Stevens's proposals, including civil rights and suffrage for the freedmen, a period of military rule in the South, and even the impeachment of the President, were neces-sary for the achievement of their basic aims, they would follow Stevens—or at least move to the positions he had outlined. But Stevens failed completely in pressing for the confiscation and redistribution of the lands of the leading rebels, because he was unable to convince his party that such a policy was either an es-sential goal or an acceptable means to other ends.

The issue of confiscation had roots stretching back to the first years of the Civil War, when abolitionists and radical Re-publicans first linked the goal of landownership for southern blacks with that of emancipation. And as the war progressed, increasing numbers of Republicans were converted to the view that the confiscation of rebel property would be a legitimate war measure. The first Confiscation Act, of August 1861, was directed only against property used in aid of the rebellion, but in 1862 Congress enacted a far more sweeping measure, de-claring all property of rebels liable to confiscation. President Lincoln, who strongly opposed widespread confiscation, forced Congress to pass an explanatory resolution, limiting the seizure of land to the lifetime of the owner. Only a handful of Republicans, Stevens among them, voted in opposition. The debates of 1862 indicated that while a majority of Republicans were willing to use confiscation as a war measure and a way of attacking slavery, far fewer envisioned a sweeping revolution of land tenure in the South.[8]

As the war progressed, however, the idea of permanent land confiscation gained wider support. In 1864 and 1865, Stevens and the veteran land reformer George W. Julian led a fight in Congress to repeal the joint resolution of 1862 and authorize the permanent seizure of rebel lands. By the end of the war both Houses, by narrow margins and in votes on different measures, had repealed the 1862 resolution. But no joint measure was ever enacted. The Freedmen's Bureau bill, passed in March 1865, did contain a provision assigning to freedmen and white refugees forty acres of confiscated or abandoned land, although the land was to be rented for three years and there was no promise of permanent ownership. Meanwhile, though the Lincoln administration had left the Confiscation Act of 1862 virtually unenforced, thousands of acres of abandoned land had fallen into government hands, and General Sherman's famous order settling freedmen on such land in South Carolina and Georgia seemed to some to presage a general policy of establishing the blacks on homesteads.[9]

At the outset of Reconstruction, therefore, the Republican party had taken some steps toward Stevens's goal of providing land to the freedmen from the estates of the planter aristocracy. But even in wartime the party had not overcome its inhibitions about such a policy, and once Union victory had been achieved, the notion to many Republicans became unthinkable. For confiscation flew in the face of too many basic tenets of the ideology which had carried the Republicans into the Civil War and which had emerged unchanged, even strengthened, by the war experience.[10] To a party which believed that a free laborer, once accorded equality of opportunity, would rise or fall in the social scale on the strength of his own diligence, frugality, and hard work, confiscation seemed an unwarranted interference with the rights of property and an unacceptable example of special privilege and class legislation.

And yet there were values and aspirations, shared by most Republicans, to which Stevens could and did appeal in an attempt to build a pro-confiscation coalition. Republicans were committed to restricting the power of the planters, protecting the rights of the freedmen, and transforming the South into a democratic (and Republican) society. During the congressional debates of 1865–67 most radical Republicans, and an increasing number of moderates, viewed black suffrage as the most effective means of achieving these goals and of obviating the need for massive federal intervention in the South. Stevens, however, challenged the idea that the impoverished and despised former slaves could immediately become independent voters. As he admitted to the House early in 1866, Stevens did not want Negro suffrage enacted for a few years. If the southern states were readmitted to the Union before the federal Constitution was altered to guarantee black rights and before the freedmen were given the economic wherewithal to establish their independence from economic coercion, the verdict of the Civil War would be undone: "They will give the suffrage to their menials, their house servants, those that they can control, and elect whom they please to make our laws. This is not the kind of suffrage I want."[11]

Stevens thus insisted that it was unrealistic to expect the freedmen to challenge effectively the political dominance of the South's traditional ruling class. John Andrew, the war governor of Massachusetts, who shared Stevens's perception, drew from it the inference that the only stable basis of reunion was an understanding between Republican leaders and "the natural leaders of opinion in the South"—a preview of the policy which would end Reconstruction in 1877. Stevens drew precisely the opposite conclusion. Realizing that emancipation had not destroyed the planter class, whose wealth rested not only on slaveholding but on control of prime black belt lands, he urged that such lands be confiscated.[12] The franchise by itself, he insisted, would not really touch the blacks' basic problems: "homesteads to them are far more valuable than the immediate right of suffrage, though both are their due." Most Republicans would reverse the proposition, as did the radical Congressman James Ashley of Ohio. "If I were a black man," Ashley declared, "with the chains just stricken from my limbs, without home to shelter me or mine, and you should offer me the ballot, or a cabin and forty acres of cotton land, I would take the ballot." Only George Julian, Wendell Phillips, and, occasionally, Benjamin F. Butler and Charles Sumner, stressed the land question, and none did so as consistently and forcefully as Stevens. Phillips, indeed, did not come around to this view until 1866, though when he did, he argued it much in the way Stevens had done:[13] "You cannot govern the South against its educated classes, with their social prestige. If they cannot be hung nor exiled, they must be flanked. . . . Four millions of uneducated negroes, with none of that character which results from position, with none of that weight which comes from one or two generations of recognized manhood, cannot outweigh that element at the South."

Confiscation, for Stevens, thus had two related goals. One was to destroy the power of the planter class; the other, to create a new class of black and white yeomen as the basis of future southern political and social power, and as allies of the Republican middle class of the North. Revolutionary as such a proposal may have been, it could be defended as the corollary of a traditional, widely shared value—the conviction that democratic institutions must rest on an industrious middle class. Stevens had always paid homage to the ideal of the yeoman republic. As he declared in 1850, "the middling classes who own the soil, and work it with their own hands, are the main support of every free government." Stevens's complete lack of racial prejudice was evident in his assumption that distributing land to blacks would make them middle-class yeomen; that their social position, morals, and psychology were the outgrowth of slavery, not of racial inferiority, and could therefore be altered.

But he also recognized that in view of the legacy of slavery and the hostility of southern whites, the traditional American ideal of success through thrift and hard work simply could not apply while the former slaves remained under their present disadvantages. But confiscation, he argued, could achieve a whole panoply of results central to the Republican ethos:[14]

> Nothing is so likely to make a man a good citizen as to make him a freeholder. Nothing will so multiply the productions of the South as to divide it into small farms. Nothing will make men so industrious and moral as to let them feel that they are above want and are the owners of the soil which they till. . . . No people will ever be republican in spirit and practice where a few own immense manors and the masses are landless. Small independent landholders are the support and guardians of republican liberty.

There were other arguments as well as confiscation. For one thing, the seizure of planter lands would be a fitting punishment for the architects of the rebellion, those "who have murdered our brothers, our fathers, and our children." If the lands of the planter class, moreover, were seized and forty acres allotted to each freedman, there would still remain hundreds of millions of acres—90 per cent of the land, in fact—which could be sold to help pay the national debt, reduce taxes, and provide pensions for Union soldiers and reimbursement for loyal citizens whose property had been destroyed during the war (of whom there were many in Stevens's home area of southern Pennsylvania). It would be, moreover, in Wendell Phillips's words, merely "naked justice to the former slave," whose uncompensated labor had cleared and cultivated the southern land and who was certainly entitled to "a share of his inheritance." But Stevens's basic appeal was to the remodeling of southern society: the transformation of an alien, undemocratic, severely stratified social order into a prosperous, democratic, and loyal republic. "The whole fabric of southern society," he declared in 1865, "*must* be changed, and never can it be done if this opportunity is lost."[15]

Stevens seems to have assumed that such a desire was widely shared in the Republican party. And there was certainly some evidence for that assumption. Long before the Civil War, anti-slavery northerners had developed an extensive critique of the southern social order and had declared their wish that the South might be transformed into a society more akin to that of the North and West. And most Republicans in the early years of Reconstruction shared Carl Schurz's view that "a free labor society must be established and built up on the ruins of the slave labor society." But far fewer were prepared to accept confiscation as the means to this end, both because Stevens's plan conflicted with some basic Republican values and because the creation of a black yeoman middle class was not what important elements of the party had in mind for the economic future of the South. Republicans in Boston, New York, and Philadelphia (the ante-bellum centers of the cotton trade), as well as other northerners who hoped to invest in the post-war South, tended to favor the speedy revival of the cotton plantation system, with northern capital and migrants supplanting the former slave-holders. Blacks would remain an essentially propertyless plantation labor force, whose basic legal rights would be recognized but who would hardly be in a position to challenge propertied whites for political and economic dominance. When the New York *Times*, the leading spokesman for this view, spoke of the South's need for a "prosperous yeomanry," it was quick to add, "very many of them will be northerners."[16]

Another group of Republicans, more willing to grant complete legal and political equality to the freedmen, looked to a wider economic transformation of the South, including the creation of a diversified, industrializing economy. But again, the South was to be rebuilt under the auspices of northern capital and settlers. This was the view, for instance, of Horace Greeley's New York *Tribune*, the *Nation*, and spokesmen for Pennsylvania's iron industry. Greeley insisted that what the South needed most was not talk of confiscation, which would paralyze investment and economic development, but an influx of northern capital, settlers, and industrial skills. And Congressman William "Pig Iron" Kelley of Pennsylvania, after touring the South in 1867 and extolling the region's economic resources and latent wealth, concluded, "The South must be regenerated, and we of the North must do it."[17]

Stevens was never able to make confiscation palatable to such Republicans. He feared, indeed, that the quick economic reconstruction of the South under northern auspices was likely to leave the freedmen no better off than under continued planter domination. He may have been influenced by the arguments of George Julian, who in 1864 and 1865 repeatedly pointed to the danger that confiscated and abandoned lands would be swallowed up by northern speculators. In Louisiana, under the direction of General Nathaniel P. Banks, freedmen had been put to work on plantations controlled by such men in "a system of enforced and uncompensated labor." If this was any indication of the economic future of the South, it appeared that "in place of the slaveholding landowner . . . we shall have the grasping monopolist of the North, whose dominion over the freedmen and poor whites will be more galling than slavery itself."[18]

That Stevens was less interested than other Republicans in speedy southern economic development under northern auspices was amply demonstrated during Reconstruction. He fought unsuccessfully in 1866 for a constitutional amendment authorizing an export tax on cotton—hardly the sort of measure investors in southern cotton plantations were likely to support. When Kelley pleaded for aid to a northern-owned railroad, on the ground that railroad development would aid the destitute freedmen of the region, Stevens scoffed: "May I ask my friend how many of these starving people he thinks are stockholders in this road?" And in 1868 he and Julian endorsed a measure, which passed the House but was killed in the Senate, declaring federal land grants to railroads in four southern states forfeited and open to black and white settlers.[19]

Because he was an iron manufacturer and supporter of a protective tariff, many historians have pictured Stevens as a conscious agent of northern capitalism, bent on establishing the North's economic hegemony over the South. But northern business interests did not see it that way. As one Philadelphia businessman complained, after learning of Stevens's opposition to a federal bankruptcy law to aid business in the South, "he seems to oppose any measure that will not benefit the *nigger*."[20]

The combination of ideological and economic obstacles to confiscation became fully apparent after Stevens, in September 1865, outlined his views on Reconstruction in a widely reprinted speech. Only a handful of Republicans endorsed his program, the most cordial reaction being that of an editor who told Stevens that the speech itself had been well received, "with the exception of your extreme views on confiscation. Some object to going as far in that measure as you purpose." Stevens, however, was not the sort to be disheartened by criticism. When Congress convened in December 1865, he introduced and the House quickly passed a resolution directing General O. O. Howard, superintendent of the Freedmen's Bureau, to report how much property under his jurisdiction had been returned to its owners, and "under what pretense of authority." Stevens's purpose was to make plain that President Johnson's lenient pardon and amnesty policies and his insistence that all land which had not been sold be returned to its pardoned owners were leading to wholesale evictions of blacks from abandoned lands on which they had been settled. Howard's reply, which was not ready until April, made the impact of Johnson's policies plain: virtually all the land under Bureau authority had been restored to the former rebels, while the amount in black hands was minuscule.[21]

Even before Howard's report had been received, Stevens introduced a confiscation measure in the House. The occasion was the bill extending the life of the Freedmen's Bureau. Introduced by the moderate Senator Lyman Trumbull, the bill had wide support among Republicans, and Johnson's eventual veto of it would be a decisive step in his break with the party. As drafted by Trumbull, the bill set aside three million acres of public land in the South for homesteading by freedmen and white refugees, affirmed for three years the title of freedmen to the lands set aside for them by General Sherman, and authorized the Bureau to buy lands for resale to blacks. In Stevens's view, none of these provisions was satisfactory. The public domain in the southern states consisted largely of hill and swamp lands, and the impoverished freedmen did not possess the capital necessary to establish homes and farms there, or to buy land from the Bureau. And there was no promise of permanent ownership of the Sherman lands. The bill did not touch the economic power of the planters, nor did it give freedmen access to the black belt land which was the key to the southern economy. When it came to the House, Stevens declared, "I say that this bill is a robbery."

When the Trumbull bill reached the House floor early in February 1886, Stevens proposed a substitute measure, adding "forfeited estates of the enemy" to the land open to settlement, making certain that the land could be purchased by blacks on easy terms, and making permanent their possession of the Sherman lands. When this substitute came to a vote it was overwhelmingly defeated, 126 to 37; Republicans divided 37 in favor, 86 opposed, with 10 abstentions, and many of the House's leading radicals, including Ashley of Ohio and Kelley of Pennsylvania, opposed it.

The tangled complexities of the land question were further illustrated two days after Steven's substitute was rejected and the Freedmen's Bureau bill passed, when the House with virtually unanimous Republican support passed Julian's Southern Homestead Act, opening all public land in the South to settlement and giving blacks and loyal whites preferential treatment until 1867. Republicans were thus quite willing to offer freedmen the same opportunity to acquire land which whites had received under the Homestead Act of 1862; they simply refused to take land from the planters to make farmers of blacks. As Stevens had foreseen, the Julian bill was a dismal failure. The land involved was so inferior, and the freedmen so lacking in capital, that by 1869 only four thousand black families had even attempted to take advantage of the Act, and many of these subsequently lost their land.[22]

These votes of February 1866 posed a dilemma for Stevens. He could have accepted them as defining for all practical purposes the limits to which Republicans were willing to move toward providing blacks with land and reorganizing southern society. As William McFeely has pointed out, the Freedmen's Bureau bill despite its limitations did hold out the possibility of a gradual but far-reaching change in the South's land system. It established federal responsibility for giving blacks access to land, and for assisting them in purchasing it on credit. Because the policy did not involve severe punishment of the planters, a complete upheaval of southern society, or special privilege for the blacks, it commanded wide support in Republican ranks. Had Stevens thrown his weight behind the measure as an acceptable alternative to massive confiscation, it might have become, in effect, official Republican policy on the land question. Yet Stevens's whole experience in the 1860s predisposed him not to accept these votes as a final verdict. The conservative New York *Herald* could exult over his defeat ("thus we see . . . the real strength of the Jacobins in the House"), but Stevens might have retorted that when he first proposed a measure for the use of black troops it had received only thirty votes. He had always been ahead of his party, he once remarked during the war, but "I have never been so far ahead . . . but that the members of the party have overtaken me."[23]

Stevens's strategy was based on the judgment that a prolongation of the national crisis would push the Republican party to the left. The longer the crisis lasted, he thought, the more radical the final settlement was likely to be. Throughout 1866 and 1867, Stevens bided his time on the land question, devoting his energies to the Fourteenth Amendment and Negro suffrage, while trying to delay a final settlement. The leftward drift which Stevens counted on as the dynamic element of the political situation was explained by the *Nation* during the hectic debates of February 1867: "Six years ago, the North would have rejoiced to accept any mild restrictions upon the spread of slavery as a final settlement. Four years ago, it would have accepted peace upon the basis of gradual emancipation. Two years ago, it would have been content with emancipation and equal civil rights for the colored people without the extension of suffrage. One year ago, a slight extension of the suffrage would have satisfied it."[24] Now, in March 1867, the Republicans succeeded in passing the first Reconstruction Act, temporarily forcing the planter class from participation in politics and imposing Negro suffrage on the South. And, just as southern intransigence had swelled the ranks of the Republican party in the 1850s and forced it to embrace emancipation and the arming of the slaves during the Civil War, Stevens could hope that if southern whites again obstructed northern goals, the party would move to an even more radical measure— confiscation. Yet the passage of the Act revealed the weakness of Stevens's strategy. As the *New York Times* had observed in 1866, Stevens's program "presupposes the continuance during peace of a public opinion which acquired force under the excitement and perils of war."[25] Inevitably, however, the impulse for a return to normal, for an end to the crisis, had grown in the Republican party—and Stevens, though unhappy with the new Reconstruction measure, had been powerless to block it. Now, the political initiative in effect passed to southern whites. If they accepted the new situation "in good faith," they could destroy whatever chance Stevens's more radical policies might have had.

Although most historians of Reconstruction have not emphasized the fact, confiscation was very much a live political issue in the spring and summer of 1867. But while the debate was very animated, it soon became clear that the fears aroused by Stevens's proposals far outweighed any attractions the plan contained. When Congress reconvened in March 1867, Stevens, ill and too weak to speak, had a colleague read a long speech and a bill providing forty acres to freedmen from confiscated land.

"To this issue," he announced, "I desire to devote the small remnant of my life." At the same time, Charles Sumner pressed the issue in the Senate, and outside of Congress Benjamin Butler, Wendell Phillips, and the American Anti-Slavery Society endorsed Stevens's proposals.

The moderate majority of Republicans, however, were determined that Congress should embark upon no new Reconstruction experiments until the success or failure of the recently enacted measures had become clear. Stevens's bill was postponed to December, and Sumner's resolutions were handily defeated. William P. Fessenden, perhaps the most powerful Senate Republican, informed Sumner, "This is more than we do for white men." To which Sumner responded, "White men have never been in slavery." The farthest some Republicans would go was a warning to the South. If the recently adopted Reconstruction plan did not achieve satisfactory results, several highly respectable Republican journals declared, confiscation would be the logical next policy. Surprisingly, only the generally conservative Philadelphia *North American,* a self-proclaimed spokesman for the manufacturing interests of Pennsylvania, seemed genuinely sympathetic to confiscation. The key question of Reconstruction, the *North American* announced, was the fate of the "plantation oligarchy," and those who opposed Stevens's proposals "must find some other means of destroying this landed aristocracy." The journal also emphasized that the creation of a yeoman class in the South would greatly benefit northern industry (which in 1867 was suffering from the postwar recession). "Just in proportion as the freedmen rise in the social scale will they consume more of the fabrics we sell to the South. Just in proportion as the South refuses to let them rise . . . do we suffer in our trade." If small farms replaced plantations as the basis of southern agriculture, the South would "buy ten dollars of merchandise off us for every one it now takes."[26]

Despite the discouraging response, Stevens continued to press the land issue. In June, he made public a letter addressed to the county assessors of southern Pennsylvania, informing them of his intention to "prosecute the claims for confiscation at the next session of Congress," and requesting a detailed list of Civil War losses which might be reimbursed from the proceeds of confiscated lands. He specifically instructed the assessors to omit his own property from the list, since some opponents charged that his real aim was to secure compensation for his Caledonia Iron Works, destroyed by the Confederates in 1863. "Feeble as my own powers are," Stevens concluded, "if I had five years more added to my life, I should not doubt that this would become an accomplished fact."[27]

By the end of July, the influential Cincinnati *Commercial* could report the existence of "a considerable number of decided advocates of the confiscation of rebel property" in Republican ranks. By then, however, the opponents of confiscation were marshaling their forces. The sudden prominence of the confiscation question forced Republicans to take sides, and most made it clear that Stevens's proposals were incompatible with their basic beliefs. Respected radical journals like the *Nation* insisted that while possession of property would be eminently desirable for the freedmen, for the government to give them land would suggest that "there are other ways of securing comfort or riches than honest work." "No man in America," it added, "has any right to anything which he has not honestly earned, or which the lawful owner has not thought proper to give him." At the same time, more conservative Republicans denounced Stevens for adding to "the distrust which already deters capitalists from embarking in [the South's] enterprises." The New York *Times* printed dispatches from correspondents in the South, reporting that *"the fear of confiscation"* was paralyzing business. When investors in plantations went to southern banks for loans, declared a letter from South Carolina, they were met with the query, "How can you give security against Thaddeus Stevens?" From Georgia it was reported that gloom hung over the men of "intelligence, influence, and property," because they believed that as long as the confiscation question was agitated, "neither capital nor emigration will flow this way."[28]

Perhaps even more threatening, in the *Times*'s view, was the precedent which might be set by the confiscation of southern property. Others might also warn that the "process of division," once begun in the South, would not be confined there, but it was the *Times* that expressed most clearly the fears felt by northern men of property:

> If Congress is to take cognizance of the claims of labor against capital . . . there can be no decent pretense for confining the task to the slave-holder of the South. It is a question, not of humanity, not of loyalty, but of the fundamental relation of industry to capital; and sooner or later, if begun at the South, it will find its way into the cities of the North. . . . An attempt to justify the confiscation of Southern land under the pretense of doing justice to the freedmen, strikes at the root of all property rights in both sections. It concerns Massachusetts quite as much as Mississippi.[29]

These fears were exaggerated by confiscation's being only one of a series of what the *Nation* called "schemes for interference with property or business" which were agitating the public scene in the spring of 1867. Labor activity seemed to have reached a new peak, with "strikes among the workmen of every kind throughout the country," and demands for federal and state laws to enact the eight-hour day.[30] In June, the radical Senator Ben Wade delivered a widely reported speech in Kansas, declaring that with the slavery issue settled, a new political question—the relations of capital and labor—was about to emerge. "Property," said Wade, "is not equally divided, and a more equal distribution of capital must be wrought out." Though Wade quickly backtracked when his speech aroused a furor in Republican circles, the *Times* insisted that it was now "perfectly clear that we are to have a political party based on the broadest and plainest doctrines of agrarianism. A war on property is to succeed the war on Slavery."[31]

Complicating the political scene—and the confiscation question—still further was the relation between the land issue and the development of the Republican party in the South. Despite black suffrage, most Republicans still envisioned their nascent southern coalition as an alliance of southern merchants, business interests, Whiggish planters, and black voters, with the white propertied elements in control. Republicans, of course, expected most of the newly enfranchised blacks to align with their party, but it was the southern whites who seemed to possess the attributes—"knowledge, character, intelligence, and ability"—necessary for political leadership. The confiscation plan seemed certain to alienate the support of propertied whites, and would create instead a class-oriented party of poor blacks and whites in which a solid black vote would be the controlling element. This fear was succinctly expressed by the *Times:* "Mr. Stevens and General Butler are determined to build up a Southern Party called Republican, on the scheme of confiscation. They expect to get by that bribe the whole negro vote and enough of the white vote to control the Southern States." [32]

In a sense the *Times* was right, although Stevens would hardly have called confiscation a "bribe." He certainly knew, however, that as one newspaper reported in 1867, "these black voters are overwhelmingly in favor of confiscation," and that support for the plan had been growing among white southerners as well. As early as January 1866, Stevens had received letters from southern loyalists endorsing his plans as being the only way to break planter domination. By 1867, such prominent organs of southern Republicanism as the Raleigh *Standard* were speaking in favor of it, and the Philadelphia *Press* reported from Alabama that if confiscation were submitted to a vote in that state, "a majority both of blacks and whites would vote for it." Southern white Republicans seemed to be coming to the realization that if the planters' economic hegemony were not broken, they would eventually "be sure to control the policy of the community." In Stevens's view, moreover, the confiscation plan would allow southern Republicans to transcend the troublesome race issue by uniting freedmen and poor whites on an economic basis. As the Washington *Daily Morning Chronicle,* Stevens's leading newspaper supporter, explained, "the great question of Reconstruction is not a question of race supremacy . . . but . . . is really and truly a question of the rights of labor."[33]

The prospect of the confiscation and redistribution of planter lands, the Boston *Advertiser* reported in June 1867, "has taken possession to a large extent of the mind of the loyal population of the South—the poor whites and land-lack negroes." This was hardly to say, however, that there were not strong Republican elements in the South which opposed such a measure. As each southern state went through the process of organizing a Republican party in the spring of 1867, virtually every convention found itself divided between "confiscation radicals" and more moderate Whiggish elements. The results were not comforting to moderate and conservative northern Republicans. In Alabama the Union League resolved that if former rebels did not accept the new political situation "in good faith," Congress should confiscate their lands. In North Carolina a Republican mass meeting called on Congress to enact Stevens's latest measure. Most disturbing was the situation in Virginia, where black delegates at the state convention almost to a man demanded a confiscation plank. Most white Republicans, led by the venerable John Minor Botts and other one-time Whig Unionists, opposed the plan, but the blacks were supported by certain white radicals such as the Reverend James Hunnicutt, the editor of a Richmond newspaper. In the end, an uneasy compromise was reached, in a resolution threatening confiscation if planters tried to intimidate black voters.[34]

Northern Republicans, including many radicals, were alarmed at the apparent influence of men like Hunnicutt among the freedmen. "Nothing could be more ominous of disaster," declared the Boston *Advertiser,* ". . . than such an array of class against class in the Southern States" as Hunnicutt and others sought. To counteract pro-confiscation influence, three Republican orators, all considered radical in the North, visited the South in the late spring, addressing gatherings of freedmen. Horace Greeley spoke at a large meeting at Richmond's African Church. "I beg you to believe," Greeley told the blacks, "that you are more likely to earn a home than get one by any form of confiscation. . . . Confiscation shrivels and paralyzes the industry of the whole community subjected to its influence." Senator Henry Wilson brought the same message to Virginia and South Carolina, and William D. Kelley also visited the South, praising its potential for economic development and informing the freedmen that "they can have homes of their own by working hard and saving what they earn—not otherwise."[35]

From Washington, Stevens looked on as the gospel of work was brought to the freedmen. Late in April, he denounced Wilson's Virginia speech and warned that "no man should make promises for the party. . . . Who authorized any orator to say that there would be no confiscation?" In May, he reiterated his criticism of the "Republican meteors" pursuing their "erratic . . . course" through the South, and in June he announced his intention of pushing the confiscation plan at the next session of Congress. But by the end of May it had become apparent that Greeley, Wilson, and Kelley were far closer to the mainstream of Republican opinion than was Thaddeus Stevens. Speaker of the House Schuyler Colfax and Senate leader Fessenden publicly supported Wilson against Stevens's criticisms, and a committee of Congressmen charged by the Republican caucus with overseeing political developments in the South declared that the rights of property would not be infringed (although it did piously urge landholders to offer land for sale to blacks at reasonable rates). It was apparent, in short, that whatever southern Republicans desired, the party in the North was hardly prepared to embrace confiscation.[36] Consequently, as the summer progressed, talk of confiscation subsided in southern Republican conventions.[37]

By the end of 1867, the leftward drift which had characterized the Republican party since the beginning of the Civil War had definitely come to an end. The party suffered a series of reverses in the state elections of 1867, which many Republican leaders blamed squarely on Stevens, the radicals, and their "extreme theories." The election returns greatly strengthened the hand of Republicans like the Ohio banker Henry Cooke and Boston's liberal industrialist Edward Atkinson, who were determined to "put down" the "ultra infidelic radicals" and "prevent the creation of an exclusive black man's party [in the South] and also kill the scheme of confiscation." As the party turned toward respectability, conservatism, and Grant, it appeared certain that, as an Ohio politician observed, "the Negro will be less prominent for some time to come."[38]

By August 1868, when he died, Stevens's political influence was at low ebb. In his characteristically cynical way he had told an interviewer, "I have no history. My life-long regret is that I have lived so long and so uselessly." He died aware that planters were already beginning to use economic intimidation to counter black voting power and that sharecropping and the crop lien—a new "system of peonage," as he called it—were spreading in the black belts, threatening to keep the freedmen permanently dependent on the planters. Stevens was nonetheless still a formidable figure, venerated by the freedmen and by millions of other Republicans, and his death produced a public expression of grief second only to the funeral of Lincoln. It marked in some ways the end of an era, symbolizing the transition from ideology to political expediency as the guiding force of the Republican party. Though the Philadelphia *Press* declared, "He dies at the moment when the truths for which he fought a long and doubtful battle have permanently and almost universally triumphed," James G. Blaine, one of the rising politicos who would control the party's destinies in the 1870s, saw it differently. "The death of Stevens," Blaine observed, "is an emancipation for the Republican party."[39]

Between 1860 and 1868 revolutionary changes had taken

place, changes for which contemporaries gave Stevens more than an average share of the credit. Slavery had been abolished, the freedmen granted civil and political equality, and democratic institutions established in all the southern states. But the final step of the Second American Revolution, the provision of an economic underpinning to the blacks' newly won freedom, had not been taken. The failure of Stevens's campaign for confiscation, his demand that society confront the basic economic questions which the abolition of slavery had entailed, exposed the limitations of the Republican party's middle-class ideology. At the same time, it exposed the vulnerability of Stevens's anomalous position as a radical in politics. Lacking a political base outside the Republican party, Stevens could be successful only so long as his proposals posed no fundamental challenge to the values and interests of the Republican mainstream. Possibly a more flexible man than Stevens, one willing to talk less flamboyantly of punishing traitors, revolutionizing southern society, and destroying social classes, one prepared to accept some form of limited, compensated expropriation of land and its sale on credit, might have achieved more for the cause of black landowning than did Stevens. Probably, however, the very idea of confiscation violated too many of the basic Republican verities for the party ever to become reconciled to it.[40]

Stevens's failure, indeed, revealed the limits to what a bourgeois capitalist culture, even in its most radical phase, will voluntarily yield to radicalism. What is actually most striking about the confiscation debate is the way it prefigured the disillusionment which would soon overtake radical Reconstruction. The same fears aroused by confiscation—special privilege, corruption, black domination, dramatic social upheaval by government fiat, a general undermining of the principles of good government—would shortly come to be associated with Reconstruction itself. The arguments used against Stevens between 1865 and 1867 would eventually justify the entire abandonment of Reconstruction.

EIGHT

Class, Ethnicity, and Radicalism in the Gilded Age: The Land League and Irish-America

On February 2, 1884, Wendell Phillips, the "golden trumpet" of the abolitionist movement and a towering champion of nineteenth-century reform, died in Boston. In the memorial meetings and tributes that followed, Irish-Americans played a prominent part. Organizations ranging from the Wolfe Tone Club of Washington, D.C., to the Ancient Order of Hibernians eulogized Phillips's memory, and the usually secretive Clan na Gael held a special open meeting to laud his principles of "universal liberty and equal rights of all men." Seven years later another veteran of the crusade against slavery, James Redpath, died in New York after being run down by a bus on Broadway. Irish-Americans mourned his passing as well. On the day of his funeral, Irish and American flags flew side by side at Redpath's home.[1]

We are accustomed to thinking of nineteenth-century Irish-Americans as implacably hostile to the major currents of native Protestant reform. Allegedly, abolitionists like Phillips and Red-

Originally published in *Marxist Perspectives*, I (Summer 1978), 6-55. Reprinted by permission of Cliomar Corporation.

path were anathema in the Irish community. Yet, the history of the Irish National Land League, in whose service Phillips and Redpath won the esteem of the Irish community, reveals a conjunction of Irish-America with the Protestant reform tradition. Although the Land League existed for only three years, it introduced thousands of Irish-Americans to modern reform and labor ideologies and helped to transform specifically Irish grievances and traditions into a broader critique of American society in the Gilded Age. The Land League both reflected and helped to shape the traditions of the Irish-American working class, and illuminated the complex interplay of class, ethnicity, and radicalism in industrializing America.

I

Between 1845 and 1889, three million Irish immigrants arrived in the United States, nearly half of whom were "refugees from disaster" fleeing the devastation of the Great Famine. These impoverished agricultural laborers and small farmers brought neither the capital nor skills necessary to acquire a secure place in the rapidly industrializing American economy. Congregating in the great cities of the Northeast, they became the "first genuine American proletariat," working at the low-paying unskilled jobs native-born Americans sought to avoid. The Irish immigrants built America's railroads, performed the work of common laborer, porter, domestic servant, and longshoreman, and inhabited urban ghettos notorious for poverty, crime, and disease. And, although post-Famine migrants came from an Ireland in which capitalist agriculture, literacy, and education were expanding rapidly, they too generally entered the marketplace as unskilled urban laborers. By 1880 the Irish-born population, including both Famine and post-Famine migrants, had risen to over 1.8 million with unskilled labor still the largest single occupation. In New York City 20 per cent of the Irish-born worked as laborers, compared with only 4 per cent of the native population.[2]

"The Irish in America," an English observer wrote in 1880, "are a great floating population of migratory labourers" who "haunt the great cities." Yet, this formulation obscures the large number of Irish-Americans settled in such smaller industrial cities as Fall River, Troy, and Scranton, as well as the increasingly differentiated class structure of the Irish-American community. Beginning as helpers in rolling mills and as laborers in mines and construction, thousands had by this time become plumbers, carpenters, and bricklayers in cities large and small, skilled molders in iron works, and craftsmen and foremen in textile mills. Second-generation Irish-Americans, who by 1880 comprised half the "Irish" community, had rapidly advanced to the status of skilled workmen. In Philadelphia some 30 per cent of the immigrant Irish worked as laborers in 1880, compared with only 15 per cent of those born in the United States of Irish parents. The second generation numbered twice as many as the first as ironworkers, bricklayers, and machinists.[3]

By this time, moreover, a significant middle class had made its appearance. Its most prosperous and respectable members, the "lace curtain" Irish, were mostly merchants and professionals whose offices were located in modern downtown business districts catering to a non-Irish clientele. These "lace curtain" Irish enjoyed less political and social influence in the larger society than economic status. Not fully integrated into the established urban bourgeoisie, they also formed no part of the emerging elite of industrial and finance capitalists. Nevertheless, their lives were far removed from those of their poorer countrymen. Living in non-working-class neighborhoods, they belonged to fraternal organizations limited primarily to persons like themselves. More numerous were the countless saloon keepers and grocers whose enterprises depended on working-class patronage, and the ubiquitous building contractors who required little capital to gain a foothold in business. These petty entrepreneurs often shared the experiences and sympathies of their working-class customers and neighbors. With its large number of merchants, lawyers, clerks, editors, and political office-holders, New York City was the center of the Irish-American middle class. The election in 1880 of William R. Grace as the first Irish Catholic mayor of New York symbolized the stability of Irish-America, the decline of the virulent nativism of the 1850s, and the success of a visible portion of the Irish community.

Nevertheless, Irish-America remained overwhelmingly working class. By far the most common form of social advancement—from unskilled to skilled positions—lay within the working class itself. And such advancement was always precarious: the depression of the 1870s reduced many skilled Irish workers to the ranks of common labor and filled relief rolls with the unemployed. Irish-America had come a long way since impoverished laborers fled the Famine, but poverty still stalked the Irish community. The bitter experience of the 1870s revealed profound class divisions within Irish-America and helped make it fertile soil for radical criticism of Gilded Age America.[4]

II

Charles Stewart Parnell, the foremost nationalist leader of late nineteenth-century Ireland, believed that Irish-Americans were "even more Irish than the Irish themselves in the true spirit of patriotism." In America nativism and anti-Catholicism reinforced an ethnic identity nourished by centuries of English rule and the horrors of the Famine years. "I have met men of the second generation," said one visitor to America, "sons of Irish parents, American in voice and appearance, who have never set foot on Irish soil, with as ardent an affection for Ireland" as any native-born rebel.[5]

The first organization to tap Irish-American nationalism effectively was the Fenian Brotherhood, organized in 1858 with distinct but coordinated branches in Ireland and America. A secret, oath-bound movement devoted to the establishment of an Irish republic through force of arms, the Fenians organized

an ill-fated "invasion" of Canada in 1866 and then rapidly succumbed to internal divisions. In the 1870s its successor, the
secret Clan na Gael, organized military units for action in case
England became embroiled in a European war. In Ireland the
Fenians' membership consisted, in the words of a British official, of "the lowest part of the Irish Roman Catholic population—urban craftsmen, shopkeepers' assistants, and agricultural laborers in the countryside." In America too, the Clan na
Gael, numbering perhaps 10,000 at its peak, was recruited almost entirely from the working class, although it did contain a
sprinkling of petty entrepreneurs. By and large the "best class
of Irishmen" held aloof. By 1877 the Clan had succeeded in
raising a considerable sum for its Skirmishing Fund to promote
armed conflict and terrorism in Ireland, but its membership
had declined to the point that the British consul in New York
exulted it was "now only the skeleton of what it once was"—an
assessment with which old Fenian leaders reluctantly agreed.[6]

It is easy to ridicule the Fenian movement. Riddled by British
informers, its few attempts at insurrection were hopelessly mis-
managed. It suffered from constant intrigues among its
leaders, and its obsession with secrecy led it to adopt a code in
which each letter of the alphabet was replaced by the one that
succeeded it, Ireland becoming Jsfmboe, and England, Fohm-
boe. It combined nineteenth-century republicanism with a fantastic rigamarole of passwords, oaths, and initiations which
sometimes seemed to take precedence over its political purposes. The Clan na Gael, equally obsessed with secrecy, nonetheless held an annual fancy-dress ball in Tammany Hall. Yet,
the Fenians raised the first mass nationalist movement in Ireland independent of middle-class leadership and owing nothing to the Catholic Church. A class movement, the Fenians not
only lacked but openly disdained a class program. Most of the
leaders believed that resolution of Ireland's social problems
must await independence.[7]

By 1878 the most far-sighted nationalists had concluded that
the mass of Irishmen and Irish-Americans would never sup-

port a secret organization whose republicanism was devoid of a social program. In October the Fenian exile John Devoy and another leader, Michael Davitt, visiting the United States after his release from prison in Britain, agreed to a policy of supporting the Irish Parliamentary party coupled with a reform of the Irish land system. Here lay the origins of the famous "New Departure"—the attempt to merge Fenianism into a mass, public movement and to bridge the gap separating nationalist leaders from the rural masses.[8]

For Devoy the New Departure did not alter the primacy of the goal of Irish independence. But, as he later recalled, while the politicians debated, "the forces of nature intervened and pushed the agrarian question to the front." Poor weather and massive American agricultural imports produced an agrarian crisis throughout western Europe in the late 1870s. In 1879, after two successive crop failures in Ireland, the prospect of a third revived memories of the Great Famine. That summer, tenants in the West of Ireland organized to demand a reduction of rents. The West, the most backward region of the island, had changed little from a traditional subsistence economy of diminutive holdings and exclusive reliance on the potato. Its tenant farmers displayed an "almost total indifference" to Home Rule: "All their ideas are dominated by the single one of land." Davitt quickly channeled spontaneous protest into a structured organization, the Land League, of which Parnell assumed leadership. By the end of 1879 the League had spread throughout the island, demanding not simply relief for tenants in distress and a halt to evictions, but "the land for the people"—transfer of ownership of the land of Ireland from a few thousand aristocratic families to tenant farmers. Within a year it had over one thousand branches and 200,000 members. "In Ireland," reported Chief Secretary William Forster in 1881, "the Land League is supreme. . . . I am forced to acknowledge that to a great extent the ordinary law is powerless."[9]

Early in 1880 Parnell traveled to America to raise funds and organize American branches. His tour was an unprecedented success. Not only did he arouse unbounded enthusiasm among Irish-Americans, but the non-Irish community welcomed him as well. At every stop he was received by mayors, judges, and prominent businessmen. He became the first foreigner to address the House of Representatives since Louis Kossuth in 1851. The Fenians had been denounced by respectable American opinion, but in Boston and New York substantial Protestant citizens received Parnell into their homes and pledged assistance to the cause of the Irish tenant farmers.

With Parnell called back to Ireland for a general election in March, Davitt continued to tour from New England to California, organizing branches wherever he went. In March 1880 a conference of prominent Irish-Americans founded the American Land League, choosing, perhaps because of factional jealousies, the virtually unknown James McCaffrey of Massachusetts as president. (His only qualification, according to Davitt, was that "he was supposed to be the handsomest man in New England"; he later became president of a college in Argentina.) By September 1881 the Land League had more than 1,500 branches organized in America and, by the fall of 1882, had collected over half a million dollars from American sources.[10]

The Land League was the first nationalist organization to unite the Irish-American community. The land issue had an impact no other could rival. As Devoy explained, commenting on the reception of a group of speakers from Ireland in 1881:

> Perhaps fully seventy-five per cent of that immense throng were men and women born under the dark shadow of landlordism, and not a few were victims of its exterminating operations. Most Irish-American audiences are so, and this explains the readiness with which they grasp the Land Question and the impulse which made them flock to the Land League standard.

Or, as one financial contributor from Michigan explained, he was "red-hot for driving the landlords out of Ireland, as that accursed system was the cause of [my] own emigration."[11]

The wealthy and prominent Irish-Americans, so strikingly absent from the Fenian Brotherhood, found the Land League easier to support, their usual caution outweighed by the respectability conferred on it by Parnell's visit. The founding conference gathered a cross-section of the Irish-American middle class, including twelve merchants, seven lawyers and public officials, and three physicians. The Catholic hierarchy had condemned the Fenians, but bishops and priests played a leading role in the League. Eleven priests attended the founding conference, and priests often played a prominent part in the meetings, rallies, and picnics of the local branches, which often took place at parish churches and schools.[12] In the Land League the three great strands of protest that had emerged in nineteenth-century Ireland finally coalesced: the revolutionary republicanism of the Fenians, the constitutional and parliamentary protest of Daniel O'Connell and Parnell, and the agrarian grievances hitherto expressed in rural secret societies.

Of the various figures associated with the American Land League, none was so controversial as Patrick Ford. Born in Galway in 1837, he had been brought to Boston by his parents at the age of eight. At fifteen he worked as printer's devil on William Lloyd Garrison's *The Liberator*, and at twenty-four edited a short-lived anti-slavery journal in Boston. After serving in the Union army and publishing a Republican newspaper in Charleston during Reconstruction, Ford moved to New York City where he founded the *Irish World* in 1870. By the early 1880s it had become the most important Irish-American newspaper, with a weekly circulation of 35,000.[13]

A small, retiring man who lacked the gift of oratory, Ford, one nationalist recalled, was "probably the only man who ever exercised any considerable influence over the Irish race, who has never made a public speech." His prominence derived from the fact that the *Irish World* had become the voice of the politically conscious Irish-American working class, read, according to Ford, by "every reform advocate in the land." Certainly its influence on the labor movement was considerable. "It circulates in every city and town in the Republic," said one observer, "and is read not merely by the Irish, but by the 'proletariat' of all nationalities." Its New York offices served as a kind of headquarters for labor leaders and Irish nationalists, ranging from Samuel Gompers to J. P. McDonnell. Gompers later recalled that New York's cigarmakers, who paid to have books and newspapers read aloud as they worked, often listened to excerpts from Ford's paper. When a Philadelphia labor editor launched a new newspaper, he declared his ambition was to create "the paper of the country second only to the *Irish World.*" [14]

From the outset Ford viewed his journal as the voice of the nationalist, Catholic, and social aspirations of the Irish-American working class. Its full title reflected the breadth of his concerns: *The Irish World and Industrial Liberator.* Readers received a weekly education in the trans-Atlantic radical tradition. Typical issues contained articles on anti-monopoly, land nationalization, strikes, women's rights, and temperance, as well as such pieces as "How Labor Is Robbed," and "Value—What Is It?" Ford declared the French Revolution "one of the first great victories of labor," and the principles of America in 1776 "the cause of Ireland in 1876." He called Thomas Paine "an infidel" but praised him as an "advocate of political liberty," and one article recounted the life and ideas of the "social giant," Proudhon.

Employing the traditional language of American radicalism, Ford insisted that "labor is the one great motive power of production," and blamed the plight of workers on an economic system in which "non-producers" appropriated most of the fruits of labor. The same message was conveyed in the regular articles by John F. Bray and Thomas Devyr, two immigrant radicals whose long careers illustrated the connection between the Chartists and the Jacksonian labor movement, and the labor and land reform movements of the 1870s and 1880s. [15]

Through the *Irish World,* Ford attempted to bridge the gap that had separated much of the Irish-American community from the reform tradition. But the heritage with which he wished his readers to identify was abolition. The crusade against slavery had acted as a central terminus from which men and ideas flowed into virtually every effort to change post-bellum society.[16] Ford's own career reflected its influence, and he always regretted that Irish-Americans had adopted "an attitude of seeming hostility to the friends of human freedom." He never tired of singing the praises of his former employer Garrison, and he consistently sought to counteract racial prejudice within the Irish community. "Welcome the colored brother in the Land League," Ford wrote in 1881. "He is a marked example of a defrauded workingman." The history of Reconstruction proved conclusively, he insisted, that "there is no liberty without the soil."[17]

The depression of the 1870s, which propelled Ford into the ranks of the labor-reform movement, convinced him of "The Total Depravity of Our Political and Economic System." The two major parties, he insisted, were hopelessly corrupt and controlled by "a privileged and non-producing class, which [has] for years fattened on labor." Along with extensive coverage of Irish news, the *Irish World* devoted increasing attention to the Greenback-Labor party, which Ford supported in the presidential campaigns of 1876 and 1880. Although no socialist, Ford did call for "a change in our economic system," including such specific measures as the income tax, an eight-hour day, an end to interest on money, the issuance of Federal greenbacks, and the nationalization of the land. Ford was more comfortable lashing out at the emerging industrial order than providing a blueprint for a new society, but he did speak of a future cooperative commonwealth in which the wage system, profit-taking, competition, and the existence of "distinctive classes" would all disappear.[18]

Although the *Irish World*'s litany of demons ranged over the entire capitalist order—encompassing the "new Slave Power" of "railroad thieves," "monopolist kings," bankers, and "stock-gambling millionaires"—Ford viewed land monopoly as "the prime evil" of American life. The *Irish World* reprinted Thomas Spence, Louis Blanc, and, later, Henry George on the evils of private property in land. Week after week Ford reiterated that "the natural gifts of God—land, air, light, and water—are things not to be bought or sold." "Nothing is a man's own property," he insisted, "except it be the result of his labor." The land question assumed decisive importance for urban workers, for "with the land to fall back upon, the worker would have a potential voice in making his bargain both for hours and for wages." In Ireland and America the "land robbers" stood as the foremost social enemy.[19]

Years before the Land League adopted the slogan, "the land for the people" had become the motto of the *Irish World*. The basis of Ford's critique of American society, it explained his dissatisfaction with most Irish nationalists. Too many Fenians, he believed, ignored social issues in their preoccupation with Irish independence. Establishing an Irish republic, however laudable, was not enough: "We have a republic here in America, and here in America, too, we have Pittsburg riots, and Land Grabbers, and Usurers, and slow starvation." To Irish tenant farmers "the right to live like a free man without the accursed shadow of a land thief" was as important as independence from England. The weekly dispatches of "Trans-Atlantic," Ford's European correspondent and a veteran nationalist since the days of O'Connell, condemned all moderate proposals for tenant right and asked, "Is there no man in Ireland advanced enough . . . to call out boldly for *the land to the cultivator?*" According to John Devoy, "Trans-Atlantic"'s articles were "the chief attraction of the paper." Many readers believed him "the apostle of a new and regenerated Ireland."[20]

As land meetings swept the West of Ireland in the summer of 1879, the *Irish World* hailed the "Daybreak in the Irish sky." "Fenianism saw only a green flag," Ford exulted, "but the men of today have discovered that there is such a thing as land." And, he boasted, his paper, more than any other single influence, had spread "the true gospel of the Land Question" in

Ireland. Ford established a "Spread the Light Fund" to finance the free distribution of thousands of copies each week in Ireland.[21]

The *Irish World* brought what one observer called "a vast propaganda to American ideas" to Ireland during the land war. The rapid expansion of literacy since the Famine made possible its wide circulation. In Cork, blacksmiths and shoemakers were said to "gather evenings to read and have it read to them." At one Land League gathering, a voice from the crowd called for three cheers for Ford's newspaper, and many local branches distributed copies "with avidity." "There was scarcely a cabin in the West," William O'Brien later recalled, "to which some relative in America did not despatch a weekly copy of the Irish World. . . . It was as if some vast Irish-American invasion was sweeping the country with new and irresistible principles of Liberty and Democracy."[22]

What made the *Irish World*'s approach to the Land League distinct was that Ford consistently sought to link the land struggle in Ireland with social issues in the United States. And not only in America: at moments he perceived the League as the opening battle in "the war of the great army of the disinherited, in all lands, for their Heaven-willed possessions." When Parnell resorted to the rhetorical device, so familiar among European reformers, of contrasting the egalitarian, democratic United States with aristocratic Ireland, Ford observed that land monopoly was spreading as rapidly in America as in the Old World. Immense land grants to railroads, the spread of bonanza farming in the West, and the monopolization of urban real estate, were threatening the "Europeanization" of American society. The principle "the land for the people" applied in America as in Ireland, for "if an Irish landlord cannot take rent, how can an American landlord?" The *Irish World* suggested that the activities of "heartless speculators and rent-hounds" in America ought to be resisted by a "Tenant League." The land issue in Ireland and social reform in the United States were two dimensions of the same issue.[23]

If the *Irish World* addressed itself to the Irish-American working class, the Boston *Pilot* may be described, in the words of the Irish nationalist T. M. Healy, as "the organ of the wealthier and more cultured portion" of Irish-America. The oldest Catholic newspaper in the country, it had become the official organ of the Archdiocese of Boston in 1876, partially owned by Archbishop John Joseph Williams. A majority of the *Pilot*'s readers were workingmen, but substantial numbers of "priests and prosperous businessmen" were also among its readers.

The *Pilot*'s editor, John Boyle O'Reilly, was "the most distinguished Irishman in America." A poet praised by Whittier, a friend of Phillips and Garrison, and an accepted figure in Boston Brahmin circles, he had been born in County Meath in 1844 and had joined the Fenian movement in the 1860s. Imprisoned in Australia for Fenian activities, he had been rescued and brought to America, where he joined the *Pilot* in 1870. Although he abandoned the Fenians at the behest of Archbishop Williams, he remained a fervent nationalist and became a supporter of the Land League.[24]

Like Patrick Ford, O'Reilly had a bent for reform. Outraged by the poverty of so many Irish-American workers, he often supported strikes. He also criticized the treatment of blacks and Indians, and wrote the poem for the dedication of the Crispus Attucks monument in 1888. Unlike Ford, however, O'Reilly published few articles on labor issues and maintained a much less critical attitude toward American society. He criticized the labor movement for exacerbating social tensions and stressed westward migration rather than social reform as a solution to workingmen's problems. And unlike Ford, he drew a sharp contrast between European society, with its conflict between fixed social classes, and the fluid, egalitarian United States. Wary of violent rhetoric and radical ideas, he made the *Pilot* a far more sedate—indeed a more boring—journal than the *Irish World*.[25]

While Ford castigated both major political parties and often criticized the attitude of the Catholic Church on labor questions, O'Reilly tied the *Pilot* closely to the Democratic party and the Archdiocese of Boston. Ford disdained "the swell mob of Irish 'society' "; O'Reilly published a list of the two hundred wealthiest Boston Irish families. O'Reilly, without doubt a reformer, tempered his ideas for fear of creating dissension within Irish-America. As Arthur Mann suggests, O'Reilly was "uncompromisingly radical as regards England, but moderate with respect to the United States."[26]

A third element in the Land League were the Fenian and Clan na Gael nationalists, for whom the land movement's importance lay only in its ability to stimulate nationalist sentiment in Ireland and undermine British authority. Irish Fenians like Patrick Egan and Thomas Brennan played prominent roles in the Land League from the beginning. But a small group of Irish nationalists, including the Dublin Fenian journal *The Irishman*, opposed the League altogether, fearing establishment of a rival organization competing for funds and influence. "I say it is a pernicious course to put the claims of a class—even though it be so great and influential a class—above the claims of the nation," said one Fenian. "It is not a thing to be wished, by those who love Ireland," declared another, "that class feuds should arise and increase in intensity, so as to dissever those who might be united, and to withdraw to class-disputes the interest which should be concentrated on the National Question."[27]

The most flamboyant critic of the Land League in America was the iconoclastic Fenian exile Jeremiah O'Donovan Rossa, who insisted that only violence could undermine English rule. Rossa's obscure journal, *United Irishman*, published in New York, incited the murder of British officials and the dynamiting of English cities. "The wrongs and injuries of seven centuries of oppression may yet be avenged by the conflagration of London," he wrote. "Liverpool might blaze like another Moscow, or Manchester redden the midnight skies like another Chicago." Particularly intrigued by the possibilities of dynamite, Rossa announced in 1882 that "Professor Mezzroff, the great Russian chemist," would conduct a "school of explosives" in New York City. Such rhetoric thoroughly alarmed British diplomats in America, who forwarded copious extracts from his journal to London, but most Irish-American nationalists considered Rossa a crank. Behind the bombast, however, lay some shrewd political perceptions. Rossa denied that the Land League was a "national movement" at all, since it did not aim at "equal rights on Irish soil for priest and parson, peer and peasant—independent altogether of English government." And he warned that not only would most Irishmen—agricultural and town laborers—not benefit from the land movement, but that making the Irish farmers proprietors of the soil would simply reinforce their traditional conservatism and make it impossible to achieve Irish independence.[28]

Much more influential than Rossa and more representative of Fenian opinion was John Devoy, editor of New York's *Irish Nation* and probably the most important nationalist ideologue on either side of the Atlantic. As one of the fathers of the New Departure, Devoy supported the nationalists' alliance with Parnell and viewed the Land League as an important step toward Irish independence. Participation in the League would help overcome the "isolation from the public life of the country" that had plagued the Irish Fenians for twenty years.

Devoy, who had come to the United States in 1871 after a stint in the French foreign legion and a prison sentence for Fenian activities, was the quintessential political exile. "I respectfully decline the honour of being classed as an 'American,'" he wrote in 1878: American issues were of interest to him only in so far as they served Irish ends. Thanks largely to his efforts, most American members of the Clan na Gael went into the Land League, believing that landlords were "the strongest bulwark of English domination in Ireland."[29]

A final element in Irish-American society taking part in the Land League was the Democratic party, especially New York's Tammany Hall. Tammany's influence rested on its leaders' participation in the daily life of Irish-America: They attended funerals, club meetings, and parties and helped constituents with jobs, rent, and personal problems. Tammany provided a "miniature, private welfare state" for New York City's poor. Boss Tweed, driven from his throne in 1871, was remembered in the popular Irish ballads of the 1870s as an urban Robin Hood, "poverty's best screen," and a friend of the workingman "no matter who may you condemn." Closely linked to the Catholic Church, Tammany made "rich contributions" to parish activities and schools. Tweed's successor, the immensely popular "Honest John" Kelly, was an in-law of New York's Cardinal McCloskey.[30]

The *Irish World* described Tammany Hall as an alliance of "the ten thousand dollar politicians" and "the ninety cents laborers." To which one should add the New York business establishment, for which Tammany performed invaluable services. Kelly helped elect a series of wealthy businessmen mayors of New York and generally opposed political and social radicalism. His house organ, the New York *Star*, claiming a daily circulation of 100,000, did declare its sympathy for "the industrious workingman," but condemned "the so-called labor champions" who set class against class; it insisted that the cause of deteriorating conditions among workers lay not in the economic order per se, but in high taxes and the high tariff enacted during the Civil War. Conveniently, both these measures could be blamed on the Republican party. The *Star* spoke out strongly against such manifestations of independent labor politics as the California Workingmen's party and the Greenback-Labor movement.[31]

Honest John Kelly fully endorsed the Land League movement. Tammany functionaries served on the committee to receive Parnell in 1880, and Kelly set up his own "Tammany Hall Irish Relief Fund" to assist the League. According to one account, the New York delegation to the 1881 Irish National Convention in Chicago was recruited from Tammany's ward clubs. One Fenian leader remarked that in America "societies gotten up in the name of Ireland" were often "used for local or

personal politics." But, Tammany's involvement in the Land
League simply meant that, as usual, its finger was on the pulse
of the Irish community.[32]

John Devoy, though never cordial toward Patrick Ford, acknowledged that the *Irish World* was generally considered "the
organ of the movement." Yet, neither in Ireland nor America
did the Land League leadership follow policies acceptable to
Ford. Parnell, a Protestant revered as the uncrowned king of a
Catholic nation and a landlord leading a movement of tenant
farmers, steered the Irish Land League on a much more moderate course than the *Irish World* desired. Throughout 1881
Ford urged Parnell to spurn Gladstone's Land Act, which offered concessions in rent and security of tenure to Irish
farmers, but the League agreed to "test" the act in the newly
created land courts. Long before the ill-fated No-Rent Manifesto was issued at the end of 1881, Ford had called for a rent
strike in Ireland, whereas Parnell adopted the policy only as a
desperate resort, probably knowing it would fail. The *Irish
World* insisted on the common interest of "the Irish serf and
the English factory slave" in a struggle against landlordism in
both countries, but, with the notable exception of Davitt, the
Irish leadership evinced little interest in such an alliance. And
throughout the history of the League, while Ford urged Irish
leaders not to ignore the claims of landless agricultural laborers, their demands received little real sympathy from their
tenant-farmer employers.[33] Although the land movement had
begun in the poorest section of the island, its social center of
gravity came to rest with the more substantial tenant farmers.
Such men had prospered from the rapid spread of capitalist
agriculture during the thirty years since the Famine as pasture
replaced tillage and the number of farmers on tiny potato plots
and of landless agricultural laborers declined sharply. These
tenants were determined to preserve their recent economic
gains and to win proprietorship of the land from the great
landlords. The old agrarian secret societies, in effect primitive
trade unions of the poorest agrarian classes, had used threats

and violence to regulate rents paid *to* the tenant farmers; the Land League aimed at abolishing rents paid *by* them.[34]

In America, too, the national Land League was tightly controlled by an alliance of nationalists and moderate, respectable representatives of the middle class. O'Reilly, Devoy, and Patrick Collins—"the recognized leader of . . . the Conservative elements in the American League"—were the leading spirits at national conventions. At the January 1881 convention O'Reilly headed the Committee on Resolutions and Collins was elected president.[35] The various elements of the Irish community represented by these three men united against what one conservative called the *Irish World*'s "pernicious doctrines of communism." In Ireland anti-Land League Fenians denounced the *Irish World* for "socialism." In America, Devoy and O'Reilly became alarmed at the spread of Ford's social beliefs. O'Reilly, indeed, suggested at the end of 1881 that the land struggle give way to a renewed agitation for Home Rule, since the issue of social reform would permanently divide both Ireland and Irish-America. An emphasis on Home Rule would win "instant and thorough approval and support" from the two elements of Irish-American life most important to O'Reilly: "the Catholic hierarchy and priests" and "intelligent and conservative men." The Chicago nationalist John Finerty agreed in a letter to Collins: "We do not want to be crusaders for utopian principles."[36]

Even more emphatically, Devoy demanded that the Land League identify its primary purpose:

> Are we men who have undertaken to effect a great and radical change in the tenure of land that will embrace the whole world? . . . Do we propose a great social revolution that will alter the present constitution of human society? . . . Or are we Irishmen struggling for the welfare of our own people?

He answered: "We are fighting for the Irish people and for the Irish people alone." Devoy condemned the "humanitarian cant" of Ford and others: "men who want to use Ireland as a means of working out a social revolution in other countries" and employ "the Land League in America for American purposes."[37]

In contrast to Ford, the more moderate elements were struck by the divergence between social conditions in Ireland and America, not the similarity. The conservative New York *Irish-American*, the New York counterpart to O'Reilly's Boston *Pilot*, described the United States as a "land of plenty," peopled by "free, untrammeled workers," who had no need of the "radical reforms" necessary in Ireland. Landlordism in America, said the *Irish-American*, was a thing of the past: "It exists no longer." Here, indeed, was a line of division cutting through the ideological debates in the American League. Those Ford called the "conservative element," whatever their disagreements, concurred in one thing: "In their heart of hearts they do not relish this land question with its logical deductions applicable to America as well as Ireland."[38]

III

Despite Ford's inability to determine Land League policy, the *Irish World*'s wide circulation on both sides of the Atlantic and its ability to channel funds to Ireland made it indispensable to the movement. Although the Land League established a central treasury overseen by the Rev. Lawrence Walsh of Connecticut, a majority of local branches forwarded their money to the New York offices of the *Irish World*. Ford claimed to have sent $350,000 to Ireland by mid-1882, while receipts for the central office of Father Walsh, through April of that year, amounted to $180,000.[39]

Not every dollar forwarded to the *Irish World*, of course, represented an endorsement of Ford's political principles. The New York office was simply convenient. For many branches, however, the destination of funds was a conscious political decision. At one, in Titusville, Pennsylvania, a motion to dispatch one hundred dollars to the national headquarters failed to receive a second, whereupon the entire body voted for the *Irish*

World. In April 1881, $107 came in from Big Mine Run, Pennsylvania, accompanied by a note: "We recognize in the *Irish World,* the leading light to the great movement which is at present agitating the world," and "admire the stand taken by it against [Patrick] Collins."[40]

The *Irish World*'s weekly list of contributions to its Land League Fund provides a profile of Ford's constituency—the grass roots of Irish-American radicalism. "The money that has kept the Land League together," the New York *Times* sneered in 1881, "has come mostly from the day laborers and servant maids of America." Ford agreed that most contributions were from workers. Men of substance, he wrote, were "very scarce at Land League meetings. . . . Fully nineteen-twentieths were poor and unpretentious workingmen." Reports from local branches, at least those associated with the *Irish World,* bear out this judgment. The average contribution listed was less than a dollar. In 1881, for example, 140 members of the Binghamton, New York, branch raised $50; sixty-six workers at the Rhode Island Locomotive Works in Providence, $16.25; and nine "hard-working sons of toil" in Troy, $6.[41]

Significantly, a large number of branches arose at places of work. The *Irish World*'s pages in 1880 and 1881 were filled with such contributions as: $270.50 from workers of the Denver and Rio Grande Railroad in southern Colorado; $15.50 from those at the Pawtucket Gas Co., Central Falls, Rhode Island; $314 from those of the Atchison, Topeka and Santa Fe Railroad in New Mexico (to which "Irishmen, Americans and even our Mexican brothers" contributed); and $11 from those in a New York City shoemakers' shop, to "hammer down" landlordism. Pittsburgh's branches were composed overwhelmingly of skilled puddlers and common laborers in the iron and steel works, along with some clerks and saloon keepers, and funds were often collected in the mills. Elsewhere, branches often united workers of different trades in the same vicinity. As the Davitt branch of Chicago reported in 1881, "Our club is composed of men chiefly employed in our South Side Rolling Mill blast furnaces and packing houses." In marked contrast were branches reporting their activities to the Boston *Pilot.* "Our ranks are in the main, sturdy farmers and the substantial business men of the town," said the St. Mary's, Kansas, branch, and a list of officers from Lewiston, Maine, was followed by the statement, "These gentlemen are prominent in business and social circles."[42]

A detailed but incomplete list published by Ford in September 1881 revealed the local sources of funds sent to the *Irish World.* (See table.) New York City and Boston, the centers of Irish-American middle-class respectability, contributed little, most of their money going to Father Walsh. Philadelphia and Chicago, where the middle class was weaker and which lacked the conservative local Irish newspapers and powerful Irish political machines of New York and Boston, sent the largest sums.[43] The center of Ford's constituency, however, lay not in the large eastern and midwestern cities, but in the mining regions of Pennsylvania and the West and in the smaller industrial centers. Here, where Irish workers had taken part in bitter struggles in the 1870s, the *Irish World*'s passion for social change found a fertile soil, and the Land League reflected and helped to shape a developing labor consciousness.

The most remarkable concentration of branches oriented toward the *Irish World* lay in the anthracite coal region of northeastern Pennsylvania, which also included the industrial centers of Scranton and Wilkes-Barre. Five counties accounted for no fewer than forty-seven branches, one-third the number for the state as a whole. This region of closely knit communities had experienced an almost steady deterioration in wages and working conditions since mid-century. A state report of the early 1870s spoke of workers and employers as "completely separated in feeling, habit of thought, purposes, interest and sympathy as if they were separate peoples." Violence wracked labor disputes, culminating in the famous Molly Maguire trials of 1876 and 1877.

A persistent quest for collective organization by anthracite

Funds Collected for Land League via *Irish World,* January 1, 1880—
September 13, 1881

Total: $150,434.97

Largest State Totals

Pennsylvania	$16,753.78
New York	12,860.19
Massachusetts	7,401.31
Rhode Island	7,099.01
Illinois	6,322.96
New Jersey	5,989.29
Missouri	5,106.02
Colorado	4,221.05
California	4,109.65

Largest City Totals

		Number of Branches
Philadelphia	$2,008.02	15
Chicago	1,912.20	11
Leadville	1,910.00	1
Troy	1,883.50	8
Albany	1,700.00	3
Providence	1,635.50	9
St. Louis	1,536.00	5
Newark	1,500.00	1
Carbondale, Pa.	1,490.12	5
Scranton	1,410.50	5
Jersey City	1,348.75	8
Fall River	1,274.61	5
New York City	500.00	2
Boston	146.00	2

Pennsylvania Anthracite Region

Carbon County

Mauch Chunk	$50.00	1

Lackawanna County

Archibald	131.00	1
Carbondale	1,490.12	5
Dunmore	390.00	1
Jermyn	228.00	1
Old Forge	14.20	1

Olyphant	30.00	1
Scranton	1,410.50	5
Winton	198.75	1

Luzerne County

Ashley	5.00	1
Drifton	51.10	1
Franklin	34.75	2
Grand Tunnel	60.00	1
Jeddo	80.00	1
Kingston	88.40	1
Milnesville	232.75	1
Mt. Pleasant	36.00	1
Nanticoke	280.00	1
Parsons	200.00	1
Pittston	650.00	3
Plains	40.00	1
Pleasant Valley	32.00	1
Sugar Notch	17.60	1
Wilkes-Barre	200.23	4

Northumberland County

Bear Valley	10.00	1
Mt. Carmel	57.00	1
Shamokin	5.76	1

Schuykill County

Ashland	14.35	1
Big Mine Run	107.09	1
Mahonoy City	90.59	1
New Castle	209.00	1

Western Mining Cities

Bodie, Cal.	$700.00	1
Butte, Mont.	467.10	1
Cherry Creek, Nev.	171.00	1
Eureka, Nev.	476.50	1
Leadville, Col.	1,910.00	1
Tombstone, Ariz.	400.00	1
Virginia City, Nev.	700.00	1

Source: *Irish World,* Sept. 24, 1881. The list is incomplete since not every branch and contribution listed individually in 1880 and 1881 appears in this accounting.

miners marked the 1870s and 1880s—a quest reflected in the formation of unions, independent political parties, and branches of the Land League, all of which, though predominantly Irish, served to unite miners across ethnic lines. The Irish immigrant John Siney founded the first broadly based anthracite miners' union, the Workingmen's Benevolent Association, in 1869. It crumbled during the "Long Strike" of 1875, which left bitter memories of the "railroad king" Franklin B. Gowan and his "gigantic corporation," the Reading Railroad—an animosity that reappeared when miners of the northern coal fields, joined by the steel workers of Scranton, took part in the national railroad strike of July 1877. Riots wracked such towns as Shamokin, Easton, and Wilkes-Barre, and federal troops occupied the area, breaking the strike in October.[44]

The events of 1877 produced an upsurge of support for the Greenback-Labor party. Three localities chose Greenback-Labor mayors and in 1878 Wilkes-Barre sent Hendrick B. Wright, an old Jacksonian renowned for giving away fresh bread on Christmas Day, to Congress as a Greenbacker. A strong supporter of the Land League, Wright believed "destitution and poverty" were as rife in America as in Ireland and declared there was "quite as much necessity for an American as an Irish Land League." At the same time, the experiences of 1875 and 1877 spurred the growth of the Knights of Labor. Local assemblies flourished in Schuykill, Lackawanna, and Luzerne counties, especially among the Irish miners.[45]

This collective organization and class consciousness nourished the phenomenal growth of the Land League. Throughout the poverty-stricken anthracite region, Irish miners banded together to send funds to Ireland via the *Irish World*. The Carbondale branch raised $1,260 at a fair and reported that more would have been contributed, but "they are working only three days a week in the mines." In Sturmerville the prizes at a Land League picnic illustrated the complex history of the region during the 1870s: a ring, a coal-drilling machine—a highly valuable item for skilled coal miners—and a revolver. Swatara, Pennsylvania, with only seventy-five families, raised $78.53 at a ball, and Mountain Top, a village so small and poor that it could not afford a Catholic church—mass was held only every two months, in the public school—raised ten dollars.[46]

By 1881 the anthracite region was alive with weekly meetings where funds were raised and the radical doctrines of the *Irish World* disseminated. The movement would not end, wrote one miner, "until the Land and its kindred monopolies are destroyed forever throughout the whole world." From Shamokin came seven dollars, in contributions of twenty-five cents, to "rouse the people to a sense of their rights, to a knowledge that the call of the children of God to the things of His creation is equal." The breadth of support indicates that the Land League united skilled miners—virtually independent subcontractors—with the larger number of unskilled mine laborers and helpers they employed. While predominantly Irish, the movement for a time eradicated ethnic divisions. Welsh, English, and Scots joined Land League meetings in Luzerne County, and in Mt. Carmel eastern Europeans, harbingers of the "slav invasion" of the 1880s, "promised to help the Land League cause." The list of contributors from Mt. Carmel—some giving as little as five cents—included, along with such Irish names as Patrick Joyce and James Flynn, Poles and Hungarians like Anthony Pulaski, Ferik Kowerlewski, Jonathan Hunkonkussie, and Anton Ferdodse. "I would like to see the Protestants and the Catholics united in the movement to free Ireland," wrote one Land Leaguer from Mauch Chunk. "Our interests are identical."[47]

The intimate connection between the Land League and the labor movement in the anthracite region is illustrated in the career of Terence V. Powderly. Born in Carbondale in 1849 of Irish-born parents, Powderly had been dismissed and blacklisted from his job as a machinist because of union activities in the early 1870s. In 1874 he joined the fledgling Knights of Labor and became a supporter and local functionary of the Greenback-Labor party. Powderly was elected mayor of Scranton in 1878 and the next year became Grand Master Workman of the Knights. At the same time he served as Finance Chairman for the Clan na Gael and in 1880 became active in Land League affairs.

Elected to the Land League Central Council in 1880, Powderly became a vice president in 1881 and spoke often on "The Irish question viewed from a labor standpoint." For Powderly the land issue was all-important for labor, in both Ireland and America. "The land," he wrote in 1882, "is the question. . . . The soil is the heritage of all men and can neither be bought or sold." At virtually every Knights of Labor convention, Powderly spoke on the land issue, insisting that an end to land monopoly was far more important than a reduction of the hours of labor or an increase in wages. As the *Irish World* observed, Powderly represented "the joining of the Land League and American labor forces."[48]

In the anthracite region the Land League functioned as a kind of surrogate for the Knights of Labor. The Knights' secrecy and oaths alienated the local Catholic clergy, already largely beholden to the coal operators for the land on which their churches were located. Hostility from parish priests impeded the Knights' growth as countless letters to Powderly attested. "All the tyrant operators," wrote one Knight, "could not crush this District Assembly half as fast as the Catholic Church." "The greatest curse to our order seems to me to be the priests," said another. By 1880 the number of Knights' assemblies in the coal region had declined precipitously. Clerical opposition had had its effect, but it also appears that Land League branches virtually took over the functions of the Knights. As Powderly later recalled:

> The Knights of Labor were then working secretly, and, as many members were Irish or sympathizers with the struggle of the Irish people for land reform, they invited me to visit cities and towns throughout the country for the purpose of speaking at Land League meetings. I accepted as many invitations as I could and when the public, or Land League, meeting would be over a secret meeting of the Knights of Labor would follow.

Powderly's activities in the League helped make him one of the most popular Catholic laymen in the country. By the mid-1880s, when he had defused clerical opposition by making the order public, he lectured for Catholic causes, and his portrait was considered a valuable prize at church fairs.[49]

Outside the anthracite region radical Land League branches were concentrated in industrial cities from New England through the middle states into the Old Northwest. Communities like Jersey City, Fall River, Troy, and Providence were high on the list of contributors to the *Irish World* Land League fund, with smaller sums coming from Cohoes and Paterson. These smaller cities were scenes of persistent conflict between capital and labor during the Gilded Age, in which much of the community, including politicians, merchants, and shopkeepers, often sided with the strikers. The Land League emerged from such heavily immigrant, self-consciously working-class communities, in which the labor movement occupied a central place.

One such center of Land League activity was the belt of southern New England textile towns stretching from Fall River, Massachusetts, down to Providence and Pawtucket in Rhode Island. Fall River had become during the 1870s the greatest textile center of America, as well as the city with the largest proportion of immigrants in its population, primarily English, Irish, and French Canadian spinners. In the "great strike" of 1875, about 15,000 weavers, spinners, and carders stayed out for two months, winning broad support among nearby Rhode Island textile workers as well. In 1879 a spinners' strike lasted four months. In 1881 the Massachusetts Bureau of Labor Statistics reported that virtually every worker it interviewed in Fall River complained of overwork, poor housing, tyrannical employers, and the general bitterness between capital and labor. For their part, manufacturers claimed their workmen were "the scum of the English and Irish," apparently laboring under a "hereditary feeling of discontent" and "filled with communistic ideas."

Fall River and Providence, with their receptive audience for the radical doctrines of the *Irish World,* contributed more than $2,900 in 1880 and 1881. The Irish workers interpreted the Land League according to their own recent experiences. At one Fall River meeting a speaker referred to the League as "a great strike" in Ireland, adding, "any man in sympathy with labor must sympathize with the Land League." Then, in words straight from the teachings of Patrick Ford, he went on: "We have the same gigantic evil in this country. The public domain is rapidly passing away into the hands of large corporations and in time the people here will be in no better condition than those of Ireland."[50]

The same symbiotic relationship between class-conscious unionism and Irish national consciousness existed in the West. The third highest urban contribution to the *Irish World* Land League fund came from the booming lead and silver mining center of Leadville, Colorado, which had grown from a collection of log huts and a population of 200 in 1877 to a city of 15,000 three years later. A bitter strike by the miners' union in 1880 was broken by the governor, who proclaimed martial law and sent in troops. Another center of the Land League was Virginia City, Nevada, site of the famous Comstock Lode. Michael Davitt received an enthusiastic reception from the miners in this birthplace of hardrock miners' unionism, but the Irish "bonanza kings" wanted nothing to do with the movement. Other mine union centers like Butte, Bodie, and Cherry Creek contributed substantial sums as well.[51]

In all these communities, a strong sense of solidarity existed among the miners, as well as a radicalism grounded in resentment over the rapid transition from the frontier to industrial civilization and from individual enterprise to absentee corporate ownership of the mines. The same feelings also marked working-class politics in San Francisco, where the Workingmen's party of 1877–78 had blamed a small group of land monopolists for transforming California from an egalitarian to an aristocratic society. When Davitt visited San Francisco in 1880, labor organizations chose the notorious Denis Kearney to welcome him. Kearney stressed that "the same system that has brought such misery to Ireland is being fastened upon us," creating a "double bond of sympathy" between Irish-American workers and the Irish movement. Davitt, who probably shared European reformers' rather sugar-coated image of nineteenth-century American life, confessed he was "astonished" at Kearney's description of California society. Davitt's education progressed when farmers, facing eviction by a California railroad, formed a Land League and asked him to address them on the Irish land system. When he returned home, he told an Irish audience that support for the Land League was growing in California in response to "a system of landlordism growing up there that bore some analogy to the system at home."[52]

Even in New York City, where anti-Ford moderates and nationalists dominated League offices, a strong connection existed between local branches and the labor movement. The relation of Irish and Irish-American issues was all too apparent in a city in which more tenants were evicted annually than in Ireland. Some "Spread the Light Clubs," "consisting of active working-men," insisted that the principle "the land for the people" be applied in New York as well—that land and homes be owned by the city, not private landlords. Tenant Leagues modeled on the Irish Land League sprang up in New York in the early 1880s. At a meeting to protest evictions, one speaker observed, "he had been thirty years in this country, and now found himself under the same yoke which caused him to flee from Ireland." The New York *Star,* organ of an alarmed Tammany Hall, solemnly insisted that "evictions in New York and evictions in Ireland are not parallel cases," reminding the "large class in the community" who appeared to disagree that "the landlord has rights and feelings" as well as the tenant.[53]

After a temporary setback in Democratic party factional politics, Honest John Kelly suddenly emerged in 1881 as an "antimonopoly" champion. "It is time that the rights of the public be made paramount to those of the corporations," he announced, and for a year or more the *Star* blasted away at railroads, "corporate monopolies," and the "privileged class" in language scarcely less extreme than Patrick Ford's. New York State, Kelly announced, was "governed by the railroads, rich corporations, and great monopolies, who have combined for the purpose of thwarting the popular will and subverting popular rule. . . . Tammany Hall today presents . . . the only rallying point around which the masses may concentrate for the perpetuation of Democratic principles." Conveniently, Tammany directed its assault primarily against such giant national corporations as Standard Oil, rather than the local business community, and it always associated "monopoly" with the Republican party. Did the anti-monopoly crusade mark a radical turn in Honest John Kelley's outlook? More likely, it reflected not only his difficulties in state Democratic politics, but also the Land League's success in spreading radical ideas in the Irish community. Wherever Irish-Americans went, Tammany could not afford to be far behind.[54]

The connection between the Irish movement and New York labor became manifest in January 1882, when 12,000 representatives of the city's unions met at Cooper Union to endorse the No-Rent Manifesto. The meeting was organized by Robert Blissert, who had been born in England of Irish parents and had emigrated after being blacklisted for his role in a London tailors' strike. Active for a time in the First International in New York, he was "one of the oldest Land Leaguers in the city." The January 30 meeting reiterated the connection between Irish and American issues. "The No Rent battle of Ireland," read a banner over the stage, "is the battle of workingmen the world over," and many of the speeches dealt with American rather than Irish conditions. George McNeill, the Massachusetts labor reformer, thought it "amazing to see the children of freemen crowding into the mills in the squalid degradation of pauper laborers." Blissert reminded the audience that "the process of land-stealing" was occurring in America as well as Ireland. And P. J. Maguire of the carpenters cautioned the audience "not to forget their wrongs in this country: . . . the monopoly of the Standard Oil Company," the railroads, and the bonanza farmers. Tammany's *Star,* still in its radical phase, was struck by the atmosphere of the gathering. "There were many thousands of Irishmen in that great assembly," it declared, who had never given "a thought to the similitude of the slave system at home and abroad," but who might begin to think differently because of the rally.[55]

Out of the meeting came New York's Central Labor Union, with Robert Blissert as its architect. At his suggestion the first plank in the CLU declaration of principles affirmed land as "the common property of the people." It immediately supported the strike of Jersey City's Irish-American freight handlers in July 1882. The freight handlers had contributed to the Land League in 1881 and the local branches formed the basis for the swift organization of a union once the strike had begun. Blissert spoke for the strikers in New York and Jersey City. That September, at New York's first Labor Day celebration, he again affirmed, "Labor today declared its right to the soil—to the land—which should belong to everyone in general and no one in particular."[56]

IV

The Land League existed for less than three years; yet, it left an indelible mark on Irish-America. Not only did it reflect and strengthen the growing role of Irish-Americans in the labor movement, but it played a significant part in overcoming the alienation between Irish-Americans and the mostly Protestant native-born reformers. During the 1840s and 1850s the first generation of Irish immigrants tended to stand aloof from the reform movements concerned with women's rights, prohibition, compulsory public education, and, most important, abolition. The galaxy of reforms and their underlying premise—that men could perfect the world—did not impress an immigrant Irish community characterized in its early years by insularity, traditionalism, and anti-intellectualism. Native reformers, for their part, viewed the Irish as a major obstacle to the achievement of reform goals—a view reinforced by their prevalent nativism and middle-class prejudices. Although some abolitionists condemned nativism on principle, Lydia Maria Child spoke for many when she observed in 1870 that the "Roman priesthood wish, and expect, to undermine our free institutions by means of the influence of Catholic voters."[57]

The Irish community was not, in fact, as intractably conservative as often alleged. We know too little about the attitude of Irish-Americans toward the anti-slavery movement to categorize it as uniformly pro-slavery. Some Famine immigrants may well have been among the tens of thousands of Irish who signed the abolitionist petitions circulated by Daniel O'Connell in the 1840s. More important, the Irish brought cultural and political traditions that merged into some expressions of native American radicalism. Many immigrants had sympathized with or taken part in the secret agrarian societies that drew strength from "the general and settled hatred for the law" permeating the Irish countryside. Much agrarian violence never transcended clan and factional feuding, but for some immigrants it represented a radical inheritance which may help explain the swiftness with which the Irish became involved in trade unionism in the United States. In the 1850s the Irish in the great eastern cities gained a reputation for labor militance at a time, significantly, when land reform held a central place in labor ideology.

A wide gap did divide the Irish community from the native reform tradition during the Civil War era, but by the late 1860s it was beginning to narrow. Irish service on the Union side dampened the fires of nativism for a time, and participation in the labor movement, by its very nature, reduced ethnic insularity. The emergence of labor leaders like John Siney of the miners and William McLaughlin of the shoemakers symbolized the new horizons opening before the post-bellum Irish community. Finally, the Fenian movement drew many Irish-Americans into contact with native reformers willing to support the cause of Irish independence. As David Montgomery has argued, Irish-American nationalism provided physically and intellectually a road out of the ghetto.[58]

Yet, the Fenians affected far fewer Irish and Irish-Americans than the Land League. Experience in the Land League first brought the Irish on both sides of the Atlantic into the mainstream of nineteenth-century reform. In Ireland it constituted a stage in the modernization of politics, educating and mobilizing the Irish countryside, and bringing the farmer onto center stage politically for the first time. As a result of the Land League, as one speaker put it, "doctrines hitherto known to be true in halls of learning only, became acceptable in the cabins of Connaught." A conservative newspaper in Dublin complained, "The wild waves of democracy are surging round the shores of Ireland." A new political language, it continued—phrases like "the cause of labor" and "rights of Man"—were now circulating freely throughout Ireland. In place of sporadic, secret, agrarian violence directed against local grievances, farmers were now demanding a thorough reform of the social order. As Davitt declared in 1879, "We do not declare war against individual landlords, not at all; we declare opposition to a system."[59]

In America the Land League caused a reciprocal intellectual reorientation in which Irish-Americans and native radicals each reconsidered their perceptions of the other. Here lies the significance of the identification of men like Wendell Phillips and James Redpath with the land movement, and the affection such men gained among Irish-Americans. Phillips, to be sure, had told the American Anti-Slavery Society as early as 1869 that overcoming the "intense prejudice" against the Irish was the next task confronting reformers. From the League's outset he offered his oratorical services, drawing on the experience and language of the anti-slavery crusade. "I said in the great rebellion, 'Give the negro a vote and forty acres of land,' " he declared in Boston, adding, "Give every Irishman a vote and forty acres of land to stand on." The Land League, Phillips went on, was "the Free Soil Party of Ireland." An active supporter of the labor movenent, Phillips added at the same time an attack on "corporate plundering" of land in the United States.[60]

James Redpath, another old abolitionist, hardly seemed a likely candidate to conduct a crusade on behalf of Ireland. As the Scottish-born Redpath said in one speech, he could not remember from his Presbyterian upbringing "a single generous or brotherly expression of regard for the Roman Catholics or for their faith. They were never called Catholics. They were 'Papists' always." When asked, early in 1880, to travel to Ireland as a correspondent for the New York *Tribune*, he held the common view that Irish poverty stemmed from the improvidence of the Irish poor. Once there, Redpath changed his mind. Convinced that the Irish land system was at fault, he perceived the Land League as an extension of the abolitionist movement. In his dispatches to the *Tribune*, in speeches in Ireland, and in more than one hundred addresses throughout America, Redpath reiterated these themes. In language reminiscent of the northern critique of slavery, he insisted that the Irish land system paralyzed industry, encouraged thriftlessness, and stifled economic progress. Irish tenants, as a result, lived in a squalor "more miserable than ever were our southern slaves." For Redpath the landlord-tenant dispute was an "irrepressible conflict," and Michael Davitt "the William Lloyd Garrison of Ireland." His advice to the Irish people recalled Garrison's rhetoric: "Let your war cry be the total and immediate abolition of Irish landlordism." Even the social ostracism of tenants who moved onto land from which others had been evicted (the boycott), stemmed in an ironic way from the abolitionist experience. Boycotting, said Redpath, who had first recommended it, had driven the carpetbaggers out of the South during Reconstruction and could be equally effective against "the renteaters" in Ireland.[61]

To the Irish authorities Redpath was "a rabid republican fanatic," whose "wild harangues have contributed so much during the past fifteen months to stir up hatred of the law." In Ireland he became an instant hero, his name, according to one priest, "a household word in every cabin." Redpath's letters to the *Tribune* won widespread sympathy for the movement among Protestant Americans and especially the inheritors of the anti-slavery mantle.[62]

The Protestant reform tradition itself was undergoing a transformation in these years. By 1880 many reformers had retreated into the genteel elitism of the "Best Men," for whom racism, nativism, and a commitment to the economic status quo had obliterated an earlier passion for social change. The editors of the New York *Tribune*, for example, did not share Redpath's enthusiasm for the Irish movement. Remarkably, many reformers did overcome their hostility to the Irish and identify with the Land League. Abolitionists like Lysander Spooner and former anti-slavery politicians like Francis Bird of Massachusetts endorsed the movement. A mutual reconsideration of long-held stereotypes and prejudices seems to have taken place. When Redpath visited Ireland in 1881, he was accompanied by David R. Locke, editor of the Toledo *Blade* and well known as "Petroleum Nasby." Locke, according to Redpath, was "one of the noblest and most steadfast workers in that great abolition of slavery movement." Because of his anti-slavery past, Locke said, he had come to Ireland "the worst prejudiced man against the Irish cause there was." But his observations led him to support the Land League and abandon those prejudices.[63]

For their part, Irish and Irish-American Land Leaguers adopted the language and idealism of the abolitionist tradition and, in a sense, redressed retroactively their past hostility toward Protestant reform. In Ireland speakers declared that the Land League followed in the footsteps of "that small voice of conscience which smote the slaveholders of the Southern states." In America it was not surprising for a man like Ford to compare the Land League to abolitionism. But it was certainly a departure for Tammany Hall to recall with pride the abolitionism of Daniel O'Connell and the support he purportedly received from "the Catholic Church and people of Ireland." And it was surprising for a speaker at the Land League national convention to recall abolition as a "most brilliant triumph." For the first time, it seemed, Ireland was "in the van of a revolution that is destined to set the world ablaze." "I was brought up to believe that there was an eternal enmity between Saxon and Celt," an Irish-American wrote the *Irish World*, "but . . . now I have none but the kindliest sympathy for the oppressed of all nations and colors."[64]

The Irish land movement, Henry George observed in 1882, "has educated a class of our people who might not for years have been reached by any other influence. . . . It was but natural that in thinking of Ireland thoughts should also be directed to the land monopoly which might be seen in the United States." George himself, more than any other individual, symbolized the link between the Irish land question, Protestant reformers, and labor radicalism. George in these years was attempting to refashion traditional republicanism to meet the immense social problems of the industrial age. "Until a few years ago," he wrote in *Progress and Poverty* (1879), "it was an article of faith with Americans . . . that the poverty of the downtrodden masses of the Old World was due to aristocratic and monarchial institutions." Such a belief had been dispelled by the emergence of "social distress of the same kind" in this country. Private property in land, George insisted, explained the coexistence of progress and poverty, material wealth and ever-increasing squalor:

> From this fundamental injustice flow all the injustices which distort and endanger modern development, which condemn the producer of wealth to poverty and pamper the nonproducer in luxury, which rear the tenement house with the palace . . . and compel us to build prisons as we open new schools.

George's theories merged three long-standing tenets of American radicalism: a safety-valve view of land, a distinction between producers and non-producers, and a labor theory of value. To George, the landlord, the greatest of monopolists and non-producers, contributed nothing to the economy but levied a tax on the earnings of capital and labor alike. "The land question and the labor question" were "but different names for the same thing."[65]

Progress and Poverty became the most widely read economic treatise ever written in this country. Jeremiah Murphey, the Irish-American head of the freight-handlers' union in Jersey City and a leading figure in the Land League, said it had educated countless workingmen in the land issue. George's appeal did not stem from his specific programs. Probably few of his readers understood the intricacies of economic rent or the supposed efficacy of a single tax on land. But, George identified the central problems of the age—the unequal distribution of wealth, the growing squalor in the cities, and the declining status of labor—and offered an apparently plausible solution. His evangelical rhetoric conveyed a passionate attachment to the cause of the poor, rare, to say the least, among economists. "The squalid poverty that festers in the heart of our civilization," he wrote in a typical passage, "the vice and degradation and ravening greed that flow from it, are the results of a treatment of land that ignores the simple law of justice."[66]

The popularity of George among Irish-Americans had even more immediate roots. In 1880 the *Irish World* printed his extended essay on the Irish land question, the basis of the book that appeared the following year. For a time the *Irish World* became George's "organ in reaching the people." Every reader, Ford wrote, should own *Progress and Poverty,* and his office printed and distributed a cheap edition. By early 1881 excerpts were being read aloud at American Land League meetings.

In 1881, having been sent by Ford to Ireland as a special correspondent, George sent back blistering attacks on British rule and on the Irish land system. Arrested, he gained instant popularity among Irish-Americans. George and Ford at this point were working together for what George called "the end we both desire—the radicalization of the movement and the people." This radicalization spelled a commitment to the abolition of the landlord system in Ireland and the mobilization of the American Land League to fight land monopoly and related social ills. "This fight is also for us," George told a Newark Land League audience. And in his book on the Irish question, he urged American branches "to announce this great principle as of universal application; to give their movement a reference to America as well as to Ireland." George's writings and speeches educated both Irish and Irish-Americans in the most recent and radical doctrines of land reform and social change.[67]

George embodied one other strain of American radicalism which, through the Land League, came to influence Irish-America in the 1880s: the social perfectionism of evangelical Protestantism. The spirit of evangelicism suffused George's speeches and writings and supplied much of his language. A devoutly religious man, he exuded the fervor of the pulpit. His utopian social vision, as expressed in the conclusion to *Progress and Poverty,* was ultimately religious: "It is the culmination of Christianity—the City of God on earth, with its walls of jasper and its gates of pearl! It is the reign of the Prince of Peace!" Christianity, George believed, could inspire the reforms needed to regenerate the world. "But it must be a Christianity that attacks vested wrongs, not that spurious thing that defends them." George's writings spurred the emergence of the social gospel among the Protestant clergy in America and reflected the wide currency of the language of Christianity among labor reformers. George McNeill, for example, described labor's goal, the vaguely defined "cooperative commonwealth," as "the Golden Rule of Christ" when "the new Pentacost will come."[68]

Historically, such language had been alien to the Catholicism of Irish-America and often associated with nativism. Before the 1880s the American Catholic Church rarely linked religion to reform. The clergy generally defined social reform as charity and moral exhortation to the poor, showing little interest in economic or social injustice. Only temperance among the galaxy of reform movements engaged the Church's support. The Knights of Labor and trade unionism met considerable hostility from the Catholic press and hierarchy.[69]

Radical Irish-Americans had long attempted to create some kind of bond between social radicalism and the Catholicism that for the Irish was not merely a religion, but almost a badge of nationality and culture. Patrick Ford insisted that the *Irish World* sought to "bear aloft the standard of the cross." During the depression of the 1870s, he did criticize the worldliness of the Church and its insensitivity to the plight of the Irish-American poor, singling out Cardinal McCloskey for riding in an elegant carriage through New York City. In 1879 Bishop Gilmour of Cleveland forbade the circulation of the *Irish World* in his diocese, while taking the opportunity to condemn unions and public education. He reminded his parishioners that poverty was no disgrace: "our master was poor." Ford replied that Gilmour's letter only lent credence to Protestant charges that the Church was "the foe of democratic institutions, of liberty of thought, and of education." Yet, when Protestants raised these same issues, Ford passionately defended the Church and reminded his readers of violations of religious liberty by Puritan New Englanders. Ford projected the ideal of America as a multiethnic, multireligious nation. He denounced Protestants who believed that they alone were true Americans, or that this was, in the current phrase, a "Protestant country." Ford envisioned America's future as a pluralistic cooperative commonwealth in which political unity and class harmony coexisted with cultural diversity.[70]

Among the Land League's most significant achievements in America lay in breaching the Church's inertia on social questions and spawning a Catholic counterpart of the Protestant social gospel. The transformation was symbolized by the emergence of Father Edward McGlynn of New York City as a major spokesman for the American Land League. Born in New York City in 1837 of Irish immigrant parents, Father McGlynn spent his first years as a priest as assistant to Father Thomas Farrell of St. Joseph's Church, a strong abolitionist who left money in his will for the establishment of a Catholic church for blacks. In 1866 Father McGlynn became pastor of St. Stephen's, "one of the largest and one of the poorest parishes" in New York City. In 1870 he ran afoul of the hierarchy for an interview with the New York *Sun* in which he defended the public schools as "one of the chief glories of America." While deprecating the use of the Protestant Bible and hymns in public schools, he believed Catholics should send their children there and said he did not intend to establish a parochial school in his parish.[71]

Father McGlynn participated in the American Land League from the outset, but only attracted attention as a speaker during Michael Davitt's visit to New York in June 1882. At a rally for Davitt, organized by the Central Labor Union, Father McGlynn won long and enthusiastic applause for his Catholic version of the social gospel: "The cause of the suffering, martyred poor in Ireland was the cause of true religion. If there seemed to be a divorce between the Church and the masses it was not the fault of the masses." Translating the image of Christ the carpenter, so common in labor circles, into terms closer to the Irish experience, he went on: "Christ himself was but an evicted peasant. . . . He came to preach a gospel of liberty to the slave, of justice to the poor, of paying the full hire to the workman, to teach the humblest, the poorest, the most benighted and enslaved the awful dignity of human nature." Throughout the summer Father McGlynn repeated this message at Land League gatherings. Most striking, he recast the evangelical rhetoric, still offensive to many Catholics, in an Irish-American vein.[72]

However atypical in his opposition to parochial education and the turbulence of his subsequent career, Father McGlynn enunciated a social Catholicism that won support from numerous younger American priests, including such lesser-known supporters of Irish-American labor radicalism as the Rev. Cornelius O'Leary, parish priest of the railroad town, DeSoto, Missouri, and Buffalo's the Rev. Patrick Cronin. During the 1880s, moreover, a powerful "liberal" group emerged in the American Church hierarchy, attempting to reassess the Church's relation to social issues and to break down the isolation of Catholics from contemporary currents of social thought. Men like Archbishop Gibbons of Baltimore, although hardly radicals, supported the Knights of Labor and effectively transmitted their working-class sympathies to Rome.[73]

The career of Father McGlynn illuminates again the conjuncture of Irish and American radicalism in the Land League. Perhaps the most compelling illustration of this conjuncture emerges not from the speeches and writings of the illustrious, but from the resolutions adopted by the Land League of the tiny Pennsylvania mining village of Swatara. Whoever in this town of seventy-five families drew up the three resolutions revealed how Irish hatred of English rule, an insistence on the dignity of labor, belief in religion as an agent of social change, and traditional American republicanism, flowed together and acquired new meaning in the Land League:

1. The present iniquitous landlord system . . . has cursed the Irish people since the final triumph of English rule. . . .
2. It is the obvious design of the Almighty that every individual man should labor, not that one portion of mankind should perform all the drudgery, slave and suffer that the other may revel in luxury.
3. We hold these truths to be self-evident: that land, like air, light, and water, are God-given gifts to His children.[74]

V

The climax of the factional and ideological disputes within the American Land League came in June 1882, during Michael Davitt's visit. Some weeks earlier, Davitt had delivered two speeches in England that caused a sensation in the Irish movement. Abandoning the official Land League program of "peasant proprietary," he adopted George's plan for the nationalization of the land as the true meaning of "the land for the people." Private property in land would be eliminated, with all farmers renting their land from the State and provision being made for access by landless agricultural and urban workers. "It is difficult to see how an increase in the number of those holding private property in land can possibly remedy evils which are so easily traceable to that institution," Davitt argued. However logical, his position flew in the face of the land hunger of the Irish tenant farmers.[75]

By the time Davitt arrived in America, rumors had swept the Land League that he intended to wrest control of the movement from Parnell, that he had been "captured" by Henry George, and that he planned to transform the League into an international alliance of land reformers in Britain, Ireland, and America. The result was a foregone conclusion. Parnell had recently concluded the "Kilmainham Treaty" with Prime Minister Gladstone, agreeing to disband the agrarian agitation and enter into a Parliamentary alliance with the Liberal party; it symbolized his shift to a more conservative nationalism and his determination to retain the good will of a portion of Britain's ruling class. He condemned land nationalization as ill-conceived and not in accord with Land League policy. Other nationalists also feared the effect of Davitt's speeches on moderate opinion. James J. O'Kelly, for instance, considered them " a stupid communistic agitation which would certainly detach from us the most important element among our people both in Ireland and America."

In America the nationalists and moderates who controlled the national Land League united against Davitt and vented their deep-seated hostility to George, Ford, and social radicalism. According to the conservative New York *Irish-American*, Ford and his followers had

> long been striving to identify the national cause of Ireland with those Communistic theories that our people have always repudiated, and to divert the efforts of those who are honestly struggling for the Irish race into those channels of hypo-sublimated revolution by which the liberation, union of all mankind . . . and the "millennium" generally are to be brought about.

The Boston *Pilot* insisted that Davitt had placed himself in "the hands of the Communists," and that men like George "care nothing for Irish nationality. They only want to see their communistic ideas put into practical operation." Tammany's *Star* joined in the denunciations.[76]

The most articulate criticisms of Davitt's new departure came from John Devoy, speaking for the extreme nationalists who snubbed their former comrade when he arrived in America. Behind Davitt's proposals, Devoy discerned the sinister influence of Ford and George, neither, he insisted, truly interested in Irish independence. Ford's intentions, said Devoy, were "not for the benefit of the Irish people, and in his tremendous plans of a universal social reform, Ireland has a very small place indeed." As for George, "Ireland is only a lever with which to stir up England. Then from England the movement is to spread to America, and the American branches of the Land League are to be the centres of the new social revolution."

Despite exaggeration, Devoy had identified the essential division within the American League. For his part, Ford hailed Davitt's speeches as "a return to the old Irish system" of collective ownership of the land, in contrast to "the Norman pattern of individual property." Father McGlynn came to the fore during these weeks by endorsing Davitt's policies. George responded: "If Davitt's trip had no other result, it were well worth this." Finally, the labor element in the Land League rallied to Davitt, and the Central Labor Union held a massive procession of trades in his honor. Banners at the rally praised land nationalization and the No-Rent Manifesto, the Clothing Cutters and Cigar Makers union bands played the Marseillaise, and one placard read, "Is slavery a thing of the past?" The ubiquitous Robert Blissert chaired the meeting, noting that the Irish slogan, "the land for the people," "had found an echo on these shores, and has supplied American workingmen with a watchword for the future."[77]

In his own remarks Davitt referred to the land movement as

"the uprising of the laborers of Ireland against a robbing system of monopoly that has confiscated the fruits of labor." He reiterated support for land nationalization. But by the time he left America, he had abandoned any idea of challenging Parnell. Isolated in Ireland and under fierce assault in America, Davitt agreed to abide by Parnell's decision on land policy. Possibly, Davitt might have taken the leadership in an independent movement of Irish agricultural laborers, who were forming autonomous Labor Leagues in 1882. But he was temperamentally and politically unwilling to challenge Parnell for leadership or to fracture the Irish movement.[78]

Perhaps the significance of the short-lived debate sparked by Davitt's 1882 visit rested less in the issue of land nationalization, which had no real chance of being adopted by the Irish movement, than in its illumination of the gap which divided those Davitt called "Tory nationalists and democratic nationalists." A seemingly subsidiary question surfaced during these weeks to clarify the difference. Davitt intended to spread the land agitation to England and to forge an alliance between the Irish movement and the British working class. His own missing right arm, the result of a childhood accident in a Lancashire factory, symbolized the grievances which could unite the poor of the two countries. Thus, he had chosen England for his land nationalization speeches and insisted that nationalist violence, which alienated all Englishmen, must cease.[79]

After all, anti-landlord sentiment had long been an integral part of both middle-class and working-class English radicalism, in both of which the non-productive landlords, who "toil not, neither do they spin," held pride of place as social villains. The tradition of land reform reached back at least as far as the writings of Thomas Spence and Thomas Paine in the 1790s, and it acquired new urgency as the number of landless urban and rural workers multiplied during the nineteenth century. From Locke to Mill, moreover, English political economy had been "continually engaged in undermining the ideas of justice and social utility" claimed for the British land system. By the second

half of the nineteenth century, glorification of "peasant proprietorship" was common in British economic writings, with English and Irish tenants compared unfavorably with the allegedly
thrifty, energetic, and productive farmers of France, Holland,
and Switzerland, who owned their own land. At mid-century
the Chartists had raised the cry, "the land belongs to the people," while middle-class reformers were demanding abolition of
entail and complex laws of settlement and the establishment of
"free trade in land." By 1882 the agricultural depression of the
late 1870s, the land war in Ireland, and the wide circulation of
the writings of Henry George all propelled the land question to
the forefront of politics. "This question of the land," said one
labor newspaper, "will bring the English and Irish people
together at last."[80]

Davitt's American supporters instantly embraced the vision
of an international radical crusade. Father McGlynn declared
the Irish people must not "hate the depressed, degraded people of England," insisting that "the miners and labourers of England are ground down quite as much as the people of Ireland,
and the poor people of both countries should make common
cause against their oppressors." Robert Blissert agreed, telling a
Land League audience, "There was no fight between the people of England and Ireland. . . . It was simply a struggle between the rich and the poor."

Such views were anathema to conservatives who wished to
see the aims of the land movement narrowly delimited, and to
nationalists like Devoy who could never overcome their hatred
of all things English. The *Irish-American* insisted that no alliance
with "the 'English Democracy' " was possible because of "the responsibility of the English people for the wrongs inflicted on
Ireland." And Devoy wrote, "We firmly believe that when any
awakening does come to the sluggish minds of the English
masses, it will take quite as anti-Irish a turn as in the days of
Cromwell." "Englishmen, whether aristocrats or democrats, are
all the same to us," said Devoy, "—foreigners." To such men,
Davitt's attempt to shatter the chains of historic hatred seemed as

radical as his scheme of land nationalization. Both obstructed a single-minded focus on Irish independence.[81]

By the end of 1882 Irish politics had been transformed. Parnell and the Parliamentary party took control of the land movement, submerging it in the new National League, for which Home Rule was the first demand and land reform—in the guise of peasant proprietorship—a distant second.

Conservatives dominated the American National League, from which Ford and his followers held aloof. "The great body of respectable and dignified Land Leaguers were present," said one account of the opening convention, "attired in black frock coats and beaver hats." The "conservative Parnell platform" of the Irish League was adopted as well, and money poured in from wealthy Irish-Americans. "A reaction has set in," the *Irish World* declared. "The class movement going on in Ireland is the very essence of Toryism." The Land League, Ford announced, no longer existed.[82]

VI

Few histories of the Irish in America contain more than a passing reference to the Land League or to such related subjects as Irish predominance in the Knights of Labor, the social theories of Patrick Ford, or Henry George's campaign for mayor of New York City in 1886. For that matter, few general histories of the Gilded Age mention the Land League or, indeed, the Catholic Church.[83] In the major exception, which has shaped the views of all subsequent students—the work of Thomas N. Brown—Irish-American nationalism emerges as a response to ethnic realities in America. A defensive reaction to nativism and discrimination, its aims were conservative despite occasionally radical rhetoric: namely, to gain a self-respecting place for Irish-Americans in American life. "Mostly," Brown writes, "the Irish wanted to be middle-class and respectable. . . . In the Lace Curtain Irishman the rebel found fulfilment." Almost a century ago the nationalist Alexander Sullivan made a similar judgment, describing the National League as "a positive Americanizing influence" that tamed the wild Irish and taught them the "self-discipline" and "business habits" they never learned in Ireland.[84]

That Irish-American nationalism and, specifically, the Land League in some sense contributed to the assimilation of Irish-Americans is beyond dispute. Yet, the Brown thesis suffers from a fatal narrowness of vision. It views working-class life simply as a transitional stage on the road to bourgeois respectability, and defines assimilation solely as acquisition of middle-class values that enabled the Irish immigrant "to accommodate . . . to an often hostile environment." Or, as William Shannon suggests, Irish-American nationalism helped the Irish enter "the larger American society that was native, Protestant, Anglo-Saxon, and middle-class in its values."

But there was another America—one not "middle-class in its values." During the Gilded Age, class conflict wracked America more fiercely than at any time in our history. The nation experienced a thorough economic revolution and the shocks associated with the development of industrial capitalism spawned massive social discontent, from the great strike of 1877, through the labor upheaval of the 1880s, to the political crisis of the 1890s. Henry George did not exaggerate when he wrote in 1883, "There is a wide-spread consciousness among the masses that there is something radically wrong in the present social organization."[85] The point is that "assimilation" could mean a merger not with the dominant culture and its values, but with a strong emergent oppositional working-class culture. The Land League and the teachings of the *Irish World* helped Americanize a large section of the Irish-American working class. But the American traditions they identified with were those of the abolitionists and Knights of Labor, of Wendell Phillips and Henry George, not those of middle-class complacency. The radical Irish-Americans wished to transform their society even as they became a more integral part of it.

Middle-class values and aspirations did not dominate Irish-

American society as thoroughly as many writers have claimed, and ethnic nationalism did not unite the Irish working and middle classes at the expense of class identification across ethnic lines. The depression of the 1870s and the Land League experience widened the gap between the classes within the Irish community and set the stage for the persistence of Irish-American radicalism during the 1880s and beyond. As one Land Leaguer in Reading, Pennsylvania, wrote to the *Irish World*, enclosing a meager $36 from a League picnic, more would have been collected but:

> The rich Irishmen of Reading do not seem to know of what is going on in Ireland or in America. If they do, the more shame for them. Not one of them ever showed his face at our meetings, or sent a dime to help the cause. Perhaps they have forgotten all about the dear old land in the hoarding of their ill-gotten wealth, which was brought them by the hard labor and hot sweat of others.[86]

Many Irish-Americans saw no contradiction between ethnic nationalism and class consciousness. The inherent tensions between these modes of looking at the world exploded more than once in the ideological struggles between those in the Land League who focused solely on Irish independence and those who sought to forge an alliance with workers in America and England. Yet, national ideas often reinforce class consciousness, and nowhere more so than in a country such as Ireland where the ruling class was of distinct religion and nationality, and in Irish-America where the center of gravity lay so solidly in the working class. In the urban centers of Gilded Age America, class and ethnic differences overlapped: the majority of workers were immigrant and the majority of the middle class, native-born. Thus, many could agree with Terence Powderly that "the American labor movement, and . . . the Irish land movement" were "almost identical."[87]

Long after the demise of the Land League, the radical impulse it embodied continued to affect Irish and Irish-American life. In Ireland, Davitt continued to pursue his dream of a grand alliance of Irish, British, and American workers, helping to organize the Irish Democratic Labor Federation in 1890 and, at the close of his life, supporting such diverse causes as the English Labor party, Indian nationalism, Zionism, and women's rights. Yet, he remained a lonely warrior. The Irish tenant farmers, for whom he had done so much, rejected his social outlook and, when they finally won possession of the land through the Wyndham Land Act of 1903, they retreated into conservatism.

The final settlement of the land issue appears as one of those tricks Ireland so regularly plays on history. Contrary to British hopes and Fenian fears, it did not destroy Irish nationalism, which had taken on a life of its own, independent of specific grievances. Nor did the overthrow of the Irish landlord class provide the lever for social revolution in England, as Marx and others had expected. "I have come to the conclusion," Marx had written in 1870, "that the decisive blow against the English ruling classes . . . cannot be delivered in England but only in Ireland." The overthrow of the Irish aristocracy was "the preliminary condition for the proletarian revolution in England."[88]

Marx, nonetheless, had a point. The English "proletarian revolution" never did take place, but the land issue, reinvigorated by the Irish land war, played havoc with British political life in the 1880s, driving a wedge between upper-class and reform elements in the Liberal party and fueling the socialist revival. Nationalization of the land became an important goal of the Social Democratic Federation founded by H. M. Hyndman in 1881, when land meetings on the Irish model swept the Scottish highlands. "The most active leaven of the present social movement," said one English observer in 1884, "is really the land question." Labor leaders like Kier Hardie found in the writings of Henry George the key to unlocking the secrets of poverty and exploitation and later moved to socialism. Yet, in the end, the British government bought out the Irish landlords, while the British working and middle classes paid the tax bill. Perhaps the most fitting epitaph for the Irish land movement was penned by Patrick Ford in 1903: "The Land war now seems to be coming to a close but whether it is to be a victory or a defeat, or a drawn battle, is something I can't figure out."[89]

In America the causes of Irish nationalism and labor reform remained deeply embedded in the labor movement long after the Land League had ceased to exist. Like the Land League, the labor movement of the 1880s and 1890s brought together Irish nationalists, reformers, and radical intellectuals like Ford and George who had been workers themselves. The labor consciousness that flowered in the 1880s, epitomized by the rapid expansion of the Knights of Labor, owed a great deal to the Ford-George wing of the Land League. Where Irish-Americans predominated, the Knights merged social radicalism and Irish nationalism as effectively as the Land League had done.

The high point of the Knights came in 1886, the year of the Great Upheaval. A large portion of New York City's Irish abandoned Tammany Hall to support Henry George's campaign for mayor, which articulated the principles of the Land League and Central Labor Union. Patrick Ford, Terence Powderly, Father McGlynn, and James Redpath, all Land League veterans, stood behind the George campaign. In 1886, too, the controversy surrounding Father McGlynn reemerged; his participation in George's campaign and subsequent refusal to explain himself in Rome led to his excommunication in 1887. The massive support the "rebel priest" received from his New York parishioners measured the deep impact his brand of social Catholicism had made on the Irish-American poor.[90]

The experience of the Land League, finally, should lead us to reexamine the entire history of the Irish in America, as well as traditional treatments of class relations and ethnic nationalism among other groups. The ideological debates in the League perhaps reflected not only differences of tactics and outlook, but the existence of two overlapping but distinct centers of power, or poles of leadership, within the Irish-

American community. Those who opposed Ford reflected the views of a nexus composed of the Catholic Church, the Democratic party, and the Irish-American middle class. The social dominance of this triple alliance was challenged in the 1880s by the organized social radicalism articulated and institutionalized in the Land League's radical branches and the Knights of Labor. Here were the only organized alternatives to the Tammany-oriented saloon and local clubhouse, as a focus for working-class social life in the Irish-American community. The discussions of political issues, the emphasis on temperance, the reading of the radical labor press, and the very process of union-building across divisions of ethnicity, skill, and craft, all embodied a social ethic that challenged the individualism of the middle class and the cautious social reformism of the Democratic party and Catholic Church.[91]

After 1890 the decline of the Knights, the retreat of Patrick Ford and Henry George from their earlier radicalism, and the continuing transformation of American capitalism combined to direct Irish-American radicalism into new channels. Historians have traditionally viewed Irish-America as becoming increasingly conservative during these years. The growing wealth and power of the Irish middle class, the increasing social importance of the Church, the Democratic party's adoption of labor reform positions on the local level, and the emergence of stable craft unionism, all helped consolidate some of the gains of the 1880s while sapping the strength of radicalism. At the same time, Irish-Americans assumed a prominent place in the labor aristocracy, propelled there by the massive influx of new immigrants. Preempting the best-paying craft and industrial employments, they dominated the American Federation of Labor as it moved toward a cautious program of incremental gains within the capitalist system. At the same time, the land issue appeared increasingly inappropriate as a focus for radical thought as American capitalism entered its modern era.[92]

It will not do, however, simply to update the myth of Irish conservatism by twenty years. Irish-Americans may have played little role in the Socialist party, but they dominated the militant Western Federation of Miners, whose first president, Ed Boyce, was an Irish immigrant. The members of the W.F.M. continued to believe that "our present social system is based upon a fundamental injustice, namely, private ownership of land." The Irish community played a significant part in the anti-imperialist movement of the 1890s and often supported factory legislation, the regulation of business, and other expressions of "urban liberalism" in the early twentieth century. And well into this century, Catholic social activists like Monsignor John A. Ryan, who had first learned of "the agrarian situation in Ireland and industrial problems in the United States" from the *Irish World,* reflected the persistence of the Ford-McGlynn brand of Irish radical thought.[93] Only when American historians have chronicled the evolution of the Irish-American working class, will the ultimate significance of the Land League and the legacy it bequeathed to Irish-America and the society at large be fully revealed.

Notes

I INTRODUCTION

1. Michael Kammen, ed., *The Past Before Us: Contemporary Historical Writing in the United States* (Ithaca, 1980).
2. Anthony Wallace, *Rockdale* (New York, 1978); E. J. Hobsbawm, "From Social History to the History of Society," *Daedalus*, C (Winter 1971), 20–45.
3. Frances FitzGerald, *America Revised: History Schoolbooks in the Twentieth Century* (Boston, 1979), 157–58.
4. Richard Hofstadter, *The Paranoid Style in American Politics* (New York, 1966), vii.
5. J. G. A. Pocock, "Virtue and Commerce in the Eighteenth Century," *Journal of Interdisciplinary History*, III (Jan. 1972), 119–34; Pocock, *The Machiavellian Moment: Florentine Political Thought and the Atlantic Republican Tradition* (Princeton, 1975), ch. 15.
6. Richard Hofstadter, *The Progressive Historians* (New York, 1968), 460–61.

II CAUSES OF THE AMERICAN CIVIL WAR

1. David Donald, "American Historians and the Causes of the Civil War," *South Atlantic Quarterly*, LIX (Summer 1960), 351–55.
2. To cite only a few of the host of works related to this point, David Brion Davis, *The Problem of Slavery in Western Culture* (Ithaca, 1966)

and Edmund S. Morgan, "Slavery and Freedom: The American Paradox," *Journal of American History,* LIX (June 1972), 5–29, stress the centrality of slavery to the American experience. Douglass North, *The Economic Growth of the United States, 1790 to 1860* (New York, 1961), shows how the profits of the cotton trade paid for the economic development of ante-bellum America. Staughton Lynd, *Class Conflict, Slavery, and the United States Constitution* (Indianapolis, 1967), Donald L. Robinson, *Slavery and the Structure of American Politics* (New York, 1971), Richard H. Brown, "The Missouri Crisis, Slavery and the Politics of Jacksonianism," *South Atlantic Quarterly,* LXV (Winter 1966), 55–72, William W. Freehling, *Prelude to Civil War* (New York, 1966), and Eric Foner, *Free Soil, Free Labor, Free Men: The Ideology of the Republican Party Before the Civil War* (New York, 1970) place slavery at the center of politics at various points in ante-bellum history. Eugene D. Genovese, *The Political Economy of Slavery* (New York, 1965), makes clear the centrality of slavery to the society of the Old South.

3. Rather than citing the scores of works on abolitionism, let me simply refer to an admirable historiographical survey: Merton L. Dillon, "The Abolitionists: A Decade of Historiography, 1959–1969," *Journal of Southern History,* XXXV (Nov. 1969), 500–522.

4. On the racism of anti-slavery advocates, see, for example, William H. Pease and Jane H. Pease, "Anti-Slavery Ambivalence: Immediatism, Expediency, Race," *American Quarterly,* XVII (Winter 1965), 682–95; Eric Foner, "Racial Attitudes of the New York Free Soilers" [essay V in this collection]; Eugene H. Berwanger, *The Frontier Against Slavery* (Urbana, 1967); and James H. Rawley, *Race and Politics* (Philadelphia, 1969). For the limitations of abolitionist radicalism, see William Appleman Williams, *The Contours of American History* (London ed., 1961), 254; Aileen Kraditor, *Means and Ends in American Abolitionism* (New York, 1969), 244–53; George F. Fredrickson, *The Black Image in the White Mind* (New York, 1971), 36–37.

5. David Potter, *The South and the Sectional Conflict* (Baton Rouge, 1968), 146.

6. The major works of "new political history" dealing with ante-bellum politics are Lee Benson, *The Concept of Jacksonian Democracy: New York as a Test Case* (Princeton, 1961); Ronald P. Formisano, *The Birth of Mass Political Parties: Michigan 1827–1861* (Princeton, 1971); Paul Kleppner, *The Cross of Culture* (New York, 1970); the essays collected in Frederick C. Luebke, ed., *Ethnic Voters and the Election of Lincoln* (Lincoln, 1971); and Michael F. Holt, *Forging a Majority: The Formation of the Republican Party in Pittsburgh, 1848–1860* (New Haven, 1969). The phrase "monistic interpretation" is quoted from Holt, 125. I should note that obviously not all these writers agree on every interpretation. Holt,

for example, tends to give anti-slavery attitudes more credence as a determinant of voting behavior than do the other writers.

7. Some of these methodological criticisms are raised in Allen G. Bogue, "United States: The 'New Political History,'" *Journal of Contemporary History*, III (Jan. 1968), 22–24; James E. Wright, "The Ethnocultural Model of Voting," *American Behavioral Scientist*, XVI (May–June 1973), 653–74; and James R. Green, "Behavioralism and Class Analysis: A Review Essay on Methodology and Ideology," *Labor History*, XIII (Winter 1972), 89–106. Among other methodological problems is the tendency of some writers to infer the behavior of voters in heterogeneous areas from the actions of those who lived in homogenous ethnic communities, and difficulties created by the use of census data on the number of church seats of each religion in a specified area, as a measure of the breakdown of religious affiliations of that area. There are also simple problems of interpreting data. Formisano, for example, presents a table of the voting of evangelical townships in Michigan in 1860. In eastern Michigan, six of eleven such townships gave Lincoln over 60 per cent of the vote, but Lincoln carried the state with 57 per cent of Michigan's ballots. The table shows that in five of eleven evangelical townships, Lincoln received less than his state-wide percentage. The figures hardly justify the conclusion that evangelical townships voted "strongly Republican" in 1860. Formisano, *Birth of Mass Political Parties*, 312–13.

8. Some of these criticisms are noted in the Wright and Green articles cited above, and in David P. Thelen, review of Kleppner, *Civil War History*, XVII (Mar. 1971), 84–86, and Thelen, review of Formisano, *Civil War History*, XVIII (Dec. 1972), 355–57. The quotation is from Wright, "The Ethnocultural Model of Voting," 664. Wright and Green questions whether these studies are adequately controlled for class and status variables. All three critics question whether class can be adequately measured by looking at units like "farmers" or "workers," or by measuring the wealth of rural and urban precincts without considering the internal class structure of these units.

9. Joel H. Silbey, "The Civil War Synthesis in American Political History," *Civil War History*, X (June 1964), 130–40; Luebke, *Ethnic Voters*, xi.

10. This incredible statement is quoted by Formisano from Philip E. Converse, "The Nature of Belief Systems in Mass Publics," in David E. Apter, *Ideology and Discontent* (New York, 1964), 245. Formisano, *Birth of Mass Political Parties*, 11–12. Cf. Leubke, *Ethnic Voters*, xiv.

11. On this last point, see Foner, *Free Soil, Free Labor, Free Men*, ch. 7.

12. Richard N. Current, *The Lincoln Nobody Knows* (New York, 1958), 58–59.

13. Lee Benson, *Toward the Scientific Study of History* (Philadelphia, 1972), 316–26.

14. See, in general, A. S. Eisenstadt, *Modernization: Protest and Change* (Englewood Cliffs, 1966), and C. E. Black, *The Dynamics of Modernization* (New York, 1966).

15. Raimondo Luraghi, "The Civil War and the Modernization of American Society: Social Structure and Industrial Revolution in the Old South Before and During the War," *Civil War History*, XVIII (Sept. 1972), 242.

16. Also relevant is Barrington Morroe, Jr., *Social Origins of Dictatorship and Democracy* (Boston, 1966), ch. 3. I should note that describing the South as "pre-modern" does not necessarily contradict the findings of Robert Fogel and Stanley Engerman that slavery was a highly profitable investment. Fogel and Engerman, *Time on the Cross: The Economics of American Negro Slavery* (Boston, 1974). George Fredrickson applies the concept of modernization to the Civil War itself, and the question of why the North was victorious, but he explicitly denies its applicability to the question of the causes of the Civil War. Fredrickson, "Blue Over Gray: Sources of Success and Failure in the Civil War," in Fredrickson, ed., *A Nation Divided: Problems and Issues of the Civil War and Reconstruction* (Minneapolis, 1975), 57–80.

17. Robert Kelley, *The Transatlantic Persuasion: The Liberal Democratic Mind in the Age of Gladstone* (New York, 1969).

18. J. R. Pole, *Abraham Lincoln and the American Commitment* (Oxford, 1966), 32; Paul Angle, ed., *Created Equal? The Complete Lincoln-Douglas Debates of 1858* (Chicago, 1958), 18. Cf. Bertram Wyatt-Brown, "Stanley Elkins' Slavery: The Antislavery Interpretation Reexamined," *American Quarterly*, XXV (May 1973), 167.

19. Richard D. Brown, "Modernization and the Modern Personality in Early America, 1600–1865: A Sketch of a Synthesis," *Journal of Interdisciplinary History*, II (Winter 1972), 201–28. E. A. Wrigeley comments on the imprecision of the modernization concept, and how it often seems to be used simply as a synonym for industrialization, in "The Process of Modernization and the Industrial Revolution in England," *Journal of Interdisciplinary History*, III (Autumn 1972), 228, 228n. The general question of the persistence of pre-industrial work habits and ideals in nineteenth-century America is raised in Herbert G. Gutman, "Work, Culture and Society in Industrializing America, 1815–1919," *American Historical Review*, LXXVIII (June 1973), 531–88.

20. Albert Soboul, *The Sans-Culottes*, trans. Remy Inglis Hall (New York, 1972), xv.

21. This point is suggested in J. H. Plumb, "Slavery, Race, and the Poor," *New York Review of Books*, Mar. 13, 1969, 4. David Brion Davis's *The Problem of Slavery in the Age of Revolution* (Ithaca, 1975) re-

lates the growth of anti-slavery in England to changes in attitudes toward labor in a way similar to my argument in the paragraphs below.

22. C. Vann Woodward, *American Counterpoint* (Boston, 1971), 6; Linda Kerber, *Federalists in Dissent* (Ithaca, 1970), 24–44; James M. Banner, *To the Hartford Convention* (New York, 1970), 99–108; Richard J. Buel, Jr., *Securing the Revolution* (Ithaca, 1972), 235.

23. Banner, *To the Hartford Convention*, 108–9; Kerber, *Federalists in Dissent*, 50, 59–63.

24. Rowland Berthoff, *An Unsettled People* (New York, 1971), 182; Stanley Elkins, *Slavery* (Chicago, 1959), ch. 4; Williams, *Contours*, 158. Cf. Fredrickson, *Black Image in the White Mind*, 19–33.

25. The highly competitive, individualistic nature of ante-bellum society also helps to explain the apparent paradox that both racism and anti-slavery thought became more pervasive in the North at the same time. As Stanley Elkins points out, "in a stratified society with strong aristocratic attitudes, there is no need to define the Negro as hopelessly inferior, because the greater portion of society is inferior in varying degrees." In America, by contrast, where freedom implied the ability to compete for advancement, the idea of freeing the slaves inevitably raised the question of social equality. Elkins, in John A. Garraty, *Interpreting American History* (2 vols.: New York, 1970), I, 188–89. Cf. Fredrickson, *Black Image in the White Mind*, 95, and David Brion Davis, "The Emergence of Immediatism in British and American Antislavery Thought," *Mississippi Valley Historical Review* (Sept. 1962), 209–30, one of the many works which relates the new anti-slavery outlook of the 1830s to a faith, engendered by evangelical religion, in the perfectibility of individual men and to a decline in deference to institutions which blocked the path to reform.

26. On notions of "free labor," see Foner, *Free Soil, Free Labor, Free Man*, ch. 1; David Montgomery, *Beyond Equality* (New York, 1965), ch. 1. Cf. the remark by sociologist Wilbert E. Moore; "If one were to attempt a one-word summary of the institutional requirements of economic development, that word would be *mobility.* Property rights, consumer goods, and laborers must be freed from traditional bonds and restraints, from aristocratic traditions, quasi-feudal arrangements, paternalistic and other multi-bonded relations." Moore, "The Social Framework of Economic Development," in Ralph Braibanti and Joseph J. Spengler, eds., *Tradition, Values and Socio-Economic Development* (Durham, 1961), 71.

27. Of course certain northern intellectuals, alienated from the more materialistic aspects of their own culture, turned to the South for the qualities lacking in northern society—"the vestiges of an old-world aristocracy, a promise of stability, and an assurance that gentility . . . could be preserved under republican institutions." William R. Taylor, *Cavalier and Yankee* (New York, 1961), xviii and

passim. I would argue, however, that by the 1840s and 1850s most northerners saw much more to criticize than to admire in southern life.

28. This argument would suggest that the process, described by George Fredrickson, in which ante-bellum radicals abandoned their position as independent critics of American institutions and uncritically identified themselves with their society—which he attributes to the Civil War experience—may have already begun during the 1850s. Fredrickson, *The Inner Civil War* (New York, 1965). John Thomas makes an argument similar to Fredrickson's in "Romantic Reform in America, 1815–1865," *American Quarterly,* XVII (Winter 1965), 656–81. However, Richard O. Curry has criticized both these works, arguing that anti-institutional radical thought persisted after the Civil War. Curry, "The Abolitionists and Reconstruction: A Critical Appraisal," *Journal of Southern History,* XXXIV (Nov. 1968), 527–45.

29. David Rothman, *The Discovery of the Asylum* (Boston, 1971), 107, 129, 214. Two works which deal with the transformation of personality and life styles required by industrial society are Herbert G. Gutman, "Work, Culture, and Society in Industrializing America, 1815–1919," and E. P. Thompson, "Time, Work Discipline and Industrial Capitalism," *Past and Present,* XXXVIII (1967), 58–97.

30. Roy F. Basler, *et al.,* eds., *The Collected Works of Abraham Lincoln* (9 vols.: New Brunswick, 1953–55), I, 108–15; IV, 268. Weld is quoted in Ronald G. Waters, "The Erotic South: Civilization and Sexuality in American Abolitionism," *American Quarterly,* XXV (May 1973), 187. Weld's statement suggests that abolitionists' "anti-institutionalism" may be interpreted as a belief that in the absence of powerful social institutions, "restraints" usually imposed by those institutions would have to be internalized by each individual. Also relevant to the above discussion is George Dennison's argument that the forcible suppression of internal disorder in the North in the 1830s and 1840s set a moral and legal precedent for the northern refusal to allow peaceable secession in 1861. Dennison, " 'The Idea of a Party System': A Critique," *Rocky Mountain Social Science Journal,* IX (Apr. 1972), 38–39n.

31. Foner, *Free Soil, Free Labor, Free Men,* 231–32; Gutman, "Work, Culture and Society," 583; Douglas V. Shaw, "The Making of an Immigrant Community: Ethnic and Cultural Conflict in Jersey City, New Jersey, 1850–1877" (Ph. D. diss., University of Rochester, 1972), 27–40, 75, 119; Formisano, *Birth of Mass Political Parties,* 146–47.

32. This is suggested in James R. Green, "Behavioralism and Class Analysis," 98.

33. This is suggested in David Donald, *Lincoln Reconsidered* (New York, 1956), 19–36, and Clifford S. Griffen, *Their Brothers' Keepers:*

Moral Stewardship in the United States 1800–1865 (New Brunswick, 1960).

34. Richards, *Gentlemen of Property and Standing* (New York, 1970), ch. 5.

35. David Brion Davis, ed., *Ante-Bellum Reform* (New York, 1967), 10. A recent study which attempts to probe this question is Joseph E. Mooney, "Antislavery in Worcester County, Massachusetts: A Case Study" (Ph. D. diss., Clark University, 1971). It is marred by the use of categories like "the common man" as units of social analysis, but its study of signers of an anti-slavery document of 1840 finds a large majority of farmers and artisans (278–79).

36. Brian Harrison, *Drink and the Victorians: The Temperance Question in England, 1815–1872* (Pittsburgh, 1971). The quotation is from page 24.

37. This is suggested in Williams, *Contours*, 280, and in Bernard Mandel, *Labor: Free and Slave* (New York, 1955). Michael Holt shows that in the mid-1850s, Know-Nothing lodge membership came disproportionately from manual workers and skilled artisans. Many of these workers presumably went into the Republican party. Holt, "The Politics of Impatience: The Origins of Know-Nothingism," *Journal of American History*, LX (Sept. 1973), 329–31.

38. William Barney, *The Road to Secession* (New York, 1972); William W. Freehling, "The Editorial Revolution, Virginia, and the Coming of the Civil War: A Review Essay," *Civil War History*, XVI (Mar. 1970), 64–72; Michael P. Johnson, *Toward a Patriarchal Republic: The Secession of Georgia* (Baton Rouge, 1977).

39. Carl Degler concludes that southern dissenters were remarkable largely for their weakness. Degler, *The Other South* (New York, 1974). Cf. Otto Olsen, "Historians and the Extent of Slave Ownership in the Southern United States," *Civil War History*, XVIII (June 1973), 101–16. On the other hand, William Barney suggests that there were severe divisions within the slaveholding class itself. The upper echelons of that class, he argues, became an increasingly closed elite in the 1850s, and younger and lesser planters found the route to upward mobility blocked by the rising price of slaves and concentration of wealth. Secession and slave expansionism, for them, was a route to renewed social mobility. Barney, *The Road to Secession*, 135.

40. [Edmund Ruffin], *Anticipations of the Future* (Richmond, 1860), viii–ix.

41. Fogel and Engerman, *Time on the Cross*, 39–40. My analysis of the situation in the British West Indies is derived from a dissertation in progress at Columbia University by George Tyson. Robert Brent Toplin shows how Brazilian slaveholders actually experienced in the 1880s what southerners may have feared in 1861—the emergence of abolitionism near plantations, slaves running away in large numbers, and the gradual disintegration of

control over the black population. Toplin, "The Spectre of Crisis: Slaveholder Reactions to Abolitionism in the United States and Brazil," *Civil War History*, XVIII (June 1973), 129–38.

42. It is perhaps appropriate to add that this disjunction exists for other periods of American history as well. Writings on the origins of the American Revolution seem to be as devoid of a clear linkage between social and political history as does Civil War historiography. For a speculative attempt to remedy this situation, see Kenneth A. Lockridge, "Social Change and the Meaning of the American Revolution," *Journal of Social History*, VI (Summer 1973), 403–39. Cf. Jack P. Greene, "The Social Origins of the American Revolution: An Evaluation and an Interpretation," *Political Science Quarterly*, LXXXVIII (Mar. 1973), 1–22.

43. Berthoff, *An Unsettled People*, 510; Michael Kammen, "Politics, Science and Society in Colonial America," *Journal of Social History*, III (Fall 1969), 63.

44. The paragraphs which follow are based on my essay, "Politics, Ideology, and the Origins of the American Civil War" [essay III in this collection].

45. Lawrence Stone, *The Causes of the English Revolution 1529–1642* (London, 1972), 10.

46. Luraghi, "Civil War and Modernization," 249. To be fair, Luraghi elsewhere observes that the Civil War "had not so much the task of making free a complete capitalistic structure yet existing, but mainly that of creating the conditions for such a structure to grow" (241).

47. For the South, see Emory Thomas, *The Confederacy as a Revolutionary Experience* (Englewood Cliffs, 1971); for the North, Allan Nevins, *The War for the Union: The Organized War 1863–64* (New York, 1971), and *The War for the Union: From Organized War to Victory, 1864–65* (New York, 1971).

III POLITICS AND IDEOLOGY

1. Seymour M. Lipset, *The First New Nation* (New York, 1963), 308–11; Frank J. Sorauf, *Political Parties in the American System* (Boston, 1964), 60–65. Distinctions between American political parties, to borrow Marvin Meyers's apt phrase, have usually been along lines of "persuasion," rather than ideology.

2. Donald L. Robinson, *Slavery and the Structure of American Politics 1765–1820* (New York, 1971), 175. See also William N. Chambers and Walter Dean Burham, eds., *The American Party Systems* (New York, 1967), 3–32, 56–89.

3. Sorauf, *Political Parties*, 61.

4. *National Intelligencer*, Oct. 6, 1855.

5. Staughton Lynd, *Class Conflict, Slavery, and the United States Consti-*

tution (Indianapolis, 1967), 161; Robinson, *Slavery and the Structure of Politics*, viii, 244.

6. James M. Banner, *To the Hartford Convention* (New York, 1970), 99–103; Glover Moore, *The Missouri Controversy 1819–1821* (Lexington, Ky., 1953), *passim;* Charles Francis Adams, ed., *Memoirs of John Quincy Adams* (12 vols; Philadelphia, 1874–77), IV, 529; William E. Ames, *A History of the National Intelligencer* (Chapel Hill, N.C., 1972), 121–22.

7. Paul Nagel, "The Election of 1824: Reconsideration Based on Newspaper Opinion," *Journal of Southern History,* XXVI (Aug. 1960), 315–29; Richard H. Brown, "The Missouri Crisis, Slavery, and the Politics of Jacksonianism," *South Atlantic Quarterly,* LXV (Winter 1966), 55–72; Robert V. Remini, *Martin Van Buren and the Making of the Democratic Party* (New York, 1959), 125–32; Richard P. McCormick, *The Second American Party System* (Chapel Hill, 1966), 338–42; Chambers and Burnham, eds., *The American Party Systems,* 21, 97–101.

8. Moore, *Missouri Controversy,* 175; James Young, *The Washington Community* (New York, 1966).

9. Robinson, *Slavery and the Structure of Politics,* 72; Linda K. Kerber, *Federalists in Dissent* (Ithaca, 1970), 24–44; Banner, *To the Hartford Convention,* 104–9; Theophilus Parsons, Jr., "A Mirror of Mens' Minds: The Missouri Compromise and the Development of an Antislavery Ideology" (unpublished seminar paper, Columbia University, 1971); *Congressional Globe,* 31 Congress, 1 Session, Appendix, 1030; 36 Congress, 2 Session, 624. C. Vann Woodward observes that patterns of derogatory sectional imagery existed far earlier than most historians have assumed. Woodward, *American Counterpoint* (Boston, 1971), 6.

10. Banner, *To the Hartford Convention,* 108–9; Kerber, *Federalists in Dissent* 50, 59–63. After the transformation of their party from a national to a regional one, New England Federalists did express their latent anti-southern feelings more openly. Richard Buel, Jr., *Securing the Revolution: Ideology in American Politics, 1789–1815* (Ithaca, 1972), 235.

11. Stanley Elkins, "Slavery and Ideology," in Ann Lane, ed., *The Debate over Slavery* (Urbana, 1971), 376n.; William W. Freehling, *Prelude to Civil War,* (New York, 1966), ch. 9, esp. 333, 358; *Congressional Globe,* 25 Congress, 2 Session, Appendix, 62.

12. Alice Felt Tyler, *Freedom's Ferment* (New York, 1962 ed.), 511; Elkins, "Slavery and Ideology," 374–77; Eric Foner, *Free Soil, Free Labor, Free Men* (New York, 1970), 87–102.

13. Gilbert H. Barnes, *The Anti-Slavery Impulse* (New York, 1964 ed.), 188–90, 195–97; James B. Stewart, *Joshua R. Giddings and the Tactics of Radical Politics* (Cleveland, 1970), ch. 4.

14. Preston King to Gideon Welles, Sept. 16, 1858, Gideon Welles Papers, Library of Congress; Eric Foner, "The Wilmot Proviso

Revisited," *Journal of American History,* LVI (Sept. 1969), 262–70; Chaplain W. Morrison, *Democratic Politics and Sectionalism* (Chapel Hill, 1967), 34–41.

15. Morrison, *Democratic Politics,* 45–51; Eric Foner, "Racial Attitudes of the New York Free Soilers" [essay V in this collection].

16. Avery Craven, *The Coming of the Civil War* (Chicago, 1942), 197; Ronald P. Formisano, *The Birth of Mass Political Parties* (Princeton, 1971), 195, 205–6; Joseph G. Rayback, *Free Soil* (Lexington, 1970), 309; Frederick W. Seward, *Seward at Washington* (2 vols.: New York 1891), I, 71.

17. Foner, *Free Soil, Free Labor, Free Men,* 188; Morrison, *Democratic Politics,* 87–91; Damon Wells, *Stephen Douglas, The Last Years, 1857–1861* (Austin, 1971) 61–67.

18. For the intentional nature of the ambiguities in popular sovereignty, see Robert W. Johannsen, *Stephen A. Douglas* (New York, 1973), 427, 440, 525.

19. Holman Hamilton, *Prologue to Conflict* (Lexington, 1964).

20. Johannsen, *Douglas,* 347, 483. For Webster's efforts to create a national consensus by compromising and suppressing the slavery issue, see Robert F. Dalzell, Jr., *Daniel Webster and the Trial of American Nationalism* (Boston, 1973), *passim,* and Major L. Wilson, "Of Time and the Union: Webster and His Critics in the Crisis of 1850," *Civil War History,* XIV (Dec. 1968), 293–306.

21. Foner, *Free Soil, Free Labor, Free Men,* 194. Of course, on the local level, the Whigs had already been eroding under the impact of such divisive issues as temperance and nativism.

22. Allan Nevins, *Ordeal of the Union* (2 vols.: New York, 1947), II, 107. Cf. Wells, *Douglas,* 64.

23. Paul M. Angle, ed., *Created Equal? The Complete Lincoln-Douglas Debates of 1858* (Chicago, 1958), 5, 17, 18, 35, 70, 202, 303, 332–34, 351. Cf. Harry Jaffa, *Crisis of the House Divided* (Garden City, 1959); Wells, *Douglas,* 110–11.

24. Angle, ed., *Created Equal?,* 22–23, 62–63; Jaffa, *Crisis,* 36. Lincoln declared that the trouble with popular sovereignty was that Douglas "looks upon all this matter of slavery as an exceedingly little thing—this matter of keeping one-sixth of the population of the whole country in a state of oppression and tyranny unequalled in the world." Angle, ed., *Created Equal?,* 35. It is hard to imagine Douglas including the slaves in any way as part of "the population of the whole country."

25. Roy F. Nichols, *The Disruption of American Democracy* (New York, 1948), esp. ch. 15. For Douglas's intentions for the territories and his expectation that popular sovereignty would result in the creation of free states in the West, see Jaffa, *Crisis,* 48; Johannsen, *Douglas,* 276, 279–80, 565; Edward L. and Frederick H. Schapsmeir, "Lincoln and Douglas: Their Versions of the West," *Journal of the West,* VII (Oct. 1968), 546. Lee Benson argues that the en-

trance of free western states into the Union was not a cause of concern for the South, since these new states, like California and Oregon in the 1850s, would likely be Democratic and pro-southern. But the 1850s clearly showed that free, Democratic states could quickly become Republican, and the Lecompton fight demonstrated that free, Democratic states were no longer accept-able to southern leaders, who insisted that Kansas be Democratic *and* slave. Lee Benson, *Toward the Scientific Study of History* (Phila-delphia, 1972), 269.

26. Foner, *Free Soil, Free Labor, Free Men,* esp. chs. 1–2.
27. Glyndon G. Van Deusen, *William Henry Seward* (New York, 1969), ch. 9; Elliot R. Barkan, "The Emergence of a Whig Persuasion: Conservatism, Democratism, and the New York State Whigs," *New York History,* LII (Oct. 1971), 370–86; Seward to James Bowen, Nov. 3, 1844, William Henry Seward Papers, University of Michigan Library; Seward to Weed, Aug. 3, 1846, Thurlow Weed Papers, University of Rochester.
28. Formisano, *Birth of Mass Political Parties,* 329; Foner, *Free Soil, Free Labor, Free Men,* 87–102; Larry Gara, "Slavery and the Slave Power: A Crucial Distinction," *Civil War History,* XV (Mar. 1969), 5–18.
29. Angle, ed., *Created Equal?,* 393. It is futile, in my opinion, to draw too-fine distinctions between various kinds of Republican anti-slavery sentiment, as Lee Benson and Ronald Formisano sometimes have a tendency to do. Though the distinctions be-tween opposition to the slave power, general anti-southernism, and what Formisano calls criticisms of "slavery as an institu-tion," or "antislavery as such" were real ones, these distinc-tions seemed pointless to the South, since even Republicans of the most moderate anti-slavery views advocated policies southerners found unacceptable. More important, the vary-ing degrees and kinds of anti-slavery sentiment fed into and reinforced one another; the Republican ideology, in other words, was much more than the sum of its parts—it must be understood in its totality. See Formisano, *Birth of Mass Political Parties,* 244, 279; Benson, *Toward the Scientific Study,* 295.
30. William W. Freehling, "The Editorial Revolution, Virginia, and the Coming of the Civil War: A Review Essay," *Civil War History,* XVI (Mar. 1970), 68–71.
31. Robert Brent Toplin, "The Specter of Crisis: Slaveholder Reac-tions to Abolitionism in the United States and Brazil," *Civil War History,* XVIII (June 1972), 129–38; John Amasa May and Joan Reynolds Faust, *South Carolina Secedes* (Columbia, 1960), 88.
32. Benjamin F. Wright, ed., *The Federalist* (Cambridge, 1961), 132–34, 357–59. Or, as C. B. MacPherson writes, the American federal theory of politics rests on the assumption "that the politi-

cally important demands of each individual are diverse and are shared with varied and shifting combinations of other individuals, none of which combinations can be expected to be a numerical majority of the electorate." MacPherson, *Democratic Theory: Essays in Retrieval* (Oxford, 1973), 190.

33. William W. Freehling, "Spoilsmen and Interests in the Thought and Career of John C. Calhoun," *Journal of American History*, LII (June 1965), 25–26; Charles M. Wiltse, *John C. Calhoun* (3 vols.; Indianapolis, 1944–51), II, 114, 195, 199, 255, 268–70; III, 416–19, 462–63; May and Faust, *South Carolina Secedes*, 81.

34. David Potter, *The South and the Sectional Conflict* (Baton Rouge, 1968), 44, 58; New York *Tribune*, Apr. 12, 1855.

IV ABOLITIONISM AND THE LABOR MOVEMENT

1. See Harvey Wish, *George Fitzhugh, Propagandist of the Old South* (Baton Rouge, 1943); Richard Hofstadter, *The American Political Tradition* (New York, 1948), ch. 4; Eugene D. Genovese, *The World the Slaveholders Made* (New York, 1969), pt. 2.

2. *Workingman's Advocate* (New York City), Mar. 13, 1830. On artisan radicalism, see Eric Foner, *Tom Paine and Revolutionary America* (New York, 1976).

3. Seth Luther, *Address to the Workingmen of New England* (Boston, 1832), 25; Philip S. Foner, *History of the Labor Movement in the United States* (New York, 1947), I, 272; John R. Commons *et al.*, eds., *A Documentary History of American Industrial Society* (10 vols.: Washington, 1910–11), V, 317; Bernard Mandel, *Labor: Free and Slave* (New York, 1955), 77; Thomas Dublin, "Women, Work and Protest in the Early Lowell Mills," *Labor History*, XVI (Winter 1975), 109–10; Lise Vogel, "Their Own Work: Two Documents from the Nineteenth-Century Labor Movement," *Signs*, I (Spring 1976), 794–800.

4. Walter Hugins, ed., *The Reform Impulse* (New York, 1972), 99–101.

5. Leon Litwack, *North of Slavery* (Chicago, 1961), 160; Joseph G. Rayback, "The American Workingman and the Antislavery Crusade," *Journal of Economic History*, III (1943), 152–63; Lorman Ratner, *Powder Keg* (New York, 1968), 62–67.

6. Alan Dawley, *Class and Community: The Industrial Revolution in Lynn* (Cambridge, 1976), 65; Leonard Richards, *Gentlemen of Property and Standing* (New York, 1970), 140–41; John B. Jentz, "Artisans, Evangelicals, and the City: A Social History of the Labor and Abolitionist Movements in Jacksonian New York" (Ph. D. diss., Graduate Center, City University of New York, 1977), 54–56, 125–35; New York *Daily Sentinel*, Sept. 17, 1831; *Workingman's Advocate*, Oct. 17, 1835; Oct. 1, 1831.

7. *The Liberator*, Jan. 1, 1831.
8. *The Liberator*, Jan. 29, 1831.
9. *The Liberator*, Sept. 5, 1846.
10. Ronald G. Walters, *The Antislavery Appeal* (Baltimore, 1976), 121.
11. Hugins, ed., *The Reform Impulse*, 168. See also Jonathan A. Glickstein, " 'Poverty Is Not Slavery': American Abolitionists and the Competitive Labor Market," *Antislavery Reconsidered: New Perspectives on the Abolitionists*, eds., Lewis Perry and Michael Fellman (Baton Rouge, 1979), 195–218. The italics in the Jay quotation are in the original.
12. George Fredrickson, *The Black Image in the White Mind* (New York, 1971), 32–34; Aileen Kraditor, *Means and Ends in American Abolitionism* (New York, 1969), 244; Gilbert Osofsky, "Abolitionists, Irish Immigrants, and the Dilemmas of Romantic Nationalism," *American Historical Review*, LXXX (Oct. 1975), 908–10.
13. See Gilbert Barnes, *The Anti-Slavery Impulse* (New York, 1933); Anne C. Loveland, "Evangelicism and Immediate Emancipation in American Anti-Slavery Thought," *Journal of Southern History*, XXXII (May 1966), 172–88.
14. Jentz, "Artisans, Evangelicals, and the City," 97, 192–93; *Workingman's Advocate*, Sept. 19, Nov. 21, 1835.
15. *Workingman's Advocate*, Jan. 30, 1830; Lewis Tappan, *Life of Arthur Tappan* (New York, 1870), 329; Bertram Wyatt-Brown, *Lewis Tappan and the Evangelical War Against Slavery* (Cleveland, 1969), 46–47.
16. Williston H. Lofton, "Abolition and Labor," *Journal of Negro History*, XXXIII (July 1948), 249–83; Mandel, *Labor: Free and Slave*, 93.
17. John L. Thomas, "Antislavery and Utopia," in *The Antislavery Vanguard*, ed., Martin B. Duberman (Princeton, 1965), 255–56; *The Liberator*, Aug. 28, 1846; *Life and Times of Frederick Douglass* (New York, 1962), 228.
18. Stephen Oates, *To Purge This Land With Blood: A Biography of John Brown* (New York, 1970), 245–46.
19. Mandel, *Labor: Free and Slave*, 77; *Herald of Freedom* (Concord), June 2, Oct. 6, 1846; Apr. 11, May 2, 1845.
20. *The Liberator*, Sept. 4, 1846; Salem *Ohio Homestead Journal*, cited in *The Liberator*, Apr. 21, 1848.
21. *The Liberator*, Sept. 25, 1846, Mar. 19, 26, Apr. 2, 1847.
22. *The Liberator*, Mar. 26, July 9, Oct. 1, 1847. On this debate, see also Kraditor, *Means and Ends*, 248–50.
23. *The Liberator*, July 9, 1847.
24. David Montgomery, "The Shuttle and the Cross: Weavers and Artisans in the Kensington Riots of 1844," *Journal of Social History*, V (Summer 1972), 411–46.
25. *Working Man's Advocate*, July 6, 1844.

26. Eric Foner, *Free Soil, Free Labor, Free Men: The Ideology of the Republican Party Before the Civil War* (New York, 1970).

27. See Eric Foner, "The Causes of the Civil War: Recent Interpretations and New Directions" [essay II in this collection].

28. David Brion Davis, *The Problem of Slavery in the Age of Revolution* (Ithaca, 1975), 347–61.

29. Davis, *Problem of Slavery*, 364, 373; Dawley, *Class and Community*, 196, 238–39.

30. Michael Fellman, *The Unbounded Frame* (Westport, 1973), 105; Mandel, *Labor: Free and Slave*, 66; Rayback, "American Workingman," 154; Foner, *History of the Labor Movement*, I, 272.

31. See Eric Foner, "Class, Ethnicity, and Radicalism in the Gilded Age: The Land League and Irish-America," [essay VIII in this collection].

32. Barry Goldberg, "Beyond Free Labor" (Ph. D. diss., Columbia University, 1978), provides compelling evidence of the persistence of the idea of "wage slavery" among labor leaders after the Civil War, as a rhetorical device for criticizing the emerging industrial society. Paradoxically, he observes, labor reformers played down the differences between chattel slavery and wage slavery, yet they identified strongly with abolitionism, ignoring that movement's response to the labor reformers of its own time. As late as 1895, the British writer John K. Ingram felt compelled to include an appendix on the "lax" use of the concept of slavery among his contemporaries, especially the term "wage slavery," in his *A History of Slavery and Serfdom* (London, 1895), 263–64.

V   RACIAL ATTITUDES

1. William Chambers, *Things As They Are in America* (London, 1854), 354; Leon F. Litwack, *North of Slavery, The Negro in the Free States, 1790–1860* (Chicago, 1961), especially chs. 1, 3–5; Allan Nevins, *Ordeal of the Union* (2 vols.: New York, 1949), I, 518–20; John C. Hurd, *The Law of Freedom and Bondage in the United States* (2 vols.: Boston, 1862), II, 131, 136, 177, 216–17; William G. Allen, *The American Prejudice Against Colour* (London, 1853), 1; Julian to Convention of Colored Citizens of Illinois, September 17, 1853, George W. Julian Papers, Indiana State Library (italics in original).

2. Charles H. Wesley, "The Participation of Negroes in Anti-Slavery Political Parties," *Journal of Negro History*, XXIX (Jan. 1944), 48; *North Star*, Sept. 1, 1848; Kirk H. Porter and Donald B. Johnson, eds., *National Party Platforms* (Urbana, 1956), 4–9; Norman D. Harris, *History of Negro Servitude in Illinois* (Chicago, 1906), 148; Hartford *Charter Oak*, Oct. 7, 28, 1847; Howard H. Bell, "A Sur-

vey of the Negro Convention Movement, 1830–1861" (Ph. D. diss., Northwestern University, 1953), 75, 82–84.

3. Dixon Ryan Fox, *The Decline of Aristocracy in the Politics of New York* (New York, 1919), 269n.; Dixon Ryan Fox, "The Negro Vote in Old New York," *Political Science Quarterly*, XXXII (June 1917), 252–75.

4. Lee Benson, *The Concept of Jacksonian Democracy* (Princeton, 1961), 320n.; New York *Tribune*, Oct. 4, 1845, Feb. 12, 1846.

5. John R. Hendricks, "The Liberty Party in New York State, 1838–1848" (Ph. D. diss., Fordham, 1959), 152–57; Works Projects Administration, ed., *Calendar of the Gerrit Smith Papers in the Syracuse University Library* (2 vols.: Albany, 1941), I, 239, 244, 260.

6. William Trimble, "The Social Philosophy of the Loco-Foco Democracy," *American Journal of Sociology*, XXVI (May 1921), 713; Frederick Merk, "A Safety Valve Thesis and Texan Annexation," *Mississippi Valley Historical Review*, XLIX (Dec. 1962), 428–36; New York *Morning News*, Mar. 13, 28, Apr. 29, 1846; Robert Gumerove, "The 'New York Morning News,' Organ of the Radical 'Barnburning' Democracy, 1844–1846" (M. A. thesis, Columbia University, 1953), 82–91; Parke Godwin, *Biography of William Cullen Bryant* (2 vols.: New York, 1883), I, 345–46; Litwack, *North of Slavery*, 89; New York *Tribune*, Jan. 12, 1852.

7. C. C. Cambreleng, John Hunter, Thomas Sears, Gouverneur Kemble, Samuel J. Tilden, Arphaxed Loomis, Michael Hoffman, Azel Danforth, William Taylor, Cyrus Kingsley, John A. Kennedy, and James Powers.

8. S. Croswell and R. Sutton, eds., *Debates and Proceedings in the New York State Convention for the Revision of the Constitution* (Albany, 1846), 788–91; cf. 783–85; *Tribune Almanac for the Years 1838 to 1868* (2 vols.: New York, 1868), I, 1847, 43; Boston (semi-weekly) *Republican*, Nov. 16, 1848; *Mr. Greeley's Record on the Questions of Amnesty and Reconstruction* (New York, 1872), 21.

9. Herbert D. A. Donovan, *The Barnburners* (New York, 1925), 92–94; Walter L. Ferree, "New York Democracy; Division and Reunion, 1847–1852" (Ph. D. diss., University of Pennsylvania, 1953), 99.

10. Michael Hoffman to Azariah C. Flagg, Mar. 25, 1845, Azariah C. Flagg Papers, New York Public Library (italics in original); *Proceedings of the Herkimer Mass Convention* (Albany, 1847), 4–8; O. C. Gardiner, *The Great Issue* (New York, 1848), 119.

11. George Rathbun, at Utica Convention: *Proceedings of the Utica Convention* (Albany, 1848), 25. Cf. *The Free Soil Question and Its Importance to the Voters of the Free States* (New York, 1848), 2–7.

12. J. Franklin Jameson, ed., "Correspondence of John C. Calhoun," *Annual Report* of American Historical Association, 1899, II, 1155; *Free Soil Question*, 7; John Bigelow, ed., *Writing and Speeches of Sam-*

uel J. Tilden (2 vols.: New York, 1885), II, 545; *National Era,* Sept. 28, 1848; Boston *Republican,* Aug. 23, 1848; Gardiner, *Great Issue,* 135; *Herkimer Convention,* 28.

13. Morgan Dix, *Memoirs of John Adams Dix* (2 vols.: New York, 1883), II, 114–17; *Congressional Globe,* 30 Congress, 1 Session, Appendix, 866ff.; Simeon B. Jewett to Dix, July 8, 1848, Dix to Thomas Hart Benton, Sept. 9, 1848, John A. Dix Papers, Columbia University Library.

14. Works Projects Administration, eds., *Calendar of the Joshua Reed Giddings Manuscripts in the Library of the Ohio State Archaeological and Historical Society* (Columbus, 1939), 222; *National Era,* July 13, 1848; Letter of Lewis H. Bishop (of Warsaw Historical Society, Warsaw, N.Y.) to author, Mar. 13, 1963; Carter G. Woodson, ed., *The Mind of the Negro As Reflected in Letters Written During the Crisis 1800–1860* (Washington, 1926), 352.

15. Ernest P. Mueller, "Preston King: A Political Biography " (Ph. D. diss., Columbia University, 1957), 335–36, 353; *Congressional Globe,* 29 Congress, 2 Session, 114–15; King to Dix, Nov. 13, 1847, Dix Papers; Thomas M. Marshall, ed., "Diary and Memoranda of William L. Marcy, 1849–1851," *American Historical Review,* XXIV (Apr. 1919), 451.

16. Charles B. Going, *David Wilmot: Free Soiler* (New York, 1942), 174–75n.; Margaret Koshinski, "David Wilmot and Free Soil" (M.A. thesis, Columbia University, 1949), 25; *Congressional Globe,* 29 Congress, 2 Session, Appendix, 317, 30 Congress, 1 Session, Appendix, 1076–79; *Herkimer Convention,* 14.

17. *Congressional Globe,* 31 Congress, 1 Session, Appendix, 943, 30 Congress, 2 Session, 406; Going, *Wilmot,* 338.

18. *Pennsylvania Freeman,* Dec. 7, 1848 (italics in original). In the same editorial, the *Freeman* addressed an eloquent appeal to the entire Free Soil party:

> The colored people . . . are calling for their rights, and contending with long-seated prejudices. We have a right to expect Free Soil men to encourage and assist them; if they will not do this, we ask them in the name of humanity, that they will not feed the popular prejudices against this outcast class.

19. Ralph V. Harlow, *Gerrit Smith* (New York, 1939), 186 (italics in original).

20. Van Buren had settled the dispute with the telling remark, "Is not the vote of Geritt [*sic*] Smith just as weighty as that of [the Barnburner] Judge Martin Grover?" Lucius E. Chittenden, *Personal Reminiscences, 1840–1890* (New York, 1893), 15–16; Oliver Dyer, *Great Senators of the United States* (New York, 1889), 95–96.

21. *Reunion of the Free Soilers of 1848, at Downer Landing, Higham, Massachusetts* (Boston, 1877), 43. Douglass confirmed the incident. *Frederick Douglass' Paper,* Aug. 20, 1852.

22. Oliver Dyer, *Phonographic Report of the Proceedings of the National Free Soil Convention* (New York, 1848), 4, 21; Edward H. Price, "The Election of 1848 in Ohio," *Ohio Archaeological and Historical Quarterly*, XXXVI (1927), 249.

23. The Western Liberty leaders had for some time been striving to broaden their party's platform, to attract anti-slavery men from the Whig and Democratic parties. Joseph G. Raybeck, "The Liberty Party Leaders of Ohio: Exponents of Anti-Slavery Coalition," *Ohio Archaeological and Historical Quarterly*, LVII (Apr. 1947), 165–78.

24. Porter and Johnson, eds. *Party Platforms*, 13–14; Harris, *Negro Servitude*, 167; Lawrence Lader, *The Bold Brahmins* (New York, 1961), 135; Boston *Republican*, Aug. 17, 1848; John Brown to Hale, Aug. 24, 1848, John P. Hale Papers, New Hampshire Historical Society.

25. Dwight Dumond, ed., *Letters of James G. Birney, 1831–1857* (2 vols.: New York, 1938), II, 623.

26. Thomas Van Rensselear to Martin Van Buren, Oct. 16, 1848, in Samuel J. Tilden Papers, New York Public Library; *Pennsylvania Freeman*, Oct. 26, 1848.

27. *North Star*, Sept. 1, 1848. Butler had been Van Buren's Attorney-General. For his views on Negro suffrage, see Butler, "Outline of the Constitutional History of New York," *Collections* of the New York Historical Society, II, Second Series (1848), 62n.

28. *North Star*, Sept. 1, 22, 1848.

29. Bell, "Negro Convention Movement," 106; *North Star*, Nov. 24, 1848, Jan. 12, 1849; (Montpelier, Vt.) *Green Mountain Freeman*, Nov. 11, 1847.

30. Ulrich B. Phillips, ed., "The Correspondence of Robert Toombs, Alexander Stephens, and Howell Cobb," *Annual Report* of American Historical Association, 1911, I, 270.

31. Henry B. Stanton, *Random Recollections* (New York, 1887), 162, 165. That many of the leading Barnburners were motivated in large part by the desire to defeat Cass is beyond question. See Chittenden, *Reminiscences*, 12–14; "Letter of William Allen Butler to George Bancroft," *Proceedings* of Massachusetts Historical Society, LX (Jan. 1927), 118–20; Azariah Flagg to Marcus Morton, June 19, 1848, Gideon Welles to Flagg, Feb. 9, 1848, Flagg Papers, Columbia University Library; John L. O'Sullivan, *Nelson Jarvis Waterbury* (New York, 1880), 11–12. For a different view, see Joseph G. Raybeck, ed., "Martin Van Buren's Desire for Revenge in the Campaign of 1848," *Mississippi Valley Historical Review*, XL (Mar. 1954), 707–16.

32. *National Era*, Nov. 15, 1849.

33. New York *Evening Post*, June 12, July 17, 19, Nov. 24, 1848, Oct. 18, 1850, May 23, July 30, 1851.

34. New York *Evening Post*, Sept. 8, 1851; Margaret Clapp, *Forgotten First Citizen: John Bigelow* (Boston, 1947), 54; John Bigelow, *Ja-*

maica in 1850 (New York, 1851), 160; Hermann Burmeister, *The Black Man* (New York, 1853), 3, 5, 13–15 (reprint from New York *Evening Post*).

35. *Tribune Almanac*, I, 1847, 44, 1849, 49; Edward M. Shepard, *Martin Van Buren*, (Boston, 1888), 427; Boston *Commonwealth*, July 27, 1852.

36. *National Era*, June 15, 1848; Philadelphia *Republic*, Dec. 22, 1848; *North Star*, Dec. 8, 1848. And contrast the Barnburners' opposition to the presence of the free Negro in the territories with the *National Era*'s position: "We are not opposed to the extension of either class of your [the South's] population, provided it be *free*, but to the existence of slavery and the migration of *slaves*." *National Era*, May 3, 1849 (italics in original).

37. Edward Channing, *A History of the United States* (6 vols.: New York, 1912–25), VI, 4; Wilfred E. Binkley, *American Political Parties* (New York, 1954), 186.

38. In virtually every northern state, Negro suffrage was viewed more favorably by the Whigs, and of course the Liberty men, then the Democrats. In states like Ohio and Massachusetts, where the Free Soilers were largely former Whigs and Liberty men, the party fought to extend the social and political rights of free Negroes. Even in these states, however, the party was plagued by the problem of racial prejudice. Emil Olbrich, "The Development of Sentiment on Negro Suffrage to 1860," *Bulletin* of the University of Wisconsin, III (1912); *National Era*, Mar. 18, 1952.

39. *Pennsylvania Freeman*, Feb. 1, 1849.

40. Charles M. Wiltse, *John C. Calhoun* (New York, 1951), 369; Chauncey S. Boucher and Robert P. Brooks, eds., "Correspondence Addressed to John C. Calhoun, 1837–1849," *Annual Report* of American Historical Association, 1929, 389; Jameson, ed., "Correspondence of Calhoun," 1183; Phillips, ed., "Correspondence of Toombs, Stephens, and Cobb," 114; Nevins, *Ordeal of the Union*, I, 255; Frederick W. Seward, *Seward at Washington* (2 vols.: New York, 1891), I, 71.

41. Porter and Johnson, eds., *Party Platforms*, 18–20; New York *Tribune*, Aug. 13, 1852; *National Era*, Aug. 12, 1852.

VI RECONSTRUCTION AND FREE LABOR

1. Howard K. Beale, "On Rewriting Reconstruction History," *American Historical Review*, XLV (July 1940), 807–27; Bernard A. Weisberger, "The Dark and Bloody Ground of Reconstruction Historiography," *Journal of Southern History*, XXV (Nov. 1959), 427–47; Vernon L. Wharton, "Reconstruction," in *Writing Southern History*, eds. Arthur S. Link and Rembert V. Patrick (Baton Rouge, 1965), 295–315; Richard O. Curry, "The Civil War and

Reconstruction, 1861–1877; A Critical Overview of Recent Trends and Interpretations," *Civil War History*, XX (Sept. 1974), 215–28.

2. W. E. B. Du Bois, *Black Reconstruction in America* (New York, 1935); William H. Trescot to Governor James L. Orr, Dec. 13, 1865, South Carolina Governors' Papers, South Carolina Archives.

3. Richard Taylor to Samuel L. M. Barlow, Dec. 13, 1865, Samuel L. M. Barlow Papers, Huntington Library; "Visit to Gowrie and East Hermitage Plantations, March 22, 1867," in Statement of Sales, Gowrie Plantation, Savannah River, Mss. volume, Manigault Family Papers, Southern Historical Collection, University of North Carolina. Taylor, apparently no historian, actually used the date " '99" in his letter, but the meaning seems clear. Manigault had visited China and the Philippines in 1850–51. Louis Manigault, Journal of Travels (typescript), South Caroliniana Library, University of South Carolina.

4. Arney R. Childs, ed., *The Private Journal of Henry William Ravenal 1859–1887* (Columbia, 1947), 269; Eliza F. Andrews, *The War-Time Journal of a Georgia Girl* (New York, 1908), 319; Capt. Isaac A. Rosekrans to James Waters, Oct. 27, 1865, Misc. Records (ser. 2767), Newberne NC Supt., Bureau of Refugees, Freedmen, and Abandoned Lands, Record Group 105, National Archives (hereafter cited as RG 105, N.A.); William A. Graham to David L. Swain, May 11, 1865, William A. Graham Papers, Southern Historical Collection, University of North Carolina; Laura Perry to Grant Perry, Feb. 3, 1869, J. M. Perry Family Papers, Atlanta Historical Society. For general discussion see James L. Roark, *Masters Without Slaves* (New York, 1977), 141–46; Robert P. Brooks, *The Agrarian Revolution in Georgia 1865–1912* (Madison, 1914), 18–26.

5. Sylvia H. Krebs, " 'Will the Freedmen Work?' White Alabamians Adjust to Free Labor," *Alabama Historical Quarterly*, XXXVI (Summer 1974), 151–63; "we the colorde people" to Governor of Mississippi, Dec. 3, 1865, F-41 (1865), Registered Letters Received (ser. 2051), Miss. Asst. Comr., RG 105, N.A.; M. Leland, "Middleton Correspondence, 1861–1865," *South Carolina Historical Magazine*, LXV (1964), 107.

6. Adam Smith, *An Inquiry into the Nature and Causes of the Wealth of Nations* (Modern Library ed.: New York, 1937), 365–66; Howard Temperly, "Capitalism, Slavery and Ideology," *Past and Present*, LXXV (May 1977), 107–9; Eric Foner, *Free Soil, Free Labor, Free Men: The Ideology of the Republican Party Before the Civil War* (New York, 1970).

7. Leon F. Litwack, *Been in the Storm So Long* (New York, 1979), 385. For criticisms of Freedmen's Bureau labor policies, see *ibid.*, 321–26, 384–91, 425; Jonathan M. Wiener, *Social Origins of the New South 1860–1885* (Baton Rouge, 1978), 47–53; William S. McFeely,

Yankee Stepfather: General O. O. Howard and the Freedmen (New Haven, 1979).

8. "Address of Capt. J. E. Bryant to Freedmen's Convention of Georgia, January 13, 1866," Mss. speech, John E. Bryant Papers, Perkins Library, Duke University.

9. Columbia *Daily Phoenix*, June 19, 1865; Augusta *Loyal Georgian*, Jan. 20, 1866.

10. Robert K. Scott to Governor James L. Orr, Dec. 13, 1866, South Carolina Governors' Papers; Kenneth B. White, "Wager Swayne—Racist or Realist?" *Alabama Review*, XXXI (Apr. 1978), 103–6.

11. Lewis C. Chartock, "A History and Analysis of Labor Contracts Administered by the Bureau of Refugees, Freedmen, and Abandoned Lands in Edgefield, Abbeville and Anderson Counties in South Carolina, 1865–1868" (Ph. D. diss., Bryn Mawr College, Graduate School of Social Work and Social Research, 1973), 43; Whitelaw Reid, *After the War* (Cincinnati, 1866), 343; Joseph H. Mahaffey, ed., "Carl Schurz's Letters from the South," *Georgia Historical Quarterly*, XXXV (Sept. 1951), 230–31.

12. *Memorial from the Cotton Planters' Convention, Which Met in Macon, September 6, 1866* (Macon, 1866), 12; Columbia *Daily Phoenix*, July 20, 1865; D. B. McLurin to N. R. Middleton, Sept. 26, 1867, Middleton Papers, Langdon Cheves Collection, South Carolina Historical Scoiety; William E. Highsmith, "Louisiana Landholding During War and Reconstruction," *Louisiana Historical Quarterly*, XXXVIII (Jan. 1955), 44; Raleigh *Semi-Weekly Record*, Aug. 23, 26, 1865.

13. John T. Trowbridge, *A Picture of the Desolated States* (Hartford, 1868), 573; Joyce Appleby, "Ideology and Theory: The Tension Between Political and Economic Liberalism in Seventeenth-Century England," *American Historical Review*, LXXXI (June 1976), 514.

14. *Indiana True Republican* (Richmond, Ind.), Sept. 14, 1865.

15. For a discussion of this point, see Eric Foner, *Tom Paine and Revolutionary America* (New York, 1976), 155–56.

16. New Orleans *Tribune*, Nov. 6, 1865; Ross H. Moore, "Social and Economic Conditions in Mississippi During Reconstruction" (Ph. D. diss., Duke University, 1937), 41; Charles Ramsdell, "Presidential Reconstruction in Texas," *Texas State Historical Association Quarterly*, XI (Apr. 1908), 301; Charles F. Ritter, "The Press in Florida, Louisiana, and South Carolina and the End of Reconstruction 1865–1877: Southern Men with Northern Interests" (Ph. D. diss., Catholic University, 1976), 66–67; Yorkville *Enquirer*, Feb. 14, 1867.

17. For a review and critique of this literature, see Harold D. Woodman, "Sequel to Slavery: The New History Views the Postbellum South," *Journal of Southern History*, XLIII (Nov. 1977), 523–54.

18. *Proceedings of the Annual Convention of the South Carolina Agricultural*

and Mechanical Society (Charleston, 1869), 7. There is a striking discussion of this point in Barbara J. Fields, "The Maryland Way from Slavery to Freedom" (Ph. D. diss., Yale University, 1978), 133–34.

19. Richard Fuke, "Black Marylanders, 1864–1868" (Ph. D. diss., University of Chicago, 1973), 26; Kemp P. Battle to Benjamin S. Hedrick, Jan. 20, 1866, Benjamin S. Hedrick Papers, Perkins Library, Duke University.

20. Fields, "The Maryland Way," 200–203; Will Martin to Governor Benjamin G. Humphreys, Dec. 5, 1865, Mississippi Governors' Papers, Mississippi Department of Archives; Reverend Samuel Agnew Diary, Nov. 3, 1865, Southern Historical Collection, University of North Carolina; Charles Colcock Jones, Jr. to Eva Jones, Nov. 7, 1865, Charles Colcock Jones, Jr. Collection, University of Georgia; Bt. Brig. Gen. Jno. B. Callis to General ?, Dec. 28, 1867, Alabama file, Letters Received by Thomas D. Eliot of House Committee on Freedmen's Affairs (ser. 18), Commissioner, RG 105, N.A.

21. Ulrich B. Phillips, ed., "The Correspondence of Robert Toombs, Alexander H. Stephens, and Howell Cobb," American Historical Association *Annual Report*, 1911, II, 684; Lt. James M. Babcock to Maj. G. D. Reynolds, Nov. 30, 1865, B-8 (1865), Registered Letters Received (ser. 2268), Actg. Asst. Comr. Southern Dist. of Miss., Natchez, RG 105, N.A.

22. Henry Watson, Jr. to Julia Watson, Dec. 16, 1865, Henry Watson, Jr. Papers, Perkins Library, Duke University; Elias H. Deas to daughter, Oct. 20, 1866, Elias H. Deas Papers, South Caroliniana Library, University of South Carolina. Cf. Roger L. Ransom and Richard Sutch, *One Kind of Freedom* (New York, 1977), 44–46.

23. *Nation*, Oct. 5, 1865; Rupert S. Holland, ed., *Letters and Diary of Laura M. Towne* (Cambridge, 1912), 9, 16–20; Elizabeth W. Pearson, ed., *Letters from Port Royal Written at the Time of the Civil War* (Boston, 1906), 181; Edward B. Heyward, undated, incomplete letter, Heyward Family Papers, South Caroliniana Library, University of South Carolina.

24. H. L. Tafft to Lt. Col. H. B. Clitz, Oct. 19, 1865, B-69 (1865), Letters Received (ser. 4109), Dept. of the South, Records of U.S. Army Continental Commands, Part 1, Record Group 393, National Archives; P. Sidney Post to "My dear Sir," Nov. 27, 1867, P. Sidney Post Papers, Knox College, Galesburg, Ill.; Willie Lee Rose, *Rehearsal for Reconstruction: The Port Royal Experiment* (Indianapolis, 1964), 37–38, 50, 128, 217–18, 301; Pearson, ed., *Letters*, 275.

25. Willard Range, *A Century of Georgia Agriculture, 1850–1950* (Athens, 1954), 7–8; H. C. Nixon, *Lower Piedmont Country* (New York, 1946), 10; Rose, *Rehearsal for Reconstruction*, 303, 382.

26. T. J. Woofter, Jr., *Black Yeomanry: Life on St. Helena Island* (New

York, 1930), 45, 117, 136–37, 140–45; Contract, Dec. 11, 1872, Albert A. Batchelor Papers, Department of Archives and Manuscripts, Louisiana State University; Brooks, *Agrarian Revolution*, 60. Cf. Ronald Davis, "Good and Faithful Labor: A Study in the Origins, Development, and Economics of Southern Sharecropping" (Ph. D. diss., University of Missouri, 1974), 123, which reports that in the Natchez District in 1880, 85 per cent of renters grew corn, while only 50 per cent of sharecroppers did.

27. Joe B. Wilkins, Jr., "Window on Freedom: The South's Response to the Emancipation of the Slaves in the British West Indies, 1833–1861" (Ph. D. diss., University of South Carolina, 1977); Lewis M. Ayres to D. H. Jacques, Dec. 26, 1865, Lewis M. Ayres Papers, South Caroliniana Library, University of South Carolina; John H. Moore, ed., *The Juhl Letters to the 'Charleston Courier'* (Athens, 1974), 69–70.

28. C. Vann Woodward, "The Price of Freedom," in *What Was Freedom's Price?*, ed., David L. Sansing (Jackson, 1978), 98–106; Pete Daniel, "The Metamorphosis of Slavery, 1865–1900," *Journal of American History*, LXVI (June 1979), 88–99; Gwendolyn M. Hall, *Social Control in Slave Plantation Societies* (Baltimore, 1971), 120–22; Philip Curtin, *The Two Jamaicas* (Cambridge, 1955), 104–9; Vernon Burton, "Race and Reconstruction: Edgefield County, South Carolina," *Journal of Social History*, XII (Fall 1978), 36.

29. Edmund S. Morgan, *American Slavery, American Freedom* (New York, 1975); Louisville *Democrat* in Columbia *Daily Phoenix*, Aug. 3, 1866; James L. Owens, "The Negro in Georgia During Reconstruction 1864–1872" (Ph. D. diss., University of Georgia, 1975), 63; Selma *Southern Argus*, Feb. 24, June 23, 1870; Michael S. Wayne, "Ante-Bellum Planters in the Post-Bellum South: The Natchez District, 1860–1880" (Ph. D. diss., Yale University, 1979), 86.

30. William Ivy Hair, *Bourbonism and Agrarian Protest: Louisiana Politics 1877–1900* (Baton Rouge, 1969), 46, Cf. *Rural Carolinian*, I (Oct. 1869), 52: "Land is the one thing that we have in abundance."

31. Robert A. Gilmour, "The Other Emancipation: Studies in the Society and Economy of Alabama Whites During Reconstruction" (Ph. D. diss., Johns Hopkins University, 1972), 119; Sam Nostlethwaite to James A. Gillespie, Mar. 14, 1869, James A. Gillespie Papers, Department of Archives and Manuscripts, Louisiana State University.

32. See Pearson, ed., *Letters*, 147.

33. Robert W. Fogel and Stanley L. Engerman, *Time on the Cross* (2 vols: Boston, 1974); Eugene D. Genovese, *The Political Economy of Slavery* (New York, 1965); Barrington Moore, Jr., *Social Origins of Dictatorship and Democracy* (Boston, 1966), 121.

34. Grady McWhiney, "The Revolution in Nineteenth-Century Alabama Agriculture," *Alabama Review*, XXXI (Jan. 1978), 3–32. See also Nixon, *Lower Piedmont*, 54–56, and the excellent discussion in

Stephen H. Hahn, "The Roots of Southern Populism: Yeoman Farmers and the Transformation of Georgia's Upper Piedmont, 1850–1890" (Ph. D. diss., Yale University, 1979).

35. Gordon B. McKinney, *Southern Mountain Republicans 1865–1900* (Chapel Hill, 1978); Otto H. Olsen, "Reconsidering the Scalawags," *Civil War History*, XII (Dec. 1966), 304–20; William C. Harris, "A Reconsideration of the Mississippi Scalawag," *Journal of Mississippi History*, XXXII (Feb. 1970), 3–42.

36. Gilmour, "The Other Emancipation," 63–68, 114, 130–44; Frank J. Huffman, "Old South, New South: Continuity and Change in a Georgia County, 1850–1880" (Ph. D. diss., Yale University, 1974), 71, 222; Joe Gray Taylor, *Louisiana Reconstructed 1863–1877* (Baton Rouge, 1974), 382; *Annual Message of Gov. J. L. Alcorn to the Mississippi Legislature, Session of 1871* (Jackson, 1871), 28; Gavin Wright, *The Political Economy of the Cotton South* (New York, 1978), 164.

37. William D. Cotton, "Appalachian North Carolina: A Political Study, 1860–1899" (Ph. D. diss., University of North Carolina, 1954), 51; John H. Cain to Governor Rufus Bullock, May 10, 1870, Rufus Bullock Papers, Georgia Department of Archives and History; T. W. Alexander *et al.* to Herschel V. Johnson, Feb. 11, 1868, Herschel V. Johnson Papers, Perkins Library, Duke University. Cf. Kenneth E. St. Clair, "Debtor Relief in North Carolina During Reconstruction," *North Carolina Historical Review*, XVIII (July 1941), 215–35.

38. Carol K. R. Bleser, *The Promised Land* (Columbia, 1970); William C. Harris, *The Day of the Carpetbagger: Republican Reconstruction in Mississippi* (Baton Rouge, 1979), 507.

39. William C. Carson *et al.* to General George G. Meade, Jan. 1868, C55 (1868), Letters Received (ser. 5783), Third Military District, Record Group 393, National Archives; Harold D. Woodman, "Post-Civil War Southern Agriculture and the Law," *Agricultural History*, LIII (Jan. 1979), 21; Peter Kolchin, *First Freedom* (Westport, 1972), 45; Joel Williamson, *After Slavery* (Chapel Hill, 1965), 148–59; Jackson *Weekly Mississippi Pilot*, Aug. 29, 1870, Jan. 23, 1875; R. H. Woody, "The Labor and Immigration Problems of South Carolina During Reconstruction," *Mississippi Valley Historical Review*, XVIII (Sept. 1931), 200; *Rural Carolinian*, III (Mar. 1872), 335.

40. Thomas Holt, *Black Over White* (Urbana, 1977), 152–53; Burton, "Race and Reconstruction," 38–39; Ralph I. Middleton to Henry A. Middleton, Aug. 24, 1869, Middleton Papers, Langdon Cheves Collection; W. H. Robert to Governor Daniel H. Chamberlain, Dec. 9, 1874, South Carolina Governor's Papers.

41. James W. Garner, *Reconstruction in Mississippi* (New York, 1901), 307–8; Selma *Southern Argus*, Feb. 3, 1870; Range, *Century of Georgia Agriculture*, 73; Frances Butler Leigh, *Ten Years on a Georgia Plantation Since the War* (London, 1883), 131–32. Cf. M. W.

Hungerford to Governor Rufus Bullock, Dec. 6, 1868, Georgia Governors' Papers, Georgia Department of Archives and History, for an instance of a white justice of the peace ruling for a black in a dispute concerning the division of a crop.

42. Beale, "Rewriting Reconstruction History," 827; Hiram Cassidy to Oscar J. Stuart, Aug. 23, 1871, Oscar J. Stuart Papers, Mississippi Department of Archives; *A Statement of Dr. Bratton's Case* (London, Ont., 1872), 8; James C. Mohr, ed., *Radical Republicans in the North* (Baltimore, 1976), xiv.

43. Charleston *Daily Republican*, July 28, 1870; *The Republican Platform!* (broadside, Savannah, 1873), Bryant Papers.

44. Eric Foner, "Thaddeus Stevens, Confiscation, and Reconstruction" [essay VII in this collection]; Edmund L. Drago, "Black Georgia During Reconstruction" (Ph. D. diss., University of California, Berkeley, 1975), 133–44; Charles Vincent, *Black Legislators in Louisiana During Reconstruction* (Baton Rouge, 1976), 98–101; Charleston *Daily Republican*, Nov. 30, 1869, Feb. 17, 1871; W. H. Robert to Governor Daniel H. Chamberlain, Dec. 9, 1874, South Carolina Governors' Papers.

45. Wiener, *Social Origins;* Kenneth G. Greenberg, "The Civil War and the Redistribution of Land: Adams County, Mississippi, 1860–1870," *Agricultural History*, XXV (Apr. 1978), 292–307; A. Jane Townes, "The Effect of Emancipation on Large Landholdings, Nelson and Goochland Counties, Virginia," *Journal of Southern History*, XLV (Aug. 1979), 403–12.

46. *Rural Carolinian*, II (Jan. 1871), 195, III (Jan. 1872), 173; Selma *Southern Argus*, Feb. 17, 1870. Cf. Jeffrey M. Paige, *Agrarian Revolution* (New York, 1975), 17.

47. *Rural Carolinian*, II (July 1871), 573; *Southern Field and Factory*, I (Mar. 1871), 116; Kolchin, *First Freedom*, 47; Selma *Southern Argus*, Feb. 17, 1870; Brooks, *Agrarian Revolution*, 52–54 (but see Drago, "Black Georgia," 246–56, challenging Brooks's contention); Savannah *Morning News*, Jan. 30, 1869; J. Carlyle Sitterson, *Sugar Country* (Lexington, 1953), 243–44; Harris, *Day of the Carpetbagger*, 277; Frank B. Conner to Lemuel P. Conner, Feb. 3, 1867, Lemuel P. Conner Family Papers, Department of Archives and Manuscripts, Louisiana State University; Charleston *News and Courier*, July 8, 1873.

48. Wiener, *Social Origins*, 71; Ralph I. Middleton to Henry A. Middleton, Feb. 8, 1870, May 2, 1872, Middleton Papers, Langdon Cheves Collection; *Rural Carolinian*, II (Mar. 1871), 324, III (Feb. 1872), 229.

49. Selma *Southern Argus*, Feb. 3, 1870; *Rural Carolinian*, I (Nov. 1869), 71; Yorkville *Enquirer*, Apr. 2, 1868; Frank B. Conner to Lemuel P. Conner, May 16, 1867, Lemuel P. Conner Family Papers; George W. Hagins to Henry Watson, Jr., Sept. 8, 1867, Henry Watson, Jr. Papers.

50. W. R. Jones to Governor William H. Smith, Aug. 9, 1870, Alabama Governors' Papers, Alabama Department of Archives and History; Affidavit of Eli Barnes, Nov. 20, 1869, Georgia Governors' Papers; P. C. Cudd to Governor Robert K. Scott, May 17, 1867, South Carolina Governors' Papers. Cf. J. C. A. Stagg, "The Problem of Klan Violence: The South Carolina Up-Country, 1868–1871," *Journal of American Studies*, VIII (1974), 303–18.

51. Harris, *Day of the Carpetbagger*, 482; Wayne, "Natchez District," 288; Nellie Morton to Rev. Gustavus D. Pike, Apr. 7, 1871, American Missionary Association Archives, Amistad Research Center, Dillard University.

52. *Proceedings of the Tax-Payers' Convention of South Carolina* (Charleston, 1874), 12–13, 51.

53. J. G. deRoulhac Hamilton, ed., *The Correspondence of Jonathan Worth* (2 vols.: Raleigh, 1909), II, 1155–56, 1185, 1217–18; Elizabeth McPherson, ed., "Letters from North Carolina to Andrew Johnson," *North Carolina Historical Review*, XXIX (Jan. 1952), 110–11.

54. S. S. Ashley to Bro. Woodworth, Jan. 1, 1869 (dated 1868), American Missionary Association Archives; Daniel E. Huger Smith *et al.*, eds., *Mason Smith Family Letters 1860–1868* (Columbia, 1950), 236; Rev. Samuel Agnew Diary, Nov. 3, 1865. Ironically, this new, truncated definition of freedom as simply self-ownership had already been promoted by certain abolitionists before the Civil War. See Eric Foner, "Abolitionism and the Labor Movement in Antebellum America" [essay III in this collection].

55. *Address of the Democratic White Voters of Charleston to the Colored Voters of Charleston, The Seaboard, and of the State Generally* (Charleston, 1868), 3–4; Mrs. C. M. Cheves to Henry A. Middleton, Aug. 26, 1868, Middleton Papers, Langdon Cheves Collection; "Letter of William Henry Trescot on Reconstruction in South Carolina, 1867," *American Historical Review*, XV (Apr. 1910), 574–82; Sarah Woolfolk Wiggins, *The Scalawag in Alabama Politics, 1865–1881* (University, Ala., 1977), 34; Savannah *Morning News*, Aug. 19, 1873.

56. C. Vann Woodward, *The Strange Career of Jim Crow* (New York, 1955); Savannah *Advertiser and Republican*, Aug. 17, 1873; Beaufort *Tribune*, May 10, 1877.

57. Alrutheus A. Taylor, *The Negro in South Carolina During the Reconstruction* (Washington, 1924), 263–64; Frenise A. Logan, *The Negro in North Carolina 1876–1894* (Chapel Hill, 1964), 49–50; William W. Rogers, *The One-Gallused Rebellion* (Baton Rouge, 1970), 28; William Cohen, "Negro Involuntary Servitude in the South, 1865–1940: A Preliminary Analysis," *Journal of Southern History*, XLII (Feb. 1976), 34–35; Woodman, "Post Civil War Southern Agriculture," 319–37; *Address to the Voters of North Carolina* (Raleigh, 1875).

58. Powhaten Lockett to Joseph Wheeler, Jan. 1, 1876, Joseph Wheeler Papers, Alabama Department of Archives and History; William Eaton to David S. Reid, Sept. 20, 1875, David S. Reid Papers, North Carolina Department of Archives; E. Merton Coulter, *Negro Legislators in Georgia During the Reconstruction Period* (Athens, 1968), 143–70 (an account strongly biased against Campbell); *Sufferings of the Rev. T. G. Campbell and His Family, in Georgia* (Washington, 1877); New York *Commercial and Financial Chronicle*, in *Appleton's Annual Cyclopedia*, n. s., II (1877), 231.
59. New York *Times*, Apr. 26, 1875; Robbins Little to John E. Bryant, July 10, 1875, Bryant Papers.
60. Mohr, *Radical Republicans*, xv; A. W. Spies to Governor James L. Orr, Nov. 30, 1866, South Carolina Governors' Papers; New York *Commercial and Financial Chronicle*, Jan. 18, 1868; Robbins Little to John E. Bryant, July 10, 1875, Bryant Papers. Cf. the classic analysis by William D. Hesseltine, "Economic Factors in the Abandonment of Reconstruction," *Mississippi Valley Historical Review*, XXII (1935), 191–210.
61. See David Montgomery, *Beyond Equality* (New York, 1967); Alfred D. Chandler, *The Visible Hand: The Managerial Revolution in American Business* (Cambridge, 1977); John G. Sproat, *"The Best Men"* (New York, 1968). Relevant to the breakup of the Radical coalition is Ellen DuBois, *Feminism and Suffrage* (Ithaca, 1978).
62. Morgan, *American Slavery, American Freedom;* Charleston *News and Courier*, July 28, 1877. Herbert G. Gutman, *Work, Culture, and Society in Industrializing America* (New York, 1976), suggests the centrality of the problem of labor discipline in the North in these years.

VII THADDEUS STEVENS

1. "The American Constitution and the Impeachment of the President," *Blackwood's Edinburgh Magazine*, CIII (June 1868), 717; Springfield *Weekly Republican*, Aug. 15, 1868. Young Georges Clemenceau, reporting American events for a Paris newspaper, was much taken with Stevens, describing him as the "Robespierre" of one of the "most radical revolutions known to history." Clemenceau, *American Reconstruction 1865–1870*, ed. Fernand Baldensperger (New York, 1928), 77, 79, 165, 227.
2. For descriptions of Stevens's personality, see George Fort Milton, *The Age of Hate* (New York, 1930), 263–64; J. W. Binckley, "The Leader of the House," *The Galaxy*, I (July 1866), 494; *The Reminiscences of Carl Schurz* (3 vols.: New York, 1907–8), III, 213–14. Ms biographical sketch, probably by Edward McPherson, Thaddeus Stevens Papers, Library of Congress. For his pre-war political career, see Richard N. Current, *Old Thad Stevens: A Story of Am-*

bition (Madison, 1942), chs. 2–9; Fawn Brodie, *Thaddeus Stevens, Scourge of the South* (New York, 1959), chs. 4–12.

3. Roy F. Basler *et al.*, eds., *The Collected Works of Abraham Lincoln* (9 vols.: New Brunswick, 1953–55), V, 49; J. A. Woodburn, "The Attitude of Thaddeus Stevens Toward the Conduct of the Civil War," *American Historical Review*, XII (Apr. 1907), 567–68; *Congressional Globe*, 37 Congress, 1 Session, 414; 3 Session, 239; 38 Congress, 1 Session, 316; 2 Session, 126; Alexander K. McClure, *Abraham Lincoln and Men of War-Times* (Philadelphia, 1892), 265.

4. William A. Dunning, *Reconstruction, Political and Economic, 1865–1877* (New York, 1907), 64; Justin S. Morrill, "Notable Letters from My Political Friends," *The Forum*, XXIV (1897–98), 141; James G. Blaine, *Memorial Address on the Life and Character of James Abram Garfield* (Washington, 1882), 10–11; W. R. Brock, *An American Crisis* (London, 1963), 62–68, *Congressional Globe*, 37 Congress, 2 Session, 2054.

5. Brooks M. Kelley, "Simon Cameron and the Senatorial Nomination of 1867," *Pennsylvania Magazine of History and Biography*, LXXXVII (Oct. 1963), 366–67, 388–89; Boston *Advertiser*, Aug. 13, 1868; David Donald, *The Politics of Reconstruction, 1863–1867* (Baton Rouge, 1965), 81; Eric L. McKitrick, *Andrew Johnson and Reconstruction* (Chicago, 1960), 260–68, and *passim*.

6. Cincinnati *Commercial*, Jan. 1, 1866; *Congressional Globe*, 39 Congress, 1 Session, 2544; Woodburn, "Stevens and the Conduct of the War," 571–72; Lancaster *Express*, Sept. 8, 1865. Cf. the assessments of Stevens's leadership in New York *Tribune*, Dec. 19, 1865; New York *Evening Post*, Apr. 3, 1866; *Nation*, Jan. 24, 1867.

7. McKitrick, *Andrew Jackson and Reconstruction*, 268; Charles R. Williams ed., *Diary and Letters of Rutherford Burchard Hayes*, (5 vols.: Columbus, 1922–26), III, 9.

8. Walter L. Fleming, " 'Forty Acres and a Mule,' " *North American Review*, CLXXXIII (May 1906), 721–37; T. Harry Williams, *Lincoln and the Radicals* (Madison, 1941), 26–27; James G. Randall, *Constitutional Problems Under Lincoln*, rev. ed. (Urbana, 1964), 276–80; Leonard P. Curry, *Blueprint for Modern America* (Nashville, 1968), 85, 95–99; *Congressional Globe*, 37 Congress, 2 Session, 3400.

9. *Congressional Globe*, 38 Congress, 1 Session, 19, 519; 2 Session, 1025–26; LaWanda Cox, "The Promise of Land for the Freedmen," *Mississippi Valley Historical Review*, XLV (Dec. 1958), 413–19, 431–35; Patrick W. Riddleberger, "George Washington Julian: Abolitionist Land Reformer," *Agricultural History*, XXIX (July 1955), 109–10; Fleming, " 'Forty Acres,' " 722–25; Randall, *Constitutional Problems*, 284–86, 316–17.

10. Eric Foner, *Free Soil, Free Labor, Free Men: The Ideology of the Republican Party Before the Civil War* (New York, 1970).

11. *Congressional Globe*, 39 Congress, 1 Session, 536.

12. George S. Merriam, *The Life and Times of Samuel Bowles*, (2 vols.: New York, 1885), II, 125; Benjamin B. Kendrick, *The Journal of the Joint Committee of Fifteen on Reconstruction* (New York, 1914), 92–105; *Congressional Globe*, 39 Congress, 1 Session, 2460, 2544.

13. *Congressional Globe*, 39 Congress, 1 Session, 2459; 40 Congress, 1 Session, 205; Benjamin W. Arnett, ed., *Duplicate Copy of the Souvenir from the Afro-American League of Tennessee to Hon. James M. Ashley of Ohio* (Philadelphia, 1894), 407–8; Riddleberger, "Julian," 108–114; Benjamin F. Butler, *Butler's Book* (Boston, 1892), 908–9, 961; *National Anti-Slavery Standard*, Nov. 17, 1866. For Sumner's complex views on the relative importance of land and the suffrage, see David Donald, *Charles Sumner and the Rights of Man* (New York, 1970), 119–20, 201; Edward L. Pierce, *Memoir and Letters of Charles Sumner*, (4 vols.: Boston, 1877–93), IV, 76, 229, 247–60; *The Works of Charles Sumner* (10 vols.: Boston, 1870–83), IV, 275; X, 220–25; XIII, 320–21.

14. *Congressional Globe*, 31 Congress, 1 Session, Appendix, 141–43; 40 Congress, 1 Session, 205. A self-made man himself, Stevens once described his social ideals as those of "the honest farmer, mechanic or laborer," as opposed to both the aristocrat and the "vagabond, the idle and dissipated." The prosperous yeomen of Lancaster County, Pennsylvania, were the bedrock of his political strength. Stevens assumed that black yeoman farmers would act pretty much as white farmers did. He did not view the freedmen, just emerging from slavery, as members of a distinct culture who might react in unpredictable ways to economic stimuli. Where blacks were allowed the choice, there were already signs of a reluctance to cultivate the "slave crop" cotton for the market, and a tendency to retreat into self-sufficiency. Black farmers might, in other words, have turned out to be quite different from the market-oriented farmers of the North idealized by Stevens. *Proceedings and Debates of the Convention of the Commonwealth of Pennsylvania, to Propose Amendments to the Constitution . . .* (14 vols.: Philadelphia, 1837–38), III, 167; Lancaster *Express*, Feb. 7, 1866; Joel Williamson, *After Slavery* (Chapel Hill, 1965), 44; Willie Lee Rose, *Rehearsal for Reconstruction* (Indianapolis, 1964), 82, 170, 226.

15. *Congressional Globe*, 39 Congress, 2 Session, 1317; *Reconstruction: Speech of the Hon. Thaddeus Stevens, Delivered in the City of Lancaster, September 7, 1865* (Lancaster, 1865), 2–5; *National Anti-Slavery Standard*, June 15, 1867.

16. Joseph Schafer, ed., *Intimate Letters of Carl Schurz, 1841–1869* (Madison, 1928), 341; William B. Hesseltine, "Economic Factors in the Abandonment of Reconstruction," *Mississippi Valley Historical Review*, XXII (Sept. 1935), 191–210; Philadelphia *Public Ledger*, Jan. 23, 1866; Cincinnati *Gazette*, Dec. 2, 1865; New York *Times*, Aug. 18, Nov. 2, 14, Dec. 18, 1865; Jan. 4, 15, 17, Sept. 2, 1866. Cf. Thomas Wagstaff, "Call Your Old Master—'Master': Southern

Political Leaders and Negro Labor During Presidential Reconstruction," *Labor History*, X (Summer 1969), 323–45.

17. Earle D. Ross, "Horace Greeley and the South," *South Atlantic Quarterly*, XVI (Oct. 1917), 333–34; New York *Tribune*, Sept. 12, 29, Oct. 11, 1865; *Nation*, Nov. 8, 1866; William D. Kelley, *Speeches, Addresses and Letters on Industrial and Financial Questions* (Philadelphia, 1872), 182–83; Robert Sharkey, *Money, Class, and Party* (Baltimore, 1959), 165–66.

18. *Congressional Globe*, 38 Congress, 1 Session, 1187–88, 2251. When Stevens pressed the confiscation issue in 1867, his proposal included a prohibition of the sale of lands in plots exceeding 500 acres, an attempt to prevent the engrossment of large tracts of land by northern speculators. *Congressional Globe*, 40 Congress, 1 Session, 203.

19. *Congressional Globe*, 39 Congress, 1 Session, 3240–41, 3687–88, 2 Session, 985; New York *Tribune*, Mar. 23, 1867; John J. McCarthy, "Reconstruction Legislation and Voting Alignments in the House of Representatives, 1863–1869" (Ph. D. diss., Yale University, 1970), 263.

20. J. Williamson to Thomas A. Jenckes, Feb. 16, 1866, Thomas A. Jenckes Papers, Library of Congress. For views of Stevens as an agent of northern capitalists, see Current, *Stevens*, and Williams, *Lincoln and the Radicals*. Of course, as Sharkey shows in *Money, Class and Party*, northern capitalists were hardly unanimous on political and economical questions.

21. *Reconstruction—Lancaster Speech;* J. W. McClurg to Stevens, Sept. 27, 1865; Joseph Bailey to Stevens, Sept. 22, 1865, Stevens Papers; *Congressional Globe*, 39 Congress, 1 Session, 104; 39 Congress, 1 Session, House Executive Document No. 99; New York *Times*, May 5, 1866.

22. *Congressional Globe*, 39 Congress, 1 Session, 655, 658, 748, 1966; William S. McFeely, *Yankee Stepfather, General O. O. Howard and the Freedmen* (New Haven, 1968), 213–20, 226–29; Christie Farnham Pope, "Southern Homesteads for Negroes," *Agricultural History*, XLIV (Apr. 1970), 202–5; Warren Hofnagle, "The Southern Homestead Act: Its Origins and Operation," *Historian*, XXXII (Aug. 1970), 615–29.

23. McFeely, *Yankee Stepfather*, 229–31; New York *Herald*, Feb. 8, 1866; *Congressional Globe*, 37 Congress, 2 Session, 243.

24. *Nation*, Feb. 21, 1867.

25. New York *Times*, Feb. 2, 1866.

26. *Congressional Globe*, 40 Congress, 1 Session, 49, 203; Springfield *Weekly Republican*, Mar. 23, 1867; New York *Times*, Mar. 13, June 7, 12, 1867; *Sumner Works*, XI, 124–29; *National Anti-Slavery Standard*, June 15, 22, 1867; James M. McPherson, *The Struggle for Equality* (Princeton, 1964), 411; Chicago *Tribune*, July 18, 1867; Philadelphia *Press*, Mar. 21, May 8, 1867; Boston *Advertiser*, Apr.

27, 1867; Philadelphia *North American and United States Gazette,* Mar. 14, 16, May 1, 27, 1867.

27. New York *Times,* May 29, June 2, 1867. See New York *Herald,* May 2, 1866, attributing Steven's confiscation proposals to his desire for compensation for the burning of his iron works.

28. Cincinnati *Commercial,* July 25, 1867; *Nation,* Mar. 21, May 9, 16, 1867; New York *Times,* Feb. 19, Mar. 10, Apr. 10, June 27, 1867. Cf. Springfield *Weekly Republican,* Apr. 27, June 15, 1867.

29. New York *Times,* July 9, 1867. Cf. Boston *Advertiser,* June 13, 1867; "The Agrarians—Division of Property," *De Bow's Review,* n.s., IV (Dec. 1867), 586–88.

30. *Nation,* June 27, 1867; Philadelphia *Press,* May 3, 16, 1867; Cincinnati *Commercial,* Apr. 15, June 5, 1867; E. L. Godkin, "The Labor Crisis," *North American Review,* CV (July 1867), 199. In New York, the month of May witnessed strikes involving railroad workers, masons, hod carriers, stablemen, printers, carpenters, and shoemakers. New York *Tribune,* May 13, 14, 16, 18, 1867.

31. William F. Zornow, " 'Bluff Ben' Wade in Lawrence, Kansas: The Issue of Class Conflict," *Ohio Historical Quarterly,* XLV (Jan. 1956), 44–52; New York *Times,* June 12, 20, July 1, 1867; Felice A. Bonadio, *North of Reconstruction: Ohio Politics, 1865–1870* (New York, 1970), 148–49.

32. Springfield *Weekly Republican,* Mar. 18, 1867; New York *Tribune,* Mar. 21, 23, 1867; New York *Times,* June 10, 1867. Cf. Cincinnati *Commercial,* Apr. 12, 1867; Springfield *Weekly Republican,* Apr. 27, 1867; New York *Times,* Apr. 30, May 13, 20, June 13, Aug. 21, 1867.

33. Philadelphia *North American and United States Gazette,* July 1, 1867; J. H. Rea to Stevens, Jan. 9, 1866; Henry W. McVay to Stevens, Mar. 1, 1867; P. H. Whitehurst to Stevens, Mar. 22, 1867, Stevens Papers; William Birthright to John Broomall, July 14, 1867, John Broomall Papers, Historical Society of Pennsylvania; Raleigh *Standard,* cited in New York *Times,* Apr. 10, 1867; Philadelphia *Press,* cited in New York *Times,* May 30, 1867; Boston *Advertiser,* June 25, 1867; Washington *Daily Morning Chronicle,* Dec. 13, 1867.

34. Boston *Advertiser,* June 13, 1867; New York *Times,* Apr. 8, 19, May, 2, 18, 30, June 12, 1867; New York *Tribune,* Apr. 20, 24, 1867; Hamilton J. Eckenrode, *The Political History of Virginia During the Reconstruction* (Baltimore, 1904), 67; Alrutheus A. Taylor, *The Negro in the Reconstruction of Virginia* (Washington, 1926), 209–12.

35. New York *Tribune,* Apr. 25, May 6, 17, 27, June 10, 1867; New York *Times,* Apr. 24, 1867; Chicago *Tribune,* July 17, 1867; Jack P. Maddex, *The Virginia Conservatives, 1867–1879* (Chapel Hill, 1970), 53.

36. New York *Times,* Apr. 28, May 24, 29, June 22, 1867; New York *Herald,* July 8, 1867; New York *Tribune,* May 23, 1867; Boston *Advertiser,* May 25, 1867.

37. New York *Tribune*, Mar. 26, Apr. 30, 1867; New York *Times*, June 22, July 31, Sept. 9, 19, 27, 1867; *Nation*, Aug. 8, 1867; J. G. de Roulhac Hamilton, *Reconstruction in North Carolina* (New York, 1914), 245–47.
38. Ellis P. Oberholtzer, *Jay Cooke, Financier of the Civil War*, (2 vols.: Philadelphia, 1907), II, 28; Sharkey, *Money, Class, and Party*, 95, 119; Mary L. Hinsdale, ed., *Garfield-Hinsdale Letters* (Ann Arbor, 1949), 112. Cf. Springfield *Weekly Republican*, Oct. 26, 1867; *Harper's Weekly*, Oct. 26, 1867; Philadelphia *North American and United States Gazette*, Oct. 11, 1867; Michael Les Benedict, "The Rout of Radicalism: Republicans and the Election of 1867," *Civil War History*, XVIII (Dec. 1972), 334–44.
39. New York *Tribune*, Aug. 14, 1868; *Independent*, Aug. 27, 1868; Brock, *American Crisis*, 282; Philadelphia *Press*, Aug. 12, 1868; George F. Hoar, *Autobiography of Seventy Years*, (2 vols.: New York, 1903), I, 239. Shortly before his death, Stevens predicted that in the future southern whites would bar black voting by adopting property qualifications "applicable to all classes alike, which would reach down to just about the black line," and he condemned the emerging sharecropping and crop lien systems, *Congressional Globe*, 40 Congress, 2 Session, 108, 1966, 2214.
40. In *Beyond Equality* (New York, 1967), an important contribution to the historiography of Reconstruction, David Montgomery has argued that radical Republicanism broke up in the late 1860s under the impact of forces outside Reconstruction, particularly the emergence of a class-conscious labor movement whose demands challenged the radicals' vision of a harmonious social order founded on equality before the law. Montgomery, however, ignores the fact that all the challenges he cites, from the danger of class legislation to the radicals' inability to move beyond "equality before the law," were present in an issue at the core of Reconstruction—confiscation. Cf. W. E. B. Du Bois, *Black Reconstruction* (New York, 1935), a frustrating, flawed, but monumental study which deserves careful reading by anyone interested in Reconstruction. Chapter 14 discusses the decline of radicalism.

VIII   THE LAND LEAGUE AND IRISH-AMERICA

1. *Irish World* (New York City), Feb. 16, 23, 1884; *United Irishman* (New York City), Feb. 16, 1884; Charles F. Horner, *The Life of James Redpath and the Development of the Modern Lyceum* (New York, 1926), 297–99.
2. Arnold Schrier, *Ireland and the American Emigration 1850–1900* (Minneapolis, 1958), 4–8, 160; Oliver MacDonagh, "The Irish Famine Emigration to the United States," *Perspectives in American History*, X (1976), 357–446; Stanley Aronowitz, *False Promises* (New York, 1973), 146; Robert Ernst, *Immigrant Life in New York City*

1825–1863 (New York, 1949), 69–71; Oscar Handlin, *Boston's Immigrants* (New York, 1968 ed.), 216–217; *10th Census*, 1880, I, 465, 752–55, 865, 892.

3. Philip H. Bagenal, *Parnellism Unveiled* (Dublin, 1880), 2; David Doyle, "The Irish and American Labor 1880–1929," *Saothar: Journal of the Irish History Society*, I (1975), 42–53; David Doyle, *Irish Americans, Native Rights, and National Empires* (New York, 1976), ch. 2; David Montgomery, *Beyond Equality* (New York, 1966), 36; Daniel J. Walkowitz, "Statistics and the Writing of Working Class Culture: A Statistical Portrait of the Iron Workers in Troy, New York, 1860–1880," *Labor History*, XV (1974), 422, 439; Ira Rosenwaike, *Population History of New York City* (Syracuse, 1972), 71–73; Stephan Thernstrom, *Poverty and Progress* (New York, 1969 ed.), 110; Bruce Laurie, Theodore Herschberg, and George Alter, "Immigrants and Industry: The Philadelphia Experience, 1850–1880," *Journal of Social History*, IX (1975), 235–43.

4. Victor A. Walsh, "Class, Culture, and Nationalism: The Irish Catholics of Pittsburgh, 1870–1883" (unpublished seminar paper, University of Pittsburgh, 1976), 3–6, 53–76; Thernstrom, *Poverty and Progress*, 155–60, 177, 184; *10th Census*, I, 715–43; Douglas V. Shaw, "The Making of an Immigrant City: Ethnic and Cultural Conflict in Jersey City, New Jersey, 1850–1877" (Ph. D. diss., University of Rochester, 1972), 170; Dennis J. Clark, *The Irish in Philadelphia* (Philadelphia, 1973), 129, 136–37, 166.

5. *Freedman's Journal* (Dublin), Mar. 27, 1880; Philip H. Bagenal, *The American Irish and Their Influence on Irish Politics* (London, 1882), 126.

6. William D'Arcy, *The Fenian Movement in the United States* (Washington, 1947); Sir F. Bruce to Earl of Clarendon, Dec. 4, 1865, Clarendon Deposit, Bodleian Library, Oxford; John Devoy, *Recollections of an Irish Rebel* (New York, 1929), 26–30; L. M. Cullen, *Life in Ireland* (London, 1968), 146–51; E. M. Archibald to Earl of Derby, Feb. 9, 1877, F.O. 5/1599/55, Public Record Office, London; New York *Sunday Democrat*, June 11, 1876.

7. D'Arcy, *Fenian Movement*, 26–27, 102, 151; Marcus Bourke, *John O'Leary* (Tralee, 1967), 151; E. M. Archibald to Earl of Derby, Feb. 16, 1876, F.O. 5/1556/5; "Constitution of the V.C., 1877," F.O. 5/1706/12, Public Record Office; *The Land League* (New York City), Feb. 5, 1881.

8. T. W. Moody, "The New Departure in Irish Politics, 1878–9," in H. A. Cronne *et al.*, eds., *Essays in British and Irish History in Honour of James Eadre Todd* (London, 1949), 303–33; John Devoy, *The Land of Eire* (New York, 1882), 41–43; William O. Brien and Desmond Ryan, eds., *Devoy's Post-Bag 1871–1928* (2 vols.: London, 1948–53), I, 340–47.

9. New York *Gaelic-American*, Sept. 8, 1906; Barbara L. Solow, *The Land Question and the Irish Economy, 1870–1903* (Cambridge, 1971),

114-17, 122-27; Cormac Ó Gráda, "Post-Famine Adjustment: Essays in Nineteenth-Century Irish Economic History" (Ph. D. diss., Columbia University, 1973), 24-26, 44; Bernard Becker, *Disturbed Ireland* (London, 1881), 85-86; E. Cant-Wall, *Ireland Under the Land Act* (London, 1883), 153; Samuel Clark, "The Political Mobilization of Irish Farmers," *Canadian Review of Sociology and Anthropology*, XII (1975), 484; T. Wemyss Reid, *Life of the Right Honourable William Edward Forster* (2 vols.: London, 1880), II, 294-95.

10. R. Barry O'Brien, *The Life of Charles Stewart Parnell* (2 vols.: London, 1898), I, 204; *Freeman's Journal*, Mar. 27, 1880; Barbara M. Solomon, *Ancestors and Immigrants* (Cambridge, 1956), 55; James J. Greene, "American Catholics and the Irish Land League, 1879-1882," *Catholic Historical Review*, XXXV (1949), 19-42; *Speech Delivered by Michael Davitt in Defence of the Land League* (London, 1890), 105.

11. *United Ireland* (Dublin), Aug. 13, 1881; *Irish Nation* (New York City), Nov. 13, 1881; *Irish World*, Oct. 2, 1880.

12. E. M. Archibald to Foreign Secretary, May 14, 1880, F.O. 282/21/171, Public Record Office; Circular, Mar. 30, 1880, Terrence V. Powderly Papers, Catholic University of America; *The Land League*, Feb. 5, 1881; Michael F. Funchion, "Chicago's Irish Nationalists, 1881-1890" (Ph. D. diss., Loyola University of Chicago, 1973), 75-80.

13. James P. Rodechko, "Patrick Ford and His Search for America: A Case Study of Irish-American Journalism, 1870-1913" (Ph. D. diss., University of Connecticut, 1967); Rodechko, "An Irish-American Journalist and Catholicism: Patrick Ford and the Irish World," *Church History*, XLIX (1970), 524-40.

14. William O'Brien, *Recollections* (New York, 1905), 274; *Irish World*, Feb. 9, 1878; *Freeman's Journal*, Apr. 3, 1882; Samuel Gompers, *Seventy Years of Life and Labor* (2 vols.: New York, 1925), I, 80-82; II, 31-32; John M. Davis to Powderly, Apr. 26, 1880, Powderly Papers.

15. *Irish World*, Jan. 19, May 4, 25, June 15, 1878; May 29, 1879; Apr. 10, 1880; Jan. 29, July 30, Aug. 6, 1881; Mar. 4, 1882; Thomas N. Brown, *Irish-American Nationalism 1870-1890* (Philadelphia, 1966), 31.

16. The legacy of the abolitionist movement was far broader than indicated in James McPherson, *The Abolitionist Legacy* (Princeton, 1976).

17. Patrick Ford, "The Irish Vote in the Pending Presidential Election," *North American Review*, CXLVII (1888), 187; *Irish World*, Apr. 6, 1878; Jan. 15, 1881.

18. *Irish World*, Feb. 23, Apr. 27, May 4, 1878; Sept. 27, Nov. 15, Dec. 29, 1879; Feb. 21, Oct. 2, 16, Nov. 13, 20, 1880.

19. *Irish World*, Feb. 2, May 4, July 13, 20, 1878; Sept. 27, 1879; Oct.

9, 1880; Michael A. Gordon, "Studies in Irish and Irish-American Thought and Behavior in Gilded Age New York City" (Ph. D. diss., University of Rochester, 1977), 434; New York *Herald*, Oct. 10, 1879; Brown, *Irish-American Nationalism*, 50.

20. *Irish World*, Mar. 2, 1878; Jan. 17, Oct. 16, 1880; Jan 28, 1882; Oct. 16, 1886; New York *Gaelic-American*, June 23, 1906.

21. *Irish World*, July 19, Aug. 30, 1879; May 22, Oct. 2, 1880.

22. Bagenal, *American Irish*, 180; *Freeman's Journal*, Aug. 15, 1881; *Irish World*, Oct. 9, Nov. 13, 1880; James S. Donnelly, Jr., *The Land and the People of Nineteenth-Century Cork* (London, 1975), 248–49; O'Brien, *Recollections*, 273.

23. *Irish World*, Aug. 2, Nov. 8, 1879; Jan. 3, Mar. 6, May 8, 1880; Jan. 29, 1881; Feb. 25, 1882; Aug. 4, 1883; U.S. Senate, Committee on Education and Labor, *Report of the Committee of the Senate Upon Capital and Labor* (3 vols.: Washington, 1885), I, 843.

24. *Freeman's Journal*, Apr. 3, 1882; Robert F. Walsh, "The Boston Pilot: A Newspaper for the Irish Immigrant, 1829–1908" (Ph. D. diss., Boston University, 1968); New York *Gaelic-American*, June 23, 1906; William L. Joyce, "Editors and Ethnicity: A History of the Irish-American Press, 1848–1883" (Ph. D. diss., University of Michigan, 1974), 5, 161; Francis G. McManamin, "John Boyle O'Reilly, Social Reform Editor," *Mid-America*, XLIII (1961), 36–54; Devoy, *Recollections*, 152, 159.

25. Katherine E. Conway, "John Boyle O'Reilly," *The Catholic World*, LIII (1891), 211–16; James B. Cullen, *The Story of the Irish in Boston* (Boston, 1893), 310–13; Boston *Pilot*, June 28, 1879; Aug. 14, 1880; Brown, *Irish-American Nationalism*, 53–54; Joyce, "Editors and Ethnicity," 157–58, 187–88.

26. Arthur Mann, *Yankee Reformers in the Urban Age* (Cambridge, 1954), 27–39, 50; *Irish World*, Mar. 25, 1882.

27. F. S. L. Lyons, *Charles Stewart Parnell* (New York, 1977), 98; *The Irishman* (Dublin), May 1, 1880; Oct. 4, 1879.

28. Funchion, "Chicago," 126; O'Brien and Ryan, eds., *Devoy's Post-Bag*, I, 517, 520; *United Irishman*, Apr. 16, 23, 30, May 14, 1881; Mar. 18, 1882.

29. *Freeman's Journal*, Dec. 27, 1878; Thomas N. Brown, "The Origins and Character of Irish-American Nationalism," *Review of Politics*, XVIII (1956), 351–52; O'Brien and Ryan, eds., *Devoy's Post-Bag*, I, 10; II, 106; Devoy, *Recollections*, 25; *Irish Nation*, Mar. 11, June 24, 1882.

30. Gustavus Myers, *The History of Tammany Hall* (2nd ed., New York, 1917), 251–52; J. Fairfax McLaughlin, *The Life and Times of John Kelly, Tribune of the People* (New York, 1885); Alexander B. Callow, Jr., *The Tweed Ring* (New York, 1966), 62–75; Gordon, "Studies in Irish-American Thought," 387–88; Melvyn Dubofsky, *When Workers Organize* (Amherst, 1968), 21; New York *Times*, June 8, 1879.

31. *Irish World*, Oct. 25, 1879; Nathan Glazer and Daniel P. Moyni-

han, *Beyond the Melting Pot* (Cambridge, 1963), 229; Alfred Connable and Edward Silberfarb, *Tigers of Tammany* (New York, 1967), 188, 192; William V. Shannon, *The American Irish* (New York, 1966), 72–73; Matthew P. Breen, *Thirty Years of New York Politics* (New York, 1899), 623; New York *Star,* Mar. 3, 30, Apr. 1, May 9, 11, Nov. 15, 1880.

32. New York *Star,* Mar. 6, 1880; *Liberty* (New York City), Dec. 24, 1881; Joseph Denieffe, *A Personal Narrative of the Irish Revolutionary Brotherhood* (Shannon, 1969), 28.

33. *Irish Nation,* June 10, 1882; Michael Davitt, *The Fall of Feudalism in Ireland* (London and New York, 1904), 652–57; Eric Strauss, *Irish Nationalism and British Democracy* (New York, 1951), 173; Conor Cruise O'Brien, *Parnell and His Party* (Oxford, 1957), 59–74; *Irish World,* May 4, 1878; Feb. 22, 1879; Nov. 20, Dec. 18, 1880; Feb. 19, Apr. 23, 1881. On the issue of agricultural laborers, see Philip H. Bagenal, " 'Uncle Pat's Cabin,' " *The Nineteenth Century,* XII (1882), 925–38; Charlotte G. O'Brien, "The Irish 'Poor Man,' " *The Nineteenth Century,* VIII (1880), 876–87.

34. Donnelly, *Cork,* 4–7, 119, 130–31; Clark, "Political Mobilization," 494–95; T. Desmond Williams, ed., *Secret Societies in Ireland* (Dublin, 1973), 34. On the social base of the League, see also Sam Clark, "The Social Composition of the Land League," *Irish Historical Studies,* XVII (1971), 447–69; and for a convincing analysis of the relationship between famine and the development of capitalist agriculture, Claude Meillassoux, "Development or Exploitation: Is the Sahel Famine Good Business?," *Review of African Political Economy,* I (1974), 27–33.

35. Davitt, *Fall of Feudalism,* 257; *Speech by Davitt,* 106; Funchion, "Chicago," 129–32; Cullen, *Irish in Boston,* 331–33.

36. New York *Irish-American,* Jan. 28, 1882; *The Irishman,* Sept. 18, 1880; James J. Roche, *Life of John Boyle O'Reilly* (New York, 1891), 207–12; Boston *Pilot,* Nov. 5, Dec. 17, 1881; John Finerty to Patrick Collins, Nov. 9, 1881, Special Irish Collection, Boston College.

37. *Irish Nation,* Dec. 17, 1881; Feb. 25, Mar. 4, 11, 1882.

38. Joyce, "Editors and Ethnicity," 6–7; New York *Irish-American,* Aug. 23, 1879; Jan. 10, June 12, 1880; *Irish World,* Apr. 16, Dec. 3, 1881.

39. *Irish World,* Oct. 14, 1882; *Second Annual Convention of the Irish National Land League of the United States* (Buffalo, 1882), 19–20.

40. *Irish World,* Oct. 23, 1880; Apr. 16, 1881. The Irish Nationalist leader T. P. O'Connor believed that "a dollar sent through the *Irish World* is a significant endorsement of the principles enunciated by the *Irish World.*" C.O. 904/15/1, Public Record Office.

41. New York *Times,* June 24, 1881; *Irish World,* Jan. 15, May 21, July 30, Aug. 27, 1881; Oct. 7, Nov. 11, 1882.

42. *Irish World,* May 29, Dec. 11, 1880; Jan. 15, Apr. 16, May 5, 1881;

Boston *Pilot,* Feb. 5, 1881; Walsh, "Class, Culture and National-ism," 127–36.

43. Funchion, "Chicago," 20, 55–56, 83–87; Clark, *Irish in Philadelphia,* 101, 171–72.

44. Wayne G. Broehl, Jr., *The Molly Maguires* (Cambridge, 1964), 97–98, 208; Clifton K. Yearley, Jr., *Enterprise and Anthracite* (Baltimore, 1961), 172–75, 215; Robert V. Bruce, *1877: Year of Violence* (Indianapolis, 1959), 294–95; John R. Commons *et al., History of Labor in the United States* (2 vols.: New York, 1918), II, 189–91.

45. Ralph J. Ricker, *The Greenback-Labor Movement in Pennsylvania* (Bellefonte, Pa., 1966), 39–43, 64, 73; Hendrick B. Wright to Powderly, Mar. 11, 1881, Powderly Papers; Jonathan Garlock, "A Structural Analysis of the Knights of Labor" (Ph. D. diss., University of Rochester, 1974), 65–79; Victor R. Greene, *The Slavic Community on Strike* (South Bend, 1968), 81, 87; Terence V. Powderly, *Thirty Years of Labor, 1859–1889* (New York, 1967 ed.), 102–4.

46. *Irish World,* Nov. 6, 1880; Jan. 22, 29, Apr. 9, May 28, 1881.

47. *Irish World,* July 24, Oct. 9, 1880; Apr. 16, 1881; Broehl, *Molly Maguires,* 83, 361.

48. Vincent J. Falzone, "Terrence V. Powderly: Mayor and Labor Leader, 1849–1893" (Ph. D. diss., University of Maryland, 1970); O'Brien and Ryan, eds., *Devoy's Post-Bag,* II, 60; Patrick Collins to Powderly, May 10, 1880, Powderly Papers; Buffalo *Daily Courier,* Jan. 14, 1881; *Irish World,* Mar. 5, 1881; Apr. 29, 1882; Powderly, *Thirty Years,* 184.

49. Henry J. Browne, *The Catholic Church and the Knights of Labor* (Washington, 1949), 55–63, 229; Peter Ward to Powderly, May 10, 1881; W. J. Hudson to Powderly, May 13, 1881, Powderly Papers; Terence V. Powderly, *The Path I Trod,* ed., Harry J. Carman *et al.* (New York, 1940), 179.

50. Herbert G. Gutman, *Work, Culture, and Society in Industrializing America* (New York, 1976), 244, 256–57; George E. McNeill, ed., *The Labor Movement* (Boston and New York, 1887), 221–29; *Thirteenth Annual Report of the Bureau of Statistics of Labor* (Boston, 1882), 195–415; Philip T. Silva, Jr., "The Position of Workers in a Textile Community: Fall River in the Early 1880's," *Labor History,* XVI(1975), 230–48; *Irish World,* Dec. 4, 1880; Sept. 24, 1881; Paul Buhle, "The Knights of Labor in Rhode Island," *Radical History Review,* XVII (Spring 1978), 40–48.

51. Rodman Paul, *Mining Frontiers of the Far West* (New York, 1963), 69, 76–80, 128; Richard E. Lingenfelter, *The Hardrock Miners* (Berkeley, 1974), 131–56; Brown, *Irish-American Nationalism,* 169; Vernon H. Jensen, *Heritage of Conflict* (Ithaca, 1950), 17–21.

52. Lingenfelter, *Hardrock Miners,* 166; Melvyn Dubofsky, *We Shall Be All* (New York, 1969), 19–22; Neil L. Shumsky, "San Francisco's Workingmen Respond to the Modern City," *California Historical*

Quarterly, LV (1976), 51–52; *Irish World*, Oct. 16, 1880; *Freeman's Journal*, Nov. 22, 1880.

53. Michael A. Gordon, "The Labor Boycott in New York City, 1880–1886," *Labor History*, XVI (1975), 184–229; *Liberty*, Dec. 24, 1881; Mathew Maguire *et al.*, to Henry George, Apr. 17, 1881, Henry George Papers, New York Public Library; *Irish World*, May 6, 1882; New York *Star*, Aug. 24, 1880; Apr. 4, 1881.

54. New York *Star*, Dec. 17, 1880; Jan. 18, Feb. 8, 11, 25, Mar. 7, 12, Aug. 31, Sept. 2, 4, Oct. 4, 9, 1881; New York *Tribune*, Jan. 5, 1882; Leonard Dinnerstein, "The Impact of Tammany Hall on State and National Politics in the Eighteen-Eighties," *New York History*, XLII (1961), 242–44.

55. *Irish World*, Feb. 11, Oct. 28, 1882; United Irishman, Feb. 18, 1882; Gordon, "Labor Boycott," 196–98; U.S. Senate, *Report of the Committee on Capital and Labor*, 805, 840; Peter A. Speek, *The Single Tax and the Labor Movement* (Madison, 1915), 24; New York *Star*, Jan. 31, 1882.

56. *John Swinton's Paper* (New York City), Feb. 28, 1886; *Irish World*, Jan. 1, 1881; May 6, Sept. 16, 1882; Gordon, "Studies in Irish-American Thought," 541–47; Douglas V. Shaw, "Labor, Irish Nationalism and Anti-Monopoly: Jersey City in 1882" (paper delivered at annual meeting, American Historical Association, 1974), 10–14.

57. Handlin, *Boston's Immigrants*, 126–42; Jay P. Dolan, *The Immigrant Church* (Baltimore, 1975), 122–27; Gilbert Osofsky, "Abolitionists, Irish Immigrants, and the Dilemma of Romantic Nationalism," *American Historical Review*, LXXX (1975), 889–912; Lydia Maria Child to Charles Sumner, July 4, 1870, Charles Sumner Papers, Harvard University.

58. Osofsky, "Abolitionists and Immigrants," 896–97; MacDonagh, "The Irish Famine Emigration," 384–86; Ernst, *Immigrant Life*, 100–101; Montgomery, *Beyond Equality*, 126–34.

59. Joseph Lee, *The Modernization of Irish Society 1848–1918* (Dublin, 1973), 65, 72, 93–95; *Freeman's Journal*, Dec. 15, 1879; Aug. 15, 1881; Norman O. Palmer, *The Irish Land League Crisis* (New Haven, 1940), 150; Dublin *Evening Mail*, Feb. 2, 1880.

60. Irving H. Bartlett, *Wendell Phillips, Brahmin Radical* (Boston, 1961), 381; *Freeman's Journal*, Dec. 17, 1879; *Irish World*, Dec. 13, 1879; Apr. 10, 1880.

61. Horner, *Redpath*, 7–12, 254–56; James Redpath, *Talks About Ireland* (New York, 1881), 31–32; *Irish World*, Apr. 17, June 5, 12, 1880; James Redpath to Patrick Collins, May 8, 1881, Special Irish Collection; *Freeman's Journal*, Aug. 18, 1880; July 27, Oct. 6, 1881; *Proceedings at a Farewell Dinner given by the Land League of New York to James Redpath* (New York, 1881), 12–13.

62. Report of the Metropolitan Police, as Regards the Irish National

Land League, Aug. 10, 1880, Carton 9, Irish Land League Police Reports, State Paper Office, Dublin Castle; *The Land League: Socialism in Ireland* (Dublin, 1880), 14; *Freeman's Journal*, Sept. 13, 1880; Devoy, *Land of Eire*, 87.

63. John G. Sproat, *"The Best Men"* (New York, 1968); New York *Tribune*, Nov. 22, 1879; Nov. 25, 1880; [Lysander Spooner], *Revolution* (New York, 1880); O'Brien and Ryan, eds., *Devoy's Post-Bag*, I, 509; *Freeman's Journal*, Jan. 30, 1880; Sept. 26, 1881.

64. *Freeman's Journal*, Sept. 19, 1881; New York *Star*, Aug. 1, 1880; Buffalo *Daily Courier*, Jan. 14, 1881; *Irish World*, Mar. 5, 1881.

65. Cork *Examiner*, Oct. 4, 1882; Henry George, *Progress and Poverty* (4th ed., New York, 1884), 270, 305; *The Times* (London), Sept. 6, 1882; *Freeman's Journal*, June 12, 1882; Stuart Bruchey, "Twice Forgotten Man: Henry George," *American Journal of Economics and Sociology*, XXXI (1972), 113–38.

66. *Irish World*, Oct. 28, 1882; J. A. Hobson, "The Influence of Henry George in England," *The Fortnightly Review*, n.s., LXII (1897), 837; Henry George, Jr., ed., *Complete Works of Henry George* (10 vols.: New York, 1906–11), III, 82.

67. Charles A. Barker, *Henry George* (New York, 1955), 320–55; U.S. Senate, *Report of the Committee on Capital and Labor*, I, 244; *Irish World*, May 1, Dec. 11, 1880; Jan. 22, 1881; Jan. 6, 1883; Henry George to Patrick Ford, Nov. 9, 1881, Letterbook, George Papers, George, Jr., ed., *Complete Works*, III, 8–12, 73–74, 107–8.

68. George, *Progress and Poverty*, 496; George, Jr., ed., *Complete Works*, III, 96; George R. Geiger, *The Philosophy of Henry George* (New York, 1933), 336–37; Henry F. May, *Protestant Churches and Industrial America* (New York, 1949), 154; Gutman, *Work, Culture, and Society*, 79–118.

69. Mann, *Yankee Reformers*, 24–25; Aaron I. Abell, *American Catholicism and Social Action* (Garden City, 1950), 27–29, 47–51; Dolan, *Immigrant Church*, 121–22.

70. Rodechko, "An Irish-American Journalist," 526–27; *Irish World*, Apr. 5, 1879; Nov. 13, 1880; Gordon, "Studies in Irish-American Thought," 93–94.

71. Sylvester L. Malone, *Dr. Edward McGlynn* (New York, 1918); Geiger, *Philosophy of George*, 344–46; Dolan, *Immigrant Church*, 66; New York *Sun*, Apr. 30, 1870.

72. Circular, Mar. 30, 1880, Powderly Papers; New York *Sun*, July 6, 1882; *Irish World*, July 15, Aug. 12, Sept. 2, 1882.

73. Greene, "American Catholics," 25–26; William B. Faherty, "The Clergyman and Labor Progress: Cornelius O'Leary and the Knights of Labor," *Labor History*, XI (1970), 175–89; Brenda K. Shelton, *Reformers in Search of Yesterday* (Albany, 1976), 31, 53, 161; Robert D. Cross, *The Emergence of Liberal Catholicism in America* (Cambridge, 1958); John T. Ellis, *The Life of James Cardinal Gibbons* (2 vols.: Milwaukee, 1952).

74. *Irish World,* Jan. 29, 1881.

75. Michael Davitt, *The Land League Proposal* (Glasgow, 1882); Michael Davitt, *Leaves From a Prison Diary* (2 vols.: London, 1885), II, 93, 99.

76. Charles E. Reeves, "Davitt's American Tour of 1882," *Quarterly Journal of Speech,* LIV (1968), 357–62; O'Brien and Ryan, eds., *Devoy's Post-Bag,* II, 121; New York *Irish-American,* June 17, 1882; Boston *Pilot,* cited in *Irish Nation,* June 17, 1882; Boston *Pilot,* July 1, 1882; New York *Star,* June 10, 18, 1882.

77. *Irish Nation,* June 10, 17, 1882; *Irish World,* Jan. 7, June 24, July 15, Sept. 2, 1882; George, Jr., ed., *Complete Works,* X, 384–87; *United Irishman,* Sept. 16, 1882.

78. T. W. Moody, "Michael Davitt, 1846–1906: A Survey and Appreciation," *Studies,* XXXV (1946), 437; Devoy, *Land of Eire,* 91; *Freeman's Journal,* May 31, Aug. 22, Oct. 9, 1882.

79. Algar L. Thorold, *The Life of Henry Labouchere* (London, 1913), 234; F. Sheehy-Skeffington, *Michael Davitt* (London, 1967 ed.), 18–23; T. W. Moody, "Michael Davitt and the British Labour Movement," *Transactions, Royal Historical Society,* 5 ser., III (1953), 56–58; *Speech of Michael Davitt,* 30; Lyons, *Parnell,* 232.

80. E. Eldon Barry, *Nationalisation in British Politics* (London, 1965), 17–40, 57–60; John Saville, "Henry George and the British Labour Movement," *Science and Society,* XXIV (1960), 321–33; Clive J. Dewey, "The Rehabilitation of the Peasant Proprietor in Nineteenth Century Economic Thought," *History of Political Economy,* VI (1974), 17–47; Joy McAskill, "The Treatment of 'Land' in English Social and Political Theory 1840–1885" (B. Litt thesis, Oxford University, 1959), 50–75, 156–76, 241–43; H. J. Perkin, "Land Reform and Class Conflict in Victorian Britain," in J. Butt and I. F. Clarke, eds., *The Victorians and Social Protest* (London, 1973), 191–93; *Reynolds's Newspaper* (London), June 22, 1879.

81. *Irish World,* July 1, 1882; New York *Irish-American,* July 15, 1882; *Irish Nation,* June 3, July 8, 1882.

82. Brown, *Irish-American Nationalism,* 159–66; unidentified newspaper clipping, Apr. 1883, F.O. 5/1861/187, Public Record Office; *Irish World,* Oct. 12, 1882.

83. For example, John A. Garraty's fine survey of the Gilded Age, *The New Commonwealth* (New York, 1968), contains no mention of the Land League and, more important, its chapter on social thought completely ignores the ferment within the Catholic Church during this period.

84. Brown, *Irish-American Nationalism,* 24, 41, 46; Alexander Sullivan, "The American Republic and the Irish National League of America," *American Catholic Quarterly Review,* IX (1884), 43–44.

85. Thomas N. Brown, quoted in Glazer and Moynihan, *Beyond the Melting Pot,* 241; Shannon, *American Irish,* 134–36; Henry George to Terence V. Powderly, Apr. 19, 1883, Powderly Papers.

86. *Irish World,* July 9, 1881.
87. Buffalo *Daily Courier,* Jan. 14, 1881. A too-little known discussion of the complex interplay of nationalism and class consciousness is contained in Ber Borochov, *Nationalism and the Class Struggle* (New York, 1937).
88. Moody, "Davitt and British Labour," 53–76; Solow, *Land Question,* 189–94; Karl Marx and Frederick Engels, *Ireland and the Irish Question* (New York, 1972), 284, 292–93.
89. Perkin, in Butt and Clarke, eds., *Victorians,* 179–83, 208–13; R. C. K. Ensor, "Some Political and Economic Interactions in Later Victorian England," *Transactions, Royal Historical Society,* 4 ser., XXXI (1949), 25–26; Barry, *Nationalisation,* 64–67, 138–41; James Hunter, "The Gaelic Connection: The Highlands, Ireland and Nationalism, 1873–1922," *Scottish Historical Review,* LIV (1975), 180–85; Paul R. Thompson, *Socialists, Liberals, and Labour* (London, 1967), 113; James D. Young, "Changing Images of American Democracy and the Scottish Labour Movement," *International Review of Social History,* XVIII, pt. 1 (1973), 78–81; John Rae, "Social Philosophy," *Contemporary Review,* XLV (1884), 295; Patrick Ford to William O'Brien, Mar. 11, 1903, William O'Brien Papers, National Library of Ireland.
90. Gordon, "Studies in Irish-American Thought," xxi, 335; Commons, *Labor Movement,* II, 453; New York *Sun,* Sept. 19, 1886; *John Swinton's Paper,* Sept. 19, 1886; Stephen Bell, *Rebel, Priest, and Prophet: A Biography of Dr. Edward McGlynn* (New York, 1937).
91. Garlock, "Knights of Labor," 6; Cross, *Liberal Catholicism,* 26–27; Charles Leinenweber, "Socialists in the Streets: The New York City Socialist Party in Working Class Neighborhoods, 1908–1918," *Science and Society,* XLI (1977), 161.
92. Aronowitz, *False Promises,* 146–49, 156; Philip Taylor, *The Distant Magnet* (New York, 1971), 197; Henry Merwin, "The Irish in American Life," *Atlantic Monthly,* LXXVII (1896), 293; Doyle, *Irish Americans;* David Montgomery, "The Irish and the American Labor Movement" (unpublished essay, 1976).
93. Leinenweber, "Socialists in the Streets," 164; Dubofsky, *We Shall Be All,* 24, 68; Doyle, *Irish Americans;* John D. Buenker, *Urban Liberalism and Progressive Reform* (New York, 1973), 30–45, 204–5; John A. Ryan, *Social Doctrine in Action* (New York, 1941), 8–9.

Acknowledgments

Numerous friends and colleagues generously offered their advice and criticism when the essays collected in this volume were originally published. I reiterate my appreciation, first expressed where the pieces originally appeared. I do wish, however, to take this opportunity to thank certain individuals for their invaluable contributions: Ira Berlin and Leslie Rowland for their unfailing generosity in sharing materials and ideas from the Freedmen and Southern Society Project, Fred Siegel for his ongoing intellectual stimulation and encouragement, and Lynn Garafola for a very special comradeship.

The dedication to James P. Shenton, in whose classes I first studied the many complex issues posed by the American Civil War, is a recognition of two decades of loyal friendship.

E.F.

Index

INDEX